W9-AOE-308

Issues across the Curriculum

Reading, Writing, Research

DOLORES laGUARDIA
University of San Francisco

HANS P. GUTH
Santa Clara University

FREE
PROFESSIONAL
COPY

FREE
PROFESSIONAL
COPY

Mayfield Publishing Company
Mountain View, California
London • Toronto

Copyright © 1997 by Mayfield Publishing Company

All rights reserved. No portion of this book may be reproduced in any form or by any means without written permission of the publisher.

Library of Congress Cataloging–in–Publication Data

    laGuardia, Dolores.
       Issues across the curriculum : reading, writing, research /
    Dolores laGuardia, Hans P. Guth.
       p. cm.
    Includes index.
    ISBN 1-55934-570-5
       1. College readers.   2. English language–Rhetoric–Problems,
    exercises, etc.   3. Interdisciplinary approach in education–
    Problems, exercises, etc.   4. Research–Methodology–Problems,
    exercises, etc.   5. Academic writing–Problems, exercises, etc.
    I. Guth, Hans Paul.   II. Title.
    PE1417.L32   1996
    808'.0427–dc20   96-21081
                                     CIP

Manufactured in the United States of America
10 9 8 7 6 5 4 3 2 1

Mayfield Publishing Company
1280 Villa Street
Mountain View, California 94041

Sponsoring editor, James Bull; production editor, Carla White; text designer, Linda Robertson; cover designer, Jeanne Schreiber; cover image, Glen Mitsui; art manager, Robin Mouat; artists, Martha Gilman Roach and Robin Mouat; manufacturing manager, Randy Hurst. The text was set in Nofret Light by TBH Typecast and printed on 45# Chromatone Matte by Banta Book Group.

To the Instructor

We cannot in one lifetime see all that we would like to see or learn all we hunger to know.

LOREN EISELEY

Knowledge that is known only to a few can be used only by a few.

GLORIA STEINEM

This book is designed to prepare your students for reading, writing, and research in the academic community. It introduces them to ideas and issues in major areas across the curriculum. It provides intellectual equipment to help them profit from coursework in both general education and their major areas of study. The book may serve as a textbook in

- courses focusing on writing across the curriculum
- freshman English courses responding to pressures to prepare students better for college writing
- orientation courses or general education courses introducing students to college education and academic disciplines

Can we help prepare our students to deal with input from fields of study or research important to an understanding of the modern world? To be fully functioning citizens, educated people have to be to some extent generalists–equipped to understand and estimate the impact of knowledge from a range of sources. Can we help prepare our students to become knowledgeable and effective in a chosen specialty or field of study? Educated people are well equipped to become specialists or expert practitioners, becoming successful in an area of professional specialization. At the same time, they are able to see their specialty in context–they see its role and its implications as part of a larger whole.

How can we help students hold their own in the arena of academic discourse? Specialists in a field share common assumptions. They speak the same language. The newcomer's task is to learn the language of the field, to understand terms that everyone knows, to become familiar with assumptions taken for granted in a given discourse community. As Thomas Kuhn has said, a field becomes a science when a perspective or paradigm becomes widely shared. Researchers no longer argue basic assumptions that everyone accepts. Instead they focus on unsolved problems. The selections in this volume are designed to provide the newcomer with a way in.

What does it take to listen in on the conversation? The chapter-opening Perspectives essays and the reading selections in Part One of this volume introduce students to key issues, and to ways of approaching these issues, in seven areas:

SCIENCE   What does it mean to think like a scientist? How has the method of science shaped our thinking in the modern world? What questions do physicists or biologists ask? How are the applications of science in medicine, technology, and environmental science changing our world? What are the responsibilities of scientists at the turn of the century?

SOCIAL SCIENCE   What does it mean to look at human behavior from the perspective of a social scientist? What questions do political scientists, anthropologists, or psychologists ask? How do they go about answering them? How much human behavior can be quantified—measured and translated into numbers or statistics? What are the uses and abuses of social science in areas like politics or educational testing?

BUSINESS   What are basic assumptions of the business world? What is the rationale of and what are challenges to the free market? What is the relationship between business and government? between business and labor? What new challenges confront economists and business leaders in the era of global competition? What are the social responsibilities of the business community? Does the economy have a conscience?

HUMANITIES   In a technology-dominated and profit-driven society, who educates the imagination? Who educates the emotions? The humanities ask students to consider questions like the following: How do art and literature hold up the mirror to the human condition? What role has the creative imagination played in the history of civilization? What is the role of architecture, sculpture, painting, drama, or poetry in human culture? Who defines and passes on our cultural heritage?

COMMUNICATION   How do the media shape our perception of reality? Who pays the piper? Do the media merely mirror or do they help create the culture of violence? Do they challenge or do they perpetuate racist and sexist stereotypes? In our computerized world, is today already the tomorrow envisioned by futurologists and visionaries?

CAREER EDUCATION   Is the work ethic obsolete? Is our educational system preparing students to survive in the world of work? How do current trends toward downsizing and outsourcing affect job seekers? Will affirmative action cease to play a role in hiring and promotion? How are women faring in the workplace?

INTERDISCIPLINARY PERSPECTIVES   In an age of specialists, who is responsible for looking at the larger picture? At what point does specialization become a handicap? What tasks or what problems require the
cooperation of specialists from different disciplines? Where do science and
aesthetics, or science and the law, intersect? What movements–feminism,
gay rights, chaos theory–cut across traditional disciplines?

Part Two of *Issues across the Curriculum* develops the students' reading, writing,
and research skills.

READING STRATEGIES   Chapter 8 deals with close, attentive reading and
making use of one's reading. It gives hands-on guidance on note taking,
quoting and paraphrasing, and integrating material from different sources.

WRITING AS PROCESS   Chapter 9 aims at making students more knowledgeable, more resourceful, and more confident writers. It takes students
through the intermeshing, overlapping stages of the writing process–from
focusing on a topic through targeting the audience, working up material,
and structuring a paper to revising and rethinking and to final editing.

WRITING/THINKING STRATEGIES   Chapter 10 traces writing and thinking
strategies that alone or in combination structure much written work and
that have applications in many areas across the disciplines. These strategies
include tracing a process, drawing general conclusions, classifying or sorting out data, comparing/contrasting, weighing the pro and con, and arguing from principle.

PRACTICAL PROSE FORMS   Chapter 11 treats specific writing tasks, from
abstracts and reviews to proposal writing, report writing, or surveys and
questionnaires.

RESEARCH STRATEGIES   Chapter 12 deals with the formal research paper
and styles of documentation. It introduces students to research processes in
the computer age. It demystifies for the student major documentation
styles, focusing especially on the MLA and APA formats. It concludes by
suggesting possible alternatives to the traditional research paper.

Acknowledgments

We owe a special debt to colleagues who have shared with us their understanding of writing across the curriculum and their criticism of existing texts and
procedures. In particular, we wish to thank Bob Brannon, Johnson County Community College; Carolyn Hill, Towson State University; Shirley Morahan, Northeast
Missouri State University; Deborah Shaller, Towson State University; and Penny
Smith, Gannon University.

To the Student

This book is designed to help you become a more successful student both while getting a general education (becoming an educated person) and while moving toward your chosen area of specialization. What should you know about major areas of the curriculum? What does it take to help you get more out of your reading? What does it take for you to become a more confident, resourceful, and effective writer? How can you improve the research skills needed both for informal research and for formal documented papers?

PART ONE: Readings across the Curriculum

The "Perspectives" essays and reading selections in Part One of this book introduce you to seven major areas of the college curriculum. A common question underlies much of the material you will study, discuss, and write about: What is some of the basic intellectual equipment that educated people share in the modern world?

SCIENCE   What does it mean to think like a scientist? How has science shaped our thinking in the modern world? What questions do physicists or biologists ask? How are the applications of science in medicine, technology, and environmental science changing our world? What are the responsibilities of scientists at the turn of the century?

SOCIAL SCIENCE   What does it mean to look at human behavior as a social scientist? What questions do political scientists, anthropologists, or psychologists ask? How do they go about answering them? How much human behavior can be measured and translated into numbers or statistics? What are potential abuses of social science in politics, in advertising?

BUSINESS   What basic assumptions rule the business world? How does a free market work? What is the relationship between business and government? Between business and labor? What challenges confront economists and business leaders in the era of global competition? What are the social responsibilities of the business community?

HUMANITIES   Who educates the imagination? Who educates the emotions? Who helps people find meaning or a sense of direction in their lives? The humanities ask you to consider questions like the following: How do art and literature hold up the mirror to the human condition? What has been the role of the creative imagination in the history of civilization? What is the role of architecture, sculpture, painting, drama, or poetry in human culture? Who defines and passes on our cultural heritage?

COMMUNICATION   How do the media shape your perception of reality? Who controls the mass media? Do the media merely mirror or do they help create the culture of violence? Do they challenge or do they perpetuate racist and sexist stereotypes? How is the computer changing the way we think, write, and look at the world?

CAREER EDUCATION   Is our educational system preparing students to survive in the world of work? How do current trends toward downsizing and outsourcing affect job seekers? Is affirmative action dead? How are women doing in the workplace?

INTERDISCIPLINARY PERSPECTIVES   In an age of specialists, who is looking at the larger picture? At what point does a specialist become a narrow specialist? What tasks or what problems require the cooperation of specialists from different disciplines? What ideas or movements cut across traditional disciplines?

PART TWO: Reading, Writing, Research

Improved competence in reading, writing, and research boosts your performance in academic work, both in general education classes and in your vocational or professional specialty. As you aim at becoming a better reader, writer, and researcher, much of your work will fit under headings like the following:

BECOMING A RESPONSIVE READER   You will work with materials representing a full range of the best current and recent writing. Your basic resource will be the work of writers (including student writers) who have tested and proven themselves as published writers. Using effective written work as Exhibit A, you will explore the purposes writing serves–what does it do for the writer and the reader? You will study the writer's use of sources–where do writers turn for material? You will study the organizing strategies experienced writers employ–what gives writing shape and direction? You will discuss writers' strategies for influencing their readers, and you will assess possible audience reactions.

JOINING IN THE PUBLIC DIALOGUE   The spoken and the written word help shape public opinion and community action. When you write about campus speech codes, abortion restrictions, or public funding for research or the arts, you are joining in an ongoing dialogue. Much writing that is part of our public discourse fills in perceived gaps in the public's knowledge. It takes on damaging preconceptions or prejudices, or it tries to counteract a current trend. It takes into account currently fashionable arguments and key controversies of the past. To be an effective writer, you learn to keep up with current public debate. You follow the discussion of current issues in newspaper and magazine articles, editorial comment, letters to the editor, newsletters, and sites on the World Wide Web.

WRITING AS PROCESS   Writing is a creative process. The finished piece on the printed page is misleading: It does not tell the reader about the process of trial and error that produced the final document. It does not chronicle the often frustrating search for reliable information, false leads that had to be abandoned, promising working hypotheses contradicted by the facts, and late-at-night sessions when it seemed as if things would never jell–the different pieces of the puzzle would never fall into place.

Different writing teachers chart the major dimensions of the writing process in somewhat different ways. You might want to think of your writing as a seven-step process. (Always remember that the different "stages" of the process overlap and are often in progress concurrently.)

- Purpose–What sets writing in motion; what brings it on? What are you trying to accomplish? Are you trying to explain a difficult concept or bring the reader up to date on new research? Are you trying to correct a misunderstanding or a stereotype? Are you trying to change the reader's mind about a major project or an important current issue?

- Audience–What does it take to bring the subject to life for your audience? What specialized information do your readers need; what key terms do you have to explain? What assumptions or possibly hostile reactions do you have to take into account? What does it take to persuade an educated audience?

- Input–Where are you going to turn for reliable information? How good are you at telling apart biased or superficial accounts and solid, well-researched ones? Have you learned to draw on informal consultation or full-fledged interviews with insiders or people in the know? How resourceful are you in tracking down needed data in printed and electronic sources?

- Structure–What does it take to turn miscellaneous and contradictory materials into a coherent piece of writing–writing that "hangs together?" What kind of thinking goes into writing? What generalizations are justified by your data? What balanced conclusion can you reach after exploring the play of pro and con in the discussion of a controverted issue? How will you structure your argument?

- Revision–Revision and rethinking loom large in the work of professional writers. How do writers rework a rough draft to help an ugly duckling turn

into a beautiful swan? How are you going to respond to feedback and second thoughts? How good are you at reshuffling material for a better flow
and at feeding in missing links?

- Editing–What are professional, businesslike ways of editing your work to
  meet the standards of written English? What is the right middle ground
  between a stodgy, pompous hyperformal style and a too casual or slangy
  style? What special formats or guidelines for style are you expected to
  observe?

- Publication–A diary may be for our own eyes only, but generally we write
  to be read. In the real world, writers meet deadlines (or the bus leaves without them); they deal with editorial second-guessing; they hope for a warm
  favorable reception and steel themselves for hostile criticism. A writer without an audience is like a doughnut shop without customers. If at all possible,
  publish your writing in a class publication, in a departmental or school-wide
  publication, in the newsletter of a special-interest group, or as letters to the
  editor in the campus daily or the local press.

USING THE WORKSHOP FORMAT   A writing class today is typically run
as a writing workshop. You may discuss readings that can serve as both
material and as models for your writing. You may explore and develop
possible topics with your classmates. You may explore promising sources
together. You will provide feedback to others and serve as a trial audience
for finished papers. You will often revise your own work in response to
input from your instructor and from classmates. You may be asked to participate in group projects–for instance, oral class presentations on provocative issues or collaborative writing of reports on demanding subjects.
Writing grows and develops in interaction with other people–friends, editors, peers.

HONING YOUR RESEARCH SKILLS   Informal research goes into most
substantial writing. However, when working on an extended investigative
paper or a formal research paper, you will be paying special attention to
how writers research a topic and integrate material from a range of different sources. You will profit from instruction in library research, data retrieval, and research techniques. You will have to learn a documentation
style appropriate to your subject and your field. Where and how are you
expected to identify author, publication, and publisher? What other publishing data will you need to include? Where and how are you going to
specify page numbers?

A Note on Plagiarism: When you draw on other writers' work, you need to respect
other people's intellectual property. Plagiarism is to writing what shoplifting is to
shopping. When in doubt, credit the source. Acknowledge the original source when

you incorporate in your paper statements, ideas, and perspectives developed by someone else. Put all direct quotation–all material you copy word for word–in quotation marks. Plagiarism can ruin a grade; at worst, it gets people expelled from institutions or dragged into court. The best insurance against plagiarism is the full disclosure policy you practice in a workshop situation: If you talk freely with others about what materials you found, what is right or what is wrong with them, and how you are going to use them, you run little risk of trying to pass off someone's else's writing as your own.

WRITING WORKSHOP 1   A Writer's Résumé

What do you bring to your reading, your writing, your research? Prepare an informal writer's résumé to take stock of what you bring to your writing class. Give your instructor or your peers a preliminary answer to questions like the following: Who are you? What might you be able to contribute to the class? What special background or experience do you have that you could draw on in your written work? What are your special academic interests or career goals? What has been your previous experience as a writer? Write a paragraph or two under each of the following headings:

- PERSONAL BACKGROUND   What in your personal experience has helped make you the kind of person you are? For instance, how important were family ties in your growing up? Did ethnic origin or a language or culture different from the mainstream play a role? Did you have a religious upbringing? Did you experience any turning points or traumatic events?

- EDUCATION   What kind of schools did you attend? For instance, what was the social or racial mix of the students? Did any teacher make a special impression on you? Did you have favorite subjects or encounter special hurdles? What did you learn from your schooling besides academic subjects?

- WORK OR CAREER INTERESTS   What has been your exposure to the world of work? Have you had any work experience or experience as a volunteer? What are your tentative career interests and why?

- ACADEMIC SPECIALIZATION   In college, have you become involved in a field of study or major? What is its appeal to you–is there a personal connection? What special challenges or obstacles does your chosen field present? Could you initiate an outsider into the basic assumptions, procedures, or mindset of people in the field?

- PREVIOUS WRITING EXPERIENCE   Can you single out a paper or writing project that taught you something about writing? What was the topic? What did it mean to you? How did you put the paper together? What material did you use? How did you organize it? What was the main point, and what evidence or arguments did you use to support it? What feedback did you receive, and how did you respond to it?

Contents

PART TWO: READING, WRITING, RESEARCH   509

Close Reading: Responding to Clues–Taking Notes–Drawing on
a Text: Quotation and Paraphrase–Synthesis: Correlating Texts–
Reading On-Line

Discovering Your Purpose–Writing for an Audience–Working Up
Material–Shaping a First Draft–Revising and Rethinking–Editing
and Proofreading–Computer Writing, Collaborative Writing,
Interactive Writing

Tracing the Process–Generalizing: Charting the Trend–Classification:
Sorting Out–Structuring a Comparison–Cause and Effect: Problem
to Solution–Weighing Pro and Con–Defining a Key Term–Argument:
Making Your Case–Persuading Your Audience

Abstract, Condensation, Summary, Review–Interviews–Proposal
Writing–Report Writing–Surveys and Questionnaires

PART ONE

Readings across the Curriculum

1

Issues in Science

SCIENCE IN PERSPECTIVE

The great thrust of science is to uncover general principles in the chaos of life.

TED ANTON AND RICK MCCOURT

Concepts without factual content are empty; sense-data without concepts are blind. The senses cannot think. The understanding cannot see. By their union only can knowledge be produced.

IMMANUEL KANT

Science thrives on anomaly, inconsistency, controversy, and doubt.

CHRISTIAN VON BAEYER

What is science? Like many of us, you may think of science first of all as the magic wand that delivers the conveniences of modern life. Airplanes have shortened the months it took wagon trains to cross the continent to the timespan required for an airline meal and an in-flight movie. Medical science makes possible hip transplants or miracle drugs for diabetics and people with mental illnesses. Computers allow fellow researchers at MIT and in South Africa to collaborate on a daily basis. However, to understand what it means to be a scientist, you have to look not so much at the products science delivers as at the procedures of science, the methods of science.

SCIENCE AS METHOD

As moderns we assume that the world we know is a construct—it is a view of reality that we have constructed in our minds. From whatever input— direct observation, secondhand information, reading, viewing, interacting with others—our minds build up our perception of reality. We could date the beginning of the modern scientific temperament from the days when early scientists first asked: How do our minds do this? How do our minds process information? What procedures, what methods, generate our knowledge of the world? Science became science when people started to define it not as a body of knowledge but as a way of knowing. Part of the modern scientist's mindset from the beginning has been the emphasis on the *how* rather than the *what* of knowledge. How do you know this? How can we verify it? These are the two basic questions we expect scientists to ask.

The intellectual revolution of the sixteenth and seventeenth centuries put the emphasis not on content but on method. A first programmatic tract of the New Science was Sir Francis Bacon's *Novum Organum* (1620)–the "New Method." Many of the early manifestos of modern science were tracts in **epistemology**–in the theory of knowledge. How do we know what we know? What procedures produce reliable results? Even if faulty methods accidentally make us stumble onto a valuable discovery, in the long run our floundering will be damaging because in the long run our faulty methods will produce bad science. Early scientists, in fact, believed that developing the right methods of inquiry was more important than trusting to the spontaneous mind-boggling insights of the great genius.

Assumptions like the following have long been part of the ideology of modern science:

- *Science is rooted in objective observation.* Much everyday science is not inspired theorizing but patient data gathering. For example, anthropologists may devote their lives to the patient year-after-year search for fossils–until three teeth and some odd leg bones start pointing to a new missing link between tree-climbing apes and prehumans walking on two feet. Dozens if not hundreds of chemical compounds may be tested and discarded before a promising new drug is identified.

- *Science is self-correcting.* Scientific knowledge is open-ended; it is not set in cement or handed down by an unquestioned authority. For a scientist, being ready to change one's mind, far from being a weakness, is a basic intellectual duty. Theories are subject to revision in the light of new data. Ideally, scientists adjust their theories when new facts do not fit their theoretical framework. The uncritical acceptance of authorities or the worship of sage teachers is a hindrance. As Thomas Hobbes, one of the early European scientist-philosophers, said, if you unthinkingly repeat what the great Aristotle said, your science is not science but Aristotelity. A scientist has to be willing to doubt–to doubt that bubonic plague is carried by bad air (rather than by flea bites), to doubt that schizophrenia is caused by traumatic childhood experiences (rather than by biochemical disturbances of the brain).

- *Science insists on verification.* If it cannot be independently confirmed by others, it is not science. Different observers–with varying backgrounds and assumptions–must be able to observe the same phenomena. They must be able to replicate, that is, restage the same experiments. They must come up with the same or similar results. A scientific law must be valid regardless of the politics, religion, or gender of the scientist. A scientific law cannot be true only for one person claiming superior insight or privileged knowledge.

- *Scientific hypotheses are worked out through trial and error.* Scientists are theory-makers–who always remember that a theory is just that. The push of modern science has been toward finding the simple, elegant underlying principles that explain a mass of observed facts. However, the cautious formulation and refining of tentative generalizations is what distinguishes the scientist from the lay person (who is prone to jump to conclusions). Scientific theories are at first tentative, and they hold true until further notice.

- *Scientific understanding is the prerequisite to control, to manipulation.* When we understand causes and effects, we can take the steps that will produce the desired consequences. Often, scientific research is motivated by practical needs. Navigators clamor for better star charts, and astronomers oblige. However, even the findings of researchers motivated by scientific curiosity often have unexpected practical results. Pure science and applied science go hand in hand and are often difficult to disentangle. Scientists come to understand the role of insulin in human metabolism, and physicians can then make progress toward controlling diabetes. People study viruses and other microorganisms, and their knowledge becomes an urgent necessity in the race against deadly diseases. Sometimes the chicken seems to come first, and sometimes the egg.

In an idealized version of the scientific method, the investigator starts with a *tabula rasa*–a clean slate. After much patient data gathering, tentative hypotheses suggest themselves. These are then tested and gradually refined until they fit most or all of the facts. This basic model is **empirical** (experience-based) and **inductive** (generalizing from scratch).

In practice, a key question or a working hypothesis will often focus the inquiry. The role of prior assumptions, working hypotheses, lucky hunches, and intuitive leaps has been much debated. Modern students of scientific inquiry have stressed the "messy" quality of the thought processes of the scientist. For instance, one student of Charles Darwin's working out of the theory of evolution was surprised to find it "tortuous, tentative, enormously complex, full of unwarranted assumptions." This "tortuous" roundabout process assures that the scientist's generalizations are *earned* generalizations–they are the end result of a grueling process and not seductive ideas off the top of someone's head.

Many scientists, whether they openly said so or not, have assumed that scientific knowledge was the only really reliable or useful kind of knowledge. Science would eventually drive out hearsay and superstition in all major areas of human life. It would lead humanity toward a more rational future.

Regardless of the personal humility or dedication of the individual scientist, scientists as a group have often been considered guilty of hubris, the overreaching pride of the scientist who denies other sources of knowledge or inspiration.

Today, you may encounter critics of science who go to the opposite extreme. They may ask you to revise conventional assumptions about its superiority and universality. According to such revisionist critics, Western science, science in the European tradition, tends to cut us off from our roots in nature. It makes us see nature as the adversary, to be tamed and controlled. Rather than seeing ourselves as part of nature, we make nature the object of human manipulation, exploitation, or consumption. The dryly analytical mindset of science threatens to cause the more emotional or intuitive parts of our being to atrophy. In many areas of modern intellectual life, we see a search for alternatives to a dominant scientific mindset. In our modern world, in fact, science and other forms of knowing–religious, artistic, literary, intuitive, imaginative–often seem to coexist uneasily side by side.

ASTRONOMY AS MASTER SCIENCE

Who were the patron saints of modern science? The modern scientific mindset goes back to the glory years of modern astronomy in the sixteenth and seventeenth centuries. As the master science of a world emerging from the Middle Ages, the new astronomy generated intense controversy and revolutionized the world view of educated people. The Polish scientist Nicolaus Copernicus (1473–1542) developed a new model to replace the Ptolemaic universe (named after the Egyptian Ptolemy). In the Ptolemaic system, the earth was at the center of the world, with the sun, the moon, and the planets moving around it in circular orbits. To account better for the observable facts of planetary motion, the Copernican theory put the sun at the center of our solar system, replacing the traditional geocentric with a heliocentric model. The earth rotated on its axis while traveling around the sun along with the other planets. The moon in turn rotated around the earth.

The astronomers adhered to the basic procedures of what was to become the New Science: They worked from careful observation–discounting hearsay, tradition, and approved doctrine. They insisted on verification–testing new theories against observable results. They were open to radical new hypotheses that could account for all or most of the observable facts. Observing the moon through the newly invented telescope, the Italian Galileo Galilei (1564–1642) observed its jagged circumference, its rough irregular surface, and the dots of light gradually becoming larger as sunrise on the moon illuminated first the mountain tops until sunlight eventually flooded the lunar valleys. Galileo and his contemporaries concluded that the moon was not part of a perfect heavens, different from our own planet subject to change and decay. The moon had an irregular surface and reflected borrowed light like the earth. It was a heavenly body in basic ways similar to the earth. Galileo discovered the moons circling around Jupiter, providing another parallel between the earth, with its lunar satellite, and other heavenly bodies.

Verification was crucial because the Ptolemaic model, even when tinkered with to account for apparent complications, did not accurately predict eclipses—causing stargazers, as the poet Edmund Spenser said, to "damn their lying books." The shift to the new theory began to pay off fully when the German Johannes Kepler (1571–1630) persuaded astronomers to try elliptical orbits rather than circles as a better approximation of the path of the planets around the sun. The British Isaac Newton (1642–1727) eventually worked out the mathematics of planetary motion that accounted for variations in speed. Mathematics became the language of modern science, as if it had been the programming language of the physical universe

The new theory of our earth as a spinning traveler in the void seemed to defy common sense for tradition-bound contemporaries. (Why didn't we all hurtle off into space?) Just as challenging was the new view of the distant stars as a myriad blazing suns in the far reaches of outer space. For many traditional thinkers, putting human beings on a minor planet in one of many sun systems meant a drastic downgrading of humankind as the glory of creation. Our earth was a mere speck in the vast galactic spaces. For many researchers and scholars, however, the new thinking opened up new vistas, leading to one of the great ferments of scientific discovery in history. To advocates of the new science, it seemed as if God had created the universe as a great learning machine to teach humanity physics and mathematics. God came to be seen as the Supreme Intelligence and master mathematician.

REEXAMINING THE NEWTONIAN UNIVERSE

When your science teachers today talk about the limitations of Newtonian physics, they are reexamining a tradition that provided the dominant model for the "hard sciences" for over two centuries. The eighteenth century saw the application of the new scientific spirit in many areas, including anatomy and mechanics. Isaac Newton, who discovered the spectrum and developed a new theory of light, had been one of the discoverers of calculus (*Principles of Mathematics*, 1687). Newton became a guiding spirit for what was later called Newtonian science. Said the poet Alexander Pope,

Nature and all its works lay hid in night.
God said, "Let Newton be," and all was light.

Physicists defined life as matter in motion (death occurs when all motion stops). The Newtonian universe was a mechanistic universe—it was a finely attuned machine that had its frictions but that made our life possible on this planet. It worked according to fixed physical laws that did not make exceptions for any one individual. Seen from the larger perspective, it worked for the benefit of all. The divine clockmaker had created the "best of all possible worlds"–a mechanism like a finely balanced Swiss watch, although on an infinitely larger and more magnificent scale.

Admirers of the new science early began to believe that much that was still a mystery would eventually be explained in physical or material terms. For instance, we poetically speak of the human heart or the human spirit. But obviously our thoughts and emotions correspond to physical, material events in the human brain. Thomas Hobbes had already pointed toward a materialistic psychology by showing how often our language about human motives suggests the push and pull of physical forces. We are *attracted* to another person; we *incline* to a course of action; we are *repelled* by what is ugly. It is as if our thoughts already mimic or anticipate the actions or motions that would act them out.

Critics of Newtonian science early rebelled against it as *too* mechanistic, too materialistic, too linear. The magnificent cosmic clockwork made by the supreme artificer gradually came to seem like a soulless machine. Much modern thinking–from quantum physics to chaos theory–is ammunition for critics who accuse the Newtonian tradition of giving oversimplified and one-dimensional answers to the mystery of life.

EVOLUTION AS MASTER METAPHOR

How did *evolution* become a fighting word? Why may the treatment of evolution in your high school biology textbooks have been different from what students read in other states–or in your own state a few years earlier or later? In the nineteenth century, biology, focusing on the relationships between different life forms, replaced cosmology as the great intellectual battleground. The nineteenth century saw a gradual shift from the static clockwork metaphor toward a more dynamic perspective. Becoming attuned to the idea of change and progress, people were ready to move beyond the model of a finished universe that represented perfection (or rather "the best of all possible worlds") and was operating according to fixed laws. Evolution–gradual, purposeful change–became the master metaphor, the guiding thought-provoking imaginative comparison, for the emerging modern world.

Biologists took their clue from students of geology, who were focusing on geological strata, sediments deposited over vast stretches of time. Geologists became convinced that the age of the earth was to be measured not in thousands but in millions of years, during which time vast momentous changes had taken place. The fossil record revealed the ossified remains of plants and animals that showed great changes over time–with new species appearing and others, like the dinosaurs, becoming extinct. It was a natural next step to fit the fossils of earlier plants and animal species into a framework of evolution toward higher, more complex, and more intelligent forms of life. A family tree of all living things would show life moving from the one-celled amoeba to complex multicelled organisms; from water dwellers to land dwellers; from tree-dwelling proto-apes (or ape ancestors) with low cranial capacity to upright almost humanlike creatures.

Charles Darwin, in his epochal *On the Origin of Species* (1859), identified the mechanism for evolution: Mutations in the genetic inheritance of a species could give the mutated form an advantage in the race to reproduce and perpetuate the species. A process of **natural selection** would then favor the advantaged variant. In the spirit of nineteenth-century science, Darwinians were determinists, believing that everything ultimately has a comprehensible cause, even if for a time it may escape our detection. If a feature evolves and survives, it must be because it gives the animal (or plant) an identifiable advantage in the struggle for existence.

The evolutionist's vision of slow progress toward higher life forms tied in well with nineteenth-century beliefs. People believed that progress toward a more sophisticated technology would extend human control over nature. They saw progress in sanitation and the control of disease. Many saw human history as slow progress from barbarism toward a higher plane of moral evolution, when humanity would leave war, torture, and barbaric punishments behind. In the evolutionist account, the appearance of humankind gave its true meaning and purpose to the emergence of life on this once lifeless planet. Evolution made humankind the culmination of a process that had started at the beginning of time.

Like the Copernican revolution before it, evolution did not remain a matter for scientific debate among specialists. Rather, it produced a seismic upheaval in philosophical, religious, and ethical thought. Traditionalists thought that to acknowledge our kinship with our cousins the chimpanzees was demeaning, and they fought the evolutionary theory tooth and nail. Refusal to acknowledge descent from the monkeys (actually from more primitive common ancestors of monkeys and humans) became the rallying cry of popular polemicists who were to the intellectual life of the time what talk-show hosts are to American popular culture today. At the same time, factions accepting the new theory drew drastically different conclusions concerning the relationship between human society and our animal heritage.

Nature now was no longer, as in the work of the Romantic nature poets, a healing influence and a source of unspoiled beauty. Instead, it was the arena where a merciless struggle for survival was played out. In the words of the poet Tennyson, nature was "red in tooth and claw" from creatures obeying the law of "eat or be eaten; kill or be killed." T. H. Huxley, the great popularizer of Darwin's thinking, warned against importing our human moral judgments into nature, since in the natural scheme of things wolf and lamb "are alike admirable." The wolf, in devouring the lamb, is merely acting out what its genes have programmed it to do. Nature is amoral; it does not pronounce judgment on the cruelty of the cat playing with a wounded bird or mouse.

So what does biology teach us? What can we learn from Darwinian nature about our destiny as human beings? Social Darwinists concluded that nature teaches us to be tough and strong if we want to survive. "Do-gooder" sentimentality was a weakness. Humanists, on the other hand, concluded that morality is not a natural impulse but a social and cultural phenomenon. To live in a humane and decent world, we have to *overcome* our natural tendencies to prey on others. We have to learn to control the natural impulse toward unlimited reproduction and overpopulation.

SCIENCE ETHICS IN THE NUCLEAR AGE

Twentieth-century science has produced revolutionary changes in our ways of living and thinking. It has made possible spectacular advances in such areas as agriculture, transportation, communication, and medicine. The study of microorganisms led to the discovery of viruses and made possible spectacular advances in the fight against killer diseases like polio, diphtheria, and tuberculosis. Insulin therapy, x-ray technology, heart surgery, organ transplants, hip replacements, and a myriad other advances have enabled many to live longer and more fulfilling lives. At the same time, has modern science outpaced the lay person's ability to grasp or visualize basic scientific concepts? Has it created perhaps insoluble ethical dilemmas?

The age of Einstein drastically changed our view of matter and of the relation between matter and energy. The new molecular physics dissolved solid matter and substituted jostling electrically charged particles. Physicists explored a world of subatomic particles where the laws of Newtonian physics did not seem to apply, where random movement and discontinuity were possible. Einstein's theory of relativity superseded notions of space and time as distinct dimensions extending in straight linear fashion.

Atomic physicists split the atom. They held out the promise that by replicating and taming the nuclear fire of the sun we could create an unlimited source of energy. We could make humanity independent of fossil fuels and the pollution they create. In some countries, such as France, nuclear energy fills a major portion of energy needs. However, in the former Soviet Union, obsolescent atomic reactors, such as those responsible for the catastrophe at Chernobyl in the Ukraine, represent a horrible health hazard for large populations. In the United States and other countries, ambitious multibillion dollar projects have been abandoned as the result of second thoughts on the part of the public and politicians.

At the same time, the atomic age has multiplied exponentially the human capacity for mass destruction. It has given humans the ability to erase millions of years of evolution in a blinding flash of suicidal human pride. At Hiroshima in August 1945, in a trial run of nuclear warfare, 70,000 people died in the original explosion, and another 50,000 died of radiation sickness and injuries in the weeks that followed. The nuclear arsenals of the United States, Russia, and a growing circle of other nations remain capable of destroying all life on this planet.

The specter of nuclear destruction presents largely unanswered ethical questions. Feminist scientists have asked whether the willing collaboration of physicists in the race to develop the technologies of mass destruction is related to the traditions and mindset of a male-dominated field. Is the "militarization of science" a natural result of traditions of male competitiveness and striving for dominance in a field that as late as the 1980s was more than 95 percent male?

In areas other than nuclear physics, science may also have reached the borderline between beneficial knowledge and tampering with the foundations of life. Much twentieth-century science has focused on the biochemical processes occurring in living organisms. A milestone was the discovery of the double helix—the genetic code that programs all life. By recombining genetic material from different sources, microbiologists can create new organisms useful for the purposes of agriculture or medicine. We are just beginning to ponder the moral dilemmas involved in using genetic engineering to program human offspring. Are we going to tamper with the genetic makeup of human beings? Are we going to select for male or female, for superior intelligence, or for freedom from genetic defects?

QUESTIONS FOR DISCUSSION

How familiar are you with the modern emphasis on perception as shaping our view of the world? What has been your own experience as a student of physics and mathematics? (Do you consider yourself as having an aptitude for these subjects? Why or why not?) In schools and textbooks, what seems to be the current status of the fight over the theory of evolution? (Do you think young Americans learn about the theory of evolution from textbooks?) What do you know about atomic reactors as a source of energy in different countries around the world? What firsthand experience have you had with efforts to fight pollution or environmental hazards? What have you read or heard about subjects like gene splicing and applications of genetic engineering?

RED
The Mystery of Color

Oliver Sacks

▬▬▬▬▬

Nothing is more wonderful or more to be celebrated than something that will unlock a person's capacities and allow that person to grow and think.

OLIVER SACKS

Color is the kind of everyday phenomenon that the lay person takes for granted. We live in a world of multicolored hues. Only when someone's capability for perceiving color is impaired—or when we watch a movie classic in black and white—do we realize that color is something we construct in the human mind. The challenge for the scientist is to explain how we do that. How does it work? How did the sensors evolve that make us perceive a technicolor world? What physical phenomena in the outside world make it possible for us to add color to the shapes and textures we take in through the eye? In the following interview, one of America's best-known scientists explores the mystery of color. Oliver Sacks is Professor of Clinical Neurology at the Albert Einstein College of Medicine in the Bronx in New York. He is a scientist animated by scientific curiosity, deeply involved in the application of science for purposes of human welfare, and skilled at making scientific knowledge accessible to nonspecialists. His case studies of perception and emotion became best-sellers when he published them in Awakenings *and* The Man Who Mistook His Wife for a Hat; *they provided the scenario for a Hollywood movie.*

QUESTION: Dr. Sacks, your shirt is pink, your sandals are brown, the sky today is not blue but grey, this pencil is yellow—do you agree with all these statements?

SACKS: In principle, yes. But we have to remember that colors do not exist by themselves in the world outside but are generated by our brains. We may want to say, "Sulphur is yellow; that's a fact of chemistry." Actually, that particular substance reflects light of a certain wavelength. In the outside world there are only wavelengths; it takes an eye and a brain to translate them into color.

QUESTION: As you will have guessed, our initial question takes off from the fascinating case history at the beginning of *An Anthropologist on Mars*. It's the story of a painter who turns totally color blind.

SACKS: I learned of his case when the painter wrote to me in 1986.

QUESTION: Is this the way you learn of most of the bizarre cases you write about?

SACKS: I should perhaps say here that my patients as a rule are not bizarre. I am not an exotic jet-setting neurologist, but have been working in a clinic for twenty-nine years. But occasionally my curiosity is triggered, as was the case with this letter. The writer reported that after a traffic accident he perceived the world as one might see it on a black-and-white television set.

QUESTION: At this time, Mr. I., as you call him, was sixty-five years old.

SACKS: Correct, and he asked me whether I recognized his illness and whether I could help him. But I told him that I had never encountered such a case and that I didn't know if I could be of help.

QUESTION: Because complete color blindness is an extremely rare illness?

SACKS: Yes, and cases of the condition being caused by injury to the brain are rarer still—most cases are caused by a hereditary retinal condition.

QUESTION: Did Mr. I. notice immediately after the accident that he had turned color blind?

SACKS: He was at first quite confused and could not remember the accident. He then started to think that he had overcome the effects. But as he was driving to work the next day, sensing that it was a bright sunny day, he suddenly noticed that everything looked grey, foggy, and fuzzy. The police stopped him and said that he had run two red lights.

QUESTION: For a painter like him the experience must have been particularly traumatic.

SACKS: As a painter, he had been known for his use of color. Colors for him had special meanings and emotional associations—but now his life's work had turned meaningless. He drove home and found his wife a totally different person: She also had turned grey, a "moving grey statue," as he phrased it. He was nauseated by her grey skin. And when he closed his eyes, trying to escape from this nightmare, it didn't work, because his imagination and memory had also been emptied of color.

QUESTION: All food also seemed grey and dead to him, as we read in your case history. He confused mustard with mayonnaise, and ketchup with jam. The people around him seemed to have a "ratty" color, and the world seemed like molten lead.

SACKS: It was indeed for him more than a simple loss of the ability to take in color. It was profound loss of the meaning, the imagery, even the memory of color, which had been an integral quality in his life and work.

QUESTION: Why did it seem so much more terrible to him than watching a film in black and white?

SACKS: He himself found it difficult to communicate with others about these devastating and nightmarish changes. To give us at least an inkling, he furnished a room all in grey, painting everything in shades of grey, the way he himself perceived everything. And in this room, one felt the three-dimensional all-surrounding quality of this grey world, totally unlike the confined space of a black-and-white photograph or television screen.

For patients who are *born* color blind, the situation is completely different. This has been their world from the beginning and they therefore do not perceive the world as horrifying but as rich and complete in its own way. For Mr. I., on the other hand, everything suddenly seemed repellent and dirty. A woman patient whose similar loss of color perception was caused by a brain tumor kept sending her freshly laundered things back to the laundry, until she finally noticed that even newly fallen snow seemed dirty to her—it then dawned on her that something was wrong with her perception. The problem was inside her, not in the outside world.

QUESTION: Can you imagine yourself in such a patient's place?

SACKS: Only up to a point. We can develop empathy for what jealousy is like or even madness. Of course we cannot be King Lear, but we can imagine what he is going through. However we cannot imagine what such neurological impairments are like—they are totally alien to us.

QUESTION: Did Mr. I. stop painting?

SACKS: When I first met him, he was not painting. He believed that he was finished as a painter and as a human being. Then he created a number of odd pictures to which he added colors according to the catalogue. Most of these pictures he destroyed later. They were incomprehensible and chaotic—until friends one day made black and white Polaroid pictures of them. Then they saw clear shapes, which had been distorted or covered by the arbitrarily applied colors.

QUESTION: What kind of brain injury had been suffered by this patient?

SACKS: Very specific areas of the brain, called V-4, which are about the size of an almond or small plum, had apparently been destroyed by a lack of blood flow, a tiny stroke, which left the rest of the brain unaffected. These areas of the brain are not found in dogs, but only in primates, who see things in color. These areas are where we correlate sensory information to construct colors, to imagine colors, and to dream in colors.

QUESTION: Is it possible to stimulate these areas of the brain artificially?

SACKS: Yes, perhaps so. With normal people magnetic stimulation may generate small explosions of color—colored rings and halo effects.

QUESTION: If it is possible to stimulate these areas of the brain, it must also be possible to block them.

SACKS: In theory, yes. One would then be exactly in Mr. I.'s situation.

QUESTION: Would you take the risk?

SACKS: I'm impulsive, and I'll try almost anything. But this procedure is quite experimental, and there may be unknown side effects—perhaps irreversible; no one knows. I would like to experience what goes on inside Mr. I.'s mind—for half an hour or a day. But not forever.

QUESTION: Mr. I. did not just experience the failure of certain kinds of perception; rather his illness amounted to the total collapse of his way of imagining the world.

SACKS: Quite so. And such a breakdown in perception can show us a great deal about how our brains construct experience. A colleague of mine in Munich has written about a woman who had a stroke and lost all ability to perceive motion or even to imagine it.

QUESTION: We heard of this case. When the woman pours coffee, the stream of liquid looks frozen to her. When she goes to parties, she sees people who suddenly disappear in one place abruptly appear again in another.

SACKS: Yes, this woman is truly unique. The brain area affected in her case is immediately adjacent to the area responsible for perceiving color—V-4 takes care of color, V-5 of motion. Both cases of disturbed vision remind me of something Christopher Isherwood said in his *Berlin Diaries* from the thirties: "I am a camera, with an open lens, I only record, I only register, I do not think." This statement is wrong; the whole point is that human vision is not something passive. On the contrary, perception is an active process: Everything—color as well as motion—has to be assembled in our heads.

QUESTION: In this connection, Goethe [the great German eighteenth-century poet and scholar] speaks of "the productive human genius, who creates a whole world from within."

SACKS: When working on his theory of color, Goethe was particularly interested in questions of perception. In my own book, one of the recurrent themes is the specific ways we not only generate a world of color, but create our own social, moral, and intellectual universe.

QUESTION: In your chapter dealing with Mr. I., you mention that color vision is not acquired by learning or experience but is inborn.

SACKS: The ability to recognize people and objects and to see them in their context in the world around us is developed through experience. But it is entirely possible that the ability to perceive color and motion is already "hard-wired," as neurologists would say, into the nervous systems of primates.

QUESTION: This assumption is confirmed by the story of the blind Virgil, another patient whose illness you describe.

SACKS: Virgil was blind from early childhood and had practically no visual experience until he was fifty years old, when an operation enabled him to see. But when the doctors removed his bandage and expected him to recognize a face, he saw only blurred colors and motions, without shape and without meaning.

QUESTION: He was unable to orient himself in the visual world?

SACKS: The perception of color and motion alone is not enough. We need shape and contours, recognition of things previously known, and putting things in context. Virgil couldn't translate his sense of what a glass feels like when touched into what a glass looks like. The visual areas of his brain had not been activated by experience and therefore had not developed.

QUESTION: Do you believe that Virgil's brain is roughly comparable to that of a baby?

SACKS: In a way, yes. But unlike a baby, he had already constructed his own complete picture of the world–through other senses like the senses of touch and hearing, which he had developed to a high degree. Whereas a baby greedily absorbs all new impressions, his operation left him with the problem of having to construct the world anew.

QUESTION: In your book you explain how human beings interconnect all received visual signals with other systems–even with our system of values.

SACKS: Both individuals and whole cultures show clear connections between colors, cultural assumptions, and values. Take for example the drastic change in the paintings of the seventeenth century. Suddenly painters showed nature in gloomy brownish hues. Had people developed a different way of seeing or a different way of interpreting what they saw? Earlier we talked about the brain areas V-4 and V-5, but we know that the brain has at least fifty vision centers–incredible, and all of these fifty areas are engaged in constant mutual exchanges. At the same time, parallel with this, an exchange with all the other centers of perception is taking place, as well as with the language center and the deep-rooted orientations that can be called values.

QUESTION: Scientists have proclaimed the 1990s the "decade of the brain." Biochemical, physiological, and anatomical aspects of the brain are being explored. Do you think this research will yield an even approximately complete picture of how human beings perceive their environment, how they feel and think?

SACKS: I think it is perfectly all right–indeed essential–to try to discover more and more details concerning special mechanisms and networks in the brain. But beyond that we need overarching concepts to pull these details together.

All of our subjective inner world is inherently private. Even if we were able to describe the processes of perception, recognition, contextualization, memory, language, and thinking, we would nevertheless find it impossible to enter into the personal inner world of another. We cannot explore this the same way we do the physical and therefore generally accessible world. Thus the color red, no matter how much we may have asserted concerning it, in the end remains a mystery, perhaps for all time.

QUESTION: Nevertheless you perhaps more than anyone else are always groping for a way closer to the mystery.

SACKS: I listen to people, take in their stories, look at their pictures–and try to study at the same time their neurological makeup. I think it is both the intriguing and the tantalizing part of neurology that we are always face to face with both of these dimensions. We know that these two worlds are intimately linked, but we cannot easily jump from one to the other.

QUESTION: Reading your book makes us think that you are especially fascinated by how several of your patients come to terms with their illness, however tormenting, and make it part of their lives.

SACKS: I have seen patients with all sorts of devastating conditions–strokes, heart attacks, head injuries–the life they know suddenly comes to an end. But often a new kind of life begins.

QUESTION: The color blind Mr. I., for instance, started to paint again, at first only in grey tones, but later he added a few colors, even though unable to perceive them himself. Besides, he changed his life; he became a night person. He claimed that at night he could see better and farther than others.

SACKS: What he had at first experienced as a disaster did indeed become transformed in a strange way. He developed what he called a "privileged way of seeing." He felt he was seeing more acutely, with a sharpened sense of structure, shadow, motion, and depth. Perhaps areas of his brain used normally for perceiving color, instead of atrophying, have been re-allocated for other purposes. The human organism tends to be adaptable and to construct the richest possible world with what perceptions remain available. For a long time people did not consider it possible that areas of the brain used for hearing, for instance, could be redirected for other purposes. But then we observed how people who are born deaf develop more acute vision. In the meantime we have found more and more examples of this plasticity of the nervous system–a flexibility, by the way, that can also turn negative. For example: If you tie two fingers of a monkey together with a rubber band and then remove the rubber band again the next day, the monkey's brain will have temporarily lost the ability to guide the two fingers independently of each other.

QUESTION: In connection with the adaptability of the brain, with the development of new patterns of life, you have even spoken of the "creative potential" of illness.

SACKS: I have had totally color blind people say to me: "Don't think of me as a sick person worthy of pity; I live in a rich, interesting visual world." Similarly, congenitally deaf people object to being treated as disabled; they prefer to think of themselves as a linguistic minority. Another disturbance that I consider in the same light is Tourette's syndrome, an illness that causes tics and compulsive repetitive motions, but also sudden brainstorms, jokes, inspirations, and weird ideas. A friend of mine—he is an artist in Toronto—has very severe Tourette's syndrome. It is startling to observe him—for instance, he leaps about the streets like a dog but yet with the intelligence of a highly gifted human being; he touches everything, sniffs everything, explores the world almost compulsively, you cannot help being astounded. But he refuses any kind of treatment for this, because he is afraid it could detract from his heightened powers of perception, his rich emotional range, and his imagination. On the other hand, he is fully aware of the hazards posed by his illness. He is capable of suddenly putting his foot in front of a car that is just beginning to move. Up to now he always pulled back his foot just in time. But he is leading his life at the knife's edge.

QUESTION: What do you take to be your role with such a patient? Do you consider yourself more of an observer, or do you want to help?

SACKS: I wouldn't have become a doctor if I weren't motivated by the desire to help people or at least offer assistance. But most neurological illnesses are irreversible. If I were looking for much satisfaction as a healer, I should have become a cardiologist. I am also strongly motivated by curiosity and the desire to understand connections.

QUESTION: You have on occasion criticized high-tech medicine, which relies heavily on pills and injections. Do you believe in restraint in this respect?

SACKS: That depends. When necessary, I intervene as promptly and decisively as any other physician. One time when an epileptic had swallowed a chicken bone during a seizure and already looked totally blue in the face, I did not inquire about his history as a patient. I at once cut open his esophagus. Otherwise he would have been dead within twenty seconds.

On the other hand, I knew a patient, for instance, who had migraine headaches every Sunday. I gave him pills. At first he was glad; he was doing well. But the next Sunday he was bored. He didn't know what to do with himself, because he had always devoted his Sundays to his migraine attacks. The Sunday after that he had a serious asthma attack and almost died of it. Then he said: "I want my migraine back." I said: "Don't be stupid; I'll give you something for your asthma." He said: "No, I'll then just be hit by something else." And he added: "Do you believe it possible that I simply need to be sick on Sundays?"

That was the first time—this was thirty years ago—that a patient told me in so many words: "Don't just look at my illness, take my life into account, of which you perhaps know nothing."

QUESTION: How do you reconcile your role as physician with that of the scientist?

SACKS: That's a rather complex matter. I think we are talking about a kind of double vision. Sometimes the two ways of seeing complement each other; at other times they are in conflict. At times I have to rein in my scientific curiosity to make sure the patient is not hurt.

QUESTION: In addition, you play a third role, that of the writer. In this capacity also you try to explore what you have called the inner world of the patient.

SACKS: Ever since I was very young I have always dragged along a pile of pencils, paper, and notebooks. When I was a child they called me "Inky." My perhaps compulsive but at the same time also natural need to put experiences into words is probably first of all an attempt to understand things and to clarify them in my own mind.

QUESTION: Can you explain the enormous interest in your case histories? Your books are bestsellers. One of them, *Awakenings*, was made into a movie. Another one, *The Man Who Mistook His Wife for a Hat*, was adapted for opera and stage.

SACKS: Part of it is evidently that people are tremendously interested in anything that has to do with the brain and the mind. But another major factor is that we are here concerned with the stories of other human beings. It is human nature to want to observe actual living persons—to use what moves us emotionally to help us understand an illness.

QUESTION: Your new book is called *An Anthropologist on Mars*. . . .

SACKS: I don't know if I like the title.

QUESTION: Do you feel occasionally like an anthropologist—doing comparative studies in the bizarre world of people with brain injuries?

SACKS: Yes, and I plan by the way to explore this aspect further in future work. For instance, I have encountered people with Tourette's syndrome in many places in the world, in Japan and rural America among others, and every time in a very different social context. This I want to trace. And last summer I visited a Pacific island where a large part of the population is totally color blind from birth. The normal ratio is one in 50,000; on this island it's one in fourteen.

QUESTION: So there is almost a kind of culture of the color blind?

SACKS: Perhaps. I visited the island with Bob Wasserman, a friend who is an oph-thalmologist, and Knut Nordby, a colleague from Norway, who is color blind himself. For Knut, it was terribly exciting to meet so many "brothers" and "sisters." This was the first time he had seen an entire community who shared his own rare mode of perception, his visual world, and it was very moving for all of us to witness this.

QUESTIONER: Dr. Sacks, we thank you for this conversation.

The Responsive Reader

1. Readers have been fascinated by Sacks' case histories and what they teach about the workings of the human brain. What do you learn from his case study of the color blind painter about the human brain, about perception, and about color? What for you is particularly striking, instructive, or new?

2. What do you learn from the case of the woman whose observation of motion was impaired? What do you learn from the case of the blind patient who learned to see at age fifty? What do you learn from Sacks' account of Tourette's syndrome?

3. Where does Sacks touch on the tremendous complexity of the brain, needed to coordinate and synthesize the full range of perception and consciousness?

4. Where in this interview does Sacks seem to emphasize the positive or compensating factors in the conditions of the people he describes? For you, does he blur the distinction between illness and health? (Why are deaf people a test case for our conventional categories of normalcy as against illness or disability?)

5. Sacks talks about two dimensions of his work as a neurologist–and the inability to cross over or jump from one to the other. What are the two dimensions? What is the barrier between the two?

For Discussion or Writing

6. Where or how does Sacks show that he is sensitive to human feeling as well as capable of objective scientific observation? Where does he seem to be in tune with current trends toward looking at the whole person, not only at a limited physical condition? Does he think that the emotional or human and the objective scientific parts of his work can come into conflict?

Collaborative Projects

7. Working with a group, investigate progress being made toward localizing brain functions. What is the current status of research into charting different areas of the human brain and assigning them specific responsibilities for perception, emotions, or language? (What is the current thinking on hemisphericity–allocating different functions to the two hemispheres of the brain?)

EMERGING SECRETS
Clues to Pre–Human Evolution

Carl Zimmer

—————

> *A century and a half after Darwin and his scientific colleagues argued over the mechanism of evolution, fossil hunters were still digging up tantalizing new evidence for the history of life on this planet. Students of human evolution were assembling bone and jaw fragments of creatures representing intermediate stages between tree-dwelling primates and erect bipedal tool-using almost-humans. In the following article abridged from* Discover *magazine, Carl Zimmer reports on the work of fossil hunters who look for clues to how and when now extinct life forms left the water to live on land. How could water-dwelling animals survive in a totally new environment? Were they "preadapted" in crucial ways for locomotion on land and for breathing the gases of the earth's atmosphere? The fossil record points toward fishlike creatures already breathing through lungs instead of gills and using four limbs to paddle, to walk on the bottom of wetlands, or to support themselves while waiting motionless for prey. This article focuses on the work of British paleontologists, or students of fossil remains, who stress the "waywardness of evolution." They call attention to the strange byways or lucky coincidences on the road toward what humans consider the culmination and "manifest destiny" of the evolutionary process—"the Long March toward Man."*

When you consider the years paleontologists often spend in daily and intimate   1
contact with their fossils, it's not very surprising that they come to regard their long-gone animals as pets.

Some work on the show dogs of the animal world. They brag about how fast their velociraptor ran or how efficiently their saber-toothed tiger could sever a spinal cord.

But when you listen to Jenny Clack talk about a fossil creature named Acanthostega that she has been working on for seven years, she sounds like the owner of a sweet, homely mongrel.

"It wasn't very smart," she said. "It probably spent a lot of its time sitting at the bottom of lagoons, hidden in the muck, waiting for something to come by it could eat."

Acanthostega mixes the anatomy of a newt with the charm of a mutt. But in   5
terms of evolutionary significance Acanthostega can easily go nose to nose with any of its fossilized companions.

Like velociraptors, sabertooths and humans, Acanthostega is a tetrapod—that is, each has four limbs, along with fingers and toes, hips and shoulders.

But at 360 million years old it has a special distinction: Aside from creatures suggested by a few older fossil fragments, it is the most primitive tetrapod known.

That means that Clack's sweet, unprepossessing pet holds answers to the great mystery of how our ancestors changed from fish and hauled their bodies out of the water.

Scientists don't have the hard evidence to illustrate every step in the evolutionary process, but they're still looking. Last week, for example, they hailed the discovery of 4–million–year–old bones as the earliest indication that humans' primitive predecessors walked upright. Acanthostega goes back eons earlier to another critical phase in the process.

Clack, who works at the University of Cambridge's Museum of Zoology, dis-   10
covered the bulk of Acanthostega's skeleton in 1987 and has been carefully reconstructing it ever since with fellow paleontologist Michael Coates.

They are just finishing up their monographs on the creature, and some of the conclusions they've drawn from its body are surprising other paleontologists.

For a long time it was assumed that our limbs and feet, which work so well for walking on land, evolved for that exact purpose. But Acanthostega has convinced Clack and Coates otherwise.

Tetrapod anatomy evolved while our ancestors lived exclusively underwater– and it evolved for life underwater.

The first vertebrate that walked onto land didn't crawl on fish fins. It had evolved well-turned legs millions of years beforehand.

SURPRISE STUDY

Before she found Acanthostega, Clack had studied early tetrapods for 10 years,   15
but she never expected to have the privilege of studying their actual origin.

"It's not something you build your career on," she said.

You may hear some paleontologists bemoan the rarity of dinosaurs, but compared with the first tetrapods, they're as common as gravel.

For most of this century, in fact, only one primitive specimen was known in any detail: a bulky, dog-size beast from Greenland named Ichthyostega.

Ichthyostega means "fish plate" because the roof of its skull was shaped like that of a fish.

LITTLE TO GO ON

The fossil record is silent about the 20 million years immediately following   20
Ichthyostega. All we know is that tetrapods branched off into two groups. One began coating its eggs with a hard shell; these became the reptiles, which eventually gave rise to dinosaurs, birds and mammals, such as us.

The other group, which continued to lay its unshelled eggs in water, is the amphibians.

Clack immersed herself in the enigma of how these early tetrapod branches took shape.

How had the ancestors of these animals emerged from the water? What allowed them to leave their cushioned aquatic cradle and enter a world of air and gravity?

Clack's husband thoroughly understood her fixation. Rob Clack, though a computer programmer by trade, is at heart a fossil hunter.

Rob and Jenny also share a passion for motorcycles, and so they often spent their vacations in Scotland collecting fossils. They half hoped to find an early tetrapod. They found only fish.

By the mid-1900s, the couple could hear Greenland calling, loudly. Greenland's mountains were formed near the end of the Devonian Period, which stretched from 408 million to 360 million years ago.

There are Devonian rocks around the world—including places such as Scotland, Pennsylvania, New York, Australia and Russia. The rocks have many fossils locked inside them, but most are hidden under forests and fields.

The Clacks believed that the naked mountains of Greenland, where eroded rocks simply pile into undisturbed heaps, were the best place to find primitive tetrapods.

The trip to Greenland proved to be momentous. Before the group returned home, Jenny, Rob and paleontologist Coates had discovered a treasure of Acanthostega fossils.

The first clue that they had found a truly remarkable creature came in 1989 when Acanthostega's arm was revealed. In all other tetrapods, the two bones of the forearm—the radius and ulna—are about the same size.

In Acanthostega, however, the radius was about a third longer than the ulna—a kind of proportion found in lobe-finned fish and a hint that Acanthostega was the most primitive tetrapod yet found.

Clack and Coates also recognized that with the radius bearing most of the animal's weight, the arm was poorly designed for support.

Worse, the bone was spatula-shaped: thick at the elbow but flat at the wrist. If tetrapods had evolved their limbs for walking on land, how could Acanthostega have had such weak arms?

A bigger surprise, however, was when Coates discovered that despite feeble wrists, Acanthostega bore fully evolved tetrapod fingers—eight of them.

These eight fingers were sophisticated and multijointed, yet since they were attached to an insubstantial wrist, they were virtually useless for helping Acanthostega walk on land.

How do you explain a land animal's body in an animal that couldn't survive on land?

One possibility is that the animal had once come onto the land but, like some amphibians, had subsequently returned to a life underwater, where its skeleton had gradually weakened.

That scenario seemed unlikely, though, when Clack and Coates found Acanthostega's gills.

Tetrapods simply aren't supposed to have a fish's gills.

All the amphibians that returned permanently to the water developed external   40
gills, feathery tissue that extends out from the body.

But Acanthostega had a full battery of gill struts in its neck. It even had a sheet of bone along its shoulders that supported the rear wall of an internal gill chamber.

The strong implication was that the animal still possessed an internal gill system. In other words, Acanthostega breathed like a fish.

It heard like a fish, too—or at least like a lobe-finned fish.

Our aquatic ancestors had extremely crude ears, consisting of a gill support bone that had changed into a plug in the skull.

"It wasn't invented for hearing," Clack explains. "It appears to be a supportive   45
structure, connecting different bits of the skull."

But when underwater sounds hit that bony plug in their skulls, it also turned out to be able to gently vibrate, and nerve endings could detect the vibration.

As their tetrapod descendants later explored the land, the skull plug became the stapes (the "stirrup") of the middle ear, and other gill supports turned into the other bones that help the stapes amplify airborne sound.

Acanthostega, however, had none of these intricate bones. It had only the plug.

Coates also discovered that on land, Acanthostega's ribs would probably have been too thin and small to hold up its guts. In addition, its spine was loose and soft.

It did, however, have rear legs and toes. It even had hips, which its fish ances-   50
tors didn't have.

Tetrapod hips, as a rule, are held firmly to the spine by ligaments and a group of fused ribs called the sacrum.

With hips only loosely attached to its spine, Acanthostega would probably have flopped about helplessly on dry land.

The more Clack and Coates uncovered of Acanthostega, the more they became convinced that not only was this an animal that lived underwater but also an animal whose ancestors had never left the water.

THE TAIL'S CONCLUSION

By the time they got to the tail, the case was decided. Acanthostega had a powerful, flexible tail with large fins running along the top and bottom of it.

Each vertebra in the tail tapered into a long upper and lower crest, each of   55
which connected to a rod-shaped bone. The crests and rods could bend like a finger.

Connecting to the rod, inside each fin, were rays made of dermal bone, the material that forms the scales of fish.

Together the crest, the rod and the ray (and the muscles attached to them all) allowed Acanthostega to use its tail to create underwater waves that could propel it forward or brake its momentum.

Useful as such a tail might have been in water, it was worthless on land. It may even have been dangerous–the bottom fin would have scraped along the ground and become prone to infection.

Hence it's not surprising that amphibians lost their fins once they began spending time on land.

And once they lost the complex architecture of their tail, they never re-claimed it. 60

The most elegant explanation for such a tail was the same as that for Acanthostega's gills, ears, hips and limbs: Its ancestors had never left the water.

Determining just what finally pushed or pulled tetrapods onto the land, and when, will take some time.

The Responsive Reader

1. Why is the fact that Acanthostega is a "tetrapod" a key issue in this essay? What key features–bone structure, behavior–did this 360-million-year-old aquatic creature apparently already share with today's humans? In what ways was it still like a fish?

2. This article works with familiar assumptions about how fish, dinosaurs, birds, mammals, and newts fit into our evolutionary family tree. What are these assumptions? How would you explain them to an outsider?

3. Goal-oriented humans tend to work toward a definite purpose. How does this article keep making the point that evolution did not work that way? Does the article convince you? (Why do details like shape and relative length of upper arm and forearm matter to the paleontologists? Why does the sense of hearing become a case in point?)

For Discussion or Writing

4. How much has an evolutionary perspective influenced your own thinking? For instance, do you tend to judge animals like chimpanzees or gorillas by how close they come to the human model or by how they fall short? (How close *do* they come? How *do* they fall short?)

5. What difference does it make whether the emergence of human beings was the purpose of evolution? Does speaking of the "randomness" of the evolutionary process make sense to you? Why or why not?

Collaborative Projects

6. Is the treatment of evolution in biology textbooks a dead issue? Or does the controversy over evolution versus creationism still affect textbook selection in your area or state? Working with a group, what can you find out from such sources as biology teachers, school officials, or publishers' representatives?

MICROORGANISMS
Invisible Empire

Lynn Margulis

━━━━━━

Lynn Margulis is a biologist and distinguished professor of biology at the University of Massachusetts at Amherst. She is the co-author, with Dorion Sagan, of What Is Life *(1995). She published the following review in* The Sciences, *a journal of the New York Academy of Sciences. The focus of the book she reviews is on bacteria—microorganisms that more than three billion years ago "began colonizing the earth shortly after meteoritic impacts stopped churning the planetary crust into sterilizing rock vapor." The study of microbes, invisible to the naked eye, is a prime example of how science forces you to go beyond common sense and the unaided testimony of your senses. Microbiology opened a new front in humanity's fight against disease, it put major historical events in a new light, and it has provided "a resource bin of future biotechnology engineering tricks." Margulis from the beginning takes major scientific concepts for granted (although she also carefully redefines some key terms). Photogenesis is the process that allows plants to use the energy carried by sunlight to extract carbon—a basic building block of life—from the carbon dioxide of the air. Symbiosis is the close intertwining of two different organisms dependent on each other for mutual benefit.*

POWER UNSEEN: How Microbes Rule the World
by Bernard Dixon

People are symbiotic beings, amalgams of interliving, collaborating life-forms. [1] Their mitochondria—the oxygen-using parts of their cells—come from free-living oxygen-respiring bacteria that exist in the cells of all plants, animals, fungi and even most protoctists: the algae, ciliates, amoebas, slime molds and other, lesser-known aquatic and tissue-dwelling organisms. The chloroplasts of plant cells, which are the green parts that carry out photosynthesis, are descended from cyanobacteria—the former blue-green algae—and their kin. The structure of the so-called eukaryotic cells (namely, the cells with nuclei), mitochondria and, in the case of plants, chloroplasts, testifies to their origin from consortiums of interliving bacteria. The symbiotic microbial origin of our own cells, as well as the cells of all plants and animals, is by now more than conjecture.

The microorganisms that have shaped our bodies have also shaped the world. In his new book, *Power Unseen: How Microbes Rule the World*, the science writer Bernard Dixon has assembled a powerful chronicle of the myriad repercussions of microbial activities. Of all the forms of life on earth, microorganisms are the oldest, the most numerous and the most widespread on the planet. Nevertheless, because they are invisible to the unaided eye, their impact has been as unsuspected as it is profound. When microorganisms were discovered, they were considered an amusing oddity, a kind of sideshow taking place only in the amateur naturalist's parlor. Not until the nineteenth century, with the discoveries of the German naturalist Christian Gottfried Ehrenberg, was it shown that the littler forms of life pervade every corner of the earth's crust.

The investigations of Louis Pasteur into rabies, ropy wine and yeast ferment endowed microorganisms with their formal identity as agents of infectious disease. But because of his findings, Pasteur demonized microorganisms as "the others," enemies to be destroyed. With help from the German bacteriologist Heinrich Hermann Robert Koch, he shaped the public perception of the inhabitants of the microscopic world. No longer were microorganisms amusing curiosities; now they were the attention-demanding targets of medicine men, the epitome of the enemy agent.

As the control of microbial growth became better understood, the role–especially of bacteria and yeast in food–became better appreciated. Dixon's anecdotes and the way he has structured his book reflect such historical attitudes toward "good" and "bad" microorganisms. But although Dixon does an admirable job showing the far-reaching effects of microorganisms, he fails to distinguish between the extraordinarily different forms of microbial life. He lumps the cyanobacteria with other bacteria, as well as algae, fungi and even nonliving entities such as viruses. He even declines, on the ground of not wanting to drive away the popular audience for which the book is intended, to give properly italicized names of genera and species (and, on page *xvii*, he mistakes *Salmonella* for *Saccharomyces*). Such practices only exacerbate the confusion of any exploration of microorganisms. But as a critic, I forgive him, mostly because the various short-story lines are so much fun; his vignettes of microbial lives are unique, compelling and enjoyable to read.

Dixon begins by subtly deconstructing the common understanding of microorganisms as pathogens and showing the impact, especially of bacteria, on history and civilization. Take crude oil, which clearly plays a part in nearly every aspect of planetary culture. In fact, of course, oil is a sine qua non of the modern industrial state. And where does crude oil come from? From microorganisms. The original microbial makers of oil are thought to have been algae, living off the energy of the sun and the carbon dioxide of the air. They were descended from cyanobacteria, which in turn evolved shortly after the origin of life, some three and a half billion years ago.   5

The cyanobacteria, though incidental to history and civilization, transformed the planet. Their evolutionary contribution was the development of a new metabolic pathway, which extracted hydrogen from water for photosynthesis. The oxygen left over from the water molecule was released into the atmosphere as a waste gas. That early atmosphere is known to have been poor in oxygen. Without the ancient cyanobacteria our planet would still have little or no reactive free oxygen in its atmosphere, and carbon dioxide would dominate instead, as it does in the atmospheres of Mars and Venus.

As the blue-green bacteria pulled carbon dioxide from the atmosphere, they incorporated hydrogen–carbon compounds into their bodies. The result was breathable air and the deposition of energy-rich hydrocarbon sediments. One of the key pieces of evidence in the scientific reconstruction of the story of crude oil is the bacterium *Botryococcus braunii*, identified as the source of a green scum on the surfaces of ponds in the Coorong region of South Australia. The scum coalesces to form a black elastic substance called Coorongite, which shows yellow when scratched. Furthermore, when heated, Coorongite yields hydrocarbons of the kind that make up crude oil; it is now recognized as a peat stage in the formation of oil shale. Perhaps as more is learned, it will be possible one day to grow oil-producing microorganisms in fermentation vats, transforming oil into a bona fide renewable resource.

At every turn Dixon extends the familiar medical viewpoint on microorganisms to encompass their social and historical effects. He links Pasteur's experiments with rabies, for instance, to questions about medical ethics, to the serendipitous discovery of the green mold *Penicillium notatum* and its ability to prevent bacterial growth, to the subsequent launch of the antibiotic revolution. He ties *Clostridium acetobutylicum*, a bacterium that plays a key role in the cheap synthesis of acetone (used in the production of explosives), to the establishment of Israel as the Jewish homeland. (The discoverer of the process, the chemist Chaim A. Weizmann, lobbied for the creation of Israel.)

Dixon also taps in to a predisease vision of the microworld, portraying bacteria as the pure, strange and intriguing oddities they are. *Serratia marcescens* leaves a bright-red pigment on bread that has been mistaken for blood, thereby providing living proof for transubstantiation and the miracle of Easter. *Proteus OX19* is a non-pathogenic microorganism that nonetheless produces antibodies to typhus. During the Second World War a number of Polish villages escaped the Nazis because some clever physicians injected *P. OX19* into the Jewish inhabitants. Their blood samples showed the antibodies to typhus, and the germ-frightened Gestapo doctors believed there was an epidemic and stayed away.

Each of Dixon's chapters is a short essay, only two or three pages long, a pleasurable, parsimonious form that lightly evokes the atmosphere of intrigue, surprise and adventure in the work of ferreting out the secrets of the exotic little beings. Nitrifying bacteria lead a double life, turning nitrogen in the atmosphere into a form usable by organic life, but also corroding and, in some cases, destroying stone and cement buildings. *Haloarcula* is a salt-loving bacterium that, despite all odds, takes the form of a square. The discoloration in antiquarian books, known as foxing, is the effect of a fungus that grows threadlike spores.

10

Dixon does not neglect the best-known cases of microbial impacts, namely, the bubonic plague and the ensuing Renaissance. The black death, caused by the bacterium *Yersinia pestis*, kills 50 percent of its victims within the first week of symptoms. The disease threw fourteenth-century Europe into a paranoiac turmoil and exacerbated religious and political fanaticism, as Christian believers sought causes of divine anger commensurate with the plague's harrowing vengeance. By 1351, four years after its outbreak, *Y. pestis* had wiped out more than twenty-five million Europeans—a third of the population.

In its wake, ironically, the plague left a boomtown prosperity, a wealth not only of goods but also of thought, called the Renaissance. By whittling down European populations, *Y. pestis* decreased competition for food, shelter and work, leaving the survivors to inherit the riches of the deceased. The sociocultural impact of the disease is virtually impossible to overestimate.

But occasionally Dixon's estimates of the effect of microbial activity on civilization are simplistic. For example, he traces the makings of the Kennedy presidency to *Phytophthora infestans*, the potato-famine fungus that reduced Ireland's population of eight million to five million and sent many Irish looking for better pastures in the United States or Australia. Although the immigration of the Kennedy and Fitzgerald families to the U.S. was microbially mediated, that does not make it microbially caused: many other necessary factors were at work as well. One could say (as Dixon does not) that were it not for the vitamin-producing microbiota in Rose Kennedy's gut, John F. Kennedy would not have been able to face his "sternest test against the might of the Soviet Union." My point is not to gainsay the effect of the potato pathogen on major demographic movements of the twentieth century. What is more important is to appreciate the great multiplicity and complexity of microbial interactions at work all over, all the time.

Microorganisms have played a decisive role in military campaigns. "Not the ingenuity of any of his military opponents," writes Dixon, but *Rickettsia prowazekii*, the bacterium that causes typhus fever, "broke Napoleon's power in Europe." Dixon's point is intriguing, since it is usually assumed that human beings—the master species of the planet—stand at the top of the chain of nutritional and intelligent command. In striking contrast to that bloated self-image, Dixon reminds us that the smallest beings can bring down the greatest. The microscopic life-forms ensure that life on earth and in the water never becomes a hierarchy, but remains, in the useful term of the writer Arthur Koestler, a "holarchy": a network of life-forms, each with smaller beings inside it, and larger beings outside. . . .

Dixon does keep one foot firmly planted in the traditional perspective of   15
microorganisms as agents of disease. Perhaps, strategically, that is the easiest way to inform the general public of the nonpathological role of microorganisms on earth. Keeping one foot at home allows Dixon to test the waters gingerly with the other

foot. *Power Unseen* highlights many agents of disease and even touches down on microorganisms that spoil food, cause cat-scratch disease or even lead to AIDS.

That negative, anthropocentric view of microbial life is easy to focus on. After all, all forms of life survive by paying preferential attention to threats, recognizable dangers and repeating hazards. More maturity and a broader perspective are needed to describe the smooth workings of microbial agents that go about their beneficial business when nothing is wrong. The physicist Stephen W. Hawking of the University of Cambridge has mentioned the nightmare fantasy of the ultimate disease–an airborne version of the AIDS virus that sweeps through the human population like a hot knife through butter. Such pathological possibilities are worth pondering, but it also bears remembering that life–a phenomenon three-plus billion years old–is hardly fragile in the aggregate. Killer microorganisms that destroy all they touch ultimately meet their own undoing as their hosts quickly vanish.

Successful life-forms, in fact, live together. Disease is pathological, not only in the usual, obvious sense, but also in the sense that it represents a failure of symbiosis. Life is a joint venture, a physical connection between distinct species or life-forms. Life-forms may dwell within each other's bodies or cell membranes, yet they ultimately reproduce as one. This limited review cannot explore implications of symbiogenesis. I must be content here merely to emphasize the idea as a fact of life, to be learned along with other, more prosaic notions to which every schoolchild is exposed (yet few understand): life on earth–from the bacterial consortiums that break down oil and recycle sewage, to the cells of all nonbacterial organisms such as plants and animals–is interdependent. That single lesson must resonate if humanity is to achieve any semblance of planetary maturity.

The Responsive Reader

1. Microorganisms, as Margulis says in her introduction, were once considered an "amusing oddity." From the beginning, what large claims does she make concerning the role of microorganisms in our world and in the history of human life?

2. Microorganisms first received major public attention as "pathogens," or agents of infectious disease. What do you learn in Margulis's early paragraphs about the role of microbiology in the fight against disease? (What did you already know?)

3. Where or how does Margulis first shift attention from "bad" to "good" microorganisms? What, for instance, do you learn about the biochemical processes involved in the making of crude oil?

4. Margulis frequently alludes to matters presumably familiar to readers attuned to a scientific outlook. Do these references make you feel like an insider or an outsider? For instance, what was "serendipitous" about the discovery of penicillin?

What examples does she give of the scientific explanation of miracles? What light does she shed on the corrosion of architectural monuments of the past?

5. Margulis credits the book she is reviewing with not neglecting major instances of the role of microbes in human history. For instance, what do you learn about the religious dimension, the politics, and the social and economic repercussions of the fourteenth-century "black death" or bubonic plague? Why does she have reservations about her subject's account of the role of the potato-famine fungus in Irish and Irish American history? How, according to Margulis, might a biologist rewrite the history of the French Emperor Napoleon's disastrous 1807 military campaign in Russia?

6. How does Margulis at the end return to the larger perspective she wants you to adopt toward microscopic organisms? What is "anthropocentric" about the media image of bacteria as carriers of disease?

For Discussion or Writing

7. Where in your own study or reading have you encountered scientific knowledge that seems to defy common sense or commonsense observation?

8. Are we too prone to judge other life forms in terms of how they benefit or harm human life?

Collaborative Project

9. What have been the successes and reversals in the fight against a major infectious disease, such as polio, cholera, tuberculosis, or AIDS? Working with a group, help plan an investigation and farm out assignments to members of the group.

CANCER'S BAD SEEDS

Shannon Brownlee

▬▬▬▬▬▬▬

> *From the beginnings of modern science, the curiosity to understand natural causes and the urge to make them work for the benefit of humankind have gone hand in hand. Science held out the promise of freeing humanity from its ancient scourges—to liberate human beings from back-breaking toil, to stave off famine, and to control the epidemics that had maimed and decimated humans since time immemorial. Once science understood the role of filth in the spread of disease, better sanitation and cleaner drinking water could stamp out cholera and typhus. The great bacteriologists (Robert Koch, Rudolf Virchow, Louis Pasteur) were at first ridiculed and ostracized when they traced infectious diseases to microscopic organisms; they eventually developed vaccines against tuberculosis (the white plague) and dread childhood diseases like diphtheria. Today, ongoing research confronts the great unmet challenges like cancer and AIDS. Shannon Brownlee has a master's degree in marine biology and was trained as a science writer at the University of California at Santa Cruz. She worked for* Discover *magazine,* Sports Illustrated, *and* U.S. News & World Report, *where she became a senior editor. She wrote the following article about ground-breaking cancer research by two Harvard researchers that was to win them a Nobel prize. Her work won her a science fellowship at Stanford University and the General Motors Cancer Research Award for 1990.*

Two years ago, doctors caring for an 18-month-old girl faced a difficult deci- 1
sion. The toddler was in the early stages of neuroblastoma, a rare childhood cancer of nerve cells, and had undergone surgery to remove her tumor, a procedure that cures the disease at this stage in 90 percent of cases. But a new, highly experimental test developed by Robert Seeger of Children's Hospital of Los Angeles and Garrett Brodeur of Washington University in St. Louis revealed something worrisome—multiple copies of a mutated gene in the girl's tumor cells. Despite successful surgery and what would normally be an excellent prognosis, the researchers recommended more radical, and painful, treatment.

The patient underwent chemotherapy, whole-body radiation and a bone-marrow transplant. In her marrow, Seeger found tiny new tumors, evidence that their unorthodox treatment had been correct. Alive and well today, the girl probably would have died without it.

Seeger and Brodeur based their decision on a snippet of DNA that, just a short time ago, would have had no predictive value. But in the past decade, cancer research has shifted dramatically to focus on the genes that underlie the cellular abnormalities of cancer. The disfigured fragment of DNA that alerted the researchers is just one of the many tumor-causing genes whose role in cancer is now understood. Called oncogenes, from the Greek *onkos*, for mass, these genes come in two forms. When whole and healthy, they govern the orderly growth and reproduction of cells. But when mutated–perhaps by carcinogens in cigarette smoke or a chance mishap during cell division–oncogenes wreak terrible mischief, creating proteins that cause cells to proliferate out of control.

So important are oncogenes to the understanding of human cancer that this year's Nobel Prize in medicine was awarded to J. Michael Bishop and Harold Varmus, researchers at the University of California in San Francisco, for making the first solid connection between cancer and these genes 14 years ago. Since then, more than 50 oncogenes have been extracted from a variety of animals, and it is now believed that oncogenes must work in teams to transform cells.

Researchers have just begun the painstaking experiments necessary to trace the   5
biochemical pathways leading from mutated genes to tumors, but already they are sounding atypically sanguine: "Cancer is no longer a mysterious, fully inexplicable process," says Robert Weinberg, a molecular biologist at the Whitehead Institute for Biomedical Research in Cambridge, Mass. "We are in the process of understanding almost all of it in the next decade, and when I say understanding, I mean understanding its causal forces." Indeed, researchers have not only learned to use oncogenes to make prognoses in four types of cancer, they have also worked out for the first time the structure of the protein made by an oncogene and, just this year, have found a drug that may block the protein's action.

GENETIC CORRUPTION

Oncogenes lead double lives, serving crucial roles in normal cell activity until they turn deadly–a phenomenon that scientists have been observing since Bishop and Varmus first plucked an oncogene from chicken cells in 1975. They discovered that a section of genetic material that made a virus capable of causing tumors in chickens was almost identical to a scrap of DNA belonging to a chicken's healthy cells, confirming a controversial theory that cancer-causing genes were mutated versions of perfectly normal ones. They subsequently found similar lengths of DNA in a zoo full of species, from fish to fowl to people, and concluded that in its uncorrupted form, this oncogene must be vital to the workings of cells.

The implication of this discovery was enormous, for it meant that we carry the seeds of cancer in our own genetic code. Indeed, researchers soon realized that the oncogenes do not actually need a virus to incite cancer. Like a thief who uses his victim's own gun, the virus simply pilfered a section of DNA from a cell, mangling it in the process and rendering it deadly. But the genes, they discovered, could also be mangled within the cell.

Not until 1982 did these findings appear to have any significance to human cancer, however. That year, Weinberg's lab isolated the cancer-causing gene from human-bladder cancer and showed it was the same as an oncogene teased from a rat-tumor virus. This hank of DNA, known as *ras*, would turn out to be a kingpin oncogene, one that would be found in half a dozen types of human tumor.

Most oncogenes are only bit players in the tragedy of human cancer. But a select handful are found again and again in a variety of human tumors, and researchers surmised early on that in their intact form, these key segments of genetic material must play central roles in regulating cell growth and division. Conversely, they reasoned, an oncogene in its perverted form sends cells multiplying out of control. But they did not know why.

As it happens, it takes surprisingly little to pervert some genes. *Ras*, for example, differs from its healthy cousin by a single change in its sequence of base pairs, the molecules forming the "letters" of the DNA code. A healthy *ras* gene makes a protein involved in signaling the cell to multiply by cell division–during rapid fetal growth, for instance. When enough new cells have been made, division stops. But the mutated *ras* protein screams at the cell like some Biblical command to be fruitful and multiply. The obedient progeny become a tumor.

Fortunately, it takes more than one type of oncogene to propel a cell down the path to malignancy, and the emerging view of cancer is of a chorus of oncogenes working in concert. Researchers have evidence that at least two oncogenes, and often as many as five or six, are mutated in tumors. Advanced colon cancers, for example, generally have at least five mutated oncogenes, or "hits," and almost invariably *ras* is among them.

It now appears that recessive oncogenes–genes that can do damage only when both copies have been mutated–are also necessary for cancer's ravages. The first of these recessive oncogenes, also known as tumor suppressor genes, was cloned by Weinberg's lab and Dr. Thaddeus Dryja in 1986. It is responsible for a rare and grisly childhood cancer called retinoblastoma, which produces glittering tumors on the retina and afflicts about 1 in 20,000 children a year. Eventually, the child is blinded or even killed if the eye is not removed.

Unlike most oncogenes, the one that causes retinoblastoma, called *rb*, causes cancer not by triggering uncontrollable cell division, but by failing to turn it off. A child inherits two copies of the *rb* gene, one from each parent. A healthy *rb* gene keeps cell growth in check, and when only one copy of *rb* is bad, the good copy can still maintain sovereignty over cells of the retina. But when both copies are defective or missing, tumors grow without restraint. Scientists have fished *rb* from a number of other human cancers, including colon, breast and lung cancer, which together account for two thirds of cancer deaths.

Despite the rapid progress in the field, identifying oncogenes is only the first step in preventing or curing cancer. Researchers are now launching experiments to probe the intricate biochemical reactions that cause cells to proliferate in the early stages of cancer. It appears that the loss of good copies of *rb*, or any of the six additional recessive oncogenes discovered thus far, leaves a cell with fewer of the proteins that restrict growth, thus clearing the way for oncogenes like *ras* to goad the cell into dividing madly. And recessive oncogenes, says John Minna, of the National Cancer Institute in Bethesda, Md., are turning out to be at least as important as the oncogenes that promote cell growth.

In cancer's final stages, other oncogenes may be responsible for the disease's   15 spreading. Individual cells break away from the primary tumor, floating through the blood and lymph fluid to alight in other parts of the body and sprout new tumors. To do so, the cells must penetrate other tissues, a diabolical capacity that William Hayward of Sloan-Kettering Institute for Cancer Research in New York speculates is made possible by an oncogene. Such findings will ultimately lead to more effective treatments. Just this year, researchers at the University of California at Berkeley reported that a drug developed to combat cholesterol can interfere with the mutated *ras* protein in a lab.

KEYS TO PROGNOSIS

Even before new treatments are found, doctors will use oncogenes to help predict which patients need additional treatment after surgery. Based on an analysis of more than 800 neuroblastoma tumors, Seeger believes that multiple copies of the oncogene *n-myc* are probably the best sign of a patient's prognosis. Similarly, Minna has found that lung-cancer patients with the worst outcome have multiple copies–as many as 50 per tumor cell–of *c-myc*, an oncogene in the same family, and earlier this year researchers reported that other oncogenes can accurately predict the course of breast and colon cancer.

Many questions remain concerning how genes are mutated in the first place, but increasingly researchers believe that both heredity and carcinogens are to blame. Radiation, chemicals, even sunlight can damage genes, and people are born with varying degrees of susceptibility to carcinogens' corrupting influence.

Now, evidence is mounting that people inherit defective oncogenes. Working alone in cells, one or even two inherited defective oncogenes are insufficient to trigger cancer. But if carcinogens mutate other genes in a cell, the inherited and environmentally damaged genes together can unleash cancer. A new test identifies fetuses at risk from *rb*, and other tests will identify those people who are most susceptible to other types of cancer, a prospect that raises both ethical questions–the use of genetic prognosticators by insurance companies, for instance–and the opportunity to halt tumors before they appear. As Nobel laureate Bishop has said, we now know that the seeds of our own destruction lie in our genes. So, too, will the seeds of our salvation as we learn more about the genetics of the disease.

The Responsive Reader

1. To understand Brownlee's opening story, what does the reader have to know about the spread of cancer cells, mutated genes, chemotherapy, radiation, bone-marrow transplants, or DNA? How "science literate" does the reader have to be?

2. Why does Brownlee consider the work on oncogenes a dramatic shift in cancer research? What are oncogenes? How do they work? What is their normal beneficial role, and how do they turn deadly? What does Brownlee mean when she says "we carry the seeds of cancer in our own genetic code"?

3. Cancer research is a time-consuming and far-flung undertaking because it does not deal with simple identifiable causes. How does this article show that researchers here deal with complex processes, which interact in complicated patterns and work in very different ways?

For Discussion or Writing

4. How does this article challenge or confirm what you know about the causes of cancer? Does the article hold out hope for progress toward prevention or cure?

Making Connections

5. Both Margulis and Brownlee talk about the double-faced nature–both potentially benign and deadly–of parts of our biological makeup. Can you trace the parallel?

MARIE CURIE: A LIFE by Susan Quinn

Lisbet Koerner

_____

I have been frequently questioned, especially by women, how I could reconcile family life with a scientific career.

MARIE CURIE

In the following book review, a professor of the history of science at Harvard University revisits a family question: What is the role of individual genius in scientific discovery? The Italian astronomer Galileo Galilei and the British physicist-mathematician Isaac Newton were enshrined as patron saints of modern science. Charles Darwin is associated in the public mind with the theory of evolution. Albert Einstein became the prototype of the eccentric intellectual genius. Jonas Salk, the discoverer of the vaccine against polio, became a modern folk hero. Marie Curie, subject of the biography reviewed in the following article, is linked in the popular imagination to the discovery of radioactivity that pointed forward to the atomic age.

As against our human need for myth-making and hero worship, historians of science remind us of the plodding everyday routine of science. Thomas S. Kuhn, in his Structure of Scientific Revolutions, *contrasted the patient everyday collection of data, the construction and replication of experiments that constitute "normal science," with the revolutionary breakthroughs—described by one reader as the "vertiginous intellectual upheavals through which knowledge lurches genuinely forward" (James Gleick). The great pioneers were not alone. Thomas Edison, who became an American folk hero as an inspired tinkerer, "rode a flood" of interest and speculation about the possible applications of newly discovered electricity. Many others were also tinkering with the myriad applications of electrical current, including the telegraph, electric power generators, or the telephone.*

In the case of Marie Curie, our questions about the role of the outstanding individual have a special added dimension: Why have science and mathematics been so long male domains? What kind of a role model does Curie provide for future women scientists? What obstacles stand in a woman scientist's path?

On May 20, 1921, President Harding welcomed to the White House "a noble creature, a devoted wife and loving mother who, aside from her crushing toil, has fulfilled all the duties of womanhood." He then hung around the neck of his visitor, the Polish-born chemist Marie Sklodowska Curie (1867–1934), a small gold key symbolizing a hugely expensive gift from her American female admirers: one gram of radium, the radioactive element that Marie Curie, together with her husband, had first discovered and isolated. By 1921 the 54-year-old woman had already become what she remains today: the world's most famous woman scientist.

Curie was the first woman to receive a Nobel Prize in science. In 1903 she won the prize in physics, with Pierre Curie and Henri Becquerel, for their discovery of radioactivity and two new radioactive elements, radium and polonium. And she remains the only woman to have received two Nobel Prizes; her second she received alone, in 1911 and in chemistry, for her continued work on radium and polonium. She trained her daughter Irène Curie so successfully that she, too, received a Nobel Prize, in 1935 and in physics, with her husband Frédéric Joliot-Curie, for experimentally producing artificial radioactivity. After her husband's accidental death in 1906, Marie Curie inherited his position. Thus, at the age of 39, mother of a 9-year-old and a 2-year-old, she became the first woman professor at the University of Sorbonne. She received many prestigious awards, scholarships and grants, and was elected to a host of learned societies, even if the French Academy of Science blackballed her and Harvard held out in its refusal to grant her an honorary degree, suspecting that her husband alone was responsible for their work.

Curie's scientific achievement remains important, if not theoretically earth-shattering. In 1895 the German scientist W. C. Röntgen generated (in effect by bombarding fluorescent spots in his glass tubes with streams of electrons) a mysterious "x-ray." It penetrated even flesh and blood to mark on a photographic plate the bones of his wife's hand. In 1896 alone, x-rays (which we now know to be electromagnetic waves roughly 1,000 times shorter than visible light) were the subject of 1,044 scientific papers and forty-nine books. In that same year a French scientist, Henri Becquerel, discovered that the element uranium had an hitherto unknown property: it spontaneously emitted yet another and unknown type of ray. By 1898 Pierre and his brother had devised an instrument, the pizo-electric quartz electrometer, that could be used to measure quantitatively the degree of this radiation.

With this tool, Marie Curie, who had given birth to her first daughter the year before, set out to search for new sources of radioactivity. Investigating two uranium compounds, pitchblende and chalcite, she deduced correctly that unknown and more potent radioactive elements inhabited these compounds. She then decided to purify these compounds, naming the residual elements "radium" and "polonium." Laboriously, and using as her solvents hydrochloric acids, sulphuric acids, and bisodium carbonates, she leached, washed, boiled and evaporated slurries of pitchblende. Having eventually reduced her original tonne of material into a few micrograms, she produced a near-pure radium chloride. By 1902 she was able to determine, within one half of one percent, the atomic weight of radium.

But what was the nature of radium's odd property of radiation? According to   5
the law of conservation of energy, the newly discovered radioactive elements must have absorbed energy in order to now emit these rays. But where had that energy come from? Was it a phosphorescence, a past exposure to an energy source? Or was it—as the Curies believed at least until 1903—a fluorescence, an ongoing exposure to an energy source? And if so, what was that energy source? We now know

that naturally occurring radioactivity was, apart from the heat of the earth's core, the first nonsolar form of energy discovered on earth. And in a weird sense, it *is* a phosphorescence of sorts: some 20 billion years ago, in the Big Bang, the energy now emitted as particulate and electromagnetic radiation once had indeed been stored within the atoms of these elements, but in the form of mass.

Around 1900, however, the Big Bang was unknown. Einstein had not yet related energy to mass. Not all physicists agreed even that the existence of the atom was securely proven. And some scientists who were atomists still understood the atom to be indivisible, which is what its name actually means. But then, in 1897, J. J. Thompson demonstrated the physical existence of the electron, and even calculated its mass. And beginning in 1898, Ernest Rutherford, establishing firmly the existence of the atom and–most importantly–some of its constituent parts, could show that radioactivity divided into alpha rays (helium atoms each missing two electrons), beta rays (high-speed electrons) and gamma rays (penetrating electromagnetic waves). Together with Frederick Soddy, Rutherford also showed that these rays were emitted as a by-product from the atomic nucleus (the existence of which he famously demonstrated in 1911), as radioactive elements degenerated into increasingly more stable species of atoms. It was now possible to draw up decay tables for radioactive isotopes, and it was Rutherford and his collaborators who established that radium is a daughter of the uranium-238 alpha disintegration series.

The key theoretical achievements in the new science of radioactivity thus belonged to Rutherford and his group, but Marie Curie's genius for the quantification of data (such as degrees of radiation and atomic weight of elements) played a significant role. And yet her contributions to pure physics do not explain her immense fame. In 1921 this scientist was greeted at New York Harbor by three orchestras and many thousands of people. And, typically for the period, she was frequently "immortalized" in verse. At a select gathering in her honor at the Paris Opéra–graced even by the presence of the President of the Republic–Sarah Bernhardt recited an emotional "Ode to Mme. Curie," likening her to "the sister of Prometheus." Marie Curie herself later "regret[ted] a little that I threw away the [fan] letters. . . . There were sonnets and poems on radium." And radium in turn was pitched, not least by Curie herself, as a miracle drug.

During World War I, she organized for ambulatory x-ray machines to tour trench hospitals. She also trained her teenage daughter in x-ray diagnostics. And she took great pride in "curietheraphy," as radiation treatment was called in France. And in this respect the popular imagination meshed her science and her gender. Radium was billed as a discovery peculiarly appropriate to a woman, engendered by what her daughter characterized as "a marvelous feminine curiosity." *The New York Times*, in its 1921 celebration of the "motherly looking scientist," even had a front-page header promise that "MME. CURIE PLANS TO END ALL CANCERS." And at a reception in her honor at the Waldorf Astoria that same year, the keynote speaker noted that Marie Curie was "not welcome here as a scientist, but as a woman who has done more to comfort human beings than any one who has made important discoveries in this generation." For radium was understood especially as a cure for women's cancers, such as malignant tumors of the cervix, uterus and breast. The gram of radium that a group of American women, most of them graduates of the Seven Sisters, donated to Curie in 1921 was thus primarily intended for the treatment of gynecological carcinomas.

But even as Curie proclaimed radioactivity a medical "magic bullet," her own fingers were hardening, reddening and stiffening, her eyes were clouding over with cataracts and–invisibly and slowly–her bone marrow was being destroyed. In 1934, at the age of 67, she died from radiation-induced pernicious anemia. The surprise is really that she lived as long as she did, and also that, after a late miscarriage in 1903, she could give birth to a healthy, normal child in 1905. Her husband was already invalided by radiation illness in 1906; her daughter Irène died from exposure-linked leukemia; and her son-in-law succumbed to liver failure related to radium toxicity. In the Curie laboratories, young assistants were regularly carried off in the advanced stages of fatal illness; some died within weeks, others lingered for years, pitiful cripples wracked by pain. Even today some of the Curies' laboratory notebooks, which are housed at the Bibliothèque Nationale in Paris, are so contaminated that the researcher must sign a waiver before examining them. In early self-experiments Marie and Pierre Curie had deliberately burned themselves with radium compounds, observing with interest such "lively effects" as grayish wounds, scaling skin and morbidly sensitive limbs. Yet even when, in her 50s, Marie Curie was turning blind and deaf, she would only admit that "perhaps radium has something to do with these troubles, but it cannot be affirmed with certainty."

In her day Curie was celebrated, then, as a woman scientist, or, more exactly, as a mother scientist. How she managed to be both a mother and a scientist, and how this dual achievement became the basis of a public cult, would be a promising theme for a biography. Unfortunately, it is not the focus of Susan Quinn's new life of Marie Curie. More traditionally, Quinn prefers to dissociate her subject from her surroundings. She structures her pleasant and slightly flat book more conventionally around an unmasking of Curie, for the purpose of exposing her subject's true, sexualized, Freudian self. The book becomes quite detailed when it describes Curie's affair in 1910 with her husband's former student, the French physicist Paul Langevin. At the time, the affair was publicly condemned because of the injury to his wife. It would be equally a scandal today, of course, but as a form of sexual harassment; the injured party would now be Langevin himself, recast as a younger and less institutionally secure colleague.

Quinn's book does not offer new or thought-provoking perspectives on Curie's life, let alone the wider history of women and science. The first important life of Marie Curie was written by her daughter Eve Curie in 1937, and other lives have since appeared. Like earlier biographies of Curie–the last two in English were published in 1986 and 1989–this most recent one does not greatly pretend to theoretical ingenuity or scholarly feats. Still, Quinn's biography is interesting to read. It allows us to reflect on that central question of Curie's life: How was it, in President Harding's words, that the "zeal, ambition and answering purpose of a lofty career could not bar you from splendidly doing all the plain but worthy tasks which fall to every woman's lot"? And this is not only a question about the past. Curie was not only a scientific pioneer, she was also a social pioneer.

The story of Marie Curie's life should matter to all men and women in two-career families, who watch with dazed amazement the leisure of their childless friends and are left with an intimation of mortality. These dour and sleep-deprived parents are moralists who come to believe that the pastimes of leisure are vanities, and that they have been miraculously given, in the small persons of their children, a grace so profound that they could never, in the earlier and easier lives, have imagined it. And yet they also yearn for what Marie Curie called a "lofty career." They are intrigued by the ability of a woman to combine a career with her "plain but worthy tasks." As she herself characterized this central dilemma: "It is my whole life that is at stake."

Marie Curie, in short, was what we would call a working parent. For the non-scientists among us, it is perhaps the most fascinating aspect of her life. Of course, she was not typical. She was brilliant, and she came from a family at once politically alienated and socially esteemed, and married into another such family, and so she and her kin were apt to examine critically the conventions of her day–such as the notion that women are best left unschooled. Still, reading her biography we can recognize her predicament. Indeed, like all working parents Curie obviously benefited from what we might name, in her honor, the Curie Compensation Correlation: as the hours available for research shrink, with the advent of children, the efficient output per hour of work grows.

She herself stemmed from impoverished and passionately patriotic Polish gentry. Born Marie Sklodowska in 1867 in Warsaw, she was brought up by her father, himself a teacher, to consider education a crucial mark of civilization (compared always to the barbarism of the Russians occupying her country) and her only means of support. To put an older sister through medical school she worked for five years as a governess, and her Brontë-esque first romance ended as her landlord-employers forbade their son to marry her. Her husband's family, the Curies, doctors and scientists all, belonged to the Alsatian Protestant bourgeoisie. Marie's husband, like her father-in-law, passionately identified with the communards of 1848, and later they were committed Dreyfusards. These were progressive families, profoundly committed to the education of women.

Pierre Curie never helped Marie raise their children or run the house, but in all other ways he supported her career. He scrupulously gave her credit for her scientific achievements, even warning the Nobel committee that he would accept the prize only if it was also awarded to his wife. And the couple successfully negotiated   15 with the University of Geneva and the Sorbonne for joint positions; you might say that they invented the "two-body problem" that now characterizes many hiring decisions in American academe. Marie Curie married a man who was, at least as she interpreted it, positively American in outlook. For, as she noted on her first American tour in 1921, on this blessed new continent she could discern no opposition "between feministic aspirations and masculine opposition." And she added, with the wonder typical of some Old World women, that in the United States men even "approve of these aspirations and encourage them."

The Responsive Reader

1. Drawing on the biographical data Koerner provides at the beginning and again at the end of her review, what would you include in a brief account of Marie Curie's background and the highlights and obstacles in her professional career?

2. How does Koerner place Curie in the context of the ferment of scientific research and experiment at the time? What was the state of scientific knowledge in Curie's field? Who were major players in the study of radioactivity, and what were their contributions?

3. What is Koerner's estimate of Curie's scientific achievement? What specifically was her role? What expectations helped explain her national and international fame?

4. How did Curie as well as her family and staff become martyrs to the cause of scientific progress?

5. Modern biographers tend to be schooled in the art of the exposé, looking for the human flaws or damaging secrets behind the imposing public persona. To judge from this review, did the biography being reviewed here conform to this pattern?

6. From this review, what do you learn about Marie Curie and her husband as pioneers in such areas as the career-building mother and the two-salary family?

For Discussion or Writing

7. From what you know about her, do you admire Marie Curie? Would you present her as a role model to young women or to young people generally? Why or why not?

8. Will science and medicine cease to be male-dominated? What has been your own observation of the changing role of women in science and medicine?

Collaborative Projects

9. Working with a group, study research efforts—like those aimed at finding an AIDS vaccine—that demonstrate the role of collaboration, of teamwork in scientific progress.

QUANTUM TECHNOLOGY AND COMMON SENSE

Sidney Perkowitz

Have advances in physics reached a point where educated lay persons can no longer grasp fundamental scientific concepts? When physicists first taught the structure of the atom, students were asked to visualize the atom as a miniature solar system. Like a miniature sun, the nucleus was at the center, with one or more electrons in orbit around it like miniature planets. However, modern quantum physics has drastically revised our thinking about subatomic particles whose location can be charted and that are in continuous motion. Quantum is a Latin word meaning a measure, or unit, of something. At the subatomic level, physicists use it to label the infinitely small spurts or bursts of energy that occur when energy is transferred or transmitted and that force us to abandon the idea of a continuous flow. Sidney Perkowitz is Charles Howard Candler professor of condensed matter physics at Emory University in Atlanta. His writing about science ranges from a monograph for specialists, Optical Characterization of Semiconductors, *to a book celebrating the mystery of light for general audiences,* Empire of Light *(1995). He says that the "microscopic quantum universe is full of strange and wondrous things, waiting to be explained."*

Look around the room in which you are reading this magazine. You and all   1
that surrounds you–your chair, the ink on this page, the air you breathe–are made up of atoms. And every atom–every particle out of which atoms are made–is, in turn, subject to the laws of quantum physics, mysterious rules that describe a physical reality radically different from the expectations of everyday common sense. Here is a world in which solid matter undulates. Particles ooze out of leakproof containers. Light ejects bullets of pure electricity out of hard matter as the color of the light turns from red to blue.

Intuitive judgment fails in the quantum world, because people have almost no direct experience with quanta. To catch a hard-hit ball to center field, a ballplayer relies on the fact that the ball acts in a way physicists call classical: it obeys the laws of motion Newton set forth 300 years ago. But examine your surroundings more closely, and you will find human-made systems that display decidedly nonclassical effects. Within the circle of your sight or your reach, it is not unlikely that there is a piece of electronic equipment. Whether the equipment is a commonplace digital watch or a complicated stereo system, inside it are artificial devices made from semiconducting materials. Such devices manipulate electrons and photons, the units of electricity and light, for desired ends. In contrast with the classical simplicity of the larger, macroscopic world, the physical laws that dominate those minute devices are quantum laws, and their performance is controlled and enhanced by the manipulation of the quantum world.

Earlier generations of electronic devices, such as vacuum tubes for radios and the cathode-ray picture tubes still ubiquitous in television and computer-monitor screens, can be understood without quantum theory. But the functioning of more recently developed devices depends on quantum effects in the semiconducting materials out of which the devices are made. The chips made of silicon at the heart of your computer or in the fuel-emissions controller of your car, and the silent, minuscule laser made of gallium aluminum arsenide that sends your voice through fiber-optic telephone lines, all rely on quantum effects for their operation. And new designs that take advantage of exotic quantum phenomena could make the next generation of devices even smaller, faster and more efficient. Such designs make sense because it is now feasible to fabricate systems so small that only the quantum effects are important. What are those new designs? Which of the many weird quantum effects are most likely to be useful? How can their application be expected to change our lives? There is much buzz in the air these days about nanotechnology—a technology that operates in the atomic dimensions characterized by the nanometer, a billionth of a meter. But a better term for the field might be quantum technology: a new discipline of design and engineering that can take full advantage of the strange world of the quantum.

The laws that govern the quantum universe can only be called mandates for ambiguity. Early inklings of that ambiguity came as the nineteenth century ended, when evidence mounted that the century-old model of light as an undulating wave could not explain its interaction with matter. The German physicist Max Planck first proposed that energy comes in steps, or quanta, rather than as a smooth flow. Building on Planck's work, Einstein proposed in 1905 that light is also a quantum of energy, a particle later given the name photon. That startling concept established the need to regard light—and indeed, all electromagnetic radiation—as sometimes a wave and sometimes a particle.

By a reciprocal logic, the duality of particle and wave was extended not long 5 thereafter from the description of radiation to a description of matter. In 1923 the French physicist Louis-Victor de Broglie derived a deceptively simple equation, eerily implying that every bit of matter is something more than solid, localized reality. Bits of matter also undulate: they are waves. De Broglie's equation involves momentum, which is a classical property of matter (namely, the product of a particle's mass and velocity), and wavelength, an intrinsic property of waves (the distance between two adjacent wave crests). Given a particle with a certain momentum, the equation shows how to determine the particle's wavelength. In so doing, the equation forges a baffling link between particles and waves that still haunts the quantum physics of matter.

The wave aspect of matter leads to the quantum properties applied in devices. It is the reason electrons mutually interfere, like so many water waves; it is responsible for the indeterminacy of the microscopic world that violates any sense of a clockwork universe; and it is the basis for the quantization of energy in solids. Paradoxically, for all that, it is the quantum fuzziness of matter that can so dramatically improve device performance.

The most powerful evidence for de Broglie's matter waves is the interference of electrons, first observed in 1927. Interference is the merging of two or more waves at the same time and place, and it highlights a profound difference between particles and waves. The effect of multiple particles converging in time and space is always greater than the effect of one particle. Two tennis balls hitting a racket deflect it more than one ball does; two cannon balls are better than one for battering down a castle wall. But the effect of multiple waves is much more complex, because it can be either stronger or weaker than a single wave.

Imagine waves being generated in a pool of water by a single source–say, a block of wood on a spring–then separated into two distinct channels. The moving peaks and valleys in each channel start in phase–that is, the crests and troughs of each wave train move along each channel in unison. Suppose the channels finally spill back into another pool where the waves reunite. If the channels are the same length, the crests and troughs of the wave trains are still in perfect step when the waves rejoin. The net effect is that crest adds to crest and trough adds to trough, doubling the height of each wave; the outcome is called constructive interference.

But suppose one channel is longer than the other by half a wavelength. Then when the waves recombine, the crest of one just matches the trough of the other, and the two waves cancel out–an effect known as destructive interference. Particles can never destroy each other in that way, and so the phenomenon clearly distinguishes waves from particles. Only recently has it become possible to control constructive and destructive interference in ordinary matter well enough to exploit it in devices.

The wave nature of matter is also responsible for the uncertainty principle of Werner Heisenberg. The name of the principle is its message: certain physical data are simply unknowable. For example, it is not possible to find both the position and the momentum of a particle simultaneously. In fact, the more known about one, the less known about the other. The circumstance has a certain ironic power, not unlike the tale of the "appointment in Samarra": a man's strenuous efforts to flee Death bring him to the very spot where Death finds him. Similarly, according to the uncertainty principle, the harder one tries to outwit the intrinsic elusiveness of physical reality, the more surely one will have to confront it face to face.   10

Everyday activities, of course, are not plagued by the uncertainty principle. A ballplayer instantaneously judges both the momentum and the position of a ball to make an elegant catch. No one–Ghostbusters and neutrino physicists excepted–is familiar with objects that pass through walls. But the only real reason such odd behavior is not more common is quantitative, not qualitative: the uncertainties defined by Heisenberg's principle are, by everyday standards, infinitesimal. Compared with the momentum and dimensions of any macroscopic object, from pea to pachyderm, the uncertainties are far too small to measure. But in the subatomic world they loom so large that they strongly affect electrons.

Perhaps the most important implication of matter waves for device physics is the quantization of energy. In the simplest atom, hydrogen, a single electron orbits a central proton. The crests and troughs of the orbiting electron's de Broglie wave can be imagined as waves generated on a circular loop of string. If such a loop were plucked and made to vibrate, the only wavelengths that could exist would be the ones that fitted exactly, an integral number of times, into the circumference of the loop. Other wavelengths would simply die out immediately after they were born, because the peaks and valleys of the waves would cancel one another.

Similarly, only a certain de Broglie wavelength is permitted for each electron orbit, depending on the size of the orbit. Since, in de Broglie's equation, wavelength determines momentum, and because momentum determines energy, each orbit is associated with a specific energy. The quantization of energy, in which each orbit is associated with a particular energy level, is the heart of the quantum-mechanical description of the hydrogen atom or, indeed, the atom of any other element.

The magnetic properties of electrons are quantized as well. Picture the electron, as one does in classical physics, as a minute sphere of charge. If the sphere spins on its axis, the moving charge constitutes an electric current. Flowing current makes magnetism, and so a spinning electron acts like a minuscule bar magnet whose north and south poles are oriented along its axis of spin. Any such magnet can be affected by any other magnet.

That classical picture was tested in 1925: a stream of electrons was passed   15
through a magnetic field, then their impact was detected on a screen. The electrons were magnetically deflected from their paths, but in a surprising manner. Instead of a continuous range of deviations, as one would expect from a randomly oriented swarm of spinning electrons, each electron was deflected in only one of two ways: a specific distance up from its initial line of travel, or the same distance down. In other words, the electrons acted as if their spin was quantized; their spin axis seemed to point either up or down, and never at any other angle with respect to the magnetic field.

Quantum effects rule the nanoworld. An understanding of strange quantum devices begins, however, with the classical view of electrons in a conducting medium—say, a copper wire. The atoms in the wire assemble themselves into a regular, three-dimensional array, each accompanied by a family of electrons. What makes copper a good electrical conductor is that some of the electrons in each atom are free to roam within the atomic structure.

Imagine yourself compressed by a factor of 100 billion (a shrinkage that would reduce the earth to a dot smaller than the period at the end of this sentence), and look about at the roaming electrons. Perch on a copper atom and peer in all directions at a nanoworld of static architecture combined with frenzied action. The architecture is framed by the massive copper atoms, each with a diameter of many feet relative to your imagined size. Their symmetrical arrangement, extending to the horizon, contrasts with the great random swarm of much smaller free electrons. Moving at high speed, the electrons carom off the atoms like so many billiard balls or the molecules of a gas. Classical theory explains what happens to such an electron gas if the wire that contains it is connected across a battery. The negative pole of the battery repels electrons, while its positive pole attracts them, thereby adding an ordered though surprisingly slow net velocity to the random electronic motion. The result is a flow of charge, an electric current.

To extend classical understanding into the quantum world, perch again on your copper atom, this time gazing at the electronic world through eyes informed by quantum theory. Now you see a complex atomic structure filled with undulating matter waves rather than ricocheting electrons. It is as if a long-sunken city of graceful classical arcades, Atlantis, if it ever was, were buffeted by subsurface storms that agitated the water filling its drowned plazas and marketplaces. Examine the great profusion of electronic waves for a time, and you see a subtle pattern. Just as in the quantized electronic orbits of individual atoms, certain wavelengths never appear, because the regularity of the atomic lattice imposes geometric conditions on the waves. The ones that do not exactly fit the atomic architecture undergo destructive interference and soon die out.

According to de Broglie's equation, the missing electronic wavelengths correspond to missing values of momentum, which implies that certain energies never appear. The significance of the missing energies can be appreciated if one takes another look at the quantum nature of a single atom. Each of its electrons occupies a specific orbit with a definite energy; the farther the electronic orbit is from the atomic nucleus, the higher the energy of the electron. Electrons ascend and descend among the orbital energy levels as if they were rungs on a ladder. If an electron in a low-lying inner orbit gains energy, it jumps to a higher empty orbit, leaving behind an empty track.

The same quantum idea of high- and low-energy levels, separated by a forbidden energy gap, applies to a semiconductor. But whereas each energy rung in the atom accommodates only two electrons, the energy levels in the semiconductor include all the vast number of electrons that reside in a solid of macroscopic size. The electrons below the gap occupy states of relatively low energy collectively known as the valence band. Those electrons are tightly bound to the atoms in the semiconductor and cannot contribute to the flow of electric current. Electrons above the gap reside in high-energy states called the conduction band, and those electrons are relatively mobile. Just as electrons in an atom jump from rung to

20

rung, energetic electrons in a semiconductor can leap from valence to conduction band.

The structure of band and gap defines the use of semiconductors in devices. An electron promoted from valence band to conduction band leaves behind a space, unpoetically but aptly called a hole. The hole makes room in which the remaining valence electrons can move–much like the empty space in the common children's puzzle in which fifteen tiles are to be shifted around within a square frame that has room for exactly sixteen tiles. The space left by the omitted tile is what makes motion possible, and the hole in the valence band enables the electrons that remain in that band to join in the flow of current. Since missing negative charge is the same as added positive charge, the holes act like mobile positive charges.

Semiconductors such as pure silicon can be "doped" with impurities chosen to add either extra electrons in the conduction band or holes in the valence band. When the electrons dominate, the material is called an *n*-type (for negative) semiconductor; when the holes dominate, the material is *p*-type (for positive). When the two types are butted together to make a *p-n* junction, the result is a useful device called a diode, a one-way street that resists the flow of electrons in one direction but not the other. That property can, for instance, change alternating current, the kind that comes from wall outlets, into unidirectional direct current.

A diode has two elements. More important still are arrangements of semiconductors in which the number of elements is three. The combination of three adjacent regions in the sequence *n-p-n*–like the wafers and the filling of an Oreo cookie–is one of the earliest forms of transistor, whose invention, in 1948, launched the electronic age. Its value is that a small voltage applied to the *p*-type region controls a large flow of electrons between the two *n*-type regions; in the terminology of electronics, a transistor is a three-terminal device in which the voltage applied to the gate modulates a large current between source and drain. Hence electronic information coming in to the gate at low power, such as the complex waveform of an audio or video signal, is amplified into a stronger but otherwise identical pattern in time. Transistors have thus become the basis of stereo and television receivers.

Almost any piece of electronic equipment is now so complex that it requires thousands or millions of such basic amplifiers and switches. Those parts are made as small as possible and built into a single small chip of semiconductor, usually silicon. But the technology is reaching its limits. The largest commercially available computer memory chip now holds 16 million bits (megabits) of data. To reach a billion bits (one gigabit) per chip, devices must become much smaller. But with such dense packing, even a minute amount of power supplied to each device can generate more heat than the equipment can tolerate. Another factor limiting the performance of electronic equipment is the speed of electrons within a device, or from device to device. The direct application of quantum principles offers the designer a variety of ways to enhance those measures of performance. . . .

It is ironic that, despite their nearly hundred-year history, and despite their application in devices many of us virtually take for granted, quantum phenomena and their implications remain elusive. Even scientists with the keenest insight into the physical universe, the Einsteins and the Feynmans of this world, have confessed puzzlement at the paradoxes that seem to seep into every corner of the quantum world. Those who would build quantum devices today must forge ahead despite a lack of profound understanding about that world. Yet by building such devices, there is the hope and the promise of boot-strapping the basic understanding. Along with their impact on technology, the new devices can serve as miniature laboratories in which one might learn much more about the philosophical riddles that permeate the quantum universe.

It is ironic that, despite their nearly hundred-year history, and despite their application in devices many of us virtually take for granted, quantum phenomena and their implications remain elusive. Even scientists with the keenest insight into the physical universe, the Einsteins and the Feynmans of this world, have confessed puzzlement at the paradoxes that seem to seep into every corner of the quantum world. Those who would build quantum devices today must forge ahead despite a lack of profound understanding about that world. Yet by building such devices, there is the hope and the promise of boot-strapping the basic understanding. Along with their impact on technology, the new devices can serve as miniature laboratories in which one might learn much more about the philosophical riddles that permeate the quantum universe.

To experience some of the sense of mystery that quantum phenomena can engage, I found, in seeking inspiration for this article, that there is nothing quite like experiencing the phenomena firsthand. For a small sum you can buy an assortment of millimeter-size light-emitting diodes and a battery. Connect the battery to an LED and look at the bright dot of light that glows forth. From my own collection of LEDs I could choose crisp yellow, ruby red, vibrant green and soothing red-rose-orange. Now take note: in this small device, costing mere pennies, you are contemplating nothing less than the enigmatic process whereby the particle-waves of electrons become the wave-particles of photons. Your gaze, your thought, will probably not resolve the unanswered questions, but still there is something to be learned: that the microscopic quantum universe is full of strange and wondrous things, waiting to be explained.

The Responsive Reader

1. Why does quantum physics matter? According to Perkowitz, what are the areas of practical application for quantum physics or "nanotechnology"?

2. How would you explain to a beginning physics student basic concepts of "classical" physics that apply in the larger macroscopic world—for instance, mass, momentum, velocity, inertia, and the wave theory of light?

3. Can you show the difference between particles and waves? Why is it that particles reinforce each other while waves may cancel each other out?

4. Where or how does Perkowitz clarify for you basic assumptions and puzzles of quantum physics? Why is it inherently "ambiguous"? How does it affect your understanding of light? How does the "wave nature of matter" change basic assumptions about matter?

5. What was a classical physicist's understanding of an electrical current passing through a conductor like copper? How does quantum physics change the traditional picture? Can you explain to an outsider the workings of quantum physics in diodes and transistors?

For Discussion or Writing

6. Have you seen evidence of a black-box mentality—where we utilize highly sophisticated devices without trying to understand how they work? Do you think educated citizens need a basic understanding of quantum physics, or should it be left to specialists?

Collaborative Projects

7. How successful are current popularizers in keeping educated readers abreast of quantum physics? Working with a group, organize a symposium on basic concepts as illuminated in articles in science magazines for the general reader.

EINSTEIN'S DREAM

Stephen Hawking

―――――――

> *I wanted to explain how far I felt we had come in our understanding of the universe.*
>
> STEPHEN HAWKING

Modern science has tested the capacity of the human mind to grasp concepts that go way beyond the direct evidence of our senses. For contemporaries of the sixteenth-century and seventeenth-century astronomers, it required a wrenching readjustment and a stretching of the imagination to grasp the tenets of the new astronomy: The earth was not flat but a globe. Instead of standing still at the center of the world, it was spinning through space as one of several planets circling around the sun—which was but one of myriad other suns. Modern physics has similarly outstripped the capacity of most of us to grasp new concepts: new theories about matter and energy, about space/time, about the Big Bang at the origin of the universe.

Stephen Hawking is a legendary figure in the mythology of modern science. Widely considered a mathematical genius, he suffers from a progressive degenerative muscular disease. His speech became slurred; after an operation he for a time lost the power of speech altogether. Eventually a computerized speech synthesizer enabled him to lecture to and interact with large audiences. Hawking's A Brief History of Time (1993) remained on the New York Times bestseller list for fifty-three weeks and appeared in thirty-three translated editions. Hawking does not agree with those who consider the universe a mystery that we can never fully analyze or comprehend. "There is still a great deal we don't know or understand about the universe," but "we may not be forever doomed to grope in the dark." The universe is "governed by an order that we can perceive partially now and that we may understand fully in the not-too-distant future."

In the early years of the twentieth century, two new theories completely changed the way we think about space and time, and about reality itself. More than seventy-five years later, we are still working out their implications and trying to combine them in a unified theory that will describe everything in the universe. The two theories are the general theory of relativity and quantum mechanics. The general theory of relativity deals with space and time and how they are curved or warped on a large scale by the matter and energy in the universe. Quantum mechanics, on the other hand, deals with very small scales. Included in it is what is called the uncertainty principle, which states that one can never precisely measure the position and the velocity of a particle at the same time; the more accurately you

1

―――――――

*A lecture given at the Paradigm Session of the NTT Data Communications Systems Corporation in Tokyo in July 1991.

can measure one, the less accurately you can measure the other. There is always an element of uncertainty or chance, and this affects the behavior of matter on a small scale in a fundamental way. Einstein was almost singlehandedly responsible for general relativity, and he played an important part in the development of quantum mechanics. His feelings about the latter are summed up in the phrase "God does not play dice." But all the evidence indicates that God is an inveterate gambler and that He throws the dice on every possible occasion.

In this essay, I will try to convey the basic ideas behind these two theories, and why Einstein was so unhappy about quantum mechanics. I shall also describe some of the remarkable things that seem to happen when one tries to combine the two theories. These indicate that time itself had a beginning about fifteen billion years ago and that it may come to an end at some point in the future. Yet in another kind of time, the universe has no boundary. It is neither created nor destroyed. It just is.

I shall start with the theory of relativity. National laws hold only within one country, but the laws of physics are the same in Britain, the United States, and Japan. They are also the same on Mars and in the Andromeda galaxy. Not only that, the laws are the same at no matter what speed you are moving. The laws are the same on a bullet train or on a jet airplane as they are for someone standing in one place. In fact, of course, even someone who is stationary on the earth is moving at about 18.6 miles (30 kilometers) a second around the sun. The sun is also moving at several hundred kilometers a second around the galaxy, and so on. Yet all this motion makes no difference to the laws of physics; they are the same for all observers.

This independence of the speed of the system was first discovered by Galileo, who developed the laws of motion of objects like cannonballs or planets. However, a problem arose when people tried to extend this independence of the speed of the observer to the laws that govern the motion of light. It had been discovered in the eighteenth century that light does not travel instantaneously from source to observer; rather, it goes at a certain speed, about 186,000 miles (300,000 kilometers) a second. But what was this speed relative to? It seemed that there had to be some medium throughout space through which the light traveled. This medium was called the ether. The idea was that light waves traveled at a speed of 186,000 miles a second through the ether, which meant that an observer who was at rest relative to the ether would measure the speed of light to be about 186,000 miles a second, but an observer who was moving through the ether would measure a higher or lower speed. In particular, it was believed that the speed of light ought to change as the earth moves through the ether on its orbit around the sun. However, in 1887 a careful experiment carried out by Michelson and Morley showed that the speed of light was always the same. No matter what speed the observer was moving at, he would always measure the speed of light at 186,000 miles a second.

How can this be true? How can observers moving at different speeds all   5 measure light at the same speed? The answer is they can't, not if our normal ideas of space and time hold true. However, in a famous paper written in 1905, Einstein pointed out that such observers could all measure the same speed of light if they abandoned the idea of a universal time. Instead, they would each have their own individual time, as measured by a clock each carried with him. The times measured by these different clocks would agree almost exactly if they were moving slowly with respect to each other–but the times measured by different clocks would differ significantly if the clocks were moving at high speed. This effect has actually been observed by comparing a clock on the ground with one in a commercial airliner; the clock in the airliner runs slightly slow when compared to the stationary clock. However, for normal speeds of travel, the differences between the rates of clocks are very small. You would have to fly around the world four hundred million times to add one second to your life; but your life would be reduced by more than that by all those airline meals.

How does having their own individual time cause people traveling at different speeds to measure the same speed of light? The speed of a pulse of light is the distance it travels between two events, divided by the time interval between the events. (An event in this sense is something that takes place at a single point in space, at a specified point in time.) People moving at different speeds will not agree on the distance between two events. For example, if I measure a car traveling down the highway, I might think it had moved only one kilometer, but to someone on the sun, it would have moved about 1,800 kilometers, because the earth would have moved while the car was going down the road. Because people moving at different speeds measure different distances between events, they must also measure different intervals of time if they are to agree on the speed of light.

Einstein's original theory of relativity, which he proposed in the paper written in 1905, is what we now call the special theory of relativity. It describes how objects move through space and time. It shows that time is not a universal quantity which exists on its own, separate from space. Rather, future and past are just directions, like up and down, left and right, forward and back, in something called space-time. You can only go in the future direction in time, but you *can* go at a bit of an angle to it. That is why time can pass at different rates.

The special theory of relativity combined time with space, but space and time were still a fixed background in which events happened. You could choose to move on different paths through space-time, but nothing you could do would modify the background of space and time. However, all this was changed when Einstein formulated the general theory of relativity in 1915. He had the revolutionary idea that gravity was not just a force that operated in a fixed background of space-time. Instead, gravity was a *distortion* of space-time, caused by the mass and energy in it. Objects like cannonballs and planets try to move on a straight line through space-time, but because space-time is curved, warped, rather than flat, their paths appear to be bent. The earth is trying to move on a straight line through space–time, but the curvature of space–time produced by the mass of the sun causes it to go in a circle around the sun. Similarly, light tries to travel in a straight line, but the curvature of space–time near the sun causes the light from distant stars to be bent if it passes near the sun. Normally, one is not able to see stars in the sky that are in almost the same direction as the sun. During an eclipse, however, when most of the sun's light is blocked off by the moon, one can observe the light from those stars. Einstein produced his general theory of relativity during the First World War, when conditions were not suitable for scientific observations, but immediately after the war a British expedition observed the eclipse of 1919 and confirmed the predictions of general relativity: Space–time is not flat, but is curved by the matter and energy in it.

This was Einstein's greatest triumph. His discovery completely transformed the way we think about space and time. They were no longer a passive background in which events took place. No longer could we think of space and time as running on forever, unaffected by what happened in the universe. Instead, they were now dynamic quantities that influenced and were influenced by events that took place in them.

An important property of mass and energy is that they are always positive.   10
This is why gravity always attracts bodies toward each other. For example, the gravity of the earth attracts us to it even on opposite sides of the world. That is why people in Australia don't fall off the world. Similarly, the gravity of the sun keeps the planets in orbit around it and stops the earth from shooting off into the darkness of interstellar space. According to general relativity, the fact that mass is always positive means that space–time is curved back on itself, like the surface of the earth. If mass had been negative, space–time would have been curved the other way, like the surface of a saddle. This positive curvature of space–time, which reflects the fact that gravity is attractive, was seen as a great problem by Einstein. It was then widely believed that the universe was static, yet if space, and particularly time, were curved back on themselves, how could the universe continue forever in more or less the same state as it is at the present time?

Einstein's original equations of general relativity predicted that the universe was either expanding or contracting. Einstein therefore added a further term to the equations that relate the mass and energy in the universe to the curvature of space–time. This so-called cosmological term had a repulsive gravitational effect. It was thus possible to balance the attraction of the matter with the repulsion of the cosmological term. In other words, the negative curvature of space–time produced by the cosmological term could cancel the positive curvature of space–time produced by the mass and energy in the universe. In this way, one could obtain a model of the universe that continued forever in the same state. Had Einstein stuck to his original equations, without the cosmological term, he would have predicted that the universe was either expanding or contracting. As it was, no one thought the universe was changing with time until 1929, when Edwin Hubble discovered that distant galaxies are moving away from us. The universe is expanding. Einstein later called the cosmological term "the greatest mistake of my life."

But with or without the cosmological term, the fact that matter caused space-time to curve in on itself remained a problem, though it was not generally recognized as such. What it meant was that matter could curve a region in on itself so much that it would effectively cut itself off from the rest of the universe. The region would become what is called a black hole. Objects could fall into the black hole, but nothing could escape. To get out, they would need to travel faster than the speed of light, which is not allowed by the theory of relativity. Thus the matter inside the black hole would be trapped and would collapse to some unknown state of very high density.

Einstein was deeply disturbed by the implications of this collapse, and he refused to believe that it happened. But Robert Oppenheimer showed in 1939 that an old star of more than twice the mass of the sun would inevitably collapse when it had exhausted all its nuclear fuel. Then war intervened, Oppenheimer became involved in the atom bomb project, and he lost interest in gravitational collapse. Other scientists were more concerned with physics that could be studied on earth. They distrusted predictions about the far reaches of the universe because it did not seem they could be tested by observation. In the 1960s, however, the great improvement in the range and quality of astronomical observations led to new interest in gravitational collapse and in the early universe. Exactly what Einstein's general theory of relativity predicted in these situations remained unclear until Roger Penrose and I proved a number of theorems. These showed that the fact that space-time was curved in on itself implied that there would be singularities, places where space-time had a beginning or an end. It would have had a beginning in the big bang, about fifteen billion years ago, and it would come to an end for a star that collapsed and for anything that fell into the black hole the collapsing star left behind.

The fact that Einstein's general theory of relativity turned out to predict singularities led to a crisis in physics. The equations of general relativity, which relate the curvature of space-time with the distribution of mass and energy, cannot be defined as a singularity. This means that general relativity cannot predict what comes out of a singularity. In particular, general relativity cannot predict how the universe should begin at the big bang. Thus, general relativity is not a complete theory. It needs an added ingredient in order to determine how the universe should begin and what should happen when matter collapses under its own gravity.   15

The necessary extra ingredient seems to be quantum mechanics. In 1905, the same year he wrote his paper on the special theory of relativity, Einstein also wrote about a phenomenon called the photoelectric effect. It had been observed that when light fell on certain metals, charged particles were given off. The puzzling thing was that if the intensity of the light was reduced, the number of particles emitted diminished, but the speed with which each particle was emitted remained the same. Einstein showed this could be explained if light came not in continuously variable amounts, as everyone had assumed, but rather in packets of a certain size. The idea of light coming only in packets, called quanta, had been introduced a few years earlier by the German physicist Max Planck. It is a bit like saying one can't buy sugar loose in a supermarket but only in kilogram bags. Planck used the idea of quanta to explain why a red-hot piece of metal doesn't give off an infinite amount of heat; but he regarded quanta simply as a theoretical trick, one that didn't correspond to anything in physical reality. Einstein's paper showed that you could directly observe individual quanta. Each particle emitted corresponded to one quantum of light hitting the metal. It was widely recognized to be a very important contribution to quantum theory, and it won him the Nobel Prize in 1922. (He should have won a Nobel Prize for general relativity, but the idea that space and time were curved was still regarded as too speculative and controversial, so they gave him a prize for the photoelectric effect instead–not that it was not worth the prize on its own account.)

The full implications of the photoelectric effect were not realized until 1925, when Werner Heisenberg pointed out that it made it impossible to measure the position of a particle exactly. To see where a particle is, you have to shine light on it. But Einstein had shown that you couldn't use a very small amount of light; you had to use at least one packet, or quantum. This packet of light would disturb the particle and cause it to move at a speed in some direction. The more accurately you wanted to measure the position of the particle, the greater the energy of the packet you would have to use and thus the more it would disturb the particle. However you tried to measure the particle, the uncertainty in its position, times the uncertainty in its speed, would always be greater than a certain minimum amount.

This uncertainty principle of Heisenberg showed that one could not measure the state of a system exactly, so one could not predict exactly what it would do in the future. All one could do is predict the probabilities of different outcomes. It was this element of chance, or randomness, that so disturbed Einstein. He refused to believe that physical laws should not make a definite, unambiguous prediction for what would happen. But however one expresses it, all the evidence is that the quantum phenomenon and the uncertainty principle are unavoidable and that they occur in every branch of physics.

Einstein's general relativity is what is called a classical theory; that is, it does not incorporate the uncertainty principle. One therefore has to find a new theory that combines general relativity with the uncertainty principle. In most situations, the difference between this new theory and classical general relativity will be very small. This is because, as noted earlier, the uncertainty predicted by quantum effects is only on very small scales, while general relativity deals with the structure of space-time on very large scales. However, the singularity theorems that Roger

Penrose and I proved show that space-time will become highly curved on very small scales. The effects of the uncertainty principle will then become very important and seem to point to some remarkable results.

Part of Einstein's problems with quantum mechanics and the uncertainty principle arose from the fact that he used the ordinary, commonsense notion that a system has a definite history. A particle is either in one place or in another. It can't be half in one and half in another. Similarly, an event like the landing of astronauts on the moon either has taken place or it hasn't. It cannot have half-taken place. It's like the fact that you can't be slightly dead or slightly pregnant. You either are or you aren't. But if a system has a single definite history, the uncertainty principle leads to all sorts of paradoxes, like the particles being in two places at once or astronauts being only half on the moon.

20

An elegant way to avoid these paradoxes that had so troubled Einstein was put forward by the American physicist Richard Feynman. Feynman became well known in 1948 for work on the quantum theory of light. He was awarded the Nobel Prize in 1965 with another American, Julian Schwinger, and the Japanese physicist Shinichiro Tomonaga. But he was a physicist's physicist, in the same tradition as Einstein. He hated pomp and humbug, and he resigned from the National Academy of Sciences because he found that they spent most of their time deciding which other scientists should be admitted to the Academy. Feynman, who died in 1988, is remembered for his many contributions to theoretical physics. One of these was the diagrams that bear his name, which are the basis of almost every calculation in particle physics. But an even more important contribution was his concept of a sum over histories. The idea was that a system didn't have just a single history in space-time, as one would normally assume it did in a classical non-quantum theory. Rather, it had every possible history. Consider, for example, a particle that is at a point A at a certain time. Normally, one would assume that the particle will move on a straight line away from A. However, according to the sum over histories, it can move on *any* path that starts at A. It is like what happens when you place a drop of ink on a piece of blotting paper. The particles of ink will spread through the blotting paper along every possible path. Even if you block the straight line between two points by putting a cut in the paper, the ink will get around the corner.

Associated with each path or history of the particle will be a number that depends on the shape of the path. The probability of the particle traveling from A to B is given by adding up the numbers associated with all the paths that take the particle from A to B. For most paths, the number associated with the path will nearly cancel out the numbers from paths that are close by. Thus, they will make little contribution to the probability of the particle's going from A to B. But the numbers from the straight paths will add up with the numbers from paths that are almost straight. Thus the main contribution to the probability will come from paths that are straight or almost straight. That is why the track a particle makes when going through a bubble chamber looks almost straight. But if you put something like a wall with a slit in it in the way of the particle, the particle paths can spread out beyond the slit. There can be a high probability of finding the particle away from the direct line through the slit.

In 1973 I began investigating what effect the uncertainty principle would have on a particle in the curved space-time near a black hole. Remarkably enough, I found that the black hole would not be completely black. The uncertainty principle would allow particles and radiation to leak out of the black hole at a steady rate. This result came as a complete surprise to me and everyone else, and it was greeted with general disbelief. But with hindsight, it ought to have been obvious. A black hole is a region of space from which it is impossible to escape if one is traveling at less than the speed of light. But the Feynman sum over histories says that particles can take *any* path through space-time. Thus it is possible for a particle to travel faster than light. The probability is low for it to move a long distance at more than the speed of light, but it can go faster than light for just far enough to get out of the black hole, and then go slower than light. In this way, the uncertainty principle allows particles to escape from what was thought to be the ultimate prison, a black hole. The probability of a particle getting out of a black hole of the mass of the sun would be very low because the particle would have to travel faster than light for several kilometers. But there might be very much smaller black holes, which were formed in the early universe. These primordial black holes could be less than the size of the nucleus of an atom, yet their mass could be a billion tons, the mass of Mount Fuji. They could be emitting as much energy as a large power station. If only we could find one of these little black holes and harness its energy! Unfortunately, there don't seem to be many around in the universe.

The prediction of radiation from black holes was the first nontrivial result of combining Einstein's general relativity with the quantum principle. It showed that gravitational collapse was not as much of a dead end as it had appeared to be. The particles in a black hole need not have an end of their histories at a singularity. Instead, they could escape from the black hole and continue their histories outside. Maybe the quantum principle would mean that one could also avoid the histories having a beginning in time, a point of creation, at the big bang.

The Responsive Reader

1. What science background do you bring to this article? For instance, how would you define gravity? What do you know about the speed of light, and in what contexts does it matter? What do you know about the Big Bang and the expanding universe? Were you taught that the laws of physics apply equally everywhere? (Where in his essay does Hawking insist on this basic assumption?)

2. What did you know about the theory of relativity? Does Hawking succeed in explaining to you that space and time are not separate dimensions? Does he explain to you why space and time are curved or warped? What causes or explains this effect? What are its implications for the physicist?

3. Does Hawking convince you that time is not static or uniform–the same for everyone everywhere? How does this essay make you rethink conventional concepts of time? How did measurements of the speed of light become a test of our assumptions about time?

4. How did Einstein's theory of relativity make us rethink the concept of gravity? According to Hawking, what were dilemmas or unsolved problems that troubled Einstein? What is the history of ideas about "gravitational collapse" and black holes? How were they a challenge to Einstein's theories?

5. What was Einstein's role in the development of quantum physics? What do you learn here about the "uncertainty principle"?

6. Hawking challenged the idea that nothing can travel faster than the speed of light. In what context, and with what result?

For Discussion or Writing

7. Hawking has said that today's revolutionary ideas about space–time and quantum physics "will come to seem as natural to the next generation as the idea that the world is round." Which of the ideas in his essay are becoming natural to you? Which are least accessible or most difficult?

Collaborative Projects

8. Is the Big Bang theory uncontested or widely accepted among today's scientists? Are there reputable alternative theories?

FORUM: *Scientists and Science Ethics*

In recent years, much attention has focused on the harmful side effects of scientific progress. Asbestos was at one time hailed as a great step forward in fireproofing buildings; today costly and difficult asbestos removal is necessary to protect workers against asbestos lung. New chemicals keep tomato crops from rotting, but they may also poison the buildings, close to the fields, where migrant workers live or their children go to school. (The Death of Ramón Gonzalez, a book by professor of environmental studies Angus Wright, investigated the case of a twenty-year-old farmworker who died two days after bathing in an irrigation canal.) Hormones help farmers raise meatier animals, but the meat may have deleterious effects on humans; some countries ban it, and others don't. What are the obligations of scientists as watchdogs and whistleblowers? At what point do you expect them to cease being well-funded researchers or consultants for industry and to turn into consumer advocates instead?

OUR WAR AGAINST NATURE

Rachel Carson

Rachel Carson's environmental classic Silent Spring *(1962) aroused a generation to the dangers of a heedless technology polluting the planet. DDT had become widely used as a miracle pesticide promising to rid the world of aphids, malaria-carrying mosquitos, or lice. But as DDT traveled up the food chain from bugs to birds, bird species suffered major genetic damage, silencing the warblings of songbirds. Like the canary in the coal mine who chokes first when the oxygen gives out, warning miners to save their lives, the brittle eggs and aborted hatchings of DDT-impacted bird populations served as an early warning to human beings threatened by toxins in food and the environment. Rachel Carson studied biology at the Pennsylvania College for Women and worked as a biologist at Johns Hopkins University in Baltimore and at the Marine Biological Laboratory at Woods Hole, Massachusetts. She wrote several books about the "mystery and meaning of the sea".* The Sea Around Us, Under the Sea Wind, *and* The Edge of the Sea. *She died of breast cancer two years after she published* Silent Spring.

It took hundreds of millions of years to produce the life that now inhabits the earth—eons of time in which that developing and evolving and diversifying life reached a state of adjustment and balance with its surroundings. The environment, rigorously shaping and directing the life it supported, contained elements that were hostile as well as supporting. Certain rocks gave out dangerous radiation;

even within the light of the sun, from which all life draws its energy, there were short-wave radiations with power to injure. Given time–time not in years but in millennia–life adjusts, and a balance has been reached. For time is the essential ingredient; but in the modern world there is no time.

The rapidity of change and the speed with which new situations are created follow the impetuous and heedless pace of man rather than the deliberate pace of nature. Radiation is no longer merely the background radiation of rocks, the bombardment of cosmic rays, the ultraviolet of the sun that have existed before there was any life on earth; radiation is now the unnatural creation of man's tampering with the atom. The chemicals to which life is asked to make its adjustment are no longer merely the calcium and silica and copper and all the rest of the minerals washed out of the rocks and carried in rivers to the sea; they are the synthetic creations of man's inventive mind, brewed in his laboratories, and having no counterparts in nature.

To adjust to these chemicals would require time on the scale that is nature's; it would require not merely the years of a man's life but the life of generations. And even this, were it by some miracle possible, would be futile, for the new chemicals come from our laboratories in an endless stream; almost five hundred annually find their way into actual use in the United States alone. The figure is staggering and its implications are not easily grasped–500 new chemicals to which the bodies of men and animals are required somehow to adapt each year, chemicals totally outside the limits of biologic experience.

Among them are many that are used in man's war against nature. Since the mid-1940's over 200 basic chemicals have been created for use in killing insects, weeds, rodents, and other organisms described in the modern vernacular as "pests"; and they are sold under several thousand different brand names.

These sprays, dusts, and aerosols are now applied almost universally to farms, gardens, forests, and homes–nonselective chemicals that have the power to kill every insect, the "good" and the "bad," to still the song of birds and the leaping of fish in the streams, to coat the leaves with a deadly film, and to linger on in soil–all this though the intended target may be only a few weeds or insects. Can anyone believe it is possible to lay down such a barrage of poisons on the surface of the earth without making it unfit for all life? They should not be called "insecticides," but "biocides."   5

The whole process of spraying seems caught up in an endless spiral. Since DDT was released for civilian use, a process of escalation has been going on in which ever more toxic materials must be found. This has happened because insects, in a triumphant vindication of Darwin's principle of the survival of the fittest, have evolved super races immune to the particular insecticide used, hence a deadlier one has always to be developed–and then a deadlier one than that. It has happened also because . . . destructive insects often undergo a "flareback," or resurgence, after spraying, in numbers greater than before. Thus the chemical war is never won, and all life is caught in its violent crossfire.

Along with the possibility of the extinction of mankind by nuclear war, the central problem of our age has therefore become the contamination of man's total environment with such substances of incredible potential for harm—substances that accumulate in the tissues of plants and animals and even penetrate the germ cells to shatter or alter the very material of heredity upon which the shape of the future depends.

Some would-be architects of our future look toward a time when it will be possible to alter the human germ plasm by design. But we may easily be doing so now by inadvertence, for many chemicals, like radiation, bring about gene muta-tions. It is ironic to think that man might determine his own future by something so seemingly trivial as the choice of an insect spray.

All this has been risked—for what? Future historians may well be amazed by our distorted sense of proportion. How could intelligent beings seek to control a few unwanted species by a method that contaminated the entire environment and brought the threat of disease and death even to their own kind? Yet this is precisely what we have done. We have done it, moreover, for reasons that collapse the mo-ment we examine them. We are told that the enormous and expanding use of pes-ticides is necessary to maintain farm production. Yet is our real problem not one of *overproduction?* Our farms, despite measures to remove acreages from production and to pay farmers *not* to produce, have yielded such a staggering excess of crops that the American taxpayer by 1962 is paying out more than one billion dollars a year as the total carrying cost of the surplus-food storage program. And is the situation helped when one branch of the Agriculture Department tries to reduce production while another states, as it did in 1958, "It is believed generally that re-duction of crop acreages under provisions of the Soil Bank will stimulate interest in use of chemicals to obtain maximum production on the land retained in crops."

All this is not to say there is no insect problem and no need of control. I am   10
saying, rather, that control must be geared to realities, not to mythical situations, and that methods employed must be such that they do not destroy us along with the insects.

The problem whose attempted solution has brought such a train of disaster in its wake is an accompaniment of our modern way of life. Long before the age of man, insects inhabited the earth—a group of extraordinarily varied and adaptable beings. Over the course of time since man's advent, a small percentage of the more than half a million species of insects have come into conflict with human welfare in two principal ways: as competitors for the food supply and as carriers of human disease.

Disease-carrying insects become important where human beings are crowded together, especially under conditions where sanitation is poor, as in time of natural disaster or war or in situations of extreme poverty and deprivation. Then control of some sort becomes necessary. It is a sobering fact, however, as we shall presently see, that the method of massive chemical control has had only limited success, and also threatens to worsen the very conditions it is intended to curb.

Under primitive agricultural conditions the farmer had few insect problems. These arose with the intensification of agriculture–the devotion of immense acreages to a single crop. Such a system set the stage for explosive increases in specific insect populations. Single-crop farming does not take advantage of the principles by which nature works; it is agriculture as an engineer might conceive it to be. Nature has introduced great variety into the landscape, but man has displayed a passion for simplifying it. Thus he undoes the built-in checks and balances by which nature holds the species within bounds. One important natural check is a limit on the amount of suitable habitat for each species. Obviously then, an insect that lives on wheat can build up its population to much higher levels on a farm devoted to wheat than on one in which wheat is intermingled with other crops to which the insect is not adapted.

The same thing happens in other situations. A generation or more ago, the towns of large areas of the United States lined their streets with the noble elm tree. Now the beauty they hopefully created is threatened with complete destruction as disease sweeps through the elms, carried by a beetle that would have only limited chance to build up large populations and to spread from tree to tree if the elms were only occasional trees in a richly diversified planting.

Another factor in the modern insect problem is one that must be viewed   15
against a background of geologic and human history: the spreading of thousands of different kinds of organisms from their native homes to invade new territories. This worldwide migration has been studied and graphically described by the British ecologist Charles Elton in his recent book *The Ecology of Invasions*. During the Cretaceous Period, some hundred million years ago, flooding seas cut many land bridges between continents and living things found themselves confined in what Elton calls "colossal separate nature reserves." There, isolated from others of their kind, they developed many new species. When some of the land masses were joined again, about 15 million years ago, these species began to move out into new territories–a movement that is not only still in progress but is now receiving considerable assistance from man.

The importation of plants is the primary agent in the modern spread of species, for animals have almost invariably gone along with the plants, quarantine being a comparatively recent and not completely effective innovation. The United States Office of Plant Introduction alone has introduced almost 200,000 species and varieties of plants from all over the world. Nearly half of the 180 or so major insect enemies of plants in the United States are accidental imports from abroad, and most of them have come as hitchhikers on plants.

In new territory, out of reach of the restraining hand of the natural enemies that kept down its numbers in its native land, an invading plant or animal is able to become enormously abundant. Thus it is no accident that our most troublesome insects are introduced species.

These invasions, both the naturally occurring and those dependent on human assistance, are likely to continue indefinitely. Quarantine and massive chemical campaigns are only extremely expensive ways of buying time. We are faced, according to Dr. Elton, "with a life-and-death need not just to find new technological means of suppressing this plant or that animal"; instead we need the basic knowledge of animal populations and their relations to their surroundings that will "promote an even balance and damp down the explosive power of outbreaks and new invasions."

Much of the necessary knowledge is now available but we do not use it. We train ecologists in our universities and even employ them in our governmental agencies but we seldom take their advice. We allow the chemical death rain to fall as though there were no alternative, whereas in fact there are many, and our ingenuity could soon discover many more if given opportunity.

It is not my contention that chemical insecticides must never be used. I do   20
contend that we have put poisonous and biologically potent chemicals indiscriminately into the hands of persons largely or wholly ignorant of their potentials for harm. We have subjected enormous numbers of people to contact with these poisons, without their consent and often without their knowledge. If the Bill of Rights contains no guarantee that a citizen shall be secure against lethal poisons distributed either by private individuals or by public officials, it is surely only because our forefathers, despite their considerable wisdom and foresight, could conceive of no such problem

I contend, furthermore, that we have allowed these chemicals to be used with little or no advance investigation of their effect on soil, water, wildlife, and man himself. Future generations are unlikely to condone our lack of prudent concern for the integrity of the natural world that supports all life.

The Responsive Reader

1. In her opening paragraphs, what basic contrast does Carson set up between the workings of nature and the result of human intervention? What key examples help her make her point?

2. Where does Carson state her thesis? Where in this selection do you observe her echoing or reiterating–reinforcing–it?

3. What does Carson see as the cause of the escalation–the "endless spiral"–in the use of pesticides? How does she deal with the justifications offered for increased pesticide use?

4. What major examples of human tampering with the "built-in checks and

balances of nature" does Carson cite in the central part of her essay? How do they help explain our current insect problems? What workings of cause and effect does she trace?

5. Does Carson identify or recommend alternatives to the massive use of pesticides? What alternatives are spelled out or implied in her essay?

For Discussion or Writing

6. Concluding a recent tribute to Carson, a *Mother Jones* editor asked: "Was anybody listening?" Based on what you see of environmental awareness, how would you answer this question?

7. To judge from your studies or reading, what has been the role of human tampering with nature in creating such environmental calamities as dust bowls, acid rain, global warming, and desertification?

8. The law of "unintended consequences" has become a cliché with politicians, urbanologists, educators, environmentalists, and others. Have you seen it in action?

Collaborative Projects

9. The invasion of the Brazilian fire ant led to widespread damage to livestock and wildlife in the southeastern United States. A massive chemical campaign against the ant has been called the Vietnam of entomology and helped motivate Carson to write *Silent Spring*. Working alone or with a group, what can you find out about the shift from chemical to biological warfare in the effort to control the fire ant or other pests?

THE MONKEY WARS

Deborah Blum

If you were threatened by a new lethal disease, would you rather have baboons or other apes die in experiments aimed at tracking and stopping the killer virus? Or would you rather die your- self as a martyr to the cause of animal rights? Deborah Blum is an investigative science writer who knows how to stir up the citizenry on issues such as these. She knows how to ferret out the gruesome facts about animal experiments usually kept under wraps by medical investigators scared of harassment by animal rights activists. Blum was trained in science writing at the Uni- versity of Wisconsin. She went to California to write first for the Fresno Bee *and then for the* Sacramento Bee. *The "Monkey Wars" series of articles she researched there and published in November 1991 won her the Pulitzer prize and the American Association for the Advancement of Science–Westinghouse writing award. Blum first became involved in the subject of animal experi- ments when apes used for medical research in California laboratories contracted the Ebola virus, which has proved deadly to patients and medical personnel in Africa.*

On the days when he's scheduled to kill, Allen Merritt summons up his ghosts.   1
They come to him from the shadows of a 20–year-old memory. Eleven hu- man babies, from his first year out of medical school. All born prematurely. All lost within one week when their lungs failed.

"We were virtually helpless," said Merritt, now head of the neonatal intensive care unit at the University of California–Davis Medical Center.

"There's nothing worse than being a new physician and standing there watch- ing babies die. It's a strong motivator to make things different."

On this cool morning, he needs that memory. The experiment he's doing is de-   5 ceptively simple: a test of a new chemical to help premature babies breathe. But it's no clinical arrangement of glass tubes. He's trying the drug on two tiny rhesus monkeys, each weighing barely one-third of a pound. At the end of the experi- ment, he plans to cut their lungs apart, to see how it worked.

Even his ghosts don't make that easy. Nestled in a towel on a surgical table, eyes shut, hands curled, the monkeys look unnervingly human. "The link between people and monkeys is very close," Merritt said. "Much closer than some people would like to think. There's a real sense of sadness, that we can only get the infor- mation we need if we kill them."

Once, there was no such need to justify. Once, American researchers could go through 200,000 monkeys a year, without question. Now, the numbers are less–

perhaps 20,000 monkeys will die every year, out of an estimated 40,000 used in experiments. But the pressures are greater.

These days, it seems that if researchers plan one little study–slicing the toes off squirrel monkeys, siphoning blood from rhesus macaques, hiding baby monkeys from their mothers–they face not just questions, but picket signs, lawsuits and death threats phoned in at night.

The middle ground in the war over research with monkeys and apes has become so narrow as to be nearly invisible. And even that is eroding.

Intelligent, agile, fast, but not fast enough, these non-human primates are   10 rapidly being driven from the planet, lost to heavy trapping and vanishing rain forests. Of 63 primate species in Asia–where most research monkeys come from–only one is not listed as vulnerable.

Primate researchers believe they are making the hard choice, using non-human primates for medical research because they must, because no other animal so closely mirrors the human body and brain. During the 1950s, American scientists did kill hundreds of thousands of monkeys for polio research, using the animals' organs to grow virus, dissecting their brains to track the spread of the infection. But out of those experiments came a polio vaccine. Using monkeys, scientists have created vaccines for measles, learned to fight leprosy, developed anti-rejection drugs that make organ transplants possible.

Outside the well-guarded laboratory wall, that choice can seem less obvious. Animal rights advocates draw a dark description of research. They point out that AIDS researchers have used endangered chimpanzees, without, so far, managing to help people dying of the disease. Further, conservationists fear that the research is introducing dangerous infection into the country's chimpanzee breeding program, badly needed to help counter the loss of wild animals.

"They're guzzling up money and animals, and for what?" asked Shirley McGreal, head of the non-profit International Primate Protection League. "Why not use those resources in helping sick people, why infect healthy animals?"

Her argument is that of animal advocates across the country–that scientists are sacrificing our genetic next-of-kin for their own curiosity, dubious medical gains and countless tax dollars.

No one is sure exactly how much money scientists spend experimenting on   15 monkeys, although the National Institutes of Health alone allocates almost $40 million annually to its primate research programs, including one in Davis. Overall, more than half of NIH's research grants–approaching $5 billion–involve at least some animal research.

Rats and mice are the most abundant, some 15 million are used in experiments every year. But primates are the most expensive; monkeys cost a basic $1,000, chimpanzees start at $50,000.

For people such as McGreal, these are animals in a very wrong place.

McGreal's long-term goal for monkeys is simple: out of the laboratory, back into what remains of the rain forests.

"I used to think that we could persuade those people to understand what we do," said Frederick King, director of the Yerkes Regional Primate Research Center in Atlanta. "But it's impossible. And that's why I no longer describe this as a battle. I describe it as a war."

The rift is so sharp that it is beginning to reshape science itself.

"Science has organized," marveled Alex Pacheco, founder of the country's most   20 powerful animal rights group, People for Ethical Treatment of Animals. "Researchers are out-lobbying us and outspending us. They've become so aggressive that it puts new pressure on us. We're going to have to fight tougher too."

In the past year, researchers have made it clear just how much they dislike the role of victim. If Pacheco wants to call scientists "sadistic bastards"–which he does frequently–then Fred King is more than ready to counter with his description of PETA: "Fanatic, fringe, one of the most despicable organizations in the country."

But beyond name-calling, the research community is realizing its political power. Its lobbyists are pushing for laws that would heavily penalize protesters who interfere with research projects. And this year, to the fury of animal rights groups, primate researchers were able to win a special exemption from the public records laws, shielding their plans for captive monkey care.

For researchers, the attention focused on them is an almost dizzying turn-about. Not so long ago, they could have hung their monkey care plans as banners across streets and no one would have read them.

"When I first started, 20 years ago, monkeys were $25 each," said Roy Henrickson, chief of lab animal care at the University of California, Berkeley. "You'd use one once and you'd throw it away. I'd talk to lab vets who were under pressure about dogs and I'd say, I'm sure glad I'm in non-human primates. Nobody cares about them."

He can date the change precisely, back to 1981, the year Pacheco went under-   25 cover in the laboratory of Edward Taub. Taub was a specialist in nerve damage, working in Silver Springs, Md. To explore the effects of ruined nerves, he took 17 rhesus monkeys and sliced apart nerves close to the spinal column, crippling their limbs. Then he studied the way they coped with the damage.

Pacheco left the laboratory with an enduring mistrust of scientists and an arm-load of inflammatory photographs: monkeys wrenched into vices, packed into filthy cages. Monkeys who, with no feeling in their hands, had gnawed their fingers to the bone. Some of the wounds were oozing with infection, darkening with gangrene.

Many believe those battered monkeys were the fuse, lighting the current, combative cycle of animal rights. In the fury over the Silver Springs monkeys, Pacheco was able to build People for Ethical Treatment of Animals into a national force, and across the country, the movement gained power. Today, membership in animal advocacy groups tops 12 million; the 30 largest organizations report a combined annual income approaching $70 million.

And primate researchers have suddenly found themselves under scrutiny of the most hostile kind.

There are experiments, such as Allen Merritt's work to salvage premature infants, that the critics will sometimes reluctantly accept. The compound that Merritt is testing on young monkeys is a kind of lubricant for the lungs, a slippery ooze that coats the tissues within, allowing them to flex as air comes in and out.

Without the ooze–called surfactant–the tissues don't stretch. They rip. The 30 problem for premature babies is that the body doesn't develop surfactant until late in fetal development, some 35 weeks into a pregnancy. Although artificial surfactants are now available, Merritt doesn't believe they're good enough. Two-thirds of the tiniest premature babies, weighing less than a pound at birth, still die as their lungs shred. He's trying to improve the medicine.

"There could be a scientific defense for doing that, even though it's extremely cruel," said Elliot Katz, head of In Defense of Animals, a national animal rights group, headquartered in San Rafael.

But Katz finds most of the work indefensible. He can rapidly cite examples of a different sort: a U.S. Air Force experiment, which involved draining 40 percent of the blood from rhesus macaques and then spinning them on a centrifuge, to simulate injured astronauts; a New York University study of addiction in which monkeys were strapped into metal boxes and forced to inhale concentrated cocaine fumes.

Last year, animal advocates rallied against a proposed study at the Seattle center, a plan to take 13 baby rhesus macaques from their mothers and try to drive them crazy through isolation, keeping them caged away from their mothers and without company. The scientists acknowledged that they might drive the monkeys to self-mutilation; rhesus macaques do badly in isolation, rocking, pulling out their hair, sometimes tearing their skin open.

This year, protesters have been holding candlelight vigils outside the home of a researcher at a Maryland military facility, the Uniformed Services University of the Health Sciences. That project involves cutting the toes from kittens and young squirrel monkeys and then, after they've wobbled into adjustment, killing them to look at their brains.

In both cases, there are scientific explanations. The Washington scientists 35 wanted to analyze the chemistry of a troubled brain, saying that it could benefit people with mental illness. The Maryland researchers are brain-mapping, drafting a careful picture of how the mind reorganizes itself to cope with crippling injury.

But these are not–and may never be–explanations acceptable to those crusading for animal rights. "This is just an example of someone doing something horrible to animals because he can get paid for it," said Laurie Raymond, of Seattle's Progressive Animal Welfare Society, which campaigned against the baby monkey experiment and takes credit for the fact that it failed to get federal funding.

Researchers are tired of telling the public about their work, documenting it in public records–and having that very openness used against them. The Washington protesters learned about the baby monkey experiment through a meeting of the university's animal care committee–which is public. The Maryland work came to light through a listing of military funded research–which is public.

When the U.S. Department of Agriculture, which inspects research facilities annually, complained about the housekeeping at the Tulane Regional Primate Research Center in Louisiana, the director wrote the agency a furious letter. Didn't administrators realize that the report was public and made scientists look bad?

"The point I am making is that USDA, without intending to do so, is playing into the hands of the animal rights/anti-vivisectionists whose stated goal is to abolish animal research," wrote center head Peter Gerone, arguing that the complaints could have been handled privately. "If you are trying to placate the animal rights activists by nitpicking inspections . . . you will only serve to do us irreparable harm."

When Arnold Arluke, a sociologist at Boston's Northeastern University, spent   40
six years studying lab workers and drafted a report saying that some actually felt guilty about killing animals, he found himself suddenly under pressure. "I was told putting that information out would be like giving ammunition to the enemy," he said.

He titled his first talk "Guilt Among Animal Researchers." The manager of the laboratory where he spoke changed "guilt" to stress. When he published that in a journal, the editors thought that stress was too controversial. They changed the title to "Uneasiness Among Lab Workers." When he gave another talk at a pharmaceutical company, he was told uneasiness was too strong. They changed the title to "How to Deal with Your Feelings." Arluke figures his next talk will be untitled.

"People in animal research don't even want to tell others what they do," he said. "One woman I talked to was standing in line at a grocery store, and when she told the person next to her what she did, the woman started yelling at her: 'You should be ashamed of yourself.'"

And when new lab animal care rules were published this year, it was clear that researchers were no longer willing to freely hand over every record of operation.

The new regulations resulted from congressional changes in 1985 to the Animal Welfare Act. They included a special provision for the care of laboratory primates; legislators wanted scientists to recognize that these were sociable, intelligent animals.

The provision–perhaps the most controversial in the entire act–was called   45
"psychological well-being of primates." When the USDA began drafting rules, in response to the new law, it received a record 35,000 letters of comment. And 14,000 consisted of a written shouting match over how to make primates happy. It took

six years before the agency could come up with rules that the research community could accept.

Originally, the USDA proposed firm standards: Laboratories would have to give monkeys bigger cages, let them share space, provide them with puzzles and toys from a list.

Researchers argued that was unreasonable: Every monkey species was different, the rigid standards might satisfy one animal and make another miserable. Now, each institution is asked to do what it thinks best for its monkeys; USDA inspectors will be free to study, criticize and ask for changes in those plans.

But animal rights groups will not. Research lobbyists persuaded the USDA to bypass the federal Freedom of Information Act; the president of the American Society of Primatologists told the agency that making the plans public would be like giving a road map to terrorists. Under the new rules, the plans will be kept at the individual institutions rather than filed with the federal government, as has been standard practice. That makes them institutional property–exempted from any requests for federal records.

Tom Wolfle, director of the Institute for Laboratory Animal Resources in Washington, D.C., the federal government's chief advisory division on animal issues, said the research community simply needed some clear space. "The idea was to prevent unreasonable criticism by uninformed people," he said.

Advocacy groups have sued the government over the new rules, saying they unlawfully shut the public out of research that it pays for. "In the end, they just handed everything back to the researchers and said, here, it's all yours," said Christine Stevens, an executive with the non-profit Animal Welfare Institute. 50

Stevens, daughter of a Michigan physiology researcher, finds this the ultimate contradiction, as well as "foolish and short-sighted." She thinks that science, of all professions, should be one of open ideas.

On this point, she has some unlikely allies. Frederick King, of Yerkes, no friend to the animal rights movement, is also unhappy with the research community's tendency to withdraw. "I don't know about the law," he said. "But our plans for taking care of our primates will be open.

"We are using taxpayers' money. In my judgment, we have an obligation to tell the public what we're about. And the fact that we haven't done that, I think, is one of the greatest mistakes over the last half-century, hell, the last century, that scientists have made."

Against that conflict, Allen Merritt's decision to make public an experiment in which he kills monkeys was not an easy one. His wife worried that anti-research fanatics would stalk their home. His supervisors worried that animal lovers would be alienated; one administrator even called the Davis primate center, suggesting that Merritt's work should not be publicly linked to the medical school's pediatrics department.

But Merritt, like King, believes that his profession will only lose if it remains   55
hidden from the public. "People need to understand what we're doing. If I were to
take a new drug first to a nursery, and unforeseen complications occurred, and a
baby died–who would accept that?"

So, on a breezy morning, he opens the way to the final test of lung-lubricating
surfactants that he will do this year, a 24-hour-countdown for two baby monkeys.
Those hours are critical to whether these drugs work. If human premature babies
last from their first morning to the next one, their survival odds soar.

The tiny monkeys–one male, one female–taken by C-section, are hurried into
an intensive care unit, dried and warmed with a blow drier, put onto folded towels, hooked up to ventilators, heart monitors, intravenous drip lines. During the experiment, they will never be conscious, never open their eyes.

"OK, let's treat," Merritt says. His technician gently lifts the tube from the ventilator, which carries oxygen into the monkey's lungs. A white mist of surfactant
fills the tube, spraying into the lungs. And then, through the night, the medical
team watches and waits.

The next morning, they decide to kill the female early. An intravenous line
going into her leg is starting to cause bleeding problems. The monkey is twitching
a little in her unconsciousness, as if in pain. Merritt sees no point in dragging her
through the experiment's official end.

But the male keeps breathing. As the sun brightens to midday, the scientists in-   60
ject a lethal dose of anesthesia. Still, the monkey's chest keeps moving, up and
down, up and down with the push of the ventilator. But, behind him, the heart
monitor shows only a straight green line.

For a few seconds, before they shut the machines down and begin the lung
dissection, Allen Merritt stands quietly by the small dead monkey, marshaling the
ghosts of the babies he couldn't save, a long time ago.

The Responsive Reader

1. Blum relies heavily on "anecdotal" human interest stories. Does the opening
   anecdote about the researcher and the two tiny rhesus monkeys bring the researcher's dilemma into focus for you? How or why?

2. As Blum introduces you to the opposing camps, what do you learn about the
   polarization between researchers and activists? Do you feel you are helped to
   understand the perspectives of both sides? (Do you agree with Blum that there
   is little if any middle ground?)

3. As in so much of contemporary America, dollars and cents loom large in the
   discussion of this issue. What do you learn here about the economics of animal
   research?

4. Horror stories about abuse of animals are a major weapon of the animal rights movement. What role do they play in this article? How do they affect you personally?

5. How much room is given to "scientific explanations" and to the defense of animal research in this article?

6. How and why, in this article, does government get into the act?

For Discussion or Writing

7. Journalists like Blum are often accused of sensationalism–going out of their way to make their stories, as she herself has said, "vivid and exciting." On balance, do you think her purpose is to inflame or to inform?

8. Where do *you* stand on the ethics of animal experiments?

Collaborative Projects

9. When members of your group check computerized indexes of media coverage, what do you find for key topics like animal experiments, primate research, or medical research and animal rights? What has been the media coverage of animal experiments during the last few years? Is there a general pattern–pro or con? Are there any signs of a developing consensus or middle ground?

DREAMING OF DISCONNECTING A RESPIRATOR

Elissa Ely

In 1996, a regional legislature in Australia became one of the first governmental bodies to legalize euthanasia, or assisted suicide. In the United States, ideological battles continue to be waged over the right to "die with dignity" or to put an end willingly to hopeless unbearable suffering. A 1995 study showed that regardless of the patient's or the family's expressed wishes, drastic costly futile life-prolonging measures for terminal patients were the rule in the hospitals studied. Elissa Ely, a science columnist writing about the human dimension of medical science, came to science the long way around. She majored in religion at Wesleyan College and tried her hand at playwriting in Boston. She worked in a homeless shelter and as a hospital intern. She became a practicing psychiatrist. Ely has done science columns for the Boston Globe *and science commentary for National Public Radio.*

Late one night in the Intensive Care Unit, one eye on the cardiac monitor and one on the Sunday paper, I read this story: 1

An infant lies in a hospital, hooked to life by a respirator. He exists in a "persistent vegetative state" after swallowing a balloon that blocked the oxygen to his brain. This "vegetative state," I've always thought, is a metaphor inaccurately borrowed from nature, since it implies that with only the proper watering and fertilizer, a comatose patient will bloom again.

One day his father comes to visit. He disconnects the respirator and, with a gun in hand, cradles his son until the infant dies. The father is arrested and charged with murder.

In the ICU where I read this, many patients are bound to respirators. I look to my left and see them lined up, like potted plants. Some will eventually be "weaned" back to their own lung power. Others will never draw an independent breath again.

In Bed No. 2, there is a woman who has been on the respirator for almost two   5 months. When she was admitted with a simple pneumonia, there were no clues she would come apart so terribly. On her third day, she had a sudden and enigmatic seizure. She rolled rapidly downhill. Her pneumonia is now gone, but her lungs refuse independence: she can't come off the machine.

I know little about this patient except that she is elderly and European. (It is the peculiar loss of hospital life that patients often exist here with a medical history, but not a personal one.) I sometimes try to picture her as she might have been: busy in a chintz kitchen smelling of pastries. She might have hummed, rolling dough. Now there is a portable radio by the bed, playing Top Ten, while the respirator hisses and clicks 12 times a minute.

The family no longer visits. They have already signed the autopsy request, which is clipped to the front of her thick chart. Yet in their pain, they cannot take the final step and allow us to discontinue her respirator. Instead, they have retired her here, where they hope she is well cared for, and where she exists in a state of perpetual mechanical life.

I have dreamed of disconnecting my patient's respirator. Every day I make her death impossible and her life unbearable. Each decision–the blood draws, the rectal temperatures, the oxygen concentration–is one for or against life. No action in the ICU is neutral. Yet many of these decisions are made with an eye toward legal neutrality–and this has little to do with medical truth. The medical truth is that this patient exists without being alive. The legal neutrality is that existence is all that is required.

Late at night, reading in the ICU, the story of that father–so dangerous and impassioned–puts me to shame. I would never disconnect my patient from her respirator; it is unthinkable. But this is not because I am a doctor. It is because I feel differently toward her than the father toward his son.

I do not love her enough.   10

The Responsive Reader

1. What memories of stories about comatose patients or patients in a "persistent vegetative state" do you bring to the reading of this column?

2. How does Ely use the story of the father and the comatose infant to challenge her readers' values or assumptions?

3. What role did the family play in the story of the elderly European patient? Would you have acted the same way the family did?

4. What crucial distinction does Ely make between "legal neutrality" and "medical truth"?

For Discussion or Writing

5. What side are you on in this controversy? Would you have charged the father with murder? Would you have disconnected the elderly patient's respirator? Why or why not?

Collaborative Projects

6. What is the purpose of "Living Wills"? What is their legal status? Are they honored or disregarded? How could you find out?

2

Issues in Social Science

SOCIAL SCIENCE IN PERSPECTIVE

Why has it been so difficult to be scientific about human behavior?

B. F. SKINNER

Being on time when the rest of the world is behind gives the impression of being ahead.

JEAN-LUC GODARD

What is the role of the social sciences? The social sciences have aimed at applying the same scientific perspective that physicists or chemists had applied to the physical world in turn to the world of human motives and behavior. Social scientists have worked to put our traditional assumptions, prejudices, and impressionistic surface observations about human actions and motives on a surer footing of systematic study and analysis.

DEFINING SOCIAL SCIENCE

The social sciences study human behavior. Sociology, political science, anthropology, and psychology explore questions like the following: What guides or explains human behavior in the family, on the job, or in the larger social and political arena? What general patterns of human behavior can we isolate and use as a basis for predicting future events?

Some major traditional trends or emphases can help you define the large area of the social sciences:

- *Social science has aimed at unbiased observation.* Ideally, social scientists step outside their own culture and regard it with the eye of an impartial observer. They are not caught up in what we are taught about our society or in what we are supposed to think.
- *Much fieldwork in social science involves one-on-one contact with subjects.* The student of human psychology needs to find ways to break through the

crust of clichés, alibis, and approved ways of thinking. Interviewers like Robert Coles, Studs Terkel, and Jonathan Kozol bring to the surface what people deep down really think and feel. The extended candid personal testimonies these researchers elicit illuminate attitudes toward work, race, poverty, or divorce.

• *Major branches of social science put a premium on hard data.* Impressionistic testimony or anecdotal evidence highlights individual cases that may not be typical or representative. We then feel the pressure to quantify information about human behavior. We collect statistics that give the investigators data to study, numbers to crunch. Much social science works with surveys, questionnaires, personality inventories, aptitude tests, or achievement tests. Much debate centers on the methodology and validity of such instruments as IQ tests, personality profiles, or political polls. Much effort goes into setting up experiments that control variables in order to obtain hard data on an isolated trait or specific behavior.

• *The social sciences invite use and abuse as a means of influencing behavior.* On the one hand, social scientists have often sought to use their findings to point the way to a more humane life. In studying the folkways of indigenous people in Samoa or New Guinea, the anthropologist Margaret Mead observed customary patterns teaching young people how to encounter or talk with members of the other sex. Traditional taboos protected women from rape or abuse as long as they played by the rules. Mead concluded that the abandonment of traditional taboos left women in our own culture disoriented and vulnerable and that we needed new quasi-instinctive, deeply engrained do's and don'ts for sexual behavior in mixed dorms or in the workplace.

On the other hand, the expertise of the social scientist lends itself to exploitation. Psychologists teach marketing experts how to exploit unconscious desires and fears, serving the needs of stockholders rather than of consumers. Political scientists advise campaign strategists on how to manipulate voter behavior, skewing the democratic process. Experts on the psychology of jurors advise lawyers on how to select juries favorable to their clients, tipping the scales of justice.

How scientific is social science? In recent years, social scientists have become increasingly concerned with the cultural biases that may affect their work. A new generation of social scientists has challenged the "myth of objectivity" that helped give the social sciences quasi-scientific status. For instance, white observers during the period of European colonialism were likely to bring to the study of African societies preconceptions about primitive, undeveloped peoples. They were ill-prepared to acknowledge the rich ceremonial cultures that you can study, for instance, in the Nigerian novelist Chinua Achebe's *Things Fall Apart* or the Nigerian playwright Wole Soyinka's *Death and the King's Horseman*.

Much current revisionist scholarship looks for cultural biases or private agendas in earlier work. For instance, Margaret Mead's observations of Polynesian cultures may have been colored by a desire to find an idyllic, problem-free sexuality as an antidote to the sexual inhibitions and neuroses of Western culture. As a student in a Women's Studies Program or in a course taught from a feminist perspective, you may be asked to reexamine assumptions about female psychology long held by a male-dominated establishment in psychology or psychiatry but rejected by feminist scholars.

POLITICAL SCIENCE: MACHIAVELLI TO MARX

On what terms do human beings live together in society? How do they institute authority and define its role or limitations? Who exercises effective power or enjoys privilege? The two great philosophers of ancient Greece, Plato and Aristotle, had both developed a theory of politics. They both examined the terms on which citizens of a polity, or city-state, should live as members of organized society. In his *Republic*, Plato had sketched out one of the first Utopias, a description of an ideal state conducted on rational principles and transcending petty jealousy and selfishness.

Modern political science started from a more grimly realistic perspective. Its pioneer was Niccolo Machiavelli, an Italian government official and diplomat who became the Copernicus of the modern political universe. In 1513, he finished *The Prince*, his much translated and often banned treatise on the principles of **power politics**. In the spirit of his time, Machiavelli admonished his readers not to rely on what everyone knew, or what everyone had been taught, or what people would have liked to believe. Instead, he asked them to look at the realities of what it takes to gain and hold political power. *Si vede per esperienza* – "We see from experience." Although he has been faulted for relying on fragmentary information and biased sources, he drew his conclusions from such facts as were available to him. Although we still use the term *Machiavellian* as a negative label, practitioners of power politics (that is, most politicians) have often acted on his advice.

Basic to Machiavelli's theory was the effective use of military power. (Power grows out of the barrel of a gun, said Chairman Mao.) Decisiveness and preemptive strikes were needed to prevent bad situations from getting worse. An effective leader would crush rivals for power and the leadership of conquered countries–while at the same time co-opting the conquered populations. Necessary cruelties, swiftly administered, would soon be forgotten, or they could be blamed on subordinates. Compared with anarchy or foreign conquest, the leader's harsh but effective rule would be the lesser evil. The end would justify the means. Although piety and compassion were handicaps in the struggle for power, the *appearance* of being religious and charitable was an important part of a leader's image. Machiavelli's answer to the splintered, weak condition of Italy and to foreign domination was to call for a strong charismatic leader, ruthless and cunning enough ("the lion and the fox") to unite his country.

By contrast, the dominant political theory of the Western democracies put the emphasis not on the leader but on the people. The people needed to unite and form an effective covenant, or **social contract.**

The British philosopher Thomas Hobbes, in his *Leviathan* (1651), described the state of nature as the war of all against all, with robber barons, rapacious warlords, or civil war making education, prosperity, and culture impossible. Without an effective government, he said, life was "nasty, brutish, and short." The solution was for all to surrender their arms and to submit to a higher authority that would keep the peace. The purpose of political institutions was to assure peace and security for the people.

Hobbes was pessimistic about the ability of citizens to agree voluntarily to the necessary taxes or military service, and he stipulated a strong executive—an absolute sovereign—with the power of taxation, military conscription, and censorship of subversive opinions. However, in the writings of John Locke and others, social contract theory soon shifted toward the concept of **popular sovereignty,** with those governing us being mere deputies or representatives of the sovereign people. Checks and balances had to be provided to prevent the abuse of power, and the people had to be able to recall or remove those abusing the public trust. When you see them in this context, you may decide that the emancipation of the slaves and women's right to vote were a gradual broadening of the base of representative democracy.

During the eighteenth century, the theory of the social contract acquired a strong individualistic, anti-institutional and anti-government, bias (still strong in current American politics). The French philosopher Jean-Jacques Rousseau believed in the native goodness of human beings: We were born capable of generosity and harmony, but we were corrupted by oppressive institutions. When humanity was freed of rigid schools, oppressive customs, and tyrannical governments, the full self-realization of the individual would become possible. Rousseau's optimistic view of human nature strongly influenced the tradition of American optimism. The American Revolution (1776–1783) made "life, liberty, and the pursuit of happiness"—rather than service to the state or loyalty to a royal house—the declared goals of organized society. Soon after Rousseau helped inspire the French Revolution, Mary Wollstonecraft, an early British feminist, in *A Vindication of the Rights of Woman* (1792), asked that women be emancipated from their inferior, dependent status and accorded equal rights with men.

Late in the nineteenth century, as a predatory, unchecked capitalistic system produced a large exploited working class living in slums and paid starvation wages, the theory of representative democratic government came in for drastic rethinking. The German Jewish political philosopher Karl Marx (1818– 1883), along with other early socialist or communist thinkers, claimed that representative democracy was an illusion masking the economic realities of a capitalistic society. Power was in the hands of those who owned the land, the mines, the factories—the means of production. People with money manipulated the political process, rigging the laws to allow the wealthy to exploit working people. The aim of political action became to wrest control from the bourgeoisie, or middle class, and put it in the hands of workers and peasants, who in capitalist societies were becoming an impoverished proletariat. (As French President Mitterand said shortly before he died in 1996, a class with wealth and power may be able to hold down the poor for a long time, but eventually they will march on the rich quarters of town and burn down the mansions.)

When studying the political history of the twentieth century, you may try charting the interplay of these three megatraditions of political theory. You will then be testing a **dialectic** view of history—which sees history not as gradual progress but as the marching and countermarching of powerful opposed forces.

- In totalitarian societies (fascist Italy, Nazi Germany, Stalinist Russia), the cult of the effective leader made people follow a Duce, a Führer, or a Comrade Chairman with dictatorial powers. "Lead, and we will follow" chanted Hitler's followers at his megalomaniacal party rallies.

- Moving in a diametrically opposite direction, the drive toward democratic representation transformed traditional monarchies into constitutional monarchies (like Britain) or republics (like France and Germany). It caused totalitarian societies to be made over on the democratic model. Iron curtains and ideologies that seemed set in cement have dissolved as citizens asserted the rights of the individual human being. (Grass now grows where the Berlin Wall once cut a death strip of watch towers, mine fields, and police dogs through a living city.)

- Finally, where the democratic ideal seemed to fail the masses, revolutionary movements committed to the ideology of class war have taken over political power in the name of the oppressed. They have championed the rights of exploited workers and dispossessed peasants, asserting their right to education, health care, and the fruits of their labor.

ANTHROPOLOGY: Understanding Other Culures

Can we study human cultures with the disinterested curiosity and open mind of a visitor from another planet? Anthropology studies customary patterns of behavior shaping people's lives. In the twenties and thirties, anthropologists like Margaret Mead (1901–1978) changed profoundly people's view of how the customs and taboos of a traditional culture shape behavior. Mead went to live among indigenous people still relatively untouched by Western influences for an inside view of patterns of adolescence and initiation into adulthood. She reported her findings–still debated and attacked half a century later–in *Coming of Age in Samoa* (1928) and *Growing Up in New Guinea* (1930).

The young science of anthropology provided a model for unbiased fresh observation: In a classic study, the pioneering anthropologist Bronislaw Malinowski (1884–1942) watched South Sea islanders going about their daily business of living. Like other students of culture, he noted the importance of factors going beyond the basic needs of raising crops and feeding the population. He studied the role of show and display in the islanders' laying out their gardens to reflect their importance in the community. (In a similar way, the palace and the gardens at Versailles reflected the splendor of the French king.) He studied the role of ritual or religious invocation in the islanders' agriculture. We might have assumed that so-called primitive societies operate on a subsistence level, with most energy consumed by the struggle to feed hungry mouths. We discover that this particular isolated non-Western society had sophisticated, highly developed patterns of social hierarchy, ostentatious display, and ritual observance.

An anthropological perspective broadens our outlook. Anthropology can help us cross narrow cultural borders, making us less ethnocentric. It can leave us less blinkered and less caught up in our own group's way of looking at the world. It weans us from considering everything in our own culture–patterns of courtship, marriage, child rearing, dealing with crime–as natural or universal or God-given. It counteracts our tendency to demonize people alien to us, to label other cultures "backward" or "primitive." Today, practitioners of ethnography study remaining indigenous cultures relatively untouched by Western civilization, often with a view toward helping them resist exploitation or extinction. At the same time, ethnographers study subcultures–ranging from punk rockers to the homeless to drug users–in our own developed societies from an anthropological perspective.

PSYCHOLOGY: Beyond Freud

How rational or irrational is human behavior? Psychology probes the workings of the human mind. It has profoundly influenced modern thinking by recognizing basic human drives, especially sexual energy, long hidden behind a fog of euphemisms and polite evasions. Early students of modern psychology learned to recognize a hierarchy of basic drives, including hunger, thirst, and the avoidance of bodily harm, that needed to be satisfied before more sophisticated human motives like empathy for others or artistic creativity could come into play. However, the major contribution of early modern psychology was to go beyond overt or easily verifiable motives to probe the true range of often puzzling, complex, and apparently irrational human behavior.

Among major early trends in psychology, the most provocative and controversial was depth psychology in the tradition of the Austrian Sigmund Freud (1856–1939), founder of psychoanalysis. Taking his clue from the study of dreams, Freud delved beyond the conscious surface of human thought and feeling to probe repressed impulses and traumas in the subconscious. According to Freud, much of people's instinctual life–the id–was frowned upon by a moralistic, guilt-ridden society, the superego. Such phenomena as the young male's love of the mother and jealousy of the father (the Oedipus complex) were taboo. They were hidden not only from others but even from the conscious self. Such repressed impulses caused the distortions, frustrations, phobias, and traumas of our neurotic modern world. A basic assumption of Freudian psychotherapy was that by bringing repressed impulses or unconscious motives to the surface, patients could exorcise the demons of the mind and become psychically whole.

Today, many of Freud's specific theories have been challenged or superseded. Nevertheless, the influence of Freudian categories and perspectives remains pervasive in literature, in the media, and in popular culture. Seen from the Freudian perspective, dreams act out psychosexual impulses in symbolic disguise, since our minds censor our dreams even while we are asleep. Art and much other human endeavor sublimate the powerful sexual forces that cannot find a direct outlet. Libido (the all-pervasive sexual energy or sex drive), infant sexuality, castration anxiety, penis envy, and sibling rivalry continue to be part of the modern vocabulary for explaining human behavior. Patterns of transference and identification, making people identify with or model themselves on others, remain part of the psychodrama of everyday life. Where our sexuality traditionally had to be hidden from a prudish society, today sex is openly explored and discussed in a thousand therapy sessions, talk shows, sex education sessions, magazine articles, and books.

On the negative side, much of the Freudian psychological approach to mental illness has in recent years given way to a new physiological perspective. Powerful new medications correct malfunctions or imbalances in the biochemistry of the brain. Depression, for instance, may as often as not be physiologically rather than psychologically based. Among Freud's many critics, feminists have strongly condemned Freud's treatment of women patients and his ascribing memories of childhood sexual abuse to female sexual fantasies. In 1995, vehement protests against an exhibit planned by the Library of Congress as a tribute testified to the extent that Freud, like Darwin and Marx, is still seen as a threat and a challenge.

The psychoanalytic movement split into feuding branches as Freud's disciples parted company with him. One of these rival branches has had a profound effect on students of myth, of literature, and generally of culture. Followers of the Swiss psychoanalyst Carl Jung (1875–1961) study patterns of thought and feeling that they see recurring in many different situations and cultural contexts. Jung described recurrent dream figures as archetypes embedded in the collective unconscious of the human species. They represent a kind of collective wisdom that survives in age-old myths and fairy tales and surfaces in dreams and works of art to guide and inspire us. For instance, many cultures have had myths or rituals centering on the charismatic leader who is defeated and killed–but who returns in a different guise as part of an age-old pattern of rebirth or resurrection.

After Freud and Jung, psychoanalysts from Karen Horney to Erich Fromm and Jacques Lacan have continued to probe the workings of the human mind. Horney broke out of the traditional male frame of reference by studying the unconscious psychological mechanisms that she claimed caused women to turn romantic love or sexual fulfillment into an unattainable Holy Grail, programming them for inevitable frustration and disappointment. Self-defeating idealized expectations would prove impossible for a chosen partner to meet, with women as a result finding themselves caught in cycles of depression, helplessness, and hostility toward men.

EXPERIMENTAL PSYCHOLOGY AND BEHAVIORISM

Can psychology emulate the scientific model of controlled experiments, with careful control of variables and with verifiable results? Current work in experimental psychology discourages theoretical speculation. Researchers set up rigorously controlled experiments with clearly defined parameters. For instance, two groups of children are exposed to different kinds of cartoons–one kind heavy on aggressive and violent acts, the other stressing nonviolent plot lines. The experimenter then observes and registers incidents of aggressive, pushy playground behavior. The working hypothesis is that aggressive behavior observed in our fantasy lives will carry over into everyday reality. According to this particular study, it does.

In the fifties and sixties, a major movement in psychology put special emphasis on overt observable behavior. Behaviorists, followers of Harvard psychologist B. F. Skinner (1904–1990), were wary of unverifiable speculation about motives and human feelings. Skinner aimed at building a science of behavior on the stimulus–response model. Whether we are dealing with a pigeon picking up a stick or a child picking up a block to build a tower, we are observing an organism interacting with its environment. A stimulus or set of stimuli generates an observable response. Positive reinforcement tends to encourage repetition of the behavior; negative reinforcement tends to discourage it.

In educational psychology, behaviorists put the emphasis on performance–on observable, testable learning outcomes. They aimed at "operationalizing" instruction: After a given unit of instruction, what would the student be able to do? The behaviorist model tended to break up teaching into discrete blocks of instruction or learning modules. It stressed applying what is learned to the student's performance in real-life situations.

As a student, you may have seen firsthand evidence of a test-oriented, "show-me-what-you-can-do" philosophy. You may have observed strong reliance on proficiency tests and SAT scores (with teachers "teaching to the test"). However, many teachers and educational reformers push for a more **holistic** approach, which sees meaningful learning as taking place in a larger context. Students mature over the years, at their own pace, with lulls and leaps forward that do not show on tests. Holistically defined, true learning means the ability to see ideas as part of a larger whole; it means the ability to see the connections between ideas. It is then not enough to teach limited skills; the test of survival in the modern world is quickness in learning *new* skills and responding to new situations. Picking the right answers on a multiple-choice test is not the same as thinking through a challenging new situation.

SOCIAL SCIENCE TODAY

Much work on current trends and future directions in our society is done by interested parties. Pollsters in the pay of candidates word questions in such a way as to obtain results pleasing to who pays the piper. Experts in audience manipulation test slogans on focus groups. Psychologists school advertisers in the appeals most effective with specified segments of the youth market or the senior market.

At the same time, social science research continues to aim at a better understanding of the social forces that shape our lives. For instance, researchers have been studying the dynamics of social and political movements. A movement like the civil rights movement or the women's movement may be galvanized by a seminal event (Rosa Parks refusing to move to the back of the bus). It may be radicalized as extreme, militant elements abandon an earlier stance of nonviolence. It may be co-opted by the establishment as everyone starts to talk the talk (but not all of them walk the walk). The means serving the ends of

the movement may include consciousness-raising workshops, grass roots organization, informal networking, letter-writing campaigns, protests, boycotts, or
legislative campaigns.

QUESTIONS FOR DISCUSSION

What were you taught about the ideology of the American Revolution
or about the ideas and ideals of the founders? (What do you know about
the ideology of the French Revolution of 1789 or the Russian Revolution of
1917?) How much do you know about Marx and Marxists? (Would you classify yourself as upper class, middle class, or lower class?) What have you read
or heard about the work of Western ethnographers with the indigenous people
of the Amazon Basin, the aborigines of Australia, the Maoris of New Zealand,
or similar populations? What ideas or associations do the terms *Freud* or *Freudian* bring to mind? Have you encountered evidence of the Jungian concern
with myth, ritual, or archetypes? Have you read about or participated in controlled psychological experiments? What do you know about the history or
key ideas of feminism or the women's movement?

JOE GUTIERREZ
On the Job

Studs Terkel

——

> *How do researchers get a handle on the social realities of our world? Grassroots interviewers like Robert Coles, Studs Terkel, and Jonathan Kozol are famous for their fieldwork. They go into the streets, the factories, the low-income neighborhoods, the homeless encampments and elicit personal testimony. Their interviewing brings out not what teachers, preachers, or social workers may want to hear but what actually motivates people. Studs Terkel became known through a series of books in which Americans talked about the real issues in their lives:* America *(1967),* Hard Times *(1970),* Working *(1972),* American Dreams: Lost and Found *(1980), and* The Great Divide *(1988). Much of Terkel's work is focused on the city of Chicago, where he was born, and which he calls "America's metaphor." Here they came looking for work: the immigrants from Eastern Europe and the Mediterranean, the Appalachians from border states, and the African Americans from the deep South, "seeking, as the others, a better life." In 1992, Terkel published* Race: How Blacks and Whites Think and Feel about the American Obsession. *The conversations recorded in this book probed race relations at a time when the gains of the Civil Rights movement were being called into question. Jobs for low-income people were disappearing, whites were developing a siege mentality, and blacks found themselves the victims of stereotyping and resurgent racism.*
>
> *Joe Gutierrez, the person speaking in the following interview, was one of fifteen children of an immigrant from Mexico and a woman from Georgia who married at age fourteen. Joe, who grew up knowing no Spanish, spent four years in a seminary studying to be a priest before he went to work in the steel mills like his father before him.*

I didn't identify with Mexicans until people started throwing racism around.   1
My name is José but I've always been called Little Joe. The whites didn't know my last name and thought I was Italian or Greek. So they let out their true feelings.

I was not accepted by the Mexicans because I couldn't speak the language: "You look white, so you don't want to be a Mexican." I forced myself to learn the language so at least I could get by.

We were the only Mexican family in the neighborhood. The Mexicans, Puerto Ricans, and blacks lived on the East Chicago side by the mills. Now it's all changed. You've got a neighbor that's black, another Puerto Rican, another something else. All on our street.

We were about eight years old, my brother, Vince, and I when we went to a public swimming pool in a park in East Chicago. We took a black kid with us. This was 1948. As soon as we dove in the pool, everybody got out. The lifeguard got out, too, a female. They shut down the pool. I was never raised to be a racist, so I didn't know what it was all about.

There's a certain amount of racism among Mexicans against blacks, and Mexicans against Puerto Ricans. But I see more racism with the blacks than with the white or Latin.

We went through a union election. We're about thirty percent black. Every time I ran for office, there was a solid black vote for the black, regardless of the person. It made no difference. Over the years, I felt it would change because people would look at the person's qualifications. For the most part, it hasn't changed. That's true among Latins also. They'll vote Latin just because he's Latin. Whites? Yeah, pretty much the same.

A good friend of mine, a white from Kentucky, just got elected griever in the metal-plate department. I said, "The black griever we have is simply unqualified; he's done a terrible job. I don't expect the blacks to vote for him. He won't get over twenty votes." He said, "The guy's gonna get a hundred votes." He was right. For three years, the guy did an awful job. They still came out and backed him. I understand the past injustices, but . . .

The guys who are honest say, "Look, we've been down so long, the first time we get somebody to represent the black community, he projects an image of leadership and we overlook the bad. We just want a black there."

It baffles my mind because I've had an ongoing fight in the mills: I don't care if you're black, brown, or white, we're all workers. I sometimes get chastised by the so-called leaders of the Latin community because I don't stand up and say we should all go for *la raza.* There are some Latins who always vote that way. I voted that way before I got involved with the union. I didn't know people. If I saw a Sánchez or Gonzalez or Rodríguez, I voted for him. I met a Cisneros who couldn't write his own name and didn't give a damn about the union, was a company guy. I said nah, nah, nah. He may be Latin but he doesn't represent the interests of working people. I don't care about image.

With whites, what comes first is my pocketbook. I can work with a black, with a Latin, but as soon as I leave that steel mill, I get on South 41 and go back to my world. Here it's a temporary world for eight hours a day, five days a week. When you park your car and walk into that plant, you walk into another world. All your prejudices, all your hates, you leave in the parking lot.

At the workplace, there's not much tension. You still have people who feel they're treated unfairly because they're black or Latin. When some whites get disciplined, they say, "I'm white, you didn't discipline the black guy." It's a crutch. But in general, it's not there. You're working around heavy equipment and you've got to look out for your buddy. It's very easy to get hurt in a steel mill.

As for whites, there's still a lot of prejudice out there. I know how to erase it. If you give other people a chance—if you give me the opportunity to present my views, maybe you'll get to know me and like me. Look, there's some people you just don't like. It's got nothing to do with color; it's got a lot to do with personality.

Latins are right in the middle. For the longest time, they were classified as blacks. You go to Texas, and Latinos are treated like blacks.

With people losing jobs, there's always got to be somebody to blame. We had nineteen thousand people at Inland Steel. Now we're below ten thousand. For years, whites had all the better jobs. In 1977, the government came in and said you've got to do something about discrimination in the workplace or we'll do it for you. They signed a Memorandum of Understanding that implemented plantwide seniority. It was good for everybody. Now a black or Latino as well as a white could transfer in any department and utilize seniority.

At the time, whites ran the trains, Latins worked on the tracks, and blacks worked in the coke plants. When the changes took place, there was a lot of hatred among whites against minorities in general. "I've worked in this mill for twenty-five years, and here's one of them coming over and bumping me out of a job." It didn't happen that way for the most part, because you still had contract language to go by. You couldn't leapfrog over somebody.

We had an election the other day and won by a landslide. I acted as a watcher. Some voted only for Latins, others only for blacks, and some whites only for whites. Our slate had a president who's white, a Latin who's vicepresident, and two black trustees. It was a mix all around. We voted for the person. We represented the rank-and-file against the old guys. For the most part, we're forty, forty-one years old. You don't have a younger crop because there are no jobs for them.

What's ahead doesn't look good. With a new power plant, a lot of departments will shut down. The coke plants will go. You'll see some of the old hatred coming back. Blacks will say, "You gave us the rotten jobs whites wouldn't take, working on batteries, causing cancer and so forth, and when things get bad, we're the first to go." We're hearing it now. With fewer and fewer jobs, it'll get worse.

I don't like racists–white, black, Latin, anybody. Life's too short for meanness. There was a lot in the army when I was in it. Sometimes it comes out of people you don't expect it from. There's a guy who's decent, a hard worker, a good family man, and he'll say, "That fuckin' nigger." It's like getting hit in the gut. I stop him: "Why do you say that?" He just shrugs. He's Mexican, a deacon in the church. I'm a lector there. I tell this guy, "If a white guy says nigger, the word you use, I bet he calls you spic, taco-bender. Cut out this bullshit."

What's happened is that people were getting tired of the sixties. There was a legitimate grievance among the blacks in this country and a lot of us took part in the marches. But about twelve, fifteen years ago, younger blacks started coming into the steel mills. The older guys found allies among the Latins on the shop floor. But the younger guys came in with one thought in mind: We've been screwed and if we don't keep on their backs, they're gonna screw us again. To them, we're no different than the whites. It started backfiring.

Those of us who were sympathetic are less that way today. I had won over a   20
lot of blacks because I did a good job. But there are some blacks, I swear to God, I
don't care what you did, it made no difference. All they saw was black. It's damaging to themselves. What more can a boss wish for?–divide and conquer!

When the government came down with a consent decree, Inland Steel ignored
it. Every other company–LTV, Bethlehem, USX–paid minorities monies–two, three
thousand dollars apiece–on the basis of years of discrimination at work. Inland
Steel paid not a penny. They had a sharp lawyer who said, "Look, people are tired
of civil rights, of marches, of busing, of affirmative action. The mood of the country is changing. Let's fight it." The government didn't follow through, and they didn't
pay a penny. . . .

I don't think the company is racist. That's too simple. It's the bottom line, the
dollar. They don't care about you, no matter what your color is. You're nothing to
them. If you're black or Latin or white, if they can set you up against the other
workers, they're going to use you. They don't give a damn what color you are. It's
the profit.

We have to keep working together, and when we hear the word nigger or
spic–or cracker–stand up and say, "I don't appreciate that. Enough of this bullshit!"

The Responsive Reader

1. This interview touches on issues that have been the subject of much controversy and conflicting information. Would you consider Joe Gutierrez a reliable
   witness? Does he sound sincere–where and why? What limits his point of view
   or perspective?

2. What has shaped Joe's views on race? What has he observed about the way
   race affects job assignments? How does it affect union politics? What are his
   views on race relations in the workplace and in society at large?

3. What is Joe's attitude toward management? What does he see as company policy on the subject of race?

4. Does Joe have prejudices? Would you call him biased or racist? Would you call
   him a person of good will?

For Discussion or Writing

5. Would you call Joe Gutierrez a typical working-class American? Why or why
   not?

6. What has shaped your own views on race or race relations? Have you had experiences comparable to those of Joe Gutierrez? Or have your own observations
   been different?

7. Do you think the trend is toward continued segregation by race or ethnicity, or will Americans of mixed descent like Joe Gutierrez be more of a factor in our society?

Collaborative Projects

8. Working with a group, you may want to help plan some interviews with working-class or low-income Americans. What is their view of race relations in the workplace?

CULTURAL PATTERNS OF THE MAASAI

Lisa Skow AND *Larry A. Samovar*

> *Anthropologists search for patterns in behavior that may at first seem strange to the out-sider. They formulate generalizations on the basis of long periods of patient observation. Ideally, they try not to let their own culturally conditioned ideas of what is natural or logical or ethical influence their research. They guard against labeling non-Western ways of looking at the world as backward or primitive. They approach indigenous populations not in a missionary spirit, trying to convert them to "civilized" ways, but in the spirit of scientists, trying to empathize and under-stand. The following article was prepared for a textbook called* Intercultural Communication *(1991). Lisa Skow is a former Peace Corps volunteer and a graduate of San Diego State University. Larry Samovar teaches at San Diego State University. The subject of their study, the Maasai of Kenya and Tanzania in East Africa, early entered into the folklore of the West as a proud people of herders and warriors.*

For many years critics of intercultural communication have charged that the field focuses on a handful of cultures while seriously neglecting others. For ex-ample, the literature abounds with material concerning Japan and Mexico, but there is very little to be found if one seeks to understand the cultures of India or black Africa. As economics and politics force a global interdependence, it behooves us to examine cultures that were previously excluded from our scrutiny.

The motivation for such analysis can take a variety of forms. Our desire for more information might be altruistic, as we learn that 40,000 babies die of starva-tion each day in developing countries. Or we may decide that we need to know about other cultures for more practical reasons. Strong ties with African countries can lead to economic, educational, and technological exchanges beneficial to indi-viduals on both sides of the globe. Regardless of our motives, the 1990s and be-yond will offer countless examples that demand that we look at cultures that we have ignored in the past. This article is an attempt to explore one of those cultures, specifically, that of the Maasai of East Africa.

If we accept the view of culture held by most anthropologists, it becomes nearly impossible to discover all there is to know about any one group of people. That is to say, how does one decide what is important about a culture if Hall (1976) is correct when he writes, "there is not one aspect of human life that is not touched and altered by culture" (p. 14)? The decision as to what to include and exclude in any analysis of a culture is usually based on the background of the researcher. Someone interested in the music of a culture would obviously look at the portion of the culture relating to that specific topic and, in a sense, abstract only part of the total phenomenon called culture.

A researcher interested in intercultural communication is also faced with the problem of what to select from the total experiences of a people. What, in short, do we need to know if our goal is to understand the behavior of another culture? One answer to this question is found in the work of Samovar and Porter (1988). They have proposed a model of intercultural communication that can be used as a guide in selecting what aspects of culture need to be incorporated into any discussion of intercultural communication. This article will address the three major components of that model: perception, verbal processes, and nonverbal processes.

BACKGROUND

The East African countries of Kenya and Tanzania know firsthand about West-   5
ern culture. They have lived through Western government, language, culture, and, unfortunately, oppression. Even today, more than two decades after each country received its independence, Western culture still has a profound influence on the people of Kenya and Tanzania. However, because there are so many different ethnic groups in these countries, it has not had the same impact and influence on each group. The Kikuyu of Kenya have adopted Western culture with such enthusiasm that one wonders what are "proper" Kikuyu traditions and customs and what are Western influences. On the other end of the Western continuum are the Maasai of southern Kenya and northern Tanzania, who have, for a number of reasons, rejected much of the culture presented by the West. They have largely shunned Western forms of government, dress, language, music, religion, and frequently even assistance. The Maasai are often referred to as "true Africans" because of their "purity"—a purity of which they are very proud.

Africa may be changing at an extraordinarily fast pace, but the Maasai are one group of people who seem content to continue their own way of life. This article hopes to offer some insight into that way of life.

PERCEPTION

One of the basic axioms of intercultural communication, and one that is part of the Samovar and Porter (1988) intercultural model, is that culture and perception work in tandem. That is to say, our cultural experiences determine, to a large extent, our view of the world. Those experiences that are most important are transmitted from generation to generation as a means of assuring that the culture will survive beyond the lifetime of its current members. Therefore, to understand any culture it is necessary to examine those experiences that are deemed meaningful enough to be carried to each generation. One way to study those experiences is through the history of a culture. The history of any culture can offer insight into the behaviors of the culture as well as explain some of the causes behind those behaviors. Let us therefore begin our analysis of the Maasai people by looking at those aspects of their history that link current perceptions to the past.

History

While the history of any culture is made up of thousands of experiences, there are often a few significant ones that serve to explain how that culture might view the world. In the case of the Maasai, there are three historical episodes that have greatly influenced their perception of themselves, other people, and events. These historical occurrences center on their creation, fierceness, and reaction to modernization.

The history of the Maasai is the history of a people with an oral tradition. Like all cultures who practice the oral tradition, the content and customs that are transmitted are largely found within the stories, poetry, and songs of the people. To the outsider they appear vague and only loosely based on facts. Some historians, along with the aid of Maasai elders, have attempted to link the stories and folklore with the available information about the Maasai's past, a past that helps explain many of the perceptions and values held by the Maasai.

Most accounts of the origin of the Maasai as a unique culture begin with the   10 belief that they were part of a larger group that was migrating south during a severe drought (Kipury, 1983). The group found themselves trapped in a deep valley so they constructed a bridge that was to transport them out of the valley. Folk tales and history go on to tell the story of how the bridge collapsed before all the people escaped. Those who were left behind are now thought to be the Somali, Borana, and Rendile peoples. Those who managed to escape the dryness of the valley went on to be the true Maa–speaking people.

While the above rendition of early Maasai history is uncertain in answering questions regarding the origins of the Maasai, it does reveal one very important aspect of how history and perception are linked. This story helps explain how the Maasai perceive themselves compared to other tribes. It also helps an outsider understand the strong feelings of pride that are associated with the Maasai culture. For the Maasai, the story of their origin, even if it is speculation, tells them they are better than other tribes of East Africa who did not come from the north nor escape across the bridge–regardless of how long ago that arrival might have been.

The Maasai's history of warfare and conflict is yet another source of knowledge about the perception of themselves and non-Maasai. Before the advent of colonialism in the latter part of the nineteenth century, other tribes in Kenya such as the Kikuyu, Akamba, and Kalenjin were often attacked by the Maasai. The attacks were fierce and usually resulted in their enemies being forced from their lands. Some Maasai, particularly the elders, still see themselves as the conquerors of other tribes, and even today, the Maasai still have the reputation of being war-like. Non-Maasai Kenyans may warn visitors of the "terrible" Maasai and their propensity for violence. A former colleague of one of the authors often expressed her distrust of the Maasai, believing that they would harm her simply because she was from the Kikuyu tribe. She had heard about the Maasai's fierceness and their dislike of other tribes who dressed in Western clothes. Whether entirely accurate or not, this perception of them as warlike influences both the behavior of the Maasai and the behavior of those who come in contact with them.

A third historical period that has shaped the perceptions of the Maasai is the preindependence period of Kenya. Because the Maasai occupied vast areas of land in Kenya, the British colonialists turned an eye toward acquiring this valuable property. Through numerous agreements, great parcels of land were turned over to the colonialists. The Maasai were settled on new tracts of land that were much less desirable than the ones they were leaving, and they soon began to realize that not only were they giving up their prime land but they were also seeing a number of promises made by the colonialists being broken. In response to these two conclu-sions, the Maasai adopted an attitude of passive resistance to all Western innova-tions and temptations to become "modern." While most other parts of Kenya were altering their culture through education and technology, the Maasai had become disillusioned with those who were seeking to alter their way of life, and hence they refused to change (Sankan, 1971).

The rejection of cultural conversion by the Maasai has had immense conse-quences on them and the people around them. On one hand it has caused the government and other tribes to perceive them as stubbornly traditional, backward, uneducated, and isolated. However, for the Maasai, resistance to change is yet an-other indication of their strength and long history of power. Other more Western-ized tribes, such as the Kikuyu, feel the Maasai are backward and not in tune with changing Kenya. Ironically, the Kikuyu seem to have a love-hate relationship with the Maasai: scorn for their refusal to be more modern yet respect for their retain-ing their traditional customs.

Values

What a culture values, or doesn't value, also helps determine how that culture perceives the world. Therefore, understanding what the Maasai regard as good or bad, valuable or worthless, right or wrong, just or unjust, and appropriate or inap-propriate can help explain the communication behavior of their culture.

Children   For a Maasai man or woman to be without children is a great mis-fortune. The Maasai strongly believe that children continue the race, and more important, they will preserve the family–hence, children are highly valued. The Maasai embrace the idea that a man can "live" even after death if he has a son who can carry on his name, enjoy his wealth, and spread his reputation. In addition, they value children because they offer the senior Maasai a continuous supply of workers. The Maasai have a saying that illustrates this point: "More hands make light the work." Children supply those hands. Unfortunately, this value is in direct conflict with the Kenyan government's family planning program to curb Kenya's dangerously high population growth. While the central government tries to emphasize the need to control the population, for the Maasai the man with the most children, no matter how poor he is, is the wealthiest and happiest of all men.

Cattle   The Maasai culture revolves around the cow, on which they greatly depend for their food, clothing, housing, fuel, trade, medicine, and ceremonies. Cattle have given the Maasai their traditionally nomadic life style. The more cattle a man has the more respected he is. Cattle are usually killed only on designated occasions such as for marriage and circumcision ceremonies or when special guests visit. The Maasai believe that all cattle were originally given to them by God. There is even a folk tale that tells of the Maasai descending to earth with cattle by their sides. This belief justifies their taking cattle from other tribes, even if it is in violation of the law.

Groups   Families and life-stage groups are at the core of the Maasai community. Because children are so highly valued, the family must be strong and central in their lives. An overwhelming portion of a Maasai child's education is still carried out in the home, with the grandparents, not the schools, providing the content of the culture.

Life-stage groups are specifically defined periods in the lives of all Maasai, particularly males. Traditionally, all men must go through four stages of life: childhood, adolescence (circumcision), moranship (warriorhood—junior and senior), and elderhood (junior and senior). Women must pass through childhood, circumcision, and then marriage. Each of these stages places a strong emphasis on the group. Attempts to get Maasai students to raise their hands and participate in formal classrooms are often futile. Drawing attention to oneself in a group setting is unacceptable because the tribe and the life-stage group are far more valuable than the individual (Johnstone, 1988).

Elders: Male and Female   Maasai children must give respect to any person older   20
than themselves, whether a sibling, grandmother, or older member of the community. They must bow their heads in greeting as a sign of humility and inferiority. Even young circumcised men and women (aged fifteen to twenty-five years) must bow their heads to male elders, particularly if the elders are highly respected in the community.

The Maasai believe the older you become the wiser you become and that a wise individual deserves a great deal of deference and respect. Part of the strong emphasis placed on elders is that the Maasai hold their history in such high regard, and it is the oldest members of the tribe who know most of the history. Young people cannot know the "truth" until they progress through each of the life-stage groups.

For Maasai youths getting older indicates a change in social status. When male Maasai students return from a school holiday with their heads shaved, this indicates that they have just gone through circumcision and initiation into another life-stage. They have become men and are instantly perceived by other students and themselves as different, even older, and deserving of more respect.

Pride   Pride for the Maasai means having the virtues of obedience, honesty, wisdom, and fairness. A man may be an elder in name only, for if he does not exhibit these characteristics, he is not a respected man in the community. A woman's pride is often defined by how well she keeps her home, by whether she is an obedient wife, and by the number of children she has.

Outsiders, whether black or white, perceive the Maasai loftiness and pride as a kind of arrogance. The Maasai themselves, because they are traditionally pastoralists, still look down on strictly agricultural tribes such as the Kikuyu.

Their strong sense of pride is also fueled by their view of themselves as warriors. As noted earlier, they have always been feared by other tribes and the colonialists. Their folklore is replete with tales of their fighting with incredible fearlessness, even when their primitive weapons faced their enemies' modern bullets. For them the battles were to preserve the "true African" way of life and to protect their cattle.

Beauty   Beauty is yet another value that is important to the Maasai. Both men and women adorn themselves with elaborate beads, body paint, and other jewelry. Maasai children, especially girls, begin wearing jewelry almost from the moment of birth. One of the primary duties a woman has is to make necklaces, bracelets, bangles, belts, and earrings for her husband, children, friends, and herself. Adornment is also a way for a woman to attract a husband, and Maasai women are very meticulous in selecting jewelry for special celebrations. Maasai warriors still spend much of their day painting themselves with red ochre, and they also plait and braid their hair, which is grown long as a sign of warriorhood.

Beauty and bodily adornment are so valued in the Maasai culture that they have distinctive jewelry and dress to wear during certain periods of each life-stage. For example, one can tell if a boy has just recently been circumcised because he wears a crown of bird carcasses. Thus, we can conclude that beauty is more than superficial for the Maasai; it is a reflection of a very important value that often steers perception in one direction or another.

World View

The world view of a culture is yet another factor that greatly modifies perception. In the Samovar and Porter (1988) model, world view deals with a culture's orientation toward such things as God, humanity, the universe, death, nature, and other philosophical issues that are concerned with the concept of being. In short, it is that perception of the world that helps the individual locate his or her place and rank in the universe. It influences nearly every action in which an individual engages. Our research would tend to agree with this observation. The Maasai's world view has three components that greatly control their life and hence their perception of the universe: coexistence with nature, religion, and death.

Nature   For the Maasai, nature must always be held in the highest regard. They believe that their very existence depends solely on nature's benevolence. Their life style is one that sees them interacting with the elements: Without rain their cattle will die, and in a sense so will they, for as we pointed out earlier, cattle supply most of the basic needs of the Maasai.

The Maasai also embrace the view that nature cannot be changed; it is too   30
powerful. But they do acknowledge that nature itself changes without their intervening, and what they must do is change as nature fluctuates. Adapting to nature is most evident in the Maasai's seminomadic life style. They carry coexistence to the point where they will not kill or eat wild animals unless they pose a threat or there is a severe drought. For the Maasai cultivating and hunting are seen as destructive to nature: Cultivation forces humans to deal directly with nature, changing and altering it to their specifications and needs; hunting for food is seen as something even worse, for then nature is not only being changed but it is being destroyed (Rigby, 1985).

Religion   The second aspect of world view, religion, is closely tied to the Maasai perception of nature. The Maasai have one god called "Engai," but this god has two very distinct personalities and therefore serves two purposes: "Engai Narok," the black god, is benevolent and generous and shows himself through rain and thunder; "Engai Nanyokie," the red god, is manifested in lightning. To the Maasai, God encompasses everything in nature, friendly or destructive (Saitoti and Beckwith, 1980). In fact, the word "Engai" actually means "sky." Cattle accompanied the Maasai people to earth from the sky and thus cattle are seen as mediators between humans and God as well as between humans and nature. Therefore, herding is traditionally the only acceptable livelihood, since it is God's will. Not to herd would be disrespectful to Engai and demeaning to a Maasai (Salvadon and Fedders, 1973).

There is a Maasai proverb that states, "The one chosen by God is not the one chosen by people" (Rigby, 1985, p. 92). Thus, not surprisingly, the Maasai have no priests or ministers; there is no one who represents God or purports to speak for God. There are "laiboni" who are considered the wisest of the elders and often cast curses and give blessings, but they do not represent God or preach. The Maasai have no religious writings, only oral legends, therefore the elders are important in the religious life of the people.

What is most significant is that God (Engai) is found in nature. Some Maasai households rise at dawn to pray to the sun, which is seen as a manifestation of Engai. God is found in many other forms in nature for the Maasai: rain, grass, and even a particularly beautiful stone. God *is* nature and cannot be artificially symbolized in a cross or a building. Since nature is God, people must live in harmony with God and the Maasai must work together. This is a different view of God than the one offered by Christianity, in which God is separate from humans and is even from a different world. . . .

VERBAL PROCESSES

In the most basic sense, language is an organized, generally agreed upon, learned symbol system used to represent human experiences within a geographic or cultural community. Each culture places its individual imprint on words—how they are used and what they mean.

Language is the primary vehicle by which a culture transmits its beliefs, values, and norms. Language gives people a means of interacting with other members of their culture and a means of thinking, serving both as a mechanism for communication and as a guide to social reality. Anyone interested in studying another culture must therefore look at the way a culture uses language and also the experiences in their environment they have selected to name. Research on the Maasai culture reveals two language variables that offer a clue into the workings of this particular group of people: their use of metaphors and their reliance on proverbs.

Metaphors

Wisdom in the Maasai culture is marked not just by age and prudence but also by language use. Elders make decisions at tribal meetings based on speeches offered by various members of the group. The most successful speakers are those whose eloquence is embellished and ornate. The metaphor offers the gifted speaker a tool to demonstrate his mastery of words. Heine and Claudi (1986) explain the importance of metaphor to the Maasai when they write:

> Maa people frequently claim that their language is particularly rich in figurative speech forms. Non-literal language, especially the use of metaphors, is in fact encouraged from earliest childhood on, and the success of a political leader depends to quite a large extent on the creative use of it (p. 17).

TABLE 1.

Category	Maasai Word	Basic Meaning	Metaphorical Meaning
Object + Animal	Olmotonyi	Large bird	Eagle shoulder cape
Person + Animal	Enker	Sheep	Careless, stupid person
Person + Object	Sotua	Umbilical cord	Close friend
Quality + Object	Olpiron	Firestick	Age-set generation

Because of the value placed on metaphors, Johnstone (1988) writes, "Whenever there were big meetings to decide important matters, the men always spoke in proverbs, metaphors, and other figurative language." Messages are full of elaborate symbolism–blunt and simple words are rarely used.

The information in Table 1, developed by Heine and Claudi (1986), helps clarify some of the types of metaphors employed by the Maasai. These few examples demonstrate how most of the metaphors in the Maa language reflect what is important in their culture. For example, the use of the umbilical cord to refer to a very close friend is indicative of the value placed on childbirth and of the strong bonds between members of the same age-set. In addition, an age-set generation is formally established when a select group of elders kindles the fire on the day that a new generation of boys will be circumcised (Heine & Claudi, 1986). These age-sets form both a unique governing body and a social hierarchy in all Maasai communities.

Proverbs

Like metaphors, proverbs are an integral part of the Maasai language. Massek and Sidai (1974) noted that "a Maasai hardly speaks ten sentences without using at least one proverb" (p. 6). These proverbs have common elements and themes that are directly related to the Maasai value system.

Proverbs convey important messages to the members of a culture because they often deal with subjects that are of significance. Therefore, the assumption behind examining the proverbs is a simple one–discover the meaning of the proverb and you will understand something of what is important to its user. This axiom is exceptionally true for the Maasai, for here one encounters proverbs focusing on respect, parents, children, wisdom, and proper conduct. Let us look at some of these proverbs as a way of furthering an understanding of the Maasai culture.   40

1. "Meeta enkerai olopeny." (The child has no owner.) Maasai children are expected to respect all elders, not just those in the immediate family. It is very common for children to refer to older men as "Father" and to older women as "Mother."

2. "Memorataa olayoni oataa menye." (One is never a man while his father is

still alive.) Even as junior elders, Maasai men do not always leave their father's homestead. It is not until a man attains the full status of senior elder that he usually establishes his own home with his wife (wives) and children. In addition, the very name of male children is indicated with the word "ole," which means "son of," placed between the first and last names. A Maasai male is very often characterized by his father's name and reputation.

3. "Eder olayioni o menye, neder entito o notanye." (A boy converses with his father while a girl converses with her mother.) This proverb is representative of both the restricted relationships between the opposite sexes in a family and the strict divisions of labor found in the Maasai culture. Young girls learn to do household chores at an early age, and by age seven their brothers are responsible for tending the family herd. . . .

NONVERBAL PROCESSES

Nonverbal systems represent yet another coding system that individuals and cultures use as a means of sharing their realities. Like verbal symbols, nonverbal codes are learned as part of the socialization process–that is, each culture teaches its members the symbol and the meaning for the symbol. In the case of the Maasai, there are a number of nonverbal messages that, when understood, offer the outsider some clues as to the workings of this foreign culture.

Movement and Posture

The Maasai show their pride and self-regard by the way they carry themselves. They are tall and slender and have a posture that reflects an appearance of strength and vigor. There is, at first glance, a regal air about them and at times they appear to be floating. "The morans [warriors], especially, walk very erect and relatively slowly. It's like they are in so much command of their environment that they are absolutely at ease" (Johnstone, personal correspondence, 1988).

The posture and movement of Maasai women also mirrors an attitude of pride and self-assurance. They are also tall and slender and have a gait that is slow and self-confident. Their heads are held high as a way of emphasizing their confidence and superiority over other tribes. . . .

Touching

While public touching between the sexes among the Maasai is usually limited to a light handshake, same-sex touching is common. Simple greetings between the sexes consist of a very light brush of the palms; in fact, so light is the touch, the hands appear barely to touch. If two women are good friends, however, they may greet each other with a light kiss on the lips. If they have not seen each other recently, they may embrace and clutch each other's upper arms. Men will frequently drape their arms around each other while conversing. When children greet an elder, they bow their heads so that the elder may place his or her hand on the young person's head, which is a sign of both respect and fondness. There is a great deal of affection to be found among the Maasai, and touching is one way of displaying that affection.

Time

The meaning cultures attach to time also reveals something of their view toward life and other people. The Maasai are unique in their treatment of time. Unlike the Westerner, for the Maasai there is always enough time: Their life is not governed by the clock; they are never in a hurry. This casual attitude produces a people who are self-possessed, calm, and most of all, *patient*.   45

Children are taught very early that there is never a need to rush. The vital chore of tending the family cattle requires that children stay alert and attentive to the herd's needs and safety, but such a chore also requires eight to ten hours of patient solitude.

This endless display of patience by the Maasai people is in direct contrast to time-conscious Americans. For example, public transportation in Kenya is not run on a firm schedule; buses and "matatus" (covered pick-up trucks) leave for their destinations when they are full. As do most Kenyans, the Maasai understand this. Inquiries from Americans as to when a vehicle will be departing are often answered with "just now." "Just now," however, can mean anywhere from five minutes to an hour.

Even though the present is fully enjoyed, the Maasai culture is very past-oriented. This strong tie to the past stems from the view that wisdom is found not in the present or the future, but rather in the past. The future is governed by the knowledge of the elderly, not by the discoveries of the young. The insignificance of the future is apparent in how the Maasai perceive death: There is nothing after death unless one is a "laiboni" (wise man). . . .

CONCLUSION

It has been the intent of this article to offer some observations about the Maasai culture. It is our contention that by knowing something about the perceptions and language systems of a culture, one can better understand that culture. This increased understanding provides us with a fund of knowledge that can be helpful in formulating messages directed to a group of people different from ourselves. It can also aid in interpreting the meanings behind the messages we receive from people who appear quite different from us. As Emerson wrote, "All persons are puzzles until at last we find some word or act, the key to the man, to the woman; straightaway all their past words and actions lie in light before us."

REFERENCES

Hall, E. (1976). *Beyond Culture*. Garden City, N.Y.: Anchor Books.

Heine, B., and Claudi, U. (1986). *On the Rise of Grammatical Categories*. Berlin, West Germany: Dietrich Reimer Verlag.

Johnstone, J. (1988, March 30). Personal correspondence.

Kipury, N. (1983). *Oral Literature of the Maasai*. Nairobi, Kenya: Heinemann Educational Books.

Massek, A. O., and Sidai, J. O. (1974). *Eneno oo Lmaasai—Wisdom of the Maasai*. Nairobi, Kenya: Transafrica Publishers.

Rigby, P. (1985). *Persistent Pastoralists: Nomadic Societies in Transition*. London, England: Zed Books.

Saitoti, T. O., and Beckwith, C. (1980). *Maasai*. London, England: Elm Tree Books.

Salvadon, C., and Fedders, A. (1973). *Maasai*. London, England: Collins.

Samovar, L. A., and Porter, R. E. (1988). "Approaching Intercultural Communication." In L. A. Samovar and R. E. Porter (Eds.), *Intercultural Communication: A Reader* (5th ed.). Belmont, Calif.: Wadsworth.

Sankan, S. S. O. (1971). *The Maasai*. Nairobi, Kenya: Kenya Literature Bureau.

The Responsive Reader

1. In the opening paragraphs, what do you learn about the authors' views on the motives, difficulties, and assumptions of the study of other cultures? Why did the authors choose the Maasai rather than other ethnic groups in Africa as the subject for their article?

2. According to the authors, what major stages or experiences in the history of the Maasai helped shape their culture? How did their history, as recorded in their oral tradition, shape their outlook or values?

3. What, according to Skow and Samovar, are traditional attitudes toward children, family life, livestock, life stages, or older members of the group? What role do these major facets of the people's life play in the traditional value system?

4. What do you learn about attitudes and beliefs in the areas of beauty, nature, and religion? (Are these the areas you would normally expect to loom large in discussions of culture? Why or why not?)

5. It is difficult if not impossible to understand a culture without knowing the language well—including the body language or gesture language—that is a major carrier for it. How much do you learn here about Maasai styles or patterns of verbal and nonverbal communication?

For Discussion or Writing

6. Where in this account of Maasai culture do you see parallels with our own culture? Where do you see major differences? Where would you expect Western values and traditional Maasai values to clash?

7. According to the authors, other ethnic groups in East Africa–such as the Kikuyu–were more receptive or adaptable than the Maasai when dealing with the Western influences that are a legacy of colonialism. Would you be inclined to side with the traditionalists or the modernists in such a situation? What would be your arguments to defend your choice?

8. Are you part of an ethnic or religious group whose history has in major ways shaped the outlook or values of many of its members? Can you identify major stages or key traditions that have shaped the collective outlook or mentality of the group?

Collaborative Projects

9. Is the Peace Corps ideal dead? What was the original rationale? What were major successes or failures? Working with a group, what recurrent themes do you encounter in testimonies, studies, or evaluations?

PRIVATE LIVES, PUBLIC VALUES

William J. Doherty

Who helps us understand and cope with changes in the basic living arrangements that pattern our lives? Sociologists track changes as traditional patterns of family living decline and new patterns evolve. Economists chart changes in purchasing power and buying patterns. Psychologists, psychiatrists, counselors, and therapists deal with the veterans of messy divorce battles and the children of dysfunctional families. Teachers know that the family backgrounds of children play a crucial role in their chances for achievement and in their psychological problems. In the following article, first published in Psychology Today, *William J. Doherty sorts out major types of family units and relationships at a time of changing social realities and evolving lifestyles. He charts directions for a future where the changes in the American family would be less of a source of conflict, frustration, and bitterness than they have been for the current generation.*

Settling down after two decades of tumultuous change, families are painfully   1
caught between their own needs and an indifferent culture. What could help everyone is a dose of reality—a new marriage of family values and public policy.

Whoever said that death and taxes are the only inevitable things in life was overlooking an obvious third one: family. No other social institution surrounds us more intimately from cradle to grave, so shapes our bodies and minds, remains such an emotional presence wherever we go, and gives us such generous measures of joy and frustration. Pretending that family is not important in our lives is like trying to cheat death: it doesn't work and you end up feeling foolish for trying.

Because the family is so central to human life, no one can be neutral about its future prospects. In fact, Americans have been wringing their hands about the state of the family for well over 100 years—with remarkably little change in the tenor of the worries. In the late 19th century, Americans began to focus on the changes wrought by urbanization and industrialization: smaller families, increased divorce rate, less connection to traditional kin and community networks, more child abuse and neglect, and squalid living conditions in urban slums. Sound familiar?

Faced with such changes in the American family, 19th-century professionals and community leaders divided into two groups, whose descendants are with us still. The "pessimists" believe that the American family is declining alarmingly in its ability to carry out its functions of child rearing and providing stability for adult life. The pessimists see the divorce rate—nine times higher than a century ago—as a key indicator of the deterioration of family bonds and the fragmentation of American society. They call for a return to the traditional values of commitment and responsibility, and are appalled by the proliferation of family types and forms in the late 20th century–never-married mothers, single-parent families, step-families, co-habiting couples, and gay and lesbian families.

The "optimists," on the other hand, view the family as an institution that is not   5
declining, but rather showing its flexibility and resilience. The optimists believe that
traditional family structures are no longer appropriate for the modern age, and that
these structures were too male-dominated and conformity-oriented to begin with.
Contemporary families may be less stable in the traditional sense, but most people
are still committed to being in a family. It's just that they need a larger menu of
family arrangements to choose from. The world is now more oriented to individual options, particularly for women, and the family has changed accordingly. From
this point of view, the main problems faced by contemporary families can be
traced to the failure of society to accept that the "Leave It to Beaver" family is a di-
nosaur, and to provide adequate support for the variety of post-Beaver families
that now dominate the landscape.

Depending on whether you are in the optimist or pessimist camp, the next
decade or two of family life will bring either: a) more deterioration, unless a shift in
values occurs; or b) continued creative change, troublesome only if other social institutions keep facing backwards instead of forwards. There is, however, a third orientation emerging, a both/and approach, and I believe it will become more
influential in our national discourse about family life in the next decade. This orientation agrees with the pessimists that the family is in trouble and that a transformation of values is needed. It also agrees with the optimists that changes in family
structure are inevitable and here to stay, and that both old and new family forms
should receive more community support.

We are at the threshold of a new dialogue about family life in the United
States, one that transcends the tired debates of the past and that might lead to a
workable consensus for the first time in our history. To understand this emerging
consensus on the American family, let's take a quick tour of the revolution in family forms in the 20th century.

In a breathtaking period of change, the 20th century has witnessed the demise
of one standard of family life, the birth of a second, its subsequent decline, and the
emergence of a third standard–one that we are still learning to live with. The first
two decades of the century were dominated by the Institutional Family as the ideal.
The Institutional Family represented the age old-tradition of a family organized
around economic production, kinship network, community connections, the father's authority, and marriage as a functional partnership rather than a romantic
relationship. Family tradition, loyalty, and solidarity were more important than individual goals and romantic interest. For the Institutional Family, the chief value
was RESPONSIBILITY.

The Institutional Family was doomed by the spirit of individualism that developed gradually in the Western world since the Renaissance, and that was given a

definitive boost by the breakup of rural communities in the 19th century and the emergence of the modern state. The modern world is based more on individual responsibility and achievement than on traditional family land holdings and kinship connections. In the culture of individualism, as Robert Bellah and his colleagues observed in their book, *Habits of the Heart* (University of California Press; 1985), relationships are based on "contracts"–what people can do for each other, rather than on traditional "covenants"–virtually unbreakable commitments based on loyalty and responsibility.

In the 1970 movie *Lovers and Other Strangers*, a young man, Tony, tells his traditional Italian father that he and his wife are divorcing because "we don't love each other any more." The befuddled father asks, "Tony, what's the story?" For the next several minutes, Tony keeps repeating his explanation, and his father keeps asking, "But, Tony, what's the story?" To a man from an Institutional Family, Tony's explanation did not compute as a reason to break up a family. The scene captured the generational shift from one type of family standard to another.

During the first half of this century, the Institutional Family gave way to the Psychological Family. In the 1920s, family sociologists began to write about the shift from "institutional marriage" to "component marriage." The Psychological Family was a more private affair than its predecessor–more nuclear, more mobile, less tied to extended-kin networks and the broader community. It aspired to something unprecedented in human history: a family based on the personal satisfaction and fulfillment of its individual members in a nuclear, two-parent arrangement.

Marriage was to be based on continued friendship, love, and attraction, not on economic necessity or the requirements of child rearing. Parents were to nurture their children's personalities, not just socialize them as good citizens. The Psychological Family arose during the time when the media and consumerism provided strong competition for traditional family values. If the chief value of the Institutional Family was RESPONSIBILITY, the chief value of the Psychological Family was SATISFACTION.

Within the Psychological Family lay the seeds of its own demise, as Judith Stacey points out in *Brave New Families* (Basic Books; 1990). Although the ideal Psychological Family was a mutually satisfying, intact, nuclear family, the underlying gender and generational politics were still traditional: male prerogatives were assumed, and the younger generation was to respect the authority of the older.

When the social changes in the 1960s challenged the Psychological Family under the banners of gender equality and personal freedom, the Psychological Family began to give way as a normative ideal in American society. Women began to achieve more independence through paid employment, the sexual revolution made marriage less necessary for sexual fulfillment, adolescents and young adults saw themselves as deserving more and owing less to their families, and men and women alike began opting out of their unhappy marriages in unprecedented

numbers. By the late 1980s, the Psychological Family, itself a radical shift from the
Institutional Family, had given way to its successor, the Pluralistic Family.

The Pluralistic Family (sometimes called the Postmodern Family) has not   15
broadly accepted an ideal family form. No new single family arrangement has replaced the Psychological nuclear family; instead, a plethora of family types has
emerged, including dual-career families, never-married families, post-divorce families, step-families, and gay and lesbian families. Legislative bodies and courts are
beginning to codify the Pluralistic Family by redefining the term to include arrangements considered deviant, non-family forms in the past. Tolerance and diversity, rather than a single family ideal, characterize the Pluralistic Family.

The chaotic proliferation of family types brought about by the disintegration
of the Psychological Family has stabilized now around a variety of forms that individuals move in and out of during their lives. In the Pluralistic Family of the immediate future, an average child can expect to grow up in some combination of: a
one-parent family, a two-parent family, or a step-family, and will go on in adulthood to cohabitate, marry, divorce, remarry, and perhaps redivorce.

The Pluralistic Family by definition will have room for some lingering Institutional Families, and a larger number of nuclear families representing the Psychological Family. Family forms do not arrive and evaporate overnight; they just
become more or less normative over time. In the late 20th century, the Psychological Family hasn't died; it has just become one family type among others. The chief
value–satisfaction–continues to be prominent in the Pluralistic Family, but it is
now supplemented by a new family value for the postmodern age–FLEXIBILITY.

The near future of the American family lies with the Pluralistic Family. At
its best, this completes a century-long trek toward liberation of the individual, particularly women and children, from the oppressive features of the traditional family. The Pluralistic Family offers individuals freedom to create the family forms that
fit their changing needs over life's course, with little stigma about failing to conform
to a single family structure and value system. And it fits the free-form American
social life of the late 20th century, where the pace of life requires quick adjustments
and where respect for diversity is a paramount civic virtue.

At its worst, however, the Pluralistic Family is filled with more internal contradictions and ambivalence than were the Institutional Family and the Psychological
Family in their heyday. Surveys indicate that most Americans still believe in the
traditional family values of responsibility and commitment, and most believe that
the stable, two-parent family is the best environment for raising children.

Family sociologist Dennis Orthner makes a distinction between family "values"   20
and family "norms." He notes that the traditional family values, or ideals, have not
changed much, according to national surveys, but that norms, or expectations, for
actual behavior have changed remarkably. The discrepancy between ideals for stability and permanent commitment, and the reality of instability and provisional

commitment, is one of two Achilles heels of the Pluralistic Family. Most Americans simply do not believe that the Pluralistic Family is stable and secure enough, especially for meeting the needs of children; they feel that divorce and other changes that liberate adults do not benefit their children.

The other Achilles heel of the Pluralistic Family is the lack of support from social institutions. The powerful decision makers in America tend to be men who were raised during the transition from the Institutional Family to the Psychological Family and who have lived their adult lives in gender-stereotyped, conformity-oriented Psychological Families. They believe in a "natural" split between the private world of the family and the public world of society—although such a split did not exist until the Institutional Family began to break down in the late 19th century.

When the umbilical cord connecting the family and the community is severed, both the family and the community become malnourished. Struggling families are left to their own devices. Family violence is seen as a personal failure, not a social and political problem. And the community loses its sense of moral obligation to promote and protect the welfare of children and other vulnerable citizens.

Many business and political leaders are suspicious of the Pluralistic Family, and fear that offering it economic and legal support is tantamount to undermining the American family as they know it—which, of course, is true. On the other hand, as they go through their own divorces and remarriages, and as they see the diversity of their children's families, these men are showing signs of accepting the reality of the Pluralistic Family.

In one sense, the next two decades for the American family are relatively easy to forecast: The Pluralistic Family will be the prevailing norm—and practically nobody will be happy about it. Conservatives will lament the decline of the nuclear Psychological Family, and liberals will decry the lack of community support for alternative family forms. And families will struggle to catch their collective breath following the tumultuous changes of the 1970s and '80s.

As they do so, there is palpable reappraisal about what the family revolution   25
has wrought. The divorce rate has stabilized, and there is evidence that the divorce rate after remarriage is declining. There is growing alarm that the sexual revolution has brought unacceptably high levels of sexual activity among teenagers with an increasing rate of teenage childbirth and a surge of single-parent families. A spate of new books, including Michele Weiner-Davis's *Divorce Busters* (Simon & Schuster; 1992), reflect a popular sentiment that marriage bonds need strengthening—in contrast to books on "creative divorce" of 25 years ago. And best-sellers such as Judith Wallerstein's *Second Chances* (Tichnor & Fields; 1989) tap many Americans' fears that divorce is ruining the lives of our children.

If most Americans are fearful about the family of the future, how have our political leaders responded? They generally don the century-old roles of pessimists and optimists. Pessimistic conservatives decry the lack of traditional family values and call for a values revolution. Optimistic liberals endorse flexibility in family values, although conservatives still seem to be slower to talk about policies.

Critics of this recent trend toward emphasizing family values view it as part of a conservative backlash against women's newfound freedoms and acceptance of alternative family lifestyles. For them, the battlefront for families lies only in the public arena, and the emergence of the "V" word (values) is a rear-guard action that threatens needed social change under the camouflage of conservative rhetoric.

Regardless of the merits of these criticisms, family values will clearly be on the national agenda in the next decade or two, as will family-policy issues such as parental leave, child care, divorce, and child-support laws, and support for families to provide health care for frail members. I predict that the two will become inextricably linked in the future. Family policies will make sense to most Americans only when they are couched in terms of family values such as commitment and care. And espousing values without addressing the policy agenda for families will be seen as posturing rather than helping. What we are approaching, for the first time in our history, is a public discussion about a family ethic to go hand in hand with a family policy.

The outline of this new family ethic underlying family policy is beginning to   30
emerge. A new family ethic for the next decade, I believe, will embrace several timeless values of the Institutional Family and the Psychological Family–but go beyond these to incorporate the newer values of the Pluralistic Family. Here are the elements in such an old and new family ethic that I see emerging in the next decade or two:

- **Commitment**–the sense of "covenant" that binds spouses to each other, parents to children and children to parents, and extended family members to one another. Without turning the clock back to an Institutional Family–era when marriage until death was sometimes psychologically deadly to trapped spouses, there will be a renewed emphasis on finding ways to renew troubled marriages rather than end them, especially when children are involved. After a divorce, there will be stronger expectations that both parents remain faithful to the unbreakable covenant that binds parents to their children.
- **Care**–the physical and emotional support of spouses and family members for one another. As philosopher Nel Noddings writes in her book, *Caring: A Feminine Approach to Ethics and Moral Education* (University of California Press; 1984), care builds on the sense of commitment and requires the ability to empathetically understand one another. To the Institutional Family's emphasis on physical and moral care of children, the Psychological Family added the idea that parents should understand and foster the emotional lives of their children, and that spouses should nurture each other emotionally.

These values are relatively new in human history and will require support from larger efforts for family-life education in the coming decades.

- **Community**–the importance of the family's ties with its neighborhood, local community, state, nation, and world, with responsibilities going both ways–the family to the community and the community to the family. This value reflects efforts to mend the split between the private world of the family and the public world of the community and its institutions. I believe that community leaders will increasingly see that the family can be no healthier than its community–and that communities can be no healthier than their families.

- **Equality**–the belief that women and men should have equal say in family matters and should stand as equals in the larger community, and that children should be given influence commensurate with their age and developmental abilities. This is the litmus test for the use of the new emphasis on family values. Will they become part of an effort to reverse women's gains towards equality with men, or will they instead become a vehicle for creating something entirely new in human history–namely, a family arrangement that provides commitment, care, and community support within the context of full personhood for men and women. Ultimately, such equality can be achieved only if it is embraced at both family and community levels at the same time.

- **Diversity**–the support for all family forms that embrace the values stated above and provide for the well-being of their members. This is the chief new value underlying the Pluralistic Family, and I see no way to build a new consensus on family values without incorporating the value of diversity. Such family forms as the never-married mother with children and gay and lesbian families are here to stay in a world that accepts the rights of citizens to form nontraditional family arrangements. This does not mean, however, that anything goes; all family forms should be judged by how well they provide commitment, care, and community for their members. Family arrangements that pass this test deserve greater measures of community support in the future.

This emerging family ethic is not a recipe for making complex decisions, such as whether to divorce one's spouse. But it does offer guidelines for responsible, caring, and fair actions when individuals are experiencing a problem such as severe marital distress. It also points the way for communities to support these family values with programs and policies.

Here's how this new family ethic could be applied: It could be considered irresponsible to get a divorce without consulting a marital therapist, especially when there are children involved, just as it is considered irresponsible to let someone die without consulting a physician. Communities, for their part, would ensure that marital-therapy services are available and affordable for couples, and just as important, provide funds for community-based family-life education so that more couples will be equipped to handle the rigors of contemporary marriage.

For families going through the divorce process, the new family ethic would expect parents to put their children's interests and needs first, to treat their ex-spouse fairly, and to support each other as parents. Adults would be expected to act maturely and responsibly for the welfare of their children after a divorce, including providing ongoing financial and emotional support. And the community would back these values by offering mediation services, family therapy, support groups, and a non-adversarial legal process.

In the new family ethic, these "shoulds" about post-divorce families would not be seen just as matters of private values and morality–or as nosegays spouted by public officials. They would be matters of major importance to the community. Fathers who abandon their children financially or emotionally after divorce would be subjected to the same social stigma as drunk drivers. The same would go for mothers who try to break their children's bonds with their fathers. And appropriate laws and policies would provide sanctions against these abuses of family values.

At the level of broad government policies, the best way for the government to support the new family ethic is to ensure adequate living standards for families. Almost all serious family problems are more common when income is lacking. In the lowest-income groups in our cities, marriage itself is threatened as an institution, since the majority of births are to single mothers, and the great majority of couples who do marry eventually divorce. In the face of decades of poverty and terrible living conditions, the values of commitment, care, community, and equality are nearly impossible to sustain. That is why calling for a transformation in family values without an accompanying transformation in public policies is like criticizing people for stumbling in the dark instead of offering them candles.

To echo the line from *Death of a Salesman,* most people agree that if the family is to be viable in the coming decades, "attention must be paid." There is little new about the concerns for families, but there are promising signs that we might be able to move beyond the stalemate between liberals and conservatives, that we might transcend the split between the private world of the family and the public world of the community.

This is a perfect time for discussion about a new family ethic, because the wave of changes in the family has subsided for the present. During the years of turbulence, we gained a lot of knowledge from research on families. We now know what factors contribute to better (and worse) adjustment for children after divorce. We now know much more about how to provide educational, therapeutic, and mediation services to families. Marriage and family therapy, for example, has matured in the past decades as a mental-health service and professional specialty. We have learned that value-free public policies do not achieve a broad national consensus. We have learned that both the pessimists and the optimists make good points, but that the tedious terms of the century-long debate about the American family must be set aside.

The Pluralistic Family is here to stay for an indefinite future. The forces of gen-   40
der equality, diveristy, and personal freedom may never again permit a single ideal family structure like the Institutional Family or the Psychological Family. The quality of the Pluralistic Family of the future depends, however, on whether we can create a new kind of family ethic that will help establish and maintain healthy bonds between family members in different living arrangements, and between families and their communities. Like death and taxes, some kind of family may be inevitable in human life, but the responsible, satisfying, and flexible family required for the next century–that is far from inevitable.

The Responsive Reader

1. According to Doherty, what sets apart people with a pessimistic and an optimistic perspective on the American family? Does he recognize or hint at a middle ground? (Where would you position yourself on the pessimism-optimism spectrum?)

2. What for you is striking or instructive in Doherty's analysis of major stages in the evolution of the family? What does he see as essential features of the Institutional Family, the Psychological Family, and the Pluralistic Family? What does he stress in tracing the history, the strengths, and the vulnerabilities of each?

3. What for Doherty are major trends under the general heading of the Pluralistic Family? How accurate or misleading do you find his mapping of major choices confronting young people today?

4. What new family ethic does Doherty project? What traditional values will it preserve? How will it go beyond them? How viable or realistic does it seem to you?

5. How would the new family ethic involve not only individual private choice but also public policy and community standards?

For Discussion or Writing

6. What is your own family background? Does the term *family* mean something good or bad to you? How does your own background affect your response to Doherty's article?

7. How would *you* sort out for tomorrow's generation major options or lifestyle choices they will confront with regard to family life or close relationships?

8. Conservative politicians have been attacking teenage pregnancy, single motherhood, and same-sex relationships. Do you think such negative campaigns

represent the attitudes of most Americans? Do these campaigns represent the attitudes of your generation?

Collaborative Projects

9. Progressive groups are campaigning for legal recognition of new kinds of domestic partnerships, including same-sex marriages. Working with a group, explore the current status of such initiatives. In your community or in your state, what is the legal status of new or unconventional partnerships? What have been recent skirmishes between proponents and opponents, and what has been their outcome?

Making Connections

10. For many observers of our society, the test of scientific objectivity is the ability to look at our own society as if we had just arrived here on a land rover from a different part of the continent or on a spaceship from a different planet. How does Doherty's analysis of our own current society compare in this regard with Skow and Samovar's account of the Maasai culture?

THE PARADOX OF INTEGRATION

Orlando Patterson

＿＿＿＿＿＿＿＿＿

How can we be sure that the conclusions reached by social scientists are more than subjective personal impressions? We ask observers of our changing society: Are their generalizations based on "anecdotal" or "impressionistic" evidence or on hard data? A major tool of social science has been statistical analysis. Social scientists learn to quantify—to construct questionnaires and surveys that allow the researcher to crunch numbers. Paul Samuelson, dean of American economists, said in his pioneering economics text: "Economics focuses on concepts that can actually be measured." (As one critical observer said, "If something is hard to count, it doesn't count.") Orlando Patterson, John Cowles professor of sociology at Harvard University, has been writing on the current status of African Americans. He wrote the following article at a time when powerful but conflicting media images were influencing Americans' perceptions of the black community: The Black Muslim minister Farrakhan had organized an all-male "Million Man March" on Washington. The long-drawn-out O. J. Simpson trial had reinforced in the minds of many African Americans the question whether a black man could expect justice from a white-dominated system and racist police. It had confirmed in the minds of many resentful whites the suspicion that blacks would not bring to justice one of their own. Colin Powell, a black general, had gathered impressive support among white voters as a possible presidential candidate. Patterson tries to get beyond political rhetoric and familiar rationalizations by anchoring his generalizations to statistical data. Where does Patterson most strongly rely on statistics? Which of his numbers do you find most instructive or unexpected? What generalizations does he base on them?

The traumas of the Million Man March and the O. J. Simpson verdict have   1
forced America to focus its gaze once again on its lingering racial crisis. In sharpening our focus, they have done at least one good. By casting too bright a light on the realities of our unfinished racial agenda, they have scrambled the sordid use of coded and covert racial rhetoric by conventional politicians. We must now call a spade a spade, and, while it is good old American politics to fan racial division while pretending the opposite, it is far too risky to appear clearly to be doing so. But what exactly is the crisis upon which we again gaze?

For African Americans, these are genuinely the best and worst of times, at least since the ending of formal Jim Crow laws. What is odd, however, is that, in the current rhetoric of race, the pain completely dominates the gain. "Pain and predicament is driving this march," cried Jesse Jackson in a by now familiar African American refrain. The orthodox view among blacks at nearly all points on the political spectrum is that relations between the races are disastrous, whether it is the left, focusing on the political neglect of the devastated ghettos, or the right, condemning the abuses of affirmative action and failed government policies. Paradoxically, it is precisely the considerable success of America's experiment in integration that makes it almost impossible for black Americans to recognize what they have achieved. This perceived lack of gratitude in turn fuels white resentment and gives public discourse on race today the bewildering quality of a dialogue of the deaf.

On the one hand, there is no denying the fact that, in absolute terms, African Americans, on average, are better off now than at any other time in their history. The civil rights movement effectively abolished the culture of post-juridical slavery, which, reinforced by racism and legalized segregation, had denied black people the basic rights of citizenship in the land of their birth. They are now very much a part of the nation's political life, occupying positions in numbers and importance that go well beyond mere ethnic representation or tokenism. Quite apart from the thousands of local and appointed offices around the country (including mayorships of some of the nation's largest cities), blacks have occupied positions of major national importance in what is now the dominant power in the world—as governors, senators and powerful members of Congress chairing major congressional committees, and as appointed officials filling some of the most important offices in the nation, including that of the head of the most powerful military machine on earth.

Even as I write, the Colin Powell phenomenon bedazzles. For the first time, a black man is being seriously considered for the nation's highest office, with his strongest support coming from people with conservative views on race. It would be ridiculous to dismiss these developments as mere tokens. What they demonstrate, beyond a doubt, is that being black is no longer a significant obstacle to participation in the public life of the nation.

What is more, blacks have also become full members of what may be called   5 the nation's moral community and cultural life. They are no longer in the basement of moral discourse in American life, as was the case up to about thirty or forty years ago. Until then blacks were "invisible men" in the nation's consciousness, a truly debased ex-slave people. America was assumed to be a white country. The public media, the literary and artistic community, the great national debates about major issues, even those concerning poverty, simply excluded blacks from consideration. Even a liberal thinker like John Kenneth Galbraith could write a major discourse on the affluent society without much thought to their plight.

No longer. The enormity of the achievement of the last forty years in American race relations cannot be overstated. The black presence in American life and thought is today pervasive. A mere 13 percent of the population, they dominate the nation's popular culture: its music, its dance, its talk, its sports, its youths' fashion; and they are a powerful force in its popular and elite literatures. A black music, jazz, is the nation's classical voice, defining, audibly, its entire civilizational style. So powerful and unavoidable is the black popular influence that it is now not uncommon to find persons who, while remaining racists in personal relations and attitudes, nonetheless have surrendered their tastes, and their viewing and listening habits, to black entertainers, talk-show hosts and sit-com stars. The typical Oprah Winfrey viewer is a conservative, white lower-middle-class housewife; the typical rap fan, an upper-middle-class white suburban youth. The cultural influence of so small and disadvantaged a minority on the wider society that has so harshly abused it finds few parallels in the history of civilization.

Closely related to the achievement of full political and cultural citizenship has been another great success of the post-war years: the desegregation of the military between 1948 and 1965. The extraordinary progress made in eliminating all formal discrimination, and a good deal of informal prejudice in promotions, has made the military, especially the Army, a model of successful race relations for the civilian community. With more than 30 percent of Army recruits and 10 percent of its officer corps black, the Army, and to a lesser extent the other services, stands out in American society as the only arena in which blacks routinely exercise authority over whites.

Most of these developments were helped along by another revolution in black life: the rapid growth in school enrollment and achievement at all levels. In 1940 there was a four-year gap in median years of schooling between whites and blacks; by 1991 this gap had been reduced to a few months. During the same period, the proportion of blacks aged 25 to 34 completing high school almost caught up with that of whites: 84 percent compared to 87 percent.

The record is far more mixed, and indeed troubling, in the case of higher education. After rapid growth in college completion during the '70s, the numbers fell off considerably during the '80s, especially for black men. The long-term effect has been that, while the proportion of blacks completing college has grown from less than 2 percent in 1940 to almost 12.8 percent in 1994, this is still only about half the white completion rate of almost 25 percent.

Even so, a six-fold increase in college completion is nothing to sniff at. It is great absolute progress and, compared to white populations elsewhere, great relative progress. African Americans, from a condition of mass illiteracy fifty years ago, are now among the most educated persons in the world, with median years of schooling and college completion rates higher than those of most Western Europeans. The average reader might find this statement a shocking overstatement. It is not. It only sounds like an overstatement when considered in light of the relentless insistence of the advocacy community that the miseducation of black Americans is the major source of their present dilemmas.

The rise of a genuine black middle class over the past quarter of a century is another cause for celebration, although no group of persons is less likely to celebrate it than the black establishment itself. The term "black middle class" once referred dismissively to those black persons who happened to be at the top of the bottom rung: Pullman porters, head waiters, successful barbers and street-front preachers, small-time funeral parlor owners and the like. Today the term "black middle class" means that segment of the nation's middle class which happens to be

10

black, and it is no longer dependent on a segregated economy. These are without doubt the best of times for middle-class African Americans, who own more businesses and control a greater share of the national wealth than at any other period. At the most conservative estimate, they are between a quarter and a third of the black population, which means anywhere between 8 and 10 million persons. It is a mistake to overemphasize their shaky economic base, as is routinely done. Almost all new middle classes in the history of capitalism have had precarious economic starts. Seen from a long-term perspective, the important thing to note is that the children they produce will be second- and third-generation burghers with all the confidence, educational resources and, most of all, cultural capital to find a more secure place in the nation's economy.

And yet it is also no exaggeration to say that, both subjectively and by certain objective standards, these are among the worst of times, since the ending of Jim Crow, for the African American population.

Put in the starkest terms, the bottom third of the African American population—some 10 million persons—live in dire poverty, while the bottom 10 percent or so—the so-called underclass—exist in an advanced stage of social, economic and moral disintegration. The grim statistics are now familiar to anyone who pays even the most cursory attention to the news.

Thirty-one percent of all black families (in contrast with only 8 percent of non-Hispanic whites), comprising nearly a third of all African Americans, live in poverty. This is worse than in 1969. Children disproportionately bear the brunt of impoverishment. In 1994, 46 percent of all black children lived in poverty, nearly three times that of white children, and the situation is likely to get worse. Their parents and other adult caretakers experience Depression-level unemployment. The overall unemployment rate for blacks is 14 percent, more than twice that of whites (6 percent). But this obscures the fact that unemployment is concentrated in certain areas and among the young, where it tops 40 percent.

These figures tell only part of the plight of poor children. The other, grimmer   15
aspect of the dilemma is the growing number of children born to female children with little or no social or economic support from the biological fathers or any other man, for that matter. The resulting abusive, mal-socialization of children by mothers who were themselves abused and mal-socialized is at the heart of the social and moral chaos in what is called the underclass. The situation is one of complete social anarchy and moral nihilism, reflected in the casual devaluation of human life. Kids and young adults kill for sneakers, leather jackets, cheap jewelry and drugs; worse, they kill for no other reason than having been dissed by a wrong look or misstatement. Linked to this social and moral catastrophe are the other well-known pathologies: the high drop-out rate in inner-city high schools, the epidemic of drugs and crime resulting in a horrendous incarceration rate wherein one in three of all black men aged 25 to 29 are under the supervision of

the criminal justice system. Although government action is needed, solving these problems will take considerably more than changes in government policy. Clearly, the message of the Million Man March was long overdue.

There is undoubtedly much to outrage our sense of justice, but the condition of the bottom third should not obscure the extraordinary achievements of the up-per two-thirds of the black population or the progress made in race relations over the past forty years. Black leaders' near-complete disregard of these hard-won achievements is obtuse and counterproductive.

This strange tendency to more loudly lament the black predicament the better it gets can be understood as a paradox of desegregation. When blacks and whites were segregated from each other there was little opportunity for conflict. The two groups lived in largely separate worlds, and when they did come in contact their interactions were highly structured by the perverse etiquette of racial relations. The system may have worked well in minimizing conflict, as long as both groups played by the rules, but it was clearly a pernicious arrangement for blacks since it condemned them to inferior status and excluded them from participation in the political life of their society and from nearly all the more desirable opportunities for economic advancement.

Desegregation meant partial access to the far superior facilities and opportuni-ties open previously only to whites. Hence, it entailed a great improvement in the condition and dignity of blacks. All this should be terribly obvious, but it must be spelled out because it is precisely this obvious improvement that is so often im-plicitly denied when we acknowledge one of the inevitable consequences of deseg regation: namely that, as individuals in both groups meet more and more, the possibility for conflict is bound to increase.

Whites outnumber blacks eight to one, and this simple demographic fact has an enormous social significance often unnoticed by whites. Numerous polls have shown tremendous change in white attitudes toward blacks over the last thirty years. For example, the number of whites who hold racist beliefs, measured by un-favorable attitudes toward miscegenation, integrated housing and job equality, has declined from a majority in the '50s to a quarter of the total population today. For whites this is real progress, however one may wish to quibble over the meaning of the survey data. But, even with only a quarter of all whites holding racist beliefs, it remains the case that for every black person there are two white racists.

Furthermore, the vast majority of blacks will rarely come in contact with the 20 percent of whites who are tolerant, for simple socioeconomic reasons. More educated, more prosperous and more suburban, the tolerant three-quarters tend to live exactly where blacks are least likely to be found: in the expensive suburbs. On the other hand, it is the least educated and most prejudiced whites who tend to be in closest proximity to blacks.

Further, the behavior of the tolerant three quarters of whites, and their attempts to improve the condition of blacks, tends to intensify racist feelings among the whites most likely to come in contact with blacks. The cost of racial change is disproportionately borne by those whites who have traditionally been most hostile to blacks. Black improvement is invariably perceived as competition in the once-protected economic preserves of working-class whites. Hence, not only do racist whites continue to outnumber blacks but their racist behavior also finds more frequent and intense outlets.

Of special concern here is the behavior of law-enforcement agencies. The typical big-city police officer is the white person with whom the typical lower- and working-class black person is most likely to come in contact outside the workplace. Unfortunately, white police officers tend to come from precisely the working-class urban communities most likely to be hostile to blacks. And there is also abundant psychological evidence that they tend to conform to the authoritarian personality type which most closely correlates with racist behavior. At the same time, their profession brings them into contact with the most lawless members of the black community, continuously reinforcing their prejudices.

The result is that the typical white police officer holds all blacks in suspicion and treats them in a manner that constantly threatens their dignity and most basic rights. In some urban communities this amounts to life under a virtual police state for many law-abiding working-class and poor black Americans. Middle-class status makes some difference, but only in well-defined social situations. It can sometimes even be a disadvantage. The Mark Fuhrman tapes revealed what every bourgeois black person already knew: that in unprotected contexts–driving on the highway, visiting a white suburban friend or caught in some minor traffic or other infraction–they are likely to find themselves specially targeted by white police officers and detectives who resent their success and take malignant pleasure in harassing them, especially if they are in mixed relationships.

In this context, the speedy decision of the jury in the O. J. Simpson trial makes perfect sense. The type of lower-middle and working-class black people who sat on the jury have every reason to believe that white police officers are racists only too willing to plant evidence and lie in court. All this is in direct contrast to the experience of the typical white person, who views the police officer either as a friend or acquaintance from the neighborhood or as a protector and guardian of the suburban peace.

What exists, then, is a serious mismatch in racial perception of change. Most   25
middle-class whites feel, correctly, that things have gotten much better not only in the objective socioeconomic condition of blacks but in their improved attitude toward blacks. The typical black person perceives and experiences the situation as either having not changed or having gotten worse.

The experience of Massachusetts is typical. By all objective criteria this is one of the most racially liberal areas of America. Not only was it the first state to elect a black U.S. senator since Reconstruction, but its current two senators are among the most liberal and pro-black in the Senate. And yet, among blacks of all classes, the Boston area has the unenviable reputation of being one of the most racist parts of the country. Many African Americans, put off by its racist image, still refuse to move to the area. The fears of blacks are legitimate; but so is the bewilderment of whites in middle-class Boston or in neighboring cities such as Cambridge (arguably one of the most racially liberal cities in the nation) when black colleagues insist they would rather go back South than settle anywhere near Boston. The sad truth is that, even as the number of tolerant whites rapidly increased between the '60s and '70s, the amount of contact between blacks and racist working-class whites also increased, as did the racial animosity of these whites, expressed most notoriously in the antibusing violence of South Boston.

To make matters worse, the hostile reaction of a small proportion of whites not only hurts a large proportion of blacks; but, given the adversarial and litigious nature of the culture, and the tendency of the media to highlight the exceptional, a small but active number of whites can disproportionately influence the perception of all whites, with consequences deleterious to blacks. The current political hostility to affirmative action is a perfect case in point.

Only a small proportion of whites—7 percent, according to recent opinion-poll data—claim to have been personally affected in any way by affirmative action. Yet the point of affirmative action is to bring blacks into greater contact with whites at the workplace and other sites where they were traditionally excluded. Aggrieved whites who feel they have been passed over in preference for blacks react sharply to this experience, which in turn colors the views of many whites who are in no way influenced by the policy. The result is the "angry white male" syndrome: increased hostility toward what are perceived as unreasonable black demands, and the conviction that the vast majority of whites are being hurt—78 percent of whites think so—when, in fact, only 7 percent can actually attest to such injuries from their own experience.

The experiential mismatch between blacks and whites is made still worse by what may be called the outrage of liberation. A formerly oppressed group's sense of outrage at what has been done to it increases the more equal it becomes with its former oppressors. In part, this is simply a case of relative deprivation; in part, it is the result of having a greater voice—more literate and vocal leadership, more access to the media and so on. But it also stems from the formerly deprived group's increased sense of dignity and, ironically, its embrace of the formerly oppressive Other within its moral universe.

The slave, the sharecropping serf, the black person living under Jim Crow laws administered by vicious white police officers and prejudiced judges, were all obliged, for reasons of sheer survival, to accommodate somehow to the system. One form of accommodation was to expect and demand less from the racist oppressors. To do so was in no way to lessen one's contempt, even hatred and loathing, for them. Indeed, one's diminished expectations may even have been a reflection of one's contempt.

It has often been observed that one of racism's worst consequences is the denial of the black person's humanity. What often goes unnoticed is the other side of this twisted coin: that it left most blacks persuaded that whites were less than human. Technically clever yes, powerful, well-armed and prolific, to be sure, but without an ounce of basic human decency. No one whose community of memory was etched with the vision of lynched, barbecued ancestors, no black person who has seen the flash of greedy, obsessive hatred in the fish-blue stare of a cracker's cocked eyes, could help but question his inherent humanness. Most blacks, whatever their outward style of interaction with whites, genuinely believed, as did the mother of Henry Louis Gates, that most whites were inherently filthy and evil, or as the poet Sterling Brown once wrote, that there was no place in heaven for "Whuffolks . . . being so onery," that, indeed, for most of them "hell would be good enough–if big enough."

Integration, however partially, began to change all that. By dis-alienating the Other, the members of each group came, however reluctantly, to accept each other's humanness. But that acceptance comes at a price: for whites, it is the growing sense of disbelief at what the nightly news brings in relentless detail from the inner cities. For blacks, it is the sense of outrage that someone truly human could have done what the evidence of more than three and a half centuries makes painfully clear. Like a woman chased and held down in a pitch-dark night who discovers, first to her relief, then to her disbelief, that the stranger recoiling from her in the horror of recognition had been her own brother, the moral embrace of integration is a liberation with a double take: outrage verging on incomprehension.

Increasingly exposed to the conflicts that result from integration, whites may rebel against affirmative action and other programs that bring them face to face with black anger. But resegregation is neither plausible nor desirable. Instead, whites, who dominate America's powerful institutions, must address the roots of black rage by committing to black America's socioeconomic advancement.

But, despite this imperative, a painful truth (one seemingly recognized by the participants in last week's march) emerges from the comparative sociology of group relations: except for those now-rare cases in which a minority constitutes the elite, the burden of racial and ethnic change always rests on a minority group. Although both whites and blacks have strong mutual interests in solving their racial problem, though the solution must eventually come from both, blacks must play the major role in achieving this objective–not only because they have more to gain from it but also because whites have far less to lose from doing nothing. It is blacks who must take the initiative, suffer the greater pain, define and offer the more creative solutions, persevere in the face of obstacles and paradoxical outcomes, insist that improvements are possible and maintain a climate of optimism concerning the eventual outcome. Or, to paraphrase Martin Luther King, it is they, and often they alone, who must keep the dream of a racially liberated America alive.

The Responsive Reader

1. According to Patterson, what factors make a realistic assessment of the status of African Americans difficult in our society today?

2. What claims does Patterson make concerning the progress made by African Americans? In what areas does he see enormous successes? What hard facts does he cite to support his conclusions? Why does he say that the record is more mixed in the area of education?

3. Much has been written about the emergence of the black middle class. What historical perspective does Patterson provide? What are his estimates concerning their number and economic status? What is his thinking about their future prospects?

4. What perspective does Patterson offer on the black underclass? What current statistics does he provide, and how does he interpret them? What are his conclusions concerning the nature and extent of the social pathology the underclass represents? What here is familiar? What is new or thought-provoking?

5. How does Patterson analyze the psychology of race relations? Why does he consider much of the rhetoric of black leaders counterproductive? How did desegregation produce greater "possibility for conflict"? Why are big-city police officers a major problem in race relations? How does Patterson explain growing hostility between the races?

6. What does the future hold? What advice or guidance does Patterson have for Americans concerned about the country's "lingering racial crisis"?

For Discussion or Writing

7. Do you think Patterson is too much of an optimist? How do his conclusions compare with your own firsthand personal observation or with conclusions based on your study or reading?

8. Americans have liked to think of theirs as a classless society–without the gross inequalities of social status or privilege of more traditional societies. How would you sort out for a newcomer or foreign observer the layers or strata of social class at the lower end of the class structure? What system of classification can you work out for people included under labels like the working class, the lower classes, the underclass?

9. Have you seen evidence that the African American influence dominates popular culture or, especially, the youth culture around the world?

Collaborative Projects

10. Working with a group, what statistics can you collect concerning the economic and social status of minority groups in your own community or area? What conclusions do your figures warrant?

DIVERSITY AND ITS DISCONTENTS

Arturo Madrid

―――――――

> *At a time of talk about a "color-blind" society, Arturo Madrid reminds us of the realities of a society in which full acceptance or integration of minorities remains a distant goal. He examines the contrast between the promises American society holds out to members of its minorities and the barriers—material and psychological—they encounter. He probes the contrast between the appearance and the realities of minority experience. Madrid is one of the Spanish-speaking Americans whose "ancestors' presence in what is now the United States antedates Plymouth Rock." He speaks for the Hispanics or Latinos of the Southwest who live in areas that were part of Mexico and for whom the Anglos were the newcomers, the immigrants. Madrid was born in New Mexico and was a student at the University of New Mexico and UCLA. He took his first teaching job at Dartmouth, an elitist New England college, and became founding president of the Tomas Rivera Center at the Claremont Graduate School in California. He is Murchison Distinguished Professor of the Humanities at Trinity University. The following article is excerpted from a speech Madrid gave at a national conference of the American Association of Higher Education. Madrid talks about what it means to be "the other" in a society where politicians cater to the nostalgia of Anglos and white ethnics for an ethnically and culturally more homogeneous world.*

My name is Arturo Madrid. I am a citizen of the United States, as are my parents and as were my grandparents and my great-grandparents. My ancestors' presence in what is now the United States antedates Plymouth Rock, even without taking into account any American Indian heritage I might have.

I do not, however, fit those mental sets that define America and Americans. My physical appearance, my speech patterns, my name, my profession (a professor of Spanish) create a text that confuses the reader. My normal experience is to be asked, "And where are *you* from?" My response depends on my mood. Passive-aggressive, I answer, "From here." Aggressive-passive, I ask, "Do you mean where I am originally from?" But ultimately my answer to those follow-up questions that will ask about origins will be that we have always been from here.

Overcoming my resentment I try to educate, knowing that nine times out of ten my words fall on inattentive ears. I have spent most of my adult life explaining who I am not. I am exotic, but—as Richard Rodriguez of *Hunger of Memory* fame so painfully found out—not exotic enough . . . not Peruvian, or Pakistani, or whatever. I am, however, very clearly the *other*, if only your everyday, garden-variety, domestic *other*. I will share with you another phenomenon that I have been part of, that of being a missing person, and how I came late to that awareness. But I've always known that I was the *other*, even before I knew the vocabulary or understood the significance of otherness.

I grew up in an isolated and historically marginal part of the United States, a small mountain village in the state of New Mexico, the eldest child of parents native to that region, whose ancestors had always lived there. In those vast and empty spaces people who look like me, speak as I do, and have names like mine predominate. But the *americanos* lived among us: the descendants of those nineteenth-century immigrants who dispossessed us of our lands; missionaries who came to convert us and stayed to live among us; artists who became enchanted with our land and humanscape and went native; refugees from unhealthy climes, crowded spaces, unpleasant circumstances; and, of course, the inhabitants of Los Alamos, whose sociocultural distance from us was accentuated by the fact that they occupied a space removed from and proscribed to us. More importantly, however, they–*los americanos*–were omnipresent (and almost exclusively so) in newspapers, newsmagazines, books, on radio, in movies, and, ultimately, on television.

Despite the operating myth of the day, school did not erase my otherness. It   5 did try to deny it, and in doing so only accentuated it. To this day what takes place in schools is more socialization than education, but when I was in elementary school–and given where I was–socialization was everything. School was where one became an American, because there was a pervasive and systematic denial by the society that surrounded us that we were Americans. That denial was both explicit and implicit.

Quite beyond saluting the flag and pledging allegiance to it (a very intense and meaningful action, given that the United States was involved in a war and our brothers, cousins, uncles, and fathers were on the frontlines), becoming American was learning English, and its corollary: not speaking Spanish. Until very recently ours was a proscribed language, either *de jure*–by rule, by policy, by law–or *de facto*–by practice, implicitly if not explicitly, through social and political and economic pressure. I do not argue that learning English was not appropriate. On the contrary. Like it or not, and we had no basis to make any judgments on that matter, we were Americans by virtue of having been born Americans and English was the common language of Americans. And there was a myth, a pervasive myth, to the effect that if only we learned to speak English well–and particularly without an accent–we would be welcomed into the American fellowship.

Sam Hayakawa and the official English movement folks notwithstanding, the true text was not our speech, but rather our names and our appearance, for we would always have an accent, however perfect our pronunciation, however excellent our enunciation, however divine our diction. That accent would be heard in our pigmentation, our physiognomy, our names. We were, in short, the *other*.

Being the *other* involves contradictory phenomena. On the one hand being the *other* frequently means being invisible. Ralph Ellison wrote eloquently about that experience in his magisterial novel, *Invisible Man*. On the other hand, being the *other* sometimes involves sticking out like a sore thumb. What is she/he doing here?

For some of us being the *other* is only annoying; for others it is debilitating; for still others it is damning. Many try to flee otherness by taking on protective colorations that provide invisibility, whether of dress or speech or manner or name. Only a fortunate few succeed. For the majority of us otherness is permanently sealed by physical appearance. For the rest, otherness is betrayed by ways of being, speaking, or doing.

The first half of my life I spent downplaying the significance and consequences   10
of otherness. The second half has seen me wrestling to understand its complex and deeply ingrained realities; striving to fathom why otherness denies us a voice or visibility or validity in American society and its institutions; struggling to make otherness familiar, reasonable, even normal to my fellow Americans.

I spoke earlier of another phenomenon that I am a part of: that of being a missing person. Growing up in northern New Mexico I had only a slight sense of us being missing persons. *Hispanos*, as we called (and call) ourselves in New Mexico, were very much a part of the fabric of the society, and there were *hispano* professionals everywhere about me: doctors, lawyers, schoolteachers, and administrators. My people owned businesses, ran organizations, and were both appointed and elected public officials.

My awareness of our absence from the larger institutional life of the society became sharper when I went off to college, but even then it was attenuated by the circumstances of history and geography. The demography of Albuquerque still strongly reflected its historical and cultural origins, despite the influx of Midwesterners and Easterners. Moreover, many of my classmates at the University of New Mexico were *hispanos*, and even some of my professors. I thought that would obtain at UCLA, where I began graduate studies in 1960. Los Angeles had a very large Mexican population and that population was visible even in and around Westwood and on the campus. Many of the groundskeepers and food-service personnel at UCLA were Mexican. But Mexican-American students were few and mostly invisible, and I do not recall seeing or knowing a single Mexican-American (or, for that matter, African-American, Asian, or American Indian) professional on the staff or faculty of that institution during the five years I was there. Needless to say, people like me were not present in any capacity at Dartmouth College, the site of my first teaching appointment, and of course were not even part of the institutional or individual mind-set. I knew then that we–a we that had come to encompass American Indians, Asian-Americans, African-Americans, Puerto Ricans, and women–were truly missing persons in American institutional life.

Over the past three decades the *de jure* and *de facto* types of segregation that have historically characterized American institutions have been under assault. As a consequence, minorities and women have become part of American institutional life. Although there are still many areas where we are not to be found, the missing persons phenomenon is not as pervasive as it once was. However, the presence of the *other*, particularly minorities, in institutions and in institutional life resembles what we call in Spanish a *flor de tierra* (a surface phenomenon): we are spare plants whose roots do not go deep, vulnerable to inclemencies of an economic, or political, or social, nature.

Our entrance into and our status in institutional life are not unlike a scenario set forth by my grandmother's pastor when she informed him that she and her family were leaving their mountain village to relocate to the Rio Grande Valley. When he asked her to promise that she would remain true to the faith and continue to involve herself in it, she asked why he thought she would do otherwise. "Doña Trinidad," he told her, "in the Valley there is no Spanish church. There is only an American church." "But," she protested, "I read and speak English and would be able to worship there." The pastor responded, "It is possible that they will not admit you, and even if they do, they might not accept you. And that is why I want you to promise me that you are going to go to church. Because if they don't let you in through the front door, I want you to go in through the back door. And if you can't get in through the back door, go in the side door. And if you are unable to enter through the side door I want you to go in through the window. What is important is that you enter and stay."

Some of us entered institutional life through the front door; others through the   15
back door; and still others through side doors. Many, if not most of us, came in through windows, and continue to come in through windows. Of those who entered through the front door, some never made it past the lobby; others were ushered into corners and niches. Those who entered through back and side doors inevitably have remained in back and side rooms. And those who entered through windows found enclosures built around them. For, despite the lip service given to the goal of the integration of minorities into institutional life, what has frequently occurred instead is ghettoization, marginalization, isolation.

Not only have the entry points been limited, but in addition the dynamics have been singularly conflictive. Gaining entry and its corollary, gaining space, have frequently come as a consequence of demands made on institutions and institutional officers. Rather than entering institutions more or less passively, minorities have of necessity entered them actively, even aggressively. Rather than waiting to receive, they have demanded. Institutional relations have thus been adversarial, infused with specific and generalized tensions.

The nature of the entrance and the nature of the space occupied have greatly influenced the view and attitude of the majority population within those institutions. All of us are put into the same box; that is, no matter what the individual reality, the assessment of the individual is inevitably conditioned by a perception that is held of the class. Whatever our history, whatever our record, whatever our validations, whatever our accomplishments, by and large we are perceived unidimensionally and dealt with accordingly. I remember an experience I had in this regard, atypical only in its explicitness. A few years ago I allowed myself to be persuaded to seek the presidency of a well-known state university. I was invited for an interview and presented myself before the selection committee, which included members of the board of trustees. The opening question of that brief but memorable interview was directed at me by a member of that august body. "Dr. Madrid," he asked, "why does a one-dimensional person like you think he can be the president of a multidimensional institution like ours?"

Over the past four decades America's demography has undergone significant changes. Since 1965 the principal demographic growth we have experienced in the United States has been of peoples whose national origins are non-European. This population growth has occurred both through birth and through immigration. A few years ago discussion of the national birthrate had a scare dimension: the high–"inordinately high"–birthrate of the Hispanic population. The popular discourse was informed by words such as "breeding." Several years later, as a consequence of careful tracking by government agencies, we now know that what has happened is that the birthrate of the majority population has decreased. When viewed historically and comparatively, the minority populations (for the most part) have also had a decline in birthrate, but not one as great as that of the majority.

There are additional demographic changes that should give us something to think about. African-Americans are now to be found in significant numbers in every major urban center in the nation. Hispanic-Americans now number over 15 million people, and although they are a regionally concentrated (and highly urbanized) population, there is a Hispanic community in almost every major urban center of the United States. American Indians, heretofore a small and rural population, are increasingly more numerous and urban. The Asian-American population, which has historically consisted of small and concentrated communities of Chinese-, Filipino-, and Japanese-Americans, has doubled over the past decade, its complexion changed by the addition of Cambodians, Koreans, Hmongs, Vietnamese, et al.

Prior to the Immigration Act of 1965, 69 percent of immigration was from Europe. By far the largest number of immigrants to the United States since 1965 have been from the Americas and from Asia: 34 percent are from Asia; another 34 percent are from Central and South America; 16 percent are from Europe; 10 percent are from the Caribbean; the remaining 6 percent are from other continents and Canada. As was the case with previous immigration waves, the current one consists principally of young people: 60 percent are between the ages of 16 and 44. Thus, for the next few decades, we will continue to see a growth in the percentage of non-European-origin Americans as compared to European-Americans.

To sum up, we now live in one of the most demographically diverse nations in the world, and one that is increasingly more so.

During the same period social and economic change seems to have acceler-ated. Who would have imagined at mid-century that the prototypical middle-class family (working husband, wife as homemaker, two children) would for all intents and purposes disappear? Who could have anticipated the rise in teenage pregnan-cies, children in poverty, drug use? Who among us understood the implications of an aging population?

We live in an age of continuous and intense change, a world in which what held true yesterday does not today, and certainly will not tomorrow. What change does, moreover, is bring about even more change. The only constant we have at this point in our national development is change. And change is threatening. The older we get the more likely we are to be anxious about change, and the greater our desire to maintain the status quo.

Evident in our public life is a fear of change, whether economic or moral. Some who fear change are responsive to the call of economic protectionism, others to the message of moral protectionism. Parenthetically, I have referred to the move-ment to require more of students without in turn giving them more as academic protectionism. And the pronouncements of E. D. Hirsch and Allan Bloom are, I believe, informed by intellectual protectionism. Much more serious, however, is the dark side of the populism which underlies this evergoing protectionism—the re-sentment of the *other*. An excellent and fascinating example of that aspect of popu-lism is the cry for linguistic protectionism—for making English the official language of the United States. And who among us is unaware of the tensions that underlie immigration reform, of the underside of demographic protectionism?

A matter of increasing concern is whether this new protectionism, and the   25 mistrust of the *other* which accompanies it, is not making more significant inroads than we have supposed in higher education. Specifically, I wish to discuss the question of whether a goal (quality) and a reality (demographic diversity) have been erroneously placed in conflict, and, if so, what problems this perception of conflict might present.

As part of my scholarship I turn to dictionaries for both origins and meanings of words. Quality, according to the *Oxford English Dictionary*, has multiple meanings. One set defines quality as being an essential character, a distinctive and inherent feature. A second describes it as a degree of excellence, of conformity to standards, as superiority in kind. A third makes reference to social status, particularly to per-sons of high social status. A fourth talks about quality as being a special or distin-guishing attribute, as being a desirable trait. Quality is highly desirable in both principle and practice. We all aspire to it in our own person, in our experiences, in our acquisitions and products, and of course we all want to be associated with people and operations of quality.

But let us move away from the various dictionary meanings of the word and to our own sense of what it represents and of how we feel about it. First of all we consider quality to be finite; that is, it is limited with respect to quantity; it has very few manifestations; it is not widely distributed. I have it and you have it, but they don't. We associate quality with homogeneity, with uniformity, with standardization, with order, regularity, neatness. All too often we equate it with smoothness, glibness, slickness, elegance. Certainly it is always expensive. We tend to identify it with those who lead, with the rich and famous. And, when you come right down to it, it's inherent. Either you've got it or you ain't.

Diversity, from the Latin *divertere*, meaning to turn aside, to go different ways, to differ, is the condition of being different or having differences, is an instance of being different. Its companion word, diverse, means differing, unlike, distinct; having or capable or having various forms; composed of unlike or distinct elements. Diversity is lack of standardization, of regularity, of orderliness, homogeneity, conformity, uniformity. Diversity introduces complications, is difficult to organize, is troublesome to manage, is problematical. Diversity is irregular, disorderly, uneven, rough. The way we use the word diversity gives us away. Something is too diverse, is extremely diverse. We want a little diversity.

When we talk about diversity, we are talking about the *other*, whatever that other might be: someone of a different gender, race, class, national origin; somebody at a greater or lesser distance from the norm; someone outside the set; someone who possesses a different set of characteristics, features, or attributes; someone who does not fall within the taxonomies we use daily and with which we are comfortable; someone who does not fit into the mental configurations that give our lives order and meaning.

In short, diversity is desirable only in principle, not in practice. Long live diversity . . . as long as it conforms to my standards, my mind set, my view of life, my sense of order. We desire, we like, we admire diversity, not unlike the way the French (and others) appreciate women; that is, *Vive la différence!*–as long as it stays in its place.   30

What I find paradoxical about and lacking in this debate is that diversity is the natural order of things. Evolution produces diversity. Margaret Visser, writing about food in her latest book, *Much Depends on Dinner*, makes an eloquent statement in this regard:

> Machines like, demand, and produce uniformity. But nature loathes it: her strength lies in multiplicity and in differences. Sameness in biology means fewer possibilities and therefore weakness.

The United States, by its very nature, by its very development, is the essence of diversity. It is diverse in its geography, population, institutions, technology; its social, cultural, and intellectual modes. It is a society that at its best does not consider quality to be monolithic in form or finite in quantity, or to be inherent in class. Quality in our society proceeds in large measure out of the stimulus of diverse modes of thinking and acting; out of the creativity made possible by the different ways in which we approach things; out of diversion from paths or modes hallowed by tradition.

One of the principal strengths of our society is its ability to address, on a continuing and substantive basis, the real economic, political, and social problems that have faced and continue to face us. What makes the United States so attractive to immigrants is the protections and opportunities it offers; what keeps our society together is tolerance for cultural, religious, social, political, and even linguistic difference; what makes us a unique, dynamic, and extraordinary nation is the power and creativity of our diversity.

The true history of the United States is one of struggle against intolerance, against oppression, against xenophobia, against those forces that have prohibited persons from participating in the larger life of the society on the basis of their race, their gender, their religion, their national origin, their linguistic and cultural background. These phenomena are not consigned to the past. They remain with us and frequently take on virulent dimensions.

If you believe, as I do, that the well-being of a society is directly related to the degree and extent to which all of its citizens participate in its institutions, then you will have to agree that we have a challenge before us. In view of the extraordinary changes that are taking place in our society we need to take up the struggle again, irritating, grating, troublesome, unfashionable, unpleasant as it is. As educated and educator members of this society we have a special responsibility for ensuring that all American institutions, not just our elementary and secondary schools, our juvenile halls, or our jails, reflect the diversity of our society. Not to do so is to risk greater alienation on the part of a growing segment of our society; is to risk increased social tension in an already conflictive world; and, ultimately, is to risk the survival of a range of institutions that, for all their defects and deficiencies, provide us the opportunity and the freedom to improve our individual and collective lot.

Let me urge you to reflect on these two words—quality and diversity—and on the mental sets and behaviors that flow out of them. And let me urge you further to struggle against the notion that quality is finite in quantity, limited in its manifestations, or is restricted by considerations of class, gender, race, or national origin; or that quality manifests itself only in leaders and not in followers, in managers and not in workers, in breeders and not in drones; or that it has to be associated with verbal agility or elegance of personal style; or that it cannot be seeded, nurtured, or developed.

Because diversity—the *other*—is among us, will define and determine our lives in ways that we still do not fully appreciate, whether that other is women (no longer bound by tradition, house, and family); or Asians, African-Americans, Indians, and Hispanics (no longer invisible, regional, or marginal); or our newest immigrants (no longer distant, exotic, alien). Given the changing profile of America, will we come to terms with diversity in our personal and professional lives? Will we begin to recognize the diverse forms that quality can take? If so, we will thus initiate the process of making quality limitless in its manifestations, infinite in quantity, unrestricted with respect to its origins, and more importantly, virulently contagious.

I hope we will. And that we will further join together to expand—not to close—the circle.

The Responsive Reader

1. Early in his speech, what key features does Madrid identify as making him "the other"? What makes him say he does not "fit those mental sets that define America and Americans"?

2. As seen by Madrid, what is the history of the *americanos* in the formerly Mexican Southwest? What was their relationship with Madrid's people?

3. The schools have traditionally played a key role in the process of assimilation, in Americanizing those perceived as different. How does Madrid assess the schools' role? What was the guiding myth? What were the traditional goals and procedures? How did the myth clash with reality?

4. What personal experiences reinforced Madrid's sense of being the "other"? How has he tried to cope with the experience?

5. Educators have often prided themselves on spearheading the movement to desegregate American society. What mixed or contradictory observations does Madrid record of efforts to desegregate higher education? Have women and minorities become "part of American institutional life"? How or to what extent?

6. Madrid is one of many voices asking us to take into account the changing demographics of our society in charting its future. What changes does Madrid emphasize? Where does he see evidence of the "fear of change"? What are key ideas in Madrid's plea for honoring diversity?

For Discussion or Writing

7. Have you ever felt like the outsider? Have you ever felt left out from the in-group? How did your experience compare with Madrid's?

8. Is our society moving toward a true acceptance of diversity? Or are we headed toward increasing separatism, "ghettoization," and "isolation"? On what indicators or evidence do you base your judgment?

Collaborative Projects

9. How do local schools address ethnic and cultural diversity? Do they have official policies or special programs? How successful are these? What problems or challenges confront teachers and administrators? Do any students feel they are the "other"? Working with a group, try to get answers to these questions

through such tools as informal interviews with teachers, administrators, students, and parents.

Making Connections

10. The prognosis of experts for the integration of America's minorities into the mainstream ranges from pessimistic to optimistic. How do Patterson and Madrid compare in their expectations and apprehensions concerning the future?

WAS AMERICA A MISTAKE?

Arthur Schlesinger, Jr.

━━━━━━

Is it possible for historians to step outside their cultural biases? Are we bound to see history through the lens furnished by our ethnic group, national allegiance, religion, gender, or class? Establishment historians wrote the history of the North American continent as a saga of discovery, of survival in the wilderness, of braving the dangers of the frontier, of pioneers putting the prairies to the plow, of entrepreneurs building great cities, of the railroads spanning the continent, of the white man bringing civilization and Christianity to heathen tribes. Native Americans chronicling the history of their people write of the rising, irresistible tide of white invasion; of broken treaties and heroic desperate resistance; of villages burned and women and children killed; of populations forced into death marches to territories where no white man could make a living; of forced conversion and the suppression of the religion and rituals of a conquered people; of the white man's diseases and the white man's vices decimating the survivors. Much current history is revisionist history—rewritten history now challenged as serving imperialism, colonialism, white supremacy, or America's "manifest destiny." The 500-year anniversary of Columbus' first voyage to the New World ignited a fierce controversy concerning the history of European colonization in the Americas. In the following article, a leading American historian tries to balance what is "useful and necessary" in the current rewriting of history and what he considers excessive or unfair. Arthur Schlesinger, Jr., is a Pulitzer Prize-winning historian who served as a special assistant to Presidents John F. Kennedy and Lyndon B. Johnson. Published during the Nixon years, Schlesinger's The Imperial Presidency *warned against the abuse of presidential power while defending the virtues of the American system.*

October 12, 1992, marked the five-hundredth anniversary of the most crucial   1
of all encounters between Europe and the Americas. In the contemporary global mood, however, the quincentennial of Christopher Columbus's landing in the New World—new, anyway, to the European intruders; old and familiar to its inhabitants—seemed an occasion less for celebration than for meditation. Indeed, in some quarters the call was for penitence and remorse.

Christopher Columbus has always been as much a myth as a man, a myth incorporating a succession of triumphs and guilts over what is now five long centuries. The myth has found particular lodgment in the mightiest of the nations to arise in the Western Hemisphere—a nation that may not speak Columbus's language (any of them) but has diligently revered his memory.

Though both the continent and the country bear another's name, Columbus has been surpassed in nomenclatural popularity in the United States only by the great George Washington—and Washington is itself located in the District of

Columbia. I make this observation as a native of Columbus, Ohio, the largest of many municipalities called after the great explorer. The preeminent university in the city in which I now live is Columbia—not to mention such other North American institutions as the Columbia Broadcasting System, the *Columbia Encyclopedia*, Columbia Pictures, and a variety of enterprises from banks to space shuttles.

The biography that fixed the nineteenth-century image of Columbus was published in 1828 and written by Washington Irving, Manhattan's first international man of letters, a lover of Spain, the aficionado of Granada and the Alhambra, and in later life the U.S. minister to Madrid. Half a century after, Irish-Americans named a newly founded Roman Catholic fraternal organization the Knights of Columbus. A movement to honor the day of landfall culminated in 1934, when President Franklin D. Roosevelt proclaimed October 12 a national holiday. The holiday is observed in most Latin American countries as well.

The United States also staged the most memorable celebration of the quadri-   5
centennial of what it was then widely acceptable to call the "discovery" of America. The World's Columbian Exposition took place in bustling, thrusting, midwestern Chicago, the very heart of the republic. Reconfiguring the great explorer in images of technology and modernity, the Chicago World's Fair saluted the man then regarded, in the words of President Benjamin Harrison, as "the pioneer of progress and enlightenment." In a book especially produced for the fair, the historian Meyer Kayserling summed up the prevailing assessment of Columbus: "In the just appreciation of his great services to mankind, all political, religious and social differences have vanished."

How things have changed in a century! Political, religious, and social differences, far from vanishing, place Columbus today in the center of a worldwide cultural civil war. The great hero of the nineteenth century seems well on the way to becoming the great villain of the twenty-first. Columbus, it is now charged, far from being the pioneer of progress and enlightenment, was in fact the pioneer of oppression, racism, slavery, rape, theft, vandalism, extermination, and ecological desolation.

The revisionist reaction, it must be said, has been under way for a while. As far back as the quadricentennial Justin Winsor, a historian and bibliographer of early America, published a soberly critical biography, arguing that Columbus had left the New World "a legacy of devastation and crime." George Santayana soon wrote of Columbus, in one of his *Odes*,

> He gave the world another world, and ruin
> Brought upon blameless, river-loving nations,
> Cursed Spain with barren gold, and made the Andes
> > Fiefs of Saint Peter.

Today revisionism is in full flood. Much of it is useful and necessary. "The one duty we owe to history," as Oscar Wilde said, "is to rewrite it." The very phrase "discovery of America" is under a ban. It is pointed out, not unreasonably, that America had been discovered centuries earlier by people trickling across the Bering Strait land bridge from East Asia. To call Columbus's landfall a "discovery" therefore convicts one of Eurocentrism. Certainly it is hard to object to the proposal that the arrival of Columbus be seen from the viewpoint of those who met him as well as from the viewpoint of those who sent him.

It is also well that we begin to see the man Columbus not in the nineteenth-century mode, as Benjamin Harrison's "pioneer of progress and enlightenment," but as he saw himself—as, that is, a God-intoxicated man who, for all his superb practical skills as a navigator, believed himself engaged in a spiritual rather than a geographical quest, the messenger not of rationalism and science but of the Almighty, warning that the world would end in another century and a half, prophesying, as he wrote to an intimate of Queen Isabella's, "the new heaven and the new earth which the Lord made, and of which St. John writes in the Apocalypse." We are right, I think, in beginning to read his messianic *Libro de las profecías* not as a cynical attempt to con the Queen nor as the paranoid outburst of an aging and despairing has-been but as the center of the Columbian dream.

Revisionism redresses the balance up to a point; but, driven by Western guilt,   10
it may verge on masochism. Let me cite the resolution on the quincentennial adopted by the National Council of Churches: "What some historians have termed a 'discovery' in reality was an invasion and colonization with legalized occupation, genocide, economic exploitation and a deep level of institutional racism and moral decadence." The Council of Churches' three-page statement is a stern indictment of the criminal history of the European conquest. The quincentennial, the resolution concludes, should be an occasion not for celebration but for "repentance."

The government of Canada decided not to celebrate the quincentennial at all, on the ground that the arrival of Columbus led to the destruction of the existing American cultures. Russell Means, a leader of the American Indian Movement, opines that Columbus "makes Hitler look like a juvenile delinquent." The novelist Hans Koning finds him "worse than Attila the Hun." Last year on Columbus Day protesters in Washington poured fake blood on the Union Station statue of Columbus. Marlon Brando recently demanded that his name be removed from the credits of a new movie, *Christopher Columbus: The Discovery*, on the ground that the film failed to portray Columbus as "the true villain he was," the man "directly responsible for the first wave of genocidal obliteration of the native peoples of North America." (Brando's role in the film, by the way, was Torquemada.)

In the university town of Berkeley, California, a leaflet charged Columbus with "grand theft; genocide; racism; initiating the destruction of culture; rape, torture and maiming of indigenous people; and [being the] instigator of the Big Lie"; city officials thereafter changed October 12 to Indigenous Peoples Day. When Cristobal Colon, a descendant of the explorer's, was appointed grand marshal of Pasadena's annual New Year's Day parade, the Tournament of Roses, the vice-mayor

denounced Colon as "a symbol of greed, slavery, rape, and genocide" and his appointment as an insult to American Indians. The protest was stilled only by the
naming of Ben Nighthorse Campbell, a congressman and Cheyenne chief, as co-
grand marshal.

Recently, in Havana, I asked Fidel Castro how he looks on the quincentennial.
He replied, "We are critical. Columbus brought many bad things." I said, "If it
weren't for Columbus, you wouldn't be here." Castro said, "Well, Columbus brought
good things as well as bad." This slightly schizophrenic reaction is not untypical.
North and south of the border Americans of Spanish descent are torn between
pride in their Hispanic heritage and romantic identification with indigenous Indian
traditions. In the United States some Latinos join the campaign against the Spanish
conquest; others take it as an attack on themselves. "My mother sees it as something that brought us religion and civilization," one told Patricia Duarte, of *Newsday*.
"Younger people see it as an atrocity."

Still, the "politically correct" image of Columbus as executioner dominates the
current discussion. As the art critic Hilton Kramer sums it up,

> Columbus is now vilified as a Eurocentric genocidal maniac who, in addition
> to decimating the native population of the Americas, was also responsible
> for destroying their ecology and bringing to this part of the world the most
> atrocious of all economic systems, namely, capitalism.

Had Columbus foreseen even a portion of all the sins he would be held   15
accountable for five centuries later, he might never have bothered to discover
America.

Why this sea change in attitudes? Obviously the global mood has shifted since
the exaltation of Columbus's heroic aspects at the quadricentennial. This change
reflects the end of European domination of the planet. It reflects the revolt of the
Third World against economic exploitation, against political control, against cultural despoliation, against personal and national humiliation, even, at times, against
modernity itself. It reflects the (belated) bad conscience of the West and the consequent re-examination of the Western impact on the rest of humanity.

No one can doubt the arrogance and brutality of the European invaders, their
callous and destructive ways, the human and ecological devastation they left
in their trail. Genocide—the calculated and purposeful murder of a race—may be
too harsh a term, at least for Spanish America; it applies more to British America,
which widely believed that the only good Indian was a dead Indian. Many
Spaniards wanted to keep natives alive, if only as slave labor; some, like Father
Bartolomé de Las Casas, denounced inhuman treatment in brave and searing language. In both South and North America many more Amerindians died by accident from European diseases—smallpox, cholera, measles—than by design from

European swords, harquebuses, and lashes. (And in the transatlantic exchange of diseases, the Europeans apparently received syphilis.)

Revisionists tend to portray pre-Columbian America as an Arcadia. The most readable statement of the case is by Kirkpatrick Sale, in his graceful and passionate book *The Conquest of Paradise* (1990). Sale envisages a continent where people lived in "balanced and fruitful harmony" with nature and with one another, "an untouched world, a prelapsarian Eden of astonishing plenitude . . . functioning to all intents and purposes in its original primal state," green and pure, until European violence smashed the human and ecological utopia.

The myth of innocence is an old one. "In the beginning," John Locke wrote three centuries ago, "all the world was *America*, and more so than that is now; for no such thing as *Money* was any where known." Yet the vision of an uncorrupted pre-Columbian America is in acute conflict with another part of the anti-Columbus campaign: the contention that pre-Columbian America contained elaborate and advanced civilizations that were ruthlessly obliterated by the European invasion.

One has only to recall the soaring temples, exact astronomical calculations, accurate calendars, and complex hieroglyphics of the Maya in Central America; or the wild surmise with which in 1519 stout Cortes and his tiny Spanish band confronted not the Pacific from Keats's peak in Darien but, shimmering in the distance, the Aztec city of Tenochtitlán, a metropolis as impressive as any in sixteenth-century Europe; or the contrast between the brutal Spanish thug Pizarro and the courteous and civilized Inca Emperor Atahualpa; or the wonderful grace, symmetry, and imaginative power of pre-Columbian art. 20

Yet these empires were also theocratic military collectivisms, quite as arrogant, cruel, and ethnocentric as the Europeans who demolished them. Far from living in harmony with nature, the Maya evidently brought about their own collapse by deforestation and other destructive agricultural practices that upset the rain-forest ecosystem of Central America. Far from living in harmony with one another, the Mayan city-states appear to have been engaged in constant warfare, with prisoners ritually tortured and decapitated.

The anthropologist Louis Faron describes the Mundurucú societies of the Amazon basin, whose approach to prisoners of war "ranged from the exotic mutilation of shrinking heads to eating parts of the corpse." After removing the brain and teeth and closing the eyes with beeswax, the Mundurucús parboiled the head and strung cords through the mouth and out the nostrils. The Tupinambas, along the Atlantic coast, "like the Caribs and Cubeos, considered the eating of human flesh a ritual act, part of their belief in consubstantiation."

These were primitive tribes, but the more developed Aztecs brought the processes of ritual torture and human sacrifice to exalted heights. Thousands of captives won in war or exacted in tribute would line up before the 114 steps of the great pyramid waiting for priests to plunge in the obsidian knife and tear out their bleeding hearts–a ceremony no doubt laudably designed to propitiate the sun god, but not easy to reconcile with the revisionist myth of prelapsarian harmony and innocence. Cortes conquered Mexico with such ease because Indian tribes subjugated and persecuted by the Aztecs embraced him as their liberator from unbearable tyranny. As Carlos Fuentes writes, "It was the victory of the *other Indians* over the Aztec overlord."

Given Aztec customs and methods, what, one wonders, would have become of the hapless inhabitants of Spain and Portugal if the Atlantic crossing had been reversed and the Aztecs had conquered Iberia? And those who insist that Aztecs and Incas, Mundurucús and Tupinambas, should be judged by their own values, not by ours, owe the same indulgence to the *conquistadores*.

The melancholy conclusion is that despite the dramatic clash of cultures, one finds in certain respects, as the historian Hugh Thomas argues, little difference between the Europe and the Mexico of 1492: little difference in the uses of power, in prescriptive inequalities, in coercion and torture, in imperialism and violence and destruction, in (to leap centuries forward to contemporary standards) the suppression of individual freedom and of human rights. The record illustrates less the pitiless annihilation of an idyllic culture by a wrecking crew of aliens than it does the criminality of all cultures and the universality of original sin. Cruelty and destruction are not the monopoly of any single continent or race or culture. As William James reminds us, "The trail of the human serpent is thus over everything." 25

Christopher Columbus, Mario Vargas Llosa observed at a quincentennial conference in Seville, has become a historical counter in a contemporary political game, and British America and Spanish America use him for different purposes. In North America, Columbus is just one more pretext for the already thriving assault mounted against the establishment by apostles of political correctness. The Latin American reaction, Vargas Llosa continues, is far more primary and organic. There Columbus serves not as scapegoat but as alibi. Blaming everything on the conquest provides a perpetual excuse for the failure of Latin American countries to achieve humane, stable, and progressive democracies. Latin America, Vargas Llosa says, must begin to accept responsibility for its own fate. So, too, says Carlos Fuentes: Latin Americans, confronting the questions raised by their "balkanized, fractured politics, failed economic systems, and vast social inequalities," must finally recognize that "we could only answer the questions from within ourselves."

The Responsive Reader

1. What were you taught about Columbus? What is familiar, and what is new or striking, in Schlesinger's account of the traditional Columbus myth?

2. According to Schlesinger, what are major targets and major tenets of today's "re-

visionist reaction"? How much revision of the traditional picture of Columbus does he himself accept? Where does he think revisionism goes too far? Why does he call it "masochistic"?

3. According to Schlesinger, what are the conflicting emotions or divided allegiances of Americans of Spanish descent in the current controversies concerning Columbus and the Spanish *conquistadores*?

4. According to Schlesinger, how are native Americans being idealized or romanticized today? What is an "Arcadia"? What makes current accounts "idyllic," "Utopian," or "prelapsarian"—taking us to a state before Adam's fall brought sin into the world?

5. How does Schlesinger try to counteract the current tendency to idealize the pre-Columbian past? What picture does he paint of the pre-Columbian American civilizations? How does he compare the European and American civilizations of Columbus's time?

For Discussion or Writing

6. Overall, would you call Schlesinger's account objective, balanced, and fair? Is he guilty of a "Eurocentric" bias—taking the side of or making excuses for the European invaders in the New World?

7. Revisionist historians are often accused of "presentism"—applying the moral standards of the present retroactively to the past. Do you think we today have the right to formulate moral judgments about the European and native American civilizations of Columbus' time?

8. Have you encountered evidence of a revisionist approach in your own study or reading of history?

Collaborative Projects

9. What are recurrent themes of current work on pre-Columbian America—for instance, the Maya, pre-Aztec, or Inca civilizations? What are the spirit, motivation, and results of current studies?

DISTANCING THE HOMELESS

Jonathan Kozol

▬▬▬▬▬

Many people are tired of hearing about the homeless; they do not want to be reminded of unpleasant things.

STUDENT PAPER

Some observers of today's social problems aim at detached objectivity, determined not to let emotions skew their interpretation of the data. Others write from passionate commitment, appealing to the social conscience of their readers. Jonathan Kozol first reached a large audience with his Death at an Early Age *(1967), his chronicle of a year teaching fourth grade at a mostly black school in his native Boston. His angry, bitter book, published after he was fired for using without authorization a poem by America's best-known African American poet, attacked defeatist teachers, timid administrators, and an apathetic community that had largely written off the school's predominantly black students. Active as a crusading teacher, lecturer, and government consultant, Kozol continued his radical critique of complacent middle-class America in books including* Rachel and Her Children, *about homeless families, and* Savage Inequalities, *which became a national bestseller. In 1995, Kozol published* Amazing Grace: The Lives of Children and the Conscience of a Nation, *about the children of the South Bronx, the nation's poorest congressional district. Barbara Ehrenreich said after reading this book, "Through public policy and private indifference, we have guaranteed that our poor, inner-city children will lead lives stunted by heartbreak, violence, and disease. . . . You will wonder at the end, with Kozol, why the God of love does not return to earth with his avenging sword in his hand."*

It is commonly believed by many journalists and politicians that the homeless   1
of America are, in large part, former patients of large mental hospitals who were
deinstitutionalized in the 1970s–the consequence, it is sometimes said, of misguided
liberal opinion, which favored the treatment of such persons in community–based
centers. It is argued that this policy, and the subsequent failure of society to build
such centers or to provide them in sufficient number, is the primary cause of
homelessness in the United States.

Those who work among the homeless do not find that explanation satisfactory. While conceding that a certain number of the homeless are, or have been,
mentally unwell, they believe that, in the case of most unsheltered people, the primary reason is economic rather than clinical. The cause of homelessness, they say
with disarming logic, is the lack of homes and of income with which to rent or acquire them.

They point to the loss of traditional jobs in industry (two million every year since 1980) and to the fact that half of those who are laid off end up in work that pays a poverty-level wage. They point to the parallel growth of poverty in families with children, noting that children, who represent one quarter of our population, make up forty percent of the poor: since 1968, the number of children in poverty has grown by three million, while welfare benefits to families with children have declined by thirty-five percent.

And they note, too, that these developments have coincided with a time in which the shortage of low-income housing has intensified as the gentrification of our major cities has accelerated. Half a million units of low-income housing have been lost each year to condominium conversion as well as to arson, demolition, or abandonment. Between 1978 and 1980, median rents climbed thirty percent for people in the lowest income sector, driving many of these families into the streets. After 1980, rents rose at even faster rates. In Boston, between 1982 and 1984, over eighty percent of the housing units renting below three hundred dollars disappeared, while the number of units renting above six hundred dollars nearly tripled.

Hard numbers, in this instance, would appear to be of greater help than psychiatric labels in telling us why so many people become homeless. Eight million American families now pay half or more of their income for rent or a mortgage. Six million more, unable to pay rent at all, live doubled up with others. At the same time, federal support for low-income housing dropped from $30 billion (1980) to $9 billion (1986). Under Presidents Ford and Carter, five hundred thousand subsidized private housing units were constructed. By President Reagan's second term, the number had dropped to twenty-five thousand. "We're getting out of the housing business, period," said a deputy assistant secretary of the Department of Housing and Urban Development in 1985.

One year later, the *Washington Post* reported that the number of homeless families in Washington, D.C., had grown by five hundred percent over the previous twelve months. In New York City, the waiting list for public housing now contains two hundred thousand names. The waiting is eighteen years.

Why, in the face of these statistics, are we impelled to find a psychiatric explanation for the growth of homelessness in the United States?

A misconception, once it is implanted in the popular imagination, is not easy to uproot, particularly when it serves a useful social role. The notion that the homeless are largely psychotics who belong in institutions, rather than victims of displacement at the hands of enterprising realtors, spares us from the need to offer realistic solutions to the fact of deep and widening extremes of wealth and poverty in the United States. It also enables us to tell ourselves that the despair of homeless people bears no intimate connection to the privileged existence we enjoy—when, for example, we rent or purchase one of those restored townhouses that once provided shelter for people now huddled in the street.

But there may be another reason to assign labels to the destitute. Terming economic victims "psychotic" or "disordered" helps to place them at a distance. It says that they aren't quite like us–and, more important, that we could not be like them. The plight of homeless families is a nightmare. It may not seem natural to try to banish beings from our midst, but it *is* natural to try to banish nightmares from our minds.

So the rituals of clinical contamination proceed uninterrupted by the eco-   10 nomic facts described above. Research that addresses homelessness as an *injustice* rather than as a medical *misfortune* does not win the funding of foundations. And the research which *is* funded, defining the narrowed borders of permissible debate, diverts our attention from the antecedent to the secondary cause of homelessness. Thus it is that perfectly ordinary women whom I know in New York City–people whose depression or anxiety is a realistic consequence of months and even years in crowded shelters or the streets–are interrogated by invasive research scholars in an effort to decode their poverty, to find clinical categories for their despair and terror, to identify the secret failing that lies hidden in their psyche.

Many pregnant women without homes are denied prenatal care because they constantly travel from one shelter to another. Many are anemic. Many are denied essential dietary supplements by recent federal cuts. As a consequence, some of their children do not live to see their second year of life. Do these mothers sometimes show signs of stress? Do they appear disorganized, depressed, disordered? Frequently. They are immobilized by pain, traumatized by fear. So it is no surprise that when researchers enter the scene to ask them how they "feel," the resulting reports tell us that the homeless are emotionally unwell. The reports do not tell us we have *made* these people ill. They do not tell us that illness is a natural response to intolerable conditions. Nor do they tell us of the strength and the resilience that so many of these people still retain despite the miseries they must endure. They set these men and women apart in capsules labeled "personality disorder" or "psychotic," where they no longer threaten our complacence.

Manhattan Borough President David Dinkins made the following observation on the basis of a study commissioned in 1986: "No facts support the belief that addiction or behavioral problems occur with more frequency in the homeless family population than in a similar socioeconomic population. Homeless families are not demographically different from other public assistance families when they enter the shelter system. . . . Family homelessness is typically a housing and income problem: the unavailability of affordable housing and the inadequacy of public assistance income."

In a "hypothetical world," write James Wright and Julie Lam of the University of Massachusetts, "where there were no alcoholics, no drug addicts, no mentally ill, no deinstitutionalization, . . . indeed, no personal social pathologies at all, there would still be a formidable homelessness problem, simply because at this stage in American history, there is not enough low-income housing" to accommodate the poor.

New York State's respected Commissioner of Social Services, Cesar Perales, makes the point in fewer words: "Homelessness is less and less a result of personal failure, and more and more is caused by larger forces. There is no longer affordable housing in New York City for people of poor and modest means."

Even the words of medical practitioners who care for homeless people have been curiously ignored. A study published by the Massachusetts Medical Society, for instance, has noted that the most frequent illnesses among a sample of the homeless population, after alcohol and drug use, are trauma (31 percent), upper respiratory disorders (28 percent), limb disorders (19 percent), mental illness (16 percent), skin diseases (15 percent), hypertension (14 percent), and neurological illnesses (12 percent). (Excluded from this tabulation are lead poisoning, malnutrition, acute diarrhea, and other illnesses especially common among homeless infants and small children.) Why, we may ask, of all these calamities, does mental illness command so much political and press attention? The answer may be that the label of mental illness places the destitute outside the sphere of ordinary life. It personalizes an anguish that is public in its genesis; it individualizes a misery that is both general in cause and general in application.

The rate of tuberculosis among the homeless is believed to be ten times that of the general population. Asthma, I have learned in countless interviews, is one of the most common causes of discomfort in the shelters. Compulsive smoking, exacerbated by the crowding and the tension, is more common in the shelters than in any place that I have visited except prison. Infected and untreated sores, scabies, diarrhea, poorly set limbs, protruding elbows, awkwardly distorted wrists, bleeding gums, impacted teeth, and other untreated dental problems are so common among children in the shelters that one rapidly forgets their presence. Hunger and emaciation are everywhere. Children as well as adults can bring to mind the photographs of people found in camps for refugees of war in 1945. But these miseries bear no stigma, and mental illness does.

Last summer, some twenty-eight thousand homeless people were afforded shelter by the city of New York. Of this number, twelve thousand were children and six thousand were parents living together in families. The average child was six years old, the average parent twenty-seven. A typical homeless family included a mother with two or three children, but in about one-fifth of these families two parents were present. Roughly ten thousand single persons, then, made up the remainder of the population of the city's shelters.

These proportions vary somewhat from one area of the nation to another. In all areas, however, families are the fastest-growing sector of the homeless population, and in the Northeast they are by far the largest sector already. In Massachusetts, three-fourths of the homeless now are families with children; in certain parts of Massachusetts–Attleboro and Northhampton, for example–the proportion reaches ninety percent. Two-thirds of the homeless children studied recently in Boston were less than five years old.

Of an estimated two to three million homeless people nationwide, about 500,000 are dependent children, according to Robert Hayes, counsel to the National Coalition for the Homeless. Including their parents, at least 750,000 homeless people in America are family members.

What is to be made, then, of the supposition that the homeless are primarily   20 the former residents of mental hospitals, persons who were carelessly released during the 1970s? Many of them are, to be sure. Among the older men and women in the streets and shelters, as many as one-third (some believe as many as one-half) may be chronically disturbed, and a number of these people were deinstitutionalized during the 1970s. But in a city like New York, where nearly half the homeless are small children with an average age of six, to operate on the basis of such a supposition makes no sense. Their parents, with an average age of twenty-seven, are not likely to have been hospitalized in the 1970s, either.

Nor is it easy to assume, as was once the case, that single men—those who come closer to fitting the stereotype of the homeless vagrant, the drifting alcoholic of an earlier age—are the former residents of mental hospitals. The age of homeless men has dropped in recent years; many of them are only twenty-one to twenty-eight years old. Fifty percent of homeless men in New York City shelters in 1984 were there for the first time. Most had previously had homes and jobs. Many had never before needed public aid.

A writer in the *New York Times* describes a homeless woman standing on a traffic island in Manhattan. "She was evicted from her small room in the hotel just across the street," and she is determined to get revenge. Until she does, "nothing will move her from that spot. . . . Her argumentativeness and her angry fixation on revenge, along with the apparent absence of hallucinations, mark her as a paranoid." Most physicians, I imagine, would be more reserved in passing judgment with so little evidence, but this author makes his diagnosis without hesitation. "The paranoids of the street," he says, "are among the most difficult to help."

Perhaps so. But does it depend on who is offering the help? Is anyone offering to help this woman get back her home? Is it crazy to seek vengeance for being thrown into the street? The absence of anger, some psychiatrists believe, might indicate much greater illness.

The same observer sees additional symptoms of pathology ("negative symptoms," he calls them) in the fact that many homeless persons demonstrate a "gross deterioration in their personal hygiene" and grooming, leading to "indifference" and "apathy." Having just identified one woman as unhealthy because she is so far from being "indifferent" as to seek revenge, he now sees apathy as evidence of illness; so consistency is not what we are looking for in this account. But how much less indifferent might the homeless be if those who decide their fate were less indifferent themselves? How might their grooming and hygiene be improved if they were permitted access to a public toilet?

In New York City, as in many cities, homeless people are denied the right to   25 wash in public bathrooms, to store their few belongings in a public locker, or, in certain cases, to make use of public toilets altogether. Shaving, cleaning of clothes, and other forms of hygiene are prohibited in the men's room of Grand Central Station. The terminal's three hundred lockers, used in former times by homeless people to secure their goods, were removed in 1986 as "a threat to public safety," according to a study made by the New York City Council.

At one-thirty every morning, homeless people are ejected from the station. Many once attempted to take refuge on the ramp that leads to Forty-second Street because it was protected from the street by wooden doors and thus provided some degree of warmth. But the station management responded to this challenge in two ways. The ramp was mopped with a strong mixture of ammonia to produce a noxious smell, and when the people sleeping there brought cardboard boxes and newspapers to protect them from the fumes, the entrance doors were chained wide open. Temperatures dropped some nights to ten degrees. Having driven these people to the streets, city officials subsequently determined that their willingness to risk exposure to cold weather could be taken as further evidence of mental illness.

At Pennsylvania Station in New York, homeless women are denied the use of toilets. Amtrak police come by and herd them off each hour on the hour. In June 1985, Amtrak officials issued this directive to police: "It is the policy of Amtrak to not allow the homeless and undesirables to remain. . . . Officers are encouraged to eject all undesirables. . . . Now is the time to train and educate them that their presence will not be tolerated as cold weather sets in." In an internal memo, according to CBS, an Amtrak official asked flatly: "Can't we get rid of this trash?"

I have spent many nights in conversation with the women who are huddled in the corridors and near the doorway of the public toilets in Penn Station. Many are young. Most are cogent. Few are dressed in the familiar rags suggested by the term *bag ladies*. Unable to bathe or use the toilets in the station, almost all are in conditions of intolerable physical distress. The sight of clusters of police officers, mostly male, guarding a toilet from use by homeless women speaks volumes about the public conscience of New York.

A young man who had lost his job, then his family, then his home, all in the summer of 1986, spoke with me for several hours in Grand Central Station on the weekend following Thanksgiving. "A year ago," he said, "I never thought that somebody like me would end up in a shelter. Nothing you've ever undergone prepares you. You walk into the place [a shelter on the Bowery]–the smell of sweat and urine hits you like a wall. Unwashed bodies and the look of absolute despair on many, many faces there would make you think you were in Dante's Hell. . . . What you fear is that you will be here forever. You do not know if it is ever going to end. You think to yourself: it is a dream and I will awake. Sometimes I think: it's an experiment. They are watching you to find out how much you can take. . . . I was a pretty stable man. Now I tremble when I meet somebody in the ordinary world. I'm trembling right now. . . . For me, the loss of work and loss of wife had left me rocking. Then the welfare regulations hit me. I began to feel that I would be re-duced to trash. . . . Half the people that I know are suffering from chest infections and sleep deprivation. The lack of sleep leaves you debilitated, shaky. You exagger-ate your fears. If a psychiatrist came along he'd say that I was crazy. But I was an ordinary man. There was nothing wrong with me. I lost my kids. I lost my home. Now would you say that I was crazy if I told you I was feeling sad?"

The Responsive Reader

1. What assumptions about the homeless do you bring to this essay? How do they compare with the misconceptions and stereotypes that Kozol sets out to chal-lenge? What stereotypes does he attack?

2. How would you sum up Kozol's strategy as an advocate for the homeless? How does he account for the popular misunderstandings he attacks? Why are they widespread? How are they perpetuated?

3. "Do-gooders" are often attacked for following the dictates of the heart and not the head. To what authorities does Kozol turn to support his position? How does he use statistics?

4. What is Kozol's answer to the popular belief that people with mental illnesses make up a large part of the homeless population?

5. Unlike many of us, Kozol befriends and talks with society's rejects. Which of the people and which of their testimonies will you remember? Does Kozol suc-ceed in making you think of the homeless as fellow human beings and fellow Americans?

For Discussion or Writing

6. In our affluent society, do we tend to blame the down and out for their own problems? Is our attitude basically, "It's their own fault"?

7. What is the point of the parable of the Good Samaritan? Do you think of your-self as one of those who walked by on the other side of the street? In Kozol's *Amazing Grace*, a pastor for the poor in her South Bronx parish comments on a society where "social blindness is accepted as the normal state of mind." Do you think you or people you know suffer from "social blindness"?

Collaborative Projects

8. How does your community or area deal with the homeless? What ordinances apply to them? Who speaks for them? What is the attitude of public officials? Working with a group, check out local initiatives or programs, legal challenges, recent developments.

THE OTHER BODY
Difference, Disability, and Identity Politics

Ynestra King

~~~~~~~~~~

Of all the ways of becoming "other" in our society, disability is the only one that can happen to anyone, in an instant, transforming that person's life and identity forever.

YNESTRA KING

Attitudes toward the disabled have slowly changed. Society has "come a long way" from times when physically impaired students like Ynestra King were shunted off to special classes and special buildings, segregated from "normal" children. Access to education, to public buildings, and to public transport has been greatly improved. Revolutionary new technologies hold out promise of greater independence and enhanced mobility and communication for many. King, however, writes to remind us of the unfinished agenda, of the distance we have to go to make possible human and humane ways of living with disability and to help allay "the underlying rage at the system" that she feels. Like other spokespersons for the disabled, King is an outspoken political activist. Her books include Ecofeminism and the Reenchantment of Nature *(1993). When she wrote the article, her son was one year old. Her article was first published in Ms. magazine.*

Disabled people rarely appear in popular culture. When they do, their disability must be a continuous preoccupation overshadowing all other areas of their character. Disabled people are disabled. That is what they "do." That is what they "are."

My own experience with a mobility impairment that is only minorly disfiguring is that one must either be a creature of the disability, or have transcended it entirely. For me, like most disabled people (and this of course depends on relative severity), neither extreme is true. It is an organic, literally embodied fact that will not change—like being a woman. While it may be possible to "do gender," one does not "do disability." But there is an organic base to both conditions that extends far into culture, and the meaning that "nature" has. Unlike being a woman, being disabled is not a socially constructed condition. It is a tragedy of nature, of a kind that will always exist. The very condition of disability provides a vantage point of a certain lived experience in the body, a lifetime of opportunity for the observation of reaction to bodily deviance, a testing ground for reactions to persons who are readily perceived as having something wrong or being different. It is fascinating, maddening, and disorienting. It defies categories of "sickness" and "health," "broken" and "whole." It is in between.

Meeting people has an overlay: I know what they notice first is that I am different. And there is the experience of the difference in another person's reaction who meets me sitting down (when the disability is not apparent), and standing up and walking (when the infirmity is obvious). It is especially noticeable when another individual is flirting and flattering, and has an abrupt change in affect when I stand up. I always make sure that I walk around in front of someone before I accept a date, just to save face for both of us. Once the other person perceives the disability, the switch on the sexual circuit breaker often pops off–the connection is broken. "Chemistry" is over. I have a lifetime of such experiences, and so does every other disabled woman I know.

White middle-class people–especially white men–in the so-called First World have the most negative reactions. And I always recognize studied politeness, the attempt to pretend that there's nothing to notice (this is the liberal response–Oh, you're black? I hadn't noticed). Then there's the do-gooder response, where the person falls all over her/himself, insisting on doing everything for you; later they hate you; it's a form of objectification. It conveys to you that that is all they see, rather like a man who can't quit talking with a woman about sex.

In the era of identity politics in feminism, disability has not only been an   5
added cross to bear, but an added "identity" to take on–with politically correct positions, presumed instant alliances, caucuses to join, and closets to come out of. For example, I was once dragged across a room to meet someone. My friend, a very politically correct lesbian feminist, said, "She's disabled, too. I thought you'd like to meet her." Rather than argue–what would I say? "I'm not interested in other disabled people," or "This is my night off"? (The truth in that moment was like the truth of this experience in every other moment, complicated and difficult to explain)–I went along to find myself standing before someone strapped in a wheelchair she propels by blowing into a tube with a respirator permanently fastened to the back of the chair. To suggest that our relative experience of disability is something we could casually compare (as other people stand by!) demonstrates the crudity of perception about the complex nature of bodily experience.

My infirmity is partial leg paralysis. I can walk anywhere, climb stairs, drive a car, ride a horse, swim, hang-glide, fly a plane, hike in the wilderness, go to jail for my political convictions, travel alone, and operate heavy equipment. I can earn a living, shop, cook, eat as I please, dress myself, wash and iron my own clothes, clean my house. The woman in that wheelchair can do none of these fundamental things, much less the more exotic ones. On a more basic human level I can spontaneously get my clothes off if I decide to make love. Once in bed my lover and I can forget my disability. None of this is true of the woman in the wheelchair. There is no bodily human activity that does not have to be specially negotiated, none in which she is not absolutely "different." It would take a very long time, and a highly nuanced conversation, for us to be able to share experiences as if they were common. The experience of disability for the two of us was more different than my experience is from the daily experience of people who are not considered disabled. So much for disability solidarity.

With disability, one is somewhere on a continuum between total bodily dysfunction–or death–and complete physical wholeness. In some way, this probably applies to every living person. So when is it that we call a person "disabled"? When do they become "other"? There are "minor" disabilities that are nonetheless significant for a person's life. Color blindness is one example. But in our culture, color blindness is considered an inconvenience rather than a disability.

The ostracization, marginalization, and distorted response to disability are not simply issues of prejudice and denial of civil rights. They reflect attitudes toward bodily life, an unease in the human skin, an inability to cope with contingency, ambiguity, flux, finitude, and death.

Visibly disabled people (like women) in this culture are the scapegoats for resentments of the limitations of organic life. I had polio when I was seven, finishing second grade. I had excelled in everything, and rarely missed school. I had one bad conduct notation–for stomping on the boys' blocks when they wouldn't let me play with them. Although I had leg braces and crutches when I was ready to start school the next year, I wanted desperately to go back and resume as much of the same life as I could. What I was not prepared for was the response of the school system. They insisted that I was now "handicapped" and should go into what they called "special education." This was a program aimed primarily at multiply disabled children, virtually all of whom were mentally retarded as well as physically disabled. It was in a separate wing of another school, and the children were completely segregated from the "normal" children in every aspect of the school day, including lunch and recreational activities. I was fortunate enough to have educated, articulate parents and an especially aggressive mother; she went to the school board and waged a tireless campaign to allow me to come back to my old school on a trial basis–the understanding being that the school could send me to special education if things "didn't work out" in the regular classroom.

And so began my career as an "exceptional" disabled person, not like the *other* "others." And I was glad. I didn't want to be associated with those others either. Apart from the objective limitations caused by the polio, the transformation in identity–the difference in worldly reception–was terrifying and embarrassing, and it went far beyond the necessary considerations my limitations required.

My experience as "other" is much greater and more painful as a disabled person than as a woman. Maybe the most telling dimension of this knowledge is my observation of the reactions of others over the years, of how deeply afraid people are of being outside the normative appearance (which is getting narrower as capitalism exaggerates patriarchy). It is no longer enough to be thin; one must have ubiquitous muscle definition, nothing loose, flabby, or ill defined, no fuzzy

10

boundaries. And of course, there's the importance of control. Control over aging, bodily processes, weight, fertility, muscle tone, skin quality, and movement. Disabled women, regardless of how thin, are without full bodily control.

I see disabled women fight these normative standards in different ways, but never get free of negotiating and renegotiating them. I did it by constructing my life around other values and, to the extent possible, developing erotic attachments to people who had similar values, and for whom my compensations were more than adequate. But at one point, after two disastrous but steamy liaisons with a champion athlete and a dancer (during which my friends pointed out the obvious · unkind truth and predicted painful endings), I discovered the worlds I had tried to protect myself from: the disastrous attraction to "others" to complete oneself. I have seen disabled women endure unspeakably horrible relationships because they were so flattered to have such a conventionally attractive individual in tow.

And then there's the weight issue. I got fat by refusing to pay attention to my body. Now that I'm slimming down again, my old vanities and insecurities are surfacing. The battle of dieting can be especially fraught for disabled women. It is more difficult because exercising is more difficult, as is traveling around to get the proper foods, and then preparing them. But the underlying rage at the system that makes you feel as if you *are* your body (female, infirm) and that everything else is window dressing–this also undermines the requisite discipline. A tempting response is to resort to an ideal of self as bodiless essence in which the body is completely incidental, and irrelevant.

The wish that the body should be irrelevant has been one of my most fervent lifelong wishes. The knowledge that it isn't is my most intense lifelong experience.

I have seen other disabled women wear intentionally provocative clothes, like the woman in a wheelchair on my bus route to work. She can barely move. She has a pretty face, and tiny legs she could not possibly walk on. Yet she wears black lace stockings and spike high heels. The other bus occupants smile condescendingly, or pretend not to notice, or whisper in appalled disbelief that this woman could represent herself as having a sexual self. That she could "flaunt" her sexual being violates the code of acceptable appearance for a disabled woman. This woman's apparel is no more far out than that of many other women on our bus– but she refuses to fold up and be a good little asexual handicapped person.

The well-intentioned liberal new campaigns around "hire the handicapped" are oppressive in related ways. The Other does not only have to demonstrate her competence on insider terms; she must be better, by way of apologizing for being different and rewarding the insiders for letting her in. And the happy handicapped person, who has had faith placed in her/him, must vindicate "the race" because the politics of tokenism assumes that there are in fact other qualifications than doing the job.

This is especially prejudicial in a recession, where there are few social services, where it is "every man for himself." Disabled people inevitably have greater expenses, since assistance must often be paid for privately. In the U.S., public construction of the disabled body is that one either is fully disabled and dysfunctional/unemployable (and therefore eligible for public welfare) or totally on one's own. There is no in-between–the possibility of a little assistance, or exceptions in certain areas. Disabled people on public assistance cannot work or they will lose their benefits. (In the U.S. ideology that shapes public attitudes and public policy, one is either fully dependent or fully autonomous.) But the reality of human and organic life is that everyone is different in some way; there is no such thing as a totally autonomous individual. Yet the mythology of autonomy perpetuates in terrible ways the oppression of the disabled. It also perpetuates misogyny–and the destruction of the planet.

It may be that this clear lack of autonomy–this reminder of mortal finitude and contingency and embeddedness of nature and the body–is at the root of the hatred of the disabled. On the continuum of autonomy and dependence, disabled people need help. To need help is to feel humiliated, to have failed. I think this "help" issue must be even harder for men than women. But any disabled person is always negotiating both the provisionality of autonomy and the rigidity of physical norms.

From the vantage point of disability, there are some objective and desirable aspects of autonomy. But they have to do with independence. The preferred protocol is that the attendant or friend perform the task that the disabled person needs done in the way the disabled person *asks it to be done.* Assistance from friends and family is a negotiated process, and often maddening. For that reason most disabled people prefer to live in situations where they can do all the basic functions themselves, with whatever special equipment or built-ins are required.

It's a dreadful business, this needing help. And it's more dreadful in the U.S.   20
than in any place in the world, because our heroes are dynamic overcomers of adversity, and there is an inevitable cultural contempt for weakness.

Autonomy is on a continuum toward dependency and death. And the idea that dependency could come at any time, that one could die at any time, or be dismembered or disfigured, and still have to live (maybe even *want to live*) is unbearable in a context that understands and values autonomy in the way we moderns do.

I don't want to depict this experience of unbearability as strictly cultural. The compromising of the human body before its natural time is tragic. It forces terrible hardship on the individual to whom it occurs. But the added overlay of oppression on the disabled is intimately related to the fear of death, and the acknowledgment of our embeddedness in organic nature. We are finite, contingent, dependent creatures by our very nature; we will all eventually die. We will all experience compromises to our physical integrity. The aspiration to human wholeness is an oppressive idealism. Socially, it is deeply infantilizing.

It promotes a simplistic view of the human person, a static notion of human life that prevents the maturity and social wisdom that might allow human beings to more fully apprehend the human condition. It marginalizes the "different," those perceived as hopelessly wedded to organic existence—women and the disabled. The New Age "human potential movement"—in the name of maximizing human growth—is one of the worst offenders in obscuring the kind of human growth I am suggesting.

I too believe that the potential for human growth and creativity is infinite—but it is not groundless. The common ground for the person—the human body—is a place of shifting sand that can fail us at any time. It can change shape and properties without warning; this is an essential truth of embodied existence.

Of all the ways of becoming "other" in our society, disability is the only one   25
that can happen to anyone, in an instant, transforming that person's life and identity forever.

The Responsive Reader

1. What does King mean by saying, "Unlike being a woman, being disabled is not a socially constructed condition"? Why does she object to society expecting that for disabled people "their disability must be a continuous preoccupation overshadowing all other areas of their character"?

2. King finds many typical responses to people with disabilities "fascinating, maddening, and disorienting." For instance, why are first meetings with others a special problem? Why are encounters with the other sex a special problem? What is wrong with the "liberal response," the "do-gooder response," or the added burden of disability in an area of "identity politics"?

3. What do you eventually learn about the exact nature and history of King's disability? (Why doesn't she tell the whole story at the very beginning, "up front"?) Why does she insist on the wide range of impairment and disability, and how does she drive the point home?

4. Why does King consider special education programs an instance of the "ostracization" and "marginalization" of disability in our society? What was her own experience with them?

5. How does the "normative standard" of the desirable individual in our society impose a special burden on people with disabilities—in areas like sex, weight, and dress?

6. What is King's quarrel with public policies dealing with the definition of and assistance for the disabled? (What is wrong with liberal "hire the handicapped" campaigns?)

7. According to King, why do disabled people prefer equipment to human assis-

tance? Can you explain King's ambivalent attitude toward "autonomy" or "independence"?

For Discussion or Writing

8. What attitudes or assumptions about the disabled did you bring to the reading of this essay? (On what were they based?) Does this article change some of your basic attitudes or assumptions? Why or why not?

9. Do you agree that the "norm" of what is desirable or socially approved is getting narrower, excluding more and more people?

Collaborative Projects

10. What programs or policies on the subject of disability are in place in your college? Do they work? How are they implemented, and with what success? Working with a group, how would you set about finding out?

FORUM: *How Smart Are Intelligence Tests?*

Tests everywhere regulate the traffic on the road to success or failure. According to a report published by Moseley Associates, a publishing consulting firm, government bodies at all levels look to testing as the most cost-effective assessment of schools and students. At the same time, standardized testing is under attack: Critics of the "tyranny of testing" question the test-driven nature of the American educational system, asking that we test less and teach more. They ask whether multiple-choice tests test the students' ability to read, write, and think—or their proficiency at taking multiple-choice tests. Critics of personnel policies of both public agencies and private companies question the reliance on "objective" tests for hiring and promotion. For instance, should police officers be hired and promoted on the basis of commitment, knowledge of the community, and interpersonal skill—or on the basis of culturally biased exams? Testing experts, or psychometricians, have always warned against naive overreliance on test results without regard for the limitations and caveats spelled out in the fine print. Several recent controversies have served to make the media and the public reexamine the uses and misuses of tests.

BEHIND THE CURVE

Leon J. Kamin

In 1994, The Bell Curve, a widely touted and attacked book, precipitated much controversy and soul-searching among psychologists schooled in the tradition of intelligence testing. Richard J. Herrnstein and Charles Murray published their book at a time when backlash politics was calling affirmative action programs into question. The Bell Curve passed ammunition to those who believe in the futility of "social engineering." The authors baldly stated the explosive thesis, usually muted since its trumpeting by Nazi ideologists, that some races are more intelligent than others and therefore genetically programmed for leadership and success. Others are programmed for low achievement and a life of crime. Much of the storm of criticism caused by the book faulted Herrnstein and Murray for disregarding not only the book's incendiary potential in an era of racial paranoia but also the unsavory history of theories of racial superiority. Critics accused the authors of drawing far-reaching conclusions not justified by the evidence. They violently attacked the reliability of the authors' data, accusing them of relying on biased sources. Leon J. Kamin is a professor of psychology at Northeastern University in Boston. His review, published in Scientific American, challenges Herrnstein and Murray on two counts: He questions the scientific validity of the authors' methodology. And he questions the scientific credentials of the authors' sources.

THE BELL CURVE: Intelligence and Class Structure in American Life
by Richard J. Herrnstein AND *Charles Murray*

This book, with 400,000 copies in print just two months after its publication,   1
has created an enormous stir. The authors unabashedly assert that scientific evidence demonstrates the existence of genetically based differences in intelligence
among social classes and races. They maintain further that data from some 1,000
publications in the social and biological sciences show that attributes such as employment, income, welfare dependency, divorce and quality of parental behavior
are determined by an individual's intelligence. These claims—another eruption of
the crude biological determinism that permeates the history of IQ testing—lead
Herrnstein and Murray to a number of social policy recommendations. The policies would not be necessary, or humane, even if the cited evidence were valid. But
the caliber of the data in *The Bell Curve* is, at many critical points, pathetic. Further,
the authors repeatedly fail to distinguish between correlation and causation and
thus draw many inappropriate conclusions.

I will deal first with an especially troubling example of the quality of the
data on which Herrnstein and Murray rely. They ask, "How do African-Americans
compare with blacks in Africa on cognitive tests?" They reason that low African-
American IQ scores might be the result either of a history of slavery and discrimination or of genetic factors. Herrnstein and Murray evidently assume that blacks
reared in colonial Africa have not been subjected to discrimination. In their view, if
low IQ scores of African-Americans are a product of discrimination, rather than
genes, black Africans should have higher IQs than African-Americans.

To answer the question they have posed, Herrnstein and Murray call on the
authority of Richard Lynn of the University of Ulster in Ireland, described as "a
leading scholar of racial and ethnic differences," from whose advice they have
"benefited especially." They state that Lynn, who in 1991 reviewed 11 African IQ
studies, "estimated the median black African IQ to be 75 . . . about 10 points lower
than the current figure for American blacks." Herrnstein and Murray conclude
that the "special circumstances" of African-Americans cannot explain their low
average IQ relative to whites. That leaves genetics free to explain the black-white
difference.

But why do black Americans have higher scores than black Africans? Herrnstein and Murray, citing "Owen 1992," write that "the IQ of 'coloured' students in
South Africa—of mixed racial background—has been found to be similar to that of
American blacks." The implication is clear: the admixture of Caucasian and African
genes, both in South Africa and in the U.S., boosts "coloured" IQ 10 points above
that of native Africans. But the claims made regarding African and coloured IQs
cannot withstand critical scrutiny.

Lynn's 1991 paper describes a 1989 publication by Ken Owen as "the best   5
single study of the Negroid intelligence." The study compared white, Indian and

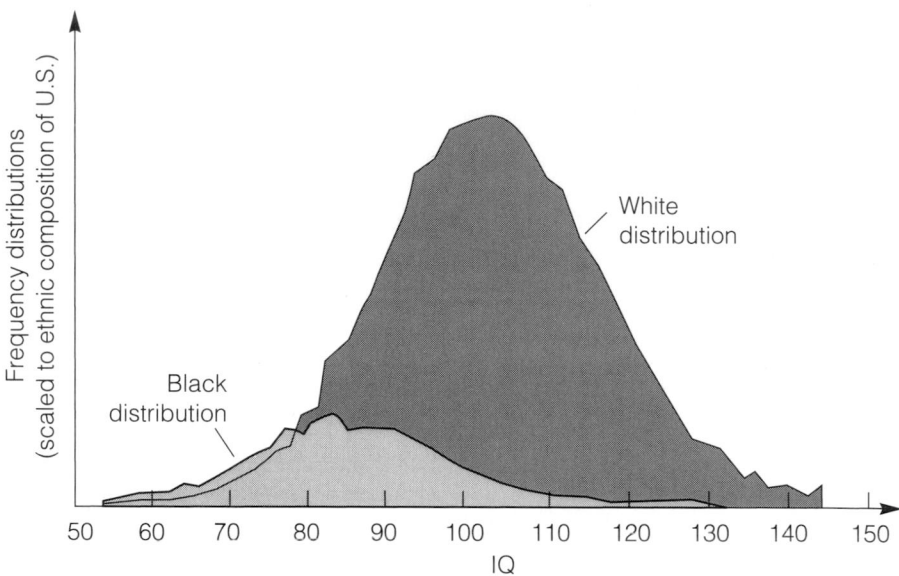

BELL CURVE, adapted from an illustration in the book, shows the distribution of white and black IQ scores. What it does not show is why the scores are different. (*Source:* National Longitudinal Survey of Labor Market Experience of Youth, 1980–1990)

black pupils on the Junior Aptitude Tests; no coloured pupils were included. The mean "Negroid" IQ in that study, according to Lynn, was 69. But Owen did not in fact assign IQs to any of the groups he tested; he merely reported test-score differences between groups, expressed in terms of standard deviation units. The IQ figure was concocted by Lynn out of those data. There is, as Owen made clear, no reason to suppose that low scores of blacks had much to do with genetics: "the knowledge of English of the majority of black testees was so poor that certain [of the] tests . . . proved to be virtually unusable." Further, the tests assumed that Zulu pupils were familiar with electrical appliances, microscopes and "Western type of ladies' accessories."

In 1992 Owen reported on a sample of coloured students that had been added to the groups he had tested earlier. The footnote in *The Bell Curve* seems to credit this report as proving that South African coloured students have an IQ "similar to that of American blacks," that is, about 85 (the actual reference does not appear in the book's bibliography). That statement does not correctly characterize Owen's work. The test used by Owen in 1992 was the "nonverbal" Raven's Progressive Matrices, which is thought to be less culturally biased than other IQ tests. He was able to compare the performance of coloured students with that of the whites, blacks and Indians in his 1989 study because the earlier set of pupils had taken the Progressive Matrices in addition to the Junior Aptitude Tests. The black pupils, recall, had poor knowledge of English, but Owen felt that the instructions for the Matrices "are so easy that they can be explained with gestures."

Owen's 1992 paper again does not assign IQs to the pupils. Rather he gives the mean number of correct responses on the Progressive Matrices (out of a possible 60) for each group: 45 for whites, 42 for Indians, 37 for coloureds and 28 for blacks. The test's developer, John Raven, repeatedly insisted that results on the Progressive Matrices tests cannot be converted into IQs. Matrices scores, unlike IQs, are not symmetrical around their mean (no "bell curve" here). There is thus no meaningful way to convert an average of raw Matrices scores into an IQ, and no comparison with American black IQs is possible.

The remaining studies cited by Lynn, and accepted as valid by Herrnstein and Murray, tell us little about African intelligence but do tell us something about Lynn's scholarship. One of the 11 entries in Lynn's table of the intelligence of "pure Negroids" indicates that 1,011 Zambians who were given the Progressive Matrices had a lamentably low average IQ of 75. The source for this quantitative claim is given as "Pons 1974; Crawford-Nutt 1976."

A. L. Pons did test 1,011 Zambian copper miners, whose average number of correct responses was 34. Pons reported on this work orally; his data were summarized in tabular form in a paper by D. H. Crawford-Nutt. Lynn took the Pons data from Crawford-Nutt's paper and converted the number of correct responses into a bogus average "IQ" of 75. Lynn chose to ignore the substance of Crawford-Nutt's paper, which reported that 228 black high school students in Soweto scored an average of 45 correct responses on the Matrices—*higher* than the mean of 44 achieved by the same-age white sample on whom the test's norms had been established and well above the mean of Owen's coloured pupils.

Seven of the 11 studies selected by Lynn for inclusion in his "Negroid" table reported only average Matrices scores, not IQs; the other studies used tests clearly dependent on cultural content. Lynn had earlier, in a 1978 paper, summarized six studies of African pupils, most using the Matrices. The arbitrary IQs concocted by Lynn for those studies ranged between 75 and 88, with a median of 84. Five of those six studies were omitted from Lynn's 1991 summary, by which time African IQ had, in his judgment, plummeted to 69.

Lynn's distortions and misrepresentations of the data constitute a truly venomous racism, combined with scandalous disregard for scientific objectivity. Lynn is widely known among academics to be an associate editor of the racist journal *Mankind Quarterly* and a major recipient of financial support from the nativist, eugenically oriented Pioneer Fund. It is a matter of shame and disgrace that two eminent social scientists, fully aware of the sensitivity of the issues they address, take Lynn as their scientific tutor and uncritically accept his surveys of research.

I turn now to a revealing example of Herrnstein and Murray's tendency to ignore the difference between mere statistical associations (correlations) and cause-and-effect relationships. The authors lament that "private complaints about the incompetent affirmative-action hiree are much more common than scholarly ex-amination of the issue." They then proceed to a scholarly and public discussion of "teacher competency examinations." They report that such exams have had "gener-ally beneficial effects," presumably by weeding out incompetent affirmative-action hirees. That view of tests for teachers is not shared by those who argue that be-cause blacks tend to get lower scores, the tests are a way of eliminating competent black teachers. But Herrnstein and Murray assure us that "teachers who score higher on the tests have greater success with their students."

To support that statement, they cite a single study by two economists who an-alyzed data from a large number of North Carolina school districts. The re-searchers obtained average teacher test scores (a measure of "teacher quality") and pupil failure rates for each district. They reported that a "1% increase in teacher quality . . . is accompanied by a 5% decline in the . . . rate of failure of students"–that is, there were fewer student failures in districts where teachers had higher test scores. It does not follow from such a correlation, however, that hiring teachers with higher test scores will reduce the rate of student failure. The same researchers found, to their surprise, that "larger class size tends to lead to improved average [pupil] performance." Does it follow that increasing the pupil-to-teacher ratio would further improve student performance? That policy might please many tax-payers, just as firing teachers with lower test scores would please some. But neither policy derives logically from the observed correlations.

To understand why, consider the following. The average proportion of black students across the North Carolina school districts was 31 percent. Suppose–it does not stretch credulity–that black teachers (who have lower test scores) tend to work in districts with large proportions of black pupils (who have higher failure rates). Such nonrandom assignment of teachers would produce a correlation be-tween teacher test scores and pupil failure rates, but one cannot then conclude that the teachers' test scores have any causal relation to student failure. To argue that, one would have to show that for a group of black teachers and for a separate group of white teachers, teachers' test scores predicted the failure rates of their stu-dents. No such information was available to the original researchers or to Herrn-stein and Murray.

What about the finding that high pupil-to-teacher ratios are associated with   15 good pupil performance? There is no way to be certain, but suppose deprived black children tended to be in small, de facto segregated rural schools, whereas more privileged whites were in larger classrooms. Would cramming more pupils into the rural schools promote academic excellence?

There is an important and general lesson buried in this example: the arithmeti-cal complexity of the multitude of correlations and logistic regressions stuffed into *The Bell Curve* does not elevate their status from mere associations to causes and effects.

The confusion between correlation and causation permeates the book's largest section, which consists of an interminable series of analyses of data taken from the National Longitudinal Survey of Labor Market Experience of Youth (NLSY). Those data, not surprisingly, indicate that there is an association within each race between IQ and socioeconomic status. Herrnstein and Murray labor mightily to show that low IQ is the cause of low socioeconomic status, and not vice versa. The argument is decked out in all the trappings of science–a veritable barrage of charts, graphs, tables, appendices and appeals to statistical techniques that are unknown to many readers. But on close examination, this scientific emperor is wearing no clothes.

The NLSY survey included more than 12,000 youngsters, who were aged 14 to 22 when the continuing study began in 1979. At that time the respondents or their parents gave information about their educations, occupations and incomes and answered questions about themselves. Those reports are the basis for classifying the childhood socioeconomic status of the respondents. The teenagers also took the Armed Forces Qualification Test, regarded by psychometricians as essentially an IQ test. As they have grown older, the respondents have provided more information about their own schooling, unemployment, poverty, marital status, childbearing, welfare dependency, criminality, parenting behavior and so on.

Herrnstein and Murray pick over these data, trying to show that it is overwhelmingly IQ–not childhood or adult socioeconomic status–that determines worldly success and the moral praiseworthiness of one's social behaviors. But their dismissal of socioeconomic status rests ultimately on the self-reports of youngsters, which do not form an entirely firm basis.

I do not suggest that such self-reports are entirely unrelated to reality. We know from many sources that children from differing social class backgrounds do indeed differ in measured IQ. And in the NLSY study, after all, the respondents' self-reports are correlated with the objective facts of their IQ scores. But comparing the predictive value of those self-reports with that of test scores is playing with loaded dice.

Further, the fact that self-reports are correlated with IQ scores is, like all correlations, ambiguous. For Herrnstein and Murray, the relation of their index of parental socioeconomic status to the child's IQ means that parents of high status–the "cream floating on the surface of American society"–have transmitted high-quality genes to their offspring. But other interpretations are possible. Perhaps the kinds of people who get high test scores are precisely those who are vain enough to claim exaggerated social status for themselves. That tendency could artificially inflate correlations of IQ both with parental socioeconomic status and with self-reports of success, distorting all tests of the relative predictive power of socioeconomic status and IQ. Such an explanation may seem far-fetched to some readers, but it is clearly a logical possibility. The choice between such alternative interpretations of statistical associations cannot be based on logic alone. There is plenty of elbow room for ideological bias in social science.

The core of the Herrnstein-Murray message is phrased with a beguiling simplicity: "Putting it all together, success and failure in the American economy, and all that goes with it, are increasingly a matter of the genes that people inherit." Income is a "family trait" because IQ, "a major predictor of income, passes on sufficiently from one generation to the next to constrain economic mobility." Those at the bottom of the economic heap were unlucky when the genes were passed out, and they will remain there.

The correlations with which Herrnstein and Murray are obsessed are of course real: the children of day laborers are less likely than the children of stockbrokers to acquire fortunes or to go to college. They are more likely to be delinquent, to receive welfare, to have children outside of marriage, to be unemployed and to have low-birth-weight babies. The children of laborers have lower average IQs than do the children of brokers, and so IQ is also related to all these phenomena. Herrnstein and Murray's intent is to convince us that low IQ causes poverty and its attendant evils–not, as others hold, vice versa.

For eight dense chapters, the authors of *The Bell Curve* wrestle with data from the NLSY survey, attempting to disentangle the roles of IQ and of socioeconomic status. They employ a number of quantitative tools, most prominently logistic regression, a technique that purports to specify what would happen if one variable were "held constant" while another variable were left free to vary. When socioeconomic status is statistically held constant by Herrnstein and Murray, IQ remains related to all the phenomena described. When IQ is held constant, the effect of socioeconomic status is invariably reduced, usually substantially, and sometimes eliminated.

There are a number of criticisms to be made regarding the ways in which   25 Herrnstein and Murray analyze these data. But for argument's sake, let us suppose that their analyses are appropriate and accurate. We can also grant that, rightly or wrongly, disproportionate salaries and wealth accrue to those with high IQ scores. What then do the Herrnstein–Murray analyses tell us?

The socioeconomic status of one's parents cannot in any immediate sense "cause" one's IQ to be high or low. Family income obviously cannot directly determine a child's performance on an IQ test. But income and the other components of an index of socioeconomic status can serve as rough indicators of the rearing environment to which a child has been exposed. With exceptions, a child of a well-to-do broker is more likely to be exposed to book learning earlier and more intensively than is a child of a laborer. And extensive practice at reading and calculating does affect, very directly, one's IQ score. That is one plausible way of interpreting the statistical link between parental socioeconomic status and a child's IQ.

The significant question is not whether socioeconomic status, as defined by Herrnstein and Murray, is more or less statistically associated with success than is their measure of IQ. Different measures of socioeconomic status, or different IQ tests, might substantially affect the results they obtained; other scholars, using other indices and tests, have in fact achieved quite different results. The significant question is, why don't the children of laborers acquire the skills that are tapped by IQ tests?

Herrnstein and Murray answer that the children of the poor, like their laborer parents before them, have been born with poor genes. Armed with that conviction, the authors hail as "a great American success story" that after "controlling for IQ," ethnic and racial discrepancies in education, wages and so forth are "strikingly diminished." They reach this happy conclusion on the questionable basis of their regression analyses. But the data, even if true, allow another reading. We can view it as a tragic failure of American society that so few black and low-socioeconomic status children are lucky enough to be reared in environments that nurture the skills needed to obtain high IQ scores. For Herrnstein and Murray, it is only fair that the race should go to the swift, who are blessed with good genes and high IQs. The conception that our society hobbles most of the contestants at the starting line does not occur to them.

In the world of *The Bell Curve*, the explanatory power of IQ is ubiquitous. The authors note that among blue-collar workers who tell researchers that they have dropped out of the labor force because of physical disability or injury, low IQ is common. Why? "An answer leaps to mind: The smarter you are, the less likely that you will have accidents." That answer leapt to mind before the thought that low-IQ workers, in minimum wage jobs, have little incentive to remain in the labor force. Dull young women lack the "foresight and intelligence" to understand that the welfare system offers them a bad deal. Welfare might be a bad deal for Herrnstein and Murray, but I am not so sure that single mothers on welfare have not figured out *their* odds pretty accurately.

People who have low IQs, according to *The Bell Curve*, commit crimes because they lack foresight, and so the threat of prison does not deter them. Further, they cannot "understand why robbing someone is wrong." Then what is to be made of the fact that although "very dull" young males are stopped by the police, booked for an offense and convicted less often than "normal" males, they are nevertheless jailed more than twice as often? "It may be . . . that they are less competent in getting favorable treatment from the criminal justice system. The data give us no way to tell." Perhaps not, but some hints are available. There is no doubt that O. J. Simpson is "competent," but his ability to hire high-priced lawyers is not irrelevant to the treatment he will receive from the criminal justice system.

The Bell Curve, near its closing tail, contains two chapters concerned with affirmative action, both in higher education and in the workplace. To read those chapters is to hear the second shoe drop. The rest of the book, I believe, was written merely as a prelude to its assault on affirmative action. The vigor of the attack is astonishing.

Affirmative action "cannot survive public scrutiny." It is based on "the explicit assumption that ethnic groups do not differ in . . . abilities." Hiring and promotion

30

procedures "that are truly fair . . . will produce . . . racial disparities," and "employers are using dual standards for black and white job applicants because someone
or something . . . is making them do so." That behavior has resulted in the "degra-
dation of intellectual requirements" in recruiting police, which has affected "police
performance on the street." We learn that a veteran of the Washington, D.C., police
force has heard "about people in the academy who could not read or write." And a
former instructor saw "people diagnosed as borderline retarded graduate from the
police academy." These anecdotes take their place among the politically potent folk-
tales about welfare queens driving Cadillacs.

At long last, Herrnstein and Murray let it all hang out: "Affirmative action, in
education and the workplace alike, is leaking a poison into the American soul."
Having examined the American condition at the close of the 20th century, these
two philosopher-kings conclude, "It is time for America once again to try living
with inequality, as life is lived. . . ." This kind of sentiment, I imagine, is what led
New York Times columnist Bob Herbert to the conclusion that *The Bell Curve* "is just a
genteel way of calling somebody a nigger." Herbert is right. The book has nothing
to do with science.

The Responsive Reader

1. At the beginning, how does Kamin summarize the central claims or basic message of *The Bell Curve?* Why does he call these claims an example of "the crude
   biological determinism that permeates the history of IQ testing"?

2. On what grounds does Kamin attack Lynn as one of the authors' key authorities? How does Kamin try to convince you that "Lynn's distortions and misrepresentations constitute a truly venomous racism, combined with scandalous
   disregard for scientific objectivity"? What kind of research had Lynn drawn on?
   According to Kamin, what were basic flaws in the research and in the use Lynn
   made of it?

3. A Chinese proverb says, "When you drink of the water, think of the source."
   The same might be said of the funding for research. What kind of thinking
   would make the Pioneer fund "nativist" and "eugenically oriented"?

4. What is Kamin's central point about the difference between correlations (or
   "mere statistical associations") and cause-and-effect relationships? How does
   he use the example of "teacher competency examinations" as a case in point?
   What holes does he poke in Herrnstein and Murray's use of statistics on
   teacher test scores and pupil performance?

5. How does Kamin ask you to rethink the correlation between low IQ and low
   socioeconomic status? How do his explanations differ from those given in the
   book under review? What are major points in his discussion of the NLSY
   study?

6. Kamin zeroes in on the "core" of the Herrnstein-Murray message when he quotes them on genes versus environment–on inherited ability versus social status as a cause of poverty. Can you spell out the basic assumptions on each side of this controversy? Can you spell out some of the implications for different interpretations of history or of the class structure? What according to Kamin are some of the factors, other than native intelligence, that affect IQ scores?

7. According to Kamin, what are the implications of the genetic IQ controversy for social policy in areas like poverty, welfare, and affirmative action?

For Discussion or Writing

8. Does Kamin convince you that there is "plenty of elbow room for ideological bias in social science"?

9. To what side do you incline in the argument over heredity versus environment as predictors of achievement or success? What has influenced your views on this issue? How would you defend your position?

Collaborative Projects

10. In schools, institutions, or organizations in your area, can you find signs of a rethinking of the nature and role of tests?

THE EQ FACTOR

Nancy Gibbs

> What is left out of traditional IQ tests? Do orthodox intelligence tests measure emotion or motivation? Do they test interpersonal intelligence? Do they test aptitude for self-control? Psychologists have explored the concept of multiple intelligences—different kinds of mental aptitudes required in the whole range of interpersonal, intellectual, and creative pursuits. In Frames of Mind: The Theory of Multiple Intelligences (1983), the psychologist Howard Gardner challenged "the standard notion of intelligence as a single capacity, with which an individual is born, and which proves difficult, if not impossible, to alter." Gardner explored the kinds of intelligence enabling individuals to deal well with language, with numbers, with music, or with other people. Psychologists and teachers began to recognize linguistic intelligence and social intelligence rather than a single aptitude that could be measured by a single intelligence test. Psychologists have begun to talk about a measurement of emotional aptitude, the EQ, to supplement the traditional IQ, which focused too narrowly on intellectual ability. The following Time magazine cover story explores the kinds of intelligence that may not be measured by traditional tests but that may nevertheless be a better basis for predicting academic and professional success.

It turns out that a scientist can see the future by watching four-year-olds   1
interact with a marshmallow. The researcher invites the children, one by one, into a plain room and begins the gentle torment. You can have this marshmallow right now, he says. But if you wait while I run an errand, you can have two marshmallows when I get back. And then he leaves.

Some children grab for the treat the minute he's out the door. Some last a few minutes before they give in. But others are determined to wait. They cover their eyes; they put their heads down; they sing to themselves; they try to play games or even fall asleep. When the researcher returns, he gives these children their hard-earned marshmallows. And then, science waits for them to grow up.

By the time the children reach high school, something remarkable has happened. A survey of the children's parents and teachers found that those who as four-year-olds had the fortitude to hold out for the second marshmallow generally grew up to be better adjusted, more popular, adventurous, confident and dependable teenagers. The children who gave in to temptation early on were more likely to be lonely, easily frustrated and stubborn. They buckled under stress and shied away from challenges. And when some of the students in the two groups took the

Scholastic Aptitude Test, the kids who had held out longer scored an average of 210 points higher.

When we think of brilliance we see Einstein, deep-eyed, woolly haired, a thinking machine with skin and mismatched socks. High achievers, we imagine, were wired for greatness from birth. But then you have to wonder why, over time, natural talent seems to ignite in some people and dim in others. This is where the marshmallows come in. It seems that the ability to delay gratification is a master skill, a triumph of the reasoning brain over the impulsive one. It is a sign, in short, of emotional intelligence. And it doesn't show up on an IQ test.

For most of this century, scientists have worshipped the hardware of the brain   5 and the software of the mind, the messy powers of the heart were left to the poets. But cognitive theory could simply not explain the questions we wonder about most: why some people just seem to have a gift for living well; why the smartest kid in the class will probably not end up the richest; why we like some people virtually on sight and distrust others; why some people remain buoyant in the face of troubles that would sink a less resilient soul. What qualities of the mind or spirit, in short, determine who succeeds?

The phrase "emotional intelligence" was coined by Yale psychologist Peter Salovey and the University of New Hampshire's John Mayer five years ago to describe qualities like understanding one's own feelings, empathy for the feelings of others and "the regulation of emotion in a way that enhances living." Their notion is about to bound into the national conversation, handily shortened to EQ, thanks to a new book, *Emotional Intelligence* by Daniel Goleman. Goleman, a Harvard psychology Ph.D. and a New York *Times* science writer with a gift for making even the chewiest scientific theories digestible to lay readers, has brought together a decade's worth of behavioral research into how the mind processes feelings. His goal, he announces on the cover, is to redefine what it means to be smart. His thesis: when it comes to predicting people's success, brainpower as measured by IQ and standardized achievement tests may actually matter less than the qualities of mind once thought of as "character" before the word began to sound quaint.

At first glance, there would seem to be little that's new here to any close reader of fortune cookies. There may be no less original idea than the notion that our hearts hold dominion over our heads. "I was so angry," we say, "I couldn't think straight." Neither is it surprising that "people skills" are useful, which amounts to saying, it's good to be nice. "It's so true it's trivial," says Dr. Paul McHugh, director of psychiatry at Johns Hopkins University School of Medicine. But if it were that simple, the book would not be quite so interesting or its implications so controversial.

This is no abstract investigation. Goleman is looking for antidotes to restore "civility to our streets and caring to our communal life." He sees practical applications everywhere for how companies should decide whom to hire, how couples can increase the odds that their marriages will last, how parents should raise their children and how schools should teach them. When street gangs substitute for families and schoolyard insults end in stabbings, when more than half of marriages end in divorce, when the majority of the children murdered in this country are killed by parents and stepparents, many of whom say they were trying to discipline the child for behavior like blocking the TV or crying too much, it suggests a demand for remedial emotional education. While children are still young, Goleman argues, there is a "neurological window of opportunity" since the brain's prefrontal circuitry, which regulates how we act on what we feel, probably does not mature until mid-adolescence.

And it is here the arguments will break out. Goleman's highly popularized conclusions, says McHugh, "will chill any veteran scholar of psychotherapy and any neuroscientist who worries about how his research may come to be applied." While many researchers in this relatively new field are glad to see emotional issues finally taken seriously, they fear that a notion as handy as EQ invites misuse. Goleman admits the danger of suggesting that you can assign a numerical yardstick to a person's character as well as his intellect; Goleman never even uses the phrase EQ in his book. But he (begrudgingly) approved an "unscientific" EQ test in *USA Today* with choices like "I am aware of even subtle feelings as I have them," and "I can sense the pulse of a group or relationship and state unspoken feelings."

"You don't want to take an average of your emotional skill," argues Harvard   10 psychological professor Jerome Kagan, a pioneer in child-development research. "That's what's wrong with the concept of intelligence for mental skills too. Some people handle anger well but can't handle fear. Some people can't take joy. So each emotion has to be viewed differently."

EQ is not the opposite of IQ. Some people are blessed with a lot of both, some with little of either. What researchers have been trying to understand is how they complement each other; how one's ability to handle stress, for instance, affects the ability to concentrate and put intelligence to use. Among the ingredients for success, researchers now generally agree that IQ counts for about 20%; the rest depends on everything from class to luck to the neural pathways that have developed in the brain over millions of years of human evolution.

It is actually the neuroscientists and evolutionists who do the best job of explaining the reasons behind the most unreasonable behavior. In the past decade or so, scientists have learned enough about the brain to make judgments about where emotion comes from and why we need it. Primitive emotional responses held the keys to survival: fear drives the blood into the large muscles, making it easier to run; surprise triggers the eyebrows to rise, allowing the eyes to widen their view and gather more information about an unexpected event. Disgust wrinkles up the face and closes the nostrils to keep out foul smells.

Emotional life grows out of an area of the brain called the limbic system, specifically the amygdala, whence come delight and disgust and fear and anger. Millions of years ago, the neocortex was added on, enabling humans to plan, learn and remember. Lust grows from the limbic system; love, from the neocortex. Animals like reptiles that have no neocortex cannot experience anything like maternal love; this is why baby snakes have to hide to avoid being eaten by their parents. Humans, with their capacity for love, will protect their offspring, allowing the brains of the young time to develop. The more connections between the limbic system and the neocortex, the more emotional responses are possible.

It was scientists like Joseph LeDoux of New York University who uncovered these cerebral pathways. LeDoux's parents owned a meat market. As a boy in Louisiana, he first learned about his future specialty by cutting up cows' brains for sweetbreads. "I found them the most interesting part of the cow's anatomy," he recalls. "They were visually pleasing–lots of folds, convolutions and patterns. The cerebellum was more interesting to look at than steak." The butcher's son became a neuroscientist, and it was he who discovered the short circuit in the brain that lets emotions drive action before the intellect gets a chance to intervene.

A hiker on a mountain path, for example, sees a long, curved shape in the   15
grass out of the corner of his eye. He leaps out of the way before he realizes it is only a stick that looks like a snake. Then he calms down; his cortex gets the message a few milliseconds after his amygdala and "regulates" its primitive response.

Without these emotional reflexes, rarely conscious but often terribly powerful, we would scarcely be able to function. "Most decisions we make have a vast number of possible outcomes, and any attempt to analyze all of them would never end," says University of Iowa neurologist Antonio Damasio, author of *Descartes' Error: Emotion, Reason and the Human Brain.* "I'd ask you to lunch tomorrow, and when the appointed time arrived, you'd still be thinking about whether you should come." What tips the balance, Damasio contends, is our unconscious assigning of emotional values to some of those choices. Whether we experience a somatic response– a gut feeling of dread or a giddy sense of elation–emotions are helping to limit the field in any choice we have to make. If the prospect of lunch with a neurologist is unnerving or distasteful, Damasio suggests, the invitee will conveniently remember a previous engagement.

When Damasio worked with patients in whom the connection between emotional brain and neocortex had been severed because of damage to the brain, he discovered how central that hidden pathway is to how we live our lives. People who had lost that linkage were just as smart and quick to reason, but their lives often fell apart nonetheless. They could not make decisions because they didn't know how they felt about their choices. They couldn't react to warnings or anger in other people. If they made a mistake, like a bad investment, they felt no regret or shame and so were bound to repeat it.

If there is a cornerstone to emotional intelligence on which most other emotional skills depend, it is a sense of self-awareness, of being smart about what we feel. A person whose day starts badly at home may be grouchy all day at work without quite knowing why. Once an emotional response comes into awareness–

or, physiologically, is processed through the neocortex–the chances of handling it appropriately–improve. Scientists refer to "metamood," the ability to pull back and recognize that "what I'm feeling is anger," or sorrow, or shame.

Metamood is a difficult skill because emotions so often appear in disguise. A person in mourning may know he is sad, but he may not recognize that he is also angry at the person for dying–because this seems somehow inappropriate. A parent who yells at the child who ran into the street is expressing anger at disobedience, but the degree of anger may owe more to the fear the parent feels at what could have happened.

In Goleman's analysis, self-awareness is perhaps the most crucial ability be-   20
cause it allows us to exercise some self-control. The idea is not to repress feeling (the reaction that has made psychoanalysts rich) but rather to do what Aristotle considered the hard work of the will. "Anyone can become angry–that is easy," he wrote in the *Nicomachean Ethics*. "But to be angry with the right person, to the right degree, at the right time, for the right purpose, and in the right way–this is not easy."

Some impulses seem to be easier to control than others. Anger, not surprisingly, is one of the hardest, perhaps because of its evolutionary value in priming people to action. Researchers believe anger usually arises out of a sense of being trespassed against–the belief that one is being robbed of what is rightfully his. The body's first response is a surge of energy, the release of a cascade of neurotransmitters called catecholamines. If a person is already aroused or under stress, the threshold for release is lower, which helps explain why people's tempers shorten during a hard day.

Scientists are not only discovering where anger comes from; they are also exposing myths about how best to handle it. Popular wisdom argues for "letting it all hang out" and having a good cathartic rage. But Goleman cites studies showing that dwelling on anger actually increases its power; the body needs a chance to process the adrenaline through exercise, relaxation techniques, a well-timed intervention or even the old admonition to count to 10.

Anxiety serves a similar useful purpose, so long as it doesn't spin out of control. Worrying is a rehearsal for danger; the act of fretting focuses the mind on a problem so it can search efficiently for solutions. The danger comes when worrying blocks thinking, becoming an end in itself or a path to resignation instead of perseverance. Overworrying about failing increases the likelihood of failure; a salesman so concerned about his falling sales that he can't bring himself to pick up the phone guarantees that his sales will fall even further.

But why are some people better able to "snap out of it" and get on with the task at hand? Again, given sufficient self-awareness, people develop coping mechanisms. Sadness and discouragement, for instance, are "low arousal" states, and the dispirited salesman who goes out for a run is triggering a high arousal state that is incompatible with staying blue. Relaxation works better for high-energy moods like anger or anxiety. Either way, the idea is to shift to a state of arousal that breaks the destructive cycle of the dominant mood.

The idea of being able to predict which salesmen are most likely to prosper   25
was not an abstraction for Metropolitan Life, which in the mid-'80s was hiring 5,000 salespeople a year and training them at a cost of more than $30,000 each. Half quit the first year, and four out of five within four years. The reason: selling life insurance involves having the door slammed in your face over and over again. Was it possible to identify which people would be better at handling frustration and take each refusal as a challenge rather than a setback?

The head of the company approached psychologist Martin Seligman at the University of Pennsylvania and invited him to test some of his theories about the importance of optimism in people's success. When optimists fail, he has found, they attribute the failure to something they can change, not some innate weakness that they are helpless to overcome. And that confidence in their power to effect change is self-reinforcing. Seligman tracked 15,000 new workers who had taken two tests. One was the company's regular screening exam, the other Seligman's test measuring their levels of optimism. Among the new hires was a group who flunked the screening test but scored as "superoptimists" on Seligman's exam. And sure enough, they did the best of all; they outsold the pessimists in the regular group by 21% in the first year and 57% in the second. For years after that, passing Seligman's test was one way to get hired as a MetLife salesperson.

Perhaps the most visible emotional skills, the ones we recognize most readily, are the "people skills" like empathy, graciousness, the ability to read a social situation. Researchers believe that about 90% of emotional communication is non-verbal. Harvard psychologist Robert Rosenthal developed the PONS test (Profile of Nonverbal Sensitivity) to measure people's ability to read emotional cues. He shows subjects a film of a young woman expressing feelings—anger, love, jealousy, gratitude, seduction—edited so that one or another nonverbal cue is blanked out. In some instances the face is visible but not the body, or the woman's eyes are hidden, so that viewers have to judge the feeling by subtle cues. Once again, people with higher PONS scores tend to be more successful in their work and relationships; children who score well are more popular and successful in school, even when their IQs are quite average.

Like other emotional skills, empathy is an innate quality that can be shaped by experience. Infants as young as three months old exhibit empathy when they get upset at the sound of another baby crying. Even very young children learn by imitation; by watching how others act when they see someone in distress, these children acquire a repertoire of sensitive responses. If, on the other hand, the feelings they begin to express are not recognized and reinforced by the adults around them, they not only cease to express those feelings but they also become less able to recognize them in themselves or others.

Empathy too can be seen as a survival skill. Bert Cohler, a University of

Chicago psychologist, and Fran Stott, dean of the Erikson Institute for Advanced Study in Child Development in Chicago, have found that children from psychically damaged families frequently become hypervigilant, developing an intense attunement to their parents' moods. One child they studied, Nicholas, had a horrible habit of approaching other kids in his nursery-school class as if he were going to kiss them, then would bite them instead. The scientists went back to study videos of Nicholas at 20 months interacting with his psychotic mother and found that she had responded to his every expression of anger or independence with compulsive kisses. The researchers dubbed them "kisses of death," and their true significance was obvious to Nicholas, who arched his back in horror at her approaching lips— and passed his own rage on to his classmates years later.

Empathy also acts as a buffer to cruelty, and it is a quality conspicuously lack-   30 ing in child molesters and psychopaths. Goleman cites some chilling research into brutality by Robert Hare, a psychologist at the University of British Columbia. Hare found that psychopaths, when hooked up to electrodes and told they are going to receive a shock, show none of the visceral responses that fear of pain typically triggers: rapid heartbeat, sweating and so on. How could the threat of punishment deter such people from committing crimes?

It is easy to draw the obvious lesson from these test results. How much happier would we be, how much more successful as individuals and civil as a society, if we were more alert to the importance of emotional intelligence and more adept at teaching it? From kindergartens to business schools to corporations across the country, people are taking seriously the idea that a little more time spent on the "touchy-feely" skills so often derided may in fact pay rich dividends.

In the corporate world, according to personnel executives, IQ gets you hired, but EQ gets you promoted. Goleman likes to tell of a manager at AT&T's Bell Labs, a think tank for brilliant engineers in New Jersey, who was asked to rank his top performers. They weren't the ones with the highest IQs; they were the ones whose E-mail got answered. Those workers who were good collaborators and networkers and popular with colleagues were more likely to get the cooperation they needed to reach their goals than the socially awkward, lone-wolf geniuses.

When David Campbell and others at the Center for Creative Leadership studied "derailed executives," the rising stars who flamed out, the researchers found that these executives failed most often because of "an interpersonal flaw" rather than a technical inability. Interviews with top executives in the U.S. and Europe turned up nine so-called fatal flaws, many of them classic emotional failings, such as "poor working relations," being "authoritarian" or "too ambitious" and having "conflict with upper management."

At the center's executive-leadership seminars across the country, managers come to get emotionally retooled. "This isn't sensitivity training or Sunday-supplement stuff," says Campbell. "One thing they know when they get through is what other people think of them." And the executives have an incentive to listen.

Says Karen Boylston, director of the center's team-leadership group: "Customers are telling businesses, 'I don't care if every member of your staff graduated with honors from Harvard, Stanford and Wharton. I will take my business and go where I am understood and treated with respect.'"

Nowhere is the discussion of emotional intelligence more pressing than in schools, where both the stakes and the opportunities seem greatest. Instead of constant crisis intervention, or declarations of war on drug abuse or teen pregnancy or violence, it is time, Goleman argues, for preventive medicine. "Five years ago, teachers didn't want to think about this," says principal Roberta Kirshbaum of P.S. 75 in New York City. "But when kids are getting killed in high school, we have to deal with it." Five years ago, Kirshbaum's school adopted an emotional literacy program, designed to help children learn to manage anger, frustration, loneliness. Since then, fights at lunchtime have decreased from two or three a day to almost none.

Educators can point to all sorts of data to support this new direction. Students who are depressed or angry literally cannot learn. Children who have trouble being accepted by their classmates are 2 to 8 times as likely to drop out. An inability to distinguish distressing feelings or handle frustration has been linked to eating disorders in girls.

Many school administrators are completely rethinking the weight they have been giving to traditional lessons and standardized tests. Peter Relic, president of the National Association of Independent Schools, would like to junk the SAT completely. "Yes, it may cost a heck of a lot more money to assess someone's EQ rather than using a machine-scored test to measure IQ," he says. "But if we don't, then we're saying that a test score is more important to us than who a child is as a human being. That means an immense loss in terms of human potential because we've defined success too narrowly."

This warm embrace by educators has left some scientists in a bind. On one hand, says Yale psychologist Salovey, "I love the idea that we want to teach people a richer understanding of their emotional life, to help them achieve their goals." But, he adds, "what I would oppose is training conformity to social expectations." The danger is that any campaign to hone emotional skills in children will end up teaching that there is a "right" emotional response for any given situation—laugh at parades, cry at funerals, sit still at church. "You can teach self-control," says Dr. Alvin Poussaint, professor of psychiatry at Harvard Medical School. "You can teach that it's better to talk out your anger and not use violence. But is it good emotional intelligence not to challenge authority?"

Some psychologists go further and challenge the very idea that emotional skills can or should be taught in any kind of formal, classroom way. Goleman's premise that children can be trained to analyze their feelings strikes Johns Hopkins' McHugh as an effort to reinvent the encounter group: "I consider that an abominable idea, an idea we have seen with adults. That failed, and now he wants to try

it with children? Good grief!" He cites the description in Goleman's book of an experimental program at the Nueva Learning Center in San Francisco. In one scene,
two fifth-grade boys start to argue over the rules of an exercise, and the teacher
breaks in to ask them to talk about what they're feeling. "I appreciate the way
you're being assertive in talking with Tucker," she says to one student. "You're not
attacking." This strikes McHugh as pure folly. "The author is presuming that someone has the key to the right emotions to be taught to children. We don't even know
the right emotions to be taught to adults. Do you really think a child of eight or
nine really understands the difference between aggressiveness and assertiveness?"

The problem may be that there is an ingredient missing. Emotional skills, like   40
intellectual ones, are morally neutral. Just as a genius could use his intellect either
to cure cancer or engineer a deadly virus, someone with great empathic insight
could use it to inspire colleagues or exploit them. Without a moral compass to
guide people in how to employ their gifts, emotional intelligence can be used
for good or evil. Columbia University psychologist Walter Mischel, who invented
the marshmallow test and others like it, observes that the knack for delaying
gratification that makes a child one marshmallow richer can help him become a
better citizen or–just as easily–an even more brilliant criminal.

Given the passionate arguments that are raging over the state of moral instruction in this country, it is no wonder Goleman chose to focus more on neutral
emotional skills than on the values that should govern their use. That's another
book–and another debate.

–Reported by SHARON E. EPPERSON and LAWRENCE MONDI/New York,
JAMES L. GRAFF/Chicago and LISA H. TOWLE/Raleigh

The Responsive Reader

1. How does the marshmallow experiment dramatize the author's point? What key
   question does it raise? What contrasting personality types does it help identify?

2. How does Gibbs define emotional intelligence early in the article? What is the
   difference between EQ and the IQ? What makes the concept of emotional intelligence controversial–what promise does it hold for a violence-ridden society,
   and why could it invite abuse?

3. According to the authorities Gibbs draws on, how did human emotions evolve?
   What was their role in helping humans survive? What are the contrasting or
   complementary roles of intellect and emotion in the workings of our minds?

4. Concepts like self-awareness, anxiety, and empathy are the small change of current pop psychology. Do you use these terms–when and where? What role do
   they play in current explorations of emotional intelligence?

5. According to Gibbs, what are potential applications of the emotional intelligence

movement in the world of business? What are potential applications in the world of education?

For Discussion or Writing

6. Do you know people whose emotional or interpersonal intelligence seems more highly developed than their intellectual skills or reasoning capacity? How can you tell? Can you draw up contrasting portraits of the two personality types— one with high intellectual ability and one with a high EQ?

7. Is the ability to express emotions culturally conditioned? Have you observed differences in the way people from different backgrounds show their feelings? How much of their expression of emotion is verbal? How much is nonverbal?

Collaborative Projects

8. Will psychometricians of the future be able to measure qualities like empathy or sensitivity? Working with a group, organize a survey or develop a questionnaire designed to measure qualities like empathy or ability to relate to others.

Making Connections

9. Drawing on the criticisms of conventional IQ testing in the articles by Kamin and Gibbs, what recommendations or guidelines for test makers would you and your classmates work out? Or, what criteria would you draw up for use in selecting tests?

3

Issues in Business

BUSINESS IN PERSPECTIVE

One of the most basic questions we can ask about human societies is how they provide for food and shelter. What is their system of incentives and rewards? Who controls the society's natural resources or means of production? The great shifts in human culture have been in the basic arrangements for providing the necessities of life. One major shift took most of humankind from the hunting and gathering stage to agricultural economies, with often elaborate systems of irrigation, tax collection, and distribution of goods. Another major shift took large numbers off the land to work in the manufacturing industries, with large populations clustered in factory towns and industrial cities. Modern business evolved as the system of production and distribution servicing the industrial world. It is now in the process of adapting to the demands of what many call the postindustrial society or the Information Age.

ECONOMIES AND ECONOMICS

Business has played a major role in determining the nature of modern societies. Economics is the science aimed at helping us understand the workings of the business world. Definitions of economics have ranged over the map: Economics is the study of how societies satisfy their need for material goods. Economics is the study of market forces. Economics is the study of human behavior that can be directly or indirectly measured in terms of money.

Capitalist countries, socialist countries, and countries with a mixed economy differ fundamentally in the role played by a market economy. The role of the free market may be minimal. For instance, workers on a collective farm may be allowed to raise produce in a little private cabbage patch in their spare time and to sell it to people tired of the empty shelves in government-operated stores. At the other extreme, in conditions approaching *laissez-faire* ("leave-business-alone") capitalism, big business may flourish largely unimpeded. Multinational corporations become powerful, fighting off government efforts at regulation and taxation. They influence legislation through lobbyists and through legislators beholden to them. They counteract the efforts of workers to unionize, finding ways to rely on cheaper nonunion labor. In mixed econo- mies (which today means most developed countries), government and busi- ness interact in complicated ways. The U.S. government, for instance, may send taxpayers' money to California wine growers to promote the sale of American wines abroad. It decides when a pharmaceutical company may start marketing a major new drug and start earning a return on a multimillion-dollar invest- ment. It may regulate how much cereal should fill a box.

Ideally, economists enable us to predict and influence economic develop- ments. However, business is an uncertain proposition. Of people who invest in restaurants, some prosper. Others lose their investment. During bull markets, stock market euphoria may drive up stock prices to levels out of proportion to company earnings. During bear markets, stock market panics may lead to a stampede of sell-offs, with prices crashing through the floor and paper for- tunes evaporating overnight. Economists labor to introduce a measure of certainty and predictability into our understanding of business and business cycles.

- Economists measure production of goods and services. The spotlight used to be on tracking output in basic industries: steel, oil, automobiles. Increasingly, in the so-called service economy, areas like health and education represent a large share of Gross National Product, whether reflected in official statistics or not.

- Economists study the workings of competition. What is meant by the law of supply and demand? What other factors affect competitiveness between individual businesses and between nations? What is meant by "unfair competition"?

- Economists study ownership or control of the means of produc- tion. What is the difference between family-owned, investor-owned, employee-owned, and state-owned enterprises (like the U.S. Post Office)?

- Economists study the distribution of wealth. How is wealth acquired and by whom? What factors cause and perpetuate poverty? Why is the gap between the rich and the poor widening in contemporary societies?

- Economists have increasingly put the spotlight on the consumer. In the consumer economy, market research looms large. Advertising techniques are grounded in the study of consumer psychology. Focus groups, test marketing of new products, and customer satisfaction surveys provide employment for experts focusing on the spending habits of the Ameri- can public.

TRADE AND CIVILIZATION

What has been your exposure to the world of production and distribution, of buying and selling, of profit and loss? How much thought have you given to the role of business in your world? Commerce has played a major role in the history of civilization from the earliest recorded times. Conventional historians used to be preoccupied with military leaders and glorious victories and defeats. Other historians, however, have emphasized that nations from the Phoenicians (rivals of the Roman empire) to the British grew prosperous and powerful through trade as much as through military might.

Corporations shipping automobiles or airplane engines from one continent to another are the modern equivalent of traders who organized caravans moving goods along century-old trade routes in Europe and Asia. Traders carried salt inland from sites where salt was obtained from ocean water. During the times of the Roman empire, thousands of trading ships plied the Mediterranean Sea, carrying olive oil, wheat, wine, pottery, timber, and other merchandise. A major impetus for the voyages of Columbus and the early Portuguese or Spanish navigators was to find new trade routes to Asia. Turkish conquests had closed the land routes from Europe to the spices and jewels of India and the Far East. Later, lucrative trade in colonial goods—natural rubber, sugar, coffee, bananas, diamonds—was a major driving force in European imperial expansion.

Trade has long been a major strand in the web of human culture. Writing systems developed to help traders (and tax collectors) to keep records. The coining of money and banking systems developed in response to the demands of trade. During the Middle Ages, the growing middle class in towns and cities provided a third force that was to supersede the age-old feudal system—the pattern of robber barons lording it over illiterate peasants. Eventually, wealthy merchants rivaled popes and princes as patrons of the arts, sitting, for instance, for individual or group portraits by painters like Rembrandt. The great parks and museums (Guggenheim, Frick) that keep our cities from turning into urban wastelands were often funded by philanthropists who had made their fortunes in banking, railroads, lumber, or retail.

THE INDUSTRIAL REVOLUTION

A major shift in human history was the movement away from manual labor to the large-scale use of machines. Backbreaking sunup-to-sundown toil had long been the lot of great masses of people. The Maya pyramids, like those of Egypt, were built by thousands of anonymous laborers. While Plato and his students discussed beauty and justice, twenty-thousand slaves labored in the silver mines of the Athenian city-state. Americans built a plantation economy on the backs of enslaved Africans, who were bought and sold like livestock and denied an education that would have enabled them to read and write.

The Industrial Revolution of the eighteenth and nineteenth centuries made people rely on mechanical devices rather than muscle to do the world's work. Pulleys and hoists had long been used in warehousing and construction to move large weights. Now coal mining, shipbuilding, and steelmaking promoted the large-scale industrial use of equipment. Technological breakthroughs like the steam engine and electricity made possible advances toward mass production. They made possible the revolution in transportation brought on by the railroads spanning the continent. The individual efforts of the traditional carpenter, shoemaker, or blacksmith could no longer compete with entrepreneurs who mass-produced furniture, shoes, and hardware. Only small pockets of "Luddites" remain in modern society–people who fight mechanization and automation, trying to make a living by peddling handmade sandals or candles or by farming on a small scale.

In demographic terms, industrialization meant massive movements of populations from the village to towns and cities. It transformed tenant farmers into workers in the manufacturing industries, with many miners and other workers living in company towns. In agriculture, the machine age brought the gradual movement away from the family farm to large units–agribusiness in the capitalist West, collective farms in the socialist East–that could finance and effectively utilize tractors, mechanical harvesters, crop-dusting planes, and chemicals used as fertilizer or pesticides.

Today a key question is what will take the place of the great manufacturing industries of the industrial age. Deindustrialization for a time threatened to turn the American industrial heartland of steel, coal, and cars into the "rust belt." In the great industrial cities like Milwaukee or Detroit, many factories closed down for good and many more moved south or overseas. The age of automation, the electronic age, and the age of service industries are rewriting many of our assumptions about how people make a living and about the foundations of prosperity.

THE FREE MARKET AND CHALLENGES TO *LAISSEZ-FAIRE*

Basic assumptions shape the thinking in today's business world. If there is an unofficial business ideology, it is the free-market tradition that goes back to the eighteenth century and Adam Smith (1723–1790), Scottish economist and author of *The Wealth of Nations*. Smith shared the basic Enlightenment belief in the "best of all possible worlds"–not the best imaginable or conceivable world, but the best that a supreme intelligence could actually design and implement. With the free play of market forces, an "invisible hand" would guide things in such a way that the uncoordinated efforts of countless individuals, bent on their own economic advancement, would promote the prosperity of all.

The cornerstone of free-market or *laissez-faire* economics is the law of supply and demand. If a potato shortage develops, there is no need for the government to prod farmers to grow more potatoes. If supply is limited, the demand for potatoes will drive prices up. More growers will find it profitable to grow tomatoes. As supply catches up with demand, prices will go back down. Supply and demand balance off, or are "in equilibrium," when enough growers furnish potatoes at prices the customers are willing to pay. In the economist's ideal world, the labor market is similarly self-regulating. When tool-and-die makers are in demand, they earn good wages. If too many people take up the trade, wages go down, and eventually some or many will look for a different kind of work.

The ideal free-market economy is to the behavior of actual economic systems as the war games played in sand boxes in military academies are to actual battles like Gettysburg or Stalingrad. Economists spend much of their time explaining "imperfections," interferences, "external" factors, and "interventions." External influences that could throw the potato market into disarray might include natural disasters like the potato blight that caused mass starvation and mass emigration in nineteenth-century Ireland. Rumors of a bad harvest might enable speculators to drive prices through the roof. Huge agribusiness corporations might conspire to curtail production and keep prices artificially high. Powerful new diet trends might demonize potatoes as excess starch, causing the bottom to drop out of the market.

Human beings do not behave like mere pawns in the labor market. They do not stop having children because their skills might not prove saleable. When wages drop to starvation levels because of an oversupply of labor, they start revolutions or join labor unions. In the heyday of the American labor movement in the thirties and forties, labor leaders like Walter Reuther organized strikes that forced General Motors and other industrial giants to negotiate improved payscales, benefits, and working conditions.

For much of the post-World War II period, conventional wisdom saw government stimulation and "fine-tuning" of the economy as the protection against a recurrence of the economic collapse of the Great Depression of the thirties. In times of an economic downturn, huge government projects–dams, super highways, space travel, a defense buildup–would help jumpstart the economy. Keynesian economics, named after the British economist John Maynard Keynes (1883–1946), encouraged government spending to stimulate the economy, to prime the pump. Sluggish consumer demand discourages investment and creates unemployment. Unemployment in turn further reduces consumer purchasing power, precipitating business failures and further sending the economy into a tailspin. The answer is to create make-work programs—preferably ambitious programs of government spending for hydroelectric dams, high-tech research, revitalized schools, and the like. Large infusions of government money are likely to heat up inflation, which in turn helps lower the true cost of the national debt, serving as a kind of indirect taxation.

In practice, defense spending has been the prime source of Keynesian economic stimulus. The arms buildup for America's entry into World War II pulled the American economy out of Depression-era doldrums. Massive infusion of American government spending under the auspices of the Marshall Plan led to an era of prodigious rebuilding and ostentatious wealth in the devastated, war-torn countries of Europe. The arms race of the Cold War helped create and maintain prosperity. However, with exceptions like the temporary flourishing of the government-financed space program, the industrial countries of the West have not found a peacetime equivalent for the financial stimulus of defense spending, so that widespread structural unemployment remains a threat to political stability and national prosperity.

Recent decades have seen the growing influence of advocates preaching a return to an unrestricted free-market economy. Keynesian economics, while still practiced by governments when the going gets rough, has been largely discredited in the minds of the followers of Milton Friedman (born 1912) and other free-market philosophers. To aggressive spokespersons of the resurgent *laissez-faire* philosophy, too many businesses have for too long been "seeking shelter in the arms of a nurturing government." Government intervention distorts competition, rewards inefficiency, and discourages individual initiative. A myriad safety and environmental regulations are adopted without regard to their economic cost. Punitive taxation eats up profits that should be plowed back into new investment; it discourages individual enterprise. Advocates of a free-market society believe that private enterprise could run the post office, garbage collection, and your local schools more efficiently and for less money than entrenched bureaucracies.

In practice, many advocates of the free-market philosophy settle for compromises that provide a safety net. The government bailed out the Chrysler corporation when it was on the ropes, unable to compete with Japanese automakers. The government rescue of the bankrupt savings and loan industry cost taxpayers in excess of $350 billion. Bankers with bonuses in the seven digits depend on the federal government to provide insurance for their customers' deposits. Multimillion government payments go to a local winery or to a local tobacco grower. The Federal Reserve intervenes to control inflation as soon as the economy heats up, workers are hired, and consumers plan to buy more homes and cars. Interest rates are raised to dry up the supply of easy money and keep the economy from overheating.

MODERN MANAGEMENT PHILOSOPHY

A major force in the American corporate culture has been a new management philosophy whose watchwords include cost-effectiveness, cost-benefit ratios, and the bottom line. Aggressive new accounting approaches are designed to measure the true return of capital and the true creation of wealth more accurately than traditional accounting methods. Management training or retraining, often conducted by outside consultants or consultant firms, is a growth industry. Workers become not so much fellow workers inspired by mutual loyalty but a major debit in the corporate balance sheet. Bonuses go to executives who shift from costly labor-intensive production to automated systems. Automatic teller machines replace bank clerks. Voicemail using computerized voices replaces telephone operators.

Major tools of the new management philosophy include "restructuring," "downsizing," and "outsourcing," with much of the hired help becoming "independent contractors" without a stake in the company. Outsourcing, as defined in an article in *Forbes* magazine, "simply means you buy from the outside services and goods that you formerly supplied internally." Although corporations like IBM do not "want to be accused of discarding people like so much wastepaper," the net result of outsourcing is that fewer people do more work at lower wages and with reduced or no benefits. The rewards for managers expert at saving substantial money per employee are substantial. According to the same article, a leading organizer of outsourced services for a major corporation owned stock valued at $125 million.

Modern management philosophy has spread beyond business into other fields. Boards of regents and college administrators talk in terms of cost-effectiveness, cutting down on courses that don't sell and students who can't pay. Conservative politicians swear by books like Peter Drucker's *The Effective Executive*. American business, with the free-market philosophy it espouses, is a major force in American politics. According to statistics cited in *Fortune* magazine, in the mid-nineties 72 percent of American chief executive officers, or CEOs, of major corporations identified themselves as Republicans, 19 percent as independents, and 7 percent as Democrats. The influence of the American free-enterprise model is also widely felt abroad. Representatives of American business preached the virtues of an unrestricted free-market philosophy in the countries of the former Soviet bloc, where the transition from a state-run economy has produced runaway inflation, a new-rich entrepreneurial elite, widespread unemployment, and the impoverishment of large segments of the population.

FREE TRADE AND THE GLOBAL ECONOMY

Today, multinational corporations do business worldwide. Shell Oil and Coca-Cola know no borders. Most Americans used to buy cars made in Detroit, cotton goods from the South, lettuce from California. Today, shirts sold at the local department store were made in Malaysia or China. Toyotas, Fords, and Volkswagens compete for the motorist's dollar here and in many countries around the world. Much of our fresh produce comes from Mexico, while farmers in the United States depend for a large share of their income on the consumption of rice, wheat, or pistachios abroad.

As well-paid workers in affluent countries soon discovered, the global economy means free movement of jobs as well as products. Companies shift production to low-wage (and often low-tax) neighbors. Jobs move from Germany to the Czech Republic, from California to Mexico, from Japan to Korea. Even made-in-America cars or textiles may utilize a large share of components made by foreign workers. Large-scale structural unemployment in Western countries can be traced in large part to the elimination of blue-collar jobs by automation and to the computerization of middle management. However, it also in large part resulted from the disappearance or trimming down of manufacturing industries that could not compete with cheap foreign labor.

While governments profess allegiance to the principle of free trade, strong protectionist impulses keep resurfacing. Governments in countries like France, Japan, Germany, and the United States are under pressure from the farm vote to subsidize and protect farmers threatened by cheap foreign produce. Trade zones or trading blocs like NAFTA and the European Common Market remove internal trade barriers while erecting external ones. Trade agreements such as these are hotly debated while advocates and opponents total up expected trade surpluses or deficits and jobs gained or lost.

THE ECOLOGICAL CHALLENGE

The myth of progress for a long time was the guiding ideology of industrial and commercial development. The opening up for homesteading of the Oklahoma Territory became a symbol of the beckoning opportunities of westward expansion. The spirit of boosterism built large bustling cities— St. Louis, Chicago, Cincinnati, Los Angeles—where there had been prairie or desert. The railroads opened up a large unexploited continent for apparently unlimited development. For a time, the vast natural resources of Siberia in the former Soviet Union provided a similar theme for a rhetoric of progress. In the capitalistic West, the driving ideology of the modern corporation has been growth—if not through new products or new markets then through acquisitions. Takeovers and mergers create blockbuster industrial, financial, or media conglomerates.

In recent decades, however, the industrialized countries of the West have experienced a slow braking and putting in reverse of the drive toward growth and development. Pondering the metaphor of Spaceship Earth, we have discovered that we inhabit a planet with finite resources. Industrial and technological development is exhausting fossil fuels. Whether peat, coal, or oil, our sources of energy are in large part decaying organic matter that is not being replenished. Pollution introduces poisonous chemicals into the air, the water, the food chain. Cancer-causing substances or carcinogens lurk in the air of our cities and in the workplace. Urban sprawl, strip mining, and massive logging destroy wildlife and ecosystems. The lure of nuclear power kept us from anticipating the failure of current nuclear technology to protect adequately against catastrophic health and environmental hazards. We lack convincing answers to the risk of meltdown or to the unsolved problem of storing radioactive waste that will be a threat to human life for thousands of years.

What is the economic cost of breathable air, drinkable water, streams with fish, nontoxic produce, uncontaminated meat? As consumers and taxpayers, will members of your generation be willing to pay the price? Are business and industry capable of putting the common good above profit?

QUESTIONS FOR DISCUSSION

How many of your classmates have had firsthand exposure to an agricultural economy or rural lifestyle? (What did they learn about this way of making a living?) How many have insiders' knowledge of an industrial area or manufacturing setting, and what has been their experience? Have you had occasion to observe considerable fluctuation in prices, and do you have ideas about the factors involved? In your community or area, is there evidence of a chamber of commerce mentality or agenda? Have you or your classmates been close to people trying to run a family business? In principle, do you favor small businesses or Big Business, and why? Do any fellow students in your class consider themselves ecologists or strong supporters of an environmental agenda? (What are their most urgent current concerns?)

SUPPLY AND DEMAND

Paul Samuelson

~~~~~~~~~~

> *In the following key excerpt from a classic economics text, Paul Samuelson, legendary American economist, isolates the dynamic that for traditional economists is the driving force in economic activity. He takes us to a simulated world of pure capitalism—where money is the key to everything and where everything has a price. Production and prices are regulated by the law of supply and demand. In principle, this law applies equally to the buying and selling of corn flakes, land, foreign coil, or German marks. In practice, as Samuelson indicates, we have to reckon with complicating factors that skew the free play of supply and demand. We have to take into account "imperfections" in the free play of competition. (For instance, subsidies or price supports for growers of wheat and tobacco muddy the play of market forces. Rumors of impending shortages or surpluses drive prices up or down.) How would supply and demand function in ideal circumstances, when not distorted by extraneous factors? How would supply and demand work in an economist's perfect world?*

The consumer, so it is said, is the king. Or rather, with everyone a king, all are voters who use their money as votes to get done what they want done. Your votes must compete with my votes; and the people with the most votes end up with the most influence on what gets produced and on where goods go.

Now our task is to see just how this spending of money votes—this system of "consumer sovereignty"—takes place under the checks and balances of economic competition.

THE MARKET MECHANISM

Let us take an example. You wake up this morning with an urge for a new pair of shoes. You would not think of saying, "I'll go down to the city hall and vote for the mayor most likely to give me a new pair of shoes. Of course, I mean a new pair of size 9, soft-leather, dark brown shoes."

Or, to take an actual case from history, suppose we begin to get prosperous enough to afford meat every day and no longer have to fill up on potatoes. How does our desire to substitute meat for potatoes get translated into action? What politicians do we tell? What orders do they in turn give to farmers to move from Maine to Texas? How much extra rent do they decide will be needed to bribe landlords to transfer land from potato production to cattle grazing? And how do they ensure that we people get what we want of pork and lamb as well as beef? And who is to get the choice cuts?

Why belabor the obvious? Everyone knows things don't work out that way at   5
all. What happens is this. Consumers begin to buy fewer potatoes and more meat.
That raises the price of meat and cuts the price of potatoes. So there soon result losses to the
potato growers and gains to the ranchers. Ranch labor finds it can hold out for
higher wages, and many potato diggers quit their jobs for better-paying work elsewhere. In time, the higher meat prices coax out larger productions of beef, pork,
and lamb. And the different parts of the cow—its horns, hide, liver, kidneys, choice
tenderloin, and tough ribs—get auctioned off for what each part will bring.

To show that it is not some important government bureaucrat or businesshead
who sets relative prices, see what actually happened when science discovered that
liver was good for anemia. Kidneys used to be dearer than liver. Now go to the
butcher shop: price liver and, if you can find any, also price kidneys. A veritable
revolution has taken place: the price of liver has risen greatly relative to the price of
kidneys, so as to *ration* the limited supply of liver among the eager demanders for
it—all through the *impersonal* workings of supply and demand.

A System of Prices

Similar revolutions are taking place in the economic marketplace all the time.
As people's desires and needs change, as engineering methods change, as supplies
of natural resources and other productive factors change, the marketplace registers changes in the prices and the quantities sold of commodities and productive
services—of tea, sugar, and beef; of land, labor, and machines. There exists a *system
of rationing by prices*, a concept that is far from obvious.

The purpose of this chapter is to show how supply and demand work themselves out in the competitive market *for one particular good.* We shall define a demand
curve and then a supply curve. Finally, we shall see how the market price reaches
its competitive equilibrium where these two curves intersect—where the forces of
demand and supply are just in balance.

THE DEMAND SCHEDULE

Let us start with demand. It is commonly observed: The quantity of a good
that people will buy at any one time depends on price. The *higher* the price charged
for an article, the *less* the quantity of it people will be willing to buy. And, other
things being equal, the lower its market price, the more units of it will be demanded.

Thus there exists at any one time a definite relation between the market   10
price of a good (such as wheat) and the quantity demanded of that good. This
relationship between price and quantity bought is called the "demand sched-
ule," or the "demand curve."

The table of Fig. 4-1 gives an example of a hypothetical demand schedule. At

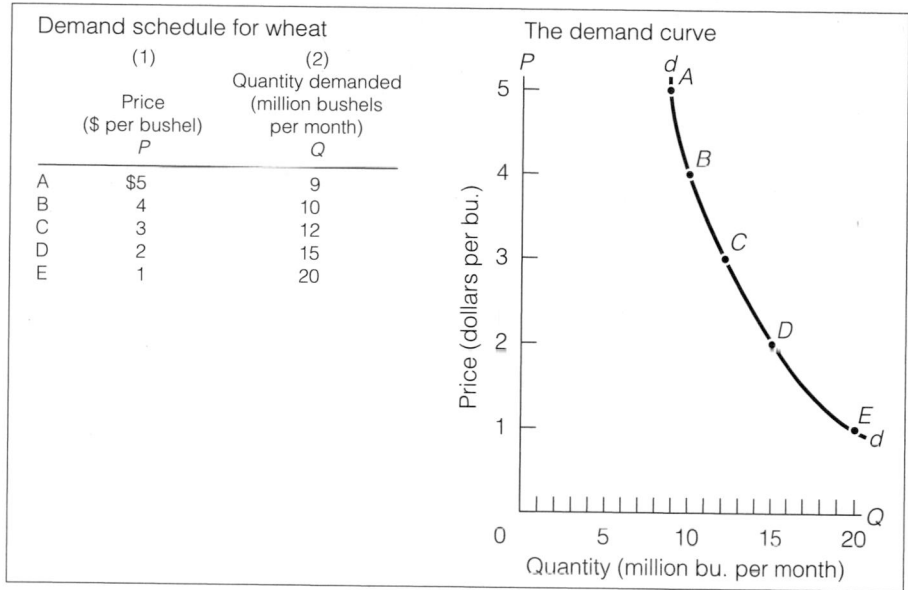

Demand schedule for wheat		
	(1)	(2) Quantity demanded (million bushels per month)
	Price ($ per bushel) P	Q
A	$5	9
B	4	10
C	3	12
D	2	15
E	1	20

FIGURE 4–1   A downward–sloping demand curve relates quantity to price

At each market price, there will be at any time a definite quantity of wheat that people will want to demand. At a lower price, the quantity demanded will go up–as more people substitute it for other goods and feel they can afford to gratify their less important wants for wheat. Compare table's Q and P at A, B, C, D, E.

In the figure, prices are measured on the vertical and quantities demanded on the horizontal axis. Each pair of Q, P numbers from the table is plotted here as a point, and a smooth curve passed through the points gives us the demand curve. The fact that dd goes downward and to the right illustrates the "law of downward-sloping demand."

any price, such as $5 per bushel, there is a definite quantity of wheat that will be demanded by all the consumers in the market–in this case 9 (million) bushels per month.

At a lower price, such as $4, the quantity bought is even greater, being 10 (million) units. At lower P of $3, quantity demanded is even greater still–namely 12 (million). By lowering P enough, we could coax out sales of more than 20 (million) units. From Fig. 4-1's table we can determine the *quantity demanded at any price*, by comparing Column (2) with Column (1).

THE DEMAND CURVE

The numerical data can also be given a graphic interpretation. The vertical scale in Fig. 4-1 represents the various alternative prices of wheat, measured in dollars per bushel. The horizontal scale measures the quantity of wheat (in terms of million bushels) that will be demanded per month by consumers.

A city corner is located as soon as we know its street and avenue. A ship's position is located as soon as we know its latitude and longitude. Similarly, to plot a point on this diagram, we must have two coordinate numbers: a price and a quantity. For our first point, *A*, corresponding to $5 and 9 million bushels, we move upward 5 units and then over to the right 9 units.

To get the next dot, at *B*, we go up only 4 units and over to the right 10 units.   15
The last dot is shown by *E*. Through the dots we draw a smooth orange curve, marked *dd*.

This picturization of the demand schedule is called the "demand curve." Note that quantity and price are *inversely* related, *Q* going up when *P* goes down. The curve slopes downward, going from northwest to southeast. This important property is given a name: the *law of downward-sloping demand*. This law is true of practically all commodities: wheat, electric razors, oil or coal, Kellogg's cornflakes, and theater tickets.

The law of downward-sloping demand: When the price of a good is raised (at the same time that all other things are held constant), less of it is demanded. Or, what is the same thing: If a greater quantity of a good is put on the market, then—other things being equal—it can be sold only at a lower price.

REASONS FOR THE LAW OF DOWNWARD-SLOPING DEMAND

This law is in accordance with common sense and has been known in at least a vague way since the beginning of recorded history. The reasons for it are not hard to identify. When the price of wheat is sky-high, only the rich will be able to afford it. The poor will have to make do with rice or coarse rye bread, just as they still must do in poorer lands. When the price of wheat is still high but not quite so high as it was before, persons of moderate means who also happen to have an especially great liking for white bread will now be coaxed into buying some wheat.

Thus a first reason for the validity of the law of downward-sloping demand comes from the fact that *lowering prices bring in new buyers*.

Not quite so obvious is a second, equally important, reason for the law's validity; namely, each reduction of price may coax out some *extra purchases by each of the good's consumers*; and—what is the same thing—a rise in price may cause any of us to buy less. Why does my quantity demanded tend to fall as price rises? For two main reasons. When the price of a good rises, I naturally try to *substitute* other goods for it (for example, rye for wheat or coal for oil). Second, when a price goes up, I find myself really poorer than I was before; and I will naturally cut down on my consumption of most normal goods when I feel poorer and have less real *income*.

Here are further examples of cases where I buy more of a good as it becomes more plentiful and its price drops. When water is very dear, I demand only enough of it to drink. Then when its price drops, I buy some to wash with. At still lower prices, I resort to still other uses. Finally, when it is really very cheap, I water flowers and use it lavishly for any possible purpose. (Note once again that people poorer than I will probably begin to use water to wash their cars only at a lower price than that at which I buy water for that purpose. Since market demand is the sum of all different people's demands, what does this mean? It means that even after *my* quantity demanded stops expanding very much with price decreases, the *total* bought in the market may still expand as new uses by new people come into effect.)

To confirm your understanding of the demand concept, imagine that there is an increase in demand for wheat brought about by a boom in people's incomes. Show that this *shifts* the whole demand curve in Fig. 4-1 rightward, and hence upward; pencil in such a new orange curve and label it *d'd'* to distinguish it from the old *dd* curve. Note that such an increase in demand means that more will now be bought at each price—as can be verified by carefully reading off points from the new curve and filling in a new Q column for Fig. 4-1's table. (Test yourself: Will a warm winter shift the *dd* curve for heating oil leftward or rightward? Why this leftward and downward shift?)

THE SUPPLY SCHEDULE

Let us now turn from demand to supply. The demand schedule related market prices and the amounts *consumers* wish to buy. How is the "supply schedule" defined?

By the *supply schedule*, or *curve*, is meant the relation between market prices and the amounts of the good that *producers* are willing to supply.

The table of Fig. 4-2 shows the supply schedule for wheat, and the diagram plots it as a supply curve. Unlike the falling demand curve, the *ss* supply curve for wheat *normally rises upward and to the right*, from southwest to northeast.

At a higher price of wheat, farmers will take acres out of corn cultivation and put them into wheat. In addition, each farmer can now afford the cost of more fertilizer, more labor, more machinery, and can now even afford to grow extra wheat on poorer land. All this tends to increase output at the higher prices offered.

As will be seen in Part Three, our old friend the law of diminishing returns provides one strong reason why the supply curve would slope upward. If society wants more wine, then more and more labor will have to be added to the same limited hill sites suitable for producing wine grapes. Even if this industry is too small to affect the general wage rate, each new worker will–according to the law of diminishing returns–be adding less and less extra

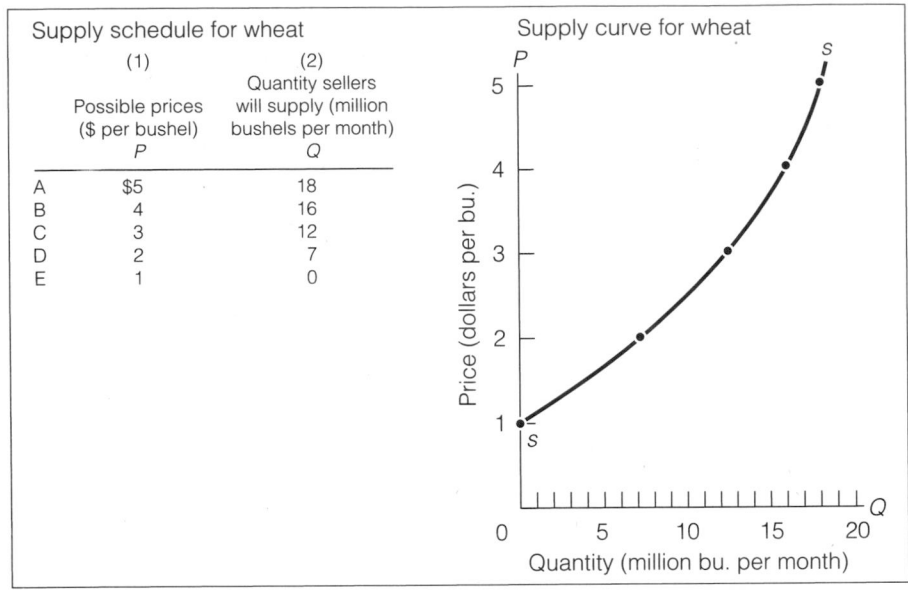

FIGURE 4-2   The supply curve relates price to the quantity produced
The table lists, for each price, the quantity that producers will want to bring to market. The diagram plots the (P, Q) pair of numbers taken from the table as the indicated black points. A smooth curve passed through these points gives the black upward–sloping supply curve, ss.

product; and hence, the necessary cost to coax out additional product will have to rise. (Cost and returns are opposite sides of the same coin, as will be shown later.[1])

How shall we depict an increase in supply? An increase in supply means an increase in the amounts that will be supplied *at each different price*. Now if you pencil the new supply curve into Fig. 4-2, you will see that it has shifted *rightward*. For an upward–sloping supply curve, this change means the new s's' curve will have shifted rightward and *downward* (not rightward and upward as in the case of a shifted downward–sloping demand curve). To verify that s's' does depict an increase in supply, fill in a new column in the table by reading off points from your new diagram carefully. TEST: An invention promotes recovery of oil from abandoned wells. Show that it shifts oil's ss rightward and downward.)

[1]Although exceptions to the law of downward–sloping demand are few enough to be unimportant in practice, Part Three gives an interesting exception to the upward–sloping supply curve. Thus, suppose that a family farmer produces wheat and its price rises so much as to bring in a much higher income. With wheat so lucrative, the farmer is at first tempted to *substitute* some leisure time

EQUILIBRIUM OF SUPPLY AND DEMAND

Let us now combine our analysis of demand and supply to see how competitive market price is determined. This is done in Fig. 4-3's table.

Thus far, we have been considering all prices as possible. We have said, "If price is so and so, Q sales will be so and so; if P is such and such, Q will be such and such; and so forth." But to which level will price *actually* go? And how much will then be produced and consumed? The supply schedule alone cannot tell us. Neither can the demand schedule alone.

Let us do what an auctioneer would do, i.e., proceed by trial and error. Can situation A in the table, with wheat selling for $5 per bushel, prevail for any period of time? The answer is a clear "No." At $5, the producers will be supplying 18 (million) bushels to the market every month [Column (3)]. But the amount demanded by consumers will be only 9 (million) bushels per month [Column (2)]. *As stocks of wheat pile up, competitive sellers will cut the price a little.* Thus, as Column (4) shows, price will tend to fall downward. But it will not fall indefinitely to zero.

To understand this better, let us try the point E with price of only $1 per bushel. Can that price persist? Again, obviously not—for a comparison of Columns (2) and (3) shows that consumption will exceed production *at that price.* Storehouses will begin to empty, *disappointed demanders who can't get wheat will tend to bid up the too-low price.* This upward pressure on P is shown by Column (4)'s rising arrow.

We could go on to try other prices, but by now the answer is obvious:

The equilibrium price, i.e., the only price that can last, is that at which the amount *willingly* supplied and amount *willingly* demanded are equal. Competitive equilibrium must be *at the intersection point* of supply and demand curves.

Only at point C, with a price of $3, will the amount demanded by consumers, 12 (million) bushels per month, exactly equal the amount supplied by producers, 12 (million). Price is at equilibrium, just as an olive at the bottom of a cocktail glass is at equilibrium, because there is no tendency for it to rise or fall. (Of course, this stationary price may not be reached at once. There may have to be an initial period of trial and error, of oscillation around the right level, before price finally settles down in balance.)

Figure 4-3's diagram shows the same equilibrium in pictorial form. The supply and demand curves, superimposed on the same diagram, cross at only one intersection point. This emphasized point C represents the equilibrium P and Q.

30

35

---

in order to produce more. But won't there reasonably come a time when the family feels comfortably enough off at the *higher income* to be able to afford to take things easier, work less, and supply less Q?

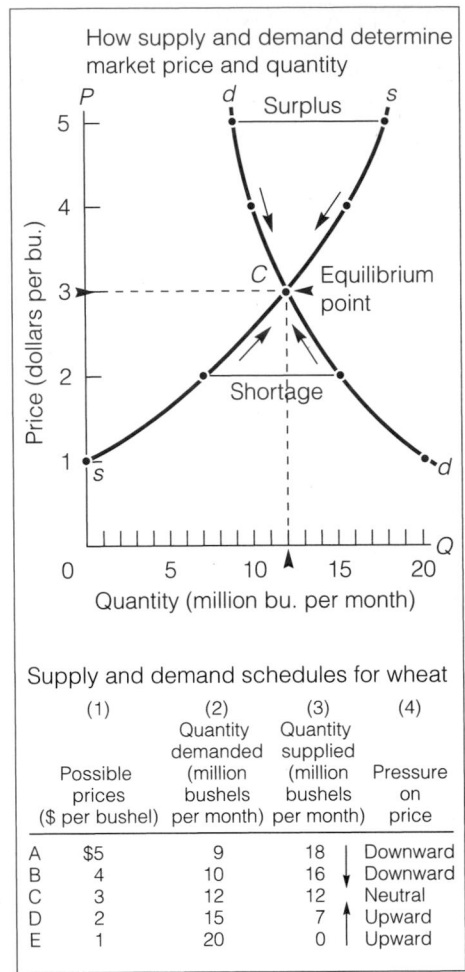

Supply and demand schedules for wheat

(1)	(2)	(3)	(4)
	Quantity	Quantity	
	demanded	supplied	
Possible	(million	(million	Pressure
prices	bushels	bushels	on
($ per bushel)	per month)	per month)	price
A $5	9	18	Downward
B 4	10	16	Downward
C 3	12	12	Neutral
D 2	15	7	Upward
E 1	20	0	Upward

FIGURE 4–3   Equilibrium price is at the intersection point where supply and de–mand match

Only at the equilibrium price of $3, shown in the orange third row, will the amount supplied just match the amount demanded.

In the diagram, at the *C* equilibrium intersection (shown by the dot), the amount supplied just matches the amount demanded. At any lower *P*, the excess amount demanded will force *P* back up; and at any *P* higher than the equilibrium, *P* will be forced back down to it.

At a higher price, the black bar shows the *surplus* of amount supplied over amount demanded. The arrows point downward to show the direction in which price will move because of the competition of excess *sellers*. At a price lower than the $3 equilibrium price, the black bar shows a *shortage*. Now the amount demanded exceeds amount supplied. Consequently, the eager bidding of excess *buyers* requires us to point the arrow indicators upward to show the pressure that they are exerting on price. Only at the point *C* will there be a balancing of forces and a stationary maintainable price.

Such is the essence of the doctrine of supply and demand.

EFFECT OF A SHIFT IN SUPPLY OR DEMAND

Now we can put the supply-and-demand apparatus to work. Gregory King, an English writer of the seventeenth century, noticed that when the harvest was bad, food rose in price. When it was plentiful, farmers got a lower price. Let us try to explain this common-sense fact by what happens in our diagrams.

Figure 4-4(a) shows how a spell of bad growing weather *reduces* the amount that farmers will supply at each and every market price and thereby raises the equilibrium point *E*. The *ss* curve has shifted to the left and has become *s's'*. The demand curve has not changed. Where does the new supply curve *s's'* intersect *dd*? Plainly at *E'*, the new equilibrium price where demand and the new reduced supply have again come into balance. Naturally, *P* has risen. And, because of the law of downward-sloping demand, *Q* has gone down.

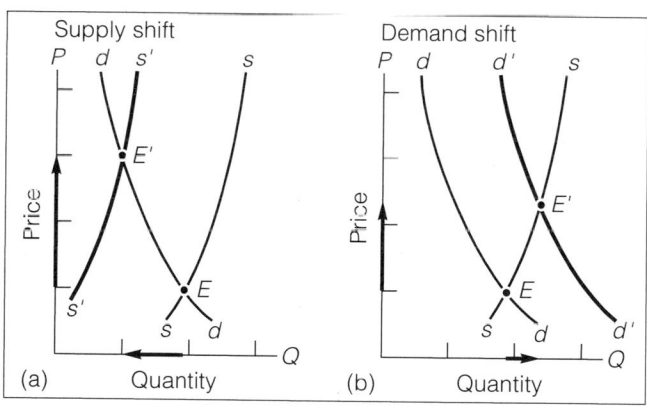

FIGURE 4-4 **When either supply or demand curve shifts, equilibrium price changes**

(a)   If supply shifts leftward for any reason, the equilibrium-price intersection will travel up the demand curve, giving higher *P* and lower *Q*.

(b)   If demand increases, the equilibrium will travel up the supply curve. *P* rises, and *Q* is also shown to rise.

Suppose the supply curve, because of good weather and cheaper fertiliz-   40
ers, had *increased*, instead. Draw in a new black equilibrium E'' with lower P and
higher Q.

Our apparatus will help us also analyze the effect of an increase in demand.
Suppose that rising family incomes make everyone want more wheat. Then at each
unchanged P, greater Q will now be demanded. The demand curve will shift rightward to $d'd'$. Figure 4-4(b) shows the resulting travel up the supply curve as enhanced demand raises competitive price to the E' intersection.

TWO STUMBLING BLOCKS

It is well to pause here to consider two minor sources of possible confusion
concerning supply and demand. These have puzzled students of economics in all
generations. The first point deals with the important fact that in drawing up a
demand schedule or curve, one always insists that "other things must be equal."
The second deals with the exact sense in which demand and supply are equal in
equilibrium.

"Other Things Equal"

To draw up a demand schedule for wheat, we vary its price and observe what
would happen to its quantity bought *at any one period of time in which no other factors are
allowed to change so as to becloud our experiment.*

Specifically, this means that, as we change wheat's P, we must not at the same
time change family income; or change the price of a competing product such as
corn; or do anything else that would tend to *shift* the demand schedule for wheat.
Why? Because, like any scientist who wants to isolate the effects of one causal factor, we must try to vary only *one* thing at a time. True enough, in economics we
cannot perform controlled experiments in a laboratory. We can rarely hold other
things constant in making statistical observations of economic magnitudes. This
limitation on our ability to experiment empirically in economics makes it all the
more important *to be clear in our logical thinking*, so that we may hope to recognize
and evaluate important *tendencies*–such as the effect of P on Q demanded–when
other tendencies are likely to be impinging on the situation at the same time.

The case of demand shift back in Fig. 4-4(b) can illustrate a common fallacy   45
based upon a failure to respect the following rule: Other things must be held equal
in defining a demand curve.

Suppose that the supply curve shifts little or not at all. But suppose the demand curve shifts up to $d'd'$ in good times when jobs are plentiful and people
have the incomes to buy more wheat. And suppose in the more depressed
phase of the business cycle, demand always shifts down to dd. Now take a piece of

graph paper and plot what would actually be recorded in the statistics of the wheat market.

> In boom times, you would record the equilibrium point shown at black E',
> and in bad times, the equilibrium point E. Take a ruler and join the black
> points E and E' in Fig. 4-4(b). The fallacy to be avoided like the plague is ex-
> pressed as follows: "I have disproved the law of downward-sloping demand;
> for note that when P was high, so too was Q–as shown by E'. And when
> P was lowered, instead of that change increasing Q, it actually lowered Q–
> as shown by E. My straight line joining E and E' represents an upward-
> sloping, not a downward-sloping, demand curve; so I have refuted a basic
> economic law."

Being alerted beforehand, one detects the fallacy in this argument. For at the same time that P went up, other things were *not* held constant; rather, income was also raised. The tendency for a rise in P to choke off purchases was more than masked by the countertendency of rising income to raise purchases. Instead of testing our economic law by moving *along* the demand curve, the beginner has measured changes that result from the *shift* of the demand curve.

Why is this bad scientific method? Because it leads to absurd results such as this: "On the basis of my revolutionary refutation of the alleged law of downward-sloping demand, I predict that, in the years when the harvest is especially big, wheat will sell for a higher rather than a lower price." Not only will such reasoning lead to absurd predictions that would lose fortunes for a speculator or a miller, but it also fails to recognize other important economic relationships–such as the fact that when family incomes go up, demand curves for goods such as wheat tend to shift upward and rightward.

Meaning of Equilibrium

The second stumbling block is a more subtle one, less likely to arise but not so easy to dispel. It is seen in the following.

"How can you say that the equality of supply and demand determines a particular equilibrium price? For, after all, *the amount one person sells is precisely what another person buys.* The quantity bought must always equal the quantity sold, no matter what the price; for that matter, whether or not the market is in equilibrium, a statistician who records the Q bought and the Q sold will always find these necessarily identical, each being a different aspect of exactly the same transaction."

The answer to this must be phrased something like this:

> You are quite right that measured Q bought and measured Q sold must be
> identical as recorded by a statistician. But the important question is this: At

50

which *P* will the amount that consumers are *willing to go on buying* be just matched by the amount that producers are *willing to go on selling*? At such a price, where there is equality between the *scheduled* amounts that suppliers and demanders want to go on buying and selling, and only at such an equilibrium *P*, will there be no tendency for price to rise or for price to fall.

At any other price, such as the case where *P* is above the intersection of supply and demand, it is a trivial fact that whatever goods change hands will show a statistical identity of measured amount bought and sold. But this measured identity does not in the least deny that suppliers are eager at so high a price to sell more than demanders will continue to buy; and that this excess of *scheduled supply* over *scheduled demand* will put downward pressure on price until it has finally reached that equilibrium level where the two curves intersect.

At that equilibrium intersection, and there alone, will everybody be happy: the auctioneer, the suppliers, the demanders–as well as the patient statistician, who always reports an identity between the measured amounts bought and sold.

WHAT SUPPLY AND DEMAND ACCOMPLISHED:
General Equilibrium

Having seen how supply and demand work, let us take stock of what has been accomplished. The scarce goods of society have been rationed out among the possible users of them. Who was it who did the rationing? A board? A committee? No. The auctioneering mechanism of competitive market price did the rationing. It was a case of "rationing by the purse."

FOR WHOM goods are destined was *partially* determined by who was willing to pay for them. If you had the money votes, you got the wheat. If you did not, you went without. Or if you had the money votes, but preferred not to spend them on wheat, you did without. The most important needs or desires–if backed by cash!–got fulfilled.

The WHAT question was being *partially* answered at the same time. The rise in market price was the signal to coax out a higher supply of wheat–the signal for other scarce resources to move into the wheat-production industry from alternative uses.

Even the HOW question was being *partially* decided in the background. For with wheat prices now high, farmers could afford expensive tractors and fertilizers and could thus bring poorer soils into use.

Why the word "partially" in this description of how the competitive market helped solve the three problems? Because this wheat market is but one market of many.

55

What is happening in the corn and rye markets also counts; and what is happening in the market for fertilizer, workers, and tractors obviously matters much.

We must note that the pricing problem is one that involves *interdependent markets*, not just the "partial equilibrium" of a single market.[2]

There are, so to speak, auctioneers operating simultaneously in the many different markets–wheat, rye, corn, fertilizer, and land; labor, wool, cotton, mutton, and rayon; bonds, stocks, personal loans, and foreign exchange in the form of English pounds or German marks. Each ends up at the equilibrium intersection point of the supply and demand schedules–wheat, rye, corn, fertilizer prices, and land rent; labor wage, wool, cotton, mutton, and rayon prices; bond price and its interest yield, stock prices and dividend yield, interest charges on personal loans, an exchange rate of $2.20 per pound or 1.8 marks to the dollar.

No market is an island unto itself. When wool P rises (because, say, of sheep disease abroad), it pulls up the Ps of domestic labor, fertilizer, and land needed for expanded domestic wool output. It raises the Ps of rival goods like cotton that some demanders will now turn to. And it might well lower the wage of wool spinners and the price of suit-company stock shares, since the latter must now pay more for its raw materials and must bid less eagerly for spinning labor.

The new "general-equilibrium set of interdependent prices" adjusts to the new situation. The price system meets the problem posed in the basic definition of economics: the study of (1) how *scarce means with alternative uses*–limited land and labor that can be switched from one industry to another–are allocated, and of (2) how to *achieve ends or goals*–as prescribed by the tastes for wool, nylon, food, and housing of those sovereign consumers who possess factors of production that give them money-income votes for the marketplace.

Each separate market, with its supply and demand curves, is doing its bit toward creating the general-equilibrium set of prices, which in a mixed economy largely resolves the basic economic problems of WHAT, HOW, and FOR WHOM.

PERFECTION AND IMPERFECTIONS OF COMPETITION

Our curves of supply and demand strictly apply only to a *perfectly competitive* market where some kind of *standardized* good such as wheat is being auctioned by an organized exchange that registers transactions of *numerous* buyers and sellers.

---

[2]The alert reader will not have to be reminded that the competitive market gives goods to those with money votes and does so efficiently. But the distribution of the money votes depends on how much you can sell your labor and property for in competitive and imperfectly competitive factor markets, and it is affected in an important way by (1) how lucky you are, (2) how lucky your parents and in-laws were, and (3) the advantages and disadvantages of your genetic and acquired skills and aptitudes. The student who writes on a final exam, "FOR WHOM is decided (in part) by how people decide to use their money votes," is not wrong. Indeed, this answer gets possibly

The Board of Trade in Chicago is one such example, and the cotton exchanges in New York or Liverpool are others. The New York Stock Exchange, while it does not auction goods and commodities or productive services rendered by factors of production, does provide a market where shares of common stocks such as those of General Motors and Royal Dutch Petroleum are auctioned at each moment of the working day. Many corporate bonds are also bought and sold on the Exchange's bond division.

The economists' curves of supply and demand are important ways of *idealizing*   65
the behavior of such markets. The curves do not pretend to give an accurate microscopic description of what is going on *during each changing moment* in such a marketplace—as various brokers mill around on the trading floor while frantically giving hand and voice signals to the specialist who serves as auctioneer for each grain or company stock. Nonetheless, the tools of supply and demand do summarize the *important average relationships resulting over a period of time* from such organized trading.

As far as these fundamental tools of supply and demand are concerned, it matters little what kind of exchange the goods are traded on: whether hand signals or slips of paper or modern computers are used; whether the auction is of the familiar kind, where the auctioneer calls out a *minimum* starting price and accepts higher and higher bids until only one high bidder is left to get the Renoir painting in question; or, alternatively, whether there is a "Dutch auction," where the price *starts high* instead of low and moves downward at stated time intervals until an eager buyer, fearing that someone else will get in the bid first, finally gives the first bid and gets the merchandise; or, as a third alternative, whether the auctioneer asks for written bids and offers in order to be able to make up a table or chart like those of Fig. 4-3 and then proceeds to find the equilibrium intersection at one fell swoop, in effect by solving two simultaneous equations.

Indeed, the market need not have a single auctioneer; all the bidding may well take place by telephone calls, as in the case of the market for United States government bonds, which is a much more nearly perfect one than the corporate bond market on the floor of the New York Stock Exchange. The same can be true of stocks listed on the so-called "over-the-counter market," a market which is conducted throughout the country completely by telephone and by computer listing of price-quotation lists of different brokers.

---

50 percent credit. However, the other 50 per cent will be lost unless the student adds, "The basic problem of FOR WHOM is the process by which the money votes *themselves* get determined, which is primarily not by supply and demand in a single good's market, but by supply and demand in the labor, land, and other interdependent factor markets of Part Four; and factor supplies depend much on distribution of ownership."

Perfection of Competition as a Limiting Pole

Needless to say, the requirements for absolutely perfect competition are as hard to meet as the requirements for a perfectly frictionless pendulum in physics. We can approach closer and closer to perfection, but can never quite reach it. Yet this fact need not do serious damage to the usefulness of our employing the idealized concept. Actually, it matters little to the economic scientist that different grades of wheat will call for slight variations from the quoted market prices. Nor does it matter in the case of standardized cotton goods that they are sold and bought in an informal way by many competing firms.

So long as there are *numerous* buyers and sellers on each side, *well informed* about quality and about each other's prices and having no reason to discriminate in favor of one merchant rather than another and no reason to expect that variations in their *own* bids and offers will have an *appreciable effect* upon the prevailing market price—so long as all this is true, the behavior of price and quantity can be expected to be much like that predicted by our supply and demand curves. . . .

To be sure, not all today's markets are anywhere near to being perfectly competitive in the economist's sense. Elements of monopoly power or of market imperfection may enter in, and these imperfections will require us to modify the competitive model. After we have learned how to handle such cases, we shall recognize that the world is a blend of competition and imperfections—which means that the competitive analysis, properly qualified, is still an indispensable tool for interpreting reality.

The Responsive Reader

1. How would you explain the basic market mechanism that is the subject of this selection? Other things being equal, how do "supply and demand work themselves out in the competitive market"? How does demand affect price, and how does price affect supply? How does supply in turn affect price, with what effect on demand? When or how are supply and demand "in equilibrium"?

2. Some of Samuelson's key examples focus on commodities like potatoes, wheat, or meat. What kind of world do these examples invoke? Do you think his graphs would have to be adjusted if the commodities bought and sold were computers, VCRs, or state-of-the-art medical equipment? Why or why not?

3. How important are some of the "imperfections" that skew the free play of supply and demand? For instance, how do monopolies interfere with the free play of market forces? (And what if anything should be done about them?) Is saturation a factor? (Even at a very low price, is there a limit to the amount of pizza people can eat or the number of computers they will buy?)

4. To judge from this selection, what is Samuelson's view of government activity in the marketplace or government intervention in the economy? Do you share it?

For Discussion or Writing

5. People in the business community often complain that American schools don't teach basic principles of economics. Do you agree? Should they?

6. To judge from your own observation and practice, do some people prefer high-priced items to low-priced ones? Do you think there are other elements of consumer psychology that don't conform to the classic laws of supply and demand?

7. Critics of capitalism have often faulted capitalists for thinking of labor as a commodity, subject to impersonal market forces. Is there evidence in this selection of that kind of thinking? Is there anything wrong with it?

Collaborative Projects

8. Does the business section of your local newspaper give much play to the theories and analyses of economists?

THE COMPETITIVE EDGE:
Japanese and Americans

William Ouchi

━━━━━━━━━

> *In the sixties and seventies, Japanese products were systematically replacing British motorcy-*
> *cles, Swiss watches, German cameras, and American cars in world markets. At first belittled as*
> *cheap and imitative, Japanese products were slowly recognized as cheaper, more sophisticated, and*
> *more reliable than what other countries had to offer. Reactions in the industrialized countries of*
> *the West ranged from panic to protectionist initiatives, with many well-established industries go-*
> *ing under. Today, the Japanese lead in customer electronics products like television sets, radios,*
> *VCRs, stereo systems, or cameras seems insurmountable. What gives the Japanese the competitive*
> *edge? William George Ouchi, a professor of management at UCLA, was one of the first researchers*
> *to study systematically the factors that put Japanese industry ahead. His* Theory Z: How
> American Business Can Meet the Japanese Challenge *(1981) was one of the first of*
> *a flood of books and articles with titles like* Japan as No. 1: Lessons for America.

Perhaps the most difficult aspect of the Japanese for Westerners to compre-   1
hend is the strong orientation to collective values, particularly a collective sense of
responsibility. Let me illustrate with an anecdote about a visit to a new factory in
Japan owned and operated by an American electronics company. The American
company, a particularly creative firm, frequently attracts attention within the business community for its novel approaches to planning, organizational design, and
management systems. As a consequence of this corporate style, the parent company determined to make a thorough study of Japanese workers and to design a
plant that would combine the best of East and West. In their study they discovered
that Japanese firms almost never make use of individual work incentives, such as
piecework or even individual performance appraisal tied to salary increases. They
concluded that rewarding individual achievement and individual ability is always
a good thing.

In the final assembly area of their new plant, long lines of young Japanese
women wired together electronic products on a piece-rate system: the more you
wired, the more you got paid. About two months after opening, the head foreladies
approached the plant manager. "Honorable plant manager," they said humbly as
they bowed, "we are embarrassed to be so forward, but we must speak to you because all of the girls have threatened to quit work this Friday." (To have this happen,
of course, would be a great disaster for all concerned.) "Why," they wanted to know,
"can't our plant have the same compensation system as other Japanese companies? When you hire a new girl, her starting wage should be fixed by her age. An

eighteen-year-old should be paid more than a sixteen-year-old. Every year on her birthday, she should receive an automatic increase in pay. The idea that any of us can be more productive than another must be wrong, because none of us in final assembly could make a thing unless all of the other people in the plant had done their jobs right first. To single one person out as being more productive is wrong and is also personally humiliating to us." The company changed its compensation system to the Japanese model.

Another American company in Japan had installed a suggestion system much as we have in the United States. Individual workers were encouraged to place suggestions to improve productivity into special boxes. For an accepted idea the individual received a bonus amounting to some fraction of the productivity savings realized from his or her suggestion. After a period of six months, not a single suggestion had been submitted. The American managers were puzzled. They had heard many stories of the inventiveness, the commitment, and the loyalty of Japanese workers, yet not one suggestion to improve productivity had appeared.

The managers approached some of the workers and asked why the suggestion system had not been used. The answer: "No one can come up with a work improvement idea alone. We work together, and any ideas that one of us may have are actually developed by watching others and talking to others. If one of us was singled out for being responsible for such an idea, it would embarrass all of us." The company changed to a group suggestion system, in which workers collectively submitted suggestions. Bonuses were paid to groups which would save bonus money until the end of the year for a party at a restaurant or, if there was enough money, for family vacations together. The suggestions and productivity improvements rained down on the plant.

One can interpret these examples in two quite different ways. Perhaps the 5 Japanese commitment to collective values is an anachronism that does not fit with modern industrialism but brings economic success despite that collectivism. Collectivism seems to be inimical to the kind of maverick creativity exemplified in Benjamin Franklin, Thomas Edison, and John D. Rockefeller. Collectivism does not seem to provide the individual incentive to excel which has made a great success of American enterprise. Entirely apart from its economic effects, collectivism implies a loss of individuality, a loss of the freedom to be different, to hold fundamentally different values from others.

The second interpretation of the examples is that the Japanese collectivism is economically efficient. It causes people to work well together and to encourage one another to better efforts. Industrial life requires interdependence of one person on another. But a less obvious but far-reaching implication of the Japanese collectivism for economic performance has to do with accountability.

In the Japanese mind, collectivism is neither a corporate or individual goal to strive for nor a slogan to pursue. Rather, the nature of things operates so that nothing of consequence occurs as a result of individual effort. Everything important in life happens as a result of teamwork or collective effort. Therefore, to attempt to assign individual credit or blame to results is unfounded. A Japanese professor of accounting, a brilliant scholar trained at Carnegie-Mellon University who teaches now in Tokyo, remarked that the status of accounting systems in Japanese industry is primitive compared to those in the United States. Profit centers, transfer prices, and computerized information systems are barely known even in the largest Japanese companies, whereas they are a commonplace in even small United States organizations. Though not at all surprised at the difference in accounting systems, I was not at all sure that the Japanese were primitive. In fact, I thought their system a good deal more efficient than ours.

Most American companies have basically two accounting systems. One system summarizes the overall financial state to inform stockholders, bankers, and other outsiders. That system is not of interest here. The other system, called the managerial or cost accounting system, exists for an entirely different reason. It measures in detail all of the particulars of transactions between departments, divisions, and key individuals in the organization, for the purpose of untangling the interdependencies between people. When, for example, two departments share one truck for deliveries, the cost accounting system charges each department for part of the cost of maintaining the truck and driver, so that at the end of the year, the performance of each department can be individually assessed, and the better department's manager can receive a larger raise. Of course, all of this information processing costs money, and furthermore may lead to arguments between the departments over whether the costs charged to each are fair.

In a Japanese company a short run assessment of individual performance is not wanted, so the company can save the considerable expense of collecting and processing all of that information. Companies still keep track of which department uses a truck how often and for what purposes, but like-minded people can interpret some simple numbers for themselves and adjust their behavior accordingly. Those insisting upon clear and precise measurement for the purpose of advancing individual interests must have an elaborate information system. Industrial life, however, is essentially integrated and interdependent. No one builds an automobile alone, no one carries through a banking transaction alone. In a sense the Japanese value of collectivism fits naturally into an industrial setting, whereas the Western individualism provides constant conflicts. The image that comes to mind is of Chaplin's silent film "Modern Times" in which the apparently insignificant hero played by Chaplin successfully fights against the unfeeling machinery of industry. Modern industrial life can be aggravating, even hostile, or natural: all depends on the fit between our culture and our technology.

The *shinkansen* or "bullet train" speeds across the rural areas of Japan giving a   10
quick view of cluster after cluster of farmhouses surrounded by rice paddies. This particular pattern did not develop purely by chance, but as a consequence of

the technology peculiar to the growing of rice, the staple of the Japanese diet. The growing of rice requires the construction and maintenance of an irrigation system, something that takes many hands to build. More importantly, the planting and the harvesting of rice can only be done efficiently with the cooperation of twenty or more people. The "bottom line" is that a single family working alone cannot produce enough rice to survive, but a dozen families working together can produce a surplus. Thus the Japanese have had to develop the capacity to work together in harmony, no matter what the forces of disagreement or social disintegration, in order to survive.

Japan is a nation built entirely on the tips of giant, suboceanic volcanoes. Little of the land is flat and suitable for agriculture. Terraced hillsides make use of every available square foot of arable land. Small homes built very close together further conserve the land. Japan also suffers from natural disasters such as earthquakes and hurricanes. Traditionally homes are made of light construction materials, so a house falling down during a disaster will not crush its occupants and also can be quickly and inexpensively rebuilt. During the feudal period until the Meiji restoration of 1868, each feudal lord sought to restrain his subjects from moving from one village to the next for fear that a neighboring lord might amass enough peasants with which to produce a large agricultural surplus, hire an army and pose a threat. Apparently bridges were not commonly built across rivers and streams until the late nineteenth century, since bridges increased mobility between villages.

Taken all together, this characteristic style of living paints the picture of a nation of people who are homogeneous with respect to race, history, language, religion, and culture. For centuries and generations these people have lived in the same village next door to the same neighbors. Living in close proximity and in dwellings which gave very little privacy, the Japanese survived through their capacity to work together in harmony. In this situation, it was inevitable that the one most central social value which emerged, the one value without which the society could not continue, was that an individual does not matter.

To the Western soul this is a chilling picture of society. Subordinating individual tastes to the harmony of the group and knowing that individual needs can never take precedence over the interests of all is repellent to the Western citizen. But a frequent theme of Western philosophers and sociologists is that individual freedom exists only when people willingly subordinate their self-interests to the social interest. A society composed entirely of self-interested individuals is a society in which each person is at war with the other, a society which has no freedom. This issue, constantly at the heart of understanding society, comes up in every century, and in every society, whether the writer be Plato, Hobbes, or B. F. Skinner.

In order to complete the comparison of Japanese and American living situations, consider flight over the United States. Looking out of the window high over the state of Kansas, we see a pattern of a single farmhouse surrounded by fields, followed by another single homestead surrounded by fields. In the early 1800s in the state of Kansas there were no automobiles. Your nearest neighbor was perhaps two miles distant; the winters were long, and the snow was deep. Inevitably, the central social values were self-reliance and independence. Those were the realities of that place and age that children had to learn to value.

The key to the industrial revolution was discovering that non-human forms of   15 energy substituted for human forms could increase the wealth of a nation beyond anyone's wildest dreams. But there was a catch. To realize this great wealth, non-human energy needed huge complexes called factories with hundreds, even thousands of workers collected into one factory. Moreover, several factories in one central place made the generation of energy more efficient. Almost overnight, the Western world was transformed from a rural and agricultural country to an urban and industrial state. Our technological advance seems to no longer fit our social structure: in a sense, the Japanese can better cope with modern industrialism. While Americans still busily protect our rather extreme form of individualism, the Japanese hold their individualism in check and emphasize cooperation.

The Responsive Reader

1. Many observers have commented on how Westernized or Americanized Japan, once a traditional "closed" society, has become. What evidence have you seen that Japan or the Japanese have become at least superficially "Westernized" in politics, business, lifestyle, or popular culture?

2. In spite of surface similarities, Ouchi builds his essay around a key contrast between the two cultures. Where does he first spell out his thesis? How does he keep reinforcing it? What are his two key examples or cases in point early in the essay?

3. How is Ouchi's discussion of the two different accounting systems relevant to his basic argument?

4. For Ouchi, the contrasting histories of the two countries do much to explain their differences in outlook or mentality. How or why?

5. What are the usual negative associations of collectivism, and how does Ouchi counter them?

6. Ouchi relates his discussion to an issue "at the heart of understanding society" and central in the work of writers from the ancient Greek philosopher Plato (*The Republic*) and the seventeenth-century British philosopher Thomas Hobbes (*Leviathan*) to the twentieth-century American psychologist B. F. Skinner (*Walden Two*). All of these constructed imaginary future societies. What is the basic issue? How is it related to Ouchi's comparison of Japanese and American culture?

For Discussion or Writing

7. In the light of Ouchi's analysis, what recommendations would you draw up for American business or American management? Can you and your classmates agree on a basic strategy?

8. Do you agree that the myth of individualism is a major force in the American ideology? Do you think it is obsolete in the modern world?

Collaborative Projects

9. In recent years, economic experts have begun to say that the end of the Japanese ascendancy is at hand, that the Japanese economy and especially its banking system are facing serious problems. Are these experts whistling in the dark? Are their predictions wishful thinking? Working with a group, study current data that can shed light on this question.

Making Connections

10. Economists may be placed on a spectrum ranging from those who like Samuelson stress purely economical factors to those who like Ouchi stress psychological and social components. How does this contrast show in the two selections? To which side do you and your classmates incline?

THE NEW ECONOMICS OF HIGH TECH

Lester C. Thurow

▬▬▬

> *Competitiveness in the global marketplace remained a central preoccupation of political and business leaders in the nineties. What undercuts America's ability to compete successfully with leading industrial nations of Europe and the Pacific Rim? In the following article, Lester C. Thurow, dean of the Sloan School of Management at MIT in Cambridge, Massachusetts, tries to give up-to-date and provocative answers to that question. This selection is from* Head to Head: The Coming Economic Battles among Japan, Europe, and America *(1992). In his book, Thurow takes on urgent current topics including global competition, trade deficits, the merger mania and hostile takeovers, and the high-tech future. He draws his conclusions from the study of a formidable array of sources, ranging from the* Wall Street Journal *and* New York Times *to the British* Economist *and* Financial Times. *What advice does he give on issues like allocating research and development (R&D) funds, reassessing the performance of American executives, or training tomorrow's workforce?*

In the past, the nations that succeeded economically were those whose busi-   1
nesses invented new products. The British in the nineteenth century and the Americans in the twentieth century got rich by doing this. In the twenty-first century,
sustainable competitive advantage will come not from new-product technologies
but from new-process technologies—those that enable industries to produce goods
and services faster, cheaper, and better.

American firms currently spend two-thirds of their R&D money on new
products and one-third on new processes. The Japanese do exactly the opposite—
one third on new products, two-thirds on new processes. Not surprisingly, both
sets of firms do well where they concentrate their talent: The Americans earn
higher rates of return on new-product technologies; the Japanese earn higher rates
of return on new processes.

Someone, however, is making a mistake. Both strategies cannot be correct. In
this case, the someone is the United States. Its spending patterns are misguided,
reflecting economic thinking that is thirty years out of date. In the early 1960s the
rate of return on investment in new-product R&D was almost always higher than
that on new-process R&D. A new product gave the inventor the monopoly power
to set higher prices and earn higher profits. With a new product, there were no
competitors.

In contrast, a new manufacturing or production process left the inventor
to fend for himself in an existing, competitive business. Competitors also knew
how to make the product, and they would always lower their prices to match the

inventor's. It was simply rational to spend most of a firm's R&D money on new-product development.

But while Americans focused on product technologies, Japan and Germany   5
focused on process technologies. They did so not because they were smarter than Americans but because the United States had such a technological advantage in the 1950s and 1960s that it was virtually impossible for either Japan or Germany to become leaders in the development of new products. They could only hope to compete in existing markets. As a result, Japan and Germany invested more heavily in process R&D. They had no choice.

But what was a good American strategy thirty years ago—a focus on product technologies—is today a poor strategy. Levels of technical sophistication in Germany, Japan, and the United States are not very different, and reverse engineering—the art of developing a new manufacturing process for an existing product—has become a highly developed art form. The nature of the change can be seen in the economic history of three of the most successful products introduced into the mass consumer market in the past two decades—the video recorder, the fax, and the CD player. Americans invented the video recorder and the fax; Europeans (the Dutch) invented the CD player. But measured in terms of sales, employment, and profits, all three have become Japanese products.

The moral of the story is clear. Those who can make a product cheaper can take it away from the inventor. In today's world it does very little good to invent a new product if the inventor is not also the cheapest producer of that product. What necessity forced upon Germany and Japan thirty years ago happens to be the right long-run R&D strategy today.

This reality will eventually force the United States to alter its R&D spending patterns, but it also requires a much more difficult shift in human-resource allocation. Over time, the pay and promotion curve for American managers and engineers in production has fallen behind that in other parts of a firm. Since production isn't seen as the key to a firm's success, it has ceased to be the route to the top. Only 4 percent of American CEOs come from production; America's best and brightest, aware of this trend, have not gone into processes. Reversing this allocation of talent is now very difficult, since traditional salary scales and promotion practices will have to be disrupted.

In order to profit from technological advancement, firms need CEOs who understand process technologies. Large investments in revolutionary technologies will only be made quickly if the man or woman at the top appreciates those technologies. Yet American CEOs are much less likely to be technologically aware than those in either Japan or Europe. In those countries 70 percent of CEOs have technical backgrounds; in the United States 30 percent do. This difference in educational background is not unrelated to the fact that in industry after industry, American firms have been slow to adopt revolutionary new-process technologies.

One striking example: Twenty-five years ago the leaders of the American steel industry failed to comprehend the technology revolution that was under way and chose not to make the massive investments in oxygen furnaces and continuous casters being made elsewhere in the world. American steel companies have been playing an unsuccessful game of catch-up ever since.

The management of technology is usually seen as something of relevance to   10
manufacturing but not to the rest of the economy. Here again, what was historically true is no longer true. In the twenty-first century there will be high-tech and low-tech products, but almost every product will be produced with high-tech processes. The automobile is a low-tech product; the robots that make it are high-tech. Gaining an edge in high-tech processes will be important in almost every industry–from fast food to textiles–and mastering process technologies will become central to the success of almost every firm.

The new information and telecommunication technologies that are being developed are also going to make more service industries into high-tech process industries. In retailing, those who survive will have the inventory-control systems that best reduce costs. Stores will be directly linked to suppliers to minimize the time lags between the customer's purchase of some particular item and the restocking of that item. Even now, American firms such as The Limited, a clothing retailer, are converting retailing into a high-tech competition. The Limited's inventory-control, telecommunication, and CAD–CAM (computer-aided design/ computer-aided manufacturing) systems allow it to know what women are buying and to put precisely those clothes in their stores within twenty-eight days; their competitors take as long as six months. The result: They win, and their slower competitors lose.

While technology creates competitive advantage, seizing that advantage requires a work force skilled from top to bottom. When the route to success is inventing new products, the education of the smartest 25 percent of the labor force is critical: Someone in that top group can be counted on to invent the new products of tomorrow. But when success depends on being the cheapest and best producer of products, the education of the bottom 50 percent of the population becomes a priority. This is the part of the population that must operate those new processes. If the bottom 50 percent cannot learn what must be learned, new high-tech processes cannot be employed.

Information technologies need to be integrated into the entire production process, from initial designs through marketing to final sales and supporting services such as maintenance. To do this requires workers in the office, the factory, the retail store, and the repair service to have levels of education and skill that they have never had to have in the past.

If sustainable competitive advantage depends on work-force skills, American firms have a problem. Human-resource management is not traditionally seen as central to the competitive survival of the firm in the United States. Skill acquisition is considered an individual responsibility. Labor is simply another factor of production to be hired–rented at the lowest possible cost–much as one buys raw materials or equipment.

The lack of importance attached to human-resource management can be seen   15
in the corporate pecking order. In an American firm the chief financial officer is almost always second in command. The post of head of human-resource management is usually a specialized job, off at the edge of the corporate hierarchy. The executive who holds it is never consulted on major strategic decisions and has no chance to move up to CEO. By way of contrast, in Japan the head of human-resource management is central–usually the second most important executive, after the CEO, in the firm's hierarchy.

While American firms often talk about the vast amounts spent on training their work forces, in fact they invest less in the skills of their employees than do either Japanese or German firms. The money they do invest is also more highly concentrated on professional and managerial employees. And the limited investments that are made in training workers are also much more narrowly focused on the specific skills necessary to do the next job rather than on the basic background skills that make it possible to absorb new technologies.

As a result, problems emerge when new breakthrough technologies arrive. If American workers, for example, take much longer to learn how to operate new flexible manufacturing stations than workers in Germany (as they do), the effective cost of those stations is lower in Germany than it is in the United States. More time is required before equipment is up and running at capacity, and the need for extensive retraining generates costs and creates bottlenecks that limit the speed with which new equipment can be employed. The result is a slower pace of technological change. And in the end the skills of the bottom half of the population affect the wages of the top half. If the bottom half can't effectively staff the processes that have to be operated, the management and professional jobs that go with these processes will disappear.

The Responsive Reader

1. What basic distinction does Thurow make between new-product technologies and new-process technologies? (What is "reverse engineering"?) What is the history of the two approaches? According to Thurow, why do they provide the key to how American economic thinking became obsolete?

2. What is the role of "human-resource allocation"? According to Thurow, what is wrong with the American executive culture–with the way this country selects and promotes executives? How does it handicap this country in global competition? What evidence or example does Thurow provide? Are they convincing?

3. What is wrong with how this country trains workers? What is wrong with the American system of education? Are Thurow's criticisms here familiar, or is his perspective different from what you would expect?

For Discussion or Writing

4. In your own observation of technological change, have you seen examples of new or improved technologies being introduced to deliver basically the same results? What technological changes have you observed that seem to satisfy genuinely new needs?

5. Do you think there is too much hyping of change in our society and especially in the business world?

Collaborative Projects

6. What do business or industry leaders in your area predict will be some of the most important changes confronting them at the beginning of the new century?

THE MARKETING OF WINDOWS 95

Amy Cortese AND *Kathy Rebello*

⸺

Classic economists describe the play of supply and demand as if it were a natural law. In-creased demand makes possible higher prices, which in turn stimulate increased production, which in turn tends to bring prices back in line. However, much current marketing strategy focuses not on satisfying existing demand but on creating demand—on making consumers feel needs they didn't know they had. An outstanding example of a marketing campaign designed to presell a product was the launching of Microsoft's Windows 95 in August 1995. Called by one journalist "the most hyped new product in history," the Windows 95 software provided a new operating sys-tem for personal computers. Microsoft launched the new product with a $200 million promo-tional campaign. During two years of development time, a steady succession of newspaper stories had fueled interest, with coverage ranging from alleged imitation of the Macintosh system to an-titrust concerns on the part of the Justice Department. The actual launch became a media event, with the spotlight on the first customer to buy the product at midnight on the launch day in New Zealand and then on the long lines of computer lovers lining up at the cash registers in time zones where midnight arrived later. Microsoft reportedly bought the Rolling Stones' song "Start Me Up" for $12 million for use in promoting the new software. Leading national and international come-dians helped multibillionaire CEO Bill Gates celebrate the momentous event. Kodak, Compaq, Coca-Cola, CompUSA, and USAir signed up as sponsors of a television "infomercial" featuring Gates and his new product. "Now software has become the center of the world," said the senior vice president of sales for Microsoft. The following article appeared in Newsweek *a few weeks before the Windows 95 launch.*

Deep in the heart of Building 5 on Microsoft Corp's sprawling campus in Red-   1
mond, Wash., hundreds of men and women hunch over PCs in dimly lit, window-less rooms. They're bug testers, and they have been toiling 'round the clock to find and fix the last glitches lurking in the 15 million lines of computer code that make up Windows 95. In a couple of weeks, the final, "golden" version of the operating system must go to manufacturing, where Win95 will be etched into CD-ROMs and recorded on diskettes.

Microsoft plans an Aug. 24 blowout in Seattle, where Bill Gates and several hundred of his closest friends will celebrate the official launch. And computer mak-ers around the world are poised to start a massive fall sales push behind the soft-ware that will, Gates says, unleash the full powers of personal-computer hardware, bring millions of new consumers into the market, and provide the bridge between the klunky PCs of the past and the intuitive, user-friendly information appliances of the 21st century. "Part of the big deal with Win95 is fixing all of the sins of the past," he says.

Things are tense around the bug room and across Microsoft's 27-acre campus in a woodsy Seattle suburb as the final countdown begins. In a hallway in Building 5, a large sheet of paper tacked to the wall bears the words: "Where do you want to go when we ship?" (a play on Microsoft's advertising tagline: "Where do you want to go today?"). Bleary-eyed programmers have scrawled dozens of responses including "Disneyland," "Home," and "To find me a husband." One employee has tacked up a picture of Gates and scribbled the boss's answer: "To the bank."

Not quite yet. There are still horrendous technical and logistic issues to tackle–checking the bug reports from 400,000 PC owners who have been testing "beta" copies since last fall, getting hundreds of PC makers ready to switch over to the new software, putting the last-minute fixes into manuals and other documentation (in some 12 languages), preparing dealers, firing up marketing campaigns, and working with other software companies, whose products will be critical to Win95's success. At the same time, a new division is gearing up for the simultaneous launch of the Microsoft Network, the software giant's online service that will be available to all Win95 users.

Nobody has ever done quite what Microsoft is attempting–to get 85 million   5
customers and a $130 billion industry to move en masse to a new technology. Hardware and software makers in all corners of the world are gearing up to build the machines that will live up to the demands of the new operating system. And they're bracing for a surge in demand for everything from memory chips to CD-ROMS as Microsoft starts spending hundreds of millions in advertising and marketing to promote Win95 and related power hungry programs.

Add to that the Win95 marketing budgets of computer and software makers, and you've got a billion-dollar blitz. "This is the biggest marketing thing we've ever done," declares Steven A. Ballimer, a Microsoft executive vice-president. "Windows 95 will be as prominent as Coca-Cola on people's minds," says Lorie Strong, vice-president for marketing services at Compaq Computer Corp.

How quickly will the world turn to Win95? For consumers, the shift will be a no-brainer: By fall, virtually every Intel Corp.-based home PC on the market will have Windows 95 as its main operating system. You'll have to special order to get Windows 3.1 or IBM's OS/2. Retailers are already gearing up for another record holiday buying season. "It's going to be a blockbuster quarter," says Peter A. Janssen, vice-president for merchandising and advertising at software retailer Egghead Inc. Microsoft has 100 employees making sure the shelves of more than 15,000 stores will be brimming with Win95 boxes–each with a suggested retail price of $209 ($109 for customers upgrading from Windows 3.1).

"JUST SOFTWARE"

In corporations, the shift will be more gradual. While Win95 has features de-signed with corporations in mind–such as built-in network connections and ad-ministrative software–the cost of installing Windows 95 on hundreds or thousands of machines and training employees is steep. Many will stick with Windows 3.1–or the more industrial-strength Windows NT–for at least a year. Even so, analysts figure Win95 shipments could hit 50 million the first year.

What can go wrong? The worst-case scenario would be a buggy–or late–Windows 95. But despite rumors of possible delays, Microsoft insists Win95 is on track. To get it right, Gates already pushed back the launch of the Windows rewrite (originally known as Chicago) from mid-1994. "It's the most in-depth, widespread testing program in the history of software," boasts Brad A. Silverberg, senior vice-president of Microsoft's Personal Systems Div. Microsoft has even jettisoned parts of the program that aren't quite ready for prime time. Some of those features, in-cluding advanced electronic-mail functions, will be sold in a $49.95 add-on pack-age later.

The biggest challenge may be living up to the massive expectations for Win95.   10 Microsoft executives spent the last year crisscrossing the globe to convince cus-tomers, consultants, and journalists that Windows 95 is truly revolutionary. And the campaign succeeded. Lately–perhaps because the company doesn't want to look too dominant–Microsoft officials are trying to bring expectations down to earth. "It's just software," says Silverberg. "It doesn't cure cancer. It doesn't grow hair. It's not a floor wax. It's Windows."

Still, by most accounts, Microsoft has another slam-dunk winner: Early re-views have praised Win95's greatly improved "user interface" and its dozens of handy new features.

If just 15% of Windows customers upgrade to the new version–the ranks of Windows users is expected to hit 100 million by the time Win95 ships–Microsoft will rake in close to $1 billion in the first year. Some analysts figure the upgrade rate could be twice that.

There's more. Microsoft, which is expected to close its June 30 year approach-ing $6 billion in sales, will get an additional $400 million to $500 million in 1996 from sales of a Win95 version of Microsoft Office, due out around the same time, figures Michael Kwatinetz, an analyst with PaineWebber Inc. Best of all, it could al-most double, to $2 billion, the revenues Microsoft makes from copies of Windows sold with new PCs–a lucrative profit stream since costs are minimal.

CHAIN REACTION

Of course, this being Microsoft, the Win95 launch is tinged with controversy. The Justice Dept. is investigating charges that by building connections to its new online service into Win95, Microsoft gives itself an insurmountable edge over on-line competitors such as CompuServe Inc. Justice investigators are also looking into terms of the contracts that Microsoft is negotiating with PC makers who will ship Win95 on their machines. Just weeks before Win95's launch, top PC makers, including Hewlett-Packard Co. and Dell Computer Corp. have not yet signed.

None of this, however, is likely to put much drag on Microsoft's bullet train. HP's business PC chief, Jacques Clay, predicts that the PC makers will sign their contracts–after negotiating better terms. And even if Justice forces Microsoft to disconnect the automatic links to the Microsoft Network, say industry insiders, it's not likely to push back the launch–or slow Windows 95's sweep of the PC industry.   15

Bottom line: While computer and software makers may privately enjoy seeing the feds make Microsoft squirm, they don't want Windows 95 to falter. They're counting on Win95 to set off a chain reaction that will sweep through the entire computer industry. Examples: PC owners who buy the Windows 95 upgrade may want to buy additional memory chips. And with an operating system that hogs 27 to 50 megabytes of storage space, you might want a bigger disk drive.

Don't want to sink more money into your old machine? PC makers will have lots of new models this fall geared specifically to the needs of Win95. Packard Bell Electronics Inc. recently announced what it says is the first officially sanctioned (by Microsoft) Win95-compatible machine, and Compaq promises an entirely Win95-ready lineup for the home market by September. "It's a chance to set off a whole new explosion," says Microsoft's Ballmer.

How big? Hard to say. But there are signs. Orders for semiconductors–a leading indicator of PC sales–are up 54% over last year. Kwatinetz of PaineWebber projects that Win95 could boost PC sales by an additional 5% in the first 12 months. "We want to sell a ton of Pentium processors in '96, and [Win95] will help," says Intel Senior Vice-President Ronald J. Whittier.

GAMES PLAYER

The cycle won't stop there. Owners of souped-up PCs will want new software programs to match. Plus, the combination of powerful Pentium PCs, multimedia technology, and Windows 95 should spur all sorts of innovative programs and launch the PC into new markets. For instance, the PC has played second fiddle to Apple Computer Inc's Macintosh in publishing circles. "People didn't take it seriously," says Jerry Barber, chief technology officer at Adobe Systems Inc., which makes desktop-publishing software. Windows 95 could change that. "We expect to sell a lot of new applications," he says.

Software developers also see a major opportunity in games for Windows 95–   20
perhaps stealing part of the multibillion-dollar video-game market now owned by Nintendo Co. and Sega Enterprises Inc. Microsoft paid special attention to making Win95 a better platform for games, speeding up graphics performance, and improving its ability to play video clips. "Win95 is a huge step forward," says Ron D.

Gilbert, co-founder and creative director at Humongous Entertainment Inc., which makes "edutainment" software. "You'll see Windows become the predominant game platform."

So what will Windows 95 do for you? For starters, it should make computing a much less frustrating experience—at least for people who haven't been spoiled by Apple's Macintoshes. The first thing you'll notice when you turn on your Windows 95 machine is a simplified graphical interface that reduces screen clutter by organizing contents into a few areas represented by icons on your screen. For instance, by clicking on an icon labeled "My Computer," you can view the contents of your disk drive. Similarly, an icon called "Network Neighborhood" offers up a graphical view of any other computers or printers you are connected to on a network.

Windows 95 also goes a long way toward making it easier to set up a system or add new devices—a modem, say, or a CD-ROM player. With a feature called plug-and-play, Windows will—in most cases—be able to identify a device and automatically figure out how to work with it. And if you've ever lost a file because you forgot what you named it, you'll love long file names. Windows 95 gets rid of the eight-character limitation for file names, so you can use more meaningful names—julysalesreport instead of july.rpt.

True, IBM's OS/2 and Apple's Mac OS have long had many of those same features—and more. So has Microsoft's Windows NT operating system. But now, these features will be built into tens of millions of home PCs. As applications software arrives to exploit some of Win95's capabilities—built-in communications that make reaching across the Internet as easy as pulling a file from your hard drive, for example—new uses for PCs will become possible. "This is a watershed event, in that the PC becomes a consumer device," says Mark Eppley, CEO of Traveling Software Inc. Win95 may provide the final nudge that makes the PC an indispensable consumer appliance—for entertainment, online communications, and interactive media. "You're looking at the PC taking more time from TV, it will cause a shift in your leisure time," says Rich Edwards, an analyst at Robertson Stephens & Co.

And guess who's geared up to take maximum advantage of the new home-PC phenomenon? That's right, from the Microsoft Network to a raft of new titles from Microsoft Consumer Div., the folks in Redmond are working overtime to think of new ways to lure you from the TV to the PC. The Microsoft Network is intended to be a giant electronic bazaar of information and online shopping—with Microsoft taking a commission on all sales. Microsoft Home is readying dozens of Win95 titles for Christmas, including updates of the popular Encarta and Cinemania CD-ROMs and Fury, a new arcade action game.

Other software makers have a lot to lose. While a new operating system gives everybody in the industry a chance to create fresh applications programs, Microsoft is often the biggest winner. Take office applications. Before Windows 3.0 came out in 1990, Microsoft trailed in two key categories: word processing and spreadsheets. But the category leaders, WordPerfect Corp. and Lotus Development Corp.,   25 were slow to ship Windows versions of their packages. Now, Microsoft Office commands 80% of the market for suites–bundles containing word-processing and spreadsheet programs.

The lesson wasn't lost on Lotus, whose declining desktop software business helped make it takeover bait for IBM. The experience with Windows 3.0 is "one reason why we decided early we would go with Windows 95," says Ilene H. Lang, senior vice-president for desktop software at Lotus. Lotus plans to update its programs for Win95 "as soon as possible," she says. Analysts figure it will be yearend at best before a version of Lotus SmartSuite for Win95 hits the streets. That will give Microsoft only a three-month head start–rather than the two years it had with Windows 3.0. Novell Inc., which acquired WordPerfect last year and is the other top competitor in suites, isn't concerned about giving Microsoft a bit of a lead. "What's the big deal if you ship in August rather than October?" asks Glen D. Mellat, vice-president for marketing at Novell.

Some companies lucked out when Microsoft decided it could not complete some things it set out to do with Win95. When the program was under development, players in niche markets–such as fax, communications, and utility programs–were spooked by reports that their bread-and-butter products would become mere features in Windows 95. Delrina Corp., a $100 million maker of communications software based in Toronto, feared that Win95's communications software would torpedo its business. But, says President Mark Skapinker, Microsoft left room for a more sophisticated package such as Delrina's Winfax program. Still, he knows better than to rest easy. "It's not Win95 I worry about now, but Win96 and Win97."

Eppley of Traveling Software likens competing with Microsoft to mountain-bike riding, his favorite sport: "You have to be focused and looking ahead at the terrain," he says. So far, Eppley has prospered by exploiting holes in Microsoft's offerings. Microsoft has built into Win95 software for transferring files between a laptop and a network back at the office–just what his flagship product, LapLink, does. But Eppley found a hole. The next version of LapLink will work between Windows 95 computers and those running older versions of Windows–something Microsoft won't do. Compaq plans to ship LapLink on all of its Windows 95 PCs. "We think [Win95] will be a boost of 20% to 30% over our existing business, at least in the first couple of months," says Eppley.

MAC ATTACK

Another survivor: Symantec Corp., a maker of utility programs that keep PCs running smoothly by sniffing out viruses, cleaning cluttered disk drives, and diagnosing problems. With each version of Windows, Microsoft adds more such capabilities, but the latest version is less ambitious than planned. Symantec CEO Gordon E. Eubanks says he still has plenty of opportunity with Win95. In fact, investors have bid up Symantec shares by 50%–from around $20 to nearly $30 this year.

Microsoft's rivals in operating systems won't get off so easily. While Mac   30
lovers say Win95 just barely catches up with the Mac os, the differences may not be apparent to most consumers. "We have better technology, a better system story, an easier migration path," contends David C. Nagel, Apple's senior vice-president for research and development. But if Apple–and its new Mac-cloning partners– can't convince customers of that, the Mac os will become a tiny minority. Already, its share of the global PC market has slipped, to around 8.3% from its peak of 9.4% in 1993. Step one will be a huge Christmas-quarter marketing blitz–with an esti- mated $100 million budget range. "Otherwise," says Nagel, "we're in danger of get- ting drowned out in a tidal wave of information coming out of Redmond."

IBM's defense appears to be to pretend Win95 doesn't exist. IBM's Personal Software Products group, which once pushed its technically superior OS/2 as a "better Windows than Windows," is sitting on the sidelines. PSP execs say they won't try to find a way for OS/2 to run Win95 applications and will focus on persuad- ing developers to write programs for OS/2. "OS/2 is everything Windows 95 hopes to be," says PSP President Lee Reiswig. But analysts say IBM will have a hard time attracting developers, with less than 10% of the desktop market.

WIN-WIN

Big Blue will continue to take on Microsoft, however–just not on the desktop. The computer giant is shifting the battle to networked computing, where Microsoft remains relatively weak. With the $3.5 billion purchase of Lotus, IBM now looks relatively strong: Lotus Notes is the leading software package for helping people work together over a network.

If IBM can capitalize on Lotus by grabbing a commanding position in net- worked applications, it may not become a Win95 loser. But if IBM doesn't make its move quickly, it could get rolled over by Microsoft's next network-computing push, centered on Windows NT. An improved, slimmed-down version of NT re- leased last year has been gaining market share–especially as a system for running network servers. It also has the industrial-strength security and dependability characteristics that corporate customers demand–and that are absent from Win95. And next year, NT will get crowd-pleasing Win95 features such as the new user interface. That's why, when it comes to Win95, "it may make sense to skip it," says Don Delson, manager for office automation and workstations standards at Nestlé USA Inc.

Either way, Microsoft wins. NT is clearly the company's long-term strategic platform, and Win95, while a major step forward, is ultimately a placeholder for bigger things to come. In fact, Windows 95's most important role could be to set up a smooth transition to NT and its successors, including Cairo, a distributed operating system based on NT that is expected in 1997. To make sure developers of applications software know the route, Microsoft is forcing them to develop for both Win95 and NT. To qualify for the "Windows-compatible" stamp, a program must now work with both operating systems.

Windows 95 "is 10 steps forward. But it's not the end of what we want to do   35 with Windows," says Brad Chase, general manager of the Personal Systems Group. Those sentiments resonate back at the bug room. In answer to "Where do you want to go when we ship?" one tester has written: "To get a cup of coffee, then start work on Win96."

By Amy Cortese in New York, with Kathy Rebello in Redmond, Wash., and bureau reports

The Responsive Reader

1. How much do you learn from the article about the new product? Disregarding the hype or the hoopla, what can you learn from this article about the actual new features designed to make Windows 95 attractive to consumers? What improvements were considered desirable, and why? In what ways was the software designed to be a step forward?

2. What do you learn here about the marketing techniques of megacorporations? How would you describe the underlying strategy? Is the article itself part of the hype?

3. How and why, according to this article, would the Justice Department (or "the feds") get involved? What legal complications did Microsoft face? How important are they made to seem in this article?

4. What was the expected effect of Windows 95 on the rest of the industry—on competitors, on suppliers, on other software companies? What were the strategy options for major players like Apple or IBM?

For Discussion or Writing

5. How much are your own buying patterns influenced by advertising? How much is your own behavior as a consumer shaped by massive promotional campaigns? Have you ever become converted to a new product or a new service by a media blitz?

6. Do you think that generally in our society quality of product is becoming less important than effectiveness of promotion?

7. What has been your own experience with "klunky" aspects of computer use? Have any developments made computers more user-friendly or more student-friendly for you?

Collaborative Projects

8. Working with a group, you may want to analyze a particularly intensive or effective promotional campaign or launching of a new or improved product. (Or you may want to study a prominent campaign that was spectacularly *unsuccessful*, like the launching of a new and improved Coca-Cola.)

TROUBLED WATERS
Regulating the Fisheries

Deborah Cramer

> *Government regulation is an ever-present facet of the business world. Zoning laws prescribe who can build what and where. Emission standards determine what automobile engines may be sold. A government agency determines what medications will be considered safe and made available to the sick. Regulation is an emotion-charged political issue: Representatives of business and industry claim that overzealous regulation skews the play of market forces and burdens business with excessive costs. It drives companies out of business and costs workers jobs. On the other hand, consumer groups and environmentalists call for stricter controls on polluters, on promoters who prey on the old and sick, or on developers who destroy natural habitats.*
>
> *Attempts to regulate commercial fishing off the nation's shores provide an object lesson in the divided loyalties regulation inspires. Much of the bountiful marine life of earlier times has been depleted. The ocean-going whaling fleets or the sardine canneries of the California coast are no more. Today, fishing towns in Canada and on the American East Coast are threatened with the loss of their livelihood and a traditional way of life. The following article from the Atlantic magazine is a classic example of writing working its way from a problem to a solution. How serious is the emergency the author describes? Is government regulation the answer? Is it politically feasible?*

The New England groundfishery is collapsing. For hundreds of years Georges Bank, one of the world's most prolific fishing grounds, has produced seemingly inexhaustible supplies of cod, haddock, and yellowtail flounder–three species of bottom-dwellers known as groundfish. Today the bank's rich waters are nearly empty of those fish, which were once a mainstay of the New England fishing industry. The National Marine Fisheries Service (NMFS) has temporarily banned groundfishing in portions of New England's offshore waters, a stopgap measure designed to halt the destruction of the three fish species while regulators put together a long-term plan to save the fishery. Whether they have the backbone to pass measures sufficiently tough to replenish fish populations is an open question. Any plan short of prohibiting groundfishing on Georges Bank and yellowtail fishing in southern New England for at least four years, and severely curtailing codfishing in the Gulf of Maine, will be like previous management efforts–too little too late.

Cycles of boom and bust have characterized the New England fishery since its inception, but the current state of western North Atlantic groundfish populations is particularly grim. Stocks of cod, haddock, and yellowtail in the waters off New England are at or near record lows. In the mid-1960s landings of groundfish peaked at more than a billion and a half pounds a year. By 1993 the catch had been reduced by 85 percent.

Fish are like a savings account or an investment. With enough capital it's possible to live off the interest. Fishermen working New England's waters have not only spent the interest but also squandered the capital, taking an average of 60 percent of the entire population of cod, haddock, and yellowtail each year. Many of the fish caught are not yet mature. Others, though mature, are young, having spawned only once or twice. As a result, according to figures compiled by scientists at NMFS, spawning populations of Georges Bank cod, haddock, and yellowtail are a tenth of those the waters have historically supported. If spawning stocks had been maintained rather than depleted, these figures suggest, Georges Bank fishermen could be catching 217 million pounds of cod, haddock, and yellowtail each year. In 1993, the last year for which figures are available, the catch was only 66 million pounds; the totals for 1994 and 1995 are expected to be even lower. Fish and fishermen are in dire straits.

The New England cod, haddock, and yellowtail fisheries are not the first to face commercial extinction. Colonists once considered the abundant halibut a trash fish, unfit for consumption. By the 1830s, however, halibut had become desirable, and the demand for it in Boston markets had skyrocketed: individual boats on Georges Bank were bringing in 20,000 pounds of halibut a day. At that rate halibut was soon fished out. Today catches of Georges Bank halibut are so rare that regulators don't even keep statistics on them; it is as if this enormous fish (surpassed in size only by swordfish, certain sharks, and tuna) no longer existed in the northwest Atlantic.

The tasty redfish is slow-growing, taking five or six years to reach maturity,   5
and thus easily susceptible to overfishing. Redfish were in great demand in the 1930s and early 1940s. The large yearly catches, peaking at 130 million pounds from the Gulf of Maine in 1942, wiped out the fishery. It has yet to recover.

The propensity to ravage the sea is by no means unique to New England fishermen. The northern cod fishery in Canada is closed indefinitely. In Newfoundland more than 20,000 fishermen and fish processors were abruptly put out of work in 1992 when the government shut down the Grand Banks, where once-vast schools of cod, numbering in the hundreds of millions, had dwindled away: the population of spawning cod was a mere three percent of its potential. The closing of many of Canada's inshore fisheries soon followed. All along the coast of Nova Scotia boats lie idle at the docks. No one knows when, or if, fish stocks will recover. In the meantime, in order to protect what's left of their fishery, Canadians have resorted to gunboat diplomacy, chasing away Spanish trawlers by seizing one boat and cutting the nets from another.

On the other side of the Atlantic the story repeats itself: 65 million people live near the edges of the North Sea, and the fishermen of at least seven European nations compete there for the haddock, cod, and sole whose abundance will soon be no more than a memory. Scientists commonly use the words "mismanaged" and "overexploited" to describe groundfish populations in the North Sea–adjectives that have been appropriate there for quite some time. Each year the mortality rate of adult cod and haddock is 65 percent, and spawning populations are too small to replenish the stocks. Fishing pressure in the North Sea is so intense that not even one percent of the one-year-old cod remain in the sea long enough to spawn. Since catches of cod now consist primarily of immature fish, the prospects for survival of the population are not good.

As the great North Atlantic fisheries disappear, fishermen cast their nets in more-distant waters, off the coast of Africa and in the Indian Ocean, their large, sophisticated fleets easily displacing the smaller boats of less industrialized nations. Half the fish caught off the coast of western Africa are taken by foreign fleets and sold in international markets at prices too high for locals to pay. While some nations are beginning to charge for the rights to take their fish, the fees are low, sometimes no more than five percent of the value of the catch. Whatever limits are placed on the size of the catch are difficult to enforce, ensuring that without more effective management the African fisheries, too, are bound to disappear.

When the fisheries go, so will a critical source of protein. In the industrialized nations of the West, where people's diets are rich, perhaps too rich, in protein, fish is a luxury. In Africa and Asia fish is a nutritional necessity, supplying 19 and 29 percent respectively of the protein in people's diets. (In North America the figure is seven percent.) International markets are siphoning fish away from those who need it to those who merely want it–a process likely to result in food shortages in years to come.

Although the Atlantic fisheries have suffered the greatest declines, others are close behind. The United Nations Food and Agriculture Organization has determined that of seventeen world fisheries, four are in a state of commercial depletion and nine more are in serious decline. The amount of fish taken from the world's oceans peaked in the late 1980s and has begun to drop. The slowness of the fall is deceiving, masking the severity of a problem that has been building for some time.

More telling than the gently declining yield is the marked change in the composition of catches. The top ten species by weight no longer include the prized cod and haddock. High on the list are species such as mackerel and pilchard, fish with low market value, which are used in the production of fish meal. Fish meal is not sold for human consumption; it is fed to livestock, pets, and, ironically, farmed fish. The Worldwatch Institute estimates that if the mackerel, pilchard, and anchovies going into fish meal were used instead to feed people, the amount of fish for human consumption would be 40 percent greater.

Unlike minerals or oil, fish is a renewable resource. Properly managed stocks could regularly supply greater quantities of fish and higher incomes for fishermen than are possible at present. Judiciously managed fisheries could yield a 23 percent increase in the fish harvest worldwide and an additional $15 billion to $30 billion a year for the industry. Steven Murawski, a fish-population biologist, and Steven Edwards, an economist, both with the NMFS, calculate that the waters off New England could support a groundfish population at least seven times as large as to-day's and an annual yield at least three times as great.

For years NMFS scientists have been warning fishery managers that unless the number of groundfish taken each year from Georges Bank was reduced, valuable groundfish stocks would disappear. First yellowtail flounder populations collapsed, then haddock. Last August scientists reported that the cod population was on the brink of collapse. If it was to be saved, the number of cod taken each year had to be reduced immediately, to as close as possible to zero.

Though the numbers that scientists use to predict fish populations and to cal-culate how many fish can safely be landed may have a large margin of error, the downward population trends, which show up in surveys year after year, are indis-putable. For more than a decade NMFS scientists predicted the crash of the Georges Bank fishery, but they were Cassandras in the tragedy enacted by fisher-men and regulators, foretelling the future to an audience unable or unwilling to hear. In New England, Canada, and Europe fishery managers have downplayed and resisted implementing recommendations from their science advisers, using the inexactness of science as an excuse to favor industry, where the political payoff is greater, rather than the resource.

Indeed, for years politics has played a central role in the management of Amer-   15
ican fisheries. In 1976 fishermen anxious to expel foreign competitors from what were traditionally considered U.S. fishing grounds successfully lobbied Congress to pre-empt the Law of the Sea negotiations by passing the Magnuson Fishery Con-servation and Management Act, which immediately and unilaterally extended U.S. jurisdiction to 200 miles offshore. Under this law regulation of the fishing industry has been in the hands of the NMFS and regional fishery-management councils. The New England council has been dominated by fishermen who tend to put the short-term economic health of their profession above the long-term health of the fishery.

In the early years of the Magnuson Act, however, the council did set quotas for the New England catch, and cod, yellowtail, and haddock populations were recov-ering. But local fishermen soon filled the niche vacated by foreign boats, and the New England fleet almost doubled. As the number of boats equipped with precision-navigation systems and high-resolution fish-finding sonar grew, fisher-men began to chafe under the quotas and to lobby for their elimination. Council members, swayed by the pleas of their colleagues, replaced the quotas with other, less direct controls. As the current abysmally low populations of cod, yellowtail, and haddock show, these measures–for example, regulating the size of mesh in nets, setting minimum sizes for fish landed, and closing spawning areas–have been decidedly ineffective.

In 1989 NMFS scientists predicted the eventual collapse of cod, haddock, and yellowtail in New England and recommended that "fishing effort"–fishermen's days at sea–on those stocks be reduced by about half. In 1991 the council, prodded by a lawsuit brought by the Conservation Law Foundation, took steps to implement that recommendation. Seeking a politically palatable solution that would not devastate the fishing industry, the council proposed to halve fishing effort at the rate of 10 percent a year over five years. Still, fishermen were angry, and took their objections directly to the New England congressional delegation.

A bill that was introduced in Congress would have further slowed the stock-rebuilding program, spreading it out over seven to ten years. Though the bill was never made into law, it undermined the council, impeding its efforts to turn its plan into regulation. By the time all compromises had been made, appeals heard, and exemptions granted, it was 1994. Yellowtail were long gone, haddock had collapsed, and cod were well on their way. The fish that the council's plan had been designed to protect were already in deep trouble.

Today the New England Fishery Management Council is in a quandary. Cod, haddock, and yellowtail stocks are so low on Georges Bank that only drastic measures will stabilize and restore them. The same is true for yellowtail in southern New England. If regulators ban all fishing on these stocks as well as the scalloping and whiting fishing on Georges Bank that take incidental bycatches of the three depleted species, then after four to ten years cod and yellowtail will be well on their way to recovery. Even under these stringent prohibitions, haddock will take ten to fifteen years to recover, and redfish and, with luck, halibut twenty to twenty-five.

In the Gulf of Maine immediately halving the number of cod taken could replenish diminishing cod stocks. Regulators dragged their feet implementing similar regulations on Georges Bank. If they do so here, in a few years Gulf of Maine cod may be as rare as Georges Bank cod is today.

20

Closing Georges Bank to groundfishing and scalloping, and limiting ground fishing in the Gulf of Maine and southern New England, will in the long run create a healthy resource and an economically healthy industry. In the short run such an action will abruptly put fishermen out of work. But half measures will do nothing to prevent the industry's slow death; the fleet will be reduced as boats are abandoned or repossessed. Short-term prospects for New England fishermen are bleak no matter what.

The costs of failing to manage a fishery for the long-term health of the resource are high. The Canadian government has spent more than $1 billion to bail out its ailing industry, and expects to spend another $1.5 billion over the next five years to develop job opportunities and provide income and retraining to the thousands of fishermen and fish processors who have lost their jobs. This subsidy far exceeds the annual value of the catch, which in Newfoundland, for example, used to be about $125 million.

It will be difficult and costly to limit groundfishing in New England. It will be equally challenging to manage fisheries wisely if stocks are ever restored. Managers will need to reinstitute direct controls, such as quotas. Nineteen years of New England fisheries management under the Magnuson Act has shown that indirect controls alone do not work. Reducing fishermen's days at sea does not necessarily result in a commensurate reduction in the number of fish harvested, particularly when gear and technology are regularly being improved. To preserve New England's fisheries, it will be essential to set quotas that are designed to protect the health of a fishery, not the short-term economic needs of fishermen. If those who set quotas are not somehow removed from the pressures of industry lobbying, the mistakes of fishery managers in the United States, Canada, and Europe will be repeated and quotas will be set too high.

Any workable management plan will require that a financial commitment be made to enforce it, with satellite trackers on boats to preclude poaching in closed spawning areas, and dockside inspections to prohibit the illegal landing of fish, and observers on boats to prevent "high-grading" (throwing quota stocks overboard to make room for more-valuable fish) and the underreporting of incidental catches.

Pressure on world fisheries can only increase. Since redfish were cleaned out of New England's fisheries fifty years ago, the world's population has nearly tripled, to 5.5 billion, and it is still rising rapidly. In the face of ever increasing demand for fish, regulators must break the long-standing, deeply rooted tendency, pervasive throughout our culture, to squander natural resources. They must have the strength to limit fishing for as long as it takes for the stocks to return. And then they must regulate the fishery to be self-sustaining, not leave it open for fishermen to exhaust again.

The Responsive Reader

1. What statistics does Cramer marshal to dramatize the current emergency? On what other evidence does she draw?

2. What regulatory remedies does Cramer recommend? Does she make a convincing case for them?

3. Does Cramer show that she is aware of the economic costs or the human costs of the solution she embraces? Where or how?

For Discussion or Writing

4. Prepare a presentation (oral or written) to a regulatory agency or to concerned legislators. Concur with or take issue with Cramer's recommendations. Is there a free-market alternative to her solutions?

5. Do you agree with Cramer that there is a "long-standing, deeply rooted tendency, pervasive in our culture, to squander natural resources"? Research a striking test case for the waste or wise management of natural resources in an area other than the fishing industry. Prepare a report on your findings.

Collaborative Projects

6. Working with a group, can you find data on a parallel situation–for instance, whaling, salmon fishing, crab fishing, lobster fishing? What is the current situation–how does it compare with what Cramer describes? What does the future hold? What is the merit of suggested solutions?

CANADA'S CULTURE COPS

Nina Munk

> *Supporters of free enterprise believe in free trade. World-wide prosperity will result when trade freely crosses borders, linking countries around the world in a global economy. In practice, however, free trade runs into obstacles: Governments impose high tariffs to protect farmers who otherwise could not compete with cheap foreign wheat or rice. Coal mines and steel mills are subsidized to save them from going under as cheap imported coal and steel flood the market. Labor unions fight the loss of jobs to low-wage countries. The American entertainment industry runs into special roadblocks to the penetration of foreign markets: Governments bent on preserving the national culture try to shield their citizens from the American popular culture that dominates the air waves around the world. Often they object particularly to the American emphasis on sex and violence— what one French critic called the "culture of brutality." However, as the following article shows, the war against American "cultural imperialism" is often fought on a broader front.*

Peter G. owns an electronics store in the Toronto area. Every two or three weeks he drives his van an hour and a half south to Buffalo, N.Y., where he loads up on 18-inch RCA brand satellite dishes from a large electronics retailer. He pays $699, plus tax, for a basic model, including the set-top receiver/decoder and remote control. On his return north he pays Canadian federal sales tax at the border, bringing his cost to $808 per dish. Back home he'll sell the dishes for about $1,100 each, plus $150 for installation.

With ten dishes in his van, that's a nice $4,420 profit for what amounts to a day's work. Peter is shopping for Toronto-area customers who want DirecTV, the new direct broadcast satellite service from GM Hughes Electronics that lets them watch U.S. channels like HBO, the Disney Channel and ESPN.

These channels are banned by the Canadian government, which deems them corrosive of Canadian culture. The Canadian culture cops have pressured El Segundo, Calif.-based DirecTV into refusing to switch on service for anyone with a Canadian address. Thomson Consumer Electronics has followed suit by cutting off deliveries of its RCA dishes to Canadian retailers.

But the law is fuzzy. It is perfectly legal for Canadians to buy dishes–or anything else–in the U.S. To get around the switch-on and billing restrictions, Peter G. charges his customers $75 a year for a U.S. address from which DirecTV's $29.95 monthly bills are automatically forwarded. To prevent DirecTV from recognizing Canadian area codes, he installs a modem that redirects outgoing telephone calls through a U.S. number.

Peter G. is by no means the only gray marketeer plying this trade. Dave Orrico, sales manager for Rosa's Superstores in upstate New York, reports that Rosa's in Niagara Falls, N.Y., just across the border from Niagara Falls, Ont., sells more 18-inch RCA dishes than the chain's five other stores combined. "We do see a lot of Ontario [license] plates in our parking lot," Orrico says.

As many as 30,000 Canadians now receive DirecTV's 150 channels of crisp digital pictures with CD-quality sound, and the number grows. "I like the American stuff for the simple reason that I can watch what I want," explains William Vanderboer, who's hooked up to DirecTV in Fort Langley, B.C., just east of Vancouver.

But the Canadian politicians still think they are living in the days when all-wise governments decided what people could read and watch. The Canadian Radio-television & Telecommunications Commission has been mandated by the Canadian Parliament to "maintain and enhance" Canadian culture—whatever that is. For every U.S. channel that goes into the home, the CRTC says there must be at least one Canadian channel. Since the number of Canadian channels is limited, so too is the number of available U.S. channels. The result is a host of copycat made-in-Canada networks: something called MuchMusic in place of the forbidden MTV; and The Sports Network, or TSN, that's ESPN in all but name—and quality.

Another CRTC rule requires that at least 60% of a conventional Canadian channel's programming qualify as "Canadian content." A program qualifies as Can-Con by receiving points, up to a maximum of ten, according to the nationality of the TV program's creative team. Six points or more and a program gets the CanCon seal of approval.

After operating in Canada for ten years, Nashville's Country Music Television channel learned firsthand of a rule that allows the CRTC to outlaw any non-Canadian TV service that competes with a Canadian service. In January Canadian officials kicked the channel off the airwaves to make way for a new, homegrown version called The Country Network.

What is this Canadian culture the government is trying to protect? A Canadian   10
from Toronto has more in common with a Bostonian than with someone from Alberta. Outside Quebec—which is largely autonomous, anyhow—it's hard to pinpoint anything distinctly Canadian. Canadian jokesters define a Canadian as an unarmed American with Medicare.

But don't try that on Ian Morrison, head of the chauvinistic lobby group Friends of Canadian Broadcasting. "A typical Canadian 10-year-old kid watches 900 hours of television a year, and more than 80% is American," says he. "That weakens the sense of belonging and identity that are the key factors in nationhood."

Is all this culture ruckus just a cover for protecting a few Canadian special interests? Of course. So, last month, after Canada shut down Nashville's Country Music Television, U.S. Trade Representative Mickey Kantor announced an investigation into Canada's denial of market access for U.S. programming services. But Peter G. couldn't care less. How else could he clear $4,420 in a single day?

The Responsive Reader

1. What is a chauvinist? According to this article, how does the Canadian government try to protect Canadian culture from American influence? Were you surprised by some of the rulings and initiatives?
2. Why does this article from *Forbes* magazine start with the story of Peter G.? What is the writer's attitude toward the Canadian government efforts? Where does it show most strongly or most clearly?
3. Do you think the Canadian government has a point? Why or why not?

For Discussion or Writing

4. Have you observed or have you read of other attempts to control the free flow of ideas or entertainment across borders? (What were the motives and results?) Do you think Americans are wary of foreign influences? In what areas?
5. Are you aware of free trade as a political and economic issue? What are current controversies or arguments? Do you feel in any way personally concerned?

Collaborative Projects

6. Many objections to American culture influence abroad center on sex and violence on the screen. Movies recognized as milestones in the history of cinematic violence include Sam Peckinpah's *The Wild Bunch* (first shown in 1969 and recently remastered), the original *Bonnie and Clyde*, and Oliver Stone's *Natural Born Killers*. Working with a group, you may want to plan a panel discussion on violence in the movies—examining such topics as the psychology of violence, the relation between violence on the screen and violence in the larger culture, or censorship issues.

THE LESSON FROM BARINGS' STRAITS

Paula Dwyer AND *William Glasgall*

Banks used to inspire confidence by doing business in buildings with classical columns and marble walls. In the great crash of 1929, neither the marble nor the dignified bearing of bankers protected customers' savings from going up in smoke. In the Savings and Loans scandal of the eighties, taxpayers bailed out the financial community to the tune of more than $350 billion. What have savers, investors, and taxpayers learned from the great disasters? In the computerized modern world of finance, little actual money changes hands. Computer programs kick in to initiate currency trades or stock trades according to preset specifications. Nameless individuals with little or no personal liability have the authority to make deals that can balloon into billion-dollar profits—or losses. In 1995, Kidder Peabody, a brokerage firm, alleged that one of its traders, Joseph Jett, had generated $350 million in phony trading profits, causing the company to declare a $210 million loss. Nick Leeson, a 28-year-old British securities trader based in Singapore, who had been given a million-dollar bonus by his employers the previous year, ran up a $1.38 billion loss in Asian future markets and forced the 233-year-old British securities house he worked for to declare bankruptcy and shut down. Leeson, the son of a plasterer, fled as the bank crumbled but was eventually extradited to Singapore to stand trial. Arriving at the Singapore airport, he wore a baseball cap turned backward.

It's a long way from the dreary public-housing complex in the London suburb of Watford, where Nick Leeson grew up as a plasterer's son, to Singapore's exclusive Orchard Road section. The cocksure head of futures trading in Barings PLC's Singapore office, Leeson earned a $1 million bonus last year, drove a Porsche, and sailed his yacht on weekends off Malaysia. But all that came crashing down with the revelation that Leeson, 28, had piled up $1.3 billion in losses on spoiled derivative deals in Singapore and Osaka.

In one humiliating blow, Leeson's huge trading loss wiped out the blue-blood investment bank's $900 million in capital and prompted the Bank of England to put Barings into bankruptcy. The collapse also sent shivers down the spines of bankers around the globe. "With so much money moving around so quickly, this is the kind of thing all of us worry about," says First Chicago Corp. CEO Richard L. Thomas. "It's stunning to think that a 233-year-old institution can be brought to its knees overnight."

EYE-POPPING

Stunning, perhaps. But not totally surprising. Over the past year or so, one financial shock after another has hit the front pages and CNN. A common thread runs through them: In the global liquidity boom of the early 1990s, when more than $1.5 trillion in U.S. mutual-fund money flooded the globe, money was so available, markets so ebullient, and profits so rich that simple safeguards and controls went by the board. Now, as interest rates rise and the margin for error narrows, many are paying a high price for inattention. Says New York economist Henry Kaufman: "Whether it's Mexico or Barings, these problems reflect inadequate monitoring and supervision."

By any standard, the list of financial accidents since 1994 is eye-popping. Hedge-fund manager George Soros, for example, dropped $600 million by misjudging the strength of the Japanese yen. Procter & Gamble Co. lost $102 million on leveraged derivatives purchased from Bankers Trust Co. The venerable investment house of Kidder, Peabody & Co. was sold off and dismembered after Joseph Jett allegedly ran up $350 million in paper profits on bogus bond deals. Wealthy Orange County, Calif., went bust when its treasurer made a spectacularly wrong bet on the direction of rates. And Mexico, the darling of emerging markets, had to seek a $53 billion international bailout after its debt-fueled economy ran out of hard cash.

Now, Barings joins the casualty list. Administrators from Ernst & Young are   5 selling off pieces of the firm. The Dutch bank ABN Amro is buying Barings' corporate finance unit, and Merrill Lynch & Co. and Dresdner Bank may bid for other parts. But long after the disposal is over, regulators and financiers will still be asking whether Barings' situation was unique. Many think not. Warns Bank of England Governor Eddie George: "What happened to Barings could happen to any financial institution in the world." Especially if one individual is given enough leeway to bet the entire store.

SLOSH OF FUNDS

In the easy-money boom, too many securities executives lost the ability or will to scrutinize high-energy traders or guard against unethical salespeople. Too many bankers and CFOs neglected to ask whether they understood the complexity–or the downside–of the highly leveraged derivatives they were using to hedge financial risks. And as an influx of some $300 billion in foreign portfolio money sent stock and bond markets soaring in developing countries, too many investors and fund managers stopped asking basic questions about disclosure, accounting, value, and risk.

Fortunately, the accidents of 1994 and '95 have not brought the financial world to its knees. Even with the Federal Reserve and some European central banks tightening, so many trillions of investment dollars are still sloshing around the globe that it's hard for any one event to disturb the momentum for long. In fact, faced with adversity, the global capital market has done a credible job of making capital flow from the basket cases to the healthy.

The affair has caused soul-searching among financiers worldwide. "If this happened at an institution that's supposed to be high quality, what's going on at lesser investment banks?" asks Henry T. C. Hu, a University of Texas professor and derivatives expert. "Perhaps we've been too complacent, and things aren't as clean as people thought."

Chastened, the world's exchange officials, central bankers, and financiers also want to know how the Barings meltdown happened and how they might prevent another one. What they are learning is nothing short of remarkable. It shouldn't be possible, but a lone trader bought enough futures and options contracts in three weeks to amass a $27 billion bet. His local bosses, the exchange regulators in three Asian cities, and Barings' managers in London stayed in the dark.

Leeson's trading-floor peers knew something was up. But they didn't sound the alarm, because Barings had been taking huge positions for years in Nikkei stock-index futures as part of a low-risk arbitrage operation that tried to profit from minute price differences in contracts traded in Singapore and Osaka. Then, around Jan. 26, Leeson mysteriously switched from arb to speculator. He converted all his contracts to buys—most likely in the belief that the destruction caused by the recent Kobe earthquake would stimulate the economy and push up the Nikkei.

When the stock market didn't cooperate, Leeson sold put and call options to raise cash for margin calls and bet that the market would settle into a narrow range. But as the Nikkei continued falling, Leeson is thought to have made one last roll of the dice on Feb. 20.

His losses had accumulated to about $700 million, and the exchanges wanted Barings to put up more cash to cover his deficit. The Bank of England says Leeson then fooled Barings officials in London into writing checks for margin calls, likely by saying the trades were on behalf of a corporate client whose funds would be deposited with Barings in a few days. When he couldn't produce the funds, Leeson fled, leaving behind a note saying: "I'm sorry."

What went wrong is simple: Barings allowed Leeson to wear too many hats. Preliminary investigations discovered that Leeson was both trader and manager, often settling his own trades. That was in violation of Osaka exchange rules and of industry practice, which keeps traders apart from back-office staffers who confirm transactions and write checks. "Leeson was the front office and the back office," says Graham Newall, head of futures trading at Barclays Bank PLC. "You can't stop someone from going berserk, but you can have a system to catch it in 24 hours."

NO RANDOM CHECKS

A Barings source says Leeson was allowed to clear trades because of his previous experience as a settlement clerk at Morgan Stanley & Co. Whatever the reason, critics say Barings clearly lacked the most elemental of security systems to keep track of its traders' activities. For example, Daniel Hodson, CEO of the London International Financial Futures Exchange, believes that Barings lacked informal, back-channel communication links with exchanges, as well as simple random checks of how well its personnel followed rules. And many outside observers say Barings management neglected to investigate why the firm's trading volume was soaring.

To catch such discrepancies, some investment banks, including Merrill Lynch, now have independent risk-management units reporting directly to the CEO. Merrill set its unit up after losing $377 million from unauthorized trading in 1987. But at Barings, says Peter Letley, deputy chairman of HSBC Investment Banking Ltd., "there were no independent controls." That's all the more dangerous when traders are dealing with derivative contracts whose value can fluctuate wildly even on small movements in stock, bond, or currency prices. Says Robert Gumerlock, managing director for risk control at Swiss Bank Corp.: "Derivatives can give you enough leverage to blow yourself up."

Paying too little heed to this reality can be a big problem for all kinds of companies. Abraham M. George, CEO of Multinational Computer Models Inc., helps international corporations manage currency and interest-rate risk. A typical portfolio these days, he notes, may contain a bewildering array of fixed and floating-rate debt, swaps that switch among currencies, options, structured notes, and more. He doubts whether many executives even know if their own treasurers understand the quirky behavior of the instruments in their portfolios. Asks George: "When you have a complex position, do senior managers know what it's worth at any given time?"   15

LURE OF LUCRE

Investors are asking much the same question of mutual funds, which moved more than $300 billion overseas in the 1990s in search of high returns in emerging markets. It may have been this flood of foreign capital, as much as economic and political reforms, that enabled emerging-market bourses to outperform those in industrial countries by nearly 3 to 1 in the early '90s.

But as markets climbed, many novice fund managers abandoned common sense for the lure of a quick buck. Eagerly acquiring Chilean bank stocks at twice book value or Thai telecom issues with price-earnings ratios of 100, "they understood how to run models, but they didn't really understand whether their earnings estimates were meaningful," says Bruce B. Bee, a veteran global money manager in

Denver. So when liquidity started to erode last year, many markets that were high on U.S. cash swiftly returned to more normal valuations.

What should be done about the oversight gap? The solution probably isn't more regulation. The Bank of England is now under fire for missing another major case of deception, having taken heat from the 1991 failure of Bank of Credit & Commerce International (BCCI). But "don't talk to me about rules," snaps central bank chief George. "We've got rules galore. Unfortunately, we've also got criminals."

Some of these will always slip through holes in the system. But as Barings executives found out too late, a far greater willingness to ask tough questions–in good times and bad–might have kept the historic investment bank alive. When the market dishes out discipline, whether because of Mexico's economic misdeeds or Barings' trading scandal, punishment can be swift and severe. By refusing to bail out Barings, the Bank of England made that point crystal clear. Not every failure can be prevented. But a good deal more skepticism would go a long way toward limiting the losses.

By Paula Dwyer in London and William Glasgall in New York, with Dean Foust in Washington and Greg Burns in Chicago

The Responsive Reader

1. What is the author's verdict on whether the Barings disaster was unique–an isolated accident, a fluke? How much of a threat do they see to the banking system in general? On what do they base their conclusions?

2. What actually happened? What banking or investment terms does the reader need to understand what was going on? (What are derivatives? What are margin calls?)

3. In what other areas do the authors see risks similar to those that brought Barings down?

4. Is there a lesson to be learned from the Barings case? To judge from this article, what safeguards are needed? What kind of supervision or restraints are possible or desirable?

For Discussion or Writing

5. How knowing or how innocent is the average person about financial dealings that make a splash in business magazines or on the business pages of newspapers? For instance, what are price-earning ratios? What have you heard about insider trading? What do you know about junk bonds? How do leveraged buy-outs work?

6. Have developments in the financial world–interest rates or credit policies, for instance–impacted your life or that of friends or family?

Collaborative Projects

7. In the early nineties, Orange County, one of the wealthiest and most conservative counties in California, declared bankruptcy after its investment manager engineered a $1.7 billion loss. According to *Business Week*, "the loss ate into operating funds badly needed by schools, water districts, and the county itself." Working with a group, you may want to investigate the nature and repercussions of one such investment debacle.

FORUM: *Business and the Consumer*

> *The customer is king, says Paul Samuelson in "Supply and Demand." Not all customers agree. Consumer groups or watchdog organizations variously picture the consumer as an easy target, as easily manipulated by savvy professionals, or as a lamb led to the slaughter. Caveat emptor is an old Roman motto—"let the buyer beware." Is this still the motto today? How much consumer education is there in our society?*

ASTROTURF LOBBYISTS SPROUT ALL OVER

Leah Garchik

> *Public relations is big business. Highly paid consultants polish the image of corporations, promote a business agenda, or influence legislation affecting business interests. Consumer groups, watchdog organizations, and whistleblowers in the media are hard put to keep up with well-funded, well-organized PR work—often traveling under the banner of public service. (Molly Ivins, columnist for the Fort Worth* Star-Telegram, *identified key members of a Coalition to Save Medicare as the National Association of Manufacturers and the U.S. Chamber of Commerce, both of which, she says, "opposed Medicare from the beginning.") Leah Garchik is a columnist with a lively sense of irony and a great sense of humor who often chronicles the foibles and fatuous pronouncements of people in the public eye. She here reports on the protective coloring public relations people and lobbyists adopt in dealing with the public.*

"It's important not to look like a Washington lobbyist," said a "grass-roots public relations" professional quoted in the newsletter PR Watch. "When I go to a zoning board meeting I wear absolutely no makeup. I comb my hair straight back in a ponytail and I wear my kid's old clothes. You don't want to look like you're someone from Washington, or someone from a corporation."

The new breed of "astroturf lobbyists," says the newsletter, are professional people motivated by professional contracts who masquerade as just plain folks motivated by their own personal interests. Many operate under the umbrella of public-spirited-sounding organizations backed by corporate interests.

"In naming your coalition . . . use words identified in your research," said public relations consultant **Blair Childs.** "There are certain words that . . . have a general positive reaction. . . . 'Fairness,' 'balance,' 'choice,' 'coalition' and 'alliance' are all words that resonate very positively."

When Philip Morris backed a California initiative that would protect the rights of smokers, for example, the company cloaked itself as "Californians for Statewide Smoking Restrictions." The following list of group names and a few of their sponsors is from PR Watch editor **John Stauber**:

- Alliance to Keep America Working, an anti-union organization financed by the U.S. Chamber of Commerce and big companies.
- American Council on Science and Health, calls environmentalists "unscientific," funded by chemical manufacturers.
- Citizens for a Sound Economy, fights health care reform and warning labels on substances such as alcohol, financed by tobacco and alcohol companies.
- Coalition for Vehicle Choice, against pollution and fuel regulations, funded by auto manufacturers.
- Institute for Justice, anti-environmental regulation, funded by Philip Morris, among others.
- National Wetlands Coalition, in favor of wetland development, funded by Chevron, Shell Oil and others.
- Safe Buildings Alliance, funded by asbestos and insulation manufacturers such as Owens Corning.
- Sea Lion Defense Fund, lobbies for increasing legal fish catch, funded by Alaskan fishing industry.
- United States Council for Energy Awareness, pro-nuclear, funded by General Electric and Westinghouse.
- Wilderness Impact Research Foundation, funded by National Cattleman's Association and other groups with mining, ranching, oil and gas investments.

Sample copies of the newsletter can be ordered from the Center for Media and Democracy, 3318 Gregory Street, Madison, Wis. 53711.

The Responsive Reader

1. What do you learn here about the strategies or ploys of PR professionals? Do you think dress is important? What's in a name? Do you perceive a common denominator or recurrent trends in the names of the organizations cited? (What would be your choices if you were a member of a jury asked to select best and worst?)

For Discussion or Writing

2. Are you an easy mark for the kind of "astroturf lobbyist" described in this article? How skeptical or how trusting are you as a target of business PR?
3. In the summer of 1995, an NRA lobbyist admitted feeding the press "The

People's Voice" contributions under an assumed, innocuous-sounding name masking his identity as a well-known lobbyist. Do you think such tactics are justified in the rough-and-tumble struggle to shape public opinion? Why or why not? Where would you draw the line?

Collaborative Projects

4. Euphemisms are part of the stock-in-trade of the PR business. Euphemisms are harmless-sounding or reassuring labels for grim facts, like "breathing your last" for death. (George Will called the trend toward low-paying temporary or part-time employment "a rearranging of jobs.") Working with a group, study the role of euphemistic language in customer service bulletins, chamber-of-commerce literature, corporate newsletters, institutional press releases, or the like.

THE RUINATION OF THE TOMATO

Mark Kramer

> *The traditional business credo asserts that business gives customers what they want. The following article examines a test case for a different theory: Businesses sell what is profitable. If what the customer wants is not profitable, the customer is out of luck. People who love tomatoes want vine-ripened, deep red, luscious tomatoes whose pungent aroma teases the nostrils and whose soft juicy meat melts on the tongue. More often than not, what the customer gets is a half-ripe, rubbery, knobby tomato without a tomato smell or taste. The following study, a classic of its kind, tries to explain why. Mark Kramer, who was a student at Brandeis University and Columbia University, is not an armchair critic who snipes at agribusiness from a distance. He became a farmer in Western Massachusetts who wrote (and made a film) about country life and the "high human costs" of the changes wrought by new technology and new business structures in American agriculture. His research for this article took him to the fields to talk to workers, supervisors, and company representatives; it made him pore over relevant research and statistics.*

Sagebrush and lizards rattle and whisper behind me. I stand in the moonlight, the hot desert at my back. It's tomato harvest time, 3 A.M. The moon is almost full and near to setting. Before me stretches the first lush tomato field to be taken this morning. The field is farmed by a company called Tejon Agricultural Partners, and lies three hours northeast of Los Angeles in the middle of the bleak, silvery drylands of California's San Joaquin Valley. Seven hundred sixty-six acres, more than a mile square of tomatoes–a shaggy, vegetable-green rug dappled with murky red dots, 105,708,000 ripe tomatoes lurking in the night. The field is large and absolutely level. It would take an hour and a half to walk around it. Yet, when I raise my eyes past the field to the much vaster valley floor, and to the mountains that loom farther out, the enormous crop is lost in a big flat world.

This harvest happens nearly without people. A hundred million tomatoes grown, irrigated, fed, sprayed, now taken, soon to be cooled, squashed, boiled, barreled, and held at the ready, then canned, shipped, sold, bought, and after being sold and bought a few more times, uncanned and dumped on pizza. And such is the magnitude of the vista, and the dearth of human presence, that it is easy to look elsewhere and put this routine thing out of mind. But that quality–of blandness overlaying a wondrous integration of technology, finances, personnel, and business systems–seems to be what the "future" has in store.

Three large tractors steam up the road toward me, headlights glaring, towing three thin-latticed towers which support floodlights. The tractors drag the towers into place around an assembly field, then hydraulic arms raise them to vertical. They illuminate a large, sandy work yard where equipment is gathering—fuel trucks, repair trucks, concession trucks, harvesters, tractor-trailers towing big open hoppers. Now small crews of Mexicans, their sunburns tinted light blue in the glare of the three searchlights, climb aboard the harvesters; shadowy drivers mount tractors and trucks. The night fills with the scent of diesel fumes and with the sound of large engines running evenly.

The six harvesting machines drift across the gray-green tomato-leaf sea. After a time, the distant ones come to look like steamboats afloat across a wide bay. The engine sounds are dispersed. A company foreman dashes past, tally sheets in hand. He stops nearby only long enough to deliver a one-liner. "We're knocking them out like Johnny-be-good," he says, punching the air slowly with his right fist. Then he runs off, laughing.

The nearest harvester draws steadily closer, moving in at about the speed of a   5
slow amble, roaring as it comes. Up close, it looks like the aftermath of a collision between a grandstand and a San Francisco tram car. It's two stories high, rolls on wheels that don't seem large enough, astraddle a wide row of jumbled and un-staked tomato vines. It is not streamlined. Gangways, catwalks, gates, conveyors, roofs, and ladders are fastened all over the lumbering rig. As it closes in, its front end snuffles up whole tomato plants as surely as a hungry pig loose in a farmer's garden. Its hind end excretes a steady stream of stems and rejects. Between the in-gestion and the elimination, fourteen laborers face each other on long benches. They sit on either side of a conveyor that moves the new harvest rapidly past them. Their hands dart out and back as they sort through the red stream in front of them.

Watching them is like peering into the dining car of a passing train. The folks aboard, though, are not dining but working hard for low wages, culling what is not quite fit for pizza sauce—the "greens," "molds," "mechanicals," and the odd tomato-sized clod of dirt which has gotten past the shakers and screens that tug tomato from vine and dump the harvest onto the conveyor.

The absorbing nature of the work is according to plan. The workers aboard this tiny outpost of a tomato sauce factory are attempting to accomplish a chore at which they cannot possibly succeed, one designed in the near past by some anonymous practitioner of the new craft of *management*. As per cannery contract, each truckload of tomatoes must contain no more than 4 percent green tomatoes, 3 percent tomatoes suffering mechanical damage from the harvester, 1 percent tomatoes that have begun to mold, and .5 percent clods of dirt.

"The whole idea of this thing," a farm executive had explained earlier in the day, "is to get as many tons as you can per hour. Now, the people culling on the machines strive to sort everything that's defective. But to us, that's as bad as them picking out too little. We're getting $40 to $47 a ton for tomatoes—a bad price this year—and each truckload is 50,000 pounds, 25 tons, 1100 bucks a load. If we're

allowed 7 or 8 percent defective tomatoes in the load and we don't have 7 or 8 percent defective tomatoes in the load, we're giving away money. And what's worse,
we're paying these guys to make the load too good. It's a double loss. Still, you
can't say to your guys, 'Hey, leave 4 percent greens and 1 percent molds when you
sort the tomatoes on that belt.' It's impossible. On most jobs you strive for perfection. They do. But you want to stop them just the right amount short of perfection–because the cannery will penalize you if your load goes over spec. So what
you do is run the belt too fast, and sample the percentages in the output from each
machine. If the load is too poor, we add another worker. If it's too good, we send
someone home."

The workers converse as they ride the machine toward the edge of the desert.
Their lips move in an exaggerated manner, but they don't shout. The few workers
still needed at harvest time have learned not to fight the machine. They speak under, rather than over, the din of the harvest. They chat, and their hands stay constantly in fast motion. . . . Just a few years ago, when harvesting of cannery
tomatoes was still done by hand, ten times the labor was required on the same
acreage to handle a harvest that yielded only a third of what growers expect these
days. The transformation of the tomato industry has happened in the course of
about twenty years.   10

Much has been written recently about this phenomenon, and with good reason. The change has been dramatic, and is extreme. Tomatoes we remember from
the past tasted rich, delicate, and juicy. Tomatoes hauled home in today's grocery
bag taste bland, tough, and dry. The new taste is the taste of modern agriculture.

The ruination of the tomato was a complex procedure. It required cooperation
from financial, engineering, marketing, scientific, and agricultural parties that used
to go their separate ways more and cross paths with less intention. Now larger institutions control the money that consumers spend on tomatoes. It is no more
possible to isolate a "cause" for this shift than it is possible to claim that it's the
spark plugs that cause a car to run. However, we can at least peer at the intricate
machinery that has taken away our tasty tomatoes and given us pale, scientific
fruit.

Let us start then, somewhat arbitrarily, with processors of tomatoes, especially
with the four canners–Del Monte, Heinz, Campbell, and Libby, McNeill & Libby–
that sell 72 percent of the nation's tomato sauce. What has happened to the quality of tomatoes in general follows from developments in the cannery tomato trade.

The increasingly integrated processors have consolidated, shifted, and "recon-
ceptualized" their plants. In the fast world of marketing processed tomatoes, the last
thing executives want is to be caught with too many cans of pizza sauce, fancy
grade, when the marketplace is starved for commercial catsup. What processors do
nowadays is capture the tomatoes and process them until they are clean and dead,
but still near enough to the head of the assembly line so they have not yet gone
past the squeezer that issues tomato juice or the sluice gate leading to the spaghetti

sauce vat, the paste vat, the aspic tank, or the cauldrons of anything in particular. The mashed stuff of tomato products is stored until demand is clear. Then it's processed the rest of the way. The new manufacturing concept is known in the trade as aseptic barreling, and it leads to success by means of procrastination.

The growers supplying the raw materials for these tightly controlled processors have contracted in advance of planting season for the sale of their crops. It's the only way to get in. At the same time, perhaps stimulated by this new guaranteed marketplace–or perhaps stimulating it–these surviving growers of tomatoes have greatly expanded the size of their planting. The interaction of large growers and large processors has thus crowded many smaller growers out of the marketplace, not because they can't grow tomatoes as cheaply as the big growers (they can) but because they can't provide large enough units of production to attract favorable contracts with any of the few canners in their area.

In turn, the increasing size of tomato-growing operations has encouraged and been encouraged by a number of developments in technology. Harvesters (which may have been the "cause" precipitating the other changes in the system) have in large part replaced persons in the fields. But the new machines became practical only after the development of other technological components–especially new varieties of tomato bred for machine harvesting, and new chemicals that make machine harvesting economical.

What is remarkable about the tomato from the grower's point of view is its rapid increase in popularity. In 1920, each American ate 18.1 pounds of tomato. These days we each eat 50.5 pounds of tomato. Half a million acres of cropland grow tomatoes, yielding nearly 9 million tons, worth over $900 million on the market. Today's California tomato acre yields 24 tons, while the same acre in 1960 yielded 17 tons and in 1940, 8 tons.

The increased consumption of tomatoes reflects changing eating habits in general. Most food we eat nowadays is prepared, at least in part, somewhere other than in the home kitchen, and most of the increased demand for tomatoes is for processed products–catsup, sauce, juice, canned tomatoes, and paste for "homemade" sauce. In the 1920s, tomatoes were grown and canned commercially from coast to coast. Small canneries persisted into the 1950s.

Tomatoes were then a labor-intensive crop, requiring planting, transplanting, staking, pruning. And, important in the tale of changing tomato technology, because tomatoes used to ripen a few at a time, each field required three or four forays by harvesting crews to recover successively ripening fruits. The forces that have changed the very nature of tomato-related genetics, farming practices, labor requirements, business configurations, and buying patterns started with the necessity, built so deeply into the structure of our economic system, for the constant perfection of capital utilization.

Some critics sometimes seem to imply that the new mechanization is a conspiracy fostered by fat cats up top to make their own lives softer. But though there

15

are, surely, greedy conspirators mixed in with the regular folks running tomato farms and tomato factories and tomato research facilities, the impulse for change at each stage of the tomato transformation–from the points of view of those effecting the change–is "the system." The system always pressures participants to *meet the competition.*

20

Even in the 1920s, more tomatoes were grown commercially for processing than for fresh consumption, by a ratio of about two to one. Today the ratio has increased to about seven to one. Fifty years ago, California accounted for about an eighth of all tomatoes grown in America. Today, California grows about 85 percent of tomatoes. Yet as recently as fifteen years ago, California grew only about half the tomato crop. And fifteen years ago, the mechanical harvester first began to show up in the fields of the larger farms.

Before the harvester came, the average California planting was about 45 acres. Today, plantings exceed 350 acres. Tomato production in California used to be centered in family farms around Merced. It has now shifted to the corporate farms of Kern County, where Tejon Agricultural Partners operates. Of the state's 4000 or so growers harvesting canning tomatoes in the late sixties, 85 percent have left the business since the mechanical harvester came around. Estimates of the number of part-time picking jobs lost go as high as 35,000.

The introduction of the harvester brought about other changes too. Processors thought that tomatoes ought to have more solid material, ought to be less acid, ought to be smaller. Engineers called for tomatoes that had tougher skins and were oblong so they wouldn't roll back down tilted conveyor belts. Larger growers, more able to substitute capital for labor, wanted more tonnage per acre, resistance to cracking from sudden growth spurts that follow irrigation, leaf shade for the fruit to prevent scalding by the hot sun, determinate plant varieties that grow only so high to keep those vines in rows, out of the flood irrigation ditches.

As geneticists selectively bred for these characteristics, they lost control of others. They bred for thickwalledness, less acidity, more uniform ripening, oblongness, leafiness, and high yield–and they could not also select for flavor. And while the geneticists worked on tomato characteristics, chemists were perfecting an aid of their own. Called ethylene, it is in fact also manufactured by tomato plants themselves. All in good time, it promotes reddening. Sprayed on a field of tomatoes that has reached a certain stage of maturity (about 15 percent of the field's tomatoes must have started to "jell"), the substance causes the plants to start the enzyme activity that induces redness. About half of the time a tomato spends between blossom and ripeness is spent at full size, merely growing red. (Tomatoes in the various stages of this ripening are called, in the trade, immature greens, mature greens, breakers, turnings, pinks, light reds, and reds.) Ethylene cuts this reddening time by a week or more and clears the field for its next use. It recovers investment sooner. Still more important, it complements the genetic work, producing plants with a determined and common ripening time so machines can harvest in a single pass. It guarantees precision for the growers. The large-scale manufacturing system that buys the partnership's tomatoes requires predictable results. On schedule, eight or ten or fourteen days after planes spray, the crop will be red and ready. The gas complements the work of the engineers, too, loosening the heretofore stubborn attachment of fruit and stem. It makes it easier for the new machines to shake the tomatoes free of the vines.

The result of this integrated system of tomato seed and tomato chemicals and tomato hardware and tomato know-how has been, of course, the reformation of tomato business.

25

According to a publication of the California Agrarian Action Project, a reform-oriented research group located at Davis (some of whose findings are reflected in this article), the effects of an emerging "low-grade oligopoly" in tomato processing are discoverable. Because of labor savings and increased efficiency of machine harvesting, the retail price of canned tomatoes should have dropped in the five years after the machines came into the field. Instead, it climbed 111 percent, and it did so in a period that saw the overall price of processed fruits and vegetables climb only 76 percent.

There are "social costs" to the reorganization of the tomato processing industry as well. The concentration of plants concentrates work opportunities formerly not only more plentiful but more dispersed in rural areas. It concentrates problems of herbicide, pesticide, and salinity pollution.

As the new age of canner tomato production has overpowered earlier systems of production, a kind of flexibility in tomato growing, which once worked strongly to the consumer's advantage, has been lost. The new high-technology tomato system involves substantial investment "up front" for seed, herbicides and pesticides, machinery, water, labor, and for the "management" of growing, marketing, and financing the crop.

Today the cannery tomato farmer has all but ceased to exist as a discrete and identifiable being. The organizations and structures that do what farmers once did operate as part and parcel of an economy functioning at a nearly incomprehensible level of integration. So much for the tasty tomato.

The Responsive Reader

1. Does Kramer give you an overview of the process that brings the tomato to the consumer's pizza? What is the process?

2. The author of this article has literally gone into the field to see modern agriculture in operation. What is particularly striking or memorable about his account of the tomato harvest? What are major facets or operations?

3. Kramer keeps reminding you that the "ruination of the tomato" was a complex phenomenon. What was the role of changing marketing patterns? What was the role of changing eating patterns? What was the role of geneticists? What was the role of the chemical industry?

4. Ultimately, Kramer seems to blame what happened to the tomato on the system. How would you sum up his view of the "system"?

For Discussion or Writing

5. What does Kramer see as the social costs or human costs of the developments he analyzes? Do you think he is too negative? Does he suggest an answer or a solution to the problems he describes?

6. Have any goods or services that matter to you been ruined or negatively affected as the result of current business practices or economic trends?

Collaborative Projects

7. In recent years, there have been movements promoting alternative produce or organic foods. Working with a group, explore whether such movements have had an impact in your area. Are they fringe phenomena or fads, or do they seem to have a future?

THE CAVE ON TOBACCO ROAD

Jonathan Alter

> *For years, packages of cigarettes have carried warnings by the U.S. Surgeon General concern-*
> *ing the health hazards of smoking. At the same time, tobacco companies have been fighting nega-*
> *tive publicity concerning alleged links between smoking and lung cancer or about the alleged*
> *addictive quality of nicotine. In August 1995, the Philip Morris Companies published full-page*
> *ads with a large "Apology accepted" headline. According to the ads, which reproduced a letter of*
> *"correction" and apology from ABC, the ABC television network had apologized for broadcasts ac-*
> *cusing tobacco companies of artificially raising the nicotine content of cigarettes for the purpose of*
> *making smoking addictive. In return, Philip Morris had dropped a $10 billion defamation suit*
> *against ABC.*

A decade ago, I covered libel suits brought by Gen. William Westmoreland [1] against CBS and by Gen. Ariel Sharon against Time magazine. More recently I wrote about "Dateline NBC's" rigged gas-tank explosions on GM cars. In these cases, news organizations were shoddy, arrogant and too slow to make amends. Was ABC's 1994 "Day One" report charging that tobacco companies adjust nicotine levels to hook smokers part of the same pattern? To the contrary. Last week's set-tlement of Philip Morris's $10 billion lawsuit against Capital Cities/ABC suggests that the American media may be moving from one extreme to the other–from underapologizing on stories that are fundamentally weak to overapologizing on stories that are fundamentally strong.

The explanation lies in the Wall Streeting of news. Deep pockets once meant that news outlets had the resources to back up investigative reporting, which often risks lawsuits. Today, deep pockets often mean a higher duty to shareholders and potential buyers than to journalists ferreting out the truth. While ABC News is still the best on TV, CEO Tom Murphy gives way to Disney's Michael Eisner on a de-pressing note. ABC caved–not entirely, but enough to send a true chill through the entire news business.

Much of ABC News was devastated by the deal. Roone Arledge helped work on the apology language but threatened to yank "Day One" anchors Diane Sawyer and Forrest Sawyer off the program in protest if forced to air it at the beginning of the broadcast. (It aired at the end, after boring rerun segments substituted at the last minute to keep ratings down.) Executive producer Tom Yellin boycotted his own show. And John Martin and Pulitzer Prize winner Walt Bogdanich, the reporters, didn't sign the apology and were given fat new contracts.

Philip Morris spun the story as a vindication, but the gist of the narrow apology was that ABC was sorry it had said that tobacco companies add significant amounts of nicotine "from outside sources." In court briefs, ABC stated that it had documents proving that Philip Morris bought nicotine-rich tobacco extract from outside sources, but the network didn't obtain documents proving that the tobacco company still *used* what it had indisputably bought. In any event, the 1994 "Day One" show let tobacco executives rebut the "spiking" charge, which left the network essentially apologizing for things it did not really say.

The whole "outside sources" argument is a canard, anyway. It's a ploy by the   5
tobacco industry to divert attention from charges that it manipulates nicotine levels—which was the focus of the "Day One" segment in the first place. ABC court filings include documents stating that Philip Morris adjusts nicotine content with its own reconstituted tobacco—from inside the company. Outside, inside—it's all a smoke screen. If you shoot someone with five bullets, how much does it matter if four were made at home and one bought "outside"?

Of course it's always easy to urge going to trial when it's not your money. But top ABC executives have been signaling a settlement all along. The Disney takeover merely accelerated what was already in the works, prompted in part by a fear of courtrooms Murphy developed a decade ago when, while serving as a Texaco board member, he was caught up in the multibillion-dollar Texaco-Pennzoil antitrust trial. Yes, if the tobacco case had gone to trial, ABC would have been cuffed around a bit for some typical TV editing practices, but they were minor and defensible infractions. And yes, holding the tobacco trial in Virginia was a huge home-court advantage; Judge T. J. Markow even has relatives on the Philip Morris payroll. But the judge indicated this year that the case would turn on motive: "If the purpose [of adding nicotine] is benign, Philip Morris wins. If to addict, it loses." Philip Morris, which continues to deny its cigarettes are addictive, was scared of a trial, too. It would have meant the release of secret documents that will now—thanks to the settlement—be returned to the company.

Murphy agreed to pay $16 million in legal fees to Philip Morris and RJR Nabisco—the real concession in the case—after consulting with, among other board members, major shareholder Warren Buffet. The Omaha billionaire, who once held a large stake in RJR Nabisco and as recently as last year invested in U.S. Tobacco, told me he wouldn't talk about any of this. But I think he might have made an excellent ABC witness about the tobacco companies' motives. During the RJR takeover fight, he was widely quoted as saying: "I'll tell you why I like the cigarette business. It costs a penny to make. Sell it for a dollar. It's addictive. And there's fantastic brand loyalty." (Of course, many of us have complicity problems when it comes to cigarettes, including *Newsweek* and all the other magazines that accept tobacco ads.)

Even after the apology, ABC corporate management was letting Philip Morris walk all over the news division. Staffers were stunned to see a gloating Philip Morris press release only minutes after the settlement; they'd been told that the deal barred such spin. But ABC general counsel Alan Braverman, who spent months keeping the news divisions in the dark (a charge he calls "absurd"), didn't exercise his right to protest. "He never said a thing to us about it," says Charles Wall of Philip Morris.

That's the inside blend. The outside problem is that real investigative reporting is easily imperiled. It takes money, guts and a willingness to back good reporters to the hilt. The "Day One" story was of historic importance. It advanced federal probes of nicotine. ABC should delete the small portions it apologized for, and rebroadcast it. But of course it never will.

The Responsive Reader

1. According to Alter, how did this case imperil investigative reporting? Why or how did it "send a chill through the entire news business"?
2. What can you glean from this article about the merits of the actual court case? What do you learn here about the exact charges, legal finer points, potentially damaging witnesses, or possible conflicts of interest?

For Discussion or Writing

3. How is what Philip Morris calls "the ongoing crusade against the tobacco companies" going at the present time? Are you taking sides in it?
4. What limits do you think are justified on the advertising of products considered harmful? Where would you draw the line? What are major test cases for you?
5. Have you see evidence of the threat of litigation having a "chilling effect"? Have you seen it skew professional or economic decisions?

Collaborative Projects

6. Working with a group, you may want to investigate the history of efforts to control cigarette advertising or to have tobacco labeled as a drug.

4

Issues in the Humanities

THE HUMANITIES IN PERSPECTIVE

The purpose of art is to lay bare the questions which have been hidden by the answers.

JAMES BALDWIN

In a data-driven society operated by automated systems, is there a department concerned with human feelings? Who teaches the language of the emotions? What branch or branches of knowledge deal with human values, anxieties, and aspirations? Where can disoriented moderns turn in their search for a sense of meaning or direction in their lives?

THE ROOTS OF CULTURE

The humanities celebrate the achievements of the human spirit. They explore the artistic and intellectual pursuits that enhance the life of the senses, educate the emotions, and give shape to the flux of experience. Before humans invented machines, cars, and computers, they invented music and dance and story. They painted images on cave walls. Prehistoric painters and potters and stone masons discovered the human delight in shapes, the hunger of the eyes for color and movement, and the delight of the human hand in textures to touch. People of many cultures have adorned the human body, their dwellings, and the resting places of their dead. They have fashioned drums and musical instruments from materials at hand.

As far as we can tell, most early cultures had storytellers who were makers of meaning. They knew creation myths about how male and female or life and death had come into the world. They chanted stories about goddesses of the harvest or about rain gods whose anger brought killer droughts. They knew stories about the firebringer who raised humans above an animal-like existence. They knew stories of human pride, like the myth of Icarus, whose wings, made of feathers and wax, melted when he flew too close to the sun. Poets recited from memory elaborately crafted poems about godlike heroes—glorious, invulnerable, although finally brought down by treachery. They promised the return of leaders betrayed, in archetypal stories of death and rebirth.

Some modern writers recreate for you the ceremonies and festivals that enhanced traditional tribal life. In *Things Fall Apart*, the Nigerian novelist Chinua Achebe recreates the marriage festivals and initiation rites–with the reunion of far-flung relatives, the elaborately prepared feasts, the drumming and dancing, the songs of recognition and praise. Achebe rekindles for his readers the spirit of ceremony and festival, enriching, celebrating life. We are not meant to spend all of our lives stooped over for labor or hunched before the computer or crawling before people with clout. We are capable of mirth, fiesta, revelry, pageantry, and other communal pursuits that lift the human spirit.

In many different cultures, art–masks, dance, music, drumming–was an integral part of the rituals that acted out vital needs, anxieties, and aspirations of the community. In communities dependent on seasonal rainfall or flooding of rivers to assure a sufficient harvest, rituals to propitiate the rain gods were a major part of the annual cycle. Age-old rituals rooted in the seasonal cycles of decay and renewal celebrated the death of winter and the return of the sun. In the later decades of the nineteenth century, the Native American populations of the Great Plains were driven to the brink of extinction by the flood of white settlers, the mass slaughter of the buffalo herds that used to sustain tribal life, and killer diseases. The ghost dances were intended to bring on a new cycle where the earth would grow a new skin, the tide of the white invaders would recede, the buffalo would return, and the ghosts of the departed ancestors would usher in a new age.

In our super-rational modern world, keeping alive the spirit of festival and myth and ritual has at times seemed a lost cause. Is it true that we have lost the sense of being active participants in a live culture and are instead turning into a race of passive spectators and couch potatoes? Has art become a frill to be cut first if the school budget or city budget is deep in the red?

If you have played an instrument, marched in a band, sung in a choir, or helped organize a music meet, you know that active participation makes you appreciate music as a performance art. It helps you know and love music from the inside. If you have drawn sketches, used water colors, created posters, made jewelry, or tie-dyed T-shirts, you know the satisfaction of making something with your hands that delights the eye. If you have been caught up in the ritual of a track meet or of a wheelchair Olympics, you know why the ancient Greeks, who founded the Olympic Games, believed that athletic competition does not only build the body but also uplifts the spirit. Alice Walker, author of *The Color Purple*, writes lovingly of the quilts and gardens that provided African American women of her grandmother's generation with an outlet for their creative abilities. Creativity is not a special gift to a few artistic geniuses; it is the birthright of every human being.

THEATER: The Human Drama

What explains the staying power of live theater? The theater is one of the oldest and most vital of the creative arts. There is a special immediacy in actors staging the human drama before a live audience. The topic may be a mortal like Oedipus struggling in vain against the will of the gods in an ancient Greek play. Or it may be an avenging student doing battle against the accused sexist professor in the war of the sexes in David Mamet's *Oleanna* on today's stage. Holding "the mirror up to nature," in the words of Shakespeare's Hamlet, live theater acts out the drama of love and hate, of human ambitions and failures, of loyalties and betrayals. Theatergoers around the world watch with grave attention as characters on the stage act out archetypal experiences and give voice to human motives.

Drama in the Western tradition first flourished 2500 years ago in ancient Greece. Greek tragedy was rooted in prehistoric religious rituals, with the priest of the god Dionysos still occupying an honored seat in front of the stage. Where the chorus alone had originally chanted myths and traditional stories, solo actors gradually started to alternate with the elaborately crafted odes and choreographed movements of the chorus to act out traditional stories. Many of the Greek plays, like true classics, speak to us urgently across gulfs of time and distance. Euripides' *The Women of Troy*, like a bulletin from the Bosnia of the mind, shows us a city in smoking ruins, the men and young boys killed, the women raped.

Sophocles' *Antigone* makes us listen to a young woman undergoing a crisis of conscience, as she pits her sense of what is right against the power of the state. The authorities, embodied in King Creon, are bent on dishonoring the corpse of her rebel brother, a traitor in their eyes. Antigone chooses to lose her life rather than disregard the gods' command to honor the dead. Although we need an interpreter to render the fast-moving ancient Greek dialogue into English, we do not need an interpreter to translate the proud defiant spirit of the heroine, the hesitations of her weak sister, or the blustering anger of the petty tyrant who realizes too late what he has wrought.

The magic of the stage transcends the theatrical conventions of a given time or place. Shakespeare, 2000 years after the Greeks, wrote scripts for a large popular theater with a frequent need for new plays. In his *Romeo and Juliet*, two young people freely commit to a union of mind and body, defying barriers of family strife, going counter to a tradition of murderous feuding that has divided their two clans. "If thou dost love, pronounce it faithfully," says Juliet during the nocturnal meeting where they declare the devoted, unconditional love that makes them defy the fiery hatred of the young hotheads on both sides and the materialism of matchmaking elders. Although the lovers go down to defeat, their loyalty to each other is a triumph over the spirit of clan or tribe with its paranoid suspicion of outsiders.

While Shakespeare's tragedies take us to the edge of despair, his comedies carry us to a joyous golden world of love games and high jinks, where good fortune befalls the deserving and idealistic youth bests age. Four hundred years after Shakespeare first wrote these plays, audiences still respond with happy liberating laughter to his gallery of bumbling lovers, pompous asses, moralizing hypocrites, and rationalizing rogues.

The theater has often been the forum for provocative new ideas, challenging the conventions of society. In the nineteenth-century play *A Doll's House*, by the Norwegian playwright Henrik Ibsen, a woman who has played the part of the flirtatious airhead wife to please her insensitive, self-righteous husband finds that her duty to herself requires her to break off a stifling marriage at the cost of losing her children. Today the American stage holds up the mirror to multicultural America, whether in Lorraine Hansberry's, ntozake shange's, and August Wilson's plays about the black community, in David Henry Whang's plays with American Chinese themes, or the Mexican American playwright Luis Valdez' biting satire in *Los Vendidos*, about Honest Sancho's Used Mexican Lot that rents token minority representatives to the white establishment.

POETRY: THE LANGUAGE OF THE EMOTIONS

Are you one of a generation that allegedly "hated poetry"–while loving the poetry of blues singers or of balladeers inspired by Bob Dylan? Poetry, which today has a limited audience, was through the centuries at the center of human culture. The earliest recorded poems chanted the exploits of tribal heroes or the creation of all living things. In early cultures, a dominant form, or **genre**, was the epic, a long elaborately crafted, strongly rhythmic poem orally recited by bards. Often, the epic commemorated a high point in the story of a people, the way Homer in the *Iliad* sang the Greek siege of the legendary city of Troy during the ten-year Trojan war:

> *As the many tribes of winged birds–*
> *The geese, the cranes, and the long-throated swans–*
> *Make their flight this way and that*
> *And then settle in fluttering swarms*
> *While a vast field echoes with their cries,*
> *So these many tribes poured out from their ships*
> *Onto the plain of Troy.*

When we talk about poetry today, we usually think of a fairly short poem communicating personal observations, thoughts, and emotions. We call such a poem the lyric, named after the lyre, or small harp, that the poets of ancient Greece played as they recited their verses. Traditionally, lyric poetry has been the voice of passion, of yearning and despair, of the joy of mutual love and the sorrow of separation. "Shall I compare thee to a summer's day?/Thou art more lovely and more temperate," says William Shakespeare in a poem he wrote toward the end of the sixteenth century (Sonnet 18). "The voice of your eyes is deeper than all roses/nobody, not even the rain, has such small hands," says the American twentieth-century poet e.e. cummings, in "somewhere I have never travelled." Poets have celebrated love as an overwhelming passion, promising fulfillment, giving meaning to otherwise meaningless lives.

Much twentieth-century poetry has been more low-key in its expression of emotions. Modern poets have tended to understate rather than to overstate their feelings. This does not mean that their poems are void of feeling. It often means that the poet trusts vivid images and incidents faithfully rendered to call up the emotions and attitudes in the reader. The following modern poem lets a thought-provoking, disturbing incident speak for itself.

Traveling through the Dark (1960)

Traveling through the dark I found a deer
dead on the edge of the Wilson River road.
It is usually best to roll them into the canyon:
that road is narrow; to swerve might make more dead.

By glow of the tail-light I stumbled back of the car
and stood by the heap, a doe, a recent killing;
she had stiffened already, almost cold.
I dragged her off; she was large in the belly.

My fingers touching the side brought me the reason—
her side was warm; her fawn lay there waiting,
alive, still, never to be born.
Beside that mountain road I hesitated.

The car aimed ahead its lowered parking lights;
under the hood purred the steady engine.
I stood in the glare of the warm exhaust turning red;
around our group I could hear the wilderness listen.

I thought hard for us all—my only swerving—
then pushed her over the edge into the river.

WILLIAM STAFFORD

What are the poet's feelings? The poem starts on an unemotional, matter-of-fact note: The deer, "a recent killing," was apparently hit by a car when crossing the road. The road is narrow, and leaving the dead deer where it is would present a hazard. It would be best to roll it into the canyon to prevent further accidents. But the poet soon makes it hard for us to stay emotionally uninvolved: The side of the killed deer is still warm; she is large with a fawn, "alive, still, never to be born." The poet hesitates, but only for a time. Then he does the right thing. However, we know he "thought hard for us all." As one student reader said, "for a brief moment, he makes us think of the impossible task of saving the fawn." He hesitates for a time—that was his "only swerving" from acting businesslike and sensible.

What are you supposed to feel? What are you supposed to think? You may be sick at heart at the thought of one of God's creatures and the burgeoning life in her womb being destroyed by a machine barreling down the highway. You may feel helpless; there seems to be no point in waving your arms or raising a fist in protest. You can "hear the wilderness listen," and perhaps you also listen. But in this poem you will hear no expressions of protest or grief; the only sound you will hear is the motor of the automobile "purring" steadily in the background.

The following poem shows something about the way poets use language to give voice to human emotions.

The Possessive (1980)

My daughter—as if I
owned her—that girl with the
hair wispy as a frayed bellpull

has been to the barber, that knife grinder,
and had the edge of her hair sharpened.

Each strand now cuts
both ways. The blade of new bangs
hangs over her red-brown eyes
like carbon steel.

> *All the little*
spliced ropes are sliced. The curtain of
dark paper-cuts veils the face that
started from next to nothing in my body—

My body. My daughter. I'll have to find
another word. In her bright helmet
she looks at me as if across a
great distance. Distant fires can be
glimpsed in the resin light of her eyes:

the watch fires of an enemy, a while before
the war starts.

Sharon Olds

How does hair become an issue in this poem? What exactly did the barber do to the girl's hair? Many of the words that answer these questions are not meant literally: The girl's hair was not literally a frayed bellpull; it merely was *like* one. We call such an imaginative comparison, signaled by *as* or *like*, a **simile.** The barber was not literally a "knife-grinder"—although he may have had his scissors or a razor sharpened like one. We call such an unmarked, unannounced imaginative comparison, treating one thing as if it *were* another, a **metaphor.** The curtain, the helmet, and the fires in the daughter's eyes are all metaphors. They all help create the feeling of separation and warlike tension that is at the heart of this poem.

The distance seems to be growing between mother and child. (On what side of the divide do you find yourself as you read this poem?) The mother used to use the possessive pronoun *my—my daughter*, as we would say *my car*. But the daughter will no longer be owned by anyone. She has moved from a nonthreatening wispy-hair or curly-hair stage to a new helmetlike hairdo, with bangs that remind the mother of sharpened blades. The poem leaves us with the sense of a coming confrontation. Parent and child are headed for a future where they will be like two armies, each waiting around its campfires on the eve of battle.

ART HISTORY: CLASSIC AND ROMANTIC

The art works you contemplate in your local art museum or on a visit to the great museums of modern art in Chicago or New York City are part of an ongoing enterprise. Art historians chronicle the manifestations of the art impulse through human history and up to the present time. They study the workings of the creative spirit in architecture, sculpture, painting, music, and the allied arts. They study wall paintings from the tombs of Egyptian pharaohs, goldsmiths' work from the Aztecs in Mexico before the Spaniards, and the stained-glass windows of medieval cathedrals. They study Italian Renaissance art that makes thousands of tourists wait for hours in long lines in front of the great museums of Florence and Rome, icons from the monasteries of Czarist Russia, and the great modern art that survived the purges and censorship binges of the twentieth century.

Art historians trace the evolution of painting—from the depiction of myth and legend on Greek vases, to the otherworldly saints and martyrs of medieval paintings, to the glorification of the human form during the Renaissance, and on to the celebration of color by nineteenth-century French impressionists like Monet and Renoir or the surreal world of dream and nightmare in the work of painters like Dali or Chagall. Scholars trace the history of Western music from the Gregorian chant of medieval monks to the complex melodic lines and many-layered harmonies of a Beethoven symphony and on to the challenges to traditional form in the work of the great early moderns like Bartok and Stravinsky.

Art history studies the great movements and countermovements of style. For instance, much art in our cultural tradition has moved between the two poles of the classic and the romantic. Classicists hark back to the great flowering of architecture, sculpture, and ceramics in ancient Greece, and especially the city state of Athens in the fifth century B.C. On the temple hill, or acropolis, Athenian builders designed structures that taught generations of future architects how to envision monumental architecture. It taught them how to envision public buildings—court buildings, stock exchanges, college libraries—that embodied grandeur and civic pride.

Approached from the front, the classic Greek temple presents a row of evenly spaced pillars holding up a cross beam, topped by a low-angled gable. This is a design of classic simplicity—a rectangle topped by a low-angled triangle—composed of three major elements: pillar, beam, and gable. This design set a standard of symmetry, harmony, and balance that future ages despaired of improving upon. (How can you improve upon perfection?) Elements of decoration complicate the design—like the friezes of the Parthenon in Athens, showing the battle with the centaurs, or half-human, half-horse creatures. But these decorative elements are subordinate to the overall composition, with its dominant impression of quasi-mathematical, quasi-geometric symmetry.

The sculptures of classic Greece give us startlingly lifelike nude warriors and athletes (and later, undraped female forms), standing at ease or concentrating on a task like throwing a discus. These sculptures celebrate the fully developed human form—human beings at their best, not stunted by starvation or scarred by disease, not marred by neuroses. For future ages, they set a dominant if not tyrannical standard of human beauty—inspiring, but also poten tially disillusioning to those looking more like Woody Allen than like a young Greek god.

The "noble simplicity and calm dignity" of the Greeks became the watchwords in periods of classical revival, periods of a dominant neo-classical style. Advocates of the classical ideal tend to play down the dark side or night side of the Greek psyche. While Apollo was the god of light, of music, and of order, Dionysos (in later Roman times Bacchus, the god of revelry and wine) was the god of passion, intoxication, and ecstasy. His worshippers, the Maenads or Bacchantes, in orgiastic nighttime rites whipped themselves into a frenzy of destructive passion. The great Greek tragedies—from Sophocles' *Oedipus Rex* to Euripides' *Medea*—are built around stories of incest, of revenge killings within the family or clan, of murderous jealousy.

Great countermovements in Western culture have been rebellions against a classicism that came to be seen as the dead hand of convention. The Romantic movement of the early nineteenth century marks a great turning point in the dialectic–the play of point and counterpoint–of our cultural tradition. Romantic poets, painters, architects, and composers rebelled against the constraints of perfectly balanced form, which to them seemed to tamp down the vital energies of nature. To the static simplicity of the classical ideal, they opposed a more dynamic ideal that made passion and energy basic principles of great art.

Romantics preferred the wild profusion of natural vegetation to the poodle cuts given to hedges and trees in trimmed neo–classical French gardens. Romantic painters and poets saw in untamed, unspoiled nature a mirror of human emotions, rejoicing equally in the healing calm of a quiet sunset and in the wild energies of a storm in the mountains or by the sea.

In architecture, the Romantics rediscovered the Gothic cathedrals of the Middle Ages, whose architects thrust rows and rows of tall arched windows, buttresses, and spires toward the heavens. The architects who built the cathedrals at Chartres, Reims, or Strasbourg broke up or abolished the horizontal lines that would suggest closure or rest. The interiors of their churches made the eye travel upward to vaulted ceilings that seemed to defy gravity. They obscured simple outlines with profuse ornamentation, covering the façades with profuse statuary ranging from the sublime to the grotesque–saints and devils, virgins and gargoyles.

Much modern art–painting, literature, music–has carried the rebellion against traditional canons of order and form several steps further. Many modern artists have seen traditional principles of order and composition as basically untrue to life. Life is chaotic, formless, threatening, uncharted. Traditional form becomes a straitjacket that constrains and distorts artistic creation. In much twentieth–century art, we see "the continuous, restless urge to experiment, the constant need to change, to innovate, to destroy the accepted styles" (A. Alvarez). The expressionism of painters like Käthe Kollwitz or Max Beckman, the cubism of Pablo Picasso, the surrealism of Marc Chagall and Salvador Dali, and the atonal music of Béla Bartók or Igor Stravinsky have been among successive waves of reaction against classic academic ideals.

PHILOSOPHY: The Self–Aware Mind

Much of Western philosophy can be seen as the story of the human reason trying to understand itself. What is the potential and what are the limitations of human reason? What can our human reason discover about the purpose or meaning of life? What guidance can reason provide in matters of ethics or morals?

At one time, philosophy ("the love of wisdom") included all of knowledge. Up into the eighteenth century, leading intellectuals were philosopher-physicist-mathematicians. Gradually the natural sciences went their own way, and philosophy concentrated on three major areas, as represented in the monumental trilogy the German philosopher Immanual Kant (1724–1804) wrote on the workings of the human reason. Logic probes the conditions under which reason operates in space/time; it establishes principles of sound reasoning and identifies the fallacies, or logical malfunctions, that lead us astray. Ethics probes the principles that guide moral conduct: What imperatives, or promptings of conscience, counteract our inclination to selfishness and violence? Aesthetics probes our judgments of what is beautiful. It explores the role of the arts in human life; it analyzes major shifts in the history of style.

The philosophers of ancient Greece (flourishing in the fifth and fourth centuries B.C.) became part of the classical heritage that helped shape our civilization. Influenced by the astronomy and mathematics of Egypt and the Middle East, the Greek philosophers developed the idea of the cosmos, their word for a universe obeying principles of order (the opposite of chaos). They developed principles of harmony and balance as the clue to the good life. Aristotle, for instance, developed the ideal of the golden mean, which finds the good at the midpoint between two harmful extremes. (Grasping greed is a vice; giving money away foolishly is a vice; spending money wisely for a worthy cause is a virtue. Taking foolish risks is a vice; shirking responsibility is a vice; taking a stand after careful thought is a virtue.) In later ages, Christian theologians adapted Aristotelian thinking in trying to work out the scholastic synthesis of reason and faith.

Artists and writers have often been Platonists (or *neo*-Platonists in times of revival of Platonic thought). They have taken their clue from Plato's *Symposium*, where the priestess Diotima instructs Plato's teacher Socrates in the meaning of love. In the imperfect world around us, we nevertheless encounter constant reminders of what is perfect and beautiful. The soaring of a hawk or the taut beauty of a startled deer makes us catch our breath. The beauty of a face or the perfect body of Michelangelo's David reminds us of what human beings are like at their best. A generous deed in a world of conniving greed reminds us of our better selves. It is as if these hints or intimations remind us of an ideal homeland of the human spirit. The yearning for the true, the good, and the beautiful is imprinted on our souls. The assignment of philosophers, teachers, and artists is to bring imperfect reality closer to the ideal.

Western philosophy since the Renaissance has been the story of currents and countercurrents in the effort to make sense of the world in which we live. Empiricism, in the tradition of John Locke (1632–1704), was the working philosophy that guided the rise of modern science. Empiricists assumed that all knowledge had to be grounded in the methodical collection and interpretation of facts. Disregarding hearsay and tradition, the human reason would process the data furnished by experience or experiment and construct a reliable mental map of our world. Taking an increasingly optimistic view of the potential of human reason, eighteenth-century rationalism stipulated that an all-knowing intelligence could identify a reason for every phenomenon. The universe seemed to be founded on rational principles, allowing us to feel at home in a world congenial to the workings of the human mind, created by a Supreme Intelligence akin to ours, although operating on an infinitely more magnificent scale.

However, the eighteenth century at the same time saw the stirrings of the skepticism that has made intellectuals increasingly doubtful of the human ability to answer the larger questions about meaning and purpose. David Hume (1711–1776), the master skeptic, challenged our presumption in assuming that the world was created by a force modeled on our puny human intelligence–as if a spider were to claim that the world was spun from the belly of a supreme super spider.

After Hume, thinkers have become increasingly skeptical of our ability to grasp an objective reality "out there." Today, it is a commonplace that reality is in the mind of the beholder. Our own perception of reality is always pieced together from partial and subjectively selected input. The frog's eye is programmed to detect movement. When a bug moves across the frog's field of vision, the frog pounces. A black-and-white television does not take in colors; in the world of black-and-white TV, colors do not exist. Dogs hear high-pitched sounds that the human ear does not register. Our contact with the outside world is limited to what our sensors are equipped to take in.

Twentieth-century trends in philosophy have continued the trend away from ambitious world views claiming to decode the larger meanings of life. For instance, pragmatism is the view that theories have to be judged by their practical consequences. What would we do differently if we accepted one theory over another? This perspective tends to make irrelevant much abstract theorizing. Not surprisingly, pragmatism is an eminently American philosophy, taught by great American philosophers including William James and John Dewey.

Existentialism is the modern answer to eighteenth-century rationalism. We live in a universe without meaning or purpose, created by the "accidental collocation of atoms" (Bertrand Russell). To give purpose or direction to our lives, we have to *create* meaning. Any purpose or meaning we intend to give to life we have to construct ourselves. We cannot turn to religious revelation (which is different for the adherents of many different faiths). Nor can we turn to innate moral principles engraved upon all human hearts. As moderns, we find ourselves in an alien universe without a compass. We must construct our own values as we deal with the challenges and test situations of existence. A leading existentialist philosopher was the French Jean-Paul Sartre (1905–1980), who wrote in an intellectual climate when the values of the traditional bourgeois society had been called into question by two world wars and by the Marxist rebellion against economic exploitation.

A symptom of the retreat from the larger metaphysical questions is the modern concern with language as the medium of thought–with the way language channels and limits perception. Ludwig Wittgenstein (1889–1951) through his ordinary-language analysis catalogued key concepts that provide the parameters of our verbal universe; it probed their workings in a web of relationships. Much modern thinking assumes that what and how we think is conditioned and limited by language.

HIGH CULTURE AND POPULAR CULTURE

Are art, literature, and philosophy the private province of a small cultural elite? It is true that princes and popes have been the patrons of the arts, building splendid palaces and art galleries while the peasants lived in hovels. It is true that art works we see at the Guggenheim Museum or the Frick Museum in New York or the Musée d'Orsay in Paris may once have been the private treasures of wealthy collectors, who could spend millions on the works of dead and living artists. Even so the resulting buildings and paintings and sculptures have often been on public view. Cities like Florence and Dresden became lived-in works of art, with their churches and public buildings and public squares all part of the organic web of the community.

It is true that people with a lifelong love of the arts will respond to the richness and challenges of works that say much less to the casual beholder or listener. But the plays of ancient Greece were performed as part of theatrical contests that were communal festivals, with much of the population of the city filling the large semi-circular open-air theaters. Shakespeare's assignment as a playwright was to fill a large popular theater with plays that sometimes closed early but sometimes had long runs. Bach wrote a cantata a week to be performed before an ordinary congregation. In Italy, opera has long been a national treasure and a public passion. Mozart and Beethoven are not the private preserve of a small cultural elite but have uplifted the spirits of millions around the world.

The modern novel, at first often serialized in popular periodicals, developed as an art form that reached a large public. Writers like Charles Dickens and the great women novelists of the nineteenth century–Emily Brontë, George Eliot, Mary Gaskell–reached a large reading audience. Millions of readers around the world have read books by Mark Twain (*Huckleberry Finn*), Harriet Beecher Stowe (*Uncle Tom's Cabin*), Ernest Hemingway (*A Farewell to Arms*), or Richard Wright (*Native Son*).

Jazz and the movies are both art forms that have bridged the gap between high culture and popular culture. American popular music from dixieland jazz and bebop to rock'n'roll and rap has spread around the world. University musicologists meet for jam sessions. Scholars write books about the great figures of American jazz, such as Charlie Parker. As for the world of the movies, film archives preserve the classics of the silent screen. Cultural historians chronicle the movie as the dominant art form of a generation. Art films by directors like Fellini show the role of the Hollywood dream factory in the lives of ordinary people at the four corners of our world. Legendary Hollywood directors peopled the imagination of millions with characters like Scarlett O'Hara, Dorothy of the *Wizard of Oz*, the gruff macho John Wayne, and Jimmy Stewart, the original sensitive male.

QUESTIONS FOR DISCUSSION

What has been your own active participation in the arts or creative activity? What have been your experiences with live theater? What character from drama or fiction has fascinated or disturbed you the most–perhaps because you saw something of yourself in the character or because you saw something of people you know well or especially care about? If you were asked to participate in a poetry reading, what poem would you choose and why? Has a painting, sculpture, building, memorial, or other art work ever made a powerful impression on you? (Have you ever followed or become involved in a controversy over an artist or a work of art?) What side would you choose in a debate over the merits of classical music and modern music? opera and musical? traditional and modern jazz? country and rap? How would you explain the lasting appeal of one of the idols of American popular culture–Laurel and Hardy, Jackie Gleason, Mary Tyler Moore, Elvis Presley, Madonna, Michael Jackson–to a visitor from another planet?

FIVE POEMS

Poetry has a reputation for being difficult, appreciated only by a few. However, many poets write poems speaking to the general reader. The following poems are relatively free of features that can make poetry demanding: unusual words rich in overtones, private symbols with a special meaning for the poet, allusions to figures in myth or history. The poems that follow do not use features that have become increasingly optional with today's poets. They do not use rhyme, that is, the bonding of two or more lines with matched words like run/sun *or* reason/season. *They do not use meter, that is, highly regularized rhythm, although each poem has a rhythm of its own. However, each poem provides the kind of experience that readers of poetry look for in a poem. The poet focuses on something worth your attention. Each poem takes shape and becomes a finished, satisfying whole.*

THE PEACE OF WILD THINGS

Wendell Berry

When the despair of the world grows in me   1
and I wake in the night at the least sound
in fear of what my life and my children's life may be,
I go and lie down where the wood drake°   °*male duck with brilliant plumage*
rests in his beauty on the water, and the
                        great heron feeds.   5
I come into the peace of wild things
who do not tax their lives with forethought
of grief. I come into the presence of still water.
And I feel above me the day-blind stars
waiting with their light. For a time   10
I rest in the grace of the world, and am free.

The Responsive Reader

1. What images or ideas about nature do you bring to this poem? What images or associations does the word *nature* call up in our mind? Do you recognize or can you visualize the nature images in this poem?

2. What do you think are the fears that keep the speaker in the poem awake at night? What does he mean by "forethought of grief"?

3. What does the poet look for in nature? What does nature do for him? How does the poem provide the antidote for what ails him? What do you think the word *grace* means in the last line of the poem? How is the poet at the end "free"?

4. How are the stars "day-blind"? For the speaker, do you think the stars were comforting or distant and cold?

For Discussion or Writing

5. If a poem works for you, it will relate in some way to something in your own experience or personality. It will stir your feelings or get you emotionally involved; it will be thought-provoking, starting you on a train of thought of your own. Can you share in the thoughts and feelings conveyed in this poem? Why or why not?

SIMPLE SONG

Marge Piercy

When we are going toward someone we say   1
You are just like me
your thoughts are my brothers
word matches word
how easy to be together.   5

When we are leaving someone we say:
how strange you are
we cannot communicate
we can never agree
how hard, hard and weary to be together.   10

We are not different nor alike
But each strange in his leather body
sealed in skin and reaching out clumsy hands
and loving is an act
that cannot outlive   15
the open hand
the open eye
the door in the chest standing open.

The Responsive Reader

1. How does the play of opposites give shape to this poem? Do you think the poet is exaggerating the contrast between the early and the closing stages of a relationship? Do you think she is too pessimistic?

2. How well do you understand the language of metaphor in this poem? What does it mean to say, "your thoughts are my brothers"? Do you recognize the feeling of being inside a "leather body," "sealed in skin," and "reaching out clumsy hands"?

3. Parallelism repeats a similar grammatical pattern or builds several sentences (or parts of sentences) on the same model. How many examples of parallel structure can you point out in this poem? Parallelism may direct your attention to several related ideas, or it may line up different ideas for contrast. Can you show both uses of parallelism in this poem?

For Discussion or Writing

4. The gesture language of the hand plays a major part in nonverbal communication. How many ways can you describe of "talking with your hands"–of using a hand or the hands to convey meaning? (For instance, how do we use the hands to signal "hurry up" or "slow down," or to signal "I don't know"?) Do you think some "hand signals" or uses of the hands vary from one group to another?

5. Do you think of yourself as a person tending to be "open" or tending to be closed off from others? How does the difference show? What do you think are some of the things that tilt people one way or the other?

A GLIMPSE

Walt Whitman

———

> A glimpse through an interstice caught,   1
> Of a crowd of workmen and drivers in a bar-room around the stove
>   late of a winter night, and I unremarked seated in a corner,
> Of a youth who loves me and whom I love, silently approaching and
>   seating himself near, that he may hold me by the hand,   5
> A long while amid the noises of coming and going, of drinking and
>   oath and smutty jest,
> There we two, content, happy in being together, speaking little,
> perhaps not a word.

The Responsive Reader

1. Walt Whitman, the nineteenth-century "poet of democracy," is often remembered for poems developed on a grand scale and celebrating the richness and sweep of the American experience. How is this poem different?

2. How does this poem go counter to stereotypes about gays or gay relationships? How does it turn the tables on heterosexuals who "do dirt" on gays?

For Discussion or Writing

3. How important do you think it is to verbalize feelings in a close relationship? Is it possible to be "content" with hardly a word?

4. What does it mean to "come out of the closet"? Do you agree with those who urge gays and lesbians to come out of the closet? What are the pros and cons?

QUESTION (1954)

May Swenson

Body my house   1
my horse my hound
What will I do
When you are fallen
Where will I sleep   5
How will I ride
What will I hunt

Where can I go without my mount
all eager and quick
How will I know   10
in thicket ahead
is danger or treasure
When Body my good
bright dog is dead

How will it be   15
to lie in the sky
without roof or door
and wind for an eye

with cloud for shift°   °*woman's shirt or chemise*
how will I hide?   20

The Responsive Reader

1. How do you read the metaphors, or imaginative comparisons, in this poem? What do they tell you about how the poet feels about her body? How is the body like a horse, or "mount"? (What qualities of a horse does the poet have in mind?) How could the body be like a dog? (What kind of dog does the poet want you to imagine?) How is the body like a house? (Where does the poet talk about what it would be like to be without it—to be "homeless"?)

2. Is there a common element or a common thread in these three body metaphors?

3. What is the question alluded to in the title to this poem? What is the central question the poem asks? Does the poem give an answer—stated or implied?

For Discussion or Writing

4. How do the poet's ways of looking at the body differ from more familiar ways? What metaphor or metaphors would *you* choose to communicate how you feel about your body?

Making Connections

5. The French have a saying about "being at ease in one's skin." You may want to compare the different ways of looking at the human body in Marge Piercy's "Simple Song" and in May Swenson's "Question."

REFUGEE SHIP

Lorna Dee Cervantes

Like wet cornstarch, I slide   1
past my grandmother's eye. Bible
at her side, she removes her glasses.
The pudding thickens.
Mama raised me without language,   5

I'm orphaned from my Spanish name.
The words are foreign, stumbling
on my tongue. I see in the mirror
My reflection: bronzed skin, black hair.

I feel I am a captive   10
aboard the refugee ship.
The ship that will never dock.
El barco que nunca atraca.

The Responsive Reader

1. What do you know about refugee ships? Of what does the refugee ship in this poem become a symbol? How is this Mexican American poet's experience like that of the passengers on the ship?

2. In what ways is the poet linked to her Hispanic or Latina heritage? In what ways is she alienated from it?

For Discussion or Writing

3. Some people can totally identify with one group, one tradition, or one shared heritage. Others are aware of divergent influences that can divide their allegiance or leave them with ambivalent feelings about their heritage. With which of these two ways of defining one's identity do you tend to identify? How or why?

YOURS

Mary Robison

A short story opens a window on the world. It creates its own small universe; it puts people in a setting and sets them in motion. The action is not likely to involve sensational car chases or serial killings. Something happens—if only a change taking place in a character's mind. But it is significant enough for us to think about, to become involved. The following selection is a short short—shorter than most short stories. But it illustrates many of the elements we expect in a short story: setting, character, plot, symbol, theme. As in much contemporary short fiction, much of what this story says is left unsaid. We have to empathize with the characters, sharing in their feelings. Pumpkins are everywhere in this story—they are still looking at us while we leave the story. Do they acquire a significance beyond themselves? Are they symbols?

Allison struggled away from her white Renault, limping with the weight of the last of the pumpkins. She found Clark in the twilight on the twig-and-leaf-littered porch behind the house.

He wore a wool shawl. He was moving up and back in a padded glider, pushed by the ball of his slippered foot.

Allison lowered a big pumpkin, let it rest on the wide floorboards.

Clark was much older—seventy-eight to Allison's thirty-five. They were married. They were both quite tall and looked something alike in their facial features. Allison wore a natural-hair wig. It was a thick blond hood around her face. She was dressed in bright-dyed denims today. She wore durable clothes, usually, for she volunteered afternoons at a children's day-care center.

She put one of the smaller pumpkins on Clark's long lap. "Now, nothing surreal," she told him. "Carve just a *regular* face. These are for kids."

In the foyer, on the Hepplewhite desk, Allison found the maid's chore list with its cross-offs, which included Clark's supper. Allison went quickly through the day's mail: a garish coupon packet, a bill from Jamestown Liquors, November's pay-TV program guide, and the worst thing, the funniest, an already opened, extremely unkind letter from Clark's relations up North. "You're an old fool," Allison read, and, "You're being cruelly deceived." There was a gift check for Clark enclosed, but it was uncashable, signed, as it was, "Jesus H. Christ."

Late, late into this night, Allison and Clark gutted and carved the pumpkins together, at an old table set on the back porch, over newspaper after soggy newspaper, with paring knives and with spoons and with a Swiss Army knife Clark used for exact shaping of tooth and eye and nostril. Clark had been a doctor, an internist, but also a Sunday watercolorist. His four pumpkins were expressive and artful. Their carved features were suited to the sizes and shapes of the pumpkins. Two looked ferocious and jagged. One registered surprise. The last was serene and beaming.

Allison's four faces were less deftly drawn, with slits and areas of distortion. She had cut triangles for noses and eyes. The mouths she had made were just wedges–two turned up and two turned down.

By one in the morning they were finished. Clark, who had bent his long torso forward to work, moved back over to the glider and looked out sleepily at nothing. All the lights were out across the ravine.

Clark stayed. For the season and time, the Virginia night was warm. Most   10
leaves had been blown away already, and the trees stood unbothered. The moon was round above them.

Allison cleaned up the mess.

"Your jack-o'-lanterns are much, much better than mine," Clark said to her.

"Like hell," Allison said.

"Look at me," Clark said, and Allison did.

She was holding a squishy bundle of newspapers. The papers reeked sweetly   15
with the smell of pumpkin guts.

"Yours are *far* better," he said.

"You're wrong. You'll see when they're lit," Allison said.

She went inside, came back with yellow vigil candles. It took her a while to get each candle settled, and then to line up the results in a row on the porch railing. She went along and lit each candle and fixed the pumpkin lids over the little flames.

"See?" she said.

The sat together a moment and looked at the orange faces.   20

"We're exhausted. It's good night time," Allison said. "Don't blow out the candles. I'll put in new ones tomorrow."

That night, in their bedroom, a few weeks earlier in her life than had been predicted, Allison began to die. "Don't look at me if my wig comes off," she told Clark. "Please."

Her pulse cords were fluttering under his fingers. She raised her knees and kicked away the comforter. She said something to Clark about the garage being locked.

At the telephone, Clark had a clear view out back and down to the porch. He wanted to get drunk with his wife once more. He wanted to tell her, from the greater perspective he had, that to own only a little talent, like his, was an awful, plaguing thing; that being only a little special meant you expected too much, most of the time, and liked yourself too little. He wanted to assure her that she had missed nothing.

He was speaking into the phone now. He watched the jack-o'-lanterns. The   25
jack-o'-lanterns watched him.

The Responsive Reader

1. What do you learn about the people in this story, their circumstances, and their relationship? What role does the age difference play in the story? How important is it? Is it treated differently from what you might expect?

2. The pumpkins are everywhere in this story. How are they described? What role do they play? Are they symbols? Of what?

3. How do you think Robison expects you to feel about these people? Do you identify with them or with one of them?

For Discussion or Writing

4. How does this story treat the subject of illness and death? Do you think this is a pessimistic story? Do you think it projects a downbeat attitude toward life?

Making Connections

5. You may want to explore the language of symbols by examining the symbolic meaning of the haircut in Sharon Olds' "The Possessive," the boat in Lorna Dee Cervantes' "Refugee Ship," and the pumpkins in Mary Robison's "Yours."

TIME

Nathan McCall

Where social scientists might rely on statistics, readers of literature trust to the power of personal testimony. They value the authentic personal voice, the truly written word. Great autobiography has always allowed readers to share in the human reality behind historical dates, survey data, or government statistics. Autobiographical testimony fills in for us the world of attitude, feeling, and human interaction that slips through the net cast by graphs and charts. For many readers, Nathan McCall's Makes Me Wanna Holler *(1994) evoked the human reality of prison life the way no statistics and no theoretical discussion could. During the Reagan and Bush presidencies, the population of America's prison Gulag archipelago climbed from half a million to an estimated million and a half human beings. McCall is a survivor who came back to tell the tale. He grew up in a black working-class neighborhood in Portsmouth, Virginia, and like many young black males, he was carrying a gun by the time he was fifteen and was in jail by the time he was twenty. After serving three years in prison for armed robbery, he studied journalism at Norfolk State University and became a reporter for the* Virginia Pilot–Ledger Star *and the* Atlanta Journal Constitution. *He moved to the prestigious* Washington Post *in 1989.*

I was standing in my cell doorway, checking out the scene on the floor below, when a white convict appeared in the doorway across from mine. He stood stark still and looked straight ahead. Without saying a word, he lifted a razor blade in one hand and began slashing the wrist of the other, squirting blood everywhere. He kept slashing, rapid-fire, until finally he dropped the razor and slumped to the floor, knocking his head against the bars as he went down.

Other inmates standing in their doorways spotted him and yelled, "Guard! Guard! Guard!" Guards came running, rushed the unconscious inmate to the dispensary, and ordered a hallboy to clean up the pool of blood oozing down the walkway. Later, when I asked the hallboy why the dude had tried to take himself out, he said, "That *time* came down on him and he couldn't take the pressure. You know them white boys can't handle time like us brothers. They weak."

It was a macho thing for a guy to be able to handle his time. Still, every once in a while, time got to everybody, no matter how tough they were. Hard time came in seasonal waves that wiped out whole groups of cats, like a monsoon. Winter was easiest on everybody. There was the sense that you really weren't missing anything on the streets because everyone was indoors. Spring and summer were hell. The Dear John letters started flowing in, sending heartbroken dudes to the fence for a clean, fast break over and into the countryside. Fall was a wash. The weather was nice enough to make you think of home, but winter was just ahead, giving you something to look forward to. Time.

I saw the lifers go through some serious changes about time. Some days, those cats carried theirs as good as anybody else, but other days, they didn't. You could look in their eyes sometimes and tell they had run across a calendar, one of those calendars that let you know what day of the week your birthday will fall on ten years from now. Or you could see in the wild way they started acting and talking that they were on the edge. Then it was time to get away from them, go to the other side of the prison yard, and watch the fireworks. They went *off.* Especially the brothers. They were determined not to go down kicking and screaming and slashing their wrists like the white boys. The brothers considered themselves too hard for that. When the time got to be too much for them, they'd go fuck with somebody and get themselves in a situation where there was no win. It was their way of saying, "Go on, kill me. Gimme a glorious way to get outta this shit."

My time started coming down on me when I realized I'd reached the one-year   5
mark and had at least two to go. I tried to cling tighter to Liz, but that didn't work. After I was transferred from the jail to Southampton, it seemed we both backed out on the marriage plans. She didn't bring it up, and neither did I. Liz's visits and letters slacked off, and I felt myself slipping out of touch with the outside world. When Liz did visit, she seemed distant and nervous, like there was something she wanted to tell me but couldn't get out. That drove me crazy, along with about a hundred thousand other irritations that constantly fucked with my head.

I thought a lot about the irony of the year 1976: It was the year Alex Haley published the slave epic *Roots* and the country was celebrating the two hundredth year of its freedom from tyranny. It seemed that every time I opened a magazine or walked past a TV set, there was talk about the yearlong bicentennial celebration. I'd heard white people brag about being free, white, and twenty-one. There I was, black, twenty-one, and in the penitentiary. It seemed I'd gotten it all wrong.

It's a weird feeling being on the edge and knowing that there's not much you can do about it but hang on. You can't get help for prison depression. You can't go to a counselor and say, "Look, I need a weekend pass. This punishment thing is taking more out of me than I think it was intended to take."

I didn't want to admit to myself that the time was getting to me that much, let alone admit it to anybody else. So I determined to do the macho thing: suffer quietly. Sometimes it got so bad I had to whisper to myself, "Hold on, Nate. Hold on."

Frustrated and depressed, I went to the prison and bought a green spiral-bound tablet and started a journal, partly out of a need to capture my fears and feelings, and partly to practice using the new words I learned. I adopted a journal theme—a quote I ran across by the writer Oliver Wendell Holmes—as encouragement to keep me pushing ahead and holding on:

I find the great thing in this world is not so much where we stand as in what direction we are moving. To reach the port of heaven, we must sail, some-times with the wind and sometimes against it–but we must sail, and not drift, nor lie at anchor.

It made me feel better sometimes to get something down on paper just like I felt it. It brought a kind of relief to be able to describe my pain. It was like, if I could describe it, it lost some of its power over me. I jotted down innermost thoughts I couldn't verbalize to anyone else, recorded what I saw around me, and expressed feelings inspired by things I read. Often, the thoughts I wrote down reflected my struggle with time.

> *Each day I inspire myself with the hope that by some miracle of God or act of legislature I will soon regain my freedom. However, from occasional conversations, I find that many other inmates have entertained the same hope–for years.*
> *May 21, 1976*

Even the guys doing less than life had a hard time. Anything in the double digits–ten years to serve, twenty, forty, sixty–could be a backbreaker. I had a buddy, Cincinnati. Real outgoing cat. Every time you saw him, he was talking beaucoup trash. But Cincinnati was doing a hard forty, and it drove him up a wall at least twice a week. He fought it by trying to keep super-busy. With a white towel hung loosely over his shoulder and several cartons of cigarettes tucked under his arm, Cincinnati (we called him that because that's where he was from) would bop briskly across the yard, intent on his missions. He'd stop and jawbone with a group of guys hanging out near the canteen, then hand a carton of cigarettes to one of them and hurry off to the next meeting.

Cincinnati was one of several major dealers at Southampton who used the drug-peddling skills they'd learned on the streets to exploit the crude prison econ-omy. In that economy, cigarettes replaced money as the medium of exchange. Favors and merchandise were negotiated in terms of their worth in packs of ciga-rettes. For twelve cartons of cigarettes, a guy could take out a contract to have somebody set up on a drug bust, or get them double-banked or shanked. Eight packs could get you a snappy pair of prison brogans from one of the brothers on the shoe-shop crew. For three packs each week, laundry workers would see to it your shirts and pants were crisply starched. Cincinnati liked to get his gray prison shirts starched so that he could turn up the collar and look real cool.

The really swift dealers found ways to convert a portion of their goods to for-bidden cash, which they used to bribe guards to get them reefer and liquor, or saved for their eventual return to the streets.

Cincinnati, who was about two years older than me and had logged a lot more street time, was penitentiary-rich. He decorated his cell with plush blue towels and stockpiled so much stuff that the rear wall of his cell looked like a convenience store. It was stacked from floor to ceiling with boxes of cookies, cigarettes, and other stuff he sold, "two for one," to inmates seeking credit until payday.

Watching cats like him, I often thought about Mo Battle and his theory about pawns. Cincinnati handled time and played chess like he lived: He failed to think far ahead and he chased pawns all over the board. In his free time off from the kitchen, where he worked, he busied himself zigzagging across the prison yard, collecting outstanding debts and treating his petty "bidness" matters like they were major business deals.

Cincinnati was playful and cheery most of the time. He was as dark as night and had a shiny gold tooth that gleamed like a coin when he smiled. Short and squat, he had a massive upper body and a low center of gravity, like Mike Tyson. In fact, his voice, high-pitched and squeaky, sounded a lot like Tyson's, too. It was the kind of voice that sounded like it belonged to a child. But nobody mistook Cincinnati for a child. He was a tank, and could turn from nice guy to cold killer in a split second.

He addressed everybody as "bro'." I'd see him on the yard and say, "Yo, Cincinnati, what's happ'nin'?" And if he was in a good mood, he'd say, "Bro' Nate, life ain't nothin' but a meatball."

But time came down on Cincinnati, like it did on everybody else. He had to do at least ten of his forty years before going up for parole. I could tell when he was thinking about it. I'd run into him on the yard and say, "What's happ'nin', Cincinnati?" He'd shake his head sadly and say, "Bro' Nate, I'm busted, disgusted, and *can't be trusted.*"

Cincinnati was so far away from home that he never got visits. On visiting days, he usually went out to the main sidewalk on the yard and looked through the fence as people visiting other inmates pulled into the parking lot.

Other times, I could tell how depressed he was by the way he handled defeat on the chessboard. I beat him all the time and taunted him, but sometimes he didn't take it well. Just before I put him in checkmate, he'd get frustrated and knock one of his big arms against the board, sending the pieces crashing to the floor. Then he'd look up with a straight face and say, "Oh, I'm sorry, Bro' Nate. I didn't mean to do that."

We were playing chess one day when Cincinnati stared at the board a long time without making a move. I got impatient. "Go on and move, man! You gonna lose anyway!"

Ignoring me, Cincinnati kept his eyes glued to the board and didn't speak for a long time. After a while, he said, "Bro' Nate, I'm gonna make a break for the fence. I been thinking about it a long time. I got a lotta money saved up. I can get outta state. You wanna come?"

Any inmate who says he's never thought about escaping is either lying or telling the sad truth. The sad truth is, the only dudes who don't think about making a break are those who are either so institutionalized that their thoughts seldom go beyond the prison gates, or who were so poor in the streets that they had been rescued and are glad to be someplace where they are guaranteed three hots and a cot.

There were a few desperate, fleeting moments when I thought half-seriously about making a run. Southampton is ringed by a tall barbed-wire fence with electrical current running through it, but everybody knew the heat was turned off much of the time. Sometimes, I'd stare at that fence and think about how to scale it. I pictured myself tossing my thick winter coat on top of the barbed wire to test the heat and protect my hands, climbing quickly to the top, and leaping to the other side to make my dash before tower guards could get off a good shot. I'd mapped an escape route based on what I'd seen of the area while traveling with the gun gang. I'd thought it through like a chess match, move for move. That's why I didn't try. When I thought it through, I always saw a great chance of getting busted or leading such a miserable life on the run that it would be another form of imprisonment.

Looking at Cincinnati, I jokingly turned down his offer to run. "Naw, brother-man. I'm gonna squat here. I'm expecting a visit from my lady this weekend. I'd hate for her to come and find me gone. Besides, I can handle my bid. You do the crime, you gotta do the time, Jack!"

I forgot about our conversation until a week or two later, when the big whistle at the guard tower sounded, signaling all inmates to go to their cells to be counted. The whistle blew at certain times every day, but on this day, it sounded at an odd hour, meaning there was something wrong. After we went to our cells, the word spread that Cincinnati had made a break. He'd hidden in the attic of the school building, then scrambled over the fence after a posse left the compound to hunt for him.

Following the count, guys in my building (I was in C-3 by then) grew real quiet. Every time someone escaped, I got quiet and privately rooted for him to get away. I sat on my bunk thinking about Cincinnati, trying to picture him out in the pitch dark, his black face sweating, ducking through bushes, hotly pursued by white men with guns and barking dogs. I imagined him low-running across some broad field, dodging lights and listening for suspicious sounds. I imagined the white country folks, alerted to the escape, grabbing their shotguns and joining the hunt.

Some weeks after Cincinnati made his break, he got caught somewhere in the state. It saddened me. He was shipped to a maximum-security prison more confining than Southampton, and he got more time tacked on to the forty years that was already giving him hell.

Prison paranoia is a dangerous thing. It can affect a person to the extent that he becomes distrustful of anyone and everyone. Even though my woman has displayed no signs of infidelity, I find myself scrutinizing her behavior each week (in the visiting room), searching her eyes for the slightest faltering trait. I search in hope that I discover none, but hope even

25

more that if there is, I will detect it before it discovers me and slithers back into some obscure
hiding place.
June 4, 1976

I walked into the crowded visiting room and took a seat at the table with Liz. My intuition told me that something was up. She'd come alone, without my parents or my son, and her brown eyes, usually bright and cheery, were sad and evasive. In a letter she'd sent to me earlier in the week, she had said there was something she wanted to discuss. I sensed what it was, and I'd come prepared.

We exchanged small talk, then there was this awkward silence. Finally, I spoke,   30
relieving her of a burden I sensed was killing her. "You're seeing someone else, aren't you?"

She nodded. "Yes."

There was a long pause as she waited for my reaction. I looked down at the floor and thought about what I'd just heard. My worst fear had come true. Liz couldn't hang. I'd have to do the time alone. I understood. She'd done the best she could. She'd been a helluva lot more supportive and reliable than I would have been under the circumstances. The best I could do was be grateful for what she'd done. Take it and grow, as she used to say. I tried to put on a brave face, and I said, "I understand, really. . . . Well, nothing I can do about that but wish you the best. I would like you to hang in there with me, but really, I don't know when I'm gettin' outta here."

She listened quietly and nodded as I talked. When I finished, she didn't say much. We sat there, bummed out, looking at each other. Mr. and Miss Manor. Liz wished me well. Her eyes watered. Then she said good-bye, and left.

I practically ran back to my cell that Saturday morning. I wanted to get back there before the tear ducts burst. It was like trying to get to the bathroom before the bladder gives out. I made it, went inside, and flopped down on a stool. I turned on the stereo, slid in one of my favorite gospel tapes, *Amazing Grace*, by Aretha Franklin, and closed my eyes. The tape opened with a song called "Mary, Don't You Weep." The deep strains of a full gospel choir, comforting the sister of Lazarus after his death, sang in a rich harmony that sent shivers through me:

Hush, Mary, don't you weep.
Hush, Mary, don't you weep.

When I heard those words, the floodgate burst and the tears started streaming   35
down my face. Streaming. The pain ran so deep it felt physical, like somebody was pounding on my chest. I'd never been hurt by a woman before. I had never cared enough to be hurt by one. I sat there, leaning on the cell door, listening to Aretha and crying. Inmates walked past and I didn't even lift my head. I didn't care who saw me or what they thought. I was crushed. Wasted. I cried until tears blurred my vision. Then I got up, picked up my washcloth, rinsed it in the sink, held it to my

face, and cried some more. Liz was gone. I remembered that she had once told me, "I'll follow you into a ditch if you lead me there." Well, I had led her there, but she'd never promised to stay.

Sometimes I'd get grinding migraines that lasted for hours on end. I figured it was caused by the pain of losing Liz, and the stress and tension hounding me. When the frequency of the headaches increased, I came up with ways to relieve the stress. I'd leave the place. I'd stretch out on my bunk, block out all light by putting a cloth over my eyes, and go into deep meditation or prayer. Starting with my toes, I'd concentrate hard and command every one of my body parts to chill. Often, by the time I reached my head the tension was gone.

Then I'd take my imagination and soar away from the prison yard. I'd travel to Portsmouth or some faraway, fictional place. Or I'd venture beyond the earth and wander through the galaxy, pondering the vastness of what God has done. I developed a hell of an imagination by doing those mental workouts, and it put me in touch with my spirit in wondrous ways. When the concentration was really good, I'd lose all feeling in my body, and my spirit would come through, making me feel at one with the universe. It was like being high: It felt so good, but I couldn't figure out a way to make it last.

> I just witnessed a brutal fight in the cafeteria. The atmosphere was certainly conducive to violence: hot, odorous air filled with noise and flies. The two combatants went at each other's throats as if their lives meant nothing to them. After being confined for an extended period of time, life does tend to lose its value. I pray that I can remember my self-worth and remain cool.
> July 21, 1976

A group of us from Tidewater were sitting around, sharing funny tales from the streets and telling war stories about crazy things we'd done. When my turn came, I told a story about a near stickup on Church Street in Norfolk. "Yeah, man, we ran across a dude who had nothing but chump change on him. We got mad 'cause the dude was broke, so we took his change and started to take his pants. He had on some yellow, flimsy-looking pants, so we made him walk with us under a streetlamp so we could get a better look at them. When we got under the streetlamp, we could see the pants were cheap. And they were dirty. So we let the dude slide, and keep his pants . . ."

Everybody was laughing. Everybody but a guy from Norfolk named Tony. Squinting his eyes, he leaned over and interrupted, "Did you say the guy had on yellow pants?"

"Yeah."

"Goddammit, that was *me* y'all stuck up that night!" he said, pointing a finger at me.

40

Everything got quiet. The guys looked at me, then at Tony, then back at me. Somebody snickered, and everybody else joined in. I laughed, too, until I looked at Tony and realized he still wasn't laughing. He was hot. He looked embarrassed and mad as hell.

To lighten the mood, I extended my hand playfully and said, "Wow, man, I'm sorry 'bout that. You know I didn't know you then."

Tony looked at my hand like he wanted to spit on it. "Naw, man. That shit ain't funny." The way he said it, I knew he wasn't going to let the thing drop. I knew that stupid macho pride had him by the throat and was choking the shit out of him.

A week or two after the exchange, he came into the library, where I was work-   45
ing, sat in a corner, and started tearing pages out of magazines. The library was filled with inmates. I walked over to the table and said, "Yo, Tony, you can't tear the pages outta the magazines, man. Other people have to read 'em."

He looked up, smiled an evil smile, then ripped out another page and said, "What you gonna do 'bout it? You ain't no killer." The room grew quiet. I felt like all eyes were on me, waiting to see what I would do. I started thinking fast. Tony was stout and muscular and I figured he'd probably do the moonwalk on me if he got his hands on me. He was sitting down and I was standing. I glanced at an empty chair near him. I thought, *I could sneak him right off the bat, grab that chair, and wrap it around his head.* Then I thought about the potential consequences of fighting at work. I could lose my job, get kicked out of the library. I thought, *I gotta let it slide. I have to.* I looked at Tony, shrugged my shoulders, and said, "I ain't gonna do nothin', man. The magazines don't belong to *me.*"

Tony sat there, staring at me, and tore more pages out of magazines. I walked away.

Later that night, I thought about it some more. I thought about how he'd come off. I thought, *He disrespected me.* I was too scared to let that man get away with disrespecting me. I felt I had faith that God would take care of me, but whenever I got that scared about something, I relied on what I knew best–faith in self. So I prayed, then set God aside for the time being and put together a shank like I'd learned to make while in the Norfolk jail. I melded a razor blade into a toothbrush handle, leaving the sharp edges sticking out, like a miniature tomahawk. I told one of my buddies what I intended to do. "I gotta get that niggah, man. He disrespected me and tried to chump me down."

The next day, we sent looking for Tony on the yard. We spotted him leaving the dispensary with a partner. While my friend kept a lookout for guards, I approached Tony. Without saying anything, I pulled the razor blade and swung it at his throat. He jumped back. I lunged at him again and he flung his arms in front of his face, blocking the blow. The razor slashed his coat. He held up his hands and said, "Hold it, hold it, hold it, man! Be cool. Everything's cool. We all right, man. I ain't got no beef with you."

I pointed the razor at him. "Niggah, don't you *never* take me to be no chump!"   50
"All right, bro', I was just playing with you yesterday."

I turned and walked away, relieved that he'd backed down and grateful that none of the guards standing on the yard had seen what went down.

My parents came to see me that afternoon. I went into the visiting room still hyper from the scene with Tony. As we talked, I looked at them and wondered what they'd say if they knew I had just risked everything I'd worked for to prove a manhood point. I wondered if Tony was going to try to get some get-back or pay somebody to try to shank me when my back was turned. I wondered if the time was coming down on me so badly that I was losing my grip.

At chow time that evening, my homie Pearly Blue came to the table and sat next to me. There was a slight smirk on his face. I sensed he was feeling a certain delight in knowing he'd warned me to hang tight with my homies to keep hassles away. "Yo, man, I heard you had a run-in with Tony."

"Yeah, a small beef."   55

"I told you these old rooty-poot niggahs will try you if they think you walk alone. . . . You know if you need to make another move on him, the homies can take care of it."

I kept looking straight ahead as I ate. "Naw, man. I got it under control."

I had no problems from Tony the remainder of the time I was at South-ampton.

The one thing that seemed to soothe everybody in the joint was music. The loud-est, most fucked-up brothers in the place chilled out when they had on a set of headphones. Some white inmates had musical instruments–guitars, saxophones, flutes–and they practiced in their cells at night. Most of the brothers didn't like hearing white music. The brothers would holler through the cell bars, "Cut that hillbilly shit out!"

But one white guy, from some rural Virginia town, was exempt from the   60
hassles. He was a fairly good guitar player, and an even better singer. Every night, before the lights went out, he calmed the building with music. He sang the same song, and it reverberated throughout the place. He strummed his guitar and sang the John Denver tune "Take Me Home, Country Roads." He sang it in a voice so clean it sounded like he was standing on a mountain crooning down into one of those luscious green valleys he was singing about:

Country rooaads,
Take me hoomme,
To the plaaace
Where I beloooonng . . .

When those lyrics floated into my cell, I'd sit quietly, lean my head against the concrete wall, and listen. That song reminded me of how lonely I was and made me think of home. It made me think of Liz. It made me think of my son, my family, my neighborhood, my life. Sometimes, when he sang that song, tears welled in my eyes and I'd wipe them away, get into bed, and think some more.

That song seemed to calm everybody in the building, even the baad-asses who were prone to yell through their cells. It had the soothing effect of a lullaby sung by a parent to a bunch of children.

The Responsive Reader

1. What kind of person is the author? What kind of human being emerges from these pages? How did the prison experience affect his outlook? How did it affect his relations with other people?

2. McCall talks about the ways different people try to deal with the burden of doing "time." How do they cope? What are you going to remember about other inmates and their stories?

3. What is the story of the author's confrontation with Tony? Is it a story of "senseless violence," or does it have a point?

4. What role does race play in this account? What images of white people do you see here through the eyes of African American inmates? Does McCall think the prison experience is different for blacks and whites?

5. What is the role of music in this account?

For Discussion or Writing

6. What attitudes, assumptions, or stereotypes about prisons and convicts did you bring to the reading of McCall's account? Does his writing challenge or change any of these? Why or why not?

7. After reading this selection, where would you place yourself on a scale going from "this could never happen to me" to "I could have been in his place"? Is your reaction "that's what happens to many of *them*" or "there but for the grace of God go *I*"? Where on the scale do your classmates place themselves? What explains your reaction? What explains theirs?

8. Some people describe prison life as an alien world of its own, with its own rules. Others describe it as a microcosm of the outside world, with similar hierarchies, and with a similar range of attitudes and behavior. To judge from this selection, which view may be closer to the truth?

Collaborative Projects

9. Inside stories of prison life range from Dennie Martin's newspaper articles from inside the California prison system to Kimberly Wozencraft's fictionalized *Rush*

(1990). Books like *The Autobiography of Malcolm X* talk about the role of the prison experience in the author's spiritual journey. You may want to work with a group on staging an "Unheard Voices" reading of selections from such accounts.

Making Connections

10. Orlando Patterson, in a part of "The Paradox of Integration," and Jonathan Kozol in "Distancing the Homeless" (both in Chapter 2) and Nathan McCall in "Time" all try to make the reader see the world from the point of view of those excluded or marginalized in our society. How successful is each? What does each make you see or understand? How do the two more general accounts and the personal autobiographical account differ in their impact on you as the reader?

CINDERELLA'S STEPSISTERS

Toni Morrison

━━━━━

Feminist writers and critics have in recent years asked us to reread familiar texts from a feminist perspective. Their reassessment of the classics has focused, for instance, on the subordinate role of women in Shakespeare's plays. It has made us reread the novels of Jane Austen (Sense and Sensibility, Pride and Prejudice) with new empathy for the struggle of intelligent and gifted women to hold their own in a male-dominated society, dealing as best they can with the callous man of wealth, the sexually predatory young bounder, and the well-meaning dullard. In the following selection, Toni Morrison, a leading African American novelist, rereads a familiar fairy tale. She finds a new and different moral in the story of Cinderella and the other women in her story. Morrison won the Nobel Prize for Literature in 1993, the first American woman in fifty-five years and the first African American writer ever to be chosen. She has written a succession of powerful novels, including The Bluest Eye *(1970),* Sula *(1973),* Song of Solomon *(1977),* Tar Baby *(1981),* Beloved *(1987) and* Jazz *(1992). Morrison is a wizard at evoking powerful contradictory feelings: nostalgia for black neighborhoods bulldozed to make way for golf courses or condominiums; her sense of the pain lurking beneath a happy-go-lucky surface of shucking, knee-slapping song and laughter; the heavy sense of misgiving of a black woman from the North as she travels back to the Old South; the terror of slave-catchers felt by a black mother who would rather kill her baby than have her grow up in slavery.*

Let me begin by taking you back a little. Back before the days at college. To   1
nursery school, probably, to a once-upon-a-time time when you first heard, or
read, or, I suspect, even saw "Cinderella." Because it is Cinderella that I want to talk
about; because it is Cinderella who causes me a feeling of urgency. What is unset-
tling about that fairy tale is that it is essentially the story of household—a world, if
you please—of women gathered together and held together in order to abuse another woman. There is, of course, a rather vague absent father and a nick-of-time
prince with a foot fetish. But neither has much personality. And there are the surrogate "mothers," of course (god- and step-), who contribute both to Cinderella's
grief and to her release and happiness. But it is her stepsisters who interest me.
How crippling it must have been for those young girls to grow up with a mother,
to watch and imitate that mother, enslaving another girl.

I am curious about their fortunes after the story ends. For contrary to recent
adaptations, the stepsisters were not ugly, clumsy, stupid girls with outsize feet. The
Grimm collection describes them as "beautiful and fair in appearance." When we
are introduced to them they are beautiful, elegant, women of status, and clearly

women of power. Having watched and participated in the violent dominion of another woman, will they be any less cruel when it comes their turn to enslave other children, or even when they are required to take care of their own mother?

It is not a wholly medieval problem. It is quite a contemporary one: feminine power when directed at other women has historically been wielded in what has been described as a "masculine" manner. Soon you will be in a position to do the very same thing. Whatever your background–rich or poor–whatever the history of education in your family–five generations or one–you have taken advantage of what has been available to you at Barnard and you will therefore leave both the economic and social status of the stepsisters *and* you will have their power.

I want not to *ask* you but to *tell* you not to participate in the oppression of your sisters. Mothers who abuse their children are women, and another woman, not an agency, has to be willing to stay their hands. Mothers who set fire to school buses are women, and another woman, not an agency, has to tell them to stay their hands. Women who stop the promotion of other women in careers are women, and another woman must come to the victim's aid. Social and welfare workers who humiliate their clients may be women, and other women colleagues have to deflect their anger.

I am alarmed by the violence that women do to each other: professional vio-   5
lence, competitive violence, emotional violence. I am alarmed by the willingness of women to enslave other women. I am alarmed by a growing absence of decency on the killing floor of professional women's worlds. You are the women who will take your place in the world where *you* can decide who shall flourish and who shall wither; you will make distinctions between the deserving poor and the undeserving poor; where you can yourself determine which life is expendable and which is indispensable. Since you will have the power to do it, you may also be persuaded that you have the right to do it. As educated women the distinction between the two is first-order business.

I am suggesting that we pay as much attention to our nurturing sensibilities as to our ambition. You are moving in the direction of freedom and the function of freedom is to free somebody else. You are moving toward self-fulfillment, and the consequences of that fulfillment should be to discover that there is something just as important as you are and that just-as-important thing may be Cinderella–or your stepsister.

In your rainbow journey toward the realization of personal goals, don't make choices based only on your security and your safety. Nothing is safe. That is not to say that anything ever was, or that anything worth achieving ever should be. Things of value seldom are. It is not safe to have a child. It is not safe to challenge the status quo. It is not safe to choose work that has not been done before. Or to do old work in a new way. There will always be someone there to stop you. But in pursuing your highest ambitions, don't let your personal safety diminish the safety of your stepsister. In wielding the power that is deservedly yours, don't permit it to enslave your stepsisters. Let your might and your power emanate from that place in you that is nurturing and caring.

Women's rights is not only an abstraction, a cause; it is also a personal affair. It is not only about "us"; it is also about me and you. Just the two of us.

The Responsive Reader

1. Can you retell the Cinderella story? Why does Morrison mention earlier versions of the story? What bothers Morrison about the story?

2. What parallel does Morrison see between the fairy tale household and the relationship between women in today's society? What kind of situations does she have in mind when she asks women not to share "in the oppression of your sisters"? Can you think of examples of conflict or rivalry relevant to her discussion?

3. Does Morrison make basic assumptions about the difference between men's values and women's? What standards and priorities is she asking women to embrace?

For Discussion or Writing

4. Do you think that ambition, competition, and success mean different things to men and women? Do you think women should conform to male standards in these areas? Do you think the growing influence of women will change prevailing attitudes in these areas?

5. What role does rivalry or solidarity among women play in books you have read or plays you have seen? What role does it play in influential popular entertainment?

Collaborative Projects

6. What image of women is projected in recent movie versions of literary classics where women play central roles? You might want to help a group arrange a symposium on this topic, exploring for instance the movies based on Alice Walker's *The Color Purple* and Jane Austen's *Sense and Sensibility*.

CULTURAL ETIQUETTE
A Guide

Amoja Three Rivers

> *Sticks and stones may break my bones,*
> *But words can never hurt me.*
>
> CHILDREN'S JINGLE

    Language is the basic tool of poets, novelists, playwrights, and biographers. People who love imaginative literature are especially sensitive to the overtones and associations of words—and may by the same token be especially sensitive to abuses of language. Students of the humanities have been prominent in recent controversies swirling around offensive or politically incorrect language. Language is not harmless or neutral. It reveals or betrays attitudes, and in turn it shapes behavior. An executive who thinks of women as dames, broads, or chicks is not likely to give women a fair shake in hiring and promotion, especially if these women are more intelligent and more capable than he is. African Americans may not expect to get justice in a court relying on testimony by white police officers who use the "N" word. Hate speech sanctions and incites hateful actions. What is the remedy? Organizations advancing the rights of women, minorities, or gays have in recent years promoted speech codes that would ban slurs or demeaning language. Opponents have argued that such restrictions abridge the right of free speech; they have a chilling effect on the open expression on which a free society depends. The following article was first published in Ms. magazine. The author is a cofounder of the Accessible African Herstory Project and was described by the editors of Ms. as a "lecturer, herstorian, and craftswoman." She zeroes in on words that, whether used thoughtlessly or intentionally, demean, denigrate, or stereotype other people.

Cultural Etiquette is intended for people of all "races," nationalities, and creeds,   1
not necessarily just "white" people, because no one living in Western society is exempt from the influences of racism, racial stereotypes, race and cultural prejudices, and anti-Semitism. I include anti-Semitism in the discussion of racism because it is simply another manifestation of cultural and racial bigotry.

All people are people. It is ethnocentric to use a generic term such as "people" to refer only to white people and then racially label everyone else. This creates and reinforces the assumption that whites are the norm, the real people, and that all others are aberrations.

"Exotic," when applied to human beings, is ethnocentric and racist.

While it is true that most citizens of the U.S.A. are white, at least four fifths of the world's population consists of people of color. Therefore, it is statistically incorrect as well as ethnocentric to refer to us as minorities. The term "minority" is used to reinforce the idea of people of color as "other."

A cult is a particular system of religious worship. If the religious practices of   5
the Yorubas constitute a cult, then so do those of the Methodists, Catholics, Episco-
palians, and so forth.

A large radio/tape player is a boom-box, or a stereo or a box or a large metallic ham sandwich with speakers. It is not a "ghetto blaster."

Everybody can blush. Everybody can bruise. Everybody can tan and get sun-
burned. Everybody.

Judaism is no more patriarchal than any other patriarchal religion.

Koreans are not taking over. Neither are Jews. Neither are the Japanese. Neither
are the West Indians. These are myths put out and maintained by the ones who really have.

All hair is "good" hair. Dreadlocks, locks, dreads, natty dreads, et cetera, is an   10
ancient traditional way that African people sometimes wear their hair. It is not
braided, it is "locked." Locking is the natural tendency of African hair to knit and
bond to itself. It locks by itself, we don't have to do anything to it to make it lock.
It is permanent; once locked, it cannot come undone. It gets washed just as regularly as anyone else's hair. No, you may not touch it, don't ask.

One of the most effective and insidious aspects of racism is cultural genocide.
Not only have African Americans been cut off from our African tribal roots, but
because of generations of whites pitting African against Indian, and Indian against
African, we have been cut off from our Native American roots as well. Consequently, most African Native Americans no longer have tribal affiliations, or know
for certain what people they are from.

Columbus didn't discover diddly-squat.

Slavery is not a condition unique to African people. In fact, the word "slave"
comes from the Slav people of Eastern Europe. Because so many Slavs were enslaved by other people (including Africans), their very name came to be synonymous with the condition.

Native Americans were also enslaved by Europeans. Because it is almost impossible to successfully enslave large numbers of people in their own land, most
enslaved Native Americans from the continental U.S. were shipped to Bermuda,
and the West Indies, where many intermarried with the Africans.

People do not have a hard time because of their race or cultural back-   15
ground. No one is attacked, abused, oppressed, pogromed, or enslaved because of
their race, creed, or cultural background. People are attacked, abused, oppressed,
pogromed, or enslaved because of racism and anti-Semitism. There is a subtle but
important difference in the focus here. The first implies some inherent fault or
shortcoming within the oppressed person or group. The second redirects the responsibility back to the real source of the problem.

Asians are not "mysterious," "fatalistic," or "inscrutable."

Native Americans are not stoic, mystical, or vanishing.

Latin people are no more hot-tempered, hot-blooded, or emotional than any-one else. We do not have flashing eyes, teeth, or daggers. We are lovers pretty much like other people. Very few of us deal with any kind of drugs.

Middle Easterners are not fanatics, terrorists, or all oil-rich.

Jewish people are not particularly rich, clannish, or expert in money matters.   20
Not all African Americans are poor, athletic, or ghetto-dwellers.

Most Asians in the U.S. are not scientists, mathematicians, geniuses, or wealthy.
Southerners are no less intelligent than anybody else.

It is not a compliment to tell someone: "I don't think of you as Jewish/Black/Asian/Latina/Middle Eastern/Native American." Or "I think of you as white."

Do not use a Jewish person or person of color to hear your confession of past   25
racist transgressions. If you have offended a particular person, then apologize di-rectly to that person.

Also don't assume that Jews and people of color necessarily want to hear about how prejudiced your Uncle Fred is, no matter how terrible you think he is.

If you are white and/or gentile, do not assume that the next Jewish person or person of color you see will feel like discussing this guide with you. Sometimes we get tired of teaching this subject.

If you are white, don't brag to a person of color about your overseas trip to our homeland. Especially when we cannot afford such a trip. Similarly, don't as-sume that we are overjoyed to see the expensive artifacts you bought.

Words like "gestapo," "concentration camp" and "Hitler" are only appropriate when used in reference to the Holocaust.

"Full-blood," "half-breed," "quarter-blood." Any inference that a person's "race"   30
depends on blood is racist. Natives are singled out for this form of bigotry and are denied rights on that basis.*

"Scalping": a custom also practiced by the French, the Dutch, and the English.*

Do you have friends or acquaintances who are terrific except they're really racist? If you quietly accept that part of them, you are giving their racism tacit approval.

As an exercise, pretend you are from another planet and you want an example of a typical human being for your photo album. Having never heard of racism, you'd probably pick someone who represents the majority of the people on the planet—an Asian person.

How many is too many? We have heard well-meaning liberals say things like "This event is too white. We need more people of color." Well, how many do you need? Fifty? A hundred? Just what is your standard for personal racial comfort?

People of color and Jewish people have been so all their lives. Further, if we   35

---

*Reprinted with permission from *The Pathfinder Directory*, by Amylee, Native American Indian Re-source Center. [Author's note] have been raised in a place where white gentiles predominate, then we have been subjected to racism/anti-Semitism all our lives. We are therefore experts on our own lives and conditions. If you do not understand or believe or agree with what someone is saying about their own oppression, do not automatically assume that they are wrong or paranoid or oversensitive.

It is not "racism in reverse" or "segregation" for Jews or people of color to come together in affinity groups for mutual support. Sometimes we need some time and space apart from the dominant group just to relax and be ourselves. If people coming together for group support makes you feel excluded, perhaps there's something missing in your own life or cultural connections.

The various cultures of people of color often seem very attractive to white people. (Yes, we are wonderful, we can't deny it.) But white people should not make a playground out of other people's cultures. We are not quaint. We are not exotic. We are not cool.

Don't forget that every white person alive today is also descended from tribal peoples. If you are white, don't neglect your own ancient traditions. They are as valid as anybody else's, and the ways of your own ancestors need to be honored and remembered.

"Race" is an arbitrary and meaningless concept. Races among humans don't exist. If there ever was any such thing as race, there has been so much constant crisscrossing of genes for the last 500,000 years that it would have lost all meaning anyway. There are no real divisions between us, only a continuum of variations that constantly change, as we come together and separate according to the movement of human populations.

Anyone who functions in what is referred to as the "civilized" world is a car-   40
rier of the disease of racism.

Does reading this guide make you uncomfortable? Angry? Confused? Are you' taking it personally? Well, not to fret. Racism has created a big horrible mess, and racial healing can sometimes be painful. Just remember that Jews and people of color do not want or need anybody's guilt. We just want people to accept responsibility when it is appropriate, and actively work for change.

The Responsive Reader

1. Have you been the target of any of the stereotyped assumptions or objectionable expressions discussed in this article? Have you used any of them yourself? In what context? For what purpose or with what results?

2. Three Rivers reminds her readers of familiar stereotypes about Latins, Asians, blacks, Jews, Middle Easterners, and other ethnic or cultural groups. Which of these do you recognize? Have they influenced your own thinking, or have you left them behind?

3. Why does Three Rivers object to the terms *minority, exotic, cult, half-breed, reverse racism*, and *race* itself? Do her objections seem justified or valid to you? Why or why not?

4. Do you find personal interaction with people of other ethnic or cultural groups awkward at times? What etiquette does Three Rivers sketch out for such situations?

For Discussion or Writing

5. Are activists like Three Rivers too thin-skinned or oversensitive? Which of her concerns would you and your classmates rate as most serious? Would you rate any of them as frivolous or misguided?

6. The author herself employs weighty, emotionally charged words like *ethnocentric, anti-Semitism, bigotry, racism*, and *genocide*. How does she use them? What do these words mean to you? What guidelines would you draw up for their use?

7. Where have you seen evidence of the power of language to antagonize, to hurt people, or to stir up conflict? Where have you seen evidence of the power of language to soothe ruffled tempers or to make peace?

Collaborative Projects

8. Does your own school or do institutions or businesses in your area have speech codes? Do they have guidelines for avoiding offensive language? Working with a group, investigate the history and effectiveness of such initiatives.

RAPE AND THE BOXING RING

Joyce Carol Oates

Culture has sometimes been narrowly defined as highbrow art and literature enjoyed by a leisured cultural elite. However, today culture is often more inclusively defined as the sum total of the images, ideas, and rituals that shape a way of life, a way of looking at the world. In American culture today, sports as a megabusiness, as a mass ritual, and as a way of looking at the world has become a major dominant force. Joyce Carol Oates is a prolific writer of fiction who has fascinated and shaken up a large readership with her disturbing close-ups of an alienated, nihilistic younger generation no longer listening to their self-righteous, materialistic elders. In the following essay, Oates addresses a key question about today's popular culture: What has brought us from the ideal of an enlightened, tolerant, humane society to a culture saturated with the pornography of violence? Oates looks in the ritual and mythology of boxing for clues to male psychology. She traces the connection between violent sports and rape as twin manifestations of the male aggressive impulse. She wrote the essay after former heavyweight champion Mike Tyson had been charged with rape by an eighteen-year-old beauty pageant contestant and sent to jail.

Mike Tyson's conviction on rape charges in Indianapolis was a minor tragedy   1
for the beleaguered sport of boxing, but a considerable triumph for women's rights. For once, though bookmakers were giving 5–1 odds that Tyson would be acquitted, and the mood of the country seemed distinctly conservative, a jury resisted the outrageous defense that a rape victim is to be blamed for her own predicament. For once, a celebrity with enormous financial resources did not escape trial and a criminal conviction by settling with his accuser out of court.

That boxing and "women's rights" should be perceived as opposed is symbolically appropriate, since of all sports, boxing is the most aggressively masculine, the very soul of war in microcosm. Elemental and dramatically concise, it raises to an art the passions underlying direct human aggression; its fundamentally murderous intent is not obscured by the pursuit of balls or pucks, nor can the participants expect help from teammates. In a civilized, humanitarian society, one would expect such a blood sport to have died out, yet boxing, sponsored by gambling casinos in Las Vegas and Atlantic City, and broadcast by cable television, flourishes: had the current heavyweight champion, Evander Holyfield, fought Mike Tyson in a title defense, Holyfield would have earned no less than $30 million. If Tyson had been still champion, and still fighting, he would have been earning more.

The paradox of boxing is that it so excessively rewards men for inflicting injury upon one another that, outside the ring, with less "art," would be punishable as aggravated assault, or manslaughter. Boxing belongs to that species of mysterious masculine activity for which anthropologists use such terms as "deep play": activity that is wholly without utilitarian value, in fact contrary to utilitarian value, so dangerous that no amount of money can justify it. Sports-car racing, stunt flying, mountain climbing, bullfighting, dueling–these activities, through history, have provided ways in which the individual can dramatically, if sometimes fatally, distinguish himself from the crowd, usually with the adulation and envy of the crowd, and traditionally, the love of women. Women–in essence, Woman–is the prize, usually self-proffered. To look upon organized sports as a continuum of Darwinian theory–in which the sports-star hero flaunts the superiority of his genes–is to see how displays of masculine aggression have their sexual component, as ingrained in human beings as any instinct for self-preservation and reproduction. In a capitalist society, the secret is to capitalize upon instinct.

Yet even within the very special world of sports, boxing is distinct. Is there any athlete, however celebrated in his own sport, who would not rather reign as the heavyweight champion of the world? If, in fantasy at least, he could be another Muhammad Ali, or Joe Louis, or indeed, Mike Tyson in his prime? Boxing celebrates the individual man in his maleness, not merely in his skill as an athlete– though boxing demands enormous skill, and its training is far more arduous than most men could endure for more than a day or two. All athletes can become addicted to their own adrenaline, but none more obviously than the boxer, who, like Sugar Ray Leonard, already a multimillionaire with numerous occupations outside the ring, will risk serious injury by coming back out of retirement; as Mike Tyson has said, "Outside of boxing, everything is so boring." What makes boxing repulsive to many observers is precisely what makes boxing so fascinating to participants.

BLOOD SACRIFICE

This is because it is a highly organized ritual that violates taboo. It flouts such   5
moral prescriptions as "Thou shalt not kill." It celebrates, not meekness, but flamboyant aggression. No one who has not seen live boxing matches (in contrast to the sanitized matches broadcast over television) can quite grasp its eerie fascination–the spectator's sense that he or she is a witness to madness, yet a madness sanctioned by tradition and custom, as finely honed by certain celebrated practitioners as an artist's performance at the highest level of genius, and, yet more disturbing, immensely gratifying to the audience. Boxing mimics our early ancestors' rite of bloody sacrifice and redemption; it excites desires most civilized men and women find abhorrent. For some observers, it is frankly obscene, like pornography; yet, unlike pornography, it is not fantasy but real, thus far more subversive.

The paradox for the boxer is that, in the ring, he experiences himself as a living conduit for the inchoate, demonic will of the crowd: the expression of their collective desire, which is to pound another human being into absolute submission. The more vicious the boxer, the greater the acclaim. And the financial reward–Tyson is reported to have earned $100 million. (He who at the age of 13 was plucked from a boys' school for juvenile delinquents in upstate New York.) Like the champion gladiators of Roman decadence, he will be both honored and despised, for, no matter his celebrity, and the gift of his talent, his energies spring from the violation of taboo and he himself is tainted by it.

Mike Tyson has said that he does not think of boxing as a sport. He sees himself as a fantasy gladiator who, by "destructing" opponents, enacts others' fantasies in his own being. That the majority of these others are well-to-do whites who would themselves crumple at a first blow, and would surely claim a pious humanitarianism, would not go unnoted by so wary and watchful a man. Cynicism is not an inevitable consequence of success, but it is difficult to retain one's boyish naiveté in the company of the sort of people, among them the notorious Don King, who have surrounded Tyson since 1988, when his comanager, Jim Jacobs, died. As Floyd Patterson, an ex-heavyweight champion who has led an exemplary life, has said, "When you have millions of dollars, you have millions of friends."

It should not be charged against boxing that Mike Tyson *is* boxing in any way. Boxers tend to be fiercely individualistic, and Tyson is, at the least, an enigma. He began his career, under the tutelage of the legendary trainer Cus D'Amato, as a strategist, in the mode of such brilliant technicians as Henry Armstrong and Sugar Ray Robinson. He was always aware of a lineage with Jack Dempsey, arguably the most electrifying of all heavyweight champions, whose nonstop aggression revolutionized the sport and whose shaved haircut and malevolent scowl, and, indeed, penchant for dirty fighting, made a tremendous impression upon the young Tyson.

In recent years, however, Tyson seems to have styled himself at least partly on the model of Charles (Sonny) Liston, the "baddest of the bad" black heavyweights. Liston had numerous arrests to his credit and served time in prison (for assaulting a policeman); he had the air, not entirely contrived, of a sociopath; he was always friendly with racketeers, and died of a drug overdose that may in fact have been murder. (It is not coincidental that Don King, whom Tyson has much admired, and whom Tyson has empowered to run his career, was convicted of manslaughter and served time in an Ohio prison.) Like Liston, Tyson has grown to take a cynical pleasure in publicly condoned sadism (his "revenge" bout with Tyrell Biggs, whom he carried for seven long rounds in order to inflict maximum damage) and in playing the outlaw; his contempt for women, escalating in recent years, is a part of that guise. The witty obscenity of a prefight taunt of Tyson's–"I'll make you into my girlfriend"–is the boast of the rapist.

Perhaps rape itself is a gesture, a violent repudiation of the female, in the assertion of maleness that would seem to require nothing beyond physical gratification of the crudest kind. The supreme macho gesture–like knocking out an opponent and standing over his fallen body, gloves raised in triumph.

In boxing circles it is said–this, with an affectionate sort of humor–that the heavyweight champion is the 300-pound gorilla who sits anywhere in the room

10

he wants; and, presumably, takes any female he wants. Such a grandiose sense of entitlement, fueled by the insecurities and emotions of adolescence, can have disastrous consequences. Where once it was believed that Mike Tyson might mature into the greatest heavyweight of all time, breaking Rocky Marciano's record of 49 victories and no defeats, it was generally acknowledged that, since his defeat of Michael Spinks in 1988, he had allowed his boxing skills to deteriorate. Not simply his ignominious loss of his title to the mediocre James (Buster) Douglas in 1990, but subsequent lackluster victories against mediocre opponents made it clear that Tyson was no longer a serious, nor even very interesting boxer.

The dazzling reflexes were dulled, the shrewd defensive skills drilled into him by D'Amato were largely abandoned: Tyson emerged suddenly as a conventional heavyweight like Gerry Cooney, who advances upon his opponent with the hope of knocking him out with a single punch–and does not always succeed. By 25, Tyson seemed already middle aged, burnt out. He would have no great fights after all. So, strangely, he seemed to invite his fate outside the ring, with sado-masochistic persistence, testing the limits of his celebrity's license to offend by ever-escalating acts of aggression and sexual effrontery.

The familiar sports adage is surely true, one's ultimate opponent is oneself.

It may be objected that these remarks center upon the rapist, and not his victim; that sympathy, pity, even in some quarters moral outrage flow to the criminal and not the person he has violated. In this case, ironically, the victim, Desiree Washington, though she will surely bear psychic scars through her life, has emerged as a victor, a heroine: a young woman whose traumatic experience has been, as so few traumas can be, the vehicle for a courageous and selfless stand against the sexual abuse of women and children in America. She seems to know that herself, telling *People* magazine, "It was the right thing to do." She was fortunate in drawing a jury who rejected classic defense ploys by blaming the victim and/or arguing consent. Our criminal-justice system being what it is, she was lucky. Tyson, who might have been acquitted elsewhere in the country, was unlucky.

'POOR GUY'

Whom to blame for this most recent of sports disgraces in America? The culture that flings young athletes like Tyson up out of obscurity, makes millionaires of them and watches them self-destruct? Promoters like Don King and Bob Arum? Celebrity hunters like Robin Givens, Tyson's ex-wife, who seemed to have exploited him for his money and a means of promoting her own acting career? The indulgence generally granted star athletes when they behave recklessly? When they abuse drugs and alcohol, and mistreat women?   15

I suggest that no one is to blame, finally, except the perpetrator himself. In Montieth Illingworth's cogently argued biography of Tyson, "Mike Tyson: Money,

Myth and Betrayal," Tyson is quoted, after one or another public debacle: "People say 'Poor guy.' That insults me. I despise sympathy. So I screwed up. I made some mistakes. 'Poor guy,' like I'm some victim. There's nothing poor about me."

The Responsive Reader

1. For Oates, what is the link between boxing and rape? What for her makes boxing a revealing symbol of the male psyche? What other sports for her are similarly revealing or instructive?

2. Does Oates attack boxing as an outsider, or does she know the sport? According to her, what taboos does the sport violate? What explains the chemistry between the boxer and the fans?

3. For Oates, is Tyson just a convenient Exhibit A for her indictment of men? Or does she try to understand him as a human being? How does she analyze his decline as a champion? Does she see extenuating circumstances in his background, in his entourage, or in the role of the larger society?

4. Men discussing rape cases are often accused of blaming the victim. What is Oates' view of the victim? How does she describe her role? How does she explain the outcome of the trial?

For Discussion or Writing

5. Do you agree that violent sports contribute to the epidemic of violence in contemporary American society? Or do you think athletes and sports fans are being made scapegoats? Why or why not?

6. Do you think that Oates' line of argument stirs up antagonism between men and women? Do you think she is fueling the war between the sexes? Do you think she is a divisive influence?

7. In the Tyson case, both the accused aggressor and the victim were African American. Does the question of race enter into Oates' discussion? Should it?

Collaborative Projects

8. Do judges and juries today tend to favor men or women in cases involving rape or violent abuse? Is there a presumption of guilt or innocence in typical cases? Or is each case different? Working with a group, study recent court cases that could shed light on these questions.

FORUM: *Government and the Arts*

Hard-nosed "practical" people have often talked as if art and culture were frills, irrelevant to the serious business of society. Literature, music, or painting were for longhairs, while the movers and shakers went about the business of stepping up the Gross National Product. Paradoxically, however, political and legal establishments have often kept a wary eye on artists, writers, and intellectuals. In the West, major works of leading writers—James Joyce, D. H. Lawrence—were for years available only in plain brown wrappers. The Nazi authorities conducted long-drawn out vindictive campaigns against "degenerate art," driving artists and writers into exile or suicide. Stalin's purges in the Soviet Union from the thirties on destroyed the lives of actors, directors, poets. The cultural revolution in Mao's China made it a crime to love Beethoven. In the United States in recent years, much controversy has swirled around government support for the arts. The National Endowment for the Humanities and the National Endowment for the Arts, channeling limited public funds into support for public broadcasting, museums, theaters, and symphony orchestras, or into sponsorship of individual artists, came under attack.

WHY AMERICA SHOULDN'T KILL CULTURAL FUNDING

Robert Hughes

Australian-born Robert Hughes, art critic for Time *magazine, is a sharp-eyed and sharp-tongued observer of the American cultural scene. In his* Culture of Complaint *(1993), he tore into the two PCs—the "patriotically correct" far right and the "politically correct" far left, who in recent years have been fighting pitched battles over the dead bodies of American culture and education. He wrote the following article for* Time *when a new conservative-dominated Congress was sharpening the knives for the two federal agencies that support the arts and humanities, accusing the NEA and the NEH of using taxpayers' money to promote art that was obscene, antireligious, and anti-American. The funds at stake—a fraction of the cost of a single new bomber—paled next to the billion-dollar pork just voted for by the self-described budget-cutters. Hughes is a controversialist who delights in giving the Rush Limbaughs and Newt Gingriches tit for tat. He here swings the cudgel at the "Philistines" who prefer Beavis and Butthead to Sesame Street and Big Bird. In the shortened version of his article reprinted here, some references to the short-term politics of culture have been omitted. What, according to Hughes, were the issues? Who were the players?*

"Democratic nations," wrote the ever prescient Alexis de Tocqueville in *Democracy in America*, long ago in 1840, "will habitually prefer the useful to the beautiful,   1 and they will require that the beautiful should be useful." What would Tocqueville have thought of today's assaults on the fabric of America's public culture?

The Republican leadership in Congress means to sever all links between American government and American culture. It wants the Federal Government to give no support at all to music, theater, ballet, opera, film, intelligent television, literature, history, archaeology, museum work, architectural conservation and the visual arts. It intends to abolish federal funding for the National Endowment for the Arts, the National Endowment for the Humanities and the Corporation for Public Broadcasting. And it wants to do it tomorrow.

This plan isn't economic. Even its proponents have largely given up on the absurd fiction that canceling America's meager $620 million worth of cultural programs will do anything to reduce the present budget deficit of $180 billion. Not when a Senate committee last month approved a pork load for the military of $7 billion more than the Pentagon asked for.

Fiscal discipline? In fact, the project is cultural defoliation—an attempt to destroy "liberal" habitat. If there was any doubt about its momentum, the young velociraptors in Congress—freshman ideologues, mostly, squeaking with Newtish zeal—buried it three weeks ago. These boys and girls aren't even cultural Neanderthals. They're Jurassic. On culture, the limbic forebrain can hold one sound bite at a time, courtesy of Rush Limbaugh or George Will. PBS? "Elitist welfare for the rich." The NEA? "State-subsidized porn." The NEH? "P.C. revisionist history."

Will this axman's folly put America alone among the nations of the world?   5
Well, not exactly. Little of Haiti's national budget goes to culture. Zaïre does not support a national theater, and cultural grants in Rwanda, even for victim art, may be assumed to be fairly small. No documentaries infected by liberal bias get aired on Tehran state television. Saddam Hussein's boys are not straining to underwrite feminist histories of, say, the Marsh Arabs of the Euphrates.

Clearly the American public culture imagined by Newt Gingrich and his fellow ideologues in and out of Congress, including their insatiable Fundamentalist Christian right wing, will not seem strange everywhere in the world.

But in the more civilized parts it will. And to many Americans—who are by no means the "cultural élite" that conservative rhetoric invokes with such shrill banality—it already does. Of course, the defunding of the endowments isn't going to kill off the arts in America. Painters, dancers, actors are tough as weeds and can grow in cracks in the concrete. There was great art, drama, writing and scholarship in America before 1965, when the endowments were founded. Dedicated people create ingenious strategies of survival for themselves. But why should they have to? By what meanness, through what smug Philistinism—and, above all, on what actual evidence—do our Jacks-in-office decree that the arts and humanities are beneath the interest of the American people and unworthy of their collective support?

To conservative rhetors in Congress, whatever is not blandly or angrily populist is élitist. In their resort to this weasel word, the patriotically correct on the right are as bad as the politically correct on the residual left–worse, in fact, because they have more power. How all these folk would hate Thomas Jefferson if he walked back in with his idea that democracy was meant to foster a "natural aristocracy" of talent and intelligence. Naked élitism!

Hypocrisy reigns. The right complains (with reason) about the dumbing-down of American education and then wants to kill one of the essential means of its spread and improvement, the National Endowment for the Humanities. It laments the depravity of network and cable TV, especially in the stew of commercial gunk it serves up to children, then wants to cut all federal funding for PBS, the only source of decent educational programming for children and of intelligent documentaries for grownups.

10

"As far as I'm concerned, there's nothing public about [PBS]," Gingrich crowed to a roomful of like-minded enthusiasts in Washington's Capitol Hill Club last February. "It's an élitist enterprise. Rush Limbaugh is public broadcasting." Yeah, and so is Howard Stern–and Jenny Jones is Ken Burns, and Tom Clancy is Toni Morrison. The fact is that no system with as broad and loyal an audience base as PBS repeatedly garners can be called élitist. A national poll conducted for PBS by Opinion Research Corp. indicates that fully 84% of Americans want to see PBS funding maintained or increased and that 82% of them–79% Republican–feel PBS programming content is "neither too conservative nor too liberal."

But Newt and his -oids resent PBS's small measure of independence from "market forces"–from corporate and hence, ultimately, political control. More important still, the Republicans want a carcass they can toss to their extreme right. The Christian Coalition and other Fundamentalists, such as the Rev. Donald Wildmon's religious hit squad, the American Family Association, believe PBS is a factory of pinko, homosexual, you-name-it agit-prop and want to see it abolished for love of censorship.

Some lefties they have there on PBS: William F. Buckley Jr., Ben Wattenberg and that far famed enemy of capitalism Louis Rukeyser. Like Pat Robertson's views on "creation science," this belief hinges on ignoring the fossil evidence. Sure, PBS has run programs exposing business fraud, supporting homosexual and other minority claims to rights, satirizing religion (however mildly) and questioning some government practices. Sometimes it has been guilty of "imbalance," but at least it hasn't completely succumbed to the emasculating belief that every assertion in a given program should be at once neutralized by its opposite. Compared with public television anywhere else, from England's BBC to state broadcasting outfits in France, Germany, Italy or Australia, PBS has been cautiously middle of the road in its political alignments, and its major source of funding, the Corporation for Public Broadcasting, has been dominated by conservatives ever since it was created in 1967 by the Johnson Administration. . . .

To put matters in perspective, one must first remember the comparative triviality of the sums involved–the shallowness of modern America's official commitments to culture.

The U.S. government currently spends less than five-hundredths of 1% of its national budget on all forms of cultural subsidy–the equivalent of maybe five cups of diner coffee per citizen per year. In fiscal 1995 the NEH got $172 million, the NEA got $162.4 million, and the CPB got $285.6 million. Still, these modest sums exert large leverage on private and corporate patronage through "matching grants" (to qualify, the recipient must raise as much as $3 from the private sources for every federal dollar) and by the vitally important role played by the NEA and the NEH as *Good Housekeeping* seals of approval on projects.

Besides, culture is business. Serious business. The splendid offerings of New   15
York City, from the Metropolitan Museum of Art to the New York City Ballet, generate more than $2 billion a year in tourist revenue. Not-for-profit arts, local and national, support 1.3 million jobs, yield $37 billion a year in economic activity and return $3.4 billion a year to the federal treasury through tax–some 20 times the budget of the NEA. It is ludicrous to pretend that the NEA is a drain on the American purse.

Over the past quarter-century, NEA seed money has been a boon and a blessing to America's myriad cultural outlets. It is easy to think of scores, and possible to find hundreds, of museum exhibitions, dance and drama projects, concerts and arts–education programs of real cultural value that would not have had private underwriting without the spur of public money. Corporations need reassurance and are reluctant to disgorge without it.

Some Republicans argue that since corporate and foundation support for the arts outweighs federal support–$16 to $1–the NEA and NEH would not be missed. This is an illusion. Some American businesses, like Philip Morris, have been very generous in their support of the arts. But this generosity depends on their public relations needs. (If there were no lung cancer or emphysema, the arts would get much less.) Increasingly, these needs are defined as social rather than artistic. Hence the shift, in private philanthropy, to race- and gender-based programs, meant to make art what theatrical director Robert Brustein calls "a conduit for social justice" rather than art *as art*. As the newsletter *Corporate Philanthropy Report* recently noted, "We no longer 'support' the arts. We use the arts in innovative ways to support the social causes chosen by our company."

That's exactly what Republican critics accuse the NEA and the NEH of doing. Moreover, if the flat-tax enthusiasts in the G.O.P. have their way, private and corporate arts subsidies–especially gifts to museums–will vanish as tax-deduction inducements evaporate. This will destroy the mechanism that made American museum collections great. There is no sign that anyone in Congress has thought this through. And why? Because frankly, my dear, we don't give a damn.

America's federal stinginess with the arts and humanities does it immense discredit. By contrast, every candidate in the last French election, from the socialist Lionel Jospin to the conservative victor Jacques Chirac, agreed that fully 1% of France's state budget should be set aside for culture. This will cost each taxpayer about $50 a year and is wholly uncontroversial. Nobody complains in Germany either, though federal cultural subsidies cost each taxpayer $38 and city ones even more: Berlin, for instance, will spend 1.1 billion marks ($800 million) in fiscal 1995, 2.6% of its total municipal budget, on art and culture–$225 for each of its 3.5 million residents. Berliners like this. They are proud of it.

Many people do feel they have a right to expect their government to spend   20 some of their tax money in preserving and amplifying their culture and their history, even if this effort works with less than 75% efficiency–which would still be better than the rate of the Pentagon's extravaganza. Some would argue that this is one of the criteria of political enlightenment. Why not in America?

Why not, indeed? Because in America, the arts have always had to prove how moral they are. Ever since the Puritans got to Massachusetts in the 17th century, American culture has had an iconophobic streak: prelates and politicians felt that though God (like them) spoke through the Word, the visual and performing arts were in some sense the devil's work, best left alone by a virtuous polity. This has combined with America's extreme loathing of tax–for American independence began with a tax revolt, when the tea chests were tossed into Boston Harbor in 1773. Put them together, and you get to hear House majority leader Dick Armey proclaiming, without a shred of evidence, that federal arts subsidy "offends the Constitution of the U.S."–without, of course, suggesting which clause or amendment it offends.

There is no such clause, because America's Founding Fathers had no doubt about the necessity of the arts in a democracy. They were radicals and revolutionists who believed that the arts should be available to the many, not the privileged few (as in 18th century Europe, where they were left to the élite "private sector," to whose corporate equivalents the G.O.P. wants to return them today). "I must study politics and war," wrote John Adams to his wife Abigail, "that my sons may have liberty to study mathematics and philosophy. My sons ought to study . . . navigation, commerce and agriculture, in order to give their children a right to study painting, poetry, music, architecture . . ." Their son John Quincy Adams amplified that in his *First Message to Congress.* For government to refrain, he wrote, from "promoting the improvement of agriculture, commerce, manufacture, the cultivation and encouragement of the mechanical and of the elegant arts, the advancement of literature . . . would be treachery to the most sacred of trusts."

Intelligent appreciation of the arts and the humanities was part of the democratic promise. Learning, no less surely than the Kentucky rifle, supported freedom. The case for federal interest in fostering it was plainly put by James Madison 200 years ago. Americans, he said, owed it to themselves "and to the cause of free government, to prove by their establishments . . . that their political institutions are

as favorable to the intellectual and moral improvement of Man as they are con-
formable to his individual and social rights."

Other Americans, whether ordinary, shortsighted materialists or mere yahoos,
have often opposed this noble idea. Hence tax-financed culture has always seemed
a "soft spot" in government budgets.

In 1814, after the British burned the Congressional Library and Jefferson of-   25
fered to sell Congress his own books as a replacement, angry voices in Congress
denounced the idea: it was immoral to spend federal money on "philosophical
nonsense" collected by a notorious freethinker, on volumes that were "worthless, in
languages which many cannot read, and most ought not." Wisely, Congress voted
over its seated bigots and populist lowbrows, as it should today. It bought the
books, for $23,950. This, as historian David McCullough pointed out to the House
Appropriations Subcommittee last February, "may be seen as the beginning of
federal involvement in the arts and humanities, to the everlasting benefit of the
country."

When the American history painter John Trumbull was paid $32,000 for the
four scenes of the American Revolution, including the *Declaration of Independence*
(1818), that adorn the rotunda of the Capitol in Washington, a loud outcry arose
against their cost. But does anyone alive today think it was wrong to spend public
money on jump-starting the Library of Congress with Jefferson's 6,500 books or
creating America's first monumental paintings of its own history? Was Franklin
Roosevelt's Works Progress Administration, which gave jobs to numerous good
American artists in the Depression years, a bad idea? American government has
supported the American arts–spottily, inconsistently, but always with some general
sense of obligation to a larger sense of polity–almost from its beginning. The claim
that the NEA and the NEH, founded in 1965, had no historical precedents in America is simply a lie.

Who begrudges the $1 million a year in federal funds for the upkeep of the
Lincoln Memorial, with its huge, Zeus-like figure of the dead President by Daniel
Chester French? Yet from there to Maya Lin's Vietnam Memorial–a focus of intense
collective feeling and reverence today, but bitterly denounced by many a flag-
wagging conservative as "a black gash of shame"–there has scarcely been a significant American public sculpture commemorating things Americans care about
that hasn't excited fierce opposition, usually in the name of patriotism and values.

Trying to find common public images in the midst of the pandemic discord of
American democracy has never been an easy task. Sometimes, as now, it has
seemed all but hopeless. One recalls the morose words of John Trumbull in 1793,
lamenting how "the whole American people" had become "violent partisans . . . the
whole country seemed to be changed into one vast arena . . . on which the two
parties, forgetting their national character, were wasting their time, their thoughts,
their energy . . . In such a state of things, what hope remained for the arts? None."

The atmosphere passed, but 200 years later a similar dementia prevails. Its obsessive objects this time are not the Terror in France and the war between France and England, as they were in 1793. They are moral—or, to be more exact, they are about the rhetoric of morality.

Our present "culture wars" do not exist in liberal democracies on the other sides of the Atlantic or the Pacific. The intolerance of these clashes is aggravated by the deep anguish that descended on America after it won the cold war and found itself no better off. The Manichaean universe, divided between right (us) and wrong (Soviets), dissolved. The apocalyptic scenario, so frightening and yet so consoling, fizzled. But the mind-set it fostered remains, particularly since America is the only country in the Western world with a strong, and vengeful, current of Fundamentalist apocalyptic religion. With the death of communism, new Antichrists and minor devils have to be found inside America. The two p.c.s.—patriotic correctness and political correctness—have mutually fostered this search, creating an atmosphere of inflamed accusation; scholarship and the arts then become scapegoats, grotesquely politicized culture-war stereotypes.

Thus Congress—and the nation—is now full of indignant wannabe reformers who know next to nothing about American culture but want to get tough on it. They have no idea that there is a vast, complex and valuable tract of images between Norman Rockwell's Thanksgiving turkey and Andres Serrano's photo of a crucifix in urine. Years of adroit propaganda by the religious right have convinced many of them that a vote for preserving the NEA in any form is a vote for sodomy, blasphemy and child abuse. This has become a matter of indurated faith, resistant to any insert of mere fact.

For these zealots, modern American art is summed up in the image of Robert Mapplethorpe, that slick and vastly overrated photographer, conservative in every sense except the sexual, who is now seen as a hybrid of welfare queen and Caligula, living off the NEA on your tax dollar and mine while sticking bullwhips up his bum. In fact, Mapplethorpe neither got nor asked for one cent from the NEA to make the photos that caused the offense; a museum did that, for a show of his work. And he died a multimillionaire because of the ranting queer hatred of Jesse Helms, Pat Buchanan and the religious right—not to mention the tribal loyalty of artworld homosexuals, many of whom would have you think that any criticism of his work amounts to homophobia.

Of the tens of thousands of grants that the NEA has made in its 30-year history, perhaps a dozen have excited serious controversy and only two—to the Mapplethorpe show and Serrano—have brought it to the verge of abolition. Significantly, neither case involved a direct grant by the NEA to the artist. Serrano got his $15,000 of public money as an award from the Southeastern Center for Contemporary Art, which the NEA had given a grant to distribute as it thought fit. All the same, it is obvious from this debacle that the NEA should not have set itself up as the Lady Bountiful of the so-called cutting edge, as it did in the '80s. Government is almost by definition a poor patron of the avant-garde. Artists who call themselves sociopolitical subversives, and then ask for state handouts, are either fools or hypocrites. But at the same time, it is, and plausibly should be, a legitimate function of government patronage to encourage promising forms of artistic expression that are not familiar enough to find their way in the marketplace. This is a thin rope to walk; the NEA fell off it and broke a leg. But you don't kill the endowment over that, any more than you abolish the U.S. Navy because of Tailhook.

The key is reform, without which the NEA probably won't survive at all. Its critics charge it with spending too much on grants to individual artists, but this is untrue—in fact, such grants account for only 4% of its budget. It's more important for the NEA to get rid of all its bogus democratic criteria, the therapeutic fustian of "self-esteem" and "empowerment" through art for this locality or that minority. Leave that to state arts councils (if they still want it, which they shouldn't either); in art there should be no such entitlements. The NEA should be more élitist—rigorously so, in fact—and should hand out more money to fewer projects. It should wholeheartedly embrace the dreaded Q word: quality.

To do that effectively, however, it needs to have its budget increased, not cut.   35
Give it one-quarter the cost of a B-2 each year—$550 million. Let it then compile a target list of the 500 or so performing-arts institutions, along with the instruments of historic preservation (museums, heritage and restoration groups, and so on) that matter most in American culture, across the whole social and geographical spectrum, and see what they (minimally) need.

America leads the world in dance, for instance, and yet an innovative genius like choreographer Twyla Tharp lacks the money to maintain a permanent company. This is a national embarrassment. Such people shouldn't have to go begging in corporate boardrooms. But in America, artists are always on probation.

The Responsive Reader

1. Terms like *philistinism, populism, élitism,* and *ideology* bounce back and forth in the current culture wars. What do they mean, and what role do they play in the current controversy?

2. What is Hughes' strategy in defending the NEA and NEH against charges of political bias? What are the major points he makes? (What use does he make of strategic comparisons with other countries?)

3. What do you learn here about the economics of federal support for the arts? What figures or statistics seem particularly significant? What point does Hughes make about the role of federal "seed money" in supporting the arts?

4. Both sides in the culture wars turn to American history for precedents and moral lessons. What for Hughes is the legacy of American Puritanism? (What is an "iconophobic streak"?) According to him, what was the perspective on art and culture of the founders of the country? (What evidence does he cite?) What

precedents does he cite for publicly funded American art? Why is the end of the Cold War relevant to his discussion? (What is a "Manichean universe"?)

5. Much criticism of the federal agencies has centered on their sponsorship of avantgarde artists and anti-establishment scholars seen as attacking traditional American values. How does Hughes size up the agencies' record in this respect? What test cases does he discuss, and from what perspective? What is Hughes' attitude toward the avantgarde? What are his recommendations on this subject?

6. What is Hughes' view of the relationship between the "private sector" and American culture?

For Discussion or Writing

7. Do you consider yourself an élitist? Do you consider yourself a populist? (Would you admit to being a Philistine?) How would you define and defend your chosen label?

8. Is there publicly funded art or government-supported art in your community? What role does it play? What do you think of it? Have there been controversies concerning it?

Collaborative Projects

9. Working with a group, you may want to investigate some aspect of government spending for culture from a concrete dollar-and-cents perspective. For instance, how much of public broadcasting has been taxpayer funded? For the last year or years for which figures are available, what was the percentage of government support in relation to total costs? What percentage came from listener or viewer support? What other sources of funding have supported public broadcasting?

THE SMASHING OF THE BELL

Robert Brustein

Robert Brustein is a drama critic devoted to the special magic and immediacy of live theater. By the same token, he is one of the people who are committed to supporting and promoting American culture on the grassroots level. He roots for the little theaters, local art museums, and music programs for youngsters that keep our communities from turning into spiritual wastelands. He is a knowledgeable chronicler of the American stage, and his heart is not with the glitzy high-royalty Broadway hits but the small but "invaluable" theatrical enterprises that operate with precious little help from the government or anyone else. Brustein fights the trends that make the theater serve fashionable ideological purposes, believing that the "kind of thinking that refuses to make distinctions among artists on the basis of color or nationality or gender, which insists on inclusion rather than exclusion," is the only kind of thinking that "prepares the way for great art, and builds the path to a reconciled society." He wrote the following obituary for federal support for American culture for the New Republic.

Two tiny federal agencies, the pitifully underfunded National Endowment for the Arts and the National Endowment for the Humanities, are facing imminent extinction from mutinous Republican legislators, toadying to a rampaging Christian right. On July 13, the eve of Bastille Day, modern Jacobins in the House of Representatives took an irretrievable step. They agreed to a freshmen-sponsored proposal to the Interior Appropriations bill that would make 40 percent cuts in the 1996 budgets and decapitate the endowments entirely within two years. Meetings between the House and the Senate might prolong the agony of these agencies a little longer, but, for all intents and purposes, the NEA and the NEH have been guillotined. Next on the block are the NEA- and NEH-sponsored achievements of the past thirty years. It is the end of a remarkable experiment, which for a time helped persuade the world that, in spite of itself and against all odds, our government might finally play a role in developing our civilization.

I no longer have the heart to argue the importance of government subsidy, however minimal, to the creative and intellectual life of this nation. After twenty-five years of disputation, my pen has run dry and my throat has gone hoarse. After auspicious beginnings and encouraging annual increases, we have watched the appropriations for the endowments freeze, then diminish and now disappear altogether. The mindless budget-cutting of this Republican Congress is making some of us ashamed to be Americans.

Both Chairman Sheldon Hackney of the NEH and Chairwoman Jane Alexander of the NEA are gracious and able personalities who have worked tirelessly to save their agencies from the axe. But after meeting with each of them on a recent visit to Washington, after talking to their staffs and after reading their brochures, I began to understand better why their efforts to save the endowments were ultimately doomed to failure. The fact is that for the last two decades neither of these agencies has been allowed to establish or articulate a clear-cut policy or definition. Periodic hostages to congressional authorization and re-appropriation, they were always prey to external pressures, whether from the left, in the form of multicultural panels with political agendas, or from the right, in the form of anticultural puritans with moral agendas, or simply from congressional demands to distribute funds on the basis of geography rather than merit.

Besotted with populist values, few in Congress or the nation were equipped to appreciate the intrinsic importance of the arts and the humanities. In recognition of this melancholy fact, the public testimony and published materials of endowment chairpeople were always likely to emphasize, not quality, excellence, imagination and inspiration as criteria for funding, but rather such peripheral benefits of access, dissemination, bookbinding, inner-city outreach, arts education and the impact of the arts and humanities on the local economy (hotels, parking lots and restaurants). "The NEH is about democracy," wrote Hackney in an eloquent pamphlet called *Lasting Values in a Disposable World*, "about equal access and participation by the many, not the few." One understands the necessity for such populist rhetoric, and wide distribution is, of course, the goal of every artist and thinker. But not every great creative or critical work has immediate mass appeal.

The National Institutes of Health and National Institute of Science do not have to apologize for distributing grants to scientists and researchers. Most lay people understand how they eventually benefit from basic research. But, forced to demonstrate their value to "the many, not the few," the NEH and the NEA invariably have had to trot out wide-audience programs (like television documentaries) to justify their existence. In the rare cases when individual advantages in art or intellect are mentioned, they are invariably encrypted within large invocations to the human spirit and the human heritage.

This kind of elevated verbal reinforcement is the lingua franca of cultural administrators. (I am often forced to use it myself.) But if the importance of the arts and humanities is still not clear to this nation thirty years after the creation of the endowments, then the struggle to preserve them is obviously hopeless. Who has been listening all this time? Who has been reading? Who has been thinking? In his office in the Old Post Office Building, the mild-mannered Hackney has two warning signs: "Thou Shalt Not Whine" and "No Snivelling." I believe he has every right now to whine, snivel, scream and stamp his foot. Certainly, delivering courteous speeches about the human spirit and the human heritage to people who believe the only function of government is to cut spending and reduce taxes is about as useful as reading Hegel to orangutans.

Anyway, it is clear that most legislators don't want to hear about the value of the endowments. They just want to hear about their scandals. The thousands of NEA grants to symphonies, museums, opera, dance and theater companies, are of far less interest to them than a few hundred dollars transferred from a sheltering organization to a controversial performance artist, while the accomplishments of the NEH in sponsoring scholarship, criticism and even TV documentaries fade before the single contested award for the establishment of history standards in the schools (an effort ironically initiated by the NEH's former chairwoman and fiercest critic, Lynn Cheney).

In the face of such persistent misrepresentation of their function, one wonders how Congress kept these agencies alive for so long. But a major difference between the past and now is that John F. Kennedy, Lyndon B. Johnson and even Richard Nixon were willing to speak out fervently on behalf of the arts and humanities, while Bill Clinton uses the word "arts" as infrequently as Ronald Reagan used the word "AIDS." (It is true that Hillary Clinton did make a speech about the importance of the arts to the human spirit and to the local economy that found its way onto the op-ed page of the *Times*.) Will Clinton veto the Internal Appropriations bill? Certainly not for the sake of the NEH or the NEA. The same spineless lack of principle that weakens the president's foreign policy decisions hobbles (or wobbles) his domestic actions. His every act is measured by the armies of voters it might conscript, and the arts and humanities have even fewer divisions than the pope.

Into this leadership vacuum have swarmed the budget-cutting servants of the religious right who, after the collapse of the Soviet Union, began to replace internal enemies like the communists and their fellow travelers with artists and intellectuals. In the heated fantasies of conservatives, prefaces to arts catalogs replaced *Das Kapital* as demonized texts, and avant-garde artists such as Robert Mapplethorpe, Andres Serrano and Karen Finley assumed the subversive roles once assigned to Alger Hiss and the Rosenbergs.

Considering the hatred attracted by these individual artists, it might just have   10
been possible to preserve the endowments had they agreed to shut off funding to anything considered even mildly avant-garde or controversial. This desperate strategem was actually attempted under former NEA Chairman John Frohnmayer, with his notorious anti-obscenity pledge, until the courts ruled it unconstitutional. But, aside from being an improper use of prior restraint, such an action would have effectively undermined a central purpose of the endowments, which was not only to encourage established institutions and traditional scholarship but to help nudge forward the boundaries of art and thought. It is easy enough to celebrate such custodial NEH functions as editing and publishing the papers of Franklin, Washington, Jefferson and Martin Luther King. But where is the critical reinterpretation that sheds new light on traditional texts? In the same way, "cutting-edge" artists may be identified with the Antichrist in the minds of some legislators, but without them the arts would have no future.

It is the natural consequence of experimentation in the arts that it lead to occasional failure, even to occasional scandal, though this occurred far less frequently than reported. At the NEA fewer than forty out of thousands of grants–forty!– proved even remotely controversial. Naturally, these were the ones that Donald Wildmon of the American Family Association and his letter-writing ilk seized upon to inflame the minds of right-wing members of Congress. But who has bothered to compare the magnitude of endowment sins with those of less stigmatized govern- ment agencies? Is anyone (other than a few libertarians and militia groups) calling for the abolition of the FBI because of Waco, or of the CIA because of Aldrich Ames?

Is it excessive to remind ourselves of Mao Tse-Tung's Cultural Revolution? In 1966, the People's Republic of China, also under the name of "democracy," ridiculed artistic and intellectual expression and humiliated artists and intellectuals as "elitist" bearers of foreign ideas. Losing a few dollars in federal subsidy is hardly the same as outright censorship, imprisonment or worse, but for artistic and intellectual in- stitutions in this country economic strangulation can be just as lethal. The cultural consequences will certainly be the same: the dumbing down of an entire nation.

Obviously, individual poets, novelists and scholars can always support their artistic and intellectual habits by working at other jobs. T. S. Eliot found employ- ment in a bank, Wallace Stevens ran an insurance agency, Faulkner and Fitzgerald went to Hollywood. But dance groups cannot take jobs in banks and theater com panies cannot take refuge in insurance offices. And it is nonsense to believe that private funds, which have been diminishing lately rather than increasing (and which are largely reserved for multicultural projects anyway) will compensate for the growing deficits caused by the collapse of the endowments.

It doesn't take a prophet to see that we face the imminent loss of countless artistic and intellectual institutions, particularly the smaller ones, some of which depend on endowment support for as much as 10 percent of their budgets. Oh, the dinosaurs will survive, of course–cultural bastions such as the Metropolitan Mu- seum, the Boston Symphony, the San Francisco Opera. But a relatively modest company (such as, I confess, my own American Repertory Theatre in Cambridge) will be able to sustain another major cut in subsidy only by doubling its ticket prices. (This will make the theater truly "elitist.") To justify these high prices, the fare will inevitably become more commercial, thus completing a process, already widely advanced, of erasing the distinction between the nonprofit world, which is at least nominally devoted to art, and the profit world, which is entirely driven by the market. And the effort to build an alternative cultural system–democratic in the sense of being available to anyone with an appetite for the imagination–will have come to an end.

One cannot begin to describe the climate of demoralization among those who have been trying over the years to educate the minds and stimulate the imagina- tions of American citizens. Those efforts were experiencing considerable success, even in the theater. Serious audiences were growing, serious playwrights were

15

multiplying. The endowments were essential, not just for their comparatively small grants, not just because they helped to generate private funds from sluggish foundations, corporations and individuals. They were important because at their best they served as the consciences of the field. Without them, we are left to contemplate a culture without guidance, principle or purpose.

This is a particularly squalid moment in our history, a monument of defeat and desolation. Running through my head is a passage from *Three Sisters*, in which Chekhov compares Andrei Prozorov to a beautiful expensive bell, raised with the help of countless people, then carelessly allowed to fall and smash. Lacking the financial support and the moral example of the endowments, it will take at least another thirty years to raise that bell again. But long before that time, thanks to our duly elected representatives, we will have regained our position as the dumbest and most philistine democracy in the Western world.

The Responsive Reader

1. What bird's eye view does Brustein give you of the history of government support for "the creative and intellectual life of this nation"? What changes in the political climate does he trace? (What are "Jacobins"?)

2. Brustein faults "mild-mannered" administrators trying to navigate between the political right and the political left. According to him, what was wrong with their strategy? Why was it "doomed to failure"? (Why was their situation different from people responsible for the National Institutes of Health and the National Institute of Science?)

3. Brustein blames much of the hostile climate toward federal support for the arts on the scandal-mongering common in our culture, with little emphasis on positive achievement. According to him, how did our current appetite for scandal play a role?

4. How does Brustein defend support for avantgarde or controversial art?

5. What is Brustein's prognosis for the future? Who will survive? Who will go under? What will be the effect on the morale of artists and friends of the arts?

For Discussion or Writing

6. Have you had experience with grassroots cultural activities—for instance, little theaters, music competitions, or film festivals? Who or what keeps them going? How do they survive?

Collaborative Projects

7. Voices often heard in the current culture wars include those of conservatives like William Bennett and George Will. You may want to help your class organize a debate or panel discussion confronting conservative and liberal views on federal funding for the arts or culture.

Making Connections

8. How does Brustein's analysis of the current situation compare with that of Hughes? Do they use similar terms? Do they identify similar causes?

5

Issues in Communication

COMMUNICATION IN PERSPECTIVE

Language is a uniquely human medium, infinitely more complex and versatile than the communication systems of other living beings. If you were to track uses of language you encounter or become involved in over a period of time, you might discover an astonishing range of human purposes it serves. Humans use language to warn others and ask for help, to coordinate efforts and make others do their bidding, to commemorate past achievement and make plans for the future. They use language in courtship, in marriage ceremonies, and in divorce proceedings. They use language to sell, to teach, to argue, to persuade, and to deceive. They use language to reach out to others, to voice their feelings. First writing and then print; then telephone, radio, and television; and now the computer have vastly expanded the reach of language as our central human means of communication.

FROM SPEECH TO WRITING

Language is first of all spoken language–though much of it today reaches you encoded in print or on the computer screen. **Oratory**, the art of effective public speech, has played a large role in human history. In the earliest records, like Homer's *Iliad* or the French *Song of Roland*, much space is devoted to accounts of battle, but much space also goes to palavers about war and peace, to drumming up support for warlike adventures, or to blaming the leadership when things go badly. Leading politicians of ancient Greece and Rome–Pericles, Cicero–are remembered for their eloquence. In the time of Abraham Lincoln and beyond, public debate and formal speeches before live crowds were a major dimension of the political process.

The invention of writing was to communication what the invention of the wheel was to transportation. Writing evolved from picture language like the Egyptian hieroglyphics or from marks imprinted on clay tablets to keep tab on trade transactions or taxes due. A simplified symbol for the head of an ox first stood for a head of livestock–and then for the first sound in the word for ox, as writing took the leap from picture writing to the use of an alphabet. Writing in the ancient world rapidly became a tremendous extension of the spoken language. It became a means of recording the myths and legends of the culture. It served to commemorate the triumphs and disasters of the clan, tribe, or nation. It served for recording extended speculations about the universe and the foundations of society.

The great religions became enshrined in scriptures, or sacred books–the Bible, the Koran. Christian missionaries fanning out from Greece and Rome into the rest of Europe adapted the Greek and Latin writing systems for re-tellings of Bible stories and books of prayer and meditation in the local lan-guages. In later periods, the impetus for developing writing systems for Native American or African languages often was to facilitate the missionary's work of spreading the Word.

THE PRINT AGE

Books, sometimes considered an endangered species in the computer age, are still being printed, sold, and read at an unprecedented rate. (How many books, including textbooks and reference books, have you bought or con-sulted during the last year?) Up to the Middle Ages, books were handwritten volumes, copied laboriously word for word by scribes. In the fifteenth cen-tury, the print revolution initiated by the German printer Johannes Gutenberg (1390–1468) introduced printing from movable type, producing multiple iden-tical copies at an increasingly affordable price. Printed pamphlets became weap-ons in the religious propaganda and psychological warfare of the Protestant reformation and the Catholic counter-reformation. Bible translations like the Luther Bible in Germany and the King James Version in England helped make obsolete the distinction between a literate priesthood, keepers of the mysteries of the faith, and the great mass of lay people who could not read and write.

Newspapers, pamphlets, and books from local, small-scale printing oper-ations helped implement the American ideal of an educated citizenry as the mainstay of democratic institutions. As earlier in England, the freedom of printing became a touchstone of freedom of expression and of a politically emancipated society. In the twentieth century, the banning of books was a key part of the machinery of repression of totalitarian regimes. ("Those who burn books will eventually burn people too," prophetically said the German Jewish poet Heinrich Heine.) Authors, publishers, and librarians continue to be on the front lines of the struggle against censorship today.

THE ERA OF MASS COMMUNICATION

What do you know about the mass media? What is their power for good and evil? The twentieth century saw the development of media of mass com-munication that reach into every home and represent a powerful potential for use and abuse. In spite of tremendous competition from the electronic media, newspapers continue to be a powerful political force and marketing tool. In England, the great traditional newspapers–the *London Times* and the *Guardian*–and periodicals like the *Economist* continue to be voices of the political, economic, and cultural establishment. At the other end of the spectrum, multimillion-copy peeping-Tom tabloids drool over the sex lives of princelings and cabinet ministers. In this country, the *New York Times*, the *Washington Post*, the *Chicago Tribune*, the *Los Angeles Times*, the *Christian Science Monitor*, and the *Wall Street Journal* are journalistic powerhouses that politicians and opinion makers disregard at their peril. Newsmagazines put a spin on the week's news, helping create and abort political candidates and social trends.

In the thirties and forties, radio bridged the gap between the political leadership and the nonreading populace in a remote town or village. Master politicians like Roosevelt, Churchill, and Hitler used radio the way a musical virtuoso plays an instrument. Their radio talks were major events that represented turning points in the struggle for political power or the struggle to maintain wartime morale. Later, radio for a time seemed to be relegated to an outlet for popular music. However, talk radio has in recent years given it a new lease on life, providing an outlet for raw unedited popular sentiment often glossed over by well-groomed professional journalists.

Movies churned out by the Hollywood dream factory fueled the fantasy lives of millions around the world. The humor and humanity of inspired clowns from Charlie Chaplin, Laurel and Hardy, and Buster Keaton to Woody Allen provided an antidote to a humorless world populated by bullies and natural born killers. The great movie classics–*Gone with the Wind* with Vivien Leigh and Clark Gable, *Citizen Kane* with Orson Welles, *On the Waterfront* with Marlon Brando and Lee Cobb–did more to shape people's views of Southern history, big business, or the labor movement than any college lecture.

Television early showed its potential for education and miseducation of the public. Like satellites forever orbiting in rerun heaven, Jackie Gleason of the *Honeymooners*, Lucille Ball of *I Love Lucy*, or Dick Van Dyke and Mary Tyler Moore continue to remind viewers of a whole new world of popular entertainment ushered in by the small screen. Telegenic politicians with a natural performer's talent like Presidents Kennedy and Reagan used television to do an end run around the insiders' politics of the smoke-filled room.

A more omnipresent and persistent teacher than school, church, or family, television today is under intense scrutiny for its power to create the mental universe in which young people live. Critics deplore the mindless sadistic violence of crime shows, with their unrelenting diet of mayhem, rape, and murder, making young people grow up in what a French critic has called "the culture of brutality." An NAACP broadside castigated the Fox network for representing "the worst traditions of American broadcasting–the cream-skimming, profit-taking, bottom-feeding, hormone-stimulating, child-exploiting, thought-extinguishing, and spirit-emptying 'tradition' of 'deregulated' television." Students of the political process criticize the dumbing-down effect of sound bites, which do not give a public official or citizen spokesperson more than a sentence or two to present a stand on a complex issue. Political attack ads descend to the lowest common denominator. In a television biography of a political leader, the handshake promising to end a half century of bloody strife between two hate-riven peoples rates less time than allegations of private sexual misconduct.

At the same time, television provides an unprecedented front-row seat for history in the making. Viewers watch as if from a balcony as tanks rumble toward the Russian parliament building in Moscow during a legislators' revolt or crush a students' sit-in in China. Courtroom TV and prime-time justice educate millions of viewers in the pathologies of our society, in the workings of the machinery of justice, and in the strategies of lawyers. Interviews like those on *Larry King Live* enable citizens to listen to the thinking of important political figures without the intervention of flacks or spinmeisters.

Who pays the piper? In many countries, the media are funded by governments for the purpose of disseminating establishment-approved information and culture. In this country, the media are fueled by advertising revenue, with some exceptions. Single-copy sales and subscription income cover only a fraction of the cost of print publications. The so-called public broadcasting media scrape by with listener support and contributions from affluent donors. Movies depend on ticket sales and subscription income from movie channels although part of their income comes from made-for-TV movies and reruns on commercial, advertising-financed stations.

In the main, the news media and much of the entertainment industry operate in the service of commercial promotion. The basic issue is that informing or educating the public is one thing and selling Coca-Cola is another. Can news organizations owned by large corporate interests maintain independence of editorial judgment? Can corporations that depend on advertising revenue tell the truth about the health hazards of smoking? Can networks owned by conservative shareholders tell the truth about the control of the political process by the wealthy?

THE COMPUTER REVOLUTION

How is the computer changing the way we communicate and the way we think? Answers to this question may vary widely, depending on whether you are listening to ardent converts or to skeptics sounding a "hype alert." The computer, first used by many as a glorified typewriter or calculating machine, has opened up vastly expanded new lines of communication. E-mail, making ordinary mail look like snail mail, makes possible spur-of-the-moment communication with instant replies and continuing interaction. On-line networking puts individuals in touch with others with similar interests in politics, current events, professional or occupational concerns, and a myriad of personal concerns and hobbies. Subscribing to electronic networks give students and other researchers instant access to databases, enabling them to track down and download information that used to require the footwork and frustrations of conventional library work.

On-line services transfer to the electronic medium news reports and magazine articles first collected by traditional wire services or published by traditional news organizations and publishers. They repackage already existing material. As with the use of scholarly information, thorny questions of copyright and reimbursement of the original authors and publishers remain unsettled. At the same time, trend watchers predict that megacommunications empires like the Murdoch Corporation or Microsoft will increasingly create their own news and other journalistic products to attract fee-paying customers and lure advertising revenue. A new form of cyberjournalism will compete with traditional news organizations that pride themselves on investigative reporting and editorial independence.

In many areas, the electronic revolution is taking society into uncharted territory. Rapid technological change and deregulation are breaking down traditional partitions within the communications industry–like those separating telephone companies, movie companies, and cable companies. Cyberenthusiasts predict that interactive on-line courses will supersede much traditional classroom education. Guardians of public morality worry that the citizenry is finding new means of exchanging possibly offensive material, eluding traditional means of censorship.

QUESTIONS FOR DISCUSSION

Do you consider yourself an effective speaker or presenter? (What have been some of your notable successes or failures?) How many books do you read, and what kind? Do you consider yourself a newspaper reader? (What sections of a newspaper do you turn to?) Do you get most of your information and commentary about the modern world from television? (What are some recent news stories you have followed–what did you learn? What slants or spins did you become aware of?) Has the computer changed your writing style, your reading habits, your purchasing patterns? Do you interact with others by computer? Do you cruise the Web?

THE SHAME OF THE CITY

Myron Stokes AND *David Zeman*

Is violence as American as apple pie? The body count of gun-related deaths in this country exceeds that of minor local wars. European tourists arriving in Florida are afraid of being killed before they leave the Miami perimeter. Rambo movies stage glorious bloodbaths. A movie like Natural Born Killers travels around the world to reinforce the stereotype of Americans as addicted to sadistic violence. How do the news media deal with violence? Has violence become too commonplace to be newsworthy? Ordinary murders, fights, spouse abuse, and fatal shootouts over a quarrel in a parking lot no longer make the front page. What was it about the incident reported in the following newsmagazine article that made it "front-page news around the world"? How much in the article is fact? How much is interpretation or editorial commentary? What spin did the reporters put on the incident?

They were good samaritans—two young men who saw something terrible happening and tried to help. As Lawrence Walker tells it, he and his friend Orlando Brown spotted the crowd on the Belle Isle bridge and stopped their car. They heard someone say a woman had just jumped into the Detroit River 32 feet below. They didn't know the woman had been savagely beaten, that she apparently jumped off the bridge to escape her attacker—or that the incident would be front-page news around the world. Walker told *Newsweek* that the crowd was "standing around like people taking an interest in sports." He and Brown looked down and saw the woman struggling in the current. They took off their shoes and shirts and jumped in, swimming toward her. She swam away, and Walker says he "figured she thought we were her attackers." Finally she sank beneath the surface and Walker, cold and exhausted, climbed out of the river. A Detroit cop accosted him and put him in handcuffs. "That's for jumping off the bridge," he says the cop told him.

Tough town, Detroit. Walker says the cops soon realized their error and took the cuffs off. But the death of 33-year-old Deletha Word and the arrest of a hulking 19-year-old named Martell Welch for second-degree murder has embarrassed the city. Detroit now has an international reputation as a place where dozens of bystanders did little or nothing to prevent a woman from being violently assaulted over a routine fender bender, and where at least some onlookers reportedly cheered as Word either jumped or fell to her death. The crowd looks pathologically callous—a case of the "Kitty Genovese syndrome," a theory about why most bystanders don't try to stop a crime in progress. The Detroit police look bad, too: somehow, they muffed the initial investigation and allowed the suspect and his friends to drive away. Welch in fact was arrested fully 30 hours after the event.

According to police, the incident began shortly after 2 a.m. on Aug. 19 with a minor collision between the car driven by Word and the car driven by Welch. Word drove off and Welch, accompanied by friends, followed her onto the bridge from Belle Isle to downtown Detroit. The island is a popular place to cruise on such a summer night, and there were dozens of other cars on the bridge.

Over the next several minutes, Welch and his friends allegedly caught up with Word in traffic, and Word, in what appeared to be a panicky attempt to escape, backed into Welch's car again. Police say Welch pulled Word out of her car, ripping off some of her clothes, and pushed her down on the hood to beat her. An accomplice then held her down while Welch allegedly got a car jack that he used to smash up her car. Word broke free and ran to the railing of the bridge, where, one witness says, she threatened to kill herself. Other witnesses say Welch's friends yelled, "Jump, bitch, jump!" Word dropped off the bridge, and Walker and Brown made their vain attempt to save her. Her body was recovered miles downstream later that day—minus a leg, which had apparently been cut off by the propeller of a passing boat.

Welch pleaded not guilty and will stand trial for second-degree homicide. But   5 the city is in the dock as well—and some say the crowd's failure to respond is reminiscent of the 1964 murder of Kitty Genovese, a New York barmaid. According to accounts at the time, none of several dozen neighbors called police when Genovese, who was being stabbed to death just outside her apartment building, repeatedly screamed for help. "It's a paradox," said Andre Modigliani, a University of Michigan social psychologist. "The more people who are watching an event, the less likely any of them will be to step in and help."

But the Belle Isle incident is more complicated than that. The reality was mass confusion, and those who saw the attack on Word had every reason to avoid an enraged and violent suspect who might well have had a gun. Although many onlookers seemed passive, police say several motorists used cellular phones to call 911; 26 people came forward to help police track down the suspect. Walker and Brown were heroes—and it is a sad footnote to a brutal story that they arrived too late.

The Responsive Reader

1. What are the bare-bones facts that emerge from this account? Can you piece together a step-by-step account of what happened on the Belle Isle Bridge? (When you compare notes with your classmates, do any of the facts seem to be in dispute?)

2. Why doesn't this newsmagazine article start with a chronological account of the bare facts? Where *does* it start, and why? What spin is this article putting on the incident?

3. Who's to blame? Who or what is responsible? Can you and your classmates agree on the causes of what happened here?

4. Assume you are an investigator. What unanswered questions would you want to ask witnesses and the people involved?

For Discussion or Writing

5. Assume you are a police officer filing a police report on this incident. What would you include? What would you leave out?

6. Assume you are a columnist for your local paper. What would you put in a column explaining what this incident means to you? Is this incident "typical"–of what? Is this just another example of "senseless violence"? (What do we mean by "senseless violence"?) Or is there a lesson to be learned?

ANATOMY OF A DISASTER

Richard Lacayo

*High on the list of sensational news events in the early nineties were lethal confrontations be-
tween federal agents and citizens accusing the government of abridging their constitutional right
to be armed to the teeth. In the Waco disaster in Texas, Koresh, a messianic leader of the Branch
Davidian sect, had previously been charged with weapons violations, and four federal agents were
killed as they tried to approach his stronghold. When the Feds eventually stormed the fortified
compound, a fiery inferno erupted, with both sides blaming each other for the deaths of the men,
women, and children trapped there. Many more died when a federal building including a day care
center in Oklahoma City was blown up in an act seen by many as retaliation by sympathizers of
Koresh. How do the pundits who analyze and interpret the news cope with such events? Richard
Lacayo is a journalistic professional who in the following* Time *article examines the "anatomy"
of another famous disaster in what he calls the "annals of right wing panic." Assuming Lacayo
to be a successful representative of mainstream journalism, what can you learn here about today's
news analysts and opinion makers? Do they seem likely to take a stand? Are they likely to take
sides? Do they hedge their bets?*

Before there was Waco, there was Ruby Ridge. As an episode in the annals of   1
right-wing panic, the 1992 shoot-out and siege at the Idaho cabin of white separatist Randy Weaver ranks second only to the inferno of the Branch Davidians the
following year. Federal agents in body armor and black ninja uniforms, armored
cars crashing up hillsides, even the fabled helicopters of militia nightmares–Ruby
Ridge had all the elements of a paranoid fantasy, with the difference that it was
stamped in real flesh and blood. In the 11-day standoff, Weaver's wife was shot
dead as she held their 10-month daughter in her arms. A day earlier his 14-year-
old son and a U.S. marshal had been killed.

Like Waco, Ruby Ridge will not go away. Five high-ranking FBI officials, including former Deputy Director Larry Potts, were suspended two weeks ago because the Justice Department is pursuing a criminal investigation into whether they
were part of a cover-up after the siege. An early FBI report let everyone off the
hook, both at the scene and at FBI headquarters. Another resulted in disciplines but
is now considered flawed (Potts, for example, was censured but was later promoted
to deputy director). More recent inquiries by the Justice Department have been
harsher, full of complaints about stonewalling and deadly and unconstitutional
changes in the rules of engagement. No review has been made public, though a
542-page report issued late last year has been widely leaked to the media and even
turned up on the Internet.

To settle a lawsuit filed by Weaver and his three surviving daughters, the government agreed last week to pay them $3.1 million. Their lawyer, Gerry Spence, a sagebrush sage and best-selling author, says the settlement lets his clients avoid a trial that would require them to relive memories of a "dead mother on the floor for 11 days, rotting in the sun, and a dead boy out in back in the woodshed." Meanwhile, the FBI was spared the ordeal of facing an Idaho jury that might well have awarded the Weavers even more money, to say nothing of what could have been weeks of squirming testimony on Court TV. At FBI headquarters, morale has tanked. Even during the darkest days of Watergate, says a morose agent, "we were in trouble for investigating the wrong people. We've never been accused of shooting women holding babies."

The settlement will not spare the FBI from Senate hearings scheduled for next month by Arlen Specter of Pennsylvania, a Republican presidential hopeful who wants to determine just how the attempt to arrest Weaver on a weapons charge got so spectacularly out of hand. For one thing, Specter wants to shed light on a central controversy: Who approved radically revised rules of engagement for the incident? Those orders let agents shoot to kill any armed male spotted in the open. Regulations ordinarily allow deadly force only in the face of immediate physical danger. "I bridle at the inability to find answers to these questions," says Specter. What does he plan to do at the hearings? "Raise hell."

Justice Department officials tried unsuccessfully to persuade Specter to post-   5
pone the hearings, fearful they would interfere with their investigation. An earlier department inquiry initially placed blame for the rule change on Eugene Glenn, the FBI field commander at Ruby Ridge, and Richard Rogers, chief of the FBI's hostage-rescue team, which provided the main firepower during the siege. But in May, Glenn sent a complaint to the Justice Department calling the first inquiry a sham and saying Potts was responsible. The new investigation focuses not only on Potts but also on his former assistant Danny Coulson and three lower-level officials. One of them, E. Michael Kahoe, has admitted destroying documents during earlier inquiries. Two others are suspected of knowing of the destruction, which may have been carried out to protect Potts and Coulson.

The Weaver incident started in October 1989. Weaver, 47, is a sometime logger whose convictions are roughly similar to those of the Christian Identity movement, which holds that white Americans and Northern Europeans are the chosen people of God and espouses a virulent racial separatism. He sold two illegal sawed-off shotguns to an undercover informant and was later arrested. Because of a clerk's error, a court summons ordering him to present himself before a judge in February 1991 listed the wrong date for his appearance. When Weaver failed to show on the correct date, a warrant was issued for his arrest. Months followed in which Weaver, believing that the government would seize his property and family, reportedly wrote threatening letters and sent messages through friends vowing to shoot whoever would try to take him.

On Aug. 21, 1992, U.S. marshals approaching Weaver's mountaintop cabin set the family dog barking. That brought out Weaver, his son Sammy and a family friend, Kevin Harris, all armed. When a marshal shot the dog, Sammy fired in the direction of the marshals, then turned and ran. In the ensuing fire fight, a marshal, William Degan, was killed by a gunshot in the chest. Sammy died of a gunshot wound in the back.

To rescue the marshals, who sent word they were pinned down by gunfire, the FBI's 50-member hostage-rescue team was flown in from Virginia. Though they now see Weaver as a posturing, marginal character, belligerent but not all that dangerous, the FBI commanders, working from information provided by the marshals, at first thought he was a heavily armed one-man commando squad.

On a plane en route from Washington, Agent Rogers, chief of the hostage-rescue team, drew up the fateful new rules of engagement in consultation with Potts by phone. These rules said that armed adults "could be" shot by FBI agents. During the night, the rules were amended to say armed males "should be" shot on sight. Glenn, the agent who initially took most of the blame, claims to have testified that he discussed the final version of the rules by phone with Potts and faxed the agreed-upon text to headquarters. Potts says he was at home sleeping when the fax arrived, leaving Coulson in command. Coulson insists he did not read the amended rules because the second page of the fax on which they were written never reached him. In an affidavit signed by Potts a month after the siege, which was taken as part of an FBI inquiry, he admits having approved changes that said armed adults "could be" shot on sight. How "should be" appeared and was approved is the subject of inquiry.

However the new rules were arrived at, they may not have played a role   10 in the death of Vicki Weaver. The Justice Department decided that Lon Horiuchi, the FBI sniper who shot her, killed her by accident when he was firing at Kevin Harris for reasons that were justified under the old rules of engagement. Horiuchi says he believed Harris was preparing to shoot down an FBI helicopter. As Harris was running to the cabin, Horiuchi fired. The shot went through the upper part of the open cabin door, behind which Vicki Weaver was standing with her infant daughter Elisheba in her arms. The woman fell to the floor dead, from a bullet to the head. Harris was wounded by fragments from the same shot.

Eventually, Weaver was talked off the mountain by Special Forces war hero and right-wing celebrity Bo Gritz. An Idaho jury later acquitted Weaver of murder and conspiracy charges in the death of the U.S. marshal, though he served 16 months on weapons charges. On his release, he moved to Grand Junction, Iowa, where as a single father he lives on Social Security survivor benefits from his wife. He recently told *Time*, "I'm just waiting for all of this to blow over so I can go back to my mountain." It may take a while. –**Reported by David S. Jackson/San Francisco and Elaine Shannon/Washington**

The Responsive Reader

1. The first few sentences use expressions including *right-wing panic, shoot-out, white separatist, black ninja uniforms, fabled helicopters, militia nightmare, paranoid fantasy.* How do these expressions set the tone? Where would you rate them on a scale going from objective reporting to strongly emotionally charged language? For you, do they seem to be slanted pro or con one side or the other?

2. In chronological order, the federal agent was killed first, then Weaver's son, and then the wife. Why does Lacayo reverse this chronological order in his first paragraph? A photograph accompanying the article showed the weapons seized in the Weaver cabin—an arsenal of eight or more weapons of varying designs, none of them looking like simple hunting rifles. Why doesn't Lacayo mention these weapons in his article?

3. Charges of "cover-up" loom large in many of today's political controversies. What role do they play in this article?

4. What for you are key items of information in Lacayo's eventual reconstruction of the events? Can you and your classmates agree on an impartial summary of the facts in this case?

5. For Lacayo, is there a key issue in this case? Where if anywhere does he place the blame?

For Discussion or Writing

6. If the case against the government had gone to trial and if you had been a member of a jury, would you have voted to award Weaver and his daughters $3 million? Why or why not?

7. Many Americans have strong convictions concerning the right to bear arms on the one hand or the need for stricter gun control on the other. Does the Weaver case in any way change or confirm your own convictions on this subject?

Collaborative Projects

8. Working with a group, you may want to investigate the range of editorial reaction to the Weaver case, the Waco incident, or a more recent *cause célèbre*. Do you find a wide range of opinion, or is there something approaching a consensus?

VIDEO OF "RACIST" EVENT CHALLENGED

Fox Butterfield

How much news is manipulated news? Citizens of countries with tight government control of the media take manufactured news for granted. They often tune out the official media and rely on the grapevine or foreign broadcasts instead. In this country, television networks have been accused of staging or restaging events presented as documentary footage. Campaign strategists launch last-minute accusations when the opponent is out of time and television money to refute the charges. Disinformation is the term for fake news picked up in good faith by news organizations serving as patsies for media manipulators. The following article by a well-known New York Times *reporter examines a case of alleged media manipulation.*

For several weeks last month, the news media carried reports of a rowdy, racist   1
event, an annual redneck campout in the hills of Tennessee where federal agents got drunk, made obscene jokes about black people and hung a banner warning, "Nigger checkpoint."

It was the first mention most people had ever heard of the Good Ol' Boys Roundup, an annual three-day camp-out for law enforcement officers and federal agents. The reports were disturbing enough to prompt hearings by the Senate Judiciary Committee, an investigation by the Justice Department and expressions of alarm by President Clinton.

Now, it turns out, the most damning accounts of the "Good Ol' Boys Roundup"–including a 90-second videotape showing the banner and tales of agents selling "nigger-hunting licenses"–were made for the National Rifle Association by a former Fort Lauderdale police officer after he was prevented by the Roundup's organizer from distributing David Duke campaign literature and expressing "white power" sentiments at the gatherings.

The tape–now considered widely suspect–and stories were, in turn, apparently fed to the *Washington Times* by an official of the rifle association, which has characterized agents of the Bureau of Alcohol, Tobacco and Firearms as "jackbooted thugs."

FORMER POLICE OFFICER

The source of the videotape and stories, former Fort Lauderdale, Fla., police   5
officer Richard Hayward, is a longtime supporter of David Duke, the onetime head

of the Ku Klux Klan who campaigned unsuccessfully for the U.S. Senate, governor of Louisiana and the 1992 Republican presidential nomination.

The Roundup's organizer, Gene Rightmyer, a former ATF agent, said he had had several run-ins with Hayward in recent years over Hayward's attempts to display "white power" insignias and distribute campaign literature for Duke at the Roundups.

Hayward has since had a falling-out with the rifle association, which he characterized in a recent interview as "totally unethical, a bunch of liars."

On the other hand, Hayward insists his videotape is genuine and his stories are true, although Justice Department investigators and civil rights leaders have said they have doubts about both.

Hayward said he offered the rifle association his allegations of racism at the Roundups last spring–coincidentally at the very time that the rifle association was undertaking a new membership drive with mailings that once again attacked ATF agents.

In return, Hayward said, the rifle association was to provide him with a plane   10
ticket from Birmingham, Ala., to Phoenix to meet with officials of the association shortly before its annual convention there last May, a free hotel room and cab fare and a security fence for his home.

BLAMES THE NRA

By Hayward's account, an official of the rifle association turned the videotape and allegation over to the *Washington Times*, which published an article about the Roundup, focusing on allegations of racism.

Other members of the news media, including the *New York Times*, soon followed suit, casting a shadow over the ATF just as congressional hearings were about to get under way into the agency's role in the siege of the Branch Davidian compound near Waco, Texas, in 1993.

Hayward now says he was betrayed by the rifle association, which, he said, leaked his identity to the news media and has been slow to make good on its part of the agreement, particularly on the construction of the fence.

DOUBTED FROM THE START

An NRA official says the association's leaders had doubts about the videotape from the start.

Rightmyer, the Roundups' organizer, suggested in a memo provided by his at-   15
torney, W. Thomas Dillard, of Knoxville, Tenn., that Hayward himself had helped hang the derogatory banner at the entrance to the 1990 Roundup, then videotaped it in an effort to impress Duke.

Hayward denied those suspicions. "I had absolutely nothing to do with the sign," he said in a telephone interview.

In a statement, Wesley Pruden, the editor in chief of the *Washington Times,* said: "We stand behind our story in all particulars. In putting together stories, we talk to a lot of people, like all good newspapers. This includes, when appropriate, members of the NRA, the ACLU, the ATF, or whoever else may have information."

The Responsive Reader

1. Why do you think the news media eagerly made use of the material contained in the damning videotape, bogus or not?

2. Can you sort out the charges and countercharges involved in this "media event"? Who called whom a racist? Who called whom a liar? What do you think really happened?

3. What was the official reply of the *Washington Times* to charges of having published bogus news? Does the stance of its editor in chief surprise you? What is your reaction to it?

For Discussion or Writing

4. Do you consider yourself one of those who naively consider everything they see on the evening news or read in the paper as real news? Or do you tend to be a skeptic (if not a cynic) about what is presented as news? What has influenced your attitude in this regard?

5. What evidence have you seen of a strong anti–government or anti-institutional bias in contemporary American life? Do you share it? Why or why not?

Making Connections

6. To judge from the articles by Stokes and Zeman, Lacayo, and Butterfield, what issues confront editors responsible for defining what is news? What guidelines do you think might be helpful for students in an introductory journalism class?

THE IDIOT CULTURE

Carl Bernstein

▬▬▬▬▬

> *In the following article, an investigative journalist who perfected the art of the exposé registers his second thoughts about journalism that feeds the public's appetite for scandal. As a young reporter, Carl Bernstein devoted himself to the exposure of abuses in high places and became an idol for a generation whose motto was "Question Authority." In 1972, Bernstein and his colleague Robert Woodward worked the Watergate scandal as reporters for the Washington Post. They uncovered "a tale of systematic and illegal political espionage and sabotage directed from the White House" that eventually brought down the Nixon presidency. Their best-selling All the President's Men (1974) confirmed for many the ideal of the watchdog function of the "fourth estate." Bernstein and Woodward prided themselves on doing basic journalistic grunt-work: following up leads, persistently asking questions, listening to people, interviewing minor players, or speaking off the record to participants in the events. Although accused of biased or slanted reporting, they made it their policy not to print allegations without confirmation or corroboration from a second source. According to Bernstein, these standards of responsible journalistic fact-finding have been compromised by current pressures to scoop the competition and stir up a jaded public.*

It is now nearly a generation since the drama that began with the Watergate   1
break-in and ended with the resignation of Richard Nixon, a full twenty years in which the American press has been engaged in a strange frenzy of self-congratulation and defensiveness about its performance in that affair and afterward. The self-congratulation is not justified; the defensiveness, alas, is. For increasingly the America rendered today in the American media is illusionary and delusionary–disfigured, unreal, disconnected from the true context of our lives. In covering actually existing American life, the media–weekly, daily, hourly–break new ground in getting it wrong. The coverage is distorted by celebrity and the worship of celebrity; by the reduction of news to gossip, which is the lowest form of news; by sensationalism, which is always a turning away from a society's real condition; and by a political and social discourse that we–the press, the media, the politicians, *and* the people–are turning into a sewer.

The greatest felony in the news business today (as Woodward recently observed) is to be behind, or to miss, a major story; or more precisely, to seem behind, or to seem in danger of missing, a major story. So speed and quantity substitute for thoroughness and quality, for accuracy and context. The pressure to compete, the fear that somebody else will make the splash first, creates a frenzied environment in which a blizzard of information is presented and serious questions may not be raised; and even in those fortunate instances in which such questions are raised (as happened after some of the egregious stories about the Clinton family), no one has done the weeks and months of work to sort it all out and to answer them properly.

Reporting is not stenography. It is the best obtainable version of the truth. The really significant trends in journalism have not been toward a commitment to the best and the most complex obtainable version of the truth, not toward building a new journalism based on serious, thoughtful reporting. Those are certainly not the priorities that jump out at the reader or the viewer from Page One or "Page Six" of most of our newspapers; and not what a viewer gets when he turns on the 11 o'clock local news or, too often, even network news productions.

"All right, was it really the best sex you ever had?" Those were the words of Diane Sawyer, in an interview of Marla Maples on "Prime Time Live," a broadcast of ABC News (where "more Americans get their news from . . . than any other source"). Those words marked a new low (out of which Sawyer herself has been busily climbing). For more than fifteen years we have been moving away from real journalism toward the creation of a sleazoid info-tainment culture in which the lines between Oprah and Phil and Geraldo and Diane and even Ted, between the *New York Post* and *Newsday*, are too often indistinguishable. In this new culture of journalistic titillation, we teach our readers and our viewers that the trivial is significant, that the lurid and the loopy are more important than real news. We do not serve our readers and viewers, we pander to them. And we condescend to them, giving them what we think they want and what we calculate will sell and boost ratings and readership. Many of them, sadly, seem to justify our condescension, and to kindle at the trash. Still, it is the role of journalists to challenge people, not merely to amuse them.

We are in the process of creating, in sum, what deserves to be called the idiot   5
culture. Not an idiot *sub*-culture, which every society has bubbling beneath the surface and which can provide harmless fun; but the culture itself. For the first time in our history the weird and the stupid and the coarse are becoming our cultural norm, even our cultural ideal.

In New York we witnessed a primary election in which "Donahue," "Imus in the Morning," and the disgraceful coverage of the *New York Daily News* and the *New York Post* eclipsed *The New York Times*, *The Washington Post*, the network news divisions, and the serious and experienced political reporters on the beat. Even *The New York Times* has been reduced to naming the rape victim in the Willie Smith case; to putting Kitty Kelley on the front page as a news story; to parlaying polls as if they were policies.

I do not mean to attack popular culture. Good journalism *is* popular culture, but popular culture that stretches and informs its consumers rather than that which appeals to the ever descending lowest common denominator. If, by popular culture, we mean expressions of thought or feeling that require no work of those who consume them, then decent popular journalism is finished. What is happening today, unfortunately, is that the lowest form of popular culture–lack of information, misinformation, disinformation, and a contempt for the truth or the reality of most people's lives–has overrun real journalism.

Today ordinary Americans are being stuffed with garbage: by Donahue-Geraldo-Oprah freak shows (cross-dressing in the marketplace; skinheads at your corner luncheonette; pop psychologists rhapsodizing over the airways about the minds of serial killers and sex offenders); by the Maury Povich news; by "Hard Copy"; by Howard Stern; by local newscasts that do special segments devoted to hyping hype. In supposedly sophisticated New York, the country's biggest media market, there ran a craven five-part series on the 11 o'clock news called "Where Do They Get Those People . . . ?," a special report on where Geraldo and Oprah and Donahue get their freaks (the promo for the series featured Donahue interviewing a diapered man with a pacifier in his mouth).

The point is not only that this is trash journalism. That much is obvious. It is also essential to note that this was on an NBC-owned and-operated station. And who distributes Geraldo? The Tribune Company of Chicago. Who owns the stations on which these cross-dressers and transsexuals and skinheads and lawyers for serial killers get to strut their stuff? The networks, the Washington Post Company, dozens of major newspapers that also own television stations, Times-Mirror and the New York Times Company, among others. And Ivana Trump, perhaps the single greatest creation of the idiot culture, a tabloid artifact if ever there was one, appeared on the cover of *Vanity Fair*. On the cover, that is, of Condé Nast's flagship magazine, the same Condé Nast/Newhouse/Random House whose executives will yield to nobody in their solemnity about their profession, who will tell you long into the night how seriously in touch with American culture they are, how serious they are about the truth.

Look, too, at what is on *The New York Times* best-seller list these days. *Double Cross: The Explosive Inside Story of the Mobster Who Controlled America* by Sam and Chuck Giancana, Warner Books, $22.95. (Don't forget that $22.95.) This book is a fantasy pretty much from cover to cover. It is riddled with inventions and lies, with conspiracies that never happened, with misinformation and disinformation, all designed to line somebody's pockets and satisfy the twisted egos of some fame-hungry relatives of a mobster. But this book has been published by Warner Books, part of Time Warner, a conglomerate I've been associated with for a long time. (*All the President's Men* is a Warner Bros. movie, the paperback of *All the President's Men* was also published by Warner Books, and I've just finished two years as a correspondent and contributor at *Time*.) Surely the publisher of *Time* has no business publishing a book that its executives and its editors know is a historical hoax, with no redeeming value except financial.

By now the defenders of the institutions that I am attacking will have cried the First Amendment. But this is not about the First Amendment, or about free expression. In a free country, we are free for trash, too. But the fact that trash will always find an outlet does not mean that we should always furnish it with an outlet. And the great information conglomerates of this country are now in the trash business. We all know pornography when we see it, and of course it has a right to exist. But we do not all have to be porn publishers; and there is hardly a major media company in America that has not dipped its toe into the social and political equivalent of the porn business in the last fifteen years.

Yes, we have always had a sensational, popular, yellow tabloid press; and we have always had gossip columns, even powerful ones like Hedda Hopper's and Walter Winchell's. But never before have we had anything like today's situation in which supposedly serious people—I mean the so-called intellectual and social elites of this country—live and die by (and actually believe!) these columns and these shows, and millions more rely upon them for their primary source of information. Liz Smith, *Newsday*'s gossip columnist and the best of a bad lot, has admitted blithely on more than a few occasions that she doesn't try very hard to check the accuracy of many of her items, or even give the subjects of her column the opportunity to comment on what is being said about them.

The failures of the press have contributed immensely to the emergence of a talk-show nation, in which public discourse is reduced to ranting and raving and posturing. We now have a mainstream press whose news agenda is increasingly influenced by this netherworld. On the day that Nelson Mandela returned to Soweto and the allies of World War II agreed to the unification of Germany, the front pages of many "responsible" newspapers were devoted to the divorce of Donald and Ivana Trump.

Today the most compelling news story in the world is the condition of America. Our political system is in a deep crisis; we are witnessing a breakdown of the comity and the community that has in the past allowed American democracy to build and to progress. Surely the advent of the talk-show nation is a part of this breakdown. Some good journalism is still being done today, to be sure, but it is the exception and not the rule. Good journalism requires a degree of courage in today's climate, a quality now in scarce supply in our mass media. Many current assumptions in America—about race, about economics, about the fate of our cities—need to be challenged, and we might start with the media. For, next to race, the story of the contemporary American media is the great uncovered story in America today. We need to start asking the same fundamental questions about the press that we do of the other powerful institutions in this society—about who is served, about standards, about self-interest and its eclipse of the public interest and the interest of truth. For the reality is that the media are probably the most powerful of all our institutions today; and they are squandering their power and ignoring their obligation. They—or more precisely, we—have abdicated our responsibility, and the consequence of our abdication is the spectacle, and the triumph, of the idiot culture.

The Responsive Reader

1. What is "trash journalism"? What are key points in Bernstein's indictment of it? What are his most persuasive or provocative examples?

2. What standards does Bernstein set up for responsible reporting? Do they sound like pious hopes or like workable guidelines?

3. What does Bernstein say about such journalistic sidelines as pornography, gossip columns, or talk shows?

4. Critics of the press are often treated to lectures about freedom of the press and the First Amendment. Does Bernstein anticipate such reactions? How does he counter them?

For Discussion or Writing

5. Do you agree that the media give more space to "the lurid and the loopy" than to real news? Do you see too much coverage of "trash celebrities"? What for you are some current test cases or examples?

6. Can you cite counterexamples—news coverage that was exceptionally informative or that impressed you as a model of responsible reporting?

7. How much do you personally follow the news? What do you look for—information? excitement? confirmation of your views? gossip? entertainment? Do you think media people responsible for news would consider you part of their ideal target audience or a less than ideal customer?

Collaborative Projects

8. Media watchers have often raised the specter of monolithic media of mass communication geared to the lowest common denominator and politically innocuous. In recent years, however, desktop publishing and electronic networking have vastly extended the range of alternative media of communication, often with a strong anti-establishment bias and a disregard of the proprieties of the commercial media. A myriad "zines" or informal low-circulation magazines now reach a large and varied audience. Working with a group, explore the world of zines.

MICHAEL JACKSON
Moby Dick of Pop

Stanley Crouch

―――――――

Criticism is a small but influential branch of the communications industry. Major newspapers have television critics, movie critics, music critics, drama critics, book reviewers, and perhaps architecture critics, not to mention columnists who keep a critical eye on the local cultural scene. PBS stations have programs devoted to film criticism or to evaluating new recordings. Criticism, whether of high culture or popular culture, has two faces: Critics may be friendly critics—sharing their enthusiasm, helping to make unknowns known, drumming up support for worthy undertakings, or coming to the defense of artists who are misunderstood. But critics may also be hostile critics, like the author of the following broadside aimed at one of the most successful pop idols of all time. What explains the hostility in this review? What function does this kind of article serve? Do you think it changes anyone's mind?

It used to be that if one didn't hurry up and say something about a show   1
business event, the boat train was gone, splashing egg in the face of the slowpoke commentator. Today's commercial questions center around how long a product built to super stardom can maintain a position at the top of the huckster's calculated wave. Then those questions break down into how much print and electronic media space it can attract. The final issue is whether or not the product can become a marlin pulling the ship of public gullibility on and on until—Lord have mercy on us!—it ends up on the deck, not a real fish but a motorized piece of plastic counterfeit sporting a serious price tag. Its falseness doesn't matter because so many of us, the hook actually in our own mouths, have been trained to ceaselessly admire and drool over the special effects of the marketplace. We resent anyone interrupting our freedom to pay for being duped. We wear our hooks with pride.

That is why the Michael Jackson phenomenon helps us face what has happened to our society as issues cut across all false fire walls of race, class, gender, religion. At 36, Jackson represents both the hard facts of open opportunity and the swollen vision of self-worth that have evolved in our narcissistic culture. A now-bone-colored big, big fish in the media, Jackson's every move foams up cultural essences that are at the nub of our perpetually embattled democratic grandeur and our equally persistent childishness. He is an entertainer whom we have watched rise from an itty bitty cute kid to a man remade quite remarkably by modern surgical techniques, all the while maintaining his emotional position in the yellow submarine of adolescent sensibility. That is why his work, at its core, is a summation of the inflated failure that now dominates our popular arts, where the value of youth is hysterically championed at the expense of a mature sense of life. This exploits the insecurities of young people by telling them, over and over, that never growing up is the best defense against an oppressive world where fun isn't given its proper due. That kind of exploitation made Jackson the King of Pop.

Even so, none of this came about by natural means. It was all connected to the gold rush entertainment possibilities of a country such as ours, where there are so many people that consistently hooking no more than 1 percent of the public wallet guarantees millions. That is exactly what went down. As a boy and part of the Jackson Five, he was pushed into the world of show business by his father Joe's ambition, which perfectly coincided with the slick Motown packaging of Berry Gordy and the high wind of teenage bad taste that accounts for so many blips on the sales screen. But Jackson eventually went further than anyone could have imagined.

He broke out of the Jackson Five and became a single, flipping and flopping his way into the air of international celebrity. Along the way, his looks changed. The tumbleweed afro of the past was replaced by a dark, gooey mop. His skin went from brown to beige to bone. The wide-angle nose went on a starvation diet that achieved ultra-slimness and an upward Peter Pan turn worthy of a self-willed Disney cartoon. Then the chin came clean with a cleft. The former child star was ready for another degree of prime time. As his videos and concert performances show, Jackson extended his stardom by adding to his repertoire all the basic trends of his idiom, white or black, and the slogans that pass for ideas. Always a mediocre singer given to progressively unimaginative phrasing and overstatement, Jackson delivers a shallow version of gospel, some maudlin rhythm and blues, uses the false bravado of hard rock inflection, postures as a love child reciting the pieties necessary for world peace, stoops to the vulgar gestures that are a priggish short hand for lower-class rage, alludes to the spanking that paddles under the brand name of sadomasochism and executes a few leftover Jackson Five dance steps that serve as quicksilver interludes within a choreographed synthesis of cheerleading moves, navy signaling without flags and aerobic exercises. His album *Thriller* sold more than 40 million units worldwide, 24 million in the United States, which meant that 236 million Americans didn't buy it.

Michael Jackson became more than a whale of a success. He also developed   5
into something of an entertainment blob, swallowing up whatever he came in contact with or whatever took him further into the mythology of pop aristocracy, where small but glimmering talents are elevated with an hysteria that bespeaks the swill of bad faith our culture has been guzzling since Woodstock. An eccentric jellyfish on the surface but truly a canny businessman, Jackson snatched up the Beatles catalog when it was there for the buying, startling Paul McCartney and angering Ringo Starr. He was more on top than ever.

Then, after years of seeming a goody blue suede shoes, Jackson was sucked into a whirlpool of controversy by a child molestation scandal in which he was accused of slurping a 12-year-old boy in unmentionable places. The response was dramatic: Jackson canceled a tour that was in progress, claiming addiction to pain killers. He disappeared. He reappeared. He went on television complaining that the police examined his wee wee. He lost endorsements. He settled out of court for a large but unrevealed amount. Not one to stay outside the limelight, Jackson suddenly married a Lisa Marie who was the daughter of Elvis Presley, that Tarzan of rock and roll, he who swung to ever-larger bank accounts on the vines of pop Negro rhythms and redneck sentimentality. It brought two entertainment kingdoms of swamp water together, Neverland flowing into Graceland.

At every point, the King of Pop was greatly helped by the arrival and evolution of promotional aids like "Entertainment Tonight," MTV, VH-1 and channel E! These television shows and cable stations are dedicated to nothing but the marketing of products, few serious questions asked. Hype and genuflection are their trade. For the good ship of show business, pop stars, directors, choreographers and technicians are interviewed, promotional videos are shown, films of films being made, videos of the making of videos, all tagged by the glistening barnacles of a forced enthusiasm American entertainment used to lampoon at every chance.

Such things, along with the regular venues of promotion, guarantee that we will have Michael Jackson and his latest recording, *HIStory*, pushed in our ears and faces for quite a while. In fact, Sony Entertainment has already spent $30 million on a promotional campaign planned to continue through two Christmas seasons.

Yet this kind of attention and success doesn't reduce the all-American tendencies to self-inflated melodrama and even more self-righteous bitching. While Jackson's millions allow him to build fantasy kingdoms, he also usurps the mantle of wealthy nut that Howard Hughes once wore with such unflagging madness. Like Hughes, Jackson also suffers from the distinct paranoia that those who must face legions of jealousy sometimes orchestrate into endless symphonies of plots and sub-plots, ranging from the press to the government. The alienation that comes with vast success builds upon the familiar theme of the poor little rich kid and becomes the basis for innumerable expressions of complaint.

This paranoia has not been missed, even in the world of rock criticism, where   10
posterior-licking and fantasies of aesthetic value are assiduously taught. Though there was some understandable alarm expressed when Jackson's gargantuan poor-mouthing and his lyrics were examined in the double-CD of *HIStory*, and while some rock critics even noted the fascist imagery of the video, what all of them missed was the problem at the very center of pop music, which is the function of its incantational rhythms.

Incantation always has two audience possibilities in our culture: one is the collective fused into a throbbing vitality through the repeating groove of a syncopated dance-beat; the other is the transformation of individuals into a mindless mass of putty in the hands of a band or a central figure. The distinction is important because the vital collective is the highest achievement of dance-oriented rhythm. Essential to that vitality is the expression of adult emotion. While blues might also have simple musical elements similar to those pop has derived from it, blues is fundamentally a music that fights self-pity and even holds it up to ridicule, the singer scorning all self-deceptive attempts at ducking responsibility for at least part of the bad state of affairs.

In jazz, for another example, the rhythmic phenomenon of swing is posed as an antidote to the sentimentality of the popular song, with the improvisation allowing for collective inventions that insert emotional irony and complexity into the music. The evolution of pop music is quite different because, far more often than not, the rhythm is used to *reinforce* the sentimentality of the material. Those pop rhythms now arrive in a form that has largely submitted to the mechanical, often using electronic programmed "drums" for static pulsations that never interact with the rest of the music, a supreme example of the very alienation it so successfully foments.

It is because of the subordination of everything to the beat that the lyrics so often go by, barely noticed. When they are noticed, especially when expressing the choked up, immature resentment of a demanding adult world, the words either become anthems of estrangement or bludgeons against some vision of corrupt and hypocritical authority. But, as with fascism, the authority of a mass "conspiracy"– of bankers, lawyers, politicians, educators, law enforcement and so on–is rejected through obeisance to a figure of gargantuan certitude. That is where the big beat of pop and the big idol of the rock star meet in the fascist garden of dance-oriented totalitarianism.

Michael Jackson has been evolving in this direction over the last few years, one video after another showing either the world or his opposition melting into mass chorus lines overwhelmed by his magical leadership. We see this most clearly in the video for "HIStory," where Jackson marches in front of legions of troops, children scream that they love him, and a huge statue of the King of Pop, one as ugly as any Hitler, Stalin or Mao would have appreciated, is unveiled. We understand in clear terms the assertion that Hitler was the first rock star because of the way his rallies used technology to create hypnotic rituals of enormously magnified passion.

The Indian poet and philosopher Tagore once observed that the invention of the pen knife leaped past the centuries of evolution that resulted in the claw, but that we often find ourselves in a world where those with the pen-knife mentalities of adolescents command weapons of destruction that they aren't mature enough to handle. When we make embittered little boys into idols by genuflecting before a briny charisma that has negligible adult application, we shouldn't be surprised

15

when they decide they should lead the world into a resurrection of an Eden, through which they will walk in the cool of the day, omnipotent as the jealous God of the Old Testament.

The Responsive Reader

1. How much do you learn about the artist's history as a performer and about high points in his career? (How much here is new; how much is familiar?)
2. How much of the criticism is aimed at the artist as a person? Do you consider it mean-spirited or justified?
3. After reading this review, do you feel you understand better the mass appeal of Michael Jackson nationally and around the world? According to this review, what are key features of Jackson's style or brand of entertainment? What are key objections by the reviewer?
4. What attitude toward show business as business emerges from this review? What is the reviewer's view of the audience? Does his general attitude necessarily color his attitude toward Jackson?

For Discussion or Writing

5. Do you think Crouch is personally alienated from American popular culture? Do you think being reviewed by a person with his negative attitude is unfair to the artist? Why or why not?
6. How would you defend Michael Jackson–or the author of this negative review?
7. How would you compare Michael Jackson's appeal with the appeal of other great idols of popular culture–Elvis, the Beatles, Madonna?

ASIAN WOMEN IN FILM
No Joy, No Luck

Jessica Hagedorn

A movie is never just a movie.

JESSICA HAGEDORN

One of the audience favorites of traditional Italian opera is Puccini's Madame Butterfly, *which tells the tragic story of a Japanese geisha girl who falls in love with a white male. Abandoned by the American naval officer whose exotic fantasy she was, having had to hand over their love child to his American wife, she commits suicide to richly sensuous music in the last act. Rebelling against the stereotype of the meek, submissive Asian female, the Chinese American playwright David Henry Hwang did a rewrite of the Butterfly theme in his* M. Butterfly *(1988). His central character is a male Chinese opera singer playing female roles and working for the Chinese government as a spy. In the following article, Jessica Hagedorn, who grew up in the Philippines, traces the history of her own rebellion against stereotypes of Asian womanhood. One of her test cases is the movie* The Joy Luck Club, *based on the novel by Amy Tan, that traces the story of four Chinese women and their daughters, moving between the hardships of the Chinese past and the conflicts of the American present. Hagedorn, herself author of the screenplay for* Fresh Kill, *is the author of the novel* Dogeaters *and the editor of* Charlie Chan Is Dead: An Anthology of Contemporary Asian American Fiction *(1993).*

As I was growing up in the Philippines in the 1950s, my fertile imagination was   1
colonized by thoroughly American fantasies. Yellowface variations on the exotic erotic loomed larger than life on the silver screen. I was mystified and enthralled by Hollywood's skewed representations of Asian women: sleek, evil goddesses with slanted eyes and cunning ways, or smiling, sarong-clad South Seas "maidens" with undulating hips, kinky black hair, and white skin darkened by makeup. Hardly any of the "Asian" characters were played by Asians. White actors like Sidney Toler and Warner Oland played "inscrutable Oriental detective" Charlie Chan with taped eyelids and a singsong, chop suey accent. Jennifer Jones was a Eurasian doctor swept up in a doomed "interracial romance" in *Love Is a Many Splendored Thing*. In my mother's youth, white actor Luise Rainer played the central role of the Patient Chinese Wife in the 1937 film adaptation of Pearl Buck's novel *The Good Earth*. Back

then, not many thought to ask why; they were all too busy being grateful to see anyone in the movies remotely like themselves.

Cut to 1960: *The World of Suzie Wong*, another tragic East/West affair. I am now old enough to be impressed. Sexy, sassy Suzie (played by Nancy Kwan) works out of a bar patronized by white sailors, but doesn't seem bothered by any of it. For a hardworking girl turning nightly tricks to support her baby, she manages to parade an astonishing wardrobe in damn near every scene, down to matching handbags and shoes. The sailors are also strictly Hollywood, sanitized and not too menacing. Suzie and all the other prostitutes in this movie are cute, giggling, dancing sex machines with hearts of gold. William Holden plays an earnest, rather prim, Nice Guy painter seeking inspiration in The Other. Of course, Suzie falls madly in love with him. Typically, she tells him, "I not important," and "I'll be with you until you say—Suzie, go away." She also thinks being beaten by a man is a sign of true passion, and is terribly disappointed when Mr. Nice Guy refuses to show his true feelings.

Next in Kwan's short-lived but memorable career was the kitschy 1961 musical *Flower Drum Song*, which, like *Suzie Wong*, is a thoroughly American commercial product. The female roles are typical of Hollywood musicals of the times: women are basically airheads, subservient to men. Kwan's counterpart is the Good Chinese Girl, played by Miyoshi Umeki, who was better playing the Loyal Japanese Girl in that other classic Hollywood tale of forbidden love, *Sayonara*. Remember? Umeki was so loyal, she committed double suicide with actor Red Buttons. I instinctively hated *Sayonara* when I first saw it as a child; now I understand why. Contrived tragic resolutions were the only way Hollywood got past the censors in those days. With one or two exceptions, somebody in these movies always had to die to pay for breaking racial and sexual taboos.

Until the recent onslaught of films by both Asian and Asian American filmmakers, Asian Pacific women have generally been perceived by Hollywood with a mixture of fascination, fear, and contempt. Most Hollywood movies either trivialize or exoticize us as people of color and as women. Our intelligence is underestimated, our humanity overlooked, and our diverse cultures treated as interchangeable. If we are "good," we are childlike, submissive, silent, and eager for sex (see France Nuyen's glowing performance as Liat in the film version of *South Pacific*) or else we are tragic victim types (see *Casualties of War*, Brian De Palma's graphic 1989 drama set in Vietnam). And if we are not silent, suffering doormats, we are demonized dragon ladies—cunning, deceitful, sexual provocateurs. Give me the demonic any day—Anna May Wong as a villain slithering around in a slinky gown is at least gratifying to watch, neither servile nor passive. And she steals the show from Marlene Dietrich in Josef von Sternberg's *Shanghai Express*. From the 1920s through the '30s, Wong was our only female "star." But even she was trapped in limited roles, in what filmmaker Renee Tajima has called the dragon lady/lotus blossom dichotomy.

Cut to 1985: There is a scene toward the end of the terribly dishonest but weirdly compelling Michael Cimino movie *Year of the Dragon* (cowritten by Oliver Stone) that is one of my favorite twisted movie moments of all time. If you ask a lot of my friends who've seen that movie (especially if they're Asian), it's one of their favorites too. The setting is a crowded Chinatown nightclub. There are two very young and very tough Jade Cobra gang girls in a shoot-out with Mickey Rourke, in the role of a demented Polish American cop who, in spite of being Mr. Ugly in the flesh—an arrogant, misogynistic bully devoid of any charm—wins the "good" Asian American anchorwoman in the film's absurd and implausible ending. This is a movie with an actual disclaimer as its lead-in, covering its ass in advance in response to anticipated complaints about "stereotypes."

My pleasure in the hard-edged power of the Chinatown gang girls in *Year of the Dragon* is my small revenge, the answer to all those Suzie Wong "I want to be your slave" female characters. The Jade Cobra girls are mere background to the white male foreground/focus of Cimino's movie. But long after the movie has faded into video-rental heaven, the Jade Cobra girls remain defiant, fabulous images in my memory, flaunting tight metallic dresses and spiky cock's-comb hairdos streaked electric red and blue.

> Mickey Rourke looks down with world-weary pity at the unnamed Jade Cobra girl (Doreen Chan) he's just shot who lies sprawled and bleeding on the street: "You look like you're gonna die, beautiful."
> Jade Cobra girl: "Oh yeah? [blood gushing from her mouth] I'm proud of it."
> Rourke: "You are? You got anything you wanna tell me before you go, sweetheart?"
> Jade Cobra girl: "Yeah. [pause] Fuck you."

Cut to 1993: I've been told that like many New Yorkers, I watch movies with the right side of my brain on perpetual overdrive. I admit to being grouchy and overcritical, suspicious of sentiment, and cynical. When a critic like Richard Corliss of *Time* magazine gushes about *The Joy Luck Club* being "a four-fold *Terms of Endearment*," my gut instinct is to run the other way. I resent being told how to feel. I went to see the 1993 eight-handkerchief movie version of Amy Tan's best-seller with a group that included my ten-year-old daughter. I was caught between the sincere desire to be swept up by the turbulent mother-daughter sagas and my own stubborn resistance to being so obviously manipulated by the filmmakers. With every flashback came tragedy. The music soared; the voice-overs were solemn or wistful; tears,

tears, and more tears flowed onscreen. Daughters were reverent; mothers carried dark secrets.

I was elated by the grandness and strength of the four mothers and the luminous actors who portrayed them, but I was uneasy with the passivity of the Asian American daughters. They seemed to exist solely as receptors for their mothers' amazing life stories. It's almost as if by assimilating so easily into American society, they had lost all sense of self.

In spite of my resistance, my eyes watered as the desperate mother played by Kieu Chinh was forced to abandon her twin baby girls on a country road in war-torn China. (Kieu Chinh resembles my own mother and her twin sister, who suffered through the brutal Japanese occupation of the Philippines.) So far in this movie, an infant son had been deliberately drowned, a mother played by the gravely beautiful France Nuyen had gone catatonic with grief, a concubine had cut her flesh open to save her dying mother, an insecure daughter had been oppressed by her boorish Asian American husband, another insecure daughter had been left by her white husband, and so on. . . . The overall effect was numbing as far as I'm concerned, but a man sitting two rows in front of us broken down sobbing. A Chinese Philippino writer even more grouchy than me later complained, "Must ethnicity only be equated with suffering?"

Because change has been slow, *The Joy Luck Club* carries a lot of cultural bag-   10
gage. It is a big-budget story about Chinese American women, directed by a Chinese American man, cowritten and coproduced by Chinese American women. That's a lot to be thankful for. And its box office success proves that an immigrant narrative told from female perspectives can have mass appeal. But my cynical side tells me that its success might mean only one thing in Hollywood: more weepy epics about Asian American mother-daughter relationships will be planned.

That the film finally got made was significant. By Hollywood standards (think white male; think money, money, money), a movie about Asian Americans even when adapted from a best-seller was a risky proposition. When I asked a producer I know about the film's rumored delays, he simply said, "It's still an *Asian* movie," surprised I had even asked. Equally interesting was director Wayne Wang's initial reluctance to be involved in the project; he told the New York *Times*, "I didn't want to do another Chinese movie."

Maybe he shouldn't have worried so much. After all, according to the media, the nineties are the decade of "Pacific Overtures" and East Asian chic. Madonna, the pop queen of shameless appropriation, cultivated Japanese high-tech style with her music video "Rain," while Janet Jackson faked kitschy orientalia in hers, titled "If." Critical attention was paid to movies from China, Japan, and Vietnam. But that didn't mean an honest appraisal of women's lives. Even on the art house circuit, filmmakers who should know better took the easy way out. Takehiro Nakajima's 1992 film *Okoge* presents one of the more original film roles for women in recent years. In Japanese, "okoge" means the crust of rice that sticks to the bottom of the rice pot; in pejorative slang, it means fag hag. The way "okoge" is used in the film seems a reappropriation of the term; the portrait Nakajima creates of Sayoko, the so-called fag hag, is clearly an affectionate one. Sayoko is a quirky, self-assured woman in contemporary Tokyo who does voice-overs for cartoons, has a thing for Frida Kahlo paintings, and is drawn to a gentle young gay man named Goh. But the other women's roles are disappointing, stereotypical "hysterical females" and the movie itself turns conventional halfway through. Sayoko sacrifices herself to a macho brute Goh desires, who rapes her as images of Frida Kahlo paintings and her beloved Goh rising from the ocean flash before her. She gives birth to a baby boy and endures a terrible life of poverty with the abusive rapist. This sudden change from spunky survivor to helpless, victimized woman is baffling. Whatever happened to her job? Or that arty little apartment of hers? Didn't her Frida Kahlo obsession teach her anything?

Then there was Tiana Thi Thanh Nga's *From Hollywood to Hanoi*, a self-serving but fascinating documentary. Born in Vietnam to a privileged family that included an uncle who was defense minister in the Thieu government and an idolized father who served as press minister, Nga (a.k.a. Tiana) spent her adolescence in California. A former actor in martial arts movies and fitness teacher ("Karaticize with Tiana"), the vivacious Tiana decided to make a record of her journey back to Vietnam.

From Hollywood to Hanoi is at times unintentionally very funny. Tiana includes a quick scene of herself dancing with a white man at the Metropole hotel in Hanoi, and breathlessly announces: "That's me doing the tango with Oliver Stone!" Then she listens sympathetically to a horrifying account of the My Lai massacre by one of its few female survivors. In another scene, Tiana cheerfully addresses a food vendor on the streets of Hanoi: "Your hairdo is so pretty." The unimpressed, poker-faced woman gives a brusque, deadpan reply: "You want to eat, or what?" Sometimes it is hard to tell the difference between Tiana Thi Thanh Nga and her Hollywood persona: the real Tiana still seems to be playing one of her B-movie roles, which are mainly fun because they're fantasy. The time was certainly right to explore postwar Vietnam from a Vietnamese woman's perspective; it's too bad this film was done by a Valley Girl.

The Responsive Reader

1. Many members of Hagedorn's generation have testified to the pervasive role of the Hollywood dream factory in shaping their view of the world. What major Hollywood stereotypes of Asian women does Hagedorn identify? (Do you recognize them?) What conclusions does this article suggest concerning Hollywood's treatment of "interracial romance"? Is Hollywood done with the stereotype of "the whore with a heart of gold"?

2. Do you understand Hagedorn's attitude toward the Jade Cobra girls? (Have you ever taken the side of the ostensible villains or "bad guys" in a movie?)

3. Why does Hagedorn have mixed feelings about the *Joy Luck Club* movie? What did she find inspiring? What made her uneasy? What did she find objectionable? Do you sympathize with her reactions?

4. What progress or lack of it does Hagedorn see in more recent movies on Asian themes?

For Discussion or Writing

5. The school books Hagedorn read in the Philippines had made her think that all Americans were "blond and freckled," all "ate apples, and all fair-haired children had dogs named Spot." What role does the "exotic" play in such a homogenized and sanitized cultural environment? What evidence have you observed of the cult of the exotic in American popular entertainment?

6. According to her introduction to *Charlie Chan Is Dead*, a central motive in Hagedorn's adolescence was the "aping of the mythologized Hollywood universe," where everyone "had to strive to be as American as possible." To judge from your own observation, how strong is the drive to become Americanized among the current generation of young Americans from diverse ethnic backgrounds?

Collaborative Projects

7. Conservative critics charge that Hollywood today is overcompensating for the negative stereotypes of the past. Working with a group, you may want to help organize a symposium on Hollywood's tendency to idealize or romanticize people from ethnically diverse backgrounds.

TALK TV
Tuning in to Trouble

Jean Albronda Heaton AND *Nona Leigh Wilson*

━━━━━

> *Talk shows have made media watchers revise their traditional picture of radio and television as passive media. In the age of talk radio and talk television, the audience gets in the act, with a vengeance. At first hailed for encouraging grassroots participation as an alternative to massaged and sanitized network fare, talk radio and talk TV have come under attack for feeding on sordid intimate detail, catering to raw prejudice, stirring up hostility, and treating people with problems as freak show exhibits. Of the two coauthors of the following article on talk TV, Heaton is a practicing psychologist and a teacher of psychology at Ohio University. Wilson teaches counseling and human resource development at South Dakota State University. The essay is adapted from their book* Tuning in Trouble: Talk TV's Destructive Impact on Mental Health *(1995). The authors are concerned about how TV talk shows shape the way women see themselves, their relations with other women, and their relations with men. Heaton and Wilson contrast the promising beginnings of talk television with its current state. As they see it, daytime television talk shows gave women a voice, a chance to deal with issues from a woman's point of view. What went wrong?*

In 1967, *The Phil Donahue Show* aired in Dayton, Ohio, as a new daytime talk al-   1
ternative. Donahue did not offer the customary "women's fare." On Monday of his first week he interviewed atheist Madalyn Murray O'Hair. Tuesday he featured single men talking about what they looked for in women. Wednesday he showed a film of a baby being born from the obstetrician's point of view. Thursday he sat in a coffin and interviewed a funeral director. And on Friday he held up "Little Brother," an anatomically correct doll without his diaper. When Donahue asked viewers to call in response, phone lines jammed.

For 18 years daytime talk *was* Donahue. His early guests reflected the issues of the time and included Ralph Nader on consumer rights, Bella Abzug on feminism, and Jerry Rubin on free speech. Never before had such socially and personally relevant issues been discussed in such a democratic way with daytime women viewers. But his most revolutionary contribution was in making the audience an integral part of the show's format. The women watching Donahue finally had a place in the conversation, and they were determined to be heard. The show provided useful information and dialogue that had largely been unavailable to housebound women, affording them the opportunity to voice their opinions about everything from politics to sex—and even the politics of sex.

No real competition emerged until 1985, when *The Oprah Winfrey Show* went national. Her appeal for more intimacy was a ratings winner. She did the same top-ics Donahue had done but with a more therapeutic tone. Donahue seemed driven to uncover and explore. Winfrey came to share and understand. In 1987, Winfrey's show surpassed Donahue's by being ranked among the top 20 syndicated shows. Phil and Oprah made it easier for those who followed; their successors were able to move much more quickly to the top.

At their best, the shows "treated the opinions of women of all classes, races, and educational levels as if they mattered," says Naomi Wolf in her book *Fire with Fire*: "That daily act of listening, whatever its shortcomings, made for a revolution in what women were willing to ask for; the shows daily conditioned otherwise un-heard women into the belief that they were entitled to a voice." Both Donahue and Winfrey deserve enormous credit for providing a platform for the voices of so many who needed to be heard, and for raising the nation's consciousness on many important topics, including domestic violence, child abuse, and other crucial prob-lems. But those pioneering days are over. As the number of shows increased and the ratings wars intensified, the manner in which issues are presented has changed. Shows now encourage conflict, name-calling, and fights. Producers set up under-handed tricks and secret revelations. Hosts instruct guests to reveal all. The more dramatic and bizarre the problems the better.

While more air time is given to the problems that women face, the topics are   5 presented in ways that are not likely to yield change. The very same stereotypes that have plagued both women and men for centuries are in full force. Instead of encouraging changes in sex roles, the shows actually solidify them. Women view-ers are given a constant supply of the worst images of men, all the way from garden-variety liars, cheats, and con artists to rapists and murderers.

If there is a man for every offense, there is certainly a woman for every trauma. Most women on talk TV are perpetual victims presented as having so little power that not only do they have to contend with real dangers such as sex-ual or physical abuse, but they are also overcome by bad hair, big thighs, and beautiful but predatory "other" women. The women of talk are almost always up-set and in need. The bonding that occurs invariably centers around complaints about men or the worst stereotypes about women. In order to be a part of the "sis-terhood," women are required to be angry with men and dissatisfied with them-selves. We need look no further than at some of the program titles to recognize the message. Shows about men bring us a steady stream of stalkers, adulterers, chau-vinistic sons, abusive fathers, and men who won't commit to women.

The shows provide a forum for women to complain, confront, and cajole, but because there is never any change as a result of the letting loose, this supports the mistaken notion that women's complaints have "no weight," that the only power women have is to complain, and that they cannot effect real changes. By bringing on offensive male guests who do nothing but verify the grounds for complaint, the shows are reinforcing some self-defeating propositions. The idea that women should direct their energies toward men rather than look for solutions in themselves is portrayed daily. And even when the audience chastises such behavior, nothing changes, because only arguments and justifications follow.

On *The Jenny Jones Show* a woman was introduced as someone who no longer had sex with her husband because she saw him with a stripper. Viewers got to hear how the stripper "put her boobs in his face" and then kissed him. The husband predictably defended his actions: "At least I didn't tongue her." The next few minutes proceeded with insult upon insult, to which the audience "oohed" and "aahed" and applauded. To top it all off, viewers were informed that the offense in question occurred at the husband's birthday party, which his wife arranged, *stripper and all*. Then in the last few minutes a psychologist pointed out the couple weren't wearing rings and didn't seem committed. She suggested that their fighting might be related to some other problem. Her comments seemed reasonable enough until she suggested that the wife might really be trying to get her husband to rape her. That comment called up some of the most absurd and destructive ideas imaginable about male and female relationships—yet there was no explanation or discussion.

It is not that women and men don't find lots of ways to disappoint each other, or that some women and some men don't act and think like the women and men on the shows. The problem is talk TV's fixation on gender war, with endless portrayals of vicious acts, overboard retaliations, and outrageous justifications. As a result, viewers are pumped full of the ugliest, nastiest news from the front.

When issues affecting people of color are dealt with, the stereotypes about   10
gender are layered on top of the stereotypes about race. Since most of the shows revolve around issues related to sex, violence, and relationships, they tend to feature people of color who reflect stereotypical images—in a steady stream of guests who have children out of wedlock, live on welfare, fight viciously, and have complicated unsolvable problems. While there are less than flattering depictions of white people on these shows, white viewers have the luxury of belonging to the dominant group, and therefore are more often presented in the media in positive ways.

On a *Ricki Lake* show about women who sleep with their friends' boyfriends, the majority of the guests were African American and Hispanic women who put on a flamboyant display of screaming and fighting. The profanity was so bad that many of the words had to be deleted. The segment had to be stopped because one guest yanked another's wig off. For many white viewers these are the images that form their beliefs about "minority" populations.

The shows set themselves up as reliable sources of information about what's really going on in the nation. And they often cover what sounds like common problems with work, love, and sex, but the information presented is skewed and confusing. Work problems become "fatal office feuds" and "back-stabbing coworkers." Problems concerning love, sex, or romance become "marriage with a 14-year-old," "women in love with the men who shoot them," or "man-stealing sisters." TV talk shows suggest that "marrying a rapist" or having a "defiant teen" are catastrophes about to happen to everyone.

Day in and day out, the shows parade all the myriad traumas, betrayals, and afflictions that could possibly befall us. They suggest that certain issues are more common than they actually are, and embellish the symptoms and outcomes. In actuality, relatively few people are likely to be abducted as children, join a Satanic cult in adolescence, fall in love with serial rapists, marry their cousins, hate their own race, or get sex changes in midlife, but when presented over and over again the suggestion is that they are quite likely to occur.

With their incessant focus on individual problems, television talk shows are a major contributor to the recent trend of elevating personal concerns to the level of personal rights and then affording those "rights" more attention than their accompanying responsibilities. Guests are brought on who have committed villainous acts (most often against other guests). The host and audience gratuitously "confront" the offenders about their wrongdoing and responsibilities. The alleged offenders almost always refute their accountability with revelations that they too were "victimized." On *Sally Jessy Raphael*, a man appeared with roses for the daughter he had sexually molested. He then revealed that he had been molested when he was five, and summed it up with "I'm on this show too! I need help, I'll go through therapy."

His sudden turnabout was not unusual. Viewers rarely see guests admit error   15
early in the show, but a reversal often occurs with just a few minutes remaining. This works well for the shows because they need the conflict to move steadily to a crescendo before the final "go to therapy" resolution. But before that viewers are treated to lots of conflict and a heavy dose of pseudo-psychological explanations that are really nothing more than excuses, and often lame ones at that. The guests present their problems, the hosts encourage them to do so with concerned questions and occasional self-disclosures, and the audience frequently get in on the act with their own testimonies. Anything and everything goes.

The reigning motto is "Secrets keep you sick." On a *Jerry Springer* show about confronting secrets, a husband revealed to his wife that he had been having an affair. Not only was the unsuspecting wife humiliated and speechless, but Springer upped the ante by bringing out the mistress, who kissed the husband and informed the wife that she loved them both. Conflict predictably ensued, and viewers were told this was a good idea because now the problem was out in the open. When Ricki Lake did a similar show, a man explained to his very surprised roommate that he had "finally" informed the roommate's mother that her son was gay, a secret the roommate had been hiding from his family.

Referring to these premeditated catastrophes as simply "disclosures" softens their edges and affords them a kind of legitimacy they do not deserve. On a program about bigamy, Sally Jessy Raphael invited two women who had been married to the same man at the same time to appear on the show. The man was also on, via satellite and in disguise. His 19-year-old daughter by one of the wives sat on the stage while these women and her father tore each other apart. Sally and the audience encouraged the fight with "oohs" and "aahs" and rounds of applause at the ever-increasing accusations. A "relationship therapist" was brought on to do the postmortem. Her most notable warning was that all this turmoil could turn the daughter "to women," presumably meaning that she could become a lesbian. The scenario was almost too absurd for words, but it was just one more show like so many others: founded on stereotypes and capped off with clichés. From the "catfight" to the "no-good father" to archaic explanations of homosexuality–cheap thrills and bad advice are dressed up like information and expertise.

These scenarios are often legitimized by the use of pseudopsychological explanations, otherwise known as psychobabble. This is regularly used as a "disclaimer," or as a prelude to nasty revelations, or as a new and more sophisticated way of reinforcing old stereotypes: "men are cognitive, not emotional," or "abused women draw abusive men to them." This not only leaves viewers with nothing more than platitudes to explain problems and clichés to resolve them, but it fails to offer guests with enormous conflicts and long histories of resentment and betrayals practical methods for changing their circumstances. The "four steps to get rid of your anger" may sound easy enough to implement, but what this kind of ready-made solution fails to acknowledge is that not all anger is the same, and certainly not everyone's anger needs the same treatment. Sometimes anger is a signal to people that they are being hurt, exploited, or taken advantage of, and it can motivate change.

Rather than encouraging discussion, exploration, or further understanding, psychobabble shuts it off. With only a phrase or two, we can believe that we understand all the related "issues." Guests confess that they are "codependents" or "enablers." Hosts encourage "healing," "empowerment," and "reclaiming of the inner spirit." In turn, viewers can nod knowingly without really knowing at all.

Talk TV initially had great potential as a vehicle for disseminating accurate information and as a forum for public debate, although it would be hard to know it from what currently remains. Because most of these talk shows have come to rely on sensational entertainment as the means of increasing ratings, their potential has been lost. We are left with cheap shots, cheap thrills, and sound-bite stereotypes. Taken on its own, this combination is troubling enough, but when considered against the original opportunity for positive outcomes, what talk TV delivers is truly disturbing.

20

The Responsive Reader

1. For the authors, what were promising features of the early TV talk shows, such as the Phil Donahue show and the Oprah Winfrey show? What did these two shows have in common? How did they differ?

2. Where did the talk shows take a wrong turn? What changed?

3. How do the shows exploit or fuel the gender wars? Why do the authors object to the way men are treated on the shows? Why do the authors object to the way women are treated? (What are striking examples?)

4. According to Heaton and Wilson, what is wrong with the way talk TV presents members of minorities?

5. Why are the authors critical of the way the shows bring in experts or authorities? Why do the authors object to the way the shows deal with or "resolve" personal problems? (What do the authors mean by "psychobabble"?)

For Discussion or Writing

6. Do you watch any of the current shows? Have you been aware of criticisms leveled at them? Check out several episodes of current shows. To judge from what you observe, are the charges brought against talk TV in this article justified?

7. For many social critics today, gender and race are intertwined. Do they raise similar issues for the authors of this article? Do they raise similar issues for you? Is the way society deals with them similar?

Collaborative Projects

8. Do the media stir up hostility between the sexes? In what areas? By what means? Working with a group, explore the media treatment of test cases.

FORUM: *Voyaging in Cyberspace*

> *When you're interacting with a computer, you are not conversing with another person.*
> *You are exploring another world.*

JOHN WALKER

The computer has vastly increased the range and speed of interpersonal communication. It facilitates instant contact and interaction with people with similar interests. Any hour of the day the buzz of a million electronic conversations makes the postal service and even the telephone seem like survivors from a horse-and-buggy age. How is communication by computer changing the way we talk, write, and think? Who participates, and who is left out? What lies ahead?

BARDS OF THE INTERNET

Philip Elmer-Dewitt

In the following article, a trend watcher for Time magazine examines the renaissance of the written word in the age of computer communication. Pundits had been deploring the decline of literacy—the ability to use the written word effectively for one's own purposes—in the era of the boom box and television The Canadian futurist Marshall McLuhan ("the medium is the message") had announced the end of the Print Age in several long books. Educators and culture critics deplored the hours spent by couch potatoes with idling minds in front of the small screen. Elmer-Dewitt examines the new speak-write of computer communication—written, yet closer to the flow and give-and-take of speech.

One of the unintended side effects of the invention of the telephone was that writing went out of style. Oh, sure, there were still full-time scribblers—journalists, academics, professional wordsmiths. And the great centers of commerce still found it useful to keep on hand people who could draft a memo, a brief, a press release or a contract. But given a choice between picking up a pen or a phone, most folks took the easy route and gave their fingers—and sometimes their mind—a rest.

Which makes what's happening on the computer networks all the more startling. Every night, when they should be watching television, millions of computer users sit down at their keyboards; dial into CompuServe, Prodigy, America Online or the Internet; and start typing—E-mail, bulletin-board postings, chat messages, rants, diatribes, even short stories and poems. Just when the media of McLuhan were supposed to render obsolete the medium of Shakespeare, the online world is experiencing the greatest boom in letter writing since the 18th century.

"It is my overwhelming belief that E-mail and computer conferencing is teaching an entire generation about the flexibility and utility of prose," writes Jon Carroll, a columnist at the San Francisco *Chronicle*. Patrick Nielsen Hayden, an editor at Tor Books, compares electronic bulletin boards with the "scribblers' compacts" of the late 18th and early 19th centuries, in which members passed letters from hand to hand, adding a little more at each turn. David Sewell, an associate editor at the University of Arizona, likens netwriting to the literary scene Mark Twain discovered in San Francisco in the 1860s, "when people were reinventing journalism by grafting it onto the tall-tale folk tradition." Others hark back to Tom Paine and the Revolutionary War pamphleteers, or even to the Elizabethan era, when, thanks to Gutenberg, a generation of English writers became intoxicated with language.

But such comparisons invite a question: If online writing today represents some sort of renaissance, why is so much of it so awful? For it can be very bad indeed: sloppy, meandering, puerile, ungrammatical, poorly spelled, badly structured and at times virtually content free. "HEY!!!!!" reads an all too typical message on the Internet, "I THINK METALLICA IZ REEL KOOL DOOD!!!!!"

One reason, of course, is that E-mail is not like ordinary writing. "You need to think of this as 'written speech,'" says Gerard Van der Leun, a literary agent based in Westport, Connecticut, who has emerged as one of the preeminent stylists on the Net. "These things are little more considered than coffeehouse talk and a lot less considered than a letter. They're not to have and hold; they're to fire and forget." Many online postings are composed "live" with the clock ticking, using rudimentary word processors on computer systems that charge by the minute and in some cases will shut down without warning when an hour runs out.

That is not to say that with more time every writer on the Internet would produce sparkling copy. Much of the fiction and poetry is second-rate or worse, which is not surprising given that the barriers to entry are so low. "In the real world," says Mary Anne Mohanraj, a Chicago-based poet, "it takes a hell of a lot of work to get published, which naturally weeds out a lot of the garbage. On the Net, just a few keystrokes sends your writing out to thousands of readers."

But even among the reams of bad poetry, gems are to be found. Mike Godwin, a Washington-based lawyer who posts under the pen name "mnemonic," tells the story of Joe Green, a technical writer at Cray Research who turned a moribund discussion group called rec.arts.poems into a real poetry workshop by mercilessly critiquing the pieces he found there. "Some people got angry and said if he was such a god of poetry, why didn't he publish his poems to the group?" recalls Godwin. "He did, and blew them all away." Green's *Well Met in Minnesota*, a mock-epic account of a face-to-face meeting with a fellow network scribbler, is now revered on the Internet as a classic. It begins, "The truth is that when I met Mark I was dressed as the *Canterbury Tales*. Rather difficult to do as you might suspect, but I wanted to make a certain impression."

The more prosaic technical and political discussion groups, meanwhile, have become so crowded with writers crying for attention that a Darwinian survival principle has started to prevail. "It's so competitive that you have to work on your style if you want to make any impact," says Jorn Barger, a software designer in Chicago. Good writing on the Net tends to be clear, vigorous, witty, and above all brief. "The medium favors the terse," says Crawford Kilian, a writing teacher at Capilano College in Vancouver, British Columbia. "Short paragraphs, bulleted lists and one-liners are the units of thought here."

Some of the most successful netwriting is produced in computer conferences, where writers compose in a kind of collaborative heat, knocking ideas against one another until they spark. Perhaps the best examples of this are found on the WELL, a Sausalito, California, bulletin board favored by journalists. The caliber of discussion is often so high that several publications—including the *New York Times* and the *Wall Street Journal*—have printed excerpts from the WELL.

Curiously, what works on the computer networks isn't necessarily what works   10
on paper. Netwriters freely lace their prose with strange acronyms and "smileys," the little faces constructed with punctuation marks and intended to convey the winks, grins, and grimaces of ordinary conversations. Somehow it all flows together quite smoothly. On the other hand, polished prose copied onto bulletin boards from books and magazines often seems long-winded and phony. Unless they adjust to the new medium, professional writers can come across as self important blowhards in debates with more nimble networkers. Says Brock Meeks, a Washington-based reporter who covers the online culture for *Communications Daily*: "There are a bunch of hacker kids out there who can string a sentence together better than their blue-blooded peers simply because they log on all the time and write, write, write."

There is something inherently democratizing—perhaps even revolutionary—about the technology. Not only has it enfranchised thousands of would-be writers who otherwise might never have taken up the craft, but it has also thrown together classes of people who hadn't had much direct contact before: students, scientists, senior citizens, computer geeks, grass-roots (and often blue-collar) bulletin-board enthusiasts, and most recently the working press.

"It's easy to make this stuff look foolish and trivial," says Tor Books' Nielsen Hayden. "After all, a lot of everyone's daily life is foolish and trivial. I mean, really, smileys? Housewives in Des Moines who log on as VIXEN?"

But it would be a mistake to dismiss the computer-message boards or to underestimate the effect a lifetime of dashing off E-mail will have on a generation of young writers. The computer networks may not be Brook Farm or the Globe

Theatre, but they do represent, for millions of people, a living, breathing life of letters. One suspects that the Bard himself, confronted with the Internet, might have dived right in and never logged off.

The Responsive Reader

1. How does Elmer-Dewitt highlight the contrast between the current situation and the state of the art of writing in the pre-electronic age? What precedents does he examine for the current renaissance of written communication?

2. What does Elmer-Dewitt see as major features of the evolving new style of writing? What concerns does he have about quality?

For Discussion or Writing

3. Do you agree that the spread of computer writing is having a "democratizing" effect? Or do you think it is helping create an élite in-group?

Collaborative Projects

4. Working with a group, analyze examples of computer interaction and share them with the class. Can you generalize about trends in computer writing or electronic communication?

A CYBERFEST FOR CULTURE LOVERS

Edward Baig

> *Culture on-line or on CD-ROM promises spectacularly widened access to classical music, the paintings of the masters, or avantgarde art and music, as well as a rich backdrop of biography, history, and criticism. French art lovers can buy a CD-ROM allowing them to roam the fabled Paris d'Orsay Museum, pause in front of a Manet painting and zoom in to examine details, or call up background provided by biographers and art historians. American music lovers can buy CD-ROMS guiding them through Beethoven's Ninth Symphony or taking them back to the Woodstock rock festival to watch performances and listen to interviews. How critical or uncritical a guide to computer culture is the author of the following Business Week article?*

Like most patrons of fine-art museums, I was passing from one room of masterpieces to another, pausing at regular intervals to admire the works that most captivated me. In one private collection of post–Impressionist paintings, I stopped to appreciate *The Music Lesson* by Henri Matisse. I moved in close, then retreated, to view the painting from different perspectives. A helpful guide pointed out that this was the artist's 1917 vision of domestic harmony, one of only two portraits of his family.

Such a wondrous afternoon—and I never set foot in a museum. Instead, I studied the pieces on *A Passion for Art*, a new CD-ROM from Corbis Publishing, which is owned by Microsoft Chairman Bill Gates.

Whether viewing multimedia compact disks or surfing the virtual museums of the Internet, art and music lovers can sample high culture on their computer screens. Institutions ranging from the Andy Warhol Museum in Pittsburgh to the Museum of Paleontology at the University of California at Berkeley display portions of their collections on the World Wide Web, a part of the Internet. Others are presenting bodies of work on CD-ROMS. One example: the Italian Metamorphosis exhibit shown at the Solomon R. Guggenheim Museum in New York. At the same time, devotees of Beethoven and Mozart—or the Beatles—can revel in compositions on CD-ROM while learning more about the periods in which the composers lived.

Computer culture is no substitute for a visit to a gallery or concert hall, of course. Multimedia disks, like art books, cannot reveal all the nuances that make a painting compelling, especially if the works are displayed with limited colors and poor resolution. But the right interactive disk can help people appreciate the real thing, though it helps if your computer is equipped with state-of-the-art sound and video components.

VOICE CLIPS

For now, CD-ROMS are easier to use than the Web, especially for PC neophytes.   5
American Visions, from Eden Interactive and Creative Labs, features splendid re-productions of some 200 paintings from noted 20th century artists such as Georgia O'Keefe, Jackson Pollock, and Mark Rothko. Based on the Roy R. Neuberger Col-lection in Purchase, N.Y., the disk includes more than 45 videos of Neuberger and various artists.

It figures that Bill Gates, a noted collector in his own right, would want to dominate computerized culture as he does so much of the software industry. His Corbis CD-ROM, distributed by Maxis, lets you explore the Barnes Foundation in Merion, Pa. Click on Matisses, Cézannes, and Renoirs, and zoom in for a closer view of the brushstrokes. By sliding the mouse, you can pan across the painting. Some 330 works of the 11,000-piece collection are included. They all offer written text on the painting and artist, some with voice-over commentary.

The Corbis program also lets you listen to audio clips of Dr. Albert C. Barnes or take a guided tour (the female nude, the dance) with art experts. You can browse a labyrinth of archives and find fascinating tidbits, such as a 1915 letter in which Barnes explains his decision not to buy Renoir's *Sailor Boy* because the price was too high. A few minor flaws: There are no videos, and you can't search through the text on the disk.

Gates has also put out strong titles under the Microsoft name. *Microsoft Art Gallery* features reproductions of more than 2,000 works from London's National Gallery, plus artists' biographies. You can view pictures by subject (religious im-agery, still life) or by clicking on a historical world atlas. In the "Beneath the Var-nish" tour, you see how such paintings as *The Incredulity of St. Thomas* were restored.

This spring, Voyager will unveil *Starry Night*, a disk that delves into Vincent van Gogh's famous painting. The software publisher has also teamed up with the Art Institute of Chicago on an upcoming disk, aimed at kids, called *With Open Eyes*.

INSTANT HELP

Voyager and Microsoft have joined forces on a series of multimedia music   10
disks that let you dissect the works of Beethoven, Mozart, and Schubert. As you listen to the full compositions–the *Ninth Symphony, Dissonant Quartet,* and *The Trout Quintet*–text that explains the selections being played scrolls down the screen. The CD sound is superb–provided you have decent speakers. By clicking on highlighted words, you can pause the text and music for definitions of terminology.

But *Viking Opera Guide* on CD-ROM is disappointing. It's nice to hear excerpts from the operas as you read about them, but the graphics are rudimentary and the program is hard to use. For example, a search for *La Bohème* yielded a citation for Ruggero Leoncavallo. Since the words *La Bohème* are not highlighted, you have to pore through the section on Leoncavallo before discovering that he was writing an opera similar to Puccini's.

People craving culture of a more modern sort might like the CD-ROM version of the Beatles' 1964 movie, *A Hard Day's Night.* Besides the uncut version of the film, the Voyager disk contains the trailer, original script (with deleted and improvised dialogue), and an essay on the Fab Four by critic Bruce Eder. Graphix Zone recently unveiled a CD-ROM, *Bob Dylan: Highway 61 Interactive,* featuring lyrics and liner notes from 41 albums, plus some recordings. For counterculture buffs, Time Warner Interactive's *Woodstock: 25th Anniversary* CD-ROM includes video clips of artists such as The Who, Janis Joplin, and Sly & the Family Stone.

Users of the Internet quickly learn that many museums approach the Information Age with a mix of excitement and trepidation. It's simple to serve up newsletters, catalogs, and some art. But museums are gun-shy about sharing complete collections with cybervisitors, partly over the fear that their works will be downloaded and used improperly for commercial purposes. That's why images on the Web are "restricted in resolution and the number of colors," says Scott Sayre, director of technology initiatives at the Minneapolis Institute of Arts, which offers more than 150 pages of information on the Internet.

Nonetheless, the Michael C. Carlos Museum at Emory University offers an impressive online collection. By clicking on a gallery index–ancient Americas, classical Greece and Rome–you can view works such as *Whistle in the Form of a Crocodile,* a Costa Rican ceramic from 200–500 A.D.

But culture-seeking on the Web can be daunting. You'll need graphical Web   15
browser software, such as Netscape Navigator or the program included on Prodigy's online service. What's more, unless you have a speedy Internet connection, you may be able to take a cab to the nearest museum by the time some pictures or videos are displayed. Even with a modem speed of 14.4 baud on Prodigy, it took me over 10 minutes to download a 28-second excerpt of Tchaikovsky's *Nutcracker* from the San Jose Symphony's Web server.

A good place to start your tour is by clicking on the Yahoo list, which segregates sites by categories (fine arts, music, photography). The Fine Art Forum www Resource Directory, at "http://www.msstate.edu/Fineart_Online/art-resources. html," is another excellent jumping-off point.

DIGITAL SHOWCASE

By clicking on color-coded terms and references, it's generally easy to go from one Web site to another. The Web server at the Georges Pompidou Center in Paris includes a list of Web addresses for museums around the world. New York-based

ArtNetWeb is a showcase for contemporary artists who pay a fee to display digital slides of their work. It's also linked to other sites including the Surrealism Server, which features Tristan Tzara and Salvador Dali.

So if you're trying to figure out what the painting means, you can linger as long as you want without getting nudged along or blocking someone's view.

The Responsive Reader

1. What do you know about the virtual reality movement? What have you seen, heard?

2. What is Baig's estimate of the promise of computer culture? What makes computerized culture a "multimedia" experience? What makes it "interactive"? According to Baig, what are the advantages? What are his most striking or intriguing examples?

3. What are the limitations? How serious do they sound to you?

4. Why do museum directors and artists view the prospects of computerized culture with "a mix of excitement and trepidation"?

For Discussion or Writing

5. Do you think of the computer as mainly a vehicle for electronic communication of the written word? Or do you think of it as a three-dimensional medium making full use of image and sound?

Collaborative Projects

6. You may want to collaborate with a group to prepare reviews of some recently released CD-ROMS for the culture lover. What is their coverage and their appeal? Are they rudimentary or sophisticated, klutzy or easy to use?

FLAMERS

Gary Chapman

Gary Chapman is director of The 21st Century Project at the University of Texas at Austin. In the following article from the New Republic, *he takes his readers on a guided tour of the darker side of computer communication. He is one of the skeptics sounding a "hype alert," asking us to distrust visions of a brave new electronic future of telecommuting workers, electronic town meetings, and multimedia classrooms. Writers like Chapman are warning us of a world where everyone shouts and few listen; where we all are afloat in an ocean of unedited, unfiltered data; where live teachers are shunted aside; and where we are increasingly isolated from true face-to-face human interaction.*

A joke floating around the Internet:

Q: How many Internet contributors does it take to change a lightbulb?

A: What are you trying to say, you worthless, scumbag jerk?

Computer networks are increasingly hyped as a new medium of virtuous   1
democratic and social discourse, the cyber-version of the Acropolis. A *Time* magazine reviewer recently called the Internet "the ultimate salon" of conversation, and
The Utne Reader is promising "electronic salons" to soothe the anomie and coarseness
of contemporary life. Author Howard Rheingold has celebrated the "virtual community" as a source of solace and fraternity, and columnist David Broder has written paeans to the new spirit of civic participation allegedly found on computer
networks.

Electronic conversations—if that's what they are to be called—on the Internet
and various other computer networks such as America Online, Prodigy and CompuServe, are certainly a new and interesting feature of American social life and
manners. The terabytes of gab on these systems, engaging millions of people, are
perhaps the first display of the direct voice of the American people in an ongoing,
semi-organized, public forum. People are talking about everything under the sun—
politics, pet care, even deliberate gibberish. Consequently, politicians, pollsters, reporters, marketers and social analysts are keenly interested in what our fellow
citizens are thinking and saying on-line. Electronic conversations, to our benefit, allow people to circumvent the managed public dialogue that politicians and P.R.-
types try to shape to serve their own ends.

But the evidence of public virtue in cyberspace is so far more discouraging
and alarming than noble and salutary. Electronic salons already contain broken

furniture and have mud on their walls. The notorious phenomenon of "flaming"–issuing a nasty and often profane diatribe–is now a familiar sociological curiosity. UseNet news groups–open, topical conversations accessible over the Internet and other systems–have become vast libraries of pyrotechnic insults. Mark Dery, editor of a new book, *Flame Wars*, offers a few choice examples: "You syphilitic bovine harpy." "You heaving purulent mammoth." "You twitching gelatinous yolk of rancid smegma." You get the idea. Many retorts are merely terse, obscene snarls, but Internet users have also developed a competition in rococo, smart-alecky taunts, such as this one: "Your reply was most impressive. You seem to have the ability to respond to mail with either profanity, inanity or pointless threats of physical violence. Why don't you try those pills the doctor gave you, and take a nice long rest. It may do you no good, but I am sure the remainder of the viewers would be pleased by the absence of your moronic and asinine diatribes." It's hard to imagine such exchanges at a PTA meeting or a cocktail party. Electronic communication is providing a disturbing glimpse of what may be smoldering, heretofore unsaid, in the minds of many Americans.

More generally, electronic conversations appear to be prone to misinterpretation, sudden and rapidly escalating hostility between the participants, and a weird kind of implosion when the conversants express their anger with sulking silence. This may be because, unlike in face-to-face conversation, there are no visual cues, what linguist Peter Farb calls "paralanguage." It may also be because people who are completely removed from one another physically can assault each other verbally without fear of bodily harm, a suggestion that our evolutionary heritage is still at work in restraining our behavior in everyday encounters.

Electronic anonymity also encourages fantasy life, often tilting toward the dark side. Dedicated network denizens frequently inhabit alter egos attached to their computer names. Some computer users have identities in cyberspace that correspond to exotic names, such as Phreak or Acid, two well-known hacker monikers, rather than to their prosaically named real-world personae. While a middle-class, suburban white man may tend not to adopt a *nom d'ordinateur*, millions of electronic Walter Mittys nationwide do take on a more aggressive personality behind a computer and a modem–ferociously pouring out their otherwise sublimated middle-class angst.

A cyberspace alter ego often goes beyond a new name and a release of inhibition. Network users lie, sometimes spectacularly. Pavel Curtis, a Xerox researcher who runs a fascinating Multi-User Dimension (or MUD)–a kind of a "virtual world" within the Internet with its own simulated geography, characters and interactions–reports that a significant portion of people logging into his system switch genders for the identities they assume. Most common are young men who portray themselves as women; indeed, it's become a rule of thumb that any sexually aggressive female on this MUD is really a man. Peter Lewis, *The New York Times*'s cyberspace reporter, tells a story about a man who conducted a protracted and intimate elec-

5

tronic romance over the Internet with a pen pal, who said she was a 26-year-old graduate student. When he met her in person, he learned that she was in fact a 13-year-old girl.

As the French discovered in their national Minitel system, sex often dominates electronic encounters. The majority of messages on Minitel have been advertisements for sex or sex talk, and, national character notwithstanding, Americans are no slackers in this regard. Computer communication seems to bring out the id screaming for attention. In February, a University of Michigan student, Jake Baker, was arrested for posting to the university's computer network a graphic fantasy of the rape, torture and murder of a fellow student; though such stories are common on a few news groups, Baker actually named his victim, which police interpreted as a threat. A reporter for *Computer Life* magazine posed on the Internet as a 15-year-old cheerleader and got more than thirty e-mail messages of a sexual nature, including requests for her panties and her telephone number. Harassment of women is so common that women often pretend to be men to avoid sexually suggestive e-mail.

Bigotry and misogyny are prevalent as well. As Amy Harmon noted recently in *The Los Angeles Times*, bigots are showing up on computer networks with increasing frequency because they can't get a hearing anywhere else. Networks are a cheap means for white supremacists and neo-Nazis to get their hate messages to thousands of people at once. The Simon Wiesenthal Center has protested to Prodigy about frequent anti-Semitic rants on that system. Prodigy officials are caught, to their embarrassment, in a tug-of-war between freedom of speech and the basic civilities that many users expect.

Finally, the general quality of the rhetoric on the Internet is discouraging in itself. Even without all the cranks, poseurs, charlatans, fetishists, single-issue monomaniacs, sex-starved lonely hearts, mischievous teenagers, sexists, racists and right-wing haranguers, many participants in unstructured Internet conversations have little of interest to say but a lot of room in which to say it. Goofy opinions and comical disregard for facts are rampant. Spelling is haphazard and even simple typos sometimes produce absurd flaming firefights. Nearly every reasonable discussion is sooner or later discovered by someone with a hobby horse or an abrasive personality or both, and there are few reliable ways to shunt such people elsewhere. It's pretty clear, too, that quite a few messages come from people who must be drunk; there are as yet no sobriety checkpoints on the "information superhighway." The new electronic Acropolis seems to foster rhetoric stylistically closer to Beavis and Butthead than to Pericles.

Fifteen years ago, the forerunner of the Internet, the Arpanet, was used almost exclusively by top computer scientists and other elite engineers and scientists, who tend to be a refined bunch, partial to classical music and good books. Many are now appalled by what networking has become. Some have dropped off the net altogether.

10

This suggests that the Internet may be on a path similar to that followed by television and other communications media: the introduction of the masses so alienates well-educated, cosmopolitan people that they abandon the medium or resort to a specialized class of cultural material that advertises its disdain for mass tastes. There are already signs that this is happening on the Internet: while veterans of the net have tended to narrow their presence to a select group of exclusive and low-profile mailing lists, more recent users are complaining loudly about the influx of hundreds of thousands of newcomers via America Online, "newbies" who are stumbling around the net asking greenhorn questions and committing faux pas of "netiquette." Many people with pressing schedules are starting to regard the ca-cophonous noise as a waste of time. Their exits raise the proportion of nuts, creeps and boors. Thus an inevitable backlash against the lofty hype surrounding the In-ternet is building, such as in Cliff Stoll's new book, *Silicon Snake Oil: Second Thoughts on the Information Highway.*

This all sounds like an anti-democratic trend, in contrast to the democratiza-tion that computer networks are supposed to both exemplify and support. Is cy-berspace already sorting itself into two camps, a jaded, invisible elite and a teeming mass of wrassling rubes? This image wouldn't be unusual in the history of Ameri-can popular culture. It seems clear that cultural polarization and low behavior in cyberspace reflect trends in American society as a whole, but the peculiar features of computer communication are amplifying the decline of our national mores and manners, and, at the same time, giving us an unprecedented bird's-eye view of what we've become.

Of course, we can always hope that computer networks are undergoing a metamorphosis from childhood to adolescence these days, with an anticipated maturation into adulthood sometime in the future. We'll have to develop manners in cyberspace just as we have in our everyday, real-world encounters, and that could entail a long process of evolution and refinement. If we don't develop virtual manners, cyberspace will continue to resemble a mud wrestling event. But if we can treat each other with respect over e-mail, we may go a long way toward solv-ing some of the basic dilemmas of democracy.

The Responsive Reader

1. Chapman caricatures those who hype computer networking as the answer to the anomie, or meaninglessness and purposelessness, of modern life. (What's a salon? What's a paean?) Why does he nevertheless see electronic conversation as a welcome alternative to the "managed public dialogue" of politicians and PR types?

2. What are major points in Chapman's indictment that follows the big "But" at the beginning of his second paragraph? What are "diatribes"—what form do they

take, and why, according to Chapman, are they a common feature in cyber-space? Why or how does the lack of "paralanguage" tend to favor "escalating hostility"? (Who was Walter Mitty?)

3. For what kind of fantasy life does electronic conversation seem to provide an outlet? What is the role of sex? (Why, in electronic communication, do men often pretend to be women and women pretend to be men?)

4. Why does Chapman see "unstructured Internet conversations" as a threat to reasonable or informed discussion? What lowering of the "general quality of the rhetoric" does Chapman see, and how does he explain it? What are his misgivings about the much touted "democratization" the computer age is supposed to bring? What are his predictions for the future?

For Discussion or Writing

5. Are you worried about insults on the Internet? Are you worried about sex on the Internet? Why or why not?

Collaborative Projects

6. What is the history of recent efforts to censor the flow of sexual material in electronic communication? What is the status of legal initiatives? What are the pros and cons?

6

Issues in Career Education

CAREER EDUCATION IN PERSPECTIVE

While pundits discuss the national debt or the pros and cons of immigration, the question looming large in the mind of the individual is often: How am I going to make a living? How well qualified am I for a decent job? What kind of education or training is a good investment? How well prepared am I to hold my own in the rapidly evolving high-tech society of the future?

THE WORLD OF WORK

Most people spend the major part of a lifetime at work. For most young people, a high priority is finding a career that enables them to make a living and at the same time derive personal satisfaction from what they do. Ideally, you will find a slot in the world of work that meets basic criteria: You are valued as a person. You feel needed for your expertise. You can take pride in your responsibilities and accomplishments. You receive a fair wage or salary for an honest day's work, or you make an honest profit on goods or services needed by the community.

Choosing a career at one time was simplified by the dictates of the class structure or family tradition. Miners' sons went to work in the mines. Farmers' offspring stayed on the farm; shopkeepers' offspring eventually took over the family business. Academics pushed their children toward professional careers. The great American myth of upward mobility gradually broke down these traditional patterns as education became the open sesame to a world of enlarged opportunity. Children of penniless immigrants speaking broken English became accountants, psychiatrists, or college professors. Women and minorities started moving into occupations that had been the traditional preserve of privileged white males. Today police officers, managers, judges, and lawyers are increasingly women or men and women of color.

In today's competitive job market, career counselors give different and contradictory advice. One school of thought says: Become a specialist, and you shall not want. Become good at something that others don't have the stamina or the motivation to pursue. Even in a world of downsizing and automated systems, someone has to do the programming that keeps the system running. Someone has to have the math to keep the books for modern businesses dealing with lease/purchase arrangements, financing for outsourced operations, cost of warranty service, salary increments, dividend distributions, contributions to pension funds, health insurance premiums, and a myriad other financial obligations and complications. Someone has to be able to decipher the convoluted rulings of the tax code, if only to punch the right instructions into the computer. Someone has to be there for people to call in when the computer or the automated assembly line is down.

The other school of thought says to you: Don't train for a limited specialty. Learn how to learn new specialties. Train for meeting changing needs in a world of rapidly changing technology. Get as much solid grounding as you can in lifeline subjects like math, statistics, and computer science. Learn Spanish or Japanese to give you an advantage over English-only applicants in a global economy. While you commute to school or work, listen to audio tapes on management theory or negotiating techniques. Lifelong employment in a steady job will be increasingly rare. Many people entering the workforce today should expect to change jobs half a dozen times or more. They should expect to go back to school for retraining or reentry programs.

EDUCATION FOR WORK

How well does education in our society prepare young people for the world of work? How well does it prepare students to grow and change in a world where technologies and production methods and management–labor relations change rapidly or become obsolete?

Many young people find the workplace more demanding, more complex, than they might have expected. Police officers, for instance, may realize that their training cannot be limited to the handling of suspects and evidence. They need to be better prepared to deal with domestic violence, mental illness, or gang loyalties. They need guidance in how to go into a neighborhood and defuse potentially violent situations. They need to learn how to be more supportive of rape victims. They need to be schooled in community relations, learning how to rebuild a reputation for professionalism damaged by sensational news reports of police brutality or police corruption.

Similarly, new teachers find that subject matter competence is only part of the job. In communities with large immigrant populations, dealing with bilingualism and different cultural backgrounds challenges the monolingual, monocultural teacher. Mainstreaming disabled students, dealing with drugs and weapons on school premises, and counteracting alienation among the young requires teachers to be therapists, police surrogates, and spiritual counselors.

Recognizing and helping with conditions like dyslexia and attention deficit disorder require special expertise.

You are likely to have heard predictions that the well-paying jobs of the future will be in areas dealing with information and communication. According to many forecasts, the workforce will be increasingly split into two parts. There will be a computer elite of software buffs and technical-innovation junkies. There will be others whose computer literacy is limited to running the price codes on merchandise over an electronic scanner. Regardless of a specific career choice, people who are fully computer literate will have the edge.

SCREENING STUDENTS FOR CAREERS

How does the educational system screen young people and channel them into different careers or occupational tracks? In status-conscious, class-conscious societies, an elitist system of education equips the children of the privileged with educational credentials that others find hard to match. In England, much of the political and military elite used to go from exclusive private boarding schools like Eton and Harrow to the universities of Oxford and Cambridge. Only in recent years have the best and brightest started to drift to schools like the University of Durham and other less tradition-bound places. In the United States, a similar network of Eastern prep schools, undergraduate colleges like Dartmouth and Amherst, and graduate schools at Harvard or Yale has served as the fast track in areas like top-level government work, top-level academic research, or the foreign service. Traditionally, in European countries pupils have been sorted early (age 10 or 11) into academic and nonacademic or vocational tracks. Only students selected for academic high schools and meeting stiff graduating requirements were eligible for university work and professional careers.

How does a democratic society try to level the educational playing field and make first-rate educational opportunities accessible to young people from the other side of the tracks? American education has generally been more flexible and multibranched than the traditional elitist pattern, and you may have had a chance to observe some of the alternatives that make it a more open system. There has been much argument pro and con over tracking, which allows academically gifted and motivated students to advance faster than poorly prepared and poorly motivated peers. Two-year colleges provide an alternative to four-year schools while at the same time making it possible for transfer students to join four-year degree programs later. Reentry students return to college after going to work or taking care of a family. Sixty-year-old candidates finish Ph.D.s. Extension classes and distance learning through interactive computer programs provide alternatives to traditional on-campus education.

One school district for years had on its letterhead a motto that said: "Our aim is to give all students a chance to develop their full potential." This has been the traditional humanistic goal of American educators. In practice, however, efforts to remove racial or ethnic barriers to equal educational opportunity have often met with failure. What Jonathan Kozol calls "savage inequalities" between the funding of suburban and inner-city schools persist. Forced busing to integrate schools in large urban districts produced a violent backlash. It met with violent resistance from parents. It has been blamed for massive white flight to suburbs and for swelling enrollments in private schools. It in the end disillusioned many parents of minority children. Recent court decisions reversing court orders that mandated busing are in keeping with conservative trends. Recently, affirmative action programs that brought minority students into undergraduate programs and law schools and medical schools have come under attack.

ENTERING THE WORLD OF WORK

A good job is more than a job. When you read a help-wanted ad that talks about "work in a healthy environment with a wellness orientation," you know that you will be expected to believe in ideals of fitness if you are to fit in. Many occupations and many organizations have their own mindset or mystique. Good teachers, no matter how frustrated at times with students' behavior and failure to learn, take the students' failure to learn personally. They may be driving home after work saying, as did a former school teacher who became President of the United States: "What have I really done for them today?" You know you are in good hands with a health professional when you begin to suspect that the person cares more about your health than you do. A good mechanic takes pride in identifying and solving problems that stymie someone with a nine-to-five mentality.

Advice like the following may help you in choosing and building a career:

- *Develop a career interest.* Many people used to be influenced in their choice of work by family tradition. If a parent or relative had a successful career as a nurse, doctor, medical technician, or optometrist, you may be inspired to follow in the person's footsteps. However, today many young people find their role models outside the family. Many people go into teaching because they admired a teacher who knew how to make students want to learn. During summer jobs, internships, or stints as a volunteer, you can keep your eyes open for kinds of work that might appeal to you or that you might find challenging.
- *Build on your strengths.* Are you good at relating to people, putting them at ease, making them feel you care about their needs and worries? Or

are you good with diagrams and charts? Are you good at crunching numbers? Do you have the long attention span needed for studying and absorbing large amounts of information? Are you intrigued by how things work or by how to make them work again when they break down? Develop your personal aptitudes and skills, and look for opportunities to use them to good advantage.

- *Start networking.* When you network, you develop ties with others who can become helpful sources of information or support for you–and you for them. You may meet people with interests related to yours in classes, during campus activities, at company open houses, at fitness centers, or at religious gatherings. Talk to such people, showing an interest in their concerns and getting them interested in yours. Keep in touch–by phone, e-mail, or informal notes. Networking can be a valuable source of tips about job opportunities, hiring policies, changes in corporate personnel, shifts in corporate policy, or the political climate at a company.

- *Scope opportunities.* When a field interests you, read up on it in newspapers and periodicals–which might range form *Business Week, Forbes*, or *Fortune* to *Working Woman* or *Psychology Today.* When you are getting ready to apply for a job or go for an interview, learn as much as you can about the employer–the company's or institution's history, ambitions, and key personnel. If you want to be systematic about it, request promotional literature for a major product or program, or try to get your hands on the company's annual report. Read up on the location–local history, local plans for development. Be prepared to show that you care about the job, the company, the people, the place.

- *Develop needed qualifications.* For instance, if you plan to teach in a state with large Spanish-speaking school populations (Texas, Florida, California), find out about requirements for Spanish-language proficiency and work intensively on your Spanish. Catch up with people more computer literate than you by taking special evening classes or making use of other opportunities. If it seems advisable, take a crash course in statistics. If you freeze up in front of groups, find tutoring or coursework that will help you shine during oral presentations.

- *Don't sell yourself short.* When you draw up a résumé or letter of application, make a point of coursework or fieldwork that is relevant to the job you seek. Call attention to extracurricular activities that might suggest leadership training or valuable experience with group work. Be familiar with plus points of your alma mater–departments with more than a local reputation, prestigious innovative programs, honors or achievements of the faculty, an admired track team. Remember you are entering a competitive world.

THE POLITICS OF WORK

Is it true that working people today feel apprehensive about a slipping standard of living, eroding job security, and an uncertain future for their children? In the industrialized countries of the West, the shortage of well-paid work and the loss of job security have become major political issues. In countries like France and Germany, share-work initiatives, shorter working hours, and early retirement are at the center of confrontations involving government, employers, and workers. In the United States, skilled politicians and well-organized initiative campaigns channel popular dissatisfaction into resentment against familiar targets. High taxes are said to discourage investment. Illegal immigrants are blamed for taking jobs away from Americans. Affirmative action programs are seen as making employers pass over white males in favor of less qualified women or minorities.

Political campaigns that make Americans at the lower end of the economic scale fight over shrinking job opportunities may be obscuring basic issues faced by workers regardless of whether they are male or female; whether they are black, Latino, or white. A basic problem for the job seeker or job holder today is that the individual feels powerless and irrelevant in a system dominated by megacorporations and large bureaucracies. Professions that are well-organized and well-funded, like the medical profession, make their voices heard and hold their own. Professions that are splintered, like the teaching profession, are at the bottom of the professional earnings scale.

When labor unions were strong, management, whether grudgingly or not, had to negotiate wages, health benefits, and working conditions with the people who did the work. In today's increasingly nonunion workforce, employees are relearning the Marxist maxim that there will always be someone desperate enough to do your job for less. Unorganized restaurant workers, bank tellers, airline employees, or agricultural workers find that the earnings multiple of the people they work for is at 180 or 200 times their own wages.

A major divisive factor in competition for jobs is the use of objective tests for hiring and promotion. Entry into and advancement in professions like teaching or police work often hinges on a candidate's performance on tests that are increasingly challenged as culturally biased. A middle-class white kid growing up in a world where people routinely talk in terms of percentages, percentage raises, discounts, averages, and multiples will have a better score on the applied math portion of a test than a kid from a background largely lacking that dimension. Does this mean we will be content to have large numbers of minority applicants fail tests that would allow them to become teachers, firefighters, or police officers?

Women in recent years have increasingly taken a stand against sexual harassment in the workplace. Multimillion-dollar damage awards have made employers rethink their attitudes toward condescending treatment of female coworkers or predatory sexual behavior by males in positions of authority. Hiring decisions and personnel policies are increasingly influenced by the need to avoid discrimination on the basis of gender, sexual orientation, or disability.

For Americans in the workforce, cynicism about involvement in the political process is an admission of defeat. Employers' obligations in matters of health insurance and protection of pension rights are political issues that affect the quality of life of millions of working Americans and their families. Worker safety and the new health hazards of the computerized workplace are political issues. Limiting the right of public employees to participate in political activity is a political issue. National and state policies on child care or family leave are political issues. A major challenge for working Americans today is how to make their voices heard and their influence felt.

QUESTIONS FOR DISCUSSION

What jobs have you had, and what did you learn from them? How did you develop your own career interests? Do you think your schooling is giving you the competence you need to succeed in the world of work? Have you made a study of how to do well in job interviews? How do Americans today, including especially working people, feel about unions? (Do you think teachers, nurses, bank tellers, or agricultural workers should unionize? Is unionization of the workforce a lost cause in today's America?) Do you consider yourself a nonpolitical or a politically involved person?

JOB ONE
Education

Joanne Jacobs

What is the future of the job market? Pundits projecting tomorrow's employment picture often zero in on the evolving high-tech and cyberspace industries of Silicon Valley in California, the Golden Triangle in North Carolina, the high-tech corridor of the Boston area, or Texas' answer to Silicon Valley in Austin. Silicon Valley, stretching between San Jose and San Francisco, is the home of Apple Computer, Hewlett Packard, National Semiconductor, and high-powered aerospace and software enterprises—the area where electronic tinkerers working in a garage started the personal computer business that has burgeoned into a multibillion-dollar industry. In the following article, Joanne Jacobs, an editor and columnist for the San Jose Mercury News, *asks: What kind of workforce will be needed by a high-tech economy? What kind of preparation will today's young Americans need to qualify? Is it true that many high school graduates don't have the necessary skills—leaving them unable to read technical manuals, unable to handle the math or statistics involved in quality control, lacking the work habits required for accuracy and high-grade reliability of performance? The article by Joanne Jacobs specified that you could post your own views on the subject in her Mercury Center message folder. Keyword: MC Talk, then pick Talk to the Mercury News and scroll down to her name.*

I was at McDonald's once when the cash registers went down. The kids at the counter just stood there, helpless. The assistant manager dashed from register to register, adding up the orders. That was a while back. By now, I'd guess that the assistant manager has a degree in computer science. Median pay for a high-tech worker in the valley is $56,113.

What about the kids who didn't even try to add? Where are the jobs for people who can push a button with a picture of french fries on it, but can't use basic skills to solve a problem?

Once there were jobs in this valley for people without much education. When the canneries closed, workers went from sorting fruit to sorting silicon chips. Production workers were supposed to check their brains by the door. They didn't have to think, or communicate, or calculate. If there was a problem, someone else solved it. If there was a decision to be made, someone else made it.

This has changed across Silicon Valley. There are plenty of jobs, but it takes a lot more to get in the door.

Intel isn't hiring machine operators anymore. They're being replaced by "self-sustaining technicians," who are expected to analyze data on the machine's

performance, decide whether it's operating within tolerances, troubleshoot problems, evaluate and train other workers and work in teams to implement quality
improvements. They need to understand statistics, intermediate algebra, chemistry
and physics.

"This is not your father's factory," says Tracy Koon, Intel's corporate affairs
manager.

A few years ago, the average technician had a high school education. Now the
average technician has an A.A. degree from a community college.

"Five years ago, if you told a supervisor his manufacturing workers would be
talking with design engineers about new products, he'd laugh at you," says Cheryl
Fields-Tyler, workforce excellence director for the American Electronics Association.
Now it's the norm.

Administrative support workers also are taking on new roles. "Secretaries are
becoming information systems managers," says Fields-Tyler.

People who work with their hands have to work with their brains too. To get   10
into a construction apprenticeship, "You need good reading and math skills, and
the ability to follow instructions," says John Neece, CEO of the Construction Trades
Council. "It helps to have computer skills."

By good reading skills, he means a 12th-grade reading level, or better: A
construction worker has to read blueprints and change orders, and understand
complex bid documents. By good math skills, he means algebra, geometry and, if
possible, trigonometry.

As the cost of building materials goes up, and customers demand lower costs,
workers must work faster and smarter. "You don't have a guy saying 'Do this, do
that' on construction sites. You can't waste materials, and you do not have time to
do the job twice."

"There's a false perception that if you don't do well in school, you can go into
a trade," says Bob MacLean, a National Semiconductor vice president. "If you don't
do well in school, you can't get a job."

On "Happy Days," Fonzie represented the kids who were bad with books but
good with their hands. Fonzie doesn't have much of a future, MacLean observes.
"There are no more jobs for grease monkeys. Auto mechanics have to read all that
fancy electronic equipment, diagnose the problem and fix computer things in your
car. They can't just turn a wrench."

Many of Larry Baumann's auto shop students don't read well enough to be-   15
come professional mechanics, says the Wilcox High teacher. "The GM service manual is written at a 14th-grade reading level. To fix a car, you need a two-year college
degree."

Once it was believed that technology would dumb-down 21st-century jobs.
Instead, technology eliminated the most repetitive, robotic jobs, and made everything else a lot more complex.

In the high-tech workplace, workers are responsible for continuously improving quality by analyzing statistical information, and working in teams with co-workers. Cutting across all jobs is a demand for people who can use math to solve problems and use the English language to communicate.

"In an amazing number of companies, front-line workers have some interaction with customers," says the AEA's Fields-Tyler. "Communications skill isn't a nice-to-have; it's a must have."

Solectron, a contract manufacturer that makes computer boards, is expanding rapidly, with entry-level jobs for machine operators, materials handlers, clerical and data-entry workers. A materials handler, for instance, needs good reading and writing skills and basic math. He has to calculate inventories and communicate with people on the line about their requirements. To move up to a technician's job, it helps to have algebra.

"It's not row after row of people with soldering irons," says Al Cotton, senior director of human resources. Line workers "have to work through persuasion, communicate, read and understand instructions, give presentations to sway your team members, explain a process to team members."

Team members must learn how to analyze problems, so they can contribute to solutions. "Even if they never run into an algebra problem after they leave school, it's still valuable," Cotton says. "Algebra teaches you to reason and process information, to think logically about solving problems. To do quality control you have to be able to do simple algebraic equations."

Komag, which makes hard disks, is expanding in San Jose and Milpitas, with manufacturing jobs for workers coming out of high school. But of 10 people who call about a job, only one gets hired.

Workers are on the job three 12-hour days a week, plus alternating Sundays. Base pay is $6.45 an hour, with four hours of overtime per shift.

Some applicants are automatically disqualified because they show up late at the assessment center. About 25–30 percent can't get past the basic skills test, which requires 8th-grade math and English skills.

Komag also puts applicants through a teamwork exercise: A group of five or six is given instructions on building something with a set of blocks, then observed to see how they work together. The final step is an interview with a panel including other line workers.

Once hired, workers are encouraged to take classes on-site or at community colleges to train for technician jobs.

Most large high-tech companies have extensive training programs: Intel spent $120 million in 1994, most of it on training factory workers.

Often, workers must take remedial English and math. Immigrants must learn to communicate in English, so they can participate in quality teams.

Above all, workers need the ability to keep on learning as jobs change.

Industry people and school people agree: There is a disconnect between what   30
schools are teaching and what employers are demanding.

Schools are focused almost totally on getting students into college, even though
40 percent never try college, and two-thirds will not earn a college degree.

"For so long we've said college, college, college," says Neece. "It's like, if you
don't go to college, you're not very smart."

"Everybody wants Johnny to go to college," says Jim Vice of Vi-Tec Manufacturing, chairman of the National Tooling Machine Association's apprenticeship
program. "If Johnny's not fit for college, he bums around, works at McDonald's,
and develops a bad attitude."

Meanwhile, apprenticeships go unfilled, and machine shop owners are desperate for skilled workers. An apprentice machinist averages $10 an hour with over-
time; a journeyman machinist can make $60,000 to $70,000 a year. High school
graduates need a 9th-grade reading level, algebra, geometry and preferably trig,
computer skills and mechanical aptitude.

"What's the purpose of school?" asks Richard Schorske, director of Workforce   35
Silicon Valley, which is working to link schools, community colleges and employers. "To go on in school? That's not good enough. The point is: Can they do the
work? Increasingly, they can't because they're illiterate and innumerate."

Nationwide, half of high school graduates are not prepared for skilled jobs,
according to the 1991 Labor Department SCANS (Secretary's Commission on
Achieving Necessary Skills) report.

Industry is trying to get specific about what skills new workers will need. For
an idea of how high the bar is being set, see "So you want to be a network installer"
in the box that follows. Those are the entry-level skills for the job.

SO YOU WANT TO BE A NETWORK INSTALLER

To help educators plan curricula, and help students prepare for skilled jobs, industries are developing detailed descriptions of what various jobs require. For
example, AT&T, GTE, Pacific Bell and TCI collaborated on skill standards for
entry-level telecommunications workers, working with the California Business
Roundtable and the state Department of Education.

Here are the prerequisites for jobs in network installation and
maintenance.

- Technical reading skills (circuit diagrams, on-line documentation, test data
  and specialized reference materials).
- Advanced mathematical skills (understand the concept of binary, octal,
  hexadecimal number systems and mathematical logic systems).

(Continued)

- Design knowledge (know and use computer-aided design to produce drawings)
- Electronics knowledge (understand principles of electrical theory and digital, analog, direct and alternating current circuits).
- Optical theory (understand reflection, refraction and optics).
- Communications theory (understand freespace transmission).
- Transmission knowledge (understand voice, data and video transmission principles, including Shannon's information theory).
- Analytic skills (conduct electronics problem-solving and analysis).
- Network skills (understand use of computers in data, voice and video networks).

Whether students are headed for college or a job, they need strong academic skills—and the ability to apply what they know to solve problems.

"The old line was that the fast track is the college track, the slow track is the applied track," says Schorske. "That's ridiculous. We hear complaints about college graduates too, that they can't apply what they know. The connection to the real world of work is missing big time. To make that connection is not dumbing down the curriculum; it's moving it up."

The Responsive Reader

1. The fast-food employee flipping hamburgers for a minimal wage has become a familiar symbol in the mythology of today's economy. Why? For what purposes does Jacobs invoke the image of the McDonald's employee in this article?

2. What for Jacobs is the basic difference between the production worker of yesteryear and of today? What does she specify as the changing requirements for manufacturing workers, for secretarial workers, for construction workers, and for auto mechanics in today's economy? For you, are her claims old news or new? To judge from your own experience and observation, is she right?

3. According to the sources cited by Jacobs, what are changing requirements "cutting across all jobs"? What jobs did technology eliminate, and how did it change the rest?

4. What do you learn here about the hiring practices and hiring criteria of high-tech companies? What do you learn about on-site training or in-service education?

5. What is the implied and overt criticism of the schools in this article? What attitudes or mindsets does Jacobs think need to change?

6. Can you explain the requirements for a "network installer" spelled out at the end of Jacobs' article?

For Discussion or Writing

7. How do you personally rate on the qualifications specified in this article? Where would be your strengths or weaknesses? How do you explain them in terms of your background or educational history?

8. In the same issue of the newspaper in which Jacobs' article appeared, a dissenting voice warned against overemphasis on the kind of academic preparation Jacobs endorses. Do you think something important is left out or played down in her article?

Collaborative Projects

9. What is the science and math background of your classmates or more generally of students at your college? Are the deficiencies of American students in these areas real–or exaggerated? Working with a group, you may want to develop a test instrument or a survey to help you answer these questions.

DOWNSIZING HITS HOME

Roger E. Swardson

While industry leaders and futurologists make much of the potential growth in high-tech jobs, more pessimistic voices warn of steady attrition in remunerative employment in an increasingly automated and streamlined economy. They predict a further erosion of job security as reducing the workforce becomes the key to rising shareholder profits and sky-rocketing executive salaries. Roger Swardson, a free-lance writer, does not write about these issues from the detached perspective of a government economist or from the perspective of a broker touting the performance of a company's stock. He writes from the perspective of the expendable employee, presenting his own experience as a temporary worker for an insurance company in Minnesota as an object lesson and a warning to others. Swardson is a shrewd observer of management practices and management thinking, and he knows well the mystique, the spin, that justifies and rationalizes management decisions that affect negatively large numbers of employees.

When I stand and look across the maze of beige cubicles, I see that Linda's is 1
strung with blue and white crepe paper and festooned with balloons. Vera stayed late yesterday and decorated. That's the way it usually works. And Linda most likely brought a box of bagels or doughnuts this morning. That's what you do on your birthday.

Just as the first Friday of the month is Jeans Day, when you wear casual clothes, and Chili Day, when a dozen people bring in their versions of slow-cookers for lunch. A couple of male managers judge the chili and make comments about each other's waistlines, and there is scattered laughter.

These aren't company events so much as they are the inventions of unquenchable women whose life mission seems to be to invent activities to keep the world's chin up. But as I stand here I can't stop thinking, "My God, the bus is going to hit many of these women."

That's the image I have of Gunther, the monolithic computer system that is scheduled to replace the workers who fill this office.

You and I are standing on a curb and a group of women are crossing the 5
street, just as they've been doing for years, in the crosswalk, where they're supposed to be, but there's this bus bearing down on them. Many of them don't see it until it's too late.

I'm horrified, but you're not. You are rooting for the bus. Your colleagues are on the bus. So is your future.

I'm a temporary, a transient co-worker of the women in this office, in this crosswalk. You have a promising job here where the company says it is becoming leaner (smaller), healthier (more profitable) and meaner (more competitive). You see change as exciting and have little patience with whiners who haven't smelled the fresh-ground Colombian of "quality plus" or "service excellence" and terms whose meaning relies on how often management repeats them.

But here's the other side of it. There isn't just that cluster of women in this one crosswalk at this one company. There are thousands of others. And not one careening bus but hundreds.

The obsession with boosting productivity has created widely disparate layers of working Americans. One is prosperous, whipping around chanting slogans and wondering what the hell the problem is beyond some bad attitudes; another works each day fearful that it will be the last; and another has fallen through the cracks into dislocation and a dreadful wage depression with little prospect of improvement. In the meantime, the economy does not produce jobs. And it will not as long as profit rests on downgrading or eliminating jobs, rather than creating them.

New workplace technology is wiping out jobs wholesale. That's not news–it's what it was designed to do. But tossing job creation from the foundation of our economic lives is another matter. Beyond the corporate boardrooms and crumbling union fiefdoms there is real fear and growing anger with the new social compact that says, "Hey, isn't this great? We're all on our own now." There's even a cheerful political philosophy for it, called communitarianism, which as much as says, "The government can't help you anymore. So get together and fend for yourselves. You'll love it"–a think-tank rehash of "I've upped mine. Up yours," the social policy of the 1980s.   10

Workers are being cut adrift in the publicized large layoffs, but more are quietly let go each day as their jobs simply disappear.

Here's one way it happens. This is the story of Gunther, which could be the bus we were watching but is actually a piece of equipment, a playing piece in the transition game. The game itself is not all that easy to follow, but the objective is simple: Don't get caught in the crosswalk.

We are in a service center of a major insurance company. It is the place where decisions are made on whether and how to insure thousands of clients of independent agents across the country, where policies are issued and constant updates are processed to keep them current. It is generally calm unless a woman on maternity leave brings in the new baby or it's Girl Scout cookie delivery day and blood sugar is at a seasonal high or it's midwinter and flu is rampant. There are more than 100 people here occupying almost the whole floor of a downtown office building. Eleven of us are men, one a vice president. Three men are temporaries.

There are four basic job classifications, as well as some specialist and support positions. At the entry level are policy assemblers, who convert stacks of paperwork into individual policies ready for the mail room. One step up are data-entry people pecking streams of instruction from the underwriters and assistants into video display terminals. The underwriters, assistants and, when the call is close, higher-ups consult oracles, odds and company policy and make book on medical practices, buildings, equipment and vehicles.

In my group we service eight Midwestern states. I am one of four policy as-   15
semblers. Three of us are temporary, two are men. A temp is brought in when a full-time assembler moves up or out. The job of assembler is being taken over by a machine called Gunther that will do our job automatically. When Gunther is ready, the last temps will be dismissed with a phone call to our agency, and the job of policy assembler, which has existed since this company began, will disappear.

Not that it's a great job. You start each day with stacks of paper, and you try to combine them in the right way and get them all the hell gone by day's end. There are light moments when, as a result of software permitting only so many charac-ters per slot, the computer provides collision insurance on a Volkswagen Rabbi or issues a policy to "A Partnership Composed of William," but the job is mostly rou-tine. Some people like it. More to the point, many people need this job. One said, "Hey, we can't all be rocket scientists, but we need some way to make a living."

Policy assembly is the traditional entry level to service-center work. Some un-derwriters began here. With this job going, the entry-level stakes move higher, and when the data-entry job is upgraded with the advent of the "paperless office," the first rung on the employment ladder will be out of reach for many traditional be-ginning workers. And the heap of dislocated workers will become steadily bigger.

So here we are, you and I, standing on this curb. The bus has done its work, many of the workers in the crosswalk silently whisked away. You are giving me a quizzical look, as if to say, "So? What did you think was going to happen? Some workers saw the bus coming a long time ago and made plans. Some didn't get wiped out. It's what happens."

Hold that thought.

What really happened was a committee, a task force, perhaps an adept sales-   20
person got a foothold somewhere in the company with a proposal to improve on the labor-intensive, error-prone and costly process of using people to assemble thousands of insurance policies each day. The idea was a new system. With a new machine. A Gunther.

Not a startling notion, really. Just the next step on the long road that reaches back over a century to when policies were handwritten. The company was finally ready to buy the whole automation scheme, which would combine abundant memory for countless policy details, image processing to digitize paperwork, spe-cialized equipment (such as Gunther) to churn out grunt work, powerful personal computers for super underwriters, and software that reaches out to the fingertips of far-flung independent agents.

Initial steps appeared routine, even mundane. They involved the consolidation of service offices scattered across the country into bigger regional centers to form the critical mass needed to satisfy the new system's voracious appetite. This meant uprooting people, retraining some, letting some go, not replacing others and finding a way to talk about it to secure cooperation and avoid chaos.

Few people knew the master plan. Nobody was ever told his or her job was disappearing until the last moment. There was talk of restructuring. New opportunities. The future lies ahead. Banners were run up. White ones said "quality" or "service," black ones "global competition" and "economic downturn." No widespread layoffs. Just people leaving here and there. An office moving. A department gone over time. Not much you could really see.

Of three basic ways to winnow workers, attrition is cheapest. Some people see what's coming and leave or move on for other reasons. The second winnower is "performance factors." Here stress identifies who can handle increased complexity and workload and who can't keep up. Finally, there are transfers for those who hold up and terminations for those left when time runs out. In the first year of consolidating the service centers, 234 people, 3 percent of the division's population, were terminated.

Management called this "exciting." Rapidly escalating fringe benefit costs, with   25
health care in the lead, made shrinking the work force even more attractive. The strong motivation of middle-management women, shouldering ever more work in hopes of hanging on to their gains and moving even higher, added an unexpected boon for male senior management. And, finally, the recession-driven flood of trained temporary workers (often having been laid off from similar jobs) smoothed out the final phases of the transition plan.

In St. Paul, the last step in that transition began with a job fair. It was a casting call for people with "clerical skills and career motivation." Nearly 500 applicants showed up for full-time policy assembly, data entry and clerical jobs. Implementation of the new system was speeding up.

But by the following summer, a little over a year after being recruited for "career opportunities," 18 full-time assemblers had been cut to six in the first service center where I worked. The rest were temps. It was not a happy place.

You lightened the day by inventing diversions. For example, one day I noticed an unusual stockpile of cat hair on my sport coat. A nap had clearly been taken there. The game of the day then called for including one cat hair in a number of policies selected for maximum geographic coverage. By day's end, a souvenir of a 13-year-old Maine Coon tomcat from Minnesota named Fitzgerald was on its way to policyholders in 19 states.

Pressure in the last days was intense. If it wasn't the work, which was being piled on, it was the uncertainty. Even the temporaries were jumpy. You never know, after all, when your time is up or whether your agency has another job for you. Those stories of lighthearted temps who love the freedom and wouldn't have it any other way are the rare exception. Every temporary I've ever known, except for students, craves a decent, permanent job. We read benefits material like the menus of expensive restaurants that are equally out of reach.

A temporary here gets $7 an hour, a good temp wage in St. Paul. No benefits, of course. The standard work-week, 38 hours and 45 minutes, yields a paycheck of $211.75 after deductions, or just under $850 a month if you are never ill, your job transfers are seamless and you've accrued enough hours to qualify for paid holidays. That's the absolute best you can do, and all those things rarely happen. [30]

More realistically, your monthly expenses must be covered by a variable and unpredictable wage of between $600 and $850. Try it. First single, then married, and then married with children. Now imagine there are millions of us, working, with annual incomes under $10,000.

Around Christmas I was switched over to the medical-industry service center and got through the trial period. This was the office of crepe paper and Chili Days; also of mothers on the shared phone making sure their children were home from school. Because the common phone was near my work area, I frequently answered it and got used to the fact that the departmental children out there expected us to know who they were. They would simply blurt, "Is my mom there?" And after a while you did get to know them, even to the point of responding, "Gee, I don't know, Tommy. Did you clean your room yet?"

The temps, of course, had a special rapport. There was the young guy who had worked his way through the University of Minnesota and graduated last year, never so much as taking out a student loan, and who would show up in a tie now and then because he had yet one more interview. And there was the temp about my age who had been in television production and who brought me a few jars of Dolga Crab Apple jelly. He quit after several months, after the pressure again became unreasonable as Gunther Day neared. When he left, another temp had to do his work and hers, too.

Two weeks before Gunther, the young graduate and I were let go. The next week the last temp, a woman from Ohio who had come to town hoping for work, also went. The last full-time assembler was then reassigned for training, and the job of policy assembly went the way of the buggy whip.

Improved productivity leads to improved profitability, which leads to job creation, right? The first part is working like a charm, judging from record amounts of money that management is shoving into its pockets across the country. But there has been no appreciable job creation. Why? [35]

Strange things happen in corporations. One day while looking for paper clips I found a memorandum that shouldn't have been in my desk. It described the very productivity program that produced my temporary job and would eventually take it back. In this insurance company, each piece of business, even an address change, is called a work unit. When most of the transition game is over, revenues, expressed in terms of gross work units, are projected to have tripled over the four-year transition period. Net work units, after factoring in the impact of the new office technology, are projected to be less than half of what they were in year one. In other words, the business will triple with a service mechanism that will be reduced by half. If it all works, there will never be a need to significantly increase service-center jobs. Ever. The company can even absorb acquisitions into the new service system. Think of the profitability. Think of the people who will be tossed out in those unsuspecting work forces.

So what happens to these leftover people? What happens in a nation filling up with leftover people?

Here we are on the curb, and you're still giving me a look. You've turned sardonic. Change happens, you say. And you believe that the change you're a part of can be predicted by computer model. OK. But how broad is the model? Is the shape of change out here on the street predictable? Manageable? In a nation of such size and diversity? One that is already breaking up into polarized fragments?

Recently I had the chance to ask James Tobin, a Nobel Prize–winning economist at Yale University, how he accounted for the dramatic increase in the nation's working poor and unemployed. Global competition? The terrible residue of trickle-down? A cyclical downturn?

Some of all of that, he said. But something much bigger as well: the final   40
downhill ride into a new era. The information age, or whatever term you prefer. Change on a scale not seen since farmhands were beckoned into the factories. Major upheaval. Mayhem, perhaps. But it will settle down again in a decade or so, he said. Eventually there will be new jobs, even if we don't now know where they will come from. But they will come. They have before. It's what happens, he said.

A new era. In a decade or so. And, along the way, new levels of insulated wealth and a new peasantry. Riches in isolation. Idleness and despair in the street. The classic formula for revolution. So how long does the computer model say we have until the rabble go for their pitchforks this time?

So here we stand. The temp whiner and the productivity freak. We could both be wrong, of course. Maybe none of this is happening. Or will happen. After all, I never did see Gunther. It's humming away in another building. Out in the suburbs. All I saw was the crosswalk.

The Responsive Reader

1. How effective is Swardson's analogy of the crossroads and the bus?

2. What do you learn here about the world of temporary work? What are some of the basic givens or parameters? Does Swardson's situation and that of his coworkers become real to you? Do you care?

3. Much has been written about the fashionable business philosophy of today's corporations. What do you learn from Swardson about a current business mentality, the corporate mindset, or management slogans?

4. From the point of view of the social scientist, the evidence Swardson presents is anecdotal—it's one person's story. Does he convince you that his experience is representative? For you, what makes his experience seem typical or else unusual?

For Discussion or Writing

5. What have been your own opportunities to observe the mechanisms of layoffs or of hiring cycles? Where do you see yourself in reading this article—are you one of the "productivity freaks" or one of the "whining temps"?

6. Are you inclined to think that the situation of people like Swardson is the result of impersonal economic forces and that nothing can be done? Or do you think that government or business or both have a responsibility to change the situation? How?

Collaborative Projects

7. The barometer of job loss and job creation changes with the vicissitudes of the economic cycle. Working with a group, can you identify something like a rough consensus in current estimates by economists, employer groups, or employee organizations? How do they size up the present? What do they predict for the future?

PREPARING FOR LIFE IN THE REAL WORLD

Hedrick Smith

The American educational system has had bad publicity for many years. Charges against the schools range from neglecting the classics and not teaching Shakespeare to not preparing students for the high-tech world of tomorrow. Employers complain about high school graduates without minimal reading and writing and oral communication skills. High-powered national commissions, like the one cited in the following article, deplore the "watering down" of the curriculum and the "dumbing down" of textbooks. Teacher morale is low, with teachers feeling undervalued and underpaid, while class sizes grow and support budgets for books, equipment, or counseling dry up. Art and music programs are axed, leaving gangs and drugs as extracurricular activities. The dropout rates for minorities are calamitous. Hedrick Smith, who won a Pulitzer Prize as a reporter for the New York Times, *became a fellow of the Foreign Policy Institute at the Johns Hopkins School of Advanced International Studies. He excerpted the following article from his book* Rethinking America *(1995). Smith here joins the large chorus of critics of American high school education, faulting it for its poor record in preparing students for the transition from school to work.*

For the average young people at American high schools, the educational system is stuck in the past, in a time warp.   1

Back in 1980, the American educational system fit the needs of the then-modern economy. But today, that system is as outmoded for many students, and as behind the competitive curve in education, as the mass-production system at General Motors has been behind the curve in making automobiles.

The two went hand in hand–GM's production system and the old-fashioned "general education" program of most U.S. high schools. GM mass-produced cars; it wanted workers who took orders and did assembly-line jobs by rote. American high schools mass-produced semiskilled human labor. Both did well enough–until their world changed.

Today there is a serious mismatch between what the education system tries to produce and what the job world needs, and the heart of the problem is a mind-set that ignores realities.

The curriculum and the educational priorities at most American high schools   5
are geared to the college-bound. Yet economists assert that 70 percent of the jobs in the American economy do not require a four-year college degree, and educators report that 70 percent to 75 percent of American teen-agers will not actually finish

four years of college. Despite these numbers, the non-college-bound student–the average American high school student–is low priority in most American high schools.

"The neglected majority" is the term that Bert Grover, Wisconsin's state school superintendent for 12 years, gave to these kids.

What worries Grover and a growing body of experts is that these young people in the middle–America's mid-kids–will be the backbone of our future workforce. They will provide the human resources for every business from high-tech electronics to manufacturing to banking, or else they will be a drag on the economy, doomed to lower living standards because they are no more qualified– or even less qualified–for modern business and industry than mid-kids in Malaysia or Mexico.

Preparing mid-kids for high performance in the new work world is the key to whether America's standard of living will rise in the 21st century or continue to stagnate for the majority.

"When it came to dealing with the needs of the non-college bound," declared Grover, "Wisconsin had institutional and programmatic anarchy."

One major reason for this "anarchy" is that the American way is to leave it to   10 the individual student, supported by his family, to find a path into life. And yet, without giving young people clear guidance and providing an organized structure, the adult world is often just abdicating its guiding role in education to the uncertain whims of teen-agers.

Two-thirds of American high school sophomores, juniors and seniors take jobs during the school year. Seniors work the most–an average of 20 hours or more per week, according to Professor Laurence Steinberg of Temple University. Steinberg and other scholars warn that there is a serious danger when the job load gets too heavy. Ten hours is the break point; less than 10 hours of work, and grades typically rise, Steinberg's studies show; more than 10 hours and schoolwork and grades suffer.

SAY NO TO WORK

Steinberg contends that excessive after-school work is a big reason why American high-school students compare poorly against other countries on international tests. "Everybody worries why Japanese and German and Swedish students are doing better than we are," Steinberg says. "One reason is, they're not spending their afternoons wrapping tacos."

One of the harshest indictments of the American system came from a national bipartisan commission that included former labor secretaries from the Carter and Reagan administrations, corporate CEOs and union leaders. The commission declared in 1990 that "America may have the worst school-to-work transition system of any advanced industrial country." Students not on the college track get "watered-down courses" and very little opportunity "for acquiring relevant, professional-level qualifications for occupations. The result is that typical high-school graduates mill about in the labor market, moving from one dead-end job to another until the age of 23 or 24. Then, with little more in the way of skills than they had at 18, they move into the regular labor market, no match for the highly trained German, Danish, Swedish or Swiss youth of 19."

ELITIST PRACTICES

By focusing its resources on the college-bound, America's public school system has unintentionally become undemocratic, elitist. Among others, Thomas Kean, Republican governor of New Jersey from 1982 to 1990 and now president of Drew University, warns that this trend is creating a dangerous divide in America.

"You follow them (the 70 percent who do not graduate from a four-year col-   15
lege) through, and their earnings haven't even kept pace with inflation, so they're losing every day—and they see the vision of the new house and the new car disappear," Kean asserted.

As Kean and others see it, the disparity in earning power—and in skills and the quality of education—is an issue threatening not only to America's capacity to compete economically, but to the stability and cohesion of American democracy.

"You take the kids who go to college, they're all exceeding the rate of inflation," Kean explained. "So you've got 70 percent of the kids going this way (his hand points down) and 30 percent going the other way (his hand points up), and you're not going to have that exist very long before this democracy is going to be in trouble. The 70 percent isn't going to allow the 30 percent to do that for very long."

PERILOUS CONSEQUENCES

A keen sense of the perilous consequences that Kean cites and a growing awareness of foreign educational models for average high-school students have spurred a new burst of educational reform in America in recent years. At the national level, both the Bush and Clinton administrations have promoted a campaign to raise America's national education standards through the Goals 2000 legislation passed by Congress in 1994. At the state and local levels, there are scores of effective experiments at educational reform—important pioneering efforts, though still a tiny fraction of America's 110,000 public schools in the 15,000 national school districts. So far, there is no national strategy being implemented.

Nonetheless, resistance to serious reform remains strong at most American public schools, despite a multitude of opinion polls expressing dissatisfaction with the existing system. Among the 110,000 public schools, precious few have embraced systemic change. According to the Education Commission of the States, a research organization, only 1 percent to 4 percent of America's schools have begun to undertake fundamental restructuring, and fewer than 1 percent have completed the process of change. More than 95 percent of America's schools have stuck with the status quo.

The biggest obstacle to change is the public mind-set, according to reform-minded public officials such as Kean. "The American public doesn't really understand what's going on in schools," Kean told me. "They don't recognize it's their child who isn't getting the kind of education which would enable him or her to earn the kind of living that they deserve. I don't think we've yet really energized ourselves to understand that this is a national priority. This is really a crisis." 20

The Responsive Reader

1. What parallel does Smith draw between the old-fashioned assembly-line system at General Motors and an educational system "stuck in the past"? What is the "basic mismatch" that Smith sees today?

2. What for Smith are the drawbacks or limitations of the traditional system of individual initiative and individual choice in matters of education?

3. Parents have often approved the part-time jobs high school students take as a valuable introduction to the work ethic and the value of a dollar. Why does this article ask readers to rethink this attitude?

4. How or why does this article join with those who take an anti-elitist view of American education? Where or in what context have you encountered charges of elitism before? According to this article, what "dangerous divide" does the elitist emphasis in the schools create? What are the economic and social implications?

5. Have you seen evidence of a movement to set or raise national academic standards? Are you aware of efforts to rate schools or to recognize them for achievement?

For Discussion or Writing

6. Have you seen any evidence of "effective experiments" or "fundamental restructuring" in your own career as a student? What major changes or reform initiatives have you had a chance to observe? Did your own school(s) or teachers seem married to the "status quo"?

Collaborative Projects

7. What information can you find concerning comparative test scores or measurements of academic performance used in comparing American students with students in other countries?

Making Connections

8. Do Joanne Jacobs and Hedrick Smith agree on the mismatch between the educational system and the world of work? Where do their views coincide; where do they differ?

BLACKBOARD BUNGLE

Leon Lederman

> *The need to stay attuned to a changing world is an especially urgent issue in teacher education or teacher training. How up to date or how far behind are teachers in a rapidly evolving technology-driven society? The following article examines the need for continuing education of teachers in the area of science and mathematics. How much retraining or in-service education for teachers does our educational system provide? Leon Lederman is chair of the Teachers Academy for Mathematics and Science in Chicago. He is a 1988 Nobel Laureate in physics, a former director at the National Accelerator Laboratory in Batavia, Illinois, and a professor of science at the Illinois Institute of Technology in Chicago. Lederman's article, published in* The Sciences, *was adapted from a talk he gave to the section on science education at the New York Academy of Sciences in 1994.*

In 1983 the National Commission on Excellence in Education, responding to a   1
request from the secretary of education, reported on the quality of education in America. The report was also presented as an open letter to the American public under the title: *A Nation At Risk: The Imperative of Educational Reform.* It began without mincing words:

> Our Nation is at risk. Our once unchallenged preeminence in commerce, industry, science, and technological innovation is being overtaken by competitors throughout the world. . . . We report to the American people that   the educational foundations of our society are presently being eroded by a rising tide of mediocrity that threatens our very future as a Nation and a people.

The body of the report was only slightly less chauvinistic than the introduction, but the purple prose and military metaphors of the former had the desired shock effect on the nation: its bugle call to action became front-page news, and for many weeks afterward there was a great outpouring of blame, anxiety and indignation on the editorial pages and the talk shows. The media attention generated by the crisis rhetoric kept the public focused on the educational predicament far more effectively than did the more specific, and more alarming, facts recited by the report inside.

But, of course, public attention moved on. Twelve years after *A Nation At Risk* the United States is still at risk. The educational systems at the federal, state and local levels are, by and large, dysfunctional. One cannot exaggerate the lack of preparation of primary school teachers for the teaching of mathematics and science. Less than 1 percent of the school budget in Chicago has normally been allocated to the ongoing professional enhancement of teachers, and little or no time is allowed during the school day for collegial interactions in urban schools in the U.S. Compare that with the corresponding statistic in Japan, where, by one estimate, the budget number is 40 percent: Japanese teachers spend nearly half their time in collegial activities, in improving curriculum, and in studying and advancing their knowledge of the teaching arts.

In 1989 a national convention of U.S. governors was convened by "the education president," George Bush, and a set of ambitious goals was set out to be achieved "by the year 2000." Yet by any measure one can devise, not much has been accomplished in advancing the "center of mass" of an enterprise that includes some fifty million students and two million teachers. And after personally spending the past five years immersed in the school-reform business, I can certainly understand the pessimism that most people have about the future of American schools–especially the large public school systems that serve most of the nation's disadvantaged children. Indeed, my own sobering experience has led me to conclude that the schools cannot heal themselves. Outside intervention, help and support are essential.

About five years ago I became involved in a consortium of universities to organize a new venture in Chicago, a private, not-for-profit intervention in the public school system designed to assist, if not to rescue, the schools. A board of directors was created, made up of teachers, principals, other educators, university presidents, scientists from universities and national laboratories, community group leaders and a number of strong participants from the private sector. We had the organizational backing of all the academic institutions in Chicago, including some fourteen universities and four-year colleges. The goal was professional enhancement: training the primary school teachers in Chicago to teach science and mathematics.

As a physicist, I hardly need to be persuaded of the value of an education in   5
science and mathematics. But all of us taking part in the Chicago schools intervention also care deeply about reading and writing and geography. So why the focus on science and mathematics? Experience with students from kindergarten age through fourth grade demonstrates that science and mathematics, taught in the right way, engage children, resonate with their own natural curiosity and open a door to the joy of learning. Children exposed to such teaching also develop their communications skills–a key to future learning. A positive introduction to the study of science and mathematics serves as a foundation for an interest in those topics throughout a person's lifetime. And as for the relevance of the curriculum, the engines that drive the changes in contemporary society are science and science-based technology.

Our target customers were some 17,000 teachers who teach science and mathematics, among other subjects, to students in kindergarten through the eighth grade. Our "mission possible" was to train the teachers in those disciplines as well as in new pedagogical techniques. We were encouraged at the outset by indications that there would be some financial support. And indeed, in 1990, with funding from the National Science Foundation, the U.S. Department of Energy, private philanthropy and the state of Illinois, we opened the Teachers Academy for Mathematics and Science (TAMS) on the campus of the Illinois Institute of Technology, near the south side of Chicago. That was the beginning of a learning process.

HISTORICAL ANTECEDENTS

We are, of course, not the first to embark on educational reform. Educational crises do have a history, and perhaps by reviewing that history one can learn how to make reform succeed.

In the 1860s a revolutionary educational movement emerged in the U.S. to promote "object teaching," a method introduced by the early nineteenth-century Swiss educational reformer Johann Heinrich Pestalozzi. Instead of merely lecturing to children, the teacher was to give them real objects with which to experiment and make observations. Object teaching sought to develop student thinking and deemphasize the memorization of facts. I wonder if that sounds familiar.

Also in the mid-1800s the industrialization of the U.S. led to the creation of a public high school system. Industry demanded a workforce that could read and communicate—and a workforce trained in such practical scientific subjects as technology, zoology, surveying, mechanics, mineralogy and engineering. Does that sound familiar?

In 1890, at Cornell University, a nature-study movement originated as a reaction against the growing urbanization of America. The basic fear was that city children would have no chance to learn which end of the cow to milk. Cornell leaflets of the day stressed birds, flowers, insects and trees. At about the same time science in the high schools was dominated by the needs of college curriculums—the style and content of both lectures and laboratories were essentially designed for the college bound. Then, in 1893, a national "Committee of Ten" set standards for high school science that reduced the influence of colleges. In its report the committee wrote:

> Every subject which is taught at all in secondary school should be taught in the same way and to the same extent to every pupil so long as he pursues it— no matter what the probable destination of the pupil may be, or at what point his education is to cease.

Does that, too, sound familiar?

In the early 1900s H. G. Wells, the noted English historian, novelist and futurist wrote: "More and more, the future of society is a race between education and catastrophe."

In general, efforts to reform science education in the U.S. have gotten their greatest boost after a war. The most dramatic instance was the famous report *Science, the Endless Frontier*, prepared in 1945 by Vannevar Bush, director of the Office of Scientific Research and Development under President Franklin Delano Roosevelt. Bush's report described science education as an essential component of a new relation between the state and the scientific and technological community. By the mid-1950s some of the postwar activity to reform science education had begun to fade, only to be shocked into greater frenzy by the 1957 success of the Soviet *Sputnik I*. I recall many of my colleagues and teachers pausing in their research activities at the time to write splendid high school textbooks in all fields of science. Yet as the years passed, the impact of those textbooks diminished, because their authors picked up their slide rules and resumed their research, leaving the revolution they had started to dangle and wither away.

THE NEW PEDAGOGY

As a scientist engaged in science education, I naturally relate our efforts at TAMS to science itself. I relate the future of science education to the future of science. And I relate the way children learn about the world to the way scientists learn about the world. There is a lot more here than metaphor.

Let me try to be more specific. Science is a process of observation, measurement and synthesis. That sequence has been adopted in many of the hands-on science-education programs that are known to be most successful. What we scientists observe and what we choose to measure are constrained by what we already know and by what we think we understand. The creative insight comes about when we learn to acquire intuitions and then recognize the preconceptions that limit those intuitions—which is quite similar to what children do with the intuitions they acquire and accumulate in their explorations.

Consider Galileo's great discovery, immortalized as Newton's first law of motion: an isolated body will continue its state of motion forever. Boy, if that isn't counterintuitive! Galileo's creative act was in realizing that ordinary intuition is irrelevant because in ordinary experience objects are never isolated. Balls stop rolling, horses must pull carts to keep the carts in motion. But Galileo's deeper intuition suspected simplicity in the law governing moving bodies, and his insightful surmise was that if you *could* isolate the body, it would continue moving forever. So he polished the block and he polished the table, and the block moved much farther. He knew he could not achieve complete isolation, but perhaps he could get close enough to sniff out the underlying simplicity.

But Galileo was also confronting a powerful tradition. In 1600 it was just "common sense" that rest was the natural state. Aristotle had said so almost 2,000 years earlier, and so it was—until Galileo's new intuition. But for the past 300 years Galileo and his followers have insisted that scientists must construct new intuitions in order to learn how the world works.

Now listen to the educational psychologist Howard E. Gardner of Harvard University, writing in 1994:

> We argue that, during the early years of life, children form extremely powerful theories or sets of beliefs about how the world works—theories of mind, theories of matter, theories of life. . . . These . . . become so deeply entrenched in the human mind, that they prove very difficult to eradicate in favor of the more comprehensive and more veridical views that have been painstakingly constructed in and across the disciplines.

What Gardner says about children can be said about Yale graduates, congressmen, judges . . . and schoolteachers.

Replacing the powerful misconceptions children bring with them to the classroom is the art of science education. Children need the same "intuition-modifying" experiences that scientists need, but where scientists need access to devices such as a synchrotron light source, a mass spectrometer, a particle accelerator, children need the chance to use their own hands, to consort with their own small collective in order to confront artfully contrived experiential processes.

As *they* polish the block and simonize the table, the block will go progressively farther; as they accumulate a large number of such examples, science as a way of thinking will begin to crystallize. But make no mistake: the process is difficult and time consuming. To change children's ways of thinking, one must first change teachers' ways of thinking. And even for teachers who love children and love teaching, that is a major challenge: it is literally a change in the teaching culture. The role of scientists in the task should be obvious. It is critical that we get involved.

WHAT MAKES GOOD SCHOOLS?

Anyone who has spent time working with large numbers of schools knows   20
that the struggle to improve them can seem nearly impossible. What makes that particularly frustrating is that what it takes to make schools work better is well known; good schools do exist, and those of us working with TAMS know from experience what makes them and what common attributes they share:

- a belief that all children can learn, though they may learn differently;
- an environment that is caring, personal, considerate and respectful of both children and adults;
- an educational mission that is shared by the entire school community;

- a clear set of priorities that place children's learning needs at the center of every activity;
- high expectations of everyone–children, teachers, parents and principals;
- a competent, well-trained staff of teachers who are rewarded with reasonable salaries, accorded the status of professionals, and given time for collegial interactions and professional development. Those teachers must be empowered to make decisions based on sound professional judgment;
- a basic understanding that there is a collaboration between the school, the parents, the principal and the local community, including local industry, universities and laboratories.

In the past four years we have learned that, even in the most embattled schools in the inner city, there is a love of children and a passion for teaching. Given the opportunity to be better teachers, the response is overwhelmingly enthusiastic. At TAMS we live by all the buzzwords: hand-on, minds-on, activity-based, inquiry methods, cooperative learning–the constructivist approach. The teacher is taught to confess that she does not know the answers to questions the children raise. Her approach is to help them find the answers. The students work in teams, and they learn from one another.

All our teacher training is in-service, or in other words provided to full-time teachers, during school hours as well as on weekends, in the evenings and during the summer. In the past four years we have introduced seventy-two schools and some 3,200 teachers to our program–and some of them have been with us for as many as three years. On average, they have received roughly 120 hours of instruction in science, 140 hours in mathematics and more than 140 hours of additional close teaching supervision. That leaves only . . . 420 schools and 14,000 teachers to go.

Changing culture is never easy. That so much time and effort (and money) are needed should be no surprise to the funding agencies, but it is. We estimate that to sustain the efforts we have begun in Chicago will probably take an investment of between $3,000 and $4,000 a year per teacher for perhaps three to four years. That expense includes the necessary costs of bringing in all the important groups that have a stake in education. The total is equivalent to the tuition for one year at a mid-priced university. Yet one of the curious and inexplicable frustrations of our work has been the difficulty of getting the money to sustain it.

HOPEFUL SIGNS–AND OBSTACLES

Does the program work? Yes! Teachers love it. And when it is well managed, it creates an intense, joyous learning process. Such interventions also lead to a greatly energized teaching corps, in which the new teaching style spreads to other subjects and brings with it technology that can fruitfully enhance the teacher's effectiveness.

Could it work elsewhere–in New York City, for instance? Again, yes, but it is 25 impossible to overestimate the difficulties. In number of students, New York City's school system is two and a half times the size of Chicago's, and New York administers 1,017 public schools. Yet there is a shot that this kind of intervention, suitably replicated in many styles and variations in, say, twenty-five cities, could begin to restore to the nation what was once a superb system of public schools.

Successful intervention requires the support, encouragement and commitment of those in the environment of the teacher: principal, parents, school councils, community groups. It needs leadership of competent and visionary school superintendents. It needs the collaboration of state and public school administrators in adopting the new tough standards coming out of Washington. And it will need, for a long time to come, the support of everyone who has a stake in the outcome of education: scientists and educators, future employers, college authorities.

What are the chief obstacles to educational reform? I have mentioned the difficulty of obtaining funding. That goes hand-in-hand with what seems to be the near impossibility of sustaining (expensive) interventions long enough to change the culture of teaching. Finding excellent staff people to carry out interventions can become a long and vexing process. Learning to collaborate with systemic obstacles to systemic reform, the central offices of education, the state regulators, the unions and bureaucracy in general can be slow and immensely frustrating, but it must be done with persistence determination–and humor. Finally, one can only wonder at the slowness with which the education of educators has changed.

Given those obstacles and the current crisis in the public schools, I do not believe we can fix them, even if we do know how, until we can make them a priority. Unfortunately, that has not yet been done in these United States, and there is enough blame for that truly sorry state of affairs to go all around. Furthermore, I must emphasize again that I do not think our educational systems can heal themselves. Outside intervention is essential. The interventions must be evolutionary and systemic, insofar as they involve parents, the community and indeed all the education stakeholders. Above all, the interventions must be sustained, so that it becomes clear the reform is working. Only then will the funding become politically irresistible. Time and again, solid and sensible reform has been aborted too soon.

Who can intervene? It seems to me that it comes down to a partnership of universities and the private sector. Today, few university presidents give much priority to precollege education. But a sustained effort by universities could begin to show results. The payback to the universities would be a population of scientifically literate students that would raise statues to university presidents and deans.

The Responsive Reader

1. How familiar are you with "crisis rhetoric" about American education? What made the 1983 "bugle call" a fair example? (What made it "chauvinistic"?) What made the 1989 governors' convention another example?

2. How does Lederman explain and support his charge that in his special area of interest the educational system is "by and large dysfunctional"? How does he use the comparison with Japan?

3. What were the personnel, goals, and procedures of the teacher education effort that Lederman joined in Chicago? What seems particularly instructive or relevant in earlier efforts at educational reform that Lederman reviews?

4. How does Lederman justify his special emphasis on education in science? How does he support his claim that scientific research and the way children learn are closely related? Why does he emphasize the need to counteract misconceptions and to change ways of thinking?

5. What are Lederman's assumptions about good teaching and good schools? Which seem familiar; which seem provocative or new? Which seem particularly important to you, and why? Which, if any, seem questionable?

6. What for Lederman are key obstacles to educational reform? What are the "systemic obstacles to systemic reform"?

For Discussion or Writing

7. Do you tend to agree that the teaching of science and math in American schools is a disaster area?

8. Do you tend to agree with Lederman that the schools cannot reform themselves? Do you tend to agree with Lederman that outside intervention is essential? Who would be the key players?

Collaborative Projects

9. How pessimistic or how optimistic are teachers, students, and parents about the future of your local schools? You may want to help organize a poll or survey designed to probe current attitudes.

ARE NURSES BEING PHASED OUT?

Ellen Papazian

> *Whole occupational groups at times see their livelihood endangered as their jobs disappear. Weavers who made hand-woven cloth were put out of work by machines. Welders in automobile factories have been replaced by robots. Telephone operators have been replaced by recorded voices guiding the caller through a maze of options. Is this trend toward displacement of workers accelerating today? The following article focuses on changes in the health care industry as public hospitals close and for-profit HMOs increasingly look at the bottom line. Ellen Papazian is a freelance writer based in New York City.*

In 1993, *Ms.* ran a story about the state of the U.S. nursing profession. At that point, there weren't enough nurses, leaving those who were employed overworked and often underpaid. Now nurses–the backbone of an $884.2 billion health care industry, almost two million strong, 96 percent female, and still sometimes shamefully underpaid–are facing a new crisis. Confronted with ever-tighter restrictions from health maintenance organizations, hospitals are trying to increase profits by eliminating nurses, specifically highly skilled registered nurses (R.N.s). They are being replaced with less-skilled workers, including unlicensed assistive personnel (UAP), who receive as little as four to six weeks training.

No exact figures on nursing layoffs are available, but according to a recent survey of 1,835 R.N.s conducted for the American Nurses Association, 68.4 percent of respondents reported layoffs or attrition cutbacks within the last year. The effects of these cutbacks are already being felt. State nursing associations have begun to document deaths and injuries due to hospital negligence. The California Nurses Association, meanwhile, has joined a class action suit against Alta Bates Medical Center in Berkeley, California, charging that it fraudulently misled patients about efforts to slash services and that it attempted to censor nurses who tried to publicize the changes in patient care.

In this forbidding climate, R.N.s are discovering that they have to become activists. Brenda Wolpert works in the intensive care unit at Mercy Community Hospital in Port Jervis, New York. In January 1995 she participated in a 35-day hunger strike for higher wages and assurances from the hospital that nurses wouldn't be laid off or replaced with nurse's aides. Said Wolpert: "When the hospital withdrew recognition of our union, we felt we needed to do something pretty dramatic to show our resolve." Indeed, by March 1995 the nurses got a new contract that guaranteed higher wages and job security.

The nursing crisis inspired R.N. Joyce Riley from Missouri City, Texas, to start

"Truth in Healthcare," a talk show on KFCC radio in Houston, dedicated to "what's really going on within the health care industry." The show features a hotline for nurses wishing to make complaints (anonymity guaranteed) about safety issues or health concerns.

The new nursing activism reached its peak with the first annual Nurses March   5
on Washington last spring, when 35,000 nurses from around the nation converged on the capital. R.N. Laura Gasparis Vonfrolio, the march's organizer, encouraged her colleagues' activism, insisting, "We have been quiet for too long." Next year's march will be bigger, promise the organizers—but things being what they are with nursing salaries, it will have to be funded out of Vonfrolio's savings, just as this year's was.

The Responsive Reader

1. Why has there been a drastic turnaround from the days of a "nursing shortage"? According to this article, what is happening to the nursing profession?
2. Are you surprised that nurses are 96 percent female?
3. What is the answer of "nursing activists" to current developments? What do you think are their chances for success?

For Discussion or Writing

4. Do you think writers like Papazian are alarmists? Do you think their charges against management are exaggerated? Is there any way of verifying charges of deteriorating care?
5. Do you think the health care industry should be run for profit like any other business? If not, how can or should it be different?

AFFIRMATIVE ACTION
What's Fair?

Lani Guinier AND *Karen Burstein*

Affirmative action was designed to help remedy the effects of past discrimination. It was touted as opening the doors of equal opportunity for America's minorities in the schools and on the job. It promised fair chances for advancement to the women entering the workforce in rapidly growing numbers. Whether as the result of specific programs or changing attitudes, minorities and women became gradually more visible in management, in government offices, in medical schools and law schools, and in the prestige professions. At the same time, a backlash built up among white males who saw their jobs threatened or who saw themselves passed over for college admission, hiring, or promotion. Resentful males won lawsuits claiming they had been passed over in favor of less qualified applicants. Politicians backed away from quota systems enforcing progress toward equal opportunity. Dissident minority voices rejected affirmative action because it undermined their self-esteem, stigmatizing them as "affirmative action hires" dependent on the crutch of official favoritism. Is affirmative action dead? In the following interview, two politically active women vote in the affirmative on affirmative action. Guinier is a professor of law at the University of Pennsylvania and the author of The Tyranny of the Majority. *Burstein is a former family court judge in Brooklyn and a lawyer in New York City. She oversaw the state's affirmative action policy as commissioner of the New York State Department of Civil Service from 1983 to 1987.*

KAREN BURSTEIN: The thesis of your work has been that the majority—in order not to be tyrannical—must allow the minority to win some of the time so that there's a stake in continuing to play the game. Is that a fair expression of your beliefs?

LANI GUINIER: Yes.

K.B.: Now it seems to me that one of the arguments against affirmative action has been that in allowing minorities to win, members of the majority lose. If you look at it from a great distance there may not be a win/lose result, but in any individual circumstance there may be. Can affirmative action be implemented so that no one loses?

L.G.: If you look at the big picture you can see a fundamental fairness, but if you're looking at the small picture, that is, if you feel you have to pay a disproportionate price, you see unfairness. The conventional approach has excluded women as well as underrepresented members of some minority groups. For example, the New York City Police Department used to have a height requirement that effectively excluded women and many men who are minorities. Successful challenges to the rule opened the force to women as well as Asian, Latino, and short white men. The women who came onto the force are often considered more effective at defusing domestic violence incidents. So it's not just that we're going to hire a woman instead of a man. It's that we're looking to hire a range of people because we need different skills in order to have an effective department.

K.B.: While diversity allows us new ways of seeing how human beings respond to one another and new ways of solving problems, Lani, it also underlines the most terrifying nature of affirmative action: the fear that if society were to say discrimination is wrong, major changes would occur in who would have power.

L.G.: But those with power are not being asked to give it up. People who feel insecure about their ability to provide for their families are the ones most threatened.

K.B.: But my point is that the discourse does not allow us to talk about the big picture the way we did a minute ago. How, for example, can we get white men who are frightened about their jobs to say, "Wait, we need a larger pie so there's more for all of us"?

L.G.: By not polarizing the debate. For example, Lowell High School is this magnet school in San Francisco that is under a federal court order to desegregate. To maintain diversity, the school combined students' averages with their performance on a test and established a ceiling on the number of any one group attending. Asian American kids had to score higher than African American, white, or Latino students. A group of Chinese American parents charged that the order was discriminatory. A group of African Americans and the NAACP defended the order, saying that without it Lowell would not be diverse. So, in a course I teach on race and gender, I asked the class to think of a new paradigm in which Lowell could admit students and be respectful of the legitimate concerns on both sides of the debate. The students proposed that Lowell admit applicants through a lottery. There would be a floor for admissions for everyone. However, if they needed trombone players, for example, and you played the trombone, this talent could be rewarded by your name being put in the lottery twice, thus enhancing your chances.

K.B.: But part of our politics has been to set one group against another as opposed to finding points of intersection. One of the values of affirmative action is that you've got a bunch of people from all over, and you can imagine solutions, and you can't be so dishonest. So how do you overcome the fundamental dishonesty of a system that frames the issue as a conflict?

L.G.: I coauthored a study of women at the Penn Law School that found that many women who come in with the same entry-level credentials as men are not doing as well once they get here. The culture of the law school is affirming of the ways men (and I'm generalizing) have been socialized. One way of looking at this is that we need to teach women how to play the game. But women are saying that instead of demonizing your opponent, there could also be more collaborative forms of problem-solving, and it may be that the litigation model is not always effective.

K.B: Yes, my work as a family court judge has shown me that the adversary system is absolutely inappropriate in resolving family disputes. Even when you make a decision, people don't accept it. And even though people are speaking about new paradigms, there still is a world out there framed by the old ones. So, that brings us back to this issue of how we get people talking about affirmative action in terms of a more diverse society instead of where they currently are, which is, "I lost a job 'cause a black person wanted it" or "I'm a man and they need a woman for the job."

L.G.: The great tragedy of the current debate is that it takes place in a win/lose context. Both the terms and substance of the debate need to be changed so that there are no inevitable losers. Even those who feel as if they are being denied a job unfairly have to be heard. People need to tell their stories, and then recommendations need to be made to accommodate these collective stories.

K.B.: When I ran a temporary state commission on workers' compensation in the state of New York, we were able to get a consensus because I insisted that we educate ourselves before taking sides. The same process could advance the debate on affirmative action, but we need to have two things—time and someone to facilitate.

L.G.: The answer is to find people whom others trust to facilitate. Maybe we have to ask journalists, for example, not to present the most extreme sides of each issue but to reconceptualize their roles. There is a movement for public journalism in which readers have a voice.

K.B.: There *is* an impulse toward broader involvement. And while over time that impulse will make the debate over affirmative action more relevant, in the short term, affirmative action may be in jeopardy. But whatever happens in the future, do you think that since its inception, affirmative action has made substantial changes in the U.S. social order?

L.G.: There is no doubt it's increased the number of women (primarily) and minorities in the workforce. So people need to testify that affirmative action has worked. I was interviewed once by a white female reporter, and as she escorted me out, she closed a few doors and said, "You know, I am a beneficiary of affirmative action." The fact that she had to confide this as if it were a dirty secret is part of the problem. We tend to think that giving people more opportunities somehow lowers the standards. But the current standards that look at education rather than ability aren't relevant. We need standards that predict who is best able to take advantage of the opportunity. A Harvard admissions officer has said that, assuming applicants have the minimum SATs and academic accomplishments, what the college looks for is somebody who's hungry. Studies have shown that those are the people most likely to be successful in life. And the SAT tells more about your parents than it does about you–it tells whether they are middle class and had the money to send you to a good school.

K.B.: A thread needs to be drawn between the woman who confided to you in secret that she was a beneficiary of affirmative action and the nature of our gatekeeping standards. Opponents of affirmative action have seized on the notion that its beneficiaries are less competent than those who have not benefited from it. That's rooted both in this idea that there's such a thing as an objective standard of excellence and in an absolute denial of the persistence of pure prejudice in our society. Racism is like a sore that will fester if not opened to the light.

L.G.: The TV news magazine *Day One* went to three schools and talked to nine- and ten-year-olds because we are told that that's the age when kids get a sense of race. Every kid was asked to complete the statement, "Black people are best at . . ." And most answered "sports." The kids said white people are good at math or management. And most did not have friends from other races. We limit racism and sexism to intentional discrimination, when in fact the phenomenon is structural and institutional. We need to acknowledge the way these ideas have penetrated down to our children.

K.B.: I want to go back to the female reporter who couldn't say out loud, 'Look, I was offered positions I might not have gotten if people weren't sensitive to the fact that women had been excluded from the process." In this country the myth is that you pull yourself up by your bootstraps. Another myth is that our society is colorblind. Maybe our language needs to be more precise. When I'm talking about a white person, maybe I should say she's a white person.

L.G.: On some level we all have a group identity and we should be explicit about that. And, as you say, Karen, if we don't acknowledge racism, it's going to fester like a wound. Diverse workforces make for more humane and inventive problem–solving, and so the beneficiaries of affirmative action who have transformed the workplace need to tell their stories.

The Responsive Reader

1. What perspective on minority rights shapes Guinier's views of the "tyranny of majority"? What test cases of discrimination against women and minorities play a role in this interview?

2. Guinier and Burstein discuss affirmative action as more than just a political obligation or an attempt to promote fairness. What do they see as its positive assets? In what areas, for instance, do they see the increased role of women as having beneficial results?

3. For many, the political and economic realities of affirmative action are that some win while others lose. What are the thoughts of the two speakers on this subject? Do they think it possible to keep affirmative action from hurting some while benefiting others? How?

4. What does Guinier say in answer to those who accuse affirmative action of lowering standards?

5. What does Guinier see as psychological obstacles to affirmative action? What does she say about the roots of racism or sexism? What attitudes need to be changed, and how?

For Discussion or Writing

6. Where do you stand on affirmative action? What helped shape your views? Does this interview change your attitude? Why or how? Or why not?

7. In 1993, the incoming Clinton administration tapped Guinier to be assistant attorney general for civil rights but backed away from the appointment when her views were criticized as too extreme. Does she sound like a radical to you? Why or why not?

RETHINKING THE DREAM

Evan Thomas AND *Bob Cohn*

One way to look at political leaders and mainstream journalists is to expect them to mold public opinion, to point the way. Another way is to look at them as weather vanes, reflecting changes in the political winds. Politicians who once published legislation to allow cheap labor into the country to work for agribusiness now champion initiatives designed to stem the migration of workers from south of the border. Journalists who once rooted for the civil rights movement, like the authors of the following Newsweek *article, now write articles full of second thoughts about affirmative action. Are the courts also "following the election returns"? Courts once ruling that the Constitution required affirmative steps to make Americans more nearly equal are now declaring preferential treatment on the basis of race or gender unconstitutional.*

Few white men have better civil-rights credentials. The old newspapermen   1
who had gathered for an informal reunion at the Atlanta airport Holiday Inn on a recent Saturday night had been thrown in jail and chased out of dusty delta towns during the Movement Days of the 1950s and '60s. During a night of strong drink and reminiscence, the old hands from publications like The New York Times and The Washington Post quietly recalled the clarity of the clash between peaceable black demonstrators and the Bull Connors of the then segregated South. "Hell, everything was clearer then," said Claude Sitton, who covered the region for the Times from 1958 to 1964. "Going to the back of the bus, drinking out of separate water fountains, going to segregated schools–those are the kinds of things that just hit you right between the eyes." But in the morning, the aging veterans puzzled over the current state of the civil-rights struggle–the tedious court battles over formulas and standards. "When it gets down to all of the subtleties and complexities of legal tests, well, that's much harder for the public to understand," said John Popham, a dapper octogenarian who covered the first stirrings of the movement for the Times back in the late 1940s. No one came out and said it, but there was a sense that the revolution they courageously covered may be losing its indisputable moral force.

Conservative politicians have been criticizing affirmative action for years. What's different today is that the once liberal establishment has begun, grudgingly and slowly, to have its own second thoughts. The judges and unelected executive-branch officials who have largely made affirmative-action policy for the past 25 years–and the editorial writers who have supported them–are beginning to back off. They eschew the rhetoric of Republican presidential candidates who want to make affirmative action a "wedge issue." The establishment would like to find a comfortable compromise. That's difficult, as President Clinton is discovering. Promised months ago, the administration's review of government affirmative action is still a work in progress, with no end in sight. But over time, the likely effect of such second-guessing will be to largely remove the government from handing out jobs or contracts or school admissions based on race.

In a recent decision, the U.S. Supreme Court seemed to scale back the federal government's own affirmative action. By a 5-to-4 vote, the justices fashioned a legal test that will make it very difficult, if not impossible, to preserve government programs that give an edge to minorities and women. The decision in *Adarand Constructors v. Pena* was written in the usual murky legalese. But the point was articulated by the plaintiff, Randy Pech, whose Adarand construction outfit in Colorado had lost out to a Hispanic-owned company under a program that ear-marked highway contracts for minorities. The burly Pech asked why he should be discriminated against to make up for discrimination that occurred more than a century ago.

Reaction to the decision was muted. Of course, civil-rights leaders are angry; Jesse Jackson called it a "major setback." But except for The New York Times, there was little protest on op-ed pages. A White House spokesman blandly noted that the administration was "asking many of the questions the court focused on."

The decision signals that the high court is following the election returns. For   5
more than a decade, since it ruled that race could be a "factor" in university admissions in the 1978 Bakke case involving the University of California the court had basically rebuffed challenges to affirmative action. In recent years, however, the court has shown a growing reluctance to use "race-conscious remedies"–the practice of trying to overcome the effects of past discrimination by helping minorities and women. This has been true not only in affirmative-action cases involving jobs and contracts, but in school desegregation and voting rights as well. On the same day the court handed down the Adarand decision, it also cast strong doubt, in a Kansas City, Mo., case, on whether federal courts can promote integration by requiring the state to fund inner-city "magnet schools." The court is expected to curtail the drawing of racially "gerrymandered" congressional districts designed to elect minority lawmakers.

The animating notion of affirmative action has always been that it is necessary to use race to overcome the effects of racism. In some ways, the policy has worked. Affirmative action's cultural impact is unlikely to be reversed entirely–the search for minorities for jobs is now ingrained, at least informally, in many institutions. On a pocketbook level, a 1995 study by Rutgers professor Alfred Blumrosen found that 5 million minority workers and 6 million women have better jobs today than they would have had without preferences and anti-discrimination laws. Certainly, minority contractors who stand to lose from the court's Adarand decision are understandably anxious. "The reality is that 90 percent of the work that we do is in the public sector," said Nigel Parkinson, president of a Maryland construction company. The decision, he said, will "just kill us."

"BEYOND RACISM"

At the same time, affirmative action has engendered tremendous resentment among whites, few of whom have lost jobs to minorities, but many of whom think they have. The policy that was supposed to get "beyond racism" risks creating more racists. Court-ordered busing did not produce integration; whites fled the inner cities, leaving schools more segregated than ever. The Kansas City program challenged in the Supreme Court spent $1.3 billion to lure suburban whites to urban magnet schools. But after a decade, the city schools were still two-thirds black.

The rule of unintended consequences is particularly ironic in the voting-rights area. The Voting Rights Act of 1965 guaranteed minorities the right to vote–but did little to increase the number of minority representatives in Congress. The Justice Department responded by encouraging states to draw some majority-minority districts. By 1993, this led to historic gains for the black and Hispanic caucuses. But the weird, serpentine-shaped districts siphoned off liberal voters from other districts–producing conservative congressmen likely to be unsympathetic to minorities.

Impatient with the important but inevitably slow progress of the courts, GOP leaders vow to eliminate all "racial preferences" from federal hiring and contracting. More telling of the shift in the establishment center was a recent scene in the Senate Labor Committee, where Nancy Kassebaum of Kansas, a moderate, held hearings to warn that affirmative-action requirements on business can become "harmful and unfair."

DIVERSE WORLD

The private sector's response to all this? Most Fortune 500 companies say they are committed to affirmative action. Creating a diverse work force, they say, is good business in an increasingly diverse world. But most of these companies now work under federal rules that make sure they follow through. And many companies also have federal contracts that require them to hire minorities and women in rough proportion to the local population. Even if the Feds go all the way and eliminate their requirements, some sort of affirmative action, however informal, is likely to remain. But without the standards that grew out of the '60s, affirmative action's future is a bit hazier–and diversity will depend not on clear federal action but on corporations, and people, doing the right thing.

with
VERN E. SMITH *in Atlanta*

The Responsive Reader

1. Thomas and Cohn write nostalgically about the early days of the Civil Rights movement when the choice between right and wrong seemed clear-cut. What images do you recall of Southern sheriffs and their police dogs, of nonviolent protesters being brutalized, of black churches bombed, or of black leaders assassinated? Did the Civil Rights movement help shape your own political or moral outlook? Why or why not?

2. The authors seem to take it for granted that a "conservative" would be opposed to affirmative action. (Are they right?) What evidence do the authors cite that the "once liberal establishment" is having second thoughts about civil rights?

3. The authors discuss the 1995 Supreme Court ruling in favor of a white contractor who challenged federal set-aside programs. What was involved? What did the case prove?

4. *Time* and *Newsweek* often make a point of "listening to both sides." How do the authors of this article size up the pros and cons of affirmative action? On balance, which side do they seem to support?

For Discussion or Writing

5. Do you think our society is becoming "color blind"? Do you think that the day of "race-conscious" or "gender-conscious" remedies is past?

6. Do you think that the Civil Rights movement in this country is "losing its indisputable moral force"?

Collaborative Projects

7. What has been the role of the courts in the current movement to curtail affirmative action programs? Working with a group, you may want to look at pivotal recent court decisions and their implications or repercussions.

FORUM: *Gender in the Workplace*

It is true that very often a woman's relationship to a job or career is different from a man's. Part of that difference comes from a result of external conditions—the double burden of home and child care, barriers to opportunity, as well as misogynistic attitudes and behavior. But added factors in those different relations to work reside within ourselves as women, in our own attitudes and behaviors.

Sheila Ruth

In recent decades, feminist scholars and teachers in women's studies programs have probed the status of women in the traditional patriarchal, male-dominated society. Seventy years after they gained the vote, women were still, in the words of one feminist scholar, "absurdly underrepresented" in state legislatures, in the U.S. Congress, and in high-level government positions. Government and law have traditionally been the domain of male legislators, officials, law professors, judges, and police officers. In the workplace, executives, doctors, and pilots were predominantly male, while secretaries, nurses, and flight attendants were predominantly female. Salaries in professions like teaching on the elementary and secondary levels, traditionally women's occupations, have been low compared with predominantly male occupations requiring equal or less training and expertise. Today, the number of female students and advanced degree candidates in areas like business and management, science, medicine, dentistry, and law is steadily growing and is in some areas approaching parity. How far has society moved toward affording women equal opportunity and comparable pay in the workplace? In a "society where money means power" (Shirley Bernard), to what extent have women become empowered?

WORK
Mabel Dole Haden and Marley Shebala

Katie Monagle

Americans talk much about their work ethic. They define themselves and others by what they do. Benjamin Franklin was concerned to find something useful to do during his lunch hour. The workaholic who works late at the office and then takes a batch of paperwork home has become part of American folklore. What is the work ethic of women increasingly making their way in the world of work? The following two personal snapshots are from an article in Ms. magazine that gave women successful in business, in law, or in journalism a chance to talk about their relation to work and their way of balancing job and personal life. They talked about both pitfalls and rewards.

Mabel Dole Haden
Lawyer
Washington, D.C.

There were times in my life before I became a lawyer that I made 25 cents an hour. I used to sit in my bathtub and cry because I had not a dime. Now I'm pretty proud that you can look in the law books and see cases that I have won in the court of appeals. Many times during my career I found myself the only woman. You became sort of hardened to it. When I first started practicing I worked in the criminal courts, and the authorities would get me mixed up with the prostitutes. The women lawyers had a joke: "Don't forget your briefcase!" so they could tell we were the lawyers and not the defendants.

I have a private practice, and we're just working, working, working. I work about eight hours a day, seven days a week. My husband is my accountant and he comes down with me every day except on the weekend. I work Christmases, Sundays, all days. I just work. I like the excitement of meeting people and helping them to solve their problems. I sort of feel it's my duty to help them regardless of whether they have money or not.

I really don't know what I would do without the work. Even with all of the headaches and burdens I moan about, I still like the work. I think it keeps me living, and I think it keeps me well.

Marley Shebala
Newspaper Reporter
Window Rock, Arizona

I'm the only full-time reporter on our paper, so I cover all beats on the Navajo reservation—government and community stories, crime, outstanding nurses, dog vaccinations. I have to keep five stories on the burner at all times.

During the 1970s I was involved in the Indian rights movement. Through the movement, I ended up doing a lot of writing and tape-recording events and taking pictures. I was just drawn into it.

I love my job. I was away from the reservation for a long time, and now I'm learning so much being back with my people, on the land. What I really enjoy is going out to remote areas and talking with the traditional Navajos about how they're coping with the non-Indian parts of the world.

One thing that's difficult is that our paper is a program of the tribal government. It bothers me because I'm a reporter—I'm not someone's PR person. I would like to see our paper become separate from the tribe, to become a full-fledged newspaper company. In the 1980s, when I was working for the tribal radio station under different tribal leadership, I was fired because I refused to let the chairman's office edit my news stories. I feel like I have earned my title of journalist.

The Responsive Reader

1. What images or stereotypes about lawyers do you bring to the reading of Haden's personal testimony? Does she challenge or confirm any of these? Does she convince you that being a woman lawyer is different?

2. What images or stereotypes about reservations do you bring to the reading of Shebala's personal testimony? Does she in any way change your mind? According to Shebala, what is the difference between being an advocate and a journalist? How did she deal with the dilemma?

For Discussion or Writing

3. Would you choose these two women as role models for sisters or daughters? What to you is most significant about their experiences? Is there a common thread?

4. What has been your own experience in the workplace? What has been your personal observation of women in the world of work?

Collaborative Projects

5. Working with a group, you may want to assemble a set of brief personal testimonies in which women talk about their experiences in the world of work.

THE NEXT WAVE

Barbara Ehrenreich

Has feminism been a movement by and for women from the affluent middle class? What has it done for women at the lower end of the economic scale? Barbara Ehrenreich is a sharp-eyed, outspoken trend watcher who frequently writes on topics of special interest to career women or women at work. A Ph.D. in biology from Rockefeller University and a fellow of the Washington Institute of Policy Studies, she wrote the following article as a contributing editor to Ms. maga-zine. Her books include For Her Own Good: 150 Years of the Experts' Advice to Women *(1978),* The Hearts of Men: American Dreams and the Flight from Com-mitment *(1983), and* The Worst Years of Our Lives: Irreverent Notes from a Decade of Greed *(1990). The targets of her satirical wit have ranged from the brainless celebrity cult that for people around the world has made star trivia synonymous with American civilization to the smug contempt of a me-first yuppie culture for working women and welfare mothers.*

Of all the charges leveled against feminism–that it is selfish, disruptive of the family, conducive to poor grooming, or disrespectful of the laws of biology–probably nothing rankles more than the well-worn accusation that it is "just a middle-class movement." I used to have a half-dozen rebuttals ready at hand: I'd list all the famous feminists I could think of with bona fide low-income back-grounds (not to mention all the less famous ones with certifiably low-income *foregrounds*). I'd make elaborate arguments about the inadequacy of class in under-standing women's status. (Is the wife of a doctor "middle class" if a divorce can pitch her into poverty?) Finally, I'd deliver my coup de grace: so what!

But I have begun to think that it does matter. If by middle class we mean someone who is college-educated, who expects to have a "career" rather than a job, and who enjoys a standard of living defined by credit cards and touch-tone appli-ances, then the women's movement–at least, the visible, organized women's move-ment–had indeed been disproportionately middle class. This, in itself, is no cause for shame. The abolition movement was middle class by the standards of the day; so too, on the average, is the contemporary peace movement, the environmental movement, and the resurgent student movement. In the clichéd explanation, only the middle class has the time and energy to sit in at bomb test sites or fritter away whole evenings debating bylaws and agenda items. The working class is, by defini-tion, otherwise occupied.

Only a funny thing is happening in the women's movement today. The middle-class movement, which is pretty much the movement as we've known it,

1

has been showing disturbing signs of lethargy. Meanwhile, something vast and angry and inspired seems to be brewing among the women of the pink-collar ghettos and the blue-collar suburbs, the housing developments and the trailer parks. And I think it may be nothing less than the next great wave of feminism.

To begin with what could be called, loosely but by no means pejoratively, the "middle-class" movement: one of the early signs of lethargy was Betty Friedan's 1981 book, *The Second Stage*. In some complex way, Friedan is still the mother of us all, so when she announced that the battle was over and it was time to refocus on home and husband, it was clear that we had turned a significant corner. The signs were everywhere. Among rank-and-file career women, consciousness-raising groups gave way to "networks," and even these began to unravel as the upwardly mobile discovered that the people one really needed to network with were *men*. In academe, women's studies—long the most reliable reproductive organ of middle-class feminism—began, in some quarters, to take on a remote and esoteric air. Reviewing an important new anthology of highbrow feminist scholarship, Catharine Stimpson—herself a leading pioneer of women's studies—found the contributions unaccountably tired and "uneasy in spirit." . . .

All of these may be taken as signs of simple exhaustion. In the last decade, organized feminism has faced the mortal challenge of the antifeminist right, and on the whole I believe we have done remarkably well. If we have not been able to advance our agenda as much as we would have liked to, neither has the other side. Even in the area of economic rights for low-income women, we were able to stymie the administration's efforts to all but eliminate food stamps, welfare, and Medicaid. And prominent among the "we" in this case was a loose coalition of distinctly middle-class organizations, including the League of Women Voters, the American Association of University Women, and the National Federation of Business and Professional Women's Clubs. Perhaps, after so many defensive struggles, a certain weariness is to be expected; a bit of a breather, richly earned.

But there is one disturbing sign that cannot be chalked up to battle fatigue, and that is the so-called postfeminism of young, educated, career-oriented women. I don't want to contribute to the exaggeration of this phenomenon; even the most elite campuses are still generating feminist activists as well as corporate clones. But it *is* there, especially on the elite campuses: the assured conviction that, whatever indignities women may have suffered in the remote past (for example, 1970), the way is now clear for any woman of spirit to rise straight to the top of whatever fascinating, lucrative profession she chooses.

For a long time I asked myself: where did we go wrong? Surely, considering the totality of the feminist agenda, it is too early to be exhausted, or too soon to be smug. Then it occurred to me. The problem is not that we (the organized, publicly visible, largely middle-class feminist movement) failed, but that we *succeeded*, at least in one absolutely critical area: the doors to the professions are now open to women. Not all the way, and certainly not all the way to the top, but they are open. Consider the numbers. In 1970, fewer than 8 percent of the nation's physicians were female; today, 14.6 percent are female and approximately 30 percent of our medical students are women, and the gains are of the same magnitude in law and business.

This may be, all things considered, the most momentous achievement since suffrage. A young woman who was born in the same year as this magazine [1972] will not have to secure her membership in the middle class through the tenuous pact of marriage. She doesn't have to marry a doctor; she can be one. And she knows it; and so do we who are old enough to be her mother, her chemistry professor, or her guidance counselor. In this one crucial way, we have it made.

Some of us, anyway. Because the chief beneficiaries of the opening up of the professions and upper-middle management are women who were born to the middle class. This is one of the nasty little secrets of the American class system: that the people who get ahead are, by and large, the ones who start out ahead, that is, who have the advantages of good schools, an encouraging home life, and the money and leisure for higher education. A 1976 study showed, for example, that the influx of women into medical school did not change the class composition of the medical student body. Most of the women, as well as the men, were the children of the approximately 20 percent of the population in the professions. If the recent *glasnost* in the professions has been feminism's greatest victory, it is a victory whose sweetness the majority of American women will never taste.

Now let us consider that sub-yuppie female majority–the women who are *not* M.B.A.s or surgical residents or assistant professors. It is these "average women," and especially the working women among them, who I believe hold the key to a feminist renewal. According to long-standing feminist myth, the "average" working-class woman is in the "I'm no women's libber, but . . ." category: perhaps a fellow traveler but never an actual feminist. Well, consider the results of a poll conducted by The Gallup Organization, Inc., in the spring of 1986. Asked "Do you consider yourself a feminist?" a stunning 56 percent of American women answered yes. (Incidentally, only 4 percent considered themselves "antifeminists." So if you're wondering who won the gender wars of the seventies and eighties, the score is in.)

But the result that surprised even the pollsters was that working-class women (blue and pink collar) were at least as likely to call themselves feminists as were women in the "professional and business" category. If anything, feminist consciousness appears to rise as one descends the socioeconomic scale. Fifty-five percent of women with family incomes of over $40,000 a year are self-identified feminists, compared to 57 percent of women with family incomes of under $20,000 a year. This 2-percentage point difference is not statistically significant, but it is probably significant that 41 percent of the upper-income group consider themselves *not* to be feminist, compared to only 26 percent of the lower-income group.

"Non-white" women (what a colorless, negative category) were the most feminist of all, with 64 percent declaring themselves feminist. What the statistics seem to be saying for anyone who cares to listen, is that the women who are most favorably disposed to feminism today are the ones who have gained the least from the movement so far, and hence have the most to gain from the struggles that lie ahead.

And for the working-class feminist majority, most of the victories still do lie ahead. True, there have been some gains in opening up the better-paying, blue-collar occupations to women, but one is struck at once by how minute they are when measured against women's advance into the professions. While the percentage of women in professional training rose from 10 to 30 or 40 percent, the percentage of women carpenters, machinists, and mechanics has not even risen to 10 percent. As a result, the average working woman is still pretty much where she always was: waiting on tables, emptying wastebaskets, or pounding a keyboard for an hourly wage in the mid-single-digit range. When she looks out—at television or the dressed-for-success-style magazines—she sees more fortunate women bounding ahead. But when she looks around her, she sees women like herself, going nowhere.

Somewhere in this collision of rising expectations and unchanging conditions lie the seeds of the next feminist upsurge. According to Joyce Miller, president of the Coalition of Labor Union Women,

> Thirteen years ago, when CLUW was formed, working women tended to see feminism as something for the college-educated suburban set. Since then, they've been taking up feminist ideas and translating them into economic issues. Issues like sexual harassment, pay equity, and child care have brought blue-collar women closer to feminism.

The signs are all around us. Think of the TWA flight attendants picketing with neatly printed posters announcing, WE ARE BREADWINNERS! (TWA boss Carl Icahn was reported to have suggested that flight attendants, being mostly women rather than, as he saw it, breadwinners, could stand to take a larger pay cut than other TWA workers.) Think of the strike of over 1,800 clerical and technical workers at Yale two years ago. Fighting for pay equity, the strikers reached out for support from NOW and campus women's groups. "We are coming together around our common interests as women . . ." one striker wrote, in words that could be a preamble to a feminist manifesto anywhere, anytime. Or, for a slightly different kind of example, think of the pink-collar wife of a striking meat packer from Minnesota: "At first we told our husbands, 'We're right behind you,'" she told a strike-support rally in New York, "but now we say to them, 'We're right *next* to you, all the way.'"

These examples come from strike situations, union activities, and indeed, how 15 else are most working women to seek the rapid redress of economic injustice? For now, unions are the main beneficiaries of working-class women's increasing assertiveness. Most new union members, for the past few years, have been women; and in 1985 American unions' slow decline in membership (a result of deindustrialization and the loss of blue-collar manufacturing jobs) began to turn around–mostly due to the influx of 70,000 new female members. Trade unions are notoriously masculine institutions, the home of hard hats and cigar-chomping bosses, but their future depends, for the first time in history, on the feminist consciousness of a female constituency. I think of an exchange that occurred on a clerical workers' picket line not far from where I live. A male union official asked, jokingly, if any of the "girls" wanted to go for coffee. "Hey, what d'you think we're out here for?" shot back a middle-aged woman. "We're not 'girls' and we don't get coffee!"

But the future of the feminist movement, as opposed to the trade union movement, depends on the ability and willingness of low-income women to carve out, create, or join autonomous *women's* organizations. There has already been an impressive start. Since 1980, about a half-dozen brand-new regional and state-wide organizations representing low-income women's economic interests have emerged–notably the California Women's Economic Agenda Project, Women for Economic Justice in Massachusetts, and Women's Agenda in Pennsylvania. These organizations tend to be traditional in their tactics–lobbying, public education, organizing–but distinctly nontraditional in their composition. The first national conference of the new, low-income women's organizations convened in California last spring, bringing together workplace organizers, welfare rights activists, and all-purpose community heroines from all ethnic groups and corners of the country. I was there, too, and I came away feeling I had seen the feminist future, and that it is far more richly diverse, and perhaps even more militant and deeply aggrieved, than anything in the feminist past.

But the big question may be whether the emergent working-class feminist insurgency will be able to find a home in the infrastructure of feminist institutions and organizations that have been created, to a large extent, by middle-class activists. For though feminist movements may be one of class or another at one time or another, the feminist *vision* belongs to all women–from the cleaning "lady" to the lady of leisure, from the lowest paid keyboard operator to the woman law partner. If the vision and the movement are to come together, for all women, organized feminism may have some soul searching to do. Do our issues too narrowly reflect our own economic status? Do our ways of talking and working together covertly exclude women who are poorer, who have had less formal education, or who may simply be unfamiliar with the decorum of meetings and "feminist process"? How open are *we* to new ideas, how ready to embrace new sisters without the self-indulgence of guilt or the insult of condescension?

I say "we" with a trace of embarrassment, knowing that already many of you will read it as "they." But if we are clear about differences now–and prepared to be open and sisterly–perhaps there will be no "us" and "them" in the next great wave of feminism.

The Responsive Reader

1. What is Ehrenreich's definition of "middle class"? Do you agree with it? How does she handle the issue of class and the women's movement?

2. What is Ehrenreich's take on the familiar charge that the women's movement has lost or is losing momentum? What symptoms or evidence does she cite? (What positive achievements of the movement does she stress?)

3. What does Ehrenreich mean by her paradoxical statement that the apparent failure of the movement was in large part caused by its successes?

4. Why does Ehrenreich consider working-class women "the key to a feminist renewal"? What evidence does she see of movement in that direction? What special needs does she see? What course does she chart for the future?

For Discussion or Writing

5. What evidence have you seen of social and economic strides made by middle-class women? Do you agree with Ehrenreich's estimate of women's advances in the professions?

6. Do you agree that working-class women will be or should be the next wave of the women's movement? Why or why not?

Collaborative Projects

7. How accurate have Ehrenreich's predictions proved to be? Can you update some of Ehrenreich's statistics and poll results? Working with a group, try to compile current data that could be compared with hers.

ARE WOMEN DOCTORS DIFFERENT?

Perri Klass

> *Does a woman who wants to be successful in the professions have to act like "a man in disguise"? Or can professional women be themselves, proving as good as men or better in their own way? Perri Klass graduated from Harvard Medical School in 1986 and became a pediatrician in Boston. She wrote about going to medical school and about the changing medical profession for the New York Times, she later published her observations in a book, A Not Entirely Benign Procedure. The following selection is from her book Baby Doctor: A Pediatrician's Training (1992). Klass had a child in the second year of medical school, crediting her school and changing times with her not being pressured to drop out. At one time, when her son, who knew mostly female doctors, was nervous about seeing a male doctor for his checkup, she told him: "Boys can be doctors, too, if they want to. If they go to school and learn how, boys can be very good doctors, really." Klass hopes that in the future doctors, both men and women, will have more of a chance to follow their own recommendations to patients—"reduce stress, eat a healthy diet, keep regular hours, spend time with your family."*

I told a friend—a fellow resident—that I was writing about women doctors.   1
"What are you going to say?" she wanted to know. "Are you going to say they're better? Are you going to come right out and say it?" Now, if I read an article saying that men make better doctors than women for certain reasons, I would probably be offended, even hurt. The best I might hope for would be to laugh it off as so much antediluvian their-egos-are-threatened prejudice. Now, I have known superb, brilliant, sensitive male doctors, residents my own age, teachers and attending physicians. Lots of them. The doctor who delivered my son, the pediatrician who takes care of him are men—and yet, I feel I am protesting too much, that these statements have a some-of-my-best-friends air about them. Okay, then, some of my best friends are male doctors.

When I interviewed women doctors, I came always to the point where I asked, are women doctors different? And with only a couple of exceptions, I got versions of the same response from the doctors I interviewed, young or old, avowedly feminist or not. First you get that disclaimer, the one I just offered; I've known some wonderful male doctors, I've known some awful female doctors, generalizations are impossible. And then, hesitantly, even apologetically, or else frankly and with a smile, comes the generalization. Yes, women are different as doctors: they're better.

Kansas City announces proudly in the courtesy magazine found in fancy hotel rooms: "When Procter & Gamble wants to know if people like its toothpaste, it turns to Kansas City. Market researchers call Kansas City a 'typically American' market. The label fits: Kansas Citians thrive on family, hard work, and tradition." In Kansas City, I interviewed a wide range of female doctors–residents, women just out of residency starting up private practices, academic physicians, specialists, older women, and recent graduates. I was surprised by how tight the network of women physicians was. I was immediately referred from doctor to doctor; in specialties where there were fewer women, their names were mentioned again and again by their colleagues. I was able to interview female physicians who stood on both sides of two classic relationships: a mentor and her student protégée, a doctor and her patient–who was also a doctor.

Linda Dorzab started medical school at the University of Missouri, Kansas City, when she was thirty-three years old. She had spent eleven years as a teacher, working with emotionally disturbed children. In June 1987, she finished her internal medicine residency, and is now beginning a private practice as an internist, affiliated with Menorah Medical Center. For the first month or so there were few patients, maybe only one a day, but by February it was up as high as nine a day, mostly new patients coming for their first appointments with her. Dr. Dorzab is proud to make a visitor welcome in her newly arranged office; an ebullient, friendly, informal woman, completely delighted to be starting up a new solo private practice. Ever since she started medical school, she says, she has dreamed of an office where she could make her patients comfortable, where there would be an atmosphere that would make her look forward to coming to work in the morning. Her office is a welcoming, plant-filled place, with gleaming mahogany furniture, including both a large desk and a small table designed for less threatening, more comfortable doctor-patient conversations. I, in the middle of my residency, find myself asking how she figured out the details of starting a practice–what supplies to order, how to find patients. Dr. Dorzab laughs, remembering how she sat down and made a list–"Cotton pads, tongue depressors–I ordered too many syringes and needles. And my proudest possession is my sigmoidoscope" (a device inserted up through the patient's rectum to give the doctor a good look at the lining of the colon). Given her background in working with disturbed children, Dr. Dorzab had originally considered going into psychiatry, "but they gave me a stethoscope and it was all so interesting. You can't get more interesting than medicine." She was older than most of the other students, and had a comparatively weak science background, but the art of medicine, she thinks, came more easily to her than to some of the younger students. Still, she had trouble performing on rounds, the high-pressure on-the-spot situations which can often be the traditional hazing occasions for medical students. "I still have the same personality as when I was a teacher, I tend to show my vulnerability–which is okay with my patients. But with colleagues the smile dims, I can turn on a more businesslike manner."

I asked her about role models, mentors, teachers from medical school who meant a lot to her. She names two women, saying of both of them that "they maintained femininity and class, and always looked confident." One of those women was Dr. Marjorie Sirridge, who is a dean at Dr. Dorzab's alma mater, UMKC. Marjorie Sirridge graduated from medical school in 1944. There were very few women in her class, but she never felt what she considers overt discrimination. To be sure, her academic advisers told her she'd never get to medical school–but that only made her more determined to go. "I was first in my class from grade one through high school–that gives confidence." Sure enough, she graduated from medical school first in that class too. But during residency she got pregnant and was informed that "pregnant residents were not acceptable." She dropped out of medicine for several years, then found her way back in by working for no pay and no training credit, went into private practice as a hematologist, pursued research on her own, and eventually found her way to academic medicine. Dr. Sirridge's office is decorated with pictures of her children and a poster of Marie Curie. Her white hair is bound up in a knot. She is extremely cordial, but she speaks with the authority of someone who is accustomed to giving out her opinions publicly. It is clear that she feels protective about the medical students she watches over, and that she is proud of Dr. Dorzab, who is striking out on her own, off into solo practice.

Dr. Sirridge worries that female medical students do not seem to take leadership roles as readily as their male colleagues. On the other hand, she thinks women do much better when it comes to human relationships. "For the women, relationships with patients are very important, a very positive thing. Many men also have this quality, but men in positions of power in medical education and government by and large do not."

The craving for female role models, female mentors, is very strong in medicine. You learn science in medical school–biochemistry, physiology, pathology; you learn these subjects in traditional classroom settings. Then you serve a kind of apprenticeship in the hospital for the second two years of medical school, consolidating the science you learned in the lecture hall, learning hospital logic and medical routine, and also learning how to be a doctor. How will you explain to a patient that he has to undergo a painful diagnostic procedure, how will you tell parents their child is dying, how will you help someone overcome bad habits that are crippling his health, how will you take command when someone is critically ill? Some medical schools are trying, more and more, to teach these skills, or at least to get students thinking and talking about them, instead of just piecing their styles together as they go along. But basically, since there is no single consensus on the best manner of doctoring, you pick up your style by trying to emulate the doctors you admire. And if you're female, it can be very instructive (and very inspiring) to watch women doctors, to learn your style from them. Many of the techniques used traditionally by male doctors tend not to work for women; and many female doctors have found themselves evolving new ways of interacting with patients, with nurses, with fellow doctors. So it isn't just vague inspiration that we're talking about here, it's who you're thinking of as you get ready to walk into that room and tell those parents about their baby dying. Who do you know who could do that as well as it could be done, offer comfort to the parents, inspire trust that their baby's last moments will be made as comfortable and easy as possible–how do you acknowledge their grief, the failure of medicine to help, even take part in their grief, and yet retain the authority you need as the doctor? And how much authority *do* you need as the doctor, anyway? Medicine is full of these situations, and you model yourself on the people who seem to handle them best.

Nevada Mitchell, MD, practices internal medicine. Her subspecialty is geriatrics. She was born in Kansas City, went to college at Vassar, then came back to KC, got married, started teaching–she had thought about medical school, but didn't feel she had what it would take to go. But reading in the Vassar alumnae magazine about classmates who had gone to medical school, she decided she wanted to try for it, and five years later she was in medical school. Dr. Mitchell has no doubt at all about the difference between male and female doctors. "There's a world of difference. The women I come into contact with are less aggressive, more likely to have one-on-one-type relationships with patients than men, less likely to go for high volume of patients–but also less likely to be out here in private practice." Dr. Mitchell returned several times to the issue of being "out here," explaining that many women take jobs with HMOs, which offer regular salaries and limited working hours. "You need a certain aggressiveness to choose private practice," she said, with some satisfaction.

Dr. Mitchell feels that older patients are often more receptive to women doctors, since they are looking for more than medical therapy. Her original decision to go into geriatrics was related to watching her younger colleagues in medical school trying to deal with the many elderly patients, and feeling those patients were often neglected or taken for granted. Her medical practice now includes many older patients, but she also does general internal medicine. With a smile, she ticked off the various groups on her fingers: older people are fine, younger and middle-aged women usually have no problem with a female doctor, younger men are initially hesitant, feel self-conscious about the complete physical examination.

Dr. Mitchell cannot think of a female doctor she wanted to be like. "I didn't   10 have that many examples. I developed my own style and image." She did, however, tell me that I ought to talk to the doctor who had operated on her when she needed some gynecological surgery. She felt that when she had discussed the medical issues with a male doctor, he had placed less of a priority on maintaining the option of future pregnancy. Dr. Mitchell, who is thirty-nine and has a sixteen-year-old daughter, wanted to keep her options open, and felt that a female doctor, Marilyn Richardson, had been more willing to take this seriously.

Ironically, Dr. Richardson herself thinks that's nonsense. An obstetrician-gynecologist specializing in reproductive endocrinology, she was a pianist for years before she went to medical school. She is highly professional, authoritative, and decided in her opinions. Patients who come looking for a female gynecologist, she says, are "erroneous–it's a patient's misconception that has evolved with consumer awareness, an erroneous belief that women doctors are more compassionate, more understanding. Well, I don't have menstrual cramps, I didn't have severe pain in labor. Women who come asking for a female doctor are looking for a buddy, and they're not going to find that in me."

I repeat to her what Dr. Mitchell said, and she laughs and says with affection, "Nevada Mitchell played the violin in my first piano recital." And then continues to deny that being female has anything to do with her mode of doctoring. "It was a male mentor who taught me sensitivity toward the preservation of fertility." Her style, she says, is a composite of this mentor and of her father, also in OB-GYN– and of techniques of doctoring she has developed for herself.

I mention to Dr. Richardson that one of the places I always felt a very sharp difference between male and female doctors was in the operating room. I ask whether she believes this is also erroneous. No, she agrees, the way that women run an OR is different. "Women manage more efficiently if they can strike a balance of authoritativeness and humaneness. Men are often arbitrary, demanding, and disrespectful, and the level of efficiency suffers. Women don't usually command quite as fiercely, will *ask* for an instrument . . . you get camaraderie with the other staff members."

Dr. Susan Love agrees. One of the first two female surgical residents at a major Boston teaching hospital, Dr. Love finished her training in 1980. She went into private practice in general surgery, though she initially had trouble getting a position on the staff of the hospital where she had just been chief surgical resident. In her practice, she found she was seeing many patients with breast disease, who preferred to go to a woman doctor, and she eventually decided to specialize in this field. She now has a partner, another woman surgeon, and they have as many patients as they can handle. Dr. Love feels strongly that she had to suppress many of her basic values in order to get through her surgical residency: "Most women have problems–unless they can block out their previous socialization. Surgeons don't really like having women, don't make it comfortable for them. Things that women like, talking to patients, aren't important, it's how many operations you've done, how many hours you've been up, how many notches on your belt. If you get through your five or six years of training, you can regain your values, but it's a real if. Most men never get them back."

Dr. Love runs an operating room, she says, by "treating the nurses like intelligent people, talking to them, teaching them. I'm not the big ruler." Are men always so different? "Surgery is a lot of ritual and a little science. The boys need high mass, incense, and altar boys, they need more boosting up. The women are much lower church." A concrete example of something she does differently, something no one

15

taught her: before the patient is put to sleep, she makes it a practice to hold the patient's hand. "I'm usually the only person in the room they really know, and it's the scariest time. The boys scrub, come in when the patient's asleep. I got razzed for it, but they're used to it now."

Unlike Dr. Richardson, Dr. Love does think that women doctors behave differently with their patients. "I spend more time in empathy, talking, explaining, teaching, and it's a much more equal power relationship." And then there's not taking people for granted–she tells the story of a recent patient, an eighty-four-year-old woman with breast cancer who was asked by a male surgeon, "Are you vain?" Embarrassed, the woman said she wasn't. The surgeon advised her, in that case, to have a mastectomy, rather than a more limited procedure–"But then her niece pointed out, but you bought a new bra to come to the doctor, but you combed your hair over your hearing aid." The doctor had simply assumed that an elderly woman would have no particular desire to keep her breast, no vanity left to speak of. Dr. Love's anecdotes are often sharp–she describes a male surgeon who explained that a particular implant used in breast reconstruction felt just like a normal breast; he meant, of course, that to someone touching the breast, the texture was close to natural, not that the woman actually had normal feeling in the implant. . . .

Then there is the question of how women get along with their coworkers–with other doctors and with nurses. The assumption has traditionally been that nurses resent female doctors, respond to them with a why-should-I-take-orders-from-*her* attitude, and then there are prurient little remarks about how women doctors resent nurses because of all the romantic attention the nurses supposedly receive from the male doctors.

Women doctors, of course, are often mistaken for nurses; many patients assume that a woman with a stethoscope is by definition a nurse. Some doctors mind this, others take it in stride. "You have to have a sense of humor," said Dr. Lois J. McKinley, an internist in Kansas City. "I took care of one patient for weeks, and when he was getting ready to leave, he was still saying, 'Oh, nurse, would you prop up my pillows.' Nursing people are good people; being mistaken for a nurse is not the worst thing that could happen." Dr. Mitchell agrees: "If I walk into a room and someone asks me for a bedpan, I just go ahead and put 'em on it!" She is laughing. "But when they call my office and assume I'm the nurse and ask, Dr. Mitchell, when will he be in, I tell them, '*He* will never be in!'"

It is generally agreed, among women doctors, that we have to be more polite and more careful with nurses than our male colleagues; a fairer way of putting this would probably be to say that nurses have had to take a lot of rudeness and bad behavior from doctors over the years, and that while they make some of the traditional female allowances for traditional male patterns, they are unwilling to accept these same behaviors from women. Or, to quote Dr. Richardson again, "When you make a big mess in the operating room, there's something different in your mind when you walk out and leave it for another woman to clean up." I have found in my own training that nurses generally expect me to clean up after myself (i.e., to gather up all the little alcohol pads and pieces of gauze left on the bed after I draw blood from a baby), to do a fair amount of my own secretarial work, and not to take too high-and-mighty a tone. What would be taken as normal behavior in a male (especially a male surgeon; they have the most traditional doctor-nurse power structure) is considered aggressive and obnoxious in a female. Dr. Lore Nelson, who will be chief resident in pediatrics at the University of Kansas next year, complained, half seriously, "A male surgeon can walk in to do some procedure and everything will be all ready, but if I go to draw blood, nothing's set up for me and I have to go ask a nurse, 'Can you please help me. . . .'" Dr. Sirridge agrees: "The women aren't successful at doing the things men do without criticism–it's easier if they ask politely."

This does not seem to be a bad thing–the traditional doctor-nurse relationship, like the traditional male-female relationship that it parodies (the man as authority figure, making decisions, issuing edicts, bearing ultimate responsibility on his broad shoulders; the woman as caretaker, tending to immediate needs and cleaning up messes, but without any real power) left a lot to be desired. Surely a good doctor is part caretaker; surely a good nurse's observations should be part of any decisions being made. I suspect that the more polite, more politic behavior that is demanded of female doctors may be closer to good manners and good medicine than the supposed norm–the license that we sometimes envy our male colleagues.   20

The Responsive Reader

1. What light does Klass's description of Dr. Dorzab and her mentor shed on questions like the following? Would you expect a woman doctor to create a more patient-friendly working environment and doctor-patient relationship? Would you expect "femininity" to be an asset or a liability? Would you expect women in medicine to have experienced discrimination? What would be your assumptions about a woman's ability to assert authority or assume leadership roles?

2. How does Klass describe the human dimension of doctoring–beyond a doctor's command of medical science or skill as a practitioner? Do women have the edge in treating patients and their families as feeling, caring human beings? How does Klass's discussion of Mitchell and Richardson explore conflicting views on this subject?

3. Increasingly as Klass goes on, she highlights differences in male and female perspectives, in attitudes toward medicine as a career. She underscores differences in male and female values. Do you recognize the key issues? What are key points?

4. How do women in authority get on with female coworkers? Why or how does this question become an issue? What is the role of traditional patterns of the doctor–nurse relationship? Do nurses set different standards for women doctors?

For Discussion or Writing

5. Would you prefer or insist on a male or female doctor, male or female lawyer, male or female professor, male or female judge? What difference does it make? Concentrating on one major area, explain and defend your choice.

6. Will women increasingly move up into positions of leadership or authority? Or are they bound to bump into the "glass ceiling"?

Collaborative Projects

7. Working with a group, what current statistics can you compile concerning the representation of women in positions of leadership or authority?

7

Interdisciplinary Perspectives

INTERDISCIPLINARY APPROACHES IN PERSPECTIVE

When we really need to know, we turn to the expert. We consult the expert on gene splicing, the expert on DNA as a means of positively identifying criminal suspects, the expert on new medications retarding the course of AIDS. However, the experts are not responsible for the larger picture. Many social and economic challenges require coordinated input from different disciplines. For example, how to slow down the spread of AIDS? We need to listen to medical experts on ways the virus is transmitted and on effective precautions. We may decide to listen to sociologists and social workers who can tell us what social groups are especially vulnerable and why. We should listen to educators and psychologists who can tell us what kind of appeals might be effective with young people and which are likely to fall on deaf ears. We may want to listen to people who have had experience with large successful public relations or public education campaigns. We are likely to learn much from a book like Randy Shilts' *And the Band Played On*, written by a journalist who with painstaking honesty chronicled the delays and non sequiturs in early efforts to combat AIDS.

THE AGE OF SPECIALIZATION

We live in the age of the specialist—who knows more about less. In the age of the information explosion, mastering the research literature in one limited field may prove a formidable task. Reading up on pancreatic cancer or schizophrenia, for example, may prove a daunting undertaking. A general practitioner once attended to most of a patient's medical needs. Today we have specialists for heart, lung, spine, skin, eye, ear, kidney, or the digestive tract. We have anesthesiologists, x-ray technicians, psychiatric technicians, lab technicians, and dieticians.

At the same time, however, we hear many voices warning us that everybody cannot just be a specialist. For instance, the survival or well-being of a physician's patients depends in part on psychological factors, including the feeling of being recognized as a human being. Doctors and nurses cannot just study abortion as a medical procedure. They may discover that they need to be schooled in the ethics and politics of abortion, and perhaps in the art of self-defense. Physicians and hospital administrators find they need to give thought to the ethical implications of gene splicing, surrogate motherhood, or denial of medical aid to the undocumented and the uninsured. They need to give thought to the economics of health care, studying the economic factors that are pushing doctors and patients toward systems of managed, rationed care.

Similarly, educators find that they do not operate in an aseptic environment, where three units of instruction yield a predictable increase in reading ability or mathematical skill. They become involved in educational psychology and the sociology of education. Do conventional tests automatically discriminate against minority children without the access to travel, reading, or quality education enjoyed by the children of middle-class whites? Why do some observers claim that girls attending all-girl schools or African Americans attending traditional black colleges score higher in self-esteem, academic achievement, and professional success? Why do many teachers make books like Paulo Freire's *Pedagogy of the Oppressed* or Mike Rose's *Lives on the Boundary* their educators' bible? What does it take to keep drugs and murder weapons out of our schools?

INTERDISCIPLINARY COOPERATION

Many problems facing our society—structural unemployment, drugs, teenage pregnancy, violence in the streets, dysfunctional families—are not likely to be solved by specialists. Teams of people attuned to interdisciplinary thinking will have to knock their heads together. For instance, communities often seem helpless when faced with rising crime rates. Ideally, efforts to reduce crime might draw on insights from a range of specializations:

- Sociologists study social factors that contribute to crime: poverty, the breakdown of traditional institutions, the culture of youth gangs, the drug culture, organized crime.
- Urbanologists—students of city living—describe the effects of replacing neighborhoods that were an organic web of homes, stores, churches, and bars with sterile highrise projects that prove a breeding ground for crime.
- Psychologists study the role of such factors as child abuse or racial antagonism in programming people for violence.
- Penologists study the treatment of criminals when they are in prison,

the percentage of repeat offenders, and the chances of reintegrating ex-convicts into society.

- Education specialists report on the effect such initiatives as mandatory school uniforms (and the banning of gang colors) have had on reducing gang allegiance and violence in the schools.

ARCHITECTURE: A CROSS-DISCIPLINARY PERSPECTIVE

Architecture is a prime example of a field that cannot be understood from a narrow specialist's point of view. For the builder, a building is a challenge in structural engineering. However, the history of architecture cannot be understood from a limited utilitarian perspective. Students of architecture cannot just focus on what is practical and useful–on how buildings provide shelter or storage areas for grain.

The pyramids of the Maya in pre-Columbian Mexico supported temples; the pyramids of the Egyptians were magnificent tombs. The Gothic cathedrals of the European Middle Ages rose high over the huddled houses of the towns *ad majorem Dei gloriam*–to the greater glory of God. Our courthouses and government buildings, with their columns and low-angle gabled façades, hark back to the style of Greek temples 2500 years ago. They follow a traditional style of monumental public architecture that says: "Here we are serious about the law."

Historians of architecture study engineering skills: The Romans put up multistory structures using bricks and mortar. Renaissance architects built domes for St. Peter's in Rome or the cathedral in Florence that were engineering marvels for their time. But historians of architecture at the same time study aesthetics–changing standards of what is beautiful, magnificent, or inspirational. They study changes in style, in form. These in turn are often intertwined with the goals and aspirations of the community or institution–with political and religious history.

The dominant style of much twentieth-century architecture harks back to the architects of the Bauhaus school–Gropius, Van der Miese, and others–who preached the gospel of "form follows function." No longer would architects stick on decorative elements–curlicues, cornices, and other leftovers from earlier stylistic periods–to give aesthetic appeal to an ugly building. Instead the stark outlines of the structure would show, determined by the functions the building served. Expanses of glass and steel, the materials of the modern industrial age, would replace the pastry cook adornments of earlier times.

Arguments for or against the Bauhaus style inevitably turn interdisciplinary, involving engineering, aesthetics, politics, and the human ecology of the workplace. Its early advocates aimed at an aesthetic that did justice to the factory era or machine age and the dignity of labor. The Nazis (who closed down the original Bauhaus center in Germany) countered with a pseudo-classical style, adorned by statues with fitness-magazine bodies and determined Schwarzenegger chins. Much later, a new generation of architects, for whom the glass and steel towers of Manhattan and other cities had come to seem impersonal and dehumanizing, started to bring back the curlicues and playful curving lines that the Bauhaus people had banished to architectural limbo.

INTERDISCIPLINARY PROGRAMS

Is your own college experimenting with programs that cut across traditional boundaries? Departments of Ethnic Studies, Women's Studies, or Urban Studies may bring together historians, psychologists, sociologists, linguists, and representatives of other fields. As Sheila Ruth says in her introduction to women's studies, *Issues in Feminism*, "almost all women's studies programs, curricula, and analyses are interdisciplinary." In the area of women's studies, "some sophistication" is required in areas including biology, history, literature, economics, and law among others:

- Art historians and literary critics may be studying the image of women in traditional art and literature. Why did poets through the ages put woman on the proverbial pedestal, praising her beauty, while in real life women had few legal or political rights? Besides Emily Dickinson, America's greatest poet, what other creative American women were active in the nineteenth century, and what were the obstacles in their path?

- Feminist theologians may be studying the role of women in the early Christian church, before the exclusion of women from the priesthood became accepted dogma.

- A feminist philosopher may be questioning the traditional definition of scholarly objectivity. Does it tend to discourage personally committed and emotionally engaged challenges to the established system, the status quo?

CROSS-DISCIPLINARY THINKING

Some of the most influential ideas are not limited to a particular field. They are in the air; they are part of a groundswell of opinion. Students of the history of ideas study the role of ideas or attitudes that seem to be part of the spirit of the times and that cut across professions or fields of study.

For instance, the nineteenth-century belief in progress egged on the builders of railroads, city planners, medical researchers, and founders of colleges. It made people cheer on people who put creeks underground, turned fields into parking lots, and straightened the meandering course of rivers.

Today, an ecological perspective and environmental concerns color the thinking and decisions of people in many fields. Legislatures require recycling of bottles and cans. Books and magazines are printed on recycled paper. Prodded by environmentalists, automobile companies have downsized cars and stepped up gasoline mileage. Lumber companies talk about "harvesting" trees to make them sound like a renewable resource. Communities balk at large-scale developments that would increase traffic congestion and strain the water supply. Chemists work on less toxic ways of controlling insect pests. Architects push solar heating.

The course of our common future depends on the ability of specialists from different disciplines to communicate with one another. It depends on the ability of the general public to understand specialists. It depends on the ability of voters and public officials to grasp ideas influential in our contemporary world. Issues like the following concern us all, regardless of occupational or academic specialty:

- Are there true "miracle drugs"? Are public agencies and the medical establishment too rash or too slow in implementing experimental medications and procedures?
- Are we "poisoning the planet"? Are we losing the war against polluters, or has a commitment to the environment become part of our political culture?
- How "multicultural" is our society going to be? Is multiculturalism a divisive slogan, or is a rich ethnically and culturally diverse society as American as pizza?
- Is the talk about "family values" just talk? Is it more than a mantra invoked by political candidates without concrete programs for dealing with the problems of society?
- Are we doomed to failure in our search for "role models" for the next generation? Can we think of people other than athletes, generals, and entertainers for young people to emulate?

QUESTIONS FOR DISCUSSION

Have you observed team teaching or been a student in classes team-taught by instructors from different disciplines? (Were you aware of differences in perspective? How did they affect what happened in the class?) Do you watch widely publicized trials on TV? Could you chart the role of players representing different disciplines—law, medicine, forensics, psychology or psychiatry, others? What experts get in the act when public bodies consider major issues concerning public transport, a new ballpark, antigrowth ordinances, clean air, shutdown of a public hospital, or similar matters of public concern? (Do you think public officials or the voters listen to the experts?) In your own intellectual history, have you been in situations where major differing perspectives intersect or clash–for instance, science and religion, science and the law, traditional history or economics and feminist perspectives?

EDUCATING THE GUARDIANS

Plato

▬▬▬▬▬▬▬▬

What is the relation between politics and religion? Plato, who taught in the fourth century B.C., was a leading Athenian philosopher in a culture before the age of specialization. The understanding of the physical universe, the theory of social organization, and questions about the meaning of life had not yet been parceled out to different academic disciplines. Plato's teachings have come down to us in his Socratic dialogues, in which his teacher Socrates explores philosophical issues with his disciples. The best-known passage from these dialogues is the allegory of the cave: We are like people who do not know reality directly but only from shadows projected onto the walls of a cave. We never emerge into the broad sunlight of true knowledge. In Plato's Republic, Socrates envisions an ideal society, or Utopia, ruled not by those with money or clout but by the wisest members of the community—the philosopher-kings. In the following selection, Plato focuses on the early education of the "guardians," the military and political élite who will defend the state against external enemies and maintain internal order. Upon completion of the training described here, a small number of the guardians will be chosen for further training as rulers.

Don't you think then, said I, that, for the purpose of keeping guard, a   1
young man should have much the same temperament and qualities as a well-bred watch-dog? I mean, for instance, that both must have quick senses to detect an enemy, swiftness in pursuing him, and strength, if they have to fight when they have caught him.

Yes, they will need all those qualities.

And also courage, if they are to fight well.

Of course.

And courage, in dog or horse or any other creature, implies a spirited dis-   5
position. You must have noticed that a high spirit is unconquerable. Every soul possessed of it is fearless and indomitable in the face of any danger.

Yes, I have noticed that.

So now we know what physical qualities our Guardian must have, and also that he must be of a spirited temper.

Yes.

Then, Glaucon, how are men of that natural disposition to be kept from behaving pugnaciously to one another and to the rest of their countrymen?

Reprinted from *The Republic of Plato*, translated by Francis Macdonald Cornford (1941). Oxford University Press. Reprinted by permission of the publisher.

It is not at all easy to see.   10

And yet they must be gentle to their own people and dangerous only to enemies; otherwise they will destroy themselves without waiting till others destroy them.

True.

What are we to do, then? If gentleness and a high temper are contraries, where shall we find a character to combine them? Both are necessary to make a good Guardian, but it seems they are incompatible. So we shall never have a good Guardian.

It looks like it.

Here I was perplexed, but on thinking over what we had been saying, I   15
remarked that we deserved to be puzzled, because we had not followed up the comparison we had just drawn.

What do you mean? he asked.

We never noticed that, after all, there are natures in which these contraries are combined. They are to be found in animals, and not least in the kind we compared to our Guardian. Well-bred dogs, as you know, are by instinct perfectly gentle to people whom they know and are accustomed to, and fierce to strangers. So the combination of qualities we require for our Guardian is, after all, possible and not against nature.

Evidently.

Do you further agree that, besides this spirited temper, he must have a philosophical element in his nature?

I don't see what you mean.   20

This is another trait you will see in the dog. It is really remarkable how the creature gets angry at the mere sight of a stranger and welcomes anyone he knows, though he may never have been treated unkindly by the one or kindly by the other. Did that never strike you as curious?

I had not thought of it before; but that certainly is how a dog behaves.

Well, but that shows a fine instinct, which is philosophic in the true sense.

How so?

Because the only mark by which he distinguishes a friendly and an un-   25
friendly face is that he knows the one and does not know the other; and if a creature makes that the test of what it finds congenial or otherwise, how can you deny that it has a passion for knowledge and understanding?

Of course, I cannot.

And that passion is the same thing as philosophy—the love of wisdom.

Yes.

Shall we boldly say, then, that the same is true of human beings? If a man is to be gentle towards his own people whom he knows, he must have an instinctive love of wisdom and understanding.

Agreed.   30

So the nature required to make a really noble Guardian of our commonwealth will be swift and strong, spirited, and philosophic.

Quite so.

Given those natural qualities, then, how are these Guardians to be brought up and educated? First, will the answer to that question help the purpose of our whole inquiry, which is to make out how justice and injustice grow up in a state? We want to be thorough, but not to draw out this discussion to a needless length.

Glaucon's brother answered: I certainly think it will help.

If so, I said, we must not think of dropping it, though it may be rather a   35
long business.

I agree.

Come on then. We will take our time and educate our imaginary citizens.

Yes, let us do so.

What is this education to be, then? Perhaps we shall hardly invent a system better than the one which long experience has worked out, with its two branches for the cultivation of the mind and of the body. And I suppose we shall begin with the mind, before we start physical training.

Naturally.   40

Under that head will come stories; and of these there are two kinds. some are true, others fictitious. Both must come in, but we shall begin our education with the fictitious kind.

I don't understand, he said.

Don't you understand, I replied, that we begin by telling children stories, which, taken as a whole, are fiction, though they contain some truth? Such story-telling begins at an earlier age than physical training; that is why I said we should start with the mind.

You are right.

And the beginning, as you know, is always the most important part, espe-   45
cially in dealing with anything young and tender. That is the time when the character is being molded and easily takes any impress one may wish to stamp on it.

Quite true.

Then shall we simply allow our children to listen to any stories that anyone happens to make up, and so receive into their minds ideas often the very opposite of those we shall think they ought to have when they are grown up?

No, certainly not.

It seems, then, our first business will be to supervise the making of fables and legends, rejecting all which are unsatisfactory; and we shall induce nurses and mothers to tell their children only those which we have approved, and to think more of molding their souls with these stories than they now do of rubbing their limbs to make them strong and shapely. Most of the stories now in use must be discarded.

What kind do you mean?   50

If we take the great ones, we shall see in them the pattern of all the rest, which are bound to be of the same stamp and to have the same effect.

No doubt; but which do you mean by the great ones?

The stories in Hesiod and Homer and the poets in general, who have at all times composed fictitious tales and told them to mankind.

Which kind are you thinking of, and what fault do you find in them?

The worst of all faults, especially if the story is ugly and immoral as well   55
as false—misrepresenting the nature of gods and heroes, like an artist whose picture is utterly unlike the object he sets out to draw.

That is certainly a serious fault; but give me an example.

A signal instance of false invention about the highest matters is that foul story, which Hesiod repeats, of the deeds of Uranus and the vengeance of Cronos; and then there is the tale of Cronos's doings and of his son's treatment of him. Even if such tales were true, I should not have supposed they should be lightly told to thoughtless young people. If they cannot be altogether suppressed, they should only be revealed in a mystery, to which access should be as far as possible restricted by requiring the sacrifice, not of a pig, but of some victim such as very few could afford.

It is true: those stories are objectionable.

Yes, and not to be repeated in our commonwealth, Adeimantus. We shall not tell a child that, if he commits the foulest crimes or goes to any length in punishing his father's misdeeds, he will be doing nothing out of the way, but only what the first and greatest of the gods have done before him.

I agree; such stories are not fit to be repeated.   60

Nor yet any tales of warfare and intrigues and battles of gods against gods, which are equally untrue. If our future Guardians are to think it a disgrace to quarrel lightly with one another, we shall not let them embroider robes with the Battle of the Giants or tell them of all the other feuds of gods and heroes with their kith and kin. If by any means we can make them believe that no one has ever had a quarrel with a fellow citizen and it is a sin to have one, that is the sort of thing our old men and women should tell children from the first; and as they grow older, we must make the poets write for them in the same strain. Stories like those of Hera being bound by her son, or of Hephaestus flung from heaven by his father for taking his mother's part when she was beaten, and all those battles of the gods in Homer, must not be admitted into our state, whether they be allegorical or not. A child cannot distinguish the allegorical sense from the literal, and the ideas he takes in at that age are likely to become indelibly fixed; hence the great importance of seeing that the first stories he hears shall be designed to produce the best possible effect on his character.

Yes, that is reasonable. But if we were asked which of these stories in particular are of the right quality, what should we answer?

I replied: You and I, Adeimantus, are not, for the moment, poets, but founders of a commonwealth. As such, it is not our business to invent stories ourselves, but only to be clear as to the main outlines to be followed by the poets in making their stories and the limits beyond which they must not be allowed to go.

True; but what are these outlines for any account they may give of the gods?

Of this sort, said I. A poet, whether he is writing epic, lyric, or drama,   65
surely ought always to represent the divine nature as it really is. And the truth is that that nature is good and must be described as such.

Unquestionably.

Well, nothing that is good can be harmful; and if it cannot do harm, it can do no evil; and so it cannot be responsible for any evil.

I agree.

Again, goodness is beneficent, and hence the cause of well-being.

Yes.   70

Goodness, then, is not responsible for everything, but only for what is as it should be. It is not responsible for evil.

Quite true.

It follows, then, that the divine, being good, is not, as most people say, responsible for everything that happens to mankind, but only for a small part; for the good things in human life are far fewer than the evil, and, whereas the good must be ascribed to heaven only, we must look elsewhere for the cause of evils.

I think that is perfectly true.

So we shall condemn as a foolish error Homer's description of Zeus as the   75

"dispenser of both good and ill." We shall disapprove when Pandarus' violation of oaths and treaties is said to be the work of Zeus and Athena, or when
Themis and Zeus are said to have caused strife among the gods. Nor must we
allow our young people to be told by Aeschylus that "Heaven implants guilt in
man, when his will is to destroy a house utterly." If a poet writes of the sor-
rows of Niobe or the calamities of the house of Pelops or of the Trojan war, either he must not speak of them as the work of a god, or, if he does so, he must
devise some such explanation as we are now requiring: he must say that what
the god did was just and good, and the sufferers were the better for being
chastised. One who pays a just penalty must not be called miserable, and his
misery then laid at heaven's door. The poet will only be allowed to say that the
wicked were miserable because they needed chastisement, and the punishment
of heaven did them good. If our commonwealth is to be well-ordered, we
must fight to the last against any member of it being suffered to speak of the
divine, which is good, being responsible for evil. Neither young nor old must
listen to such tales, in prose or verse. Such doctrine would be impious, self-
contradictory, and disastrous to our commonwealth.

I agree, he said, and I would vote for a law to that effect.

Well then, that shall be one of our laws about religion. The first principle
to which all must conform in speech or writing is that heaven is not responsible for everything, but only for what is good.

I am quite satisfied.

Now what of this for a second principle? Do you think of a god as a sort
of magician who might, for his own purposes, appear in various shapes, now
actually passing into a number of different forms, now deluding us into believing he has done so; or is his nature simple and of all things the least likely
to depart from its proper form?

I cannot say offhand.   80

Well, if a thing passes out of its proper form, must not the change come
either from within or from some outside cause?

Yes.

Is it not true, then, that things in the most perfect condition are the least
affected by changes from outside? Take the effect on the body of food and
drink or of exertion, or the effect of sunshine and wind on a plant: the health-
iest and strongest suffer the least change. Again, the bravest and wisest spirit is
least disturbed by external influence. Even manufactured things–furniture,
houses, clothes–suffer least from wear and tear when they are well made and
in good condition. So this immunity to change from outside is characteristic of
anything which, thanks to art or nature or both, is in a satisfactory state.

That seems true.

But surely the state of the divine nature must be perfect in every way, and would therefore be the last thing to suffer transformation from any outside cause.   85

Yes.

Well then, would a god change or alter himself?

If he changes at all, it can only be in that way.

Would it be a change for the better or for the worse?

It could only be for the worse; for we cannot admit any imperfection in divine goodness or beauty.   90

True; and that being so, do you think, Adeimantus, that anyone, god or man, would deliberately make himself worse in any respect?

That is impossible.

Then a god cannot desire to change himself. Being as perfect as he can be, every god, it seems, remains simply and forever in his own form.

That is the necessary conclusion.

If so, my friend, the poets must not tell us that "the gods go to and fro   95 among the cities of men, disguised as strangers of all sorts from far countries"; nor must they tell any of those false tales of Proteus and Thetis transforming themselves, or bring Hera on the stage in the guise of a priestess collecting alms for "the life-giving children of Inachus, the river of Argos." Mothers, again, are not to follow these suggestions and scare young children with mischievous stories of spirits that go about by night in all sorts of outlandish shapes. They would only be blaspheming the gods and at the same time making cowards of their children.

No, that must not be allowed.

But are we to think that the gods, though they do not really change, trick us by some magic into believing that they appear in many different forms?

Perhaps.

What? said I; would a god tell a falsehood or act one by deluding us with an apparition?

I cannot say.   100

Do you not know that the true falsehood—if that is a possible expression— is a thing that all gods and men abominate?

What do you mean?

This, I replied: no one, if he could help it, would tolerate the presence of untruth in the most vital part of his nature concerning the most vital matters. There is nothing he would fear so much as to harbor falsehood in that quarter.

Still I do not understand.

Because you think I mean something out of the ordinary. All I mean is the presence of falsehood in the soul concerning reality. To be deceived about the truth of things and so to be in ignorance and error and to harbor untruth in the soul is a thing no one would consent to. Falsehood in that quarter is abhorred above everything.

It is indeed.

Well then, as I was saying, this ignorance in the soul which entertains untruth is what really deserves to be called the true falsehood; for the spoken falsehood is only the embodiment or image of a previous condition of the soul, not pure unadulterated falsity. Is it not so?

It is.

This real falsehood, then, is hateful to gods and men equally. But is the spoken falsehood always a hateful thing? Is it not sometimes helpful—in war, for instance, or as a sort of medicine to avert some fit of folly or madness that might make a friend attempt some mischief? And in those legends we were discussing just now, we can turn fiction to account; not knowing the facts about the distant past, we can make our fiction as good an embodiment of truth as possible.

Yes, that is so.

Well, in which of these ways would falsehood be useful to a god? We cannot think of him as embodying truth in fiction for lack of information about the past.

No, that would be absurd.

So there is no room in his case for potential inventions. Would he need to tell untruths because he has enemies to fear?

Of course not.

Or friends who are mad or foolish?

No; a fool or a madman could hardly enjoy the friendship of the gods.

Gods, then, have no motive for lying. There can be no falsehood of any sort in the divine nature.

None.

We conclude, then, that a god is a being of entire simplicity and truthfulness in word and in deed. In himself he does not change, nor does he delude others, either in dreams or in waking moments, by apparitions or oracles or signs.

I agree, after all you have said.

You will assent, then, to this as a second principle to guide all that is to be said or written about the gods; that they do not transform themselves by any magic or mislead us by illusions or lies. For all our admiration of Homer, we shall not approve his story of the dream Zeus sent to Agamemnon; nor yet those lines of Aeschylus where Thetis tells how Apollo sang at her wedding:

Boding good fortune for my child, long life
From sickness free, in all things blest by heaven,
His song, so crowned with triumph, cheered my heart.
I thought those lips divine, with prophecy
Instinct, could never lie. But he, this guest,
Whose voice so rang with promise at the feast,
Even he, has slain my son.

If a poet writes of the gods in this way, we shall be angry and refuse him the means to produce his play. Nor shall we allow such poetry to be used in educating the young, if we mean our Guardians to be godfearing and to reproduce the divine nature in themselves so far as man may.

I entirely agree with your principles, he said, and I would have them observed as laws.

So far, then, as religion is concerned, we have settled what sorts of stories about the gods may, or may not, be told to children who are to hold heaven and their parents in reverence and to value good relations with one another.

Yes, he said; and I believe we have settled right.   125

We also want them to be brave. So the stories they hear should be such as to make them unafraid of death. A man with that fear in his heart cannot be brave, can he?

Surely not.

And can a man be free from that fear and prefer death in battle to defeat and slavery, if he believes in a world below which is full of terrors?

No.

Here again, then, our supervision will be needed. The poets must be told   130
to speak well of that other world. The gloomy descriptions they now give must be forbidden, not only as untrue, but as injurious to our future warriors. We shall strike out all lines like these:

I would rather be on earth as the hired servant of another, in the house of landless man with
little to live on, than be king over all the dead;

or these:

Alack, there is, then, even in the house of Death a spirit or a shade; but the wits dwell in it no
more.

We shall ask Homer and the poets in general not to mind if we cross out all passages of this sort. If most people enjoy them as good poetry, that is all the more reason for keeping them from children or grown men who are to be free, fearing slavery more than death.

I entirely agree.

We must also get rid of all that terrifying language, the very sound of which is enough to make one shiver: "loathsome Styx," "the River of Wailing," "infernal spirits," "anatomies," and so on. For other purposes such language may be well enough; but we are afraid that fever consequent upon such shivering fits may melt down the fine-tempered spirit of our Guardians. So we will have none of it; and we shall encourage writing in the opposite strain.

Clearly.

Another thing we must banish is the wailing and lamentations of the famous heroes. For this reason: if two friends are both men of high character, neither of them will think that death has any terrors for his comrade; and so he will not mourn for his friend's sake, as if something terrible had befallen him.

No. 135

We also believe that such a man, above all, possesses within himself all that is necessary for a good life and is least dependent on others, so that he has less to fear from the loss of a son or brother or of his wealth or any other possession. When such misfortune comes, he will bear it patiently without lamenting.

True.

We shall do well, then, to strike out descriptions of the heroes bewailing the dead, and make over such lamentations to women (and not to women of good standing either) and to men of low character, so that the Guardians we are training for our country may disdain to imitate them.

Quite right.

Once more, then, we shall ask Homer and the other poets not to represent 140 Achilles, the son of a goddess, as "tossing from side to side, now on his face, now on his back," and then as rising up and wandering distractedly on the seashore, or pouring ashes on his head with both hands, with all those tears and wailings the poet describes; nor to tell how Priam, who was near akin to the gods, "rolled in the dung as he made entreaty, calling on each man by name." Still more earnestly shall we ask them not to represent gods as lamenting, or at any rate not to dare to misrepresent the highest god by making him say: "Woe is me that Sarpedon, whom I love above all men, is fated to die at the hands of Patroclus." For if our young men take such unworthy descriptions seriously instead of laughing at them, they will hardly feel themselves, who are but men, above behaving in that way or repress any temptation to do so. They would not be ashamed of giving way with complaints and outcries on every trifling occasion; and that would be contrary to the principle we have deduced and shall adhere to, until someone can show us a better.

It would.

Again, our Guardians ought not to be overmuch given to laughter. Violent laughter tends to provoke an equally violent reaction. We must not allow poets to describe men of worth being overcome by it; still less should Homer speak of the gods giving way to "unquenchable laughter" at the sight of Hephaestus "bustling from room to room." That will be against your principles.

Yes, if you choose to call them mine.

Again, a high value must be set upon truthfulness. If we were right in saying that gods have no use for falsehood and it is useful to mankind only in the way of medicine, obviously a medicine should be handled by no one but a physician.

Obviously.   145

If anyone, then, is to practice deception, either on the country's enemies or on its citizens, it must be the Rulers of the commonwealth, acting for its benefit; no one else may meddle with this privilege. For a private person to mislead such Rulers we shall declare to be a worse offense than for a patient to mislead his doctor or an athlete his trainer about his bodily condition, or for a seaman to misinform his captain about the state of the ship or of the crew. So, if anyone else in our commonwealth "of all that practice crafts, physician, seer, or carpenter," is caught not telling the truth, the Rulers will punish him for introducing a practice as fatal and subversive in a state as it would be in a ship.

It would certainly be as fatal, if action were suited to the word.

Next, our young men will need self-control; and for the mass of mankind that chiefly means obeying their governors, and themselves governing their appetite for the pleasures of eating and drinking and sex. Here again we shall disapprove of much that we find in Homer.

I agree.

Whereas we shall allow the poets to represent any examples of self-con-   150
trol and fortitude on the part of famous men, and admit such lines as these: "Odysseus smote his breast, chiding his heart: Endure, my heart; thou hast borne worse things than these."

Yes, certainly.

Nor again must these men of ours be lovers of money, or ready to take bribes. They must not hear that "gods and great princes may be won by gifts."

No, that sort of thing cannot be approved.

If it were not for my regard for Homer, I should not hesitate to call it downright impiety to make Achilles say to Apollo: "Thou hast wronged me, thou deadliest of gods; I would surely requite thee, if I had but the power." And all those stories of Achilles dragging Hector round the tomb of Patroclus and slaughtering captives on the funeral pyre we shall condemn as false, and not let our Guardians believe that Achilles, who was the son of a goddess and of the wise Peleus, third in descent from Zeus, and the pupil of the sage Chiron, was so disordered that his heart was a prey to two contrary maladies, mean covetousness and arrogant contempt of gods and men.

You are right.   155

We have now distinguished the kinds of stories that may and may not be told about gods and demigods, heroes, and the world below. There remains the literature concerned with human life.

Clearly.

We cannot lay down rules for that at our present stage.

Why not?

Because, I suspect, we shall find both poets and prose-writers guilty of the   160 most serious misstatements about human life, making out that wrongdoers are often happy and just men miserable; that injustice pays, if not detected; and that my being just is to another man's advantage, but a loss to myself. We shall have to prohibit such poems and tales and tell them to compose others in the contrary sense. Don't you think so?

I am sure of it.

Well, as soon as you admit that I am right there, may I not claim that we shall have reached agreement on the subject of all this inquiry?

That is a fair assumption.

Then we must postpone any decision as to how the truth is to be told about human life, until we have discovered the real nature of justice and proved that it is intrinsically profitable to its possessor, no matter what reputation he may have in the eyes of the world.

That is certainly true. . . .   165

One thing is easily settled, namely that grace and seemliness of form and movement go with good rhythm, ungracefulness and unseemliness with bad.

Naturally.

And again, good or bad rhythm and also tunefulness or discord in music go with the quality of the poetry; for they will be modelled after its form, if, as we have said, metre and music must be adapted to the sense of the words.

Well, they must be so adapted.

And the content of the poetry and the manner in which it is expressed de-   170
pend, in their turn, on moral character.

Of course.

Thus, then, excellence of form and content in discourse and of musical expression and rhythm, and grace of form and movement, all depend on goodness of nature, by which I mean, not the foolish simplicity sometimes called by
courtesy "good nature," but a nature in which goodness of character has been
well and truly established.

Yes, certainly.

So, if our young men are to do their proper work in life, they must follow
after these qualities wherever they may be found. And they are to be found in
every sort of workmanship, such as painting, weaving, embroidery, architecture, the making of furniture; and also in the human frame and in all the
works of nature: in all these grace and seemliness may be present or absent.
And the absence of grace, rhythm, harmony is nearly allied to baseness of
thought and expression and baseness of character; whereas their presence
goes with that moral excellence and self-mastery of which they are the embodiment.

That is perfectly true.   175

Then we must not only compel our poets, on pain of expulsion, to make
their poetry the express image of noble character; we must also supervise
craftsmen of every kind and forbid them to leave the stamp of baseness, license, meanness, unseemliness, on painting and sculpture, or building, or any
other work of their hands; and anyone who cannot obey shall not practice his
art in our commonwealth. We would not have our Guardians grow up among
representations of moral deformity, as in some foul pasture where, day after
day, feeding on every poisonous weed they would, little by little, gather insen-
sibly a mass of corruption in their very souls. Rather we must seek out those
craftsmen whose instinct guides them to whatsoever is lovely and gracious; so
that our young men, dwelling in a wholesome climate, may drink in good
from every quarter, whence, like a breeze bearing health from happy regions,
some influence from noble works constantly falls upon eye and ear from
childhood upward, and imperceptibly draws them into sympathy and harmony with the beauty of reason, whose impress they take.

There could be no better upbringing than that.

Hence, Glaucon, I continued, the decisive importance of education in poetry and music: rhythm and harmony sink deep into the recesses of the soul
and take the strongest hold there, bringing that grace of body and mind which
is only to be found in one who is brought up in the right way. Moreover, a

proper training in this kind makes a man quick to perceive any defect or ugliness in art or in nature. Such deformity will rightly disgust him. Approving all that is lovely, he will welcome it home with joy into his soul and, nourished thereby, grow into a man of a noble spirit. All that is ugly and disgraceful he will rightly condemn and abhor while he is still too young to understand the reason; and when reason comes, he will greet her as a friend with whom his education has made him long familiar.

I agree, he said; that is the purpose of education in literature and music. . . .

Now, the ordinary athlete undergoes the rigors of training for the sake of muscular strength; but ours will do so rather with a view to stimulating the spirited element in their nature. So perhaps the purpose of the two established branches of education is not, as some suppose, the improvement of the soul in one case and of the body in the other. Both, it may be, aim chiefly at improving the soul.

How so?

Have you noticed how a life-long devotion to either branch, to the exclusion of the other, affects the mind, resulting in an uncivilized hardness in the one case, and an overcivilized softness in the other?

I have certainly noticed that unmitigated athletics produce a sort of ferocity, and a merely literary and musical education makes men softer than is good for them.

Surely that ferocity is the outcome of the spirited element in our nature. A proper training would produce courage; but if that element is overstrained, it naturally becomes hard and savage. Gentleness, on the other hand, is characteristic of the philosophic disposition. Here again, too much relaxation will result in oversoftness; the right training will produce a gentleness that is steady and disciplined. Now we agree that our Guardians must combine both these dispositions; and they will have to be harmonized so that courage and steadfastness may be united in a soul that would otherwise be either unmanly or boorish.

Certainly.

When a man surrenders himself to music, allowing his soul to be flooded through the channels of his ears with those sweet and soft and mournful airs we spoke of, and gives up all his time to the delights of song and melody, then at first he tempers the high-spirited part of his nature, like iron whose brittle hardness is softened to make it serviceable; but if he persists in subduing it to such incantation, he will end by melting it away altogether. He will have cut the sinews of his soul and made himself what Homer calls a faint-hearted warrior. Moreover, this result follows quickly in a temperament that is naturally spiritless; while a high-spirited one is rendered weak and unstable, read-

180

185

ily flaring up and dying down again on slight provocation. Such men become rather irritable, bad-tempered, and peevish.

Quite so.

On the other hand, there are the consequences of hard bodily exercise and high living, with no attempt to cultivate the mind or use the intellect in study. At first, the sense of physical fitness fills a man with self-confidence and energy and makes him twice the man he was. But suppose he does nothing else and holds aloof from any sort of culture; then, even if there was something in him capable of desiring knowledge, it is starved of instruction and never encouraged to think for itself by taking part in rational discussion or intellectual pursuits of any kind; and so it grows feeble for lack of stimulus and nourishment, and deaf and blind because the darkness that clouds perception is never cleared away. Such a man ends by being wholly uncultivated and a hater of reason. Having no more use for reasonable persuasion, he gains all his ends by savage violence, like a brute beast, and he lives in a dull stupor of ignorance with no touch of inward harmony or grace.

That is exactly what happens.

There are, then, these two elements in the soul, the spirited and the philo-   190
sophic; and it is for their sake, as I should say, and not (except incidentally) for the sake of soul and body, that heaven has given to mankind those two branches of education. The purpose is to bring the two elements into tune with one another by adjusting the tension of each to the right pitch. So one who can apply to the soul both kinds of education blended in perfect proportion will be master of a nobler sort of musical harmony than was ever made by tuning the strings of the lyre.

We may well say that, Socrates.

And our commonwealth will need the constant vigilance of such a master, to preserve its constitution.

Certainly, he will be indispensable.

So much, then, for the outlines of education and nurture. We need not go into all the details of their musical performances or of their hunting and athletic contests and races. Obviously these will follow from our principles and can easily be worked out.

Yes, easily.   195

The Responsive Reader

1. What is the puzzle that sets this Socratic dialogue in motion? How is it resolved? (Or is it?) Is this paradox still a challenge for society today?

2. In Greek mythology, Cronos destroyed his father, Uranus, and then Zeus in turn made himself king of the gods by destroying his father, Cronos. How much do you know about the Greek myths that Socrates criticizes? What do you know about stories of metamorphosis, or change of identity or appearance, that are common in Greek mythology? Why does Socrates object to them?

3. The nature or origin of evil has been a central overriding question in Western religious thought. What is the essence of Socrates' teaching here? Why is he so insistent on this subject? What were you taught or what do you believe on this subject?

4. According to Socrates, what is wrong with fiction and poetry stimulating excessive grief or laughter?

5. Socrates makes the teaching of high moral standards a central goal of education. What is his definition of "moral character"? (Why does he make an apparent exception under the heading of "truthfulness"?)

For Discussion or Writing

6. What laws do you think people with strong religious views would make today concerning what should and should not be taught to children?

7. In many cultures, politics and religion have been closely intertwined. (What striking examples can you cite?) Why did separation of church and state become a key feature of American history? Do you agree with those who claim that in this country separation of church and state, of God and country, has gone too far?

8. Do we still expect our schools to teach character? How does our definition compare with that of Socrates?

Collaborative Projects

9. You may want to collaborate with your classmates on scripting an imaginary dialogue in which Socrates advocates censorship of current popular entertainment.

GOD AND THE MACHINE AGE

Eric Hoffer

―――――――

> *Are science and religion at odds? Did the creators of modern science set out to undermine religious faith? Eric Hoffer is a student of ideas that make a difference in the lives of large numbers of ordinary people; he is admired by his followers for his ability to "convince you that assumptions you have always carelessly held are not true" (Maurice Dolbier). Hoffer is a working-class intellectual who says that he "had no schooling" but after overcoming near-blindness read "indiscriminately everything within reach." After growing up in New York, he struck out for California along with thousands of Depression-era Okies and Arkies, working as a migratory field-worker on the West Coast and as a gold miner in Nevada. While working as a longshoreman in San Francisco, he went to the University of California as a "research professor" once a week. He first became known for his book* The True Believer *(1951); he has written incisively about the lure of totalitarian ideologies for exploited workers and about the closed mental universe of converts to what they accept as the only true system of belief. The following selection from his book* The Ordeal of Change *(1963) focuses on an important chapter in the history of Western thought, predating the polarization that in the nineteenth century drove scientists and conservative theologians into opposing camps.*

I once heard a brilliant young professor of political science wonder what it   1
would be like if one were to apply the law of the diffusion of gases to the diffusion
of opinion. The idea seemed to him farfetched, yet he was eager to play with it.

It occurred to me, as I listened, that to a Galileo or a Kepler the idea would not
have seemed at all fantastic. For both Galileo and Kepler really and truly believed
in a God who had planned and designed the whole of creation—a God who was a
master mathematician and technician. Mathematics was God's style, and whether it
was the movement of the stars, the flight of a bird, the diffusion of gases, or the
propagation of opinions—they all bore God's mathematical hallmark.

It sounds odd in modern ears that it was a particular concept of God that
prompted and guided the men who were at the birth of modern science. They felt
in touch with God in every discovery they made. Their search for the mathematical laws of nature was to some extent a religious quest. Nature was God's text, and
the mathematical notations were His alphabet.

The book of nature, said Galileo, is written in letters other than those of our alphabet—"these letters being triangles, quadrangles, circles, spheres, cones, pyramids,
and other mathematical figures." So convinced was Kepler that in groping for the
laws that govern the motions of the heavenly bodies he was trying to decipher
God's text, he later boasted in exaltation that God the author had to wait six

thousand years for His first reader. Leonardo da Vinci paused in his dissection of corpses to pen a prayer: "Would that it might please the Creator that I were able to reveal the nature of man and his customs even as I describe his figure." Leonardo's interest in anatomy may have arisen from his work as an artist, but he was eventually driven mainly by the curiosity of the scientist and the mechanic. Living creatures were wondrous machines devised by a master mechanic, and Leonardo was taking them apart to discover how they were built and how they worked. By observing them and tinkering with them, man could himself become a maker of machines. One could perhaps eventually build a seeing mechanism, a hearing mechanism, a flying machine, and so on. The making of machines would be a second creation: man's way of breathing will and thought into matter.

The concept of God as a master mathematician and craftsman accounts perhaps for the striking difference between the revival of learning and the revival of science in the sixteenth and seventeenth centuries. Whereas the revival of learning was wholly dominated by the ideas and examples of antiquity, the revival of science, though profiting from Greek scientific writing, manifested a marked independence from the beginning. The vivid awareness of God's undeciphered text spread out before them kept the new scientists from expending their energies in the exegesis and imitation of ancient texts. In this case, a genuine belief in God was a factor in the emergence of intellectual independence.

It is of course conceivable that modern science and technology might have developed as they did without a particular conception of God. Yet one cannot resist the temptation to speculate on the significance of the connection. It is as if the Occident had first to conceive a God who was a scientist and a technician before it could create a civilization dominated by science and technology. It is perhaps not entirely so, though it has often been said, that man makes his God in his own image. Rather does he create Him in the image and his cravings and dreams—in the image of what man wants to be. God-making could be part of the process by which a society realizes its aspirations: it first embodies them in the conception of a particular God, and then proceeds to imitate that God. The confidence requisite for attempting the unprecedented is most effectively generated by the fiction that in realizing the new we are imitating rather than originating. Our preoccupation with heaven can be part of an effort to find precedents for the unprecedented.

For all we know, one of the reasons that other civilizations, with all their ingenuity and skill, did not develop a machine age is that they lacked a God whom they could readily turn into an all-powerful engineer. For has not the mighty Jehovah performed from the beginning of time the feats that our machine age is even now aspiring to achieve? He shut up the sea with doors and said: "Hitherto shalt thou come but no further; and here shall thy proud waves be stayed." He made pools of water in the wilderness and turned the desert into a garden. He numbered the stars and called them by name. He commanded the clouds, and told rivers whither to flow. He measured the waters in the hollow of His hand, and meted out the heavens with the span, and comprehended the dust in a measure and weighed the mountains in scales.

The momentous transition that occurred in Europe after the late Middle Ages was in some degree also a transition from the imitation of Christ to the imitation of God. The new scientists felt close to the God who had created the world and set it going. They stood in awe of Him, yet felt as if they were of His school. They were thinking God's thoughts, and whether they knew it or not aspired to be like Him.

The imitation of God was undoubtedly a factor in the release of the dynamism which marked the modern Occident from its birth, and set it off from other civilizations. Not only the new scientists, but the artists, explorers, inventors, merchants, and men of affairs felt that, in the words of Alberti, "men can do all things if they will." When Columbus exclaimed, "Il mondo è poco!" he was expressing triumph rather than despair. The momentous discoveries and achievements implied a downgrading of God. For there is vying in imitation, and the impulse is to overtake and overcome the model we imitate. With its increased mastery over things, the Occident began to feel that it was catching up with God; that it was taming God's creation and making it subservient to a man-made world. The Occident was harking back to the generation of the flood that set out to storm the heavens and felt that "nothing will be restrained from them which they have imagined to do."

The Responsive Reader

1. According to Hoffer, what was "the particular concept of God that prompted and guided the men who were at the birth of modern science"? What does it mean to say that "mathematics was God's style"? How could anatomy be part of "God's text"?

2. How could the making of machinery be seen as "a second creation"?

3. A major part of the "revival of learning" was the rediscovery of ancient Greek literature (like Homer's epics) and philosophy. Although contemporary with the beginnings of modern science, how was it different in spirit or methodology? (What is exegesis?)

4. Scientists have often been charged with overreaching, impious pride. Does Hoffer consider the early scientists and their contemporaries in art, navigation, or commerce guilty of this charge?

For Discussion or Writing

5. Have you previously encountered the idea that nature was God's true scripture or that God reveals himself through his creation? Is the idea alive today? Where or how?

6. The nineteenth century witnessed intense controversies between promoters of science and defenders of traditional religion. Is there a conflict between science education and religious teaching today? Are the two compatible? Are the two kept in separate compartments? If not, where do they clash, and with what results?

Collaborative Projects

7. What is the role of religion in secular colleges or universities today? Working with a group, you may want to collate opinions of college chaplains, professors of theology or the history of religion, or others in the know.

Making Connections

8. Was consideration of religious questions absent from the science essays in Chapter 1? For instance, was God ever mentioned or His existence implied? Does the point of view in any of the essays seem particularly compatible or incompatible with a religious point of view?

DARWIN'S IMAGERY
The "Tree of Nature"

Howard E. Gruber

▬▬▬

Modern science was not developed by minds that work like calculating machines. The early Greek intellectuals pondered the relation between science and art, between truth and beauty. Mathematicians and physicists talk of the "elegance" of the simple formulas that furnish a key to a mass of disorganized data. Albert Einstein talked about the religious awe that the mysteries of the universe inspired in modern physicists. The following is part of an article Howard Gruber contributed to a book on the relation between science and aesthetics. His article focuses on a crucial stage in Charles Darwin's working out of his theory of evolution, eventually published in Darwin's On the Origin of Species by Means of Natural Selection, or the Preservation of Favored Races in the Struggle for Life *(1859). After the five-year voyage of the* Beagle, *Darwin spent several years in working on his theory, a process he recorded in his notebooks. Gruber saw two opposed principles at work in Darwin's thinking. On the one hand, Darwin took pleasure in the spectacle of complexity, of burgeoning diversity, in the natural world. On the other hand, he was at the same time looking for the clean, elegant, simple formula to provide the key. In the following pages, Gruber talks about the scientist's imagination—the role key images play in how scientists organize their thinking.*

Recently I visited an exhibition of anamorphoses at the Brooklyn Museum: 1
Distorted images are seen as normal when viewed from a special station point or when reflected in a cone or cylinder. One may see at the center of a picture a cone with a mirrored surface, surrounded by a distorted, unrecognizable image. At first, there is a tendency to glance perfunctorily at the distorted image, say of a human face or body, and then to study attentively the "corrected" version seen from the appropriate position. After a while, however, the distortions themselves draw the attention as objects of aesthetic interest. They have their own, sometimes weird, ugly, fascination. There is more to anamorphoses than a complex game of mapping a transformation. The artists who have played this game over the centuries are telling us something serious: nature has many faces, some harmonious and pretty, others wild and ugly.

It was precisely this duality that gave Darwin's contemporaries so much difficulty. Why would the Divine Artificer deliberately endow the natural order of His Creation with so much imperfection—hatred and violence, pestilence and death? How could these inescapable facts be reconciled with the image of a harmonious and perfect order of nature, the work of an omnipotent and benevolent Creator? There were various theological answers to the puzzle, and Darwin was thoroughly exposed to them in his university education. But when he begins his notebooks on evolution, we see from the first page that he has set himself the task of finding a completely natural solution to the dilemma. "Why is life short?" (*First Notebook*, p. 2). Why the cycle of birth, growth, reproduction, and death? His answer: to eliminate imperfections acquired in the life of the individual, ". . . generation destroys the effect of accidental injuries, which if animals lived for ever would be endless . . ." (p. 4). At the same time, the reproductive cycle permits adaptation: "There may be unknown difficulty with *full grown* individual with fixed organisation thus being modified,–therefore generation to adapt and alter the race to *changing* world." (p. 4, Darwin's italics). Thus, the function of the life cycle has a double aspect, to pre-serve the near-perfect adaptation already achieved, and to permit the organism to change when necessary?

From this vantage point Darwin moved quickly to his first theory of evolution, which I have described in detail elsewhere. Monads or simple living forms arise through spontaneous generation; they evolve as they adapt to changing circum-stances. Because of the fortuitous nature of their encounters with a changing world, their evolution takes the form of an irregularly branching tree. "Organized beings represent a tree, *irregularly branched*. . . . As many terminal buds dying as new ones generated. There is nothing stranger in death of species, than individuals" (p. 21, Darwin's italics). In quick succession, he makes three tree diagrams, each capturing somewhat different features of the idea that is growing in him. The first (fig. 1, up-per diagram) emphasizes the idea of a triple branching: "Would there not be a triple branching in the tree of life owing to three elements–air, land and water, and the endeavour of each typical class to extend his domain into the other domains and subdivisions, three more, double arrangement. If each main stem of the tree is adapted for these three elements, there will be certainly points of affinity in each branch." (p. 24). This diagram and passage reflects certain general taxonomic prob-lems Darwin was hoping to solve within the framework of his theory.

The second diagram (fig. 1, lower diagram) emphasizes the long gaps in the fossil record, a long dotted line showing a continuity between hypothetical extinct (but unknown) forms and the seemingly sudden efflorescence of a later group of organisms.

In the third diagram (fig. 2) Darwin introduces a specific notation to indicate a   5
fundamental feature of his tree of life, extinction. Extinction was by no means a universally accepted idea, even among evolutionists. Lamarck had vigorously de-nied it. Darwin well knew that the fact of extinction is hard to prove, since it is founded on negative evidence–that is, the failure up to a particular moment in sci-entific time to find living specimens of an organism known to have once lived. Negative evidence is risky, counts for little. But Darwin had already begun to see that his tree image is a picture of exponential growth in the number of species, and this poses a problem for him that can only be solved by the idea of extinction. Thus he was at pains to show that extinction was not simply a fact but a formal

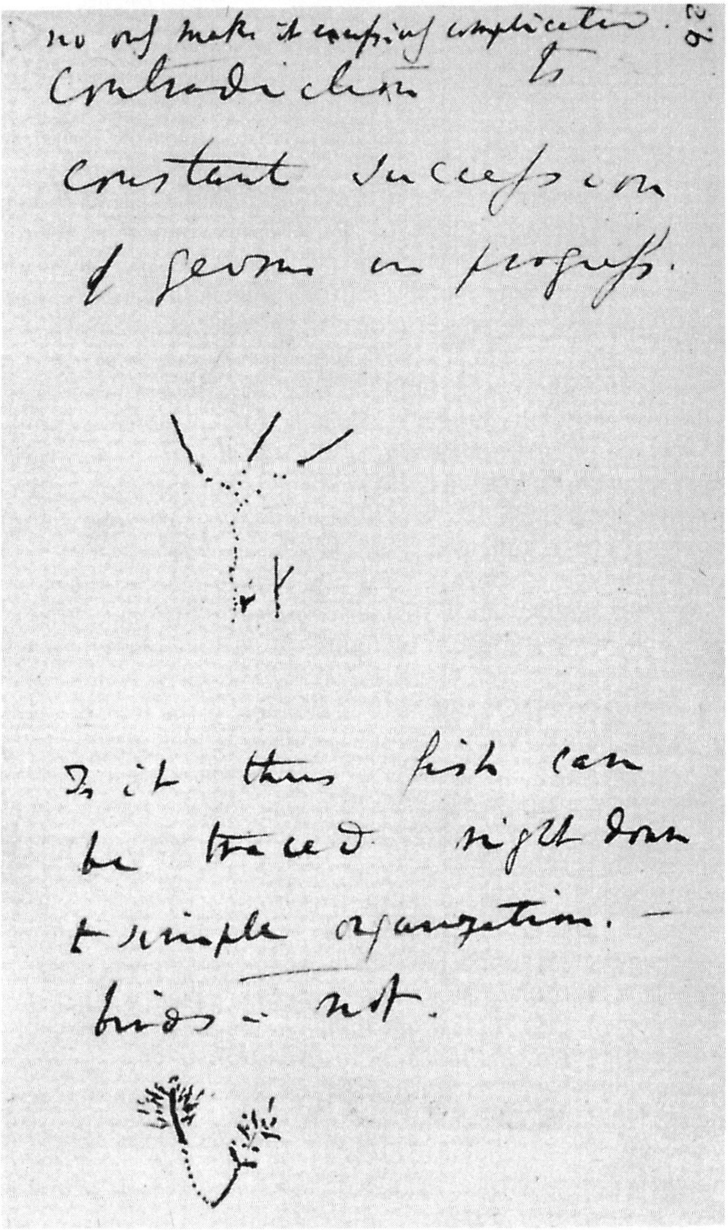
no only make it excessively complicated. 26
Contradiction to
constant succession
of germs in progress.

Is it thus fish can
be traced right down
to simple organization. —
birds — not.

FIGURE 1. Darwin's first two tree diagrams, on page 26 of the *First Notebook*. Immediately preceding the upper tree the MS reads, "The tree of life should perhaps be called the coral of life, base of branches dead; so that passages cannot be seen–[end of p. 25, beginning of p. 26] this again offers ((no only makes it excessively complicated)) contradiction to constant succession of germs in progress." Words in double parentheses were inserted above the line by Darwin. Immediately preceding the lower tree the MS reads, "Is it thus fish can be traced right down to simple organization–birds–not." (Courtesy of the Syndics of Cambridge University Library.)

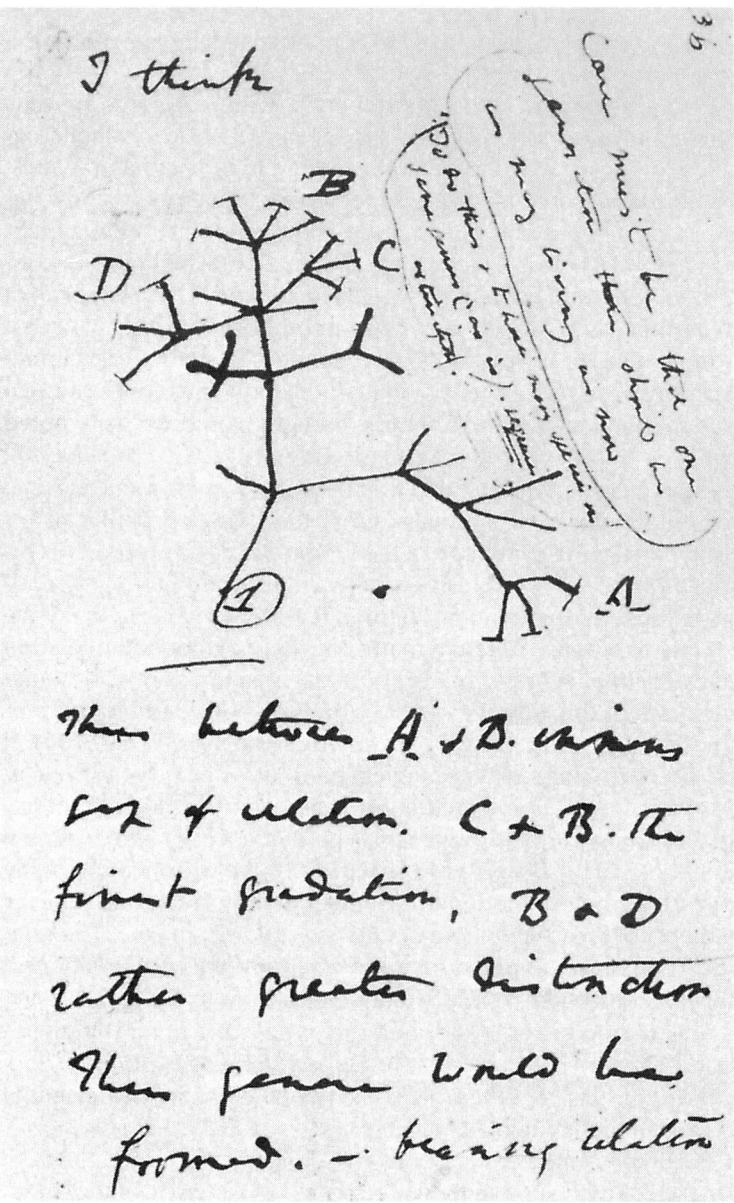

FIGURE 2.   Darwin's third tree diagram, on page 36 of the *First Notebook*. The MS reads, "I think" followed by the diagram. Then, "Thus between A & B immense gap of relation, C & B, the finest gradation, B & D rather greater distinction. Thus genera would be formed–bearing relation [end of p. 36, beginning of p. 37] to ancient types." The marginal insertion alongside the tree diagram reads, "Case must be that one generation then should have as many living as now. To do this & to have many species in same genus (as is), *requires* extinction." (Courtesy of the Syndics of Cambridge University Library.)

requirement of his system. "I think Case must be that one generation then should have as many living as now. To do this and to have as many species in same genus *requires* extinction" (p. 36, Darwin's italics).

In short, the branching model, the image of the irregularly branching tree of nature played a pivotal role very early in his thinking about evolution. It captures many points: the fortuitousness of life, the irregularity of the panorama of nature, the explosiveness of growth and the necessity to bridle it "so as to keep number of species constant" (p. 37). And most important, the fundamental duality that at any time some must live and others die.

It took about fifteen months from this point until Darwin grasped the principle of natural selection as a key operator giving the tree of life its form. While Darwin's thought changed in many ways from these earliest notes until the time, some twenty years later, when he wrote the *Origin of Species*, this image of nature remained constant. Essentially the same tree diagram as his third tree diagram appears in the *Origin*. It is the only diagram in the book, and it is referred to throughout as he exploits its theoretical richness, some of which I have indicated.

Over the years, Darwin drew and redrew the tree diagram. I have paid attention to the scraps of paper in his manuscript on which these diagrams can be found, some dateable, others not. Some of them are hasty sketches, others painstakingly drawn and delicate traceries. On one such scrap there is the remark, "Tree not good simile–endless piece of seaweed dividing." He is probably not so much correcting himself as searching for the right variant of his image to express a particular idea that has caught his attention, just as in the *First Notebook*, after his first drawing he wrote, "The tree of life should perhaps be called the coral of life, base of branches dead, so that passages cannot be seen" (p. 25).

We have seen how Darwin's view of the functional significance of the life cycle is connected with his panoramic view of nature as a whole. It is not often enough brought out that there was a certain cosmological cast to Darwin's thinking. Influenced, perhaps intimidated, by the empiricism of his day, Darwin later suggested that he worked in a "Baconian" fashion, inductively from facts to theory. His notebooks do not bear this out. He sketched his ideas with a broad brush and often drew a long bow. Thus, "Astronomers might formerly have said that God ordered each planet to move in its particular destiny. In same manner God orders each animal created with certain form in certain country, but how much more simple and sublime power let attraction act according to certain law, such are inevitable consequences–let animal be created then by the fixed laws of generation, such will be their successors. Let the powers of transportal be such, and so will be the forms of one country to another.–Let geological changes go at such a rate, so will be the number and distribution of the species!!" (pp. 101–102). In Darwin's image of the world, the life cycle and the evolving tree of life are nested in a larger view of the working of the cosmos.

It may be argued at this point that Darwin's diagrams are only conceptual   10
tools for theoretical thought and have no aesthetic significance. Then why the evident pleasure in the actual drawings, the constant search for the right metaphor, the
emotional excitement conveyed by his punctuation and frequent resort to a high-
flown style? There is exactly that combination of feeling with concern for form and
content that we have in mind when we speak of an aesthetic act. As well say that
anamorphoses are not art, or that Dürer's use of instruments or Leonardo's studies
of human anatomy have no aesthetic significance. Only if we presuppose a divorce
between art and scientific thought would we be tempted to turn a blind eye to the
aesthetic side of Darwin's imagery.

If the irregularly branching tree of life is Darwin's image of nature deployed in
evolutionary time, the "tangled bank" of his eloquent closing paragraph of the *Origin of Species* represents his image of the same explosive vitality in all its complex interconnectedness at one moment in time. It was this passage that gave the title to
Stanley Edgar Hyman's lovely book about the relation between intellectual work
and literary imagination. Although foretastes of this passage occur in the notebooks and in the preliminary sketches of the *Origin* Darwin wrote in 1842 and
1844, the precise image of the tangled bank does not. Nevertheless, Darwin's fascination with the intricate web of contemporaneous relationships among organisms is evident as early as the notebooks of the *Beagle* voyage (1831–36) and
appears in many forms long before the *Origin*. In the carefully drawn-up table of
contents of the *Origin* there occurs the striking phrase, "The relation of organism to
organism the most important of all relations." This idea is spelled out in some detail
in the text.

This is of course not an idea original with Darwin. It can be found in many
places, notably Gilbert White's *Natural History and Antiquities of Selbourne*. It is nonetheless an idea essential to Darwin's thinking.

But interconnectedness does not by itself mean *imperfection*. Among Darwin's
immediate precursors, in Lamarck's thought, in German *Naturphilosophie*, and in English Natural Theology, the idea of perfection was deeply embedded. In the first
two it took the form of a scale of increasing perfection toward some limit or ideal
type, that is, man, as in Lamarck's ladder of nature. The Natural Theologians could
not accept this formulation because it meant that some of God's creation was less
than perfect. In their view every organism was perfectly adapted to its place, seeming imperfections simply showed the limitations of our understanding of His work.
Darwin's view of the natural order as inherently irregular, incomplete, and imperfect differed as radically from his predecessors' as did his view of the process by
which this came about.

Thus two great and vital images, one of historical, the other of contemporary
relations, form the substrate for the theory of evolution by natural selection. They
are not, however, merely background, but are woven explicitly into the theory as
presented in the *Origin*.

The irregularly branching tree and the tangled bank represent the vital complexifying aspect of Darwin's thought. Other images must be sought that express the simplifying aspect. Of all those things that might occur in nature's incessant branching, some never do at all. The extinction of one evolutionary line makes impossible all the species that might have evolved from it. Of all those transient relations depicted in the tangled bank, some endure and others disappear. As we have already seen, the necessity for some principle of selection almost leaps out of these images.

In *Darwin on Man* I have carefully spelled out the slow process by which the thinker constructs the mental circumstances of his own insights. In considering even a most important moment of insight, this slow phase of construction must not be forgotten. On the other hand, such moments do occur and they deserve our attention. As is well known now, on September 25, 1838, Darwin, after reading (or perhaps rereading?) Malthus' *Essay on Population*, finally saw the principle of natural selection in a clear way. The passage in his notebook where he writes this out conveys the feeling of the moment as it was happening. It contains a striking and brutal mechanical image: "One may say there is a force like a hundred thousand wedges trying [to] force every kind of adapted structure into the gaps in the economy of nature, or rather forming gaps by thrusting out weaker ones" (*Third Notebook*, p. 135). The image reoccurs in the sketches of 1842 and 1844. In the first edition of the *Origin* it is heightened: "The face of Nature may be compared to a yielding surface, with ten thousand sharp wedges packed close together and driven inwards by incessant blows, sometimes one wedge being struck, and then another with greater force" (p. 67). This image has two features. On the one hand it emphasizes the idea that the theory deals with the interplay of a multitude of small forces rather than with the clash of Titans (in this way the theory is quite unlike Freud's depiction of struggle between Eros and Thanatos). On the other hand, the wedging image brings out the incessant rupturing of the seeming harmony of nature. Oddly, this image disappears from later editions of the *Origin*. It is as though Darwin needed to insist on this brutal rupturing but then recoiled a little from the hard mechanical nature of his image.

In the *Origin*, of course, two other well-known images occur. Human warfare, in Malthus' treatise the actual subject matter, becomes for Darwin one of the images he draws upon. For us the idea of warfare may seem to evoke the prodigal "wastefulness" of nature. For Darwin, there is a different emphasis. The image brings out the magnitude of the selection ratio of those that die to those that survive to reproduce. But Darwin's whole point is that this is not wasteful but creative, nature's way of fashioning the many ingenious contrivances embodied in every organism. Besides, if we avoid anthropocentrism, in the struggle for existence nothing is wasted. Those that die are eaten. Darwin is explicit on the way in which he intends the image of struggle to be taken: "I use the term Struggle for Existence in a large and metaphorical sense . . ." (*Origin*, p. 62)–covering many shades of meaning from actual combat between two organisms to simple dependence on conditions of life such as climate.

Finally, there is the metaphor of artificial selection. In one sense, Darwin's deep interest in artificial selection represents his desire to submit his theory to experimental test. Darwin was an inveterate experimentalist, and it must have troubled him that the theory as a whole could not be so tested. Human efforts to breed plants and animals come as close as possible. Darwin was, however, keenly aware of the many differences between artificial and natural selection, and his examination of the former, placed with poetic strategy in chapter 1 of the *Origin*, "Variation Under Domestication," has a clearly metaphoric intent. This metaphor plays a specific role in the theoretical structure, to emphasize the cumulative nature of evolutionary change. Darwin concludes the chapter by remarking that, of the several possible causes of change that he has discussed, natural selection is the most important: "Over all these causes of Change I am convinced that the accumulative action of Selection, whether applied methodically and more quickly, or unconsciously and more slowly, but more efficiently, is by far the predominant Power" (*Origin*, p. 43).

There are then at least these five images that Darwin used in developing the theory of evolution through natural selection–tree, tangled bank, wedging, war, and artificial selection. One of these, wedging, Darwin himself dropped from later editions of the *Origin*, so it is no wonder that it has been forgotten. Of the remaining four, only two are commonly referred to in discussing Darwin's theory–war and artificial selection. Both of these are simplifying images, dealing with the selective and corrective side of the process. The other two images, all too often forgotten, dramatize the principle of vitality, the explosive, irregular living material on which selection works.

For the moment, I simply want to draw attention to two points. First, the multiplicity of these images. Second, the specificity of their functions in the theoretical structure. Earlier we saw that each drawing of the tree of life had specific features highlighting one or another aspect of the theory at an early stage of its development. Now the same can be said of Darwin's use of images in the definitive construction of his theory. They are not multiplied as a display of virtuosity but used with poetic economy, each image making its point, each point finding its image.

The Responsive Reader

1. According to Gruber, what "completely natural" solution did Darwin find to the puzzle of the "imperfections," and especially disease and death in God's creation?

2. What makes the "tree of life" a good image for emphasizing the vitality of nature? Why does Gruber say at the end that the tree image is one of two images Darwin used to "dramatize the principle of vitality, the explosive, irregular living

material on which selection works"? (What other alternative images did Darwin consider and reject?)

3. As Gruber says, the image of the "tangled bank" did not become a familiar slogan of evolutionists or anti-evolutionists. What role did it play in Darwin's thinking?

4. The struggle for existence, the war of all against all, became a familiar concept as the theory of evolution was popularized. According to Gruber, how did Darwin use the metaphor of struggle? What did he have in mind? Why does the idea of the alleged "wastefulness" of nature become an issue here?

5 Why would Darwin, who developed the theory of natural selection, have been deeply interested in "artificial selection"? (IIow are the two different? What do the two have in common?)

For Discussion or Writing

6. IIow does Gruber ask us to revise the ideal of the scientist working inductively, patiently correlating data in order to produce cautious generalizations?

Collaborative Projects

7. Leonardo da Vinci, quintessential representative of the Italian Renaissance, is often described as painter, sculptor, scientist, inventor, engineer. Working alone or with a group, what can you find about the relation of art and science in his work?

SCIENCE AND THE LAW
Are Breast Implants Actually OK?

Marcia Angell

Medical experts testifying to the damages suffered by alleged victims of malpractice or unsafe products have become a familiar courtroom sight. DNA testing plays a crucial role in murder trials and paternity suits. Two different worlds meet here: the world of science and the world of law. Physicians use the tools of science to make the patient whole. Lawyers move in when something has gone wrong with the healing process. Their assignment is to fix blame—to recover damages, to put incompetent practitioners out of business, to take unsafe medications off the market. The author of the following article is a physician and the executive editor of the New England Journal of Medicine, *one of the most prestigious and influential medical journals. She is the author of* Class Action: Medical Fact, Law, and the Breast Implant Controversy (1996). *To judge from her article, is it possible for scientists and lawyers to speak the same language?*

In 1992, when FDA Commissioner David Kessler decided to ban silicone gel-filled breast implants, he generated more alarm than controversy. According to Kessler, the manufacturers had not fulfilled their responsibility to demonstrate the safety of the implants, and so he had no choice but to take them off the market. His decision brought to a close a thirty-year period during which breast implants had been easily available, at least for those who could afford them. It also spread apprehension among the 1 percent of American women who already had the implants—most to enlarge their breasts, although a minority had implants for reconstruction after mastectomy for breast cancer. Polls indicated that the great majority of women with breast implants were pleased with the results. Nevertheless, many people were jubilant about the FDA ban—including advocates of tough government regulation, women who believed breast implants had made them ill and feminists who thought it was about time someone put a stop to the pressure to conform to male fantasies.

As executive editor of the *New England Journal of Medicine* and as a woman, I was aware that breast implants were controversial on many counts, but I had not given the matter much thought until Dr. Kessler submitted an article to the *Journal* explaining his reasons for banning the devices. The article was important, and we were happy to publish it. Still, I was troubled by the likely consequences of Kessler's action, as well as by some of his arguments. He seemed disdainful of women who wanted breast implants for purely cosmetic reasons, and his decision struck me as patronizing. More importantly, it seemed likely that the million or so women who had the implants would take the FDA ban as proof that implants were extremely dangerous.

And that is exactly what happened. Despite Kessler's weak assurances that removal of the implants was unnecessary, and although no scientific studies had demonstrated their danger, women rushed to have them taken out, sometimes by the same plastic surgeons who had put them in. One woman who could not afford the fee attempted to remove her own implants with razor blades. (She survived the ordeal and was pictured in newspapers looking greatly relieved after a surgeon finished the job.) Inevitably, perhaps, given the American fervor for suing one another, and the money to be made in splashy product liability suits, the small trickle of high-stakes court cases involving breast implants that began in the early '80s soon swelled to a torrent. Sympathetic juries awarded huge damages to women with a variety of complaints that they and their lawyers attributed to breast implants.

In the two years following the FDA ban, more than 1,000 lawyers rushed to file more than 16,000 lawsuits on behalf of women with breast implants. A small display ad in the July 26, 1994, *Washington Post* exemplified the opportunistic spirit of the moment: "The law firm of Chandler, Franklin, and O'Brien is pleased to announce the opening of our new Fairfax office devoted exclusively to representing women in breast implant litigation," followed by the toll-free number, 1–800–488–4LAW. Another firm, Kresch & Kresch, could be reached at 1–800–LAW–HELP; while a Florida attorney adopted the number 1–800–RUPTURE. Even as all but two of the manufacturers got out of the implant business, the number of lawyers who belong to Public Citizen's breast implant clearinghouse increased from four in 1990 to 179 in 1992; the Breast Implant Committee of the American Trial Lawyers Association grew from twenty to 160 in just the six months leading up to the ban.

Facing one product liability case after another, the breast implant manufacturers, while maintaining that the implants were safe, eventually agreed to the largest class-action settlement in the annals of American law. In April 1994 the major manufacturers settled for $4.25 billion, a billion of which was explicitly set aside for the lawyers involved. Although nearly any woman with implants would be entitled to something under the terms of the settlement, women were permitted to opt out if they thought they could do better on their own. As of June 1, 1995, some 440,000 women (about a quarter of all women with breast implants in this country) had registered to participate in the class-action settlement but, with vigorous encouragement from plaintiffs' attorneys, about 15,000 (half of them foreigners, for whom the terms of the settlement are less generous) have opted to seek higher damages individually.

The trouble with all this is that at the time the FDA made its decision to ban breast implants there had been no systematic studies of the effects of breast implants. The suits thus proceeded in the absence of sound scientific findings. Furthermore, they helped to create an atmosphere of unnecessary wariness about medical implants in general, especially those, like the contraceptive Norplant, that make use of the dreaded silicone.

What *did* we know about the risks of breast implants? We knew, of course, that there could be complications from the surgery itself (as with any surgery), including infections and hemorrhage. We also knew that very small amounts of silicone fluid from the gel leaked through the outer envelope of the implant. (This leakage was not noticeable to the woman and tended to be contained within the capsule of scar tissue that inevitably forms around the implants.) We knew that, in many women, the capsule of scar tissue contracted excessively, distorting and hardening the breasts and often causing discomfort. And finally, we knew that in about 5 percent of women an implant ruptured, releasing silicone gel into the surrounding tissues and flattening the breast. But these local complications, unpleasant as they were, were not the basis for most of the alarm about breast implants, nor were they the focus of the multimillion-dollar lawsuits.

Instead, a growing number of Americans had come to believe that breast implants could cause devastating effects on the rest of the body. In particular, silicone gel-filled implants were said to be responsible for a constellation of disorders known as connective tissue diseases. These diseases—which include systemic lupus (SLE), rheumatoid arthritis and scleroderma—involve, or are thought to involve, a disturbance in the immune system that turns the body's protective defenses against itself. The result is an autoimmune disease—that is, a prolonged civil war within the body that can produce profound weakness and fatigue along with variable damage to the joints, skin and internal organs. One theory was that silicone, leaking slowly from the implants, provokes an immune reaction that then somehow turns into an autoimmune process—and it was this unproven theory that served as the basis for the largest lawsuits. But the question of whether silicone gel-filled breast implants cause connective tissue disease is not ultimately a matter of opinion or legal argument; it is a matter of biological fact. Either they cause connective tissue disease (alone or in conjunction with other factors), or they don't. And the only way to answer the question is through epidemiologic studies.

To be sure, there are many individual stories (some medically proven, others not) of connective tissue disease developing after the placement of breast implants, but these anecdotal reports alone do not constitute evidence that the implants caused the disease. They could well represent pure coincidence. Each year, for example, about 100 women with breast implants can be expected to come down with lupus or scleroderma, by chance alone. Since connective tissue disease can occur in women with or without implants, the only way to demonstrate that implants actually contribute to the disease is to show that the incidence is significantly higher in women with breast implants than in those without. Yet, it was not until June 16, 1994, two years after breast implants were taken off the market and two months after the class-action settlement was announced, that the first such study of the possible link between breast implants and connective tissue disease was published. And that study failed to find a link.

In the study, Mayo Clinic researchers compared a group of 749 women who   10 had received breast implants between 1964 and 1991 with 1,498 of their neighbors, matched for age. The researchers found that the implant group was no more likely to develop connective tissue disease (or related symptoms and abnormal tests) than the group without implants. This was only one study, of course, and was not large enough to rule out some increase in risk. But it did cast doubt on the link between breast implants and connective tissue disease at a time when many people assumed the theory had been proven.

Meanwhile, at least four other well-designed epidemiologic studies were underway. The largest was a retrospective cohort study of about 450,000 American women in the health professions. Although they have not been published yet, interim results indicate no association between breast implants and connective tissue diseases, with the possible exception of rheumatoid arthritis. Another large retrospective cohort study, published in the *New England Journal of Medicine* in June 1995 also found no association between implants and connective tissue disease in nearly 90,000 nurses. All three of these studies investigated a whole range of non-specific symptoms, in addition to well-defined connective tissue diseases, and so addressed the claim that disease caused by breast implants may not fulfill all the usual criteria for "classical" connective tissue disease.

The remaining two epidemiologic studies, published in 1994 and 1995, dealt just with scleroderma. Scleroderma, a disease characterized by extensive scarring of the skin and sometimes of internal organs, is the connective tissue disease most closely linked by anecdotal reports to silicone breast implants. Neither study could find an association. While all together these studies don't mean that there can be *no* link between connective tissue disease and breast implants, they do mean that any risk of connective tissue disease from implants is so small that it has been impossible to detect. So why were the courts so sure the facts were otherwise?

Partly because of the development of "expert" testimony. The kind of evidence an "expert" witness in the courtroom must adduce to claim that medical harm is caused by implants is of a different order from what scientists would normally have to offer in their work. Indeed, an expert witness isn't really expected to produce evidence so much as an educated guess. Often, an expert's field isn't even relevant to the case at hand. In many of the breast implant cases, for example, plaintiffs' attorneys have relied on pathologists or toxicologists to speculate about the mechanism by which breast implants might cause connective tissue disease, rather than calling on epidemiologists who would get to the question of whether there actually is an association. And, of course, expert witnesses are selected and paid by the contesting lawyers and their testimony worked out in advance.

The terms of the class settlement were remarkably generous and broad. All women with breast implants were entitled to compensation if they had, or within the next thirty years developed, any of ten connective tissue diseases or symptoms suggestive of such disease, provided the symptoms began or worsened after the implants were placed. Of the $4.25 billion, $1.2 billion was set aside for women claiming to have implant-related illnesses already–248,500 women of the 440,000 registered as of June 1. The amount of compensation was to be determined by the type of disorder, its severity and the woman's age at onset. A chart or grid sent to all women with breast implants showed the exact amounts. For example, a woman younger than 36 with severe scleroderma would receive $1.4 million; a woman over 56 with mild Sjogren's syndrome (dryness of the eyes and salivary glands) would receive $140,000. Claimants were not required to show that the implants were related to the illness. In addition, women who were not ill could receive lesser amounts for emotional distress. They would also be reimbursed for all uninsured medical costs related to breast implants, including evaluations, treatment of implant rupture and removal of implants. Husbands, other "significant others" and children born before April 1, 1994, were also entitled to make claims. Children, for example, could claim compensation for injuries caused by their mother's implants (a particularly mysterious provision, since no such injury has ever been demonstrated).

Women claiming current illness were required to submit substantiating medical records. If these were not sufficient to place the woman in the appropriate category on the grid, the woman's doctor was to send the diagnosis, along with copies of relevant records. Beyond this, there would be no attempt to verify the woman's medical condition. A doctor's diagnosis or the medical records would be challenged only if they failed to meet the eligibility requirements. Moreover, while many of the eligibility requirements (such as swollen joints or abnormal substances in the blood) can be objectively measured, some (such as fatigue or muscle aches) cannot. In fact, it would be possible to qualify for compensation without any objective manifestations of illness whatsoever. For example, a woman could claim joint and muscle aches, disturbed sleep, fatigue and burning pain in the chest, none of which can be objectively verified by her doctor or anyone else, and collect up to $700,000.

In the end, the class-action settlement may well unravel. In early May of this year, Judge Sam C. Pointer, the Alabama federal judge who is overseeing the settlement, announced that the size of the compensation for each woman would have to be revised downward. (You can phone Judge Pointer's information line at 1-800-887-6828 for a recorded message giving the current state of play.) It was apparent that the $1.2 billion set aside for current claims would nowhere near cover them. And if it looks like each woman will receive less, then many will opt out of the settlement and go for jury trials, leaving the manufacturers little reason to stay in. (Dow Corning, which had pledged to contribute half the amount of the settlement, has already filed for Chapter 11. The company will now have all claims against it held up in bankruptcy court for years.) A desperate Judge Pointer charged the attorneys representing both sides to try to negotiate a new agreement by August 30, presumably one involving increased contributions from the manufacturers. "There are just too many sick women," said Ralph Knowles, one of the lawyers representing the plaintiffs. "I didn't think it was going to be anything like that. If I did, we would have never agreed to the $4.25 billion."

But whatever happens to this settlement, a great deal of damage has already been done. It did not take plaintiffs' attorneys long to realize that breast implants are not the only medical devices on the market that contain silicone. Already, several class actions have been filed on behalf of the approximately 300,000 men with silicone-containing penile implants. Breast implant litigation has also contributed to new alarmism about Norplant, the (highly reliable) contraceptive that is placed under the skin of the arm in six very small, silicone-coated rods. The number of product liability lawsuits against Wyeth–Ayerst, the manufacturer of Norplant, and its parent company, American Home Products, has, according to a *New York Times* story, swelled from twenty in Norplant's first three years on the market to 180 in 1994. Forty-six class-action suits have been filed on behalf of Norplant users, and implants of the contraceptive have fallen from 800 a day to sixty. The illnesses attributed to it include autoimmune and connective tissue-like disorders. Yet, as with breast implants, there is no evidence to implicate Norplant in these disorders.

More worrisome still is the indirect threat to all medical devices–whether they contain silicone or not. Under our liability laws, plaintiffs can make claims against any party involved in the manufacture of an allegedly harmful product, no matter how remote the involvement. Suppliers of raw materials (or biomaterials) for medical devices can be sued, then, even if they have nothing to do with the design and manufacture of the product. The sale of biomaterials for medical devices is a small part of the business of most big suppliers, so the resulting revenues can quickly be offset by the legal liabilities.

Ostensibly because of such risks, three large suppliers of biomaterials have already pulled back from the market. Dow Corning, a supplier as well as a manufacturer, has drastically scaled back sales of silicone to other manufacturers of medical devices and may stop selling it altogether. The embargo will probably affect a wide variety of silicone-containing devices, ranging from the useful to the vital. Among them are cardiac pacemaker wires, artificial joints, mechanical heart valves, intraocular lenses (used after cataract surgery), implantable arteriovenous shunts for people on chronic dialysis and shunts for people with hydrocephalus (a potentially lethal condition in which fluid accumulates in the brain). Dow Chemical Company has stopped supplying a material used in pacemaker components. DuPont announced in 1993 that it would sever connections with the permanent medical implant industry. It will no longer provide medical manufacturers with Dacron polyester, which is used in vascular grafts, or a number of other materials.

In DuPont's calculus, what had happened with silicone could happen with any other constituent of medical devices.

Under these conditions, a large number of important medical products may become scarce or even unavailable. In May 1994 Senator Joseph Lieberman of Connecticut, then-chairman of the Governmental Affairs Subcommittee on Regulation and Government Information, held hearings on the impact of product liability suits on the availability of medical devices. Among those who testified was Eleanor Gackstatter, president of Meadox Medicals, a manufacturer of vascular grafts and other devices. Gackstatter said that she had tried to contact fifteen alternative suppliers of polyester yarn after DuPont announced it would no longer supply Dacron to her company. None of them, even foreign suppliers, would deal with American manufacturers because of the liability risks. Many manufacturers have a two- or three-year supply of biomaterials on hand, but when that is depleted, there may be a serious shortage. Said Lieberman, "This is a public-health time bomb, and the lives of real people are going to be lost if it explodes."

The effect of the accumulating scientific evidence on the legal situation is difficult to predict. At first, it seemed that new evidence, which so far has failed to find a connection between breast implants and systemic disease, would come too late to affect the class-action settlement. But with Dow Corning's bankruptcy and the likely collapse of the class-action settlement, the matter may very well remain in flux for years. If so, new studies failing to find a link between implants and connective tissue disease could influence the many lawsuits that will follow the collapse of the class-action settlement. Women who thought they had a choice between accepting the terms of a generous class-action settlement or trying for a larger amount individually may find themselves without either option. If that happens, there is no doubt that they will, not unreasonably, feel betrayed by the system.

What lessons can we learn from this tangled story? Any moralist who wanted to preach about the corrupting effects of money and the need for tort reform could certainly find a parable here. Rapacious attorneys who solicit business from women with breast implants, well-paid doctors who stretch the scientific and ethical limits of their profession to bolster legal cases, witnesses who eagerly tailor and sell opinions, even the many healthy women with breast implants who now want to take advantage of the furor over them—all are responding to the lure of big financial awards. Just as worrisome in this case, though, was the apparent resistance to accepting the discipline of scientific evidence, even as our world becomes increasingly dependent on it. The only way to learn the health effects of breast implants is through careful research and unbiased interpretation of the results. There are no shortcuts. Only by relying on scientific evidence can we control the greed, fear and self-indulgence that have so far dominated the breast implant story.

20

The Responsive Reader

1. What do you learn from this article about the legal dimension of the controversy? For instance, what do you learn about the basis for and the status of the lawsuits, the nature of the settlements (concluded or proposed), the motives of plaintiffs and lawyers, and the prospects for eventual financial compensation?
2. What do you learn from this article about the scientific dimension of the controversy? What can be considered as established, and what questions remain open?
3. What do you learn about the impact of the litigation on the health care industry?

For Discussion or Writing

4. If you were a juror in a lawsuit involving breast implants, what impact would this article have on your thinking?

Collaborative Projects

5. Since 1989, women in France have had access to mifepristone (often called RU486), which induces abortions resembling a spontaneous miscarriage, without surgical intervention. What is the history of this drug in the United States? What has been the role of the Food and Drug Administration in considering approval of the drug for the American market? Do you feel the FDA should use its regulatory power to ban this drug?

Making Connections

6. How does the attitude toward business or industry in Angell's essay compare with the perspective in the essays by Garchik, Kramer, and Alter in Chapter 3? Compared with these writers, would you call Angell an apologist for business, or a defender of business?

WHOLLY WRIT
Women's Spirituality

Charlene Spretnak

⎯⎯⎯⎯

> *The women's movement has made us rethink basic assumptions. Feminists have changed attitudes toward marriage and divorce, toward the economic role of women, or toward the role of women in the military or in other traditionally male occupations. More fundamentally, feminist writers have reexamined the spiritual history of our culture. They have pointed to a dominant male principle in vengeful warrior gods, like the Greek Zeus hurling his thunderbolts. They have documented and challenged the exclusion of women from church history and priestly office. They have rediscovered an alternative strand in human spirituality, represented by goddesses, priestesses, and female seers and healers. They have reconstructed prehistoric myths of the earth mother, of nature goddesses representing nature as nurturing, sustaining, and supporting rather than as a subversive force to be controlled and subdued by the dominant male. The Greek Demeter was the goddess of the harvest, of fertility and bounty. The Egyptian mother goddess Isis was seen by her worshipers as all-powerful, as the healer of the sick, and at the same time as "loving and merciful" (Sarah B. Pomeroy). Charlene Spretnak wrote the following review of books dealing with female spirituality for* Ms. *magazine. Her own latest book is* States of Grace: The Recovery of Meaning in a Postmodern Age.*
>
> *Early in her review, Spretnak defends generalizations about "women's experience" against a fashionable "deconstructionist" view. Deconstructionists question anyone's ability to establish an independent perspective transcending the culture and the language system in which we are all trapped.*

In our time women's spirituality–in both perception and expression–has been constrained by two overarching social forces: the patriarchal biases in most religions and the modern worldview that devalues and marginalizes spiritual concerns in general. Consequently, the growing presence of feminist spirituality over the past 20 years has challenged not only patriarchal religion but the underpinnings of the sterile, modern view that human life is a drama apart from the larger Earth community and the sacred whole that is the cosmos. The goal of feminist spirituality has never been the simple substitution of Yahweh-with-a-skirt. Rather, it seeks, in all its diversity, to revitalize relational, body-honoring, cosmologically grounded spiritual possibilities for women and all others.

The tensions that arose during the 1970s–between feminists who remained in mainstream religions and those who left to pursue other spiritual paths–have largely subsided. Today there is greater appreciation of common ground in many areas: recognizing the interrelatedness of all life, honoring the dignity of the female, discovering the power of creating ritual, perceiving work for ecological and social justice as a spiritual responsibility, and cultivating sensitivity to diverse multicultural experiences. Moreover, there is now greater respect for a woman's self-determination in her choice of spiritual orientation as well as in other aspects of her life.

The images and metaphors of spiritual traditions have often overshadowed the perceptions that evoked them and have fueled divisiveness among religions. At the core of each orientation is an expression of relationship to the ultimate mystery inherent in the cosmos, its self-organizing, self-regulating rhythms of creativity. The universe unfolds through an intricate play of novelty, allurement, relation, and engagement—all rising and passing away in lifetimes of a microsecond or in arcs of billions of years. Humans have only partial apprehension of this unimaginably complex web of forces, so we call on metaphor, symbol, myth, or poetry to name and portray it. We call it the divine, God, Goddess, The Way, The Great Holy, Cosmic Consciousness, or other names. Many feminists feel there is good reason to use female metaphors for the divine. First, it overturns a cornerstone of gender politics in patriarchal cultures. Second, the symbolization matches physical reality; has anyone ever seen anything spring into existence because a male finger was pointed toward it? We are not amused by mythic narratives that steal the generative power of the female; womb envy should find less aggressive outlets.

The honoring of the female body in feminist spirituality has been experienced by hundreds of thousands of women as a healing corrective. It also figures, however, in a current debate in academic circles: the argument over "essentialism." Feminists subscribing to the worldview of deconstructive postmodernism assert that (1) any talk of "women's experience" is oppressive because it generalizes and thereby denies the particular experience of individuals, and (2) any talk of the (female) body is misleading because one can know only the social concepts about the body that one's particular society puts forth. Such feminists often cite "women's spirituality" as one of the worst offenders on both counts. I feel that the debate has been framed too crudely. The issue is not belief in a universal, essential female personality structure, but this: Does the fact that females, in all our cultural and individual diversity, bleed in rhythm with the moon and have the capability to grow people from our flesh (plus transform milk into food for the newborn) affect the ways women experience life? Deconstruction slams the door on that question; women's spirituality explores it. The deconstructionist "erasure of the body" is foremost a denial of the elemental power of the female body.

These and other issues are explored in a wide variety of books on women's spirituality, which address such subjects as pastoral work, contemplative expression (prayers and poems), ritual, art, literature, cultural history, psychology, and political activism. The following is a sampling of recently published works.

The poet Muriel Rukeyser wrote that if one woman told the truth about her life, the world would split open. That seems to be the goal of *Sermons Seldom Heard:*

Women Proclaim Their Lives (Crossroad, $15.95), edited by Annie Lally Milhaven. A few years ago, it occurred to Milhaven, a former nun, that she had been listening to sermons for 50 years and had never heard one about the suffering that typically befalls women and children: surviving incest, battering, rape, depression, the financial struggles of single mothers, and unwanted divorce for middle-aged wives. She commissioned sermons on these and other topics from women with and without theological academic degrees who had lived through the particular hell discussed in each piece. The power of this collection results from the wrenching personal stories combined with the commonplace occurrence (according to statistics) of such violations. The silence of religious institutions on these topics has long protected the violators. This book is intended for two audiences: clergy, and women who find themselves in the situations described and who might be inspired by learning how other women freed themselves through spiritual self-empowerment that led to action. Each sermon is followed by a factual presentation on the syndrome or situation, a reading list, and a list of relevant organizations. I hope this book will be put into the hands of every clergy person in the country with a simple message: *Here! Pick any three and read them aloud for your next three sermons! Break the silence!*

Feminist theology's emphasis on articulating women's experience as the basis of our spiritual reflections is expressed in the full flowering of *Four Centuries of Jewish Women's Spirituality* (Beacon Press, $18), edited by Ellen M. Umansky and Dianne Ashton. The pieces are arranged in four chronological groupings: "1560–1800: Traditional Voices"; "1800–1890: Stronger Voices"; "1890–1960: Urgent Voices"; and "1960–1990: Contemporary Voices." Piety, the inculcating of spiritual values, and friendship are the informing themes that link the diversity of contributions. A related anthology is *A Ceremonies Sampler: New Rites, Celebrations, and Observances of Jewish Women* (Woman's Institute for Continuing Jewish Education, $9.95), edited by Elizabeth Resnick Levine. By inviting 22 women to describe rituals they have created to mark passages, events, or healing, Levine is providing models to inspire her Jewish sisterhood. The book succeeds in demonstrating that the creation of effective ceremonies is within the reach of grass-roots women, but the examples selected often fail to reach the poetic depth of ritual pieces in the previous book.

Woman-centered spiritual traditions are valued by Annette Van Dyke because they offer a bridge between lesbian and heterosexual feminists and because they honor "the female principle," which she defines as the force that creates, nourishes, and transmutes everything in the cosmos. In *The Search for a Woman-Centered Spirituality* (New York University Press, $13.95), she interprets novels and nonfiction by women in spiritual traditions "outside of the dominant Euro-American culture's ideas of religion": Leslie Marmon Silko, Paula Gunn Allen, the late Audre Lorde, Alice Walker, Starhawk, Marion Zimmer Bradley, Sonia Johnson, and Mary Daly. Van Dyke concludes that the works she explores by these authors are healing ceremonies, and she demonstrates an understanding of the profoundly political nature of self-defining that is core to feminist spirituality.

In *The Dancing Goddess: Principles of a Matriarchal Aesthetic* (Beacon Press, $17.95), Heide Göttner-Abendroth presents an insightful feminist rebuttal of the patriarchal assumptions embedded in both formalist and neo-Marxist theories of art. She suggests a radical conceptualization of art as cosmologically grounded processes of self-healing and "complex social counterpractice." This book was originally published in Germany in 1982. Most North American feminists would call Göttner-Abendroth's vision "postpatriarchal" and "Goddess-oriented" rather than "matriarchal." While her presentation of prepatriarchal, matrifocal cultures is too generalized and her prescription sometimes too doctrinaire, Göttner-Abendroth's analysis of contemporary feminist art and ritual practice illuminates the presence of a counterforce that "oversteps the system."

The Myth of the Goddess: Evolution of an Image (Viking Arkana, $40) is a substantive work of cultural history. Anne Baring and Jules Cashford, both Jungian analysts, set out to compile stories and images of Western goddess figures, beginning with Paleolithic sculptures from 20,000 B.C.E. They soon became absorbed in tracing the decline and disappearance of "the myth of the goddess," which they define as the vision of life as a living unity. They conclude that the diminishing influence of that myth throughout the Bronze and Iron Ages was paralleled by the rise of the myth of the god, which extols humanity's *dissociation* from nature. The authors were surprised to discover the extent to which Judaism and Christianity inherited the paradigm of Babylonian mythology: the influential story of Marduk's slaying of the goddess-creator (depicted for the first time as menacing and evil, in the form of Tiamat) established the concept of opposition between Creative Spirit and Chaotic Nature, introducing a range of dualistic thinking that is still with us. The book ends with musings on the possibility of reclaiming "'a goddess myth' without a Goddess"—recovering a sense of the Earth community as a sacred unity without having to believe in a literal divine being. Toward this end, the authors are encouraged by holistic discoveries of contemporary science. This comprehensive survey is written in an accessible style; the imposition of Jungian theory is minimal.

As Baring and Cashford note, what Heinrich Schliemann did for Troy, Marija Gimbutas has done for the Neolithic era of "Old Europe," unearthing the treasures of a culturally rich and advanced cluster of societies that flourished between 7000 and 3500 B.C.E. In *The Civilization of the Goddess* (HarperSanFrancisco, $50), Gimbutas draws together her pioneering work of several decades to present essential aspects of European prehistory that have not previously been treated on a pan-European scale. The book is a companion piece to *The Language of the Goddess* (HarperSanFrancisco, $24.95), which presents Gimbutas' interpretation of the symbol system of Old Europe. Gimbutas' text is clear and specific; unfortunately, admirers and critics alike have sometimes transformed her findings into a version resembling a Neolithic paradisiacal Disneyland.

The effect of negative images of the female in the West from the Bronze Age onward is pondered by Patricia Reis in *Through the Goddess: A Woman's Way of Healing*

(Continuum, $24.95). She presents a feminist analysis of ways in which "the patriarchal imagination" has structured much of psychology as a campaign against the ubiquitous "bad mother" and the supposedly looming threat of a domineering matriarchy. For a healthier alternative, Reis proposes a "feminist archetypal psychology" that focuses attention on the dynamics of our biological bodies as well as of "the cultural body," the ways in which "the female body-events" have been perceived and interpreted. Because her skillful use of archetypal theory is evocative rather than dogmatic, this wise and gentle book is a healing work.

The critical perspective of ecofeminism is the vantage point from which the theologian Rosemary Radford Ruether seeks to evaluate the heritage of Western Christian culture and to contribute to "a healed relationship" between women and men, between humans and the earth, and among nations and classes. In *Gaia & God: An Ecofeminist Theology of Earth Healing* (HarperSanFrancisco, $22), she proposes that the work of eco-justice and spirituality can best be viewed as the outer and inner aspects of transformation. Ruether begins by revealing the ideological biases in foundational belief systems of Western culture, which sacralized patriarchal relations of domination and projected evil onto nature. Drawing on her vision of a transformed, ecological version of both the sacramental and covenantal traditions within Christianity, she arrives at pragmatic, political suggestions for moving beyond patterns of destruction. The only problematic chapter in the book is on "the fall into patriarchy," in which Ruether dismisses a major theory about the origins of patriarchy in Europe that is supported by many feminist scholars without citing the main evidence for it.

Spiritual concerns combined with political activism are also the focus of *Ecofeminism and the Sacred* (Crossroad, $14.95), edited by Carol J. Adams. This multicultural anthology explores topics illuminated by the central insight of ecofeminism: the historical, political, and symbolic relationship between the domination of nature and the female. Some contributors discuss the effects of bringing ecofeminist values into institutionalized religion; all share their diverse visions, including "emergent Afrocentric ecowomanism." Interrelationship, solidarity, transformation, and embodiment are recurrent themes. Animal rights, nuclear power, abortion rights, and community resistance to degrading conditions in poor urban areas are some of the topics. This collection—the first devoted exclusively to ecofeminism and spirituality—is a thoughtful contribution to an evolving body of analysis and action.

Much of the cutting-edge political analysis of Italy today seeks to identify and   15
redress the "ethnocide" of the peasant cultures. Regarding these cultures with new respect, political theorists discover an ethos of justice, equality, and the rights of the poor—all symbolized by the living tradition of the black madonnas, according to Lucia Chiavola Birnbaum. In a fascinating study, *Black Madonnas: Feminism, Religion, and Politics in Italy* (forthcoming from Northeastern University Press, $35), she identifies the expression of contemporary Italian liberation theology in the beliefs and observances surrounding the dark (black, brown, or gray) madonnas of Italy,

whose worshipers are often fiercely anticlerical and antiestablishment. Birnbaum sees continuity between those earth-based images of the sacred female and their Neolithic predecessors found on or near the same sites. She asserts that Italy is currently undergoing a cultural revolution through the delegitimizing of patriarchal symbols and the rise of "heretical old/new vernacular beliefs."

The range of these books demonstrates feminist spirituality's challenge to the modern compartmentalization that limits spiritual concerns to the private realm. A full, rich unfolding of the person cannot proceed when society is distorted by a manipulative political economy in which survival depends on relentless competition, orchestrated greed, and a callous disregard for others. Women's spirituality seeks a renewed understanding that being is being-in relation and that the web of life deserves attentive care.

The Responsive Reader

1. What "common ground" underlying current writing about women's spirituality does Spretnak sketch out early in her review? Do you recognize major concerns or recurrent themes? (How does Spretnak explain that religion has often become a divisive force?) What typical or shared experiences are seen as uniting women in a book like *Sermons Seldom Heard*?

2. Traditionally, spirit and body have been seen as opposed principles in a dualistic view of human nature. (Have you seen evidence of this opposition?) How and why is this dualism revised in the writings reviewed here? What relationship to the female body is assumed or promoted by these writers?

3. What is ecofeminism? Where in this review do you see evidence of feminist views of connectedness with nature as contrasted with male views of nature as untamed or evil? What are some of the watchwords or recurrent themes invoked here under this heading? Can you help make them meaningful to your classmates?

4. To judge from this review, what are the concerns of "liberation theology"? What major charges are brought against the contemporary political and economic system toward the end of this review?

For Discussion or Writing

5. Do you agree that our modern society or the prevailing modern world view "devalues and marginalizes spiritual concerns in general"? To judge from your own experience and observation, how strong are religious or spiritual forces today?

6. To advance the cause of women, should feminists play up or play down differences between the sexes? To promote true equality, should we emphasize or deemphasize gender-specific qualities?

Collaborative Projects

7. What can you find out about prehistoric earth mothers or mother goddesses? Working with a group, what background can you assemble on female deities like Ishtar, Astarte, Isis, Demeter, Aphrodite, or Artemis? What are current feminist perspectives on the worship of the Virgin Mary?

Making Connections

8. Can you trace shared feminist concerns or an underlying feminist perspective in Spretnak's essay and in the selections by Lisbet Koerner (Chapter 1), Toni Morrison (Chapter 4), and Jessica Hagedorn (Chapter 5)? Or are there major differences in emphasis or point of view?

AMERICA'S EMERGING GAY CULTURE

Randall E. Majors

<hr>

As traditional taboos erode, society has been redefining the status of gays and lesbians in law, in the workplace, in the churches, and in the military. For politicians, employers, and the courts, sexual orientation becomes a test case of their readiness to accept or condemn evolving values. Are we as a society ready to understand and accept gay and lesbian lifestyles, rights, and responsibilities? Are we ready to leave stereotypes and prejudices behind? Or are we in for a homophobic backlash, demonizing homosexuality along with abortion and the United Nations? Randall E. Majors of the California State University at Hayward wrote the following article for a volume of readings on intercultural communication. He sees the gay community as solidifying a new sense of identity and solidarity that is an affirmation of the "American vision of freedom and opportunity."

A gay culture, unique in the history of homosexuality, is emerging in America. 1
Gay people from all walks of life are forging new self-identity concepts, discovering new political and social power, and building a revolutionary new life style. As more people "come out," identifying themselves as gay, and join with others to work and live as openly gay people, a stronger culture takes shape with each passing year.

There have always been homosexual men and women, but never before has there emerged the notion of a distinct "culture" based on being gay. A useful way to analyze this emerging gay culture is to observe the communication elements by which gay people construct their life styles and social institutions. Lesbians and gay men, hereafter considered together as gay people, are creating a new community in the midst of the American melting pot. They are building social organizations, exercising political power, and solidifying a unique sense of identity—often under repressive and sometimes dangerous conditions. The following essay is an analysis of four major communication elements of the American gay culture: the gay neighborhood, gay social groups, gay symbols, and gay meeting behavior. These communication behaviors will demonstrate the vibrancy and joy that a new culture offers the American vision of individual freedom and opportunity.

THE GAY NEIGHBORHOOD

Most cultural groups find the need to mark out a home turf. American social history has many examples of ethnic and social groups who create their own special communities, whether by withdrawing from the larger culture or by forming specialized groups within it. The utopian communities of the Amish or Shakers are examples of the first, and ghetto neighborhoods in large urban areas are examples of the latter.

This need to create a group territory fulfills several purposes for gay people. First, a gay person's sense of identity is reinforced if there is a special place that is somehow imbued with "gayness." When a neighborhood becomes the home of many gay people, the ground is created for a feeling of belonging and sharing with others. Signs of gayness, whether overt symbols like rainbow flags or more subtle cues such as merely the presence of other gay people on the street, create the feeling that a certain territory is special to the group and hospitable to the group's unique values.

How do you know when a neighborhood is gay? As with any generality, the   5
rule of thumb is that "enough gay people in a neighborhood and it becomes a gay neighborhood." Rarely do gay people want to paint the streetlamps lavender, but the presence of many more subtle factors gives a gay character to an area. The most subtle cues are the presence of gay people as they take up residence in a district. Word spreads in the group that a certain area is starting to look attractive and open to gay members. There is often a move to "gentrify" older, more affordable sections of a city and build a new neighborhood out of the leftovers from the rush to the suburbs. Gay businesses, those operated by or catering to gay people, often develop once enough clientele is in the area. Social groups and services emerge that are oriented toward the members of the neighborhood. Eventually, the label of "gay neighborhood" is placed on an area, and the transformation is complete. The Castro area in San Francisco, Greenwich Village in New York, New Town in Chicago, the Westheimer district in Houston, and West Hollywood or Silver Lake in Los Angeles are examples of the many emergent gay neighborhoods in cities across America.

A second need fulfilled by the gay neighborhood is the creation of a meeting ground. People can recognize and meet each other more easily when a higher density of like population is established. It is not easy to grow up gay in America; gay people often feel "different" because of their sexual orientations. The surrounding heterosexual culture often tries to imprint on everyone sexual behaviors and expectations that do not suit gay natures. Because of this pressure, gay people often feel isolated and alienated, and the need for a meeting ground is very important. Merely knowing that there is a specific place where other gay people live and work and play does much to anchor the psychological aspects of gayness in a tangible, physical reality. A gay person's sense of identity is reinforced by knowing that there is a home base, or a safe place where others of a similar persuasion are nearby.

Gay neighborhoods reinforce individual identity by focusing activities and events for members of the group. Celebrations of group unity and pride, demonstrations of group creativity and accomplishment, and services to individual members' needs are more easily developed when they are centralized. Gay neighborhoods are host to all the outward elements of a community–parades, demon-strations, car washes, basketball games, petition signing, street fairs, and garage sales.

A critical purpose for gay neighborhoods is that of physical and psychological safety. Subcultural groups usually experience some degree of persecution and op-pression from the larger surrounding culture. For gay people, physical safety is a very real concern–incidences of homophobic assaults or harassment are common in most American cities. By centralizing gay activities, some safeguards can be mounted, as large numbers of gay people living in proximity create a deterrence to violence. This may be informal awareness of the need to take extra precautions and to be on the alert to help other gay people in distress or in the form of actual street patrols or social groups, such as Community United Against Violence in San Fran-cisco. A sense of psychological safety follows from these physical measures. Group consciousness raising on neighborhood safety and training in safety practices cre-ate a sense of group cohesion. The security inspired by the group thus creates a psychic comfort that offsets the paranoia that can be engendered by alienation and individual isolation.

Another significant result of gay neighborhoods is the political reality of "clout." In the context of American grassroots democracy, a predominantly gay population in an area can lead to political power. The concerns of gay people are taken more seriously by politicians and elected officials representing an area where voters can be registered and mustered into service during elections. In many areas, openly gay politicians represent gay constituencies directly and voice their concerns in ever-widening forums. The impact of this kind of democracy-in-action is felt on other institutions as well: police departments, social welfare agencies, schools, churches, and businesses. When a group centralizes its energy, members can bring pressure to bear on other cultural institutions, asking for and demanding attention to the unique needs of that group. Since American culture has a strong tradition of cultural diversity, gay neighborhoods are effective agents in the larger cultural acceptance of gay people. The gay rights movement, which attempts to se-cure housing, employment, and legal protection for gay people, finds its greatest support in the sense of community created by gay neighborhoods.

GAY SOCIAL GROUPS

On a smaller level than the neighborhood, specialized groups fulfill the social   10
needs of gay people. The need for affiliation–to make friends, to share recreation, to find life partners, or merely to while away the time–is a strong drive in any group of people. Many gay people suffer from an isolation caused by rejection by other people or by their own fear of being discovered as belonging to an unpopular group. This homophobia leads to difficulty in identifying and meeting other gay

people who can help create a sense of dignity and caring. This is particularly true for gay teenagers who have limited opportunities to meet other gay people. Gay social groups serve the important function of helping gay people locate each other so that this affiliation need can be met.

The development of gay social groups depends to a large degree on the number of gay people in an area and the perceived risk factor. In smaller towns and cities, there are often no meeting places, which exacerbates the problem of isolation. In some small towns a single business may be the only publicly known meeting place for gay people within hundreds of miles. In larger cities, however, an elaborate array of bars, clubs, social groups, churches, service agencies, entertainment groups, stores, restaurants, and the like add to the substance of a gay culture.

The gay bar is often the first public gay experience for a gay person, and it serves as a central focus for many people. Beyond the personal need of meeting potential relationship partners, the gay bar also serves the functions of entertainment and social activity. Bars offer a wide range of attractions suited to gay people: movies, holiday celebrations, dancing, costume parties, live entertainment, free meals, boutiques, and meeting places for social groups. Uniquely gay forms of entertainment, such as drag shows and disco dancing, were common in gay bars before spreading into the general culture. Bars often become a very central part of a community's social life by sponsoring athletic teams, charities, community services, and other events as well as serving as meeting places.

The centrality of the bar in gay culture has several drawbacks, however. Young gay people are denied entrance because of age restrictions, and there may be few other social outlets for them. A high rate of alcoholism among urban gay males is prominent. With the spread of Acquired Immune Deficiency Syndrome (AIDS), the use of bars for meeting sexual partners has declined dramatically as gay people turn to developing more permanent relationships.

Affiliation needs remain strong despite these dangers, however, and alternative social institutions arise that meet these needs. In large urban areas, where gay culture is more widely-developed, social groups include athletic organizations that sponsor teams and tournaments; leisure activity clubs in such areas as country-and-western dance, music, yoga, bridge, hiking, and recreation; religious groups such as Dignity (Roman Catholic), Integrity (Episcopal), and the Metropolitan Community Church (MCC); volunteer agencies such as information and crisis hotlines and charitable organizations; and professional and political groups such as the Golden Gate Business Association of San Francisco or the national lobby group, the Gay Rights Task Force. A directory of groups and services is usually published in urban gay newspapers, and their activities are reported on and promoted actively. Taken together, these groups compose a culture that supports and nourishes a gay person's life.

GAY SYMBOLS

Gay culture is replete with symbols. These artifacts spring up and constantly   15
evolve as gayness moves from an individual, personal experience into a more
complex public phenomenon. All groups express their ideas and values in symbols, and the gay culture, in spite of its relatively brief history, has been quite creative in symbol making.

The most visible category of symbols is in the semantics of gay establishment
names. Gay bars, bookstores, restaurants, and social groups want to be recognized
and patronized by gay people, but they do not want to incur hostility from the
general public. This was particularly true in the past when the threat of social consequences was greater. In earlier days, gay bars, the only major form of gay establishment, went by code words such as "blue" or "other"—the Blue Parrot, the Blue
Goose, the Other Bar, and Another Place.

Since the liberalization of culture after the 1960s, semantics have blossomed
in gay place names. The general trend is still to identify the place as gay, either
through affiliation (Our Place or His 'N' Hers), humor (the White Swallow or
Uncle Charley's), high drama (the Elephant Walk or Backstreet), or sexual suggestion (Ripples, Cheeks, or Rocks). Lesbians and gay men differ in this aspect of their
cultures. Lesbian place names often rely upon a more personal or classical referent
(Amanda's Place or the Artemis Cafe), while hypermasculine referents are commonly used for gay male meeting places (the Ramrod, Ambush, Manhandlers, the
Mine Shaft, the Stud, or Boots). Gay restaurants and nonpornographic bookstores
usually reflect more subdued names, drawing upon cleverness or historical associations: Dos Hermanos, Women and Children First, Diana's, the Oscar Wilde
Memorial Bookstore, and Walt Whitman Bookstore. More commonly, gay establishments employ general naming trends of location, ownership, or identification of
product or service similar to their heterosexual counterparts. The increasing tendency of business to target and cater to gay markets strengthens the growth and
diversity of gay culture.

A second set of gay symbols are those that serve as member-recognition factors. In past ages such nonverbal cues were so popular as to become mythical: the
arched eyebrow of Regency England, the green carnation of Oscar Wilde's day, and
the "green shirt on Thursday" signal of mid-century America. A large repertoire of
identifying characteristics has arisen in recent years that serves the functions of recognizing other gay people and focusing on particular interests. In the more sexually promiscuous period of the 1970s, popular identifying symbols were a ring of
keys worn on the belt, either left or right depending upon sexual passivity or aggressiveness, and the use of colored handkerchiefs in a rear pocket coded to desired
types of sexual activity. Political sentiments are commonly expressed through buttons, such as the "No on 64" campaign against the LaRouche initiative in California

in 1986. The pink triangle as a political symbol recalls the persecution and annihilation of gay people in Nazi Germany. The lambda symbol, an ancient Greek referent, conjures up classical images of gay freedom of expression. Stud earrings for men are gay symbols in some places, though such adornment has evolved and is widely used for the expression of general countercultural attitudes. The rainbow and the unicorn, mythical symbols associated with supernatural potency, also are common signals of gay enchantment, fairy magic, and spiritual uniqueness to the more "cosmic" elements of the gay community.

Another set of gay symbols to be aware of are the images of gay people as portrayed in television, film, literature, and advertising. The general heterosexual culture controls these media forms to a large extent, and the representations of gay people in those media take on a straight set of expectations and assumptions. The results are stereotypes that often oversimplify gay people and their values and do not discriminate the subtleties of human variety in gay culture. Since these stereotypes are generally unattractive, they are often the target of protests by gay people. Various authors have addressed the problem of heterosexual bias in the areas of film and literature. As American culture gradually becomes more accepting of and tolerant toward gay people, these media representations become more realistic and sympathetic, but progress in this area is slow.

One hopeful development in the creation of positive gay role models has been   20
the rise of an active gay market for literature. Most large cities have bookstores that stock literature supportive of gay culture. A more positive image for gay people is created through gay characters, heroes, and stories that deal with the important issues of family, relationship, and social responsibility. This market is constantly threatened by harsh economic realities, however, and gay literature is not as well developed as it might be.

Advertising probably has done the most to popularize and integrate gay symbols into American culture. Since money making is the goal of advertising, the use of gay symbols has advanced more rapidly in ad media than in the arts. Widely quoted research suggests that gay people, particularly men, have large, disposable incomes, so they become popular target markets for various products: tobacco, body-care products, clothing, alcohol, entertainment, and consumer goods. Typical gay-directed advertising in these product areas includes appeals based upon male bonding, such as are common in tobacco and alcohol sales ads, which are attractive to both straight and gay men since they stimulate the bonding need that is a part of both cultures.

Within gay culture, advertising has made dramatic advances in the past ten years, due to the rise of gay-related businesses and products. Gay advertising appears most obviously in media specifically directed at gay markets, such as gay magazines and newspapers, and in gay neighborhoods. Gay products and services are publicized with many of the same means as are their straight counterparts. Homoerotic art is widely used in clothing and body-care product ads. The male and female body are displayed for their physical and sexual appeal. This eroticizing of the body may be directed at either women or men as a desirable sexual object, and perhaps strikes at a subconscious homosexual potential in all people. Prominent elements of gay advertising are its use of sexuality and the central appeal of hyper-masculinization. With the rise of sexual appeals in general advertising through double entendre, sexual punning, subliminal seduction, and erotic art work, it may be that gay advertising is only following suit in its emphasis on sexual appeals. Hugely muscled bodies and perfected masculine beauty adorn most advertising for gay products and services. Ads for greeting cards, billboards for travel service, bars, hotels, restaurants, and clothing stores tingle to the images of Hot 'N' Hunky Hamburgers, Hard On Leather, and the Brothel Hotel or its crosstown rival, the Anxious Arms. Some gay writers criticize this use of advertising as stereotyping and distorting of gay people, and certainly, misconceptions about the diversity in gay culture are more common than understanding. Gay people are far more average and normal than the images that appear in public media would suggest.

GAY MEETING BEHAVIOR

The final element of communication in the gay culture discussed here is the vast set of behaviors by which gay people recognize and meet one another. In more sexually active days before the concern for AIDS, this type of behavior was commonly called cruising. Currently, promiscuous sexual behavior is far less common than it once was, and cruising has evolved into a more standard meeting behavior that helps identify potential relationship partners.

Gay people meet each other in various contexts: in public situations, in the workplace, in gay meeting places, and in the social contexts of friends and acquaintances. Within each context, a different set of behaviors is employed by which gay people recognize someone else as gay and determine the potential for establishing a relationship. These behaviors include such nonverbal signaling as frequency and length of interaction, posture, proximity, eye contact, eye movement and facial gestures, touch, affect displays, and paralinguistic signals. The constraints of each situation and the personal styles of the communicators create great differences in the effectiveness and ease with which these behaviors are displayed.

Cruising serves several purposes besides the recognition of other gay people. 25 Most importantly, cruising is an expression of joy and pride in being gay. Through cruising, gay people communicate their openness and willingness to interact. Being gay is often compared to belonging to a universal–though invisible–fraternity or sorority. Gay people are generally friendly and open to meeting other gay people in social contexts because of the common experience of rejection and isolation they have had growing up. Cruising is the means by which gay people communicate their gayness and bridge the gap between stranger and new-found friend.

Cruising has become an integral part of gay culture because it is such a commonplace behavior. Without this interpersonal skill–and newcomers to gay life often complain of the lack of comfort or ease they have with cruising–a gay person can be at a distinct disadvantage in finding an easy path into the mainstream of gay culture. While cruising has a distinctly sexual overtone, the sexual subtext is often a symbolic charade. Often the goals of cruising are no more than friendship, companionship, or conversation. In this sense, cruising becomes more an art form or an entertainment. Much as the "art of conversation" was the convention of a more genteel cultural age, gay cruising is the commonly accepted vehicle of gay social interaction. The sexual element, however, transmitted by double meaning, clever punning, or blatant nonverbal signals, remains a part of cruising in even the most innocent of circumstances.

In earlier generations, a common stereotype of gay men focused on the use of exaggerated, dramatic, and effeminate body language–the "limp wrist" image. Also included in this negative image of gay people was cross-gender dressing, known as "drag," and a specialized, sexually suggestive argot called "camp." Some gay people assumed these social roles because that was the picture of "what it meant to be gay," but by and large these role behaviors were overthrown by the gay liberation of the 1970s. Gay people became much less locked into these restraining stereotypes and developed a much broader means of social expression. Currently, no stereotypic behavior would adequately describe gay communication style–it is far too diverse and integrated into mainstream American culture. Cruising evolved from these earlier forms of communication, but as a quintessential gay behavior, cruising has replaced the bitchy camp of an earlier generation of gay people.

The unique factor in gay cruising, and the one that distinguishes it from heterosexual cruising, is the level of practice and refinement the process receives. All cultural groups have means of introduction and meeting, recognition, assessment, and negotiation of a new relationship. In gay culture, however, the "courtship ritual" or friendship ritual of cruising is elaborately refined in its many variants and contexts. While straight people may use similar techniques in relationship formation and development, gay people are uniquely self-conscious in the centrality of these signals to the perpetuation of their culture. There is a sense of adventure and discovery in being "sexual outlaws," and cruising is the shared message of commitment to the gay life style.

CONCLUSION

These four communication elements of gay culture comprise only a small part of what might be called gay culture. Other elements have been more widely discussed elsewhere: literature, the gay press, religion, politics, art, theater, and relationships. Gay culture is a marvelous and dynamic phenomenon, driven and buffeted by the energies of intense feeling and creative effort. Centuries of cultural repression that condemned gay people to disgrace and persecution have been turned upside down in a brief period of history. The results of this turbulence have the potential for either renaissance or cataclysm. The internalized fear and hatred of repression is balanced by the incredible joy and idealism of liberation. Through the celebration of its unique life style, gay culture promises to make a great contribution to the history of sexuality and to the rights of the individual. Whether it will fulfill this promise or succumb to the pressures that any creative attempt must face remains to be seen.

The Responsive Reader

1. According to Majors, what is the culture of a gay neighborhood? What busi nesses, social groups, or civic initiatives give it its character? What patterns of friendship or socializing have evolved?

2. What role do symbols play in the gay community? Is there a shared language that insiders know and that outgroups the outsider?

3. What is the media image of gays? According to this article, do the media reinforce stereotypes, or do they promote understanding or tolerance?

4. How does the gay community cope with homophobia? How does it deal with rejection, discrimination, gay-bashing? How does homophobia affect outlook or behavior in the gay community?

5. According to Majors, what negative stereotypes is the gay community trying to leave behind?

For Discussion or Writing

6. What has shaped your own assumptions about gays and lesbians? What has been your own observation of increased acceptance or of a homophobic backlash?

7. How effective is Majors as a voice for the gay community? Is he being defensive? Is he persuasive? (Will anything change the attitudes of conservative readers?)

8. A familiar assumption of today's feminists is that the personal is also political. Is the same true for the gay community? Do you think it is possible to keep sexual orientation a matter of private choice, or does it inevitably become a social or political issue?

Collaborative Projects

9. What is the status of gays and lesbians in the churches? in the colleges? in the military? in law? Working with a group, you may want to investigate the current status of gays and lesbians in one major area of American life.

CHAOS AND COMPLEXITY
An Approaching Reality

Bryan Sun

━━━━

> *Chaos theory has become a buzzword as futurists warn us not to trust in traditional certainties in a discontinuous universe. How does chaos theory ask us to revise our thinking about the physical world? What is the appeal of chaos theory to scholars in different disciplines? The following research paper on chaos theory was first printed in a newsletter published by instructors in the writing program at Stanford University. The paper documents a paradigm shift—the kind of change in basic assumptions that makes us look at many different things from a new and perhaps revolutionary perspective. Bryan Sun, who had earlier written a paper on intergenerational expectations in a Chinese American family, said about the history of his chaos paper:*
> A year ago, I read an article in the *Scientific American* about the thoughts of several scientists who subscribed to a new type of ideology—chaos theory. I didn't think much of it until I saw the movie *Jurassic Park*, and there was that phrase again—chaos theory. Then during a dinner conversation someone mentioned computer chips, and—here's the huge surprise—chaos theory. Resolved to understand the phrase, I picked up an article about it in the library, got interested, dug up a few more articles, and before I knew it I had a research paper that almost wrote itself.

In the movie *Jurassic Park*, scientists attempt to recreate real dinosaurs from pre-   1
served DNA. To insure that the dinosaurs do not escape, the scientists develop them on a remote island near Costa Rica. When the critic and mathematician Ian Malcolm enters the scene, however, he quickly pronounces Jurassic Park doomed to failure. Malcolm, a new-age chaos theory mathematician, says "[Jurassic Park] is another apparently simple system—animals within a zoo environment—that will eventually show unpredictable behavior . . . [because of] chaos theory." He is quickly proven right, as the dinosaurs capitalize on a human mistake and begin to destroy the island.

Unfortunately, the sensational special effects of Jurassic Park obscure an important concept that arises in the movie—chaos theory. Chaos theory states that some systems are so incredibly sensitive and intricate that it is impossible to forecast or control their future. Complexity theory, a sister theory to chaos, lies at the borderline between chaos and order, and is a branch of theory that deals with systems that appear chaotic, but actually can be controlled or understood.[1] Together, these theories explain the unpredictable nature of clouds and weather, the preservation of species, and even the beating of the human heart. Yet, despite the ubiquitous nature of chaos and complexity theory, until recently no one has really discovered how to use nature's chaotic behavior to society's advantage. The emerging applications of complexity and chaos theory to contemporary economics, business, medicine, and technology represent a drastic paradigm shift from accepted modes of thought, and as a result the world marketplace of ideas and technology is not greeting them with open arms. Due to the potential power locked within these theories, people and companies that first learn to reconceptualize their work on the basis of chaos and complexity theory will advance their fields in ways that their conventional-thinking counterparts will not even dream of.

What's the most intuitive way to predict the future? Well, to most people, the logical place to start is by analyzing general trends and major events of recent history. But to the chaologist, this approach is wrong. Chaologists believe that small, seemingly insignificant events can snowball into significant events in the future. James Gleick, author of Chaos, points to an explanatory folklore example: "For the want of a nail, the shoe was lost; for the want of a shoe, the horse was lost; for want of the horse, the rider was lost . . ." In this tale, the seemingly unimportant event of losing a nail eventually leads to the downfall of the entire kingdom. Chaologists have their own term for this multiplier effect which they call the "Butterfly Effect." The Butterfly Effect says that if a butterfly flaps its wings in Brazil, it can set off a tornado in Texas.[2] Small change in initial conditions, big change in outcome. This is a central tenet of chaos theory.

The Butterfly Effect has convinced some professionals to reconceptualize the fundamental ideas of their fields. William Brian Arthur, a Stanford economist, embraced the Butterfly Effect and applied it to economics. While traditional economists analyzed markets by studying general trends, Arthur began to wonder whether or not small, "insignificant" business changes could eventually blossom into huge market effects. Traditional economists also saw the market linearly: if a company (1) discovered a way to lower production costs, then (2) they could lower market cost, which would lead to (3) greater consumer demand. Each event would be a link in the 1-2-3 causal chain, and everything seemed to work logically and chronologically. Unfortunately, the linear theory wasn't always accurate. Chaologists, like Arthur, believed that the 1-2-3 chain might not always work as planned, since small perturbations to an economic system might disrupt the overall flow. Of course, if Arthur was right, then it would be increasingly difficult to predict the actions of the market, since billions of small, disruptive changes occur daily.

Arthur's introduction of a chaotic economic paradigm represents a nascent   5
movement on Wall Street to listen to the ideas of chaos theory. Chaologists' methodology differs from traditional economics, which bases its ideas on the belief of maximum-efficiency markets. Traditional economics says that all people and business will act towards maximum efficiency and profit. Arthur disagrees, however, pointing to several examples entrenched in modern technology. The modern

QWERTY keyboard, for example, is not an efficient placement of keys; there are better ways to arrange the keys that would increase typing speed. In fact, the current keyboard design was conjured by an engineer who wanted to slow down typists because fast typing used to break old typewriters. If the world ran by the conventional, "maximum efficiency" economics, a company should have designed and marketed a more efficient keyboard–and yet, it hasn't happened.

Chaologists also disagree with conventional economics in another way. They simply point out that humans make business mistakes. Traditional economics says businessmen will almost always strive for their own benefit; they will stamp out competitors without hesitation, and they will closely follow market trends. Chaos marketing, however, tries to account for the fact that businessmen are human; that they might help fellow companies out of kindness, or that they might buy or sell stock purely out of impulse and no other motivation. This new perspective, which drastically revises traditional economics, has a strong potential to be the foundation of future economic systems. "Chaologists have the potential to revitalize the money-management industry. That's because chaos theory turns portfolio theory[3] on its ear by tossing out its central tenets–that investors act rationally and that markets are efficient" (G. Weiss 139).

Though chaos marketing sounds ideal, it is quite difficult, since it requires an economic model that can successfully predict human emotions and anticipate seemingly unpredictable behavior. However, this intimidating barrier has not stopped the economists' world from taking baby steps into actually using chaos theory. For example, J. Doyne Farmer, a former physicist at Los Alamos National Laboratory, recently founded Prediction Company, a chaos-based investment firm. Located in Albuquerque, Prediction Company uses computerized biological models of the stock market to predict stock trends. Since chaos theorists believe that nature's chaotic behavior mimics itself in many other man-made systems, the stock market to a chaologist can be modeled after a living organism. In most basic terms, a computerized biological organism will display a certain amount of chaotic fluctuation. Theoretically, an economic system should display a similar amount of chaotic behavior if the model is accurate. If chaos theory is right, biological chaos modeling has a probabilistic advantage over a conventional business predictor. As Farmer states, "'If I can be right 55% of the time, that's enough to make plenty of money'" (Lemonick 62). The "chaotic" ideas of Prediction Company have become a reality. The company has already modeled economic systems using biological models, and has easily topped a 55% success rate.

While chaos theory has the potential to change the loud business bustle of New York's Wall Street, it will also revolutionize the way people understand the tranquil life cycle of Brazilian rainforest flora. Ecologists are among the people most excited by the prospects of chaos theory in opening up new doors for their research. Nature itself doesn't perform lineally, and ecologists of the past have had trouble explaining ecological trends. For instance, one might naturally think that richer soil would naturally be able to sustain the largest yield of healthy plants. However, this is not true, as Dr. David Tilman and Dr. David Wedin argue in their 1991 study published in Nature. They found that the best soil for plants is not the richest or the poorest soil, but somewhere in between. Plants that grow on the richest soil grow rapidly and successfully for one year, but then the plants tend to die out and cover the soil, preventing light from reaching the surface of the earth beneath. As a result, the next generation of plants undergoes a population crash. Predicting the optimal fertilizer content of the soil (its richness) with a linear system is difficult because studies have shown that small initial differences in fertilizer content produce huge differences in resulting crop growth. However, chaos theorists can use computer models to simulate initial fertilizer conditions and allow the computer to predict the probable crop yields over, say, a decade. By playing with the initial conditions, chaos theorists can find an optimal fertilizer richness. Ecologists can then apply this information to predict the life of ecosystems or to improve crop yields for farmers.

The ability of ecologists to recognize a chaotic element in nature will have particularly important repercussions on the environment. If ecologists learn to successfully model an ecosystem using chaos theory and computer models, then they will learn how to successfully control ecosystems by altering select conditions. Dr. William Schaffer, a pioneer in ecological chaos, believes that ecological modeling "in principle" may be a viable possibility. Ecologists see this as an important goal, especially since the impact of humans on the environment continues to grow with the increasing population and its use of technology. In addition, more and more ecologists are seeing applications of chaos to ecological systems. As Tilman says, "There is a good chance that many ecological systems are going to have chaotic dynamics in them. In ecosystems with more than one species, he said, chaos is even more likely" (Stevens 4).

The presence of chaotic behavior in natural systems is good news for humans   10
and the rest of the flora and fauna. While many people might intuitively think that nature would thrive without humans, chaos theory disagrees. Proof of the existence of chaos in nature shows that ecosystems can have massive growth and decay swings even without the presence of humans. This provides a greater responsibility and justification for humans to try to understand ecosystems and to help them thrive. In another sense, however, chaotic behavior in nature can also help nature survive. For instance, chaos can provide a protective cushion to prevent species extinction. "[C]haos can provide significant protection against extinction by increasing the degree of asynchrony among local populations. This result is consistent with recent conclusions that subdividing a population can stabilize systems that would otherwise go extinct with probability one" (Allen 232). The concept is the same; small differences in the animal population lead to large diver-

sity in succeeding generations, which turns out to be a saving grace for animal populations.

Despite all the evidence, though, chaos is still counter–intuitive. Surely what is "natural" does not necessarily have to be "chaotic." Right? This belief in natural order has permeated the entire world for centuries. Yet when cardiologists at Harvard Medical School closely examined electrocardiograms (EKGs), they found that healthy, natural heartbeats were extremely chaotic. Their findings represent only one of the many incipient applications of chaos theory to the field of health and medicine. What cardiologist Ary Goldberger found was that "healthy hearts behave in a chaotic manner, while so–called 'abnormal' rhythms of diseased hearts reflect a loss of chaotic behavior that could herald sudden cardiac arrest" (Peterson 156). Goldberger's studies on chaotic behavior in cardiology could usher in a new method of predicting heart attacks. By monitoring the chaotic level of a person's heartbeat, one could effectively know when a heart attack is coming before it actually occurs.

Goldberger's use of chaos theory as a prevention–oriented medical tool applies directly to other health fields, most notably that of epidemiology. In the past, predicting and controlling the outbreak of diseases was difficult, because it seemed to occur so chaotically. But Dr. Schaffer, the chaos ecologist, has built successful epidemiological models that accurately explain and anticipate general rates and locations of epidemic spreading. In one study, traditional epidemiologists tried to use conventional models to explain outbreaks of chicken pox and measles, but failed to produce a satisfying model. Schaffer, however, generated a two dimensional phase-space "chaos map," called a Poincaré map, that successfully explained all the data: "Schaffer's model also predicted the consequences of damping the dynamics by mass inoculation programs–consequences that could not be predicted by standard epidemiology" (Gleick 316). If future epidemiologists expand the applications of chaos theory to their work, they may find themselves able to control once–intractable epidemics. Chaos theory may play a role in tracking and stemming the growth of AIDS and suppress resurgences of diseases such as tuberculosis. Schaffer's pioneer work clearly succeeded because of chaos theory, but his methodology and modeling still need scientific acceptance and approval before his effort makes any more than a small dent in the future of health care.

Any good trend will probably hit the consumer market, sooner or later, and chaos theory is no exception. Once chaos theory passed initial scrutiny by people of different fields, it began to show up in more commercial products. South Korea's Goldstar Company in the past few months has marketed a chaos theory-based washing machine: "Analyzing the movements of water in a standard washing machine, [Goldstar] identified those that produce cleaner, less-tangled clothes, then built a 'chaos' washer that produces these motions" (Paisley 84). Experts predict that Goldstar's lock on chaos-products will make it the leader of washing machine sales next year. The Asian appliance market can expect other chaos–products soon: "Electric fans and other electrical appliances using chaos-logic controls may appear in shops this year, [engineering professor Kazuyuki Aihara] adds. Several computer software companies are already offering services that use chaos–engineering to help predict stock prices and the weather" (Ono 41). It is important to note, however, that so far chaos theory is more of an advertising launching pad and not yet a serious engineering asset to Asian companies. Several companies promise they will market chaos products, but the actual release of such products is occurring at a moderate pace. Especially in Europe and the United States, chaos products still wait to debut in the consumer marketplace.

Though the introduction of a concept to the consumer market usually hails imminent success (or at least some consumer airtime), chaos theory is still wholly unaccepted and remains a dark horse to most of the population. Many barriers prevent chaos theory from making the larger impact on society than it could, and foremost among these is the fact that chaos theory represents a paradigm shift contrary to common sense, which makes it difficult to appreciate. People from non-scientific fields are justifiably straightforward: if a new concept seems like a complex black box that does not seem to apply to their interests, they ignore it. One meeting between CEOs and business executives placed a chaologist on the podium to explain how chaos theory could apply to the stock market. The chaologist's speech was so mathematical that business executives began quipping phrases such as "Now speak English with me" (G. Weiss 140). In other fields, chaos theory is viewed skeptically because there is no concrete proof for it: "The study of chaos in ecological systems is especially difficult because they do not behave with the crispness of, say, a chemical reaction or a flow of fluid in a tube" (Stevens 4). Chaos theory's inauguration into the scientific world eerily parallels that of the introduction of Einstein's theory of relativity: for almost 20 years, Einstein's concepts were so revolutionary and difficult to grasp that only a few select individuals recognized how momentous the discovery was. This ambiguity and complexity attached to chaos theory threatens to keep it behind a veiled curtain for the coming years.

Yet, there is definitely something there. Chaos theory contains an immense pool of potential power, but so far only a few select individuals from different disciplines have dared test the waters. There should be an interest in exploring chaos theory. It may hold the key to a successful artificial heart, the control of an entire ecosystem, the survival of a species, or even a good washing machine. Yet, for all the benefits that chaos theory has to offer, the key players in the professional fields still refuse to listen. Perhaps it will take just one small change to mark the advent of chaos theory: one small discovery that will multiply into scientific interest, then public interest, then finally widespread appreciation, like the little butterfly whose small beating wings can produce the power of a tornado. When the world does finally discover the benefits of chaos, only then will actual chaos theory change into a chaos reality, and society will be better for it.

Notes

[1] Chaos and complexity theory are relatively new concepts. Their definitions have yet to be standardized, and as a result different texts use definitions that appear to overlap. Since they are related, for the purposes of simplicity this paper will use the more popular term "chaos theory," though it is important to note that there is a distinction between the two.

[2] On December 1979, meteorologist Edward Lorenz presented the paper "Predictability: Does the Flap of a Butterfly's Wings in Brazil Set Off a Tornado in Texas?" to the American Association for the Advancement of Sciences. From this, chaologists quickly adopted the idea of the "Butterfly Effect," a term which has become a catch-phrase in the world of chaos theory.

[3] Portfolio theory is the generally accepted type of economic theory.

Works Cited

Allen, J. C., W. M. Schaffer, and D. Rosko. "Chaos Reduces Species Extinction by Amplifying Local Population Noise." *Nature* 15 July 1993: 229–232.

Crichton, Michael. *Jurassic Park*. New York: Ballantine Books, 1990.

Gleick, James. *Chaos: Making a New Science*. New York: Viking Penguin Inc., 1987.

Lemonick, Michael D. "Life, the Universe, and Everything." *Time* 22 Feb. 1993: 62–63.

Ono, Takashi. "'Chaos' is Coming." *World Press Review* April 1993: 41.

Paisley, Ed. "Out of Chaos, Profits." *Business Week* 7 Oct. 1993: 84.

Peterson, Ivars, and Carol Ezzell. "Crazy Rhythms: Confronting the Complexity of Chaos in Biological Systems." *Science News* 5 Sept. 1992: 156–158.

Stevens, William K. "Balance of Nature? What Balance is That?" *New York Times* 22 Oct. 1991: C4.

Weiss, Gary. "Chaos Hits Wall Street–The Theory, That is." *Business Week* 2 Nov. 1992: 138–140.

The Responsive Reader

1. How does Sun explain the central tenets of chaos theory? Had you heard of the "butterfly effect"? For Sun, why are chaos theory and complexity theory closely related?

2. How would chaos theory challenge conventional economics? (What makes conventional economics "linear"?) What kind of elements would chaologists cause economists to factor into their equations?

3. How would chaos theory change the thinking of ecologists? How could it affect the way we look at ecosystems? How could it be "good news" for life on this planet?

4. According to Sun, what is the promise of chaos theory in the area of medicine and health? How would it affect the way products are made and marketed?

For Discussion or Writing

5. What makes chaos theory "counterintuitive"? Faced with this kind of challenge to conventional thinking, are you likely to find yourself on the side of the pioneers or on the side of the skeptics? What do you find persuasive or doubtful in this article?

6. Where have you encountered or observed the "black box" syndrome? Do we increasingly make use of a process or product without understanding how it works? Does it matter?

Making Connections

7. Sun's essay on chaos theory and the essays on evolution by Zimmer, on microorganisms by Margulis, and on quantum technology by Perkovitz (all in Chapter 1) deal with successive challenges to commonsense thinking. Are these challenges similar in major ways? Or do they represent different kinds of challenges?

FORUM: Rethinking Nuclear War

The fiftieth anniversary of the end of World War II triggered discussions reminding us of nuclear war as the great unsolved problem of our global civilization. In August 1945, the first atomic bombs obliterated the Japanese cities of Hiroshima and Nagasaki. Eye-witness accounts and documentaries recounting the agony of the victims of the atomic furnace lit by the bomb and of radiation sickness traumatized a generation. The bomb had been developed with crucial input from scientists driven from Europe by Nazi tyranny and racism. Some of the leading players in the multibillion race to build the bomb, like the physicist J. Robert Oppenheimer, had profound misgivings about helping to develop a technology with the potential of destroying humanity. Both the United States and Russia eventually developed the H-bomb, escalating the threat of mutual annihilation. Half a century later, after the philosophy of the "nuclear deterrent" had become obsolete with the collapse of the Soviet Union, much of the nuclear arsenal remained in place. In spite of much talk about nonproliferation, countries like India, Israel, and North Korea were inching closer to the capability to produce nuclear weapons. What lessons can be learned from the events of August 1945? Who will draw these lessons for us—historians, political leaders, physicists, cultural anthropologists, military strategists?

DROPPING THE A–BOMB
The Non–Event

Alan Cranston

Half a century after the beginning of the nuclear age, scholars, politicians, and journalists were still passionately debating the ethics of dropping the bomb. The script for a planned memorial exhibit at the Smithsonian Institute was revised and re-revised as revisionist historians and veterans groups fought over how to rewrite history. In the following column, Alan Cranston, long a United States Senator and a force in liberal California politics, addresses this question from the point of view of a contemporary observer and an insider of the American political establishment. He does not see the momentous historical event as the result of any one individual's personal decision. Instead he tries to reconstruct a chain of events that "had assumed a life of its own."

Hiroshima's fiftieth anniversary has set loose a torrent of magazine covers, TV   1
specials and newspaper pull-out sections re-examining the decision to drop the atomic bomb on Japan. Many have dwelled upon the morality, strategic necessity and wisdom of the decision. But, whatever the merits of those arguments, it is a

simple but startling historical fact, still virtually unknown even after a half a century, that there was never any "decision," as such. The Truman administration simply assumed that the bomb would be used as soon as it became available. The president and his advisers discussed where, when and how to drop it, but the profound moral and ethical implications of this monstrous new weapon, which bedevil scholars and statesmen to this day, escaped scrutiny.

Franklin Roosevelt and Winston Churchill had agreed in a secret memorandum on September 18, 1944, that "when a 'bomb' is finally available it might perhaps, after mature deliberation, be used against the Japanese. . . ." But no "mature deliberation" occurred. On September 22 Roosevelt asked Vannevar Bush, head of the Office of Scientific Research and Development, whether he thought the bomb should be used against Japan or employed only as a threat. No decision was made, and they agreed to table the issue temporarily. By the time we got the bomb, FDR was dead, and the memorandum, having been misfiled in the White House, was not available to Harry Truman. Truman's role, according to General Leslie R. Groves, the head of the Manhattan Project, was "one of non-interference–basically a decision not to interfere with existing plans." David McCullough's *Truman* quotes Churchill on "the decision that was not a decision."

When some of the scientists behind the Manhattan Project tried to tell Truman they thought dropping the bomb was immoral and would set off a dangerous nuclear arms race, they were shunted off to former senator and future Secretary of State James F. Byrnes, who gave their views short shrift in his own advice to Truman. The closest Truman's top officials and advisers ever came to questioning the bomb's use was the consideration given to publicly demonstrating its capacity as a warning to Japan. Yet even this brief discussion focused on the pros and cons–mostly cons–of a demonstration; it did not fundamentally question the bombing of Japan itself.

Military planning advanced unquestioned, with cold precision, in the highest secrecy. The U.S. Air Force began to practice dropping atomic bombs in the late summer of 1944. A Target Committee was established in 1945 to consider what to bomb in Japan. Truman later said, "Let there be no mistake about it. I regarded the bomb as a military weapon and never had any doubt that it should be used."

Years of war had dulled moral sensitivities toward civilian slaughter, allowing 5 policymakers to view the terrible new weapon in purely military terms. Back in 1939, before the U.S. entered the war, Roosevelt had urged both sides to avoid the "barbarism" of civilian bombings. But the Nazi Luftwaffe and the British Royal Air Force were soon engaged in bloody tit-for-tat bombings of London, Berlin and other cities, and by early 1945 the U.S. Air Force was itself participating in incendiary assaults on Dresden and Tokyo. The atomic bombing of Hiroshima and Nagasaki was seen as a logical next step rather than a leap into a new realm. Sparing innocents was a principle long since abandoned.

Truman recollected in later years that he made "the" decision to use the bomb on his way home from the Potsdam conference after Japan had rejected the Allies' demand for "unconditional surrender." He claimed to remember calling a high-level meeting at Potsdam with Byrnes, Secretary of War Henry L. Stimson, Admiral William Leahy, Generals George C. Marshall and Dwight D. Eisenhower, Navy Secretary James C. Forrestal "and some others to discuss what should be done with this awful weapon." But, in archival records and other resources, historians have been unable to find any evidence that such a "meeting" ever took place.

On August 6 and 9, 1945, it was as if portions of the sun suddenly plummeted down on Hiroshima and Nagasaki. The world, which had known nothing of the weapon, was stunned by the instant obliteration of tens of thousands of human beings. Most Americans were jubilant, convinced that with the long war over, the lives of American troops in the Pacific would be spared. Japan did surrender a few days after Hiroshima. It will never be known whether an alternative policy could have ended the war, for none was ever considered. About this time I met Albert Einstein, who warned me, as he did others, that all-out use of nuclear weapons might extinguish all life on Earth. Truman, who stoutly defended use of the bomb to the end of his days, was nevertheless aghast at the sheer and previously unimaginable human suffering and physical devastation it wrought.

The nuclear chain of events had assumed a life of its own that dwarfed the processes that gave it birth. In Stimson's words, it forever changed "the relationship of man to the universe"–without a "decision" to do so ever having been made. All of this leads to a question for today's world: How confident are we about the processes designed to deal with the nuclear dilemmas that will arise slowly, or more likely suddenly, in the days and decades to come?

The Responsive Reader

1. What does Cranston tell you that you didn't know? What inside information does Cranston have about the historical situation, major and minor players, key events, Allied strategy, or public opinion?

2. How does Cranston deal with the question of personal involvement or personal responsibility? President Truman has been held responsible for one of the great crimes against humanity. Scientists working on the bomb have been accused of selling out their ethical principles to the political and military establishment. What is Cranston's answer to these charges?

3. Is Cranston a defeatist or fatalist concerning the threat of nuclear war? Or is he a voice of warning?

For Discussion or Writing

4. What evidence do you know that modern war, whether traditional war or guerilla war, knows no ethical inhibitions against the slaughter of civilian populations?

5. Do you personally believe that in war the end justifies the means? Does it make sense to balk at some killings but not at others? Or do you believe that even in time of war we must condemn war crimes or crimes against humanity? Where would you draw the line?

DOOMSDAYS

Paul Gray

The story of Hiroshima has been told and retold in agonizing detail by survivors, histori-
ans, and journalists trying to make the unspeakable understandable. Standing out among the
many accounts are books like Jonathan Schell's The Fate of the Earth *(1982), a pains-*
takingly researched indictment of public apathy, with shattering testimonies from survivors.
Schell said at the time that bare statistics about bomb yields and secondary effects tell us noth-
ing: "We seek a human truth and come up with a handful of figures." Does the following Time
essay succeed in making the human truth of nuclear destruction real for a new generation of
readers?

After witnessing the successful test of the first atomic bomb–a primordial burst   1
of energy on the predawn New Mexico desert, a man-made fire bright enough to
flicker in reflection off the moon–Brigadier General Thomas F. Farrell sought out
his immediate superior, Major General Leslie R. Groves. Groves was commander of
the top-secret Manhattan Project, which had been commissioned and funded–
with $2 billion–to try to build such a bomb. "When Farrell came up to me," Groves
remembered, "his first words were, 'The war is over.' My reply was, 'Yes, after we
drop two bombs on Japan.'" This was the morning of July 16, 1945; within an
amazing 30 days, both of these statements would be history.

President Truman learned of the bomb test while in Potsdam, a suburb of
burned-out and bombed-out Berlin, where he was meeting with Winston
Churchill and Joseph Stalin, leaders of the nations allied with the U.S. in the defeat
of Nazi Germany. The news that the atomic bomb actually worked promised to
solve in a flash two of Truman's most urgent problems in the Pacific: the ordering
of a heavy-casualty land invasion of the Japanese home islands, scheduled to begin Nov. 1, and the necessity of making concessions to Stalin in order to secure Soviet military intervention to help speed the defeat of Japan.

The atomic bomb held out the hope that neither action would be necessary.
Truman confided to his diary, "It is certainly a good thing for the world that Hitler's
crowd or Stalin's did not discover this atomic bomb. It seems to be the most terrible thing ever discovered, but it can be made the most useful."

The question of how to deliver and drop atomic bombs on Japanese soil had
been thoroughly studied at the highest U.S. government levels well before the test
in New Mexico. A list of prospective targets had been drawn up, with an emphasis, as Groves later wrote, on "places the bombing of which would most adversely

affect the will of the Japanese people to continue the war." A special Air Force unit–
the 509th Composite Group–had been formed in September 1944, under the command of Lieut. Colonel Paul W. Tibbets, regarded by many to be the service's best
bomber pilot. Tibbets' group would be responsible for dropping the then untested
atomic devices, although few of its 225 officers and 1,542 enlisted men were told
the exact nature of their assignment.

On Tinian, a 39-sq.-mi. island in the Marianas some 1,500 miles south of
Japan, U.S. forces had constructed the largest airport in the world, including four
parallel, 8,500-ft.-long runways designed for B-29 Superfortresses. Several of the
incendiary-bomb raids on Japanese cities staged by Major General Curtis LeMay's
XXI Bomber Command began and ended in the Marianas. Members of the 509th
unit started arriving at Tinian in June. On July 26, components of Little Boy, the
uranium-based bomb that was scheduled to be dropped first, reached Tinian
aboard the U.S. warship *Indianapolis.*

That same day, the Potsdam Declaration was issued by the U.S., Britain and
Nationalist China, the three countries at war with Japan. The document offered the
enemy "an opportunity to end this war." Its language was blunt: "Following are our
terms. We will not deviate from them. There are no alternatives. We shall brook no
delay." It concluded, "We call upon the government of Japan to proclaim now the
unconditional surrender of all Japanese armed forces. . . . The alternative for Japan
is prompt and utter destruction." Only those who had seen or heard of the atomic
bomb, including Truman and Churchill, could understand what the last words
might mean.

The Potsdam text reached Tokyo on the morning of July 27 and was debated
most of the day by the Japanese leaders. Some saw a possibility of national face
saving in that the demand for "unconditional surrender" was linked specifically to
the Japanese armed forces and made no mention of Emperor Hirohito. The one
condition the Japanese were determined to maintain, at the expense, if need be, of
total extinction, was that the revered Hirohito would never be deposed, imprisoned
or tried as a war criminal. In the end, the military advisers successfully argued that
the Potsdam Declaration must be rejected to keep up the morale of Japan's besieged
forces and civilians.

The next afternoon Japan's Prime Minister, Kantaro Suzuki, held a press conference in Tokyo at which he vowed that his government planned to ignore the
declaration and would "resolutely fight for the successful conclusion of the war."
But the previous night, the first components of Fat Man, the plutonium-based
bomb whose prototype had been tested on July 16, had arrived at Tinian.

By July 30, scrutiny of the Suzuki statement had convinced Washington that
Japan would not surrender under the Potsdam terms. Secretary of War Henry L.
Stimson cabled President Truman, who was still at the conference, asking for final
ratification of the order to drop the atomic bomb, which had been drafted on July
24 by Groves and approved by Stimson and Army Chief of Staff General George C.

Marshall. Truman wrote out in longhand a reply for transmission: "Suggestion approved. Release when ready."

Bad weather–a typhoon approached Japan on Aug. 1–only delayed what was   10
now inevitable. The skies cleared gradually. By the afternoon of Aug. 5, on Tinian, Little Boy was being winched into the specially modified bomb bay of a B-29, which Tibbets would christen–in honor of his mother's given names–*Enola Gay*. The 9,700-lb. bomb was 10 1/2 ft. long and 29 in. in diameter; it looked, one of Tibbet's crew decided, like "an elongated trash can with fins." After a midnight briefing, crews of the seven B-29s assigned to carry out the mission and various support functions had breakfast and then rode by truck to their stations. The strike plane *Enola Gay*, with Tibbets as pilot, groaned down the runway, picking up speed that would lift its 65 tons into the air. It took off at 2:45 a.m., Tinian time. Only on the way to the target did Tibbets tell his 11-man crew that they were carrying a new kind of bomb.

Monday, Aug. 6, dawned clear, hot and humid in Hiroshima, a city on the southwestern coast of the main Japanese island of Honshu. In 1942 it had had a population of 420,000, but evacuations had reduced that number this summer morning to about 280,000 civilians, 43,000 military personnel and 20,000 forced Korean laborers and volunteer workers. Hiroshima housed the headquarters of the Japanese army's Second General Headquarters.

The city had been spared the incendiary-bomb raids that were raining fire on so many Japanese cities–perhaps, some of its citizens hoped, because it made a poor target for such an attack. Situated on a broad alluvial delta, surrounded on three sides by low mountains, Hiroshima was threaded by seven tributaries of the Ota River–watery obstacles to the spread of fires–emptying into Hiroshima Bay on the Inland Sea. On this Monday morning, some 8,900 schoolchildren had been ordered to increase Hiroshima's advantage by helping clean and widen streets.

An air-raid alert sounded at 7:09–radar had picked up the approach of the 509th Group's weather plane–and an all clear followed at 7:31, after the B-29 departed. Perhaps this apparently harmless sortie lulled the city's civil-defense monitors. In any case, just before 8:15 three more B-29s–the *Enola Gay* and two escorts–could be seen and then heard flying some 30,000 ft. over Hiroshima. No alarms sounded in time. The radio announcer on duty had received word that three enemy planes had been sighted, but he had momentarily paused to check his notes instead of grabbing the microphone at once. "Military command announces three enemy planes . . ." He never finished. Outside, a teacher supervising a team of schoolgirl laborers said, "Oh, there's a B!" They looked up and saw the eye of death.

Little Boy, which had been dropped from the *Enola Gay* at 8:15:30, exploded 43 sec. later at 1,900 ft. above Hiroshima, creating a blinding bluish-white flash and, for a fraction of a second, unearthly heat. Temperatures near the hypocenter, the ground point immediately below the explosion, surged to figures ranging from 5400°F to 7200°F; within a mile of the hypocenter, the surfaces of objects instantly rose to more than 1000°F. Those caught in the middle of this maelstrom were the lucky ones. They died instantly, vaporized into puffs of smoke or carbonized into small, blackened, smoking corpses, mummified in their last living gesture.

People farther away from the source of the thermal wave were destined for longer agonies. The intense heat melted the eyeballs of some who had stared in wonder at the blast; it burned off facial features and seared skin all over the body into peeling, draping strips. The survivors who first emerged out of the roiling inferno that the center of Hiroshima had become walked like automatons, their arms held forward, hands dangling. In shock, they instinctively tried to keep their burned skin from touching anything, including themselves.

They stumbled toward the riverbanks, some crying out, *"Mizu, mizu!"* (Water, water); the temperature and their injuries had left them severely dehydrated. Because light colors reflect heat and dark ones absorb it, some bomb victims had the images of their clothing tattooed on their flesh; the pattern of a kimono on a woman's back, the unburned swath left by a sash around the waist of an otherwise charred man. "Big black flies appeared and tried to lay eggs on human flesh," says survivor Michiko Watanabe, now 65. "The injured were so weak that they couldn't brush away the flies that nestled in their hands and necks. Some were black from a blanket of flies that covered them."

The heat from Little Boy singed more than 4 sq. mi. of Hiroshima reddish-brown. In the process, it left a bizarre photographic negative of the instant of destruction. Objects, human or inanimate, that came between the blast and other objects cast their shadows as unburned patterns on the protected space: a spiral ladder was imprinted on the surface of a storage plant behind it. Survivors foraging for food in vegetable gardens later that day dug up potatoes and found they had already been baked in the ground.

Nature itself seemed deranged by the violence. Whirlwinds tore through the city. Fires jumped rivers with ease. Dark, marble-size drops of water–later called black rain–condensed off the explosion's towering smoke and fell to earth.

After the thermal heat came the blast, spreading out from the explosion center at an initial speed of 2 m.p.s. and then subsiding toward the speed of sound. Shock waves were the principal threat of conventional bombs, but Little Boy achieved a new order of destructive power. Unleashing the equivalent of 12,500 tons of TNT, it essentially flattened Hiroshima in one blow: only 6,000 of the city's 76,000 buildings were undamaged; 48,000 of them were entirely destroyed. Practically every window and mirror in the city splintered, hurling shards of glass into the bodies of anyone nearby. The explosion started more fires outside the central ring of devastation, as flammable houses collapsed onto cooking fires or sputtering electric wires. People pinned under rubble inside burning buildings cried out for help; few heard them, and even fewer were in any condition to save them from burning alive. An estimated 100,000 died that first day, and the death toll climbed to 140,000 by the end of the year.

Assistance of any kind vanished that morning in Hiroshima. All the usual 20 functions of municipal government simply stopped when the bomb exploded. Hospitals and medical centers, to which the tens of thousands of grievously wounded people swarmed, were part of the general ruin. Of the city's 150 doctors, 65 had died in the blast, and most of the rest had been seriously hurt. More than 90% of the nurses were either dead or incapacitated.

Those physicians able to function did so heroically. They could not know they would be the first medical experts to observe a new disease, the third effect, after the heat and blast, of Little Boy. On Tuesday an official of the Red Cross Hospital in Hiroshima discovered that the X-ray plates stored in a basement vault that had survived the blast and a fire had all been exposed. The bomb had spread radiation throughout central Hiroshima, with lingering, lethal effects on its survivors that would not be fully understood for years.

The outside world learned of the Hiroshima bomb—but not of its gruesome effects—from a terse White House announcement approved by President Truman, who was steaming home from Potsdam on the U.S.S. *Augusta*. The big news was saved for the beginning of the third paragraph: "It is an atomic bomb. It is a harnessing of the basic power of the universe. The force from which the sun draws its powers has been loosed against those who brought war to the Far East." This was the first public announcement anywhere indicating that nuclear weapons even existed.

Japanese radio offered its citizens, few of them presumably listening in Hiroshima, a more tentative report: "Hiroshima suffered considerable damage as the result of an attack by a few B-29s. Our enemies have apparently used a new type of bomb. The details are being investigated."

In truth, Tokyo initially knew almost nothing about what had happened in Hiroshima. As General George Marshall noted later, "What we did not take into account was that the destruction would be so complete that it would be an appreciable time before the actual facts of the case would get to Tokyo." As Washington waited impatiently for word of surrender, the Japanese Cabinet tried to find out what on earth had happened to Hiroshima. Since the first reports seemed unbelievable, some Japanese leaders wanted desperately not to believe them. Others decided that even if Truman's announcement was true—that Hiroshima was hit with an atomic bomb—Japan should continue to fight. "I am convinced," War Minister Korechika Anami told his Cabinet colleagues, "that the Americans had only one bomb, after all."

Such a response had been anticipated by General Groves, who argued all 25 along to the Manhattan Project's civilian overseers that at least two atomic bombs would be necessary to effect Japan's surrender: the first to demonstrate the awful destructive power of a nuclear weapon and the second to convince the Japanese military that there were more where that came from.

On Aug. 8, Fat Man–a bulbous bomb, nearly 12 ft. long and 5 ft. in diameter, weighing 10,000 lbs.–was loaded into another of the 509th Group's B–29s at Tinian. The plane and its escorts took off the next morning at 3:47 and headed for Kokura, a city that contained a major weapons arsenal, on the north coast of the island of Kyushu. Finding the target obscured by clouds and facing a fuel shortage on the strike plane, Major Charles W. Sweeney decided to fly over the alternate target on his way to an emergency landing on Okinawa.

Thus did Nagasaki enter history, an afterthought on the day of its ordeal and ever since a footnote. the second city to be hit by an atomic bomb. Fat Man exploded 1,650 ft. above the city of some 240,000 people on the western coast of Kyushu at 11:02 on the morning of Aug. 9. In many ways, the event was a carbon copy of the horrors of Hiroshima: flash, heat, blast, radiation; permanent shadows cast by bombshine; thirsty, mortally burned people, emerging from the smoke and dust, trailing strips of their skin behind them. Some in Nagasaki had been afraid that their city would be attacked by the new weapon. Hideo Matsuno, then 27, a reporter with the government's propaganda arm, had read an Aug. 7 intelligence report about Hiroshima. "We know about the atomic bomb," he says.

Fat Man released the equivalent of 22,000 tons of TNT, almost twice the power set forth by Little Boy. Trees had been knocked over in Hiroshima; in Nagasaki they were snapped in two. But the devastation in Nagasaki was limited, to an extent, by its topography; from the harbor, the city radiated northward in two valleys, separated by steep hills. The bomb exploded over Urakami valley, Nagasaki's north-westerly fork, and the worst of the damage was contained there. The destruction, nevertheless, was infernal. About 74,000 were killed instantly. The Urakami Catholic church, which had the country's largest Christian congregation at the time, was destroyed; more than two-thirds of the congregation died as a result of the bombing. "It was as if a giant had crushed it," says Takako Yoshida, then 18, who saw one of the church's two mammoth bell towers lying in the river below as she was being carried out on a stretcher three days later.

Japan's Supreme War Council was meeting in a military building on the grounds of the Imperial Palace in Tokyo at the moment of the Nagasaki bombing. A military aide entered the meeting at 11:30 a.m. with word of the disaster. This news was bad enough, but it only added to the council's bleak agenda, which was headed by the announcement, received in Tokyo the night before, that the U.S.S.R. had abruptly and unexpectedly declared war on Japan. Already, on the morning of Aug. 9, some of an estimated 1.6 million Soviet troops had attacked Japanese-held Manchuria.

As it had been since May, the six-member Supreme Council remained split down the middle on the questions of whether and how to end the war. One faction of three, headed by Prime Minister Suzuki and joined by Foreign Minister

Shigenori Togo and Navy Minister Mitsumasa Yonai, favored negotiating for peace on the most favorable terms still remaining; the other, led by War Minister Anami, argued that Japan must fight on. The debate continued in a Cabinet meeting that ran more than eight hours. At last, Suzuki told the deadlocked Cabinet that he would convene an Imperial Conference at 11 p.m., bringing the Supreme Council before Emperor Hirohito.

The 18-ft. by 30-ft. room in the imperial air-raid shelter was virtually unventilated and sweltering when the Emperor arrived as the meeting began and took his seat on a small dais. The assembled leaders, headed by the Supreme Council's Big Six, as they were called, listened again to a reading of the Potsdam Declaration and then began debating possible responses to the terms it imposed. One plan, favored by Suzuki and Togo, called for an acceptance of the Potsdam demands, with the sole condition that Hirohito and the imperial dynasty be retained in Japan.

More than two hours of argument only emphasized the hopeless abyss between the pacifists and the militarists. Then Kilchiro Hiranuma, president of the Privy Council, who had been specially invited to attend by Hirohito, proposed asking for the Emperor's opinion, shocking everyone into silence. Everyone, that is, except Prime Minister Suzuki, who quickly pointed out that it was the right move, given that the government was stymied and unable to act at the moment their people most needed action: "I propose, therefore, to seek the imperial guidance and substitute it for the decision of this conference."

To ask the Emperor, whom the Japanese believed ruled them from "beyond the clouds," to shape the course of earthly policymaking was unprecedented. Hirohito, who no doubt had a role in planning the scene, did not seem at all surprised and began speaking, slowly, so that everyone in the room could hear and understand. He said the time had come to accept the terms set down in Potsdam, that with the forces arrayed against them, "I have given serious thought to the situation prevailing at home and abroad and have concluded that continuing the war means destruction for the nation and a prolongation of bloodshed and cruelty in the world." Some of those present began to weep. "The time has come," Hirohito went on, "when we must bear the unbearable. I swallow my tears and give my sanction to the proposal to accept the Allied proclamation on the basis outlined by the Foreign Minister."

That proposal still insisted on "the supreme power of the Emperor" in postwar Japan. Four more days of fighting and delicate negotiations remained before all sides could agree to stop the killing. Conventional–but not atomic–bombing of Japan continued; by some estimates, more than 15,000 died in air raids during this final spasm.

Finally, at noon Japanese time on Aug. 15, a message recorded by Hirohito was   35
broadcast throughout Japan. Citizens gathered around public loudspeakers, heads bowed in reverence; they had never before heard their Emperor's voice. He told them that "the war situation has developed not necessarily to Japan's advantage,

while the general trends of the world have all turned against her interests. More-over, the enemy has begun to employ a new and most cruel bomb, the power of which to do damage is indeed incalculable, taking the toll of many innocent lives." He told them Japan had been defeated.—*With reporting by Irene M. Kunii/Hiroshima and Nagasaki*

The Responsive Reader

1. How does Gray's assessment of the role of the political and military leaders on the American side compare with that of Cranston? How does Gray see the ques-tion of personal responsibility?

2. Is there a point in retelling one more time in excruciating detail the story of what happened to the people of Hiroshima? Is all of this familiar? Or have people be-gun to forget? Does anything here make a special impact on you?

3. How does Gray chronicle the bombing and the immediate aftermath as seen from the Japanese side? War-time propaganda makes it its business to make people hate the enemy. After the end of the war in the Pacific, Japanese com-manders were tried for war crimes and executed by the victorious Allied forces. How is the enemy seen in this account? How would you describe Gray's attitude toward the Japanese leadership?

For Discussion or Writing

4. Does Gray's account change your assumptions or your thinking? How?

5. Has overexposure to atrocities numbed today's audiences? Do we suffer from "compassion fatigue"?

Collaborative Projects

6. How is the use of the atomic bomb against Japan seen in Japan today? Working with a group, what sources can you consult? Where would you turn for infor-mation? Would you expect a range of opinion?

THE CLASH OF CULTURES

Howard Chua-Eoan

> *In the following companion essay to Gray's "Doomsdays," another* Time *writer shifts the focus from the ethical questions about Hiroshima to how the world arrived there. What road took two great nations to Pearl Harbor and Hiroshima? Wars are the bloody culmination of a history—a history of conflict, of incomprehension and prejudice, of flag-waving and hate-mongering, of ideological fervor and official miscalculation. American historians still probe the events leading up to the war of the North against the secessionist South. European historians are still unraveling the tangled skein of events leading up to World War I, pitting the Kaiser's Germany against the Allies. According to Howard Chua-Eoan, if we remain ignorant of the history that led up to the war in the Pacific, what are the "parables we ignore at our peril"?*

In the end, a trinity of bombs brought the war to a close: Jumbo, the device   1
detonated in Alamagordo, New Mexico, to prove that atomic weapons could be made; Little Boy, the uranium titan that vaporized Hiroshima; and Fat Man, the plutonium monster that laid waste to Nagasaki. In the crematory light of those blasts, the world changed—so much death contained in so little; so much of the bloody business of war refined to a bloodless decision. Ultimately it all came down to science, to a matter of buttons. In a flash, Prometheus was one with Genghis Khan.

The philosophical ramifications of Hiroshima and Nagasaki have occupied humankind for half a century now. What has been obscured is the nature of the war that led to the use of the bombs, a war that possessed its own terrible clarity: that of simple, ferocious hate; of civilization pitted against civilization, race against race, blood against blood. That kind of fighting still occurs; in the Balkans, in Rwanda and Burundi, in the streets of Los Angeles and Karachi. But the imagination of the world pays little heed to the sensibilities of such conflicts. Minds have been polarized by the cold war and fascinated by the mighty mushroom clouds of 1945—by the imminence of endless death from the radiance of a thousand suns. Nevertheless, in the shadow of that terrifying splendor lurks a history of immense human hatreds, parables we ignore at our peril.

The war in Asia was waged mercilessly on all sides. Major General Curtis LeMay, the man who took charge of the B-29 bombings of Japan, once said, "I'll tell you what war is about. You've got to kill people, and when you've killed enough, they stop fighting." Eugene Sledge, then an 18-year-old Marine, remembered the abattoir of the Pacific this way in his memoirs: "I felt sickened to the depths of my soul. I asked God 'Why, why, why?' . . . I had tasted the bitterest essence of the war . . . and it filled me with disgust."

The carnage was horrific. In the China theater alone, perhaps as many as 10 million people perished. In the fighting in the central Pacific, some 20,000 U.S. soldiers died. On Saipan, Japanese women and children hurled themselves from cliffs rather than submit to the American invaders. Most Japanese soldiers there either died fighting or took their own lives: 27,040 corpses were found. The toll from Tarawa– 984 U.S. Marines and 29 Navy men killed in just 76 hours of fighting–caused normally self-censoring correspondents to send home horror stories that nearly triggered a congressional investigation. All of February 1945 saw street fighting in Manila between American soldiers and renegade Japanese troops intent on turning the Philippine capital into Stalingrad-on-the-South-China-Sea. An estimated 100,000 people, mostly civilians, died. And then came the battles for Okinawa.

Off the coast of that island, at 10 a.m. on May 10, 1945, a Japanese Zero flew in   5 low against the U.S. aircraft carrier *Bunker Hill* and crashed onto the flight deck, igniting the 30 planes waiting to fly sorties. Thirty seconds later, another Japanese suicide flight dropped out of the sky and struck the *Bunker Hill* amidships, ripping open a 40-ft. hole with the blast of its 550-lb. bomb and turning the fast carrier into an inferno for the next six hours. Of the 3,000 crewmen on board, 353 died in the smoke and flames. The kamikaze attacks were part of the Japanese navy's Ten Go (Operation Heaven), which sent some 1,465 volunteer pilots on suicide missions against Allied ships during the assault on Okinawa, then in its second month.

At the same time that the *Bunker Hill* was aflame, Lieut. General Simon Bolivar Buckner, commander of the American forces fighting to capture Okinawa, was undertaking a new offensive to seize control of the island. The Americans knew the tiny speck in the Pacific was the ultimate stepping-stone to the empire's home islands. Throughout the 83-day struggle for Okinawa, Buckner's favorite toast, over bourbon and water, was "May you walk in the ashes of Tokyo." Aware of this objective, his enemy, Lieut. General Mitsuru Ushijima, prepared a war of attrition to keep Okinawa from becoming a staging ground for the U.S. invasion of Japan. "Do your utmost," Ushijima's men were told. "The victory of the century lies in this battle." In early July, when the battles for Okinawa were finally over, more than 125,000 people were dead. Among the corpses were those of Buckner and Ushijima, the former killed by a stray bullet, the latter by his own hand.

In Japan the Imperial Army mobilized civilians to stave off the expected invasion. The defense exercises–involving mock bamboo thrusts to the bellies of invading soldiers–struck many citizens as ridiculous. But everyone took part in the drills. A student explained, "No one wanted to be blamed for quitting." In the U.S. few were for quitting either. A June 1945 Gallup poll showed 90% of Americans pressing for decisive victory rather than peace terms that would allow Japan to avoid occupation.

Though paired with the European conflicts as World War II, the immense battles in Asia traced their beginnings back to different histories, different cultures, different fears and humiliations. The Pacific was a clash of civilizations: the attempt of a modern, non-Western power to carve its place, if not establish its superiority, in a world dominated and colonized by white people. And the war's beginning came long before the attack on Pearl Harbor.

The U.S. Naval War College in Newport, Rhode Island, was preparing strategies for a war against Japan as early as 1897. The Japanese saw the war as part of a hundred-year conflict that had begun with the humiliation of the self-satisfied, isolationist Chinese empire in 1842, after the Opium War, at the hands of the British. Until 1853 Japan was a hermetic, medieval kingdom, but learning from the foibles of its neighbors and from the technological prowess of the West, it established itself by 1895 as the dominant Asian power, defeating the forces of the moribund Chinese empire. Japan wanted not only to overtake China, the source of much of its traditional culture, as the dominant regional power but also to prove that Asians need never defer to the West. By 1905 it had trounced the Russians in Manchuria, sinking the armada that Nicholas II dispatched from the Baltic Sea to retake the waters around his Pacific port of Vladivostok. Japan had become a power "of the junior first rank," as one author noted. It wanted to be more.

The quest for superiority required not only armaments but also the establishment of a biological prerogative. For a would-be master race, the rights of hegemony must by definition be present in the blood. Japan thus embarked on the creation of a mythology of a chosen people with the Emperor, descendant of the sun goddess Amaterasu, as the divine icon of the Yamato race. Biologists produced studies decrying the apish physical features of other races (hairiness, long arms) and noting the highly evolved characteristics of the Japanese (relatively flattened forehead-to-nose ratio, milder body odor). More important, however, racial purity derived from loyalty to the Emperor and the protective centuries of isolation, which fostered a spirituality the Japanese believed was possessed by no other people. Proclamations in the Emperor's name bore the weight of both legal and divine imperative. "Bear in mind that duty is weightier than a mountain, while death is lighter than a feather," proclaimed a rescript in the name of the Meiji Emperor. To disobey that dictum was a sin against heaven; it was treason and a denial of blood heritage.

The ideology dispensed with the silence that tradition once demanded in the Emperor's presence, replacing it with aggressive shouts of "Banzai!" ("May you live 10,000 years!"). At the same time, as the historian John Dower notes in his book *War Without Mercy*, the Thought Bureau of the Ministry of Education propagated the attendant doctrine that Japanese were "intrinsically quite different from the so-called citizens of Occidental countries," inculcating a sense of superiority. One industrialist said the Japanese were the "sole superior race in the world."

It was the American commodore Matthew Perry who, in 1853, persuaded

Japan to open its ports to Western trade, thus initiating an astonishing rush toward modernization. But when the Japanese began flexing their muscle in East Asia, the U.S. realized that its protégé had become a rival, with much resulting paranoia, including hysteria about Japanese designs on American territory. By 1924 an anti-Japanese immigration act had been passed. From the 1890s through the 1940s, the Hearst newspapers were especially rabid about the "yellow peril." When war did come, one of the Hearst tabloids declared, "The war in the Pacific is the World War, the War of the Oriental Races against the Occidental Races for the Domination of the World."

Throughout the early 20th century, the U.S. tried to temper its Pacific expansion with paternalism, attempting to define it as something other than a continuation of the bloody way in which it had won its Western states. It championed the "Open Door" policy in China—advocating universal trading access while respecting territorial integrity—even as Europe and Japan were dividing China into spheres of influence. Washington also promised independence to its Philippine colony by the early '40s.

Still, many of the American soldiers sent to Asia to pacify the Philippines in 1898 had fought in the Indian wars and described their new foes with white-settler terms for the old. "The only good Filipino," said a soldier, "is a dead one." Eventually, this "legacy of racial war words," as Dower writes, would lead to the American soldier's attitude toward the Japanese. A 1942 article titled "The Nips" in the New York *Times* Magazine said, "The Japanese are likened to the American Indian in their manner of making war. Our fighting men say that isn't fair to the Indian. He had honor of a sort." During the Pacific war, U.S. soldiers had reason to fear even Japanese corpses, which were sometimes rigged with explosives.

The war victories gave the Japanese a chance to avenge past humiliations. In 15 *Prisoners of the Japanese*, historian Gavan Daws tells the story of U.S. Marine Corps Major J. P. S. Devereux, captured by the Japanese on Wake Island. Devereux, wrote Daws, "would never willingly have lowered himself to talk to a yellow man on equal terms." Now he had to. Devereux could not speak Japanese—few U.S. soldiers could. And so, in a submissive voice, he asked a Japanese officer of junior rank, "Do you speak English?" The Japanese replied contemptuously, in perfect English, "No, I do not speak English. Do you speak Japanese?"

Americans and other Westerners were convinced that the Japanese were a containable threat. For example, many Westerners believed myopia was common among the Japanese (hence the bespectacled caricatures) and that it would keep them from becoming good fighter pilots. Thus when the empire's air force destroyed Douglas MacArthur's fighters on the ground in the Philippines, the general thought white mercenaries had flown the Japanese planes. Japan's astonishing successes in routing the British and Americans in the early months of the Pacific war were credited to German military advisers. Even in 1945, on Okinawa, U.S. soldiers believed the Japanese strategy of heavy bombardments was inspired by German consultants.

But the Japanese did indeed drive the Westerners out of Asia and the Pacific. They had planned the grand strategy to establish self-sufficiency in the face of what they perceived as a Soviet threat. And they had carried out the blueprint. In 1942 F.D.R.'s Chief of Staff, Admiral William Leahy, was privately worried that Japan might "succeed in combining most of the Asiatic peoples against the whites." Such paranoia led to the internment of 110,000 Americans of Japanese descent in concentration camps; the FBI also kept close surveillance on alleged Japanese attempts to turn black Americans against the U.S. government. For its part, Japanese propaganda described Americans as racist, sex-obsessed, abortion-loving *yaju* (wild beasts).

However, the doctrine of racial superiority worked very quickly against Japanese efforts to set up a harmonious new order in Asia. Indigenous leaders once sympathetic to Tokyo's presence accused the Japanese of arrogance. Civilians who did not bow to Japanese soldiers or who somehow displeased them were automatically slapped; these atrocities contributed to Japanese unpopularity. The occupation police, the Kempeitai, won a reputation for torture. Occupation forces performed medical experiments on prisoners of war–or used them for target practice. Anti-Japanese guerrilla movements proliferated.

For Americans, the Bataan death march was the most infamous example of Japanese cruelty. American and Filipino prisoners from the fall of Corregidor in 1942 were refused food and water on a six-day, 60-mile forced march to their place of confinement at Camp O'Donnell. Fingers were chopped off to get at West Point rings; decapitated bodies lined the road; by one estimate, there was a body every 10 or 15 paces. The death toll: more than 10,000.

For all its early prowess, the empire had exhausted its resources and skills to pull together its victories. Six months after Pearl Harbor, a Japanese armada steaming toward Midway Island was severely defeated and turned back. In October 1944 the Imperial Navy was routed in Leyte Gulf in the Philippines, and Japan was virtually eliminated as a sea power. By July 1945 it was cut off from its territory in Southeast and East Asia, losing the raw materials it had gone to war for. The empire in June had just 4,000 aircraft, with only 800 operational. The U.S. had 22,000 at its disposal.

While the majority of Allied soldiers shrank from atrocity, a few were not averse to inflicting on the Japanese the horrors that had been visited on their comrades. In *Tennozan*, George Feifer cites Marine memories of barbaric acts against "the Japs" on Okinawa. The dead were cut up in search of souvenirs; soldiers, surrendering unarmed, were shot. Elsewhere, hospital ships were sunk and prisoners tortured. In 1946 Edgar Jones wrote in the *Atlantic Monthly*: "What kind of war do civilians suppose we fought, anyway? We shot prisoners in cold blood, wiped out hospitals, strafed lifeboats, killed or mistreated enemy civilians, finished off the enemy wounded, tossed the dying into a hole with the dead, and in the Pacific boiled the flesh off enemy skulls to make table ornaments for sweethearts, or carved their bones into letter openers."

By June 22, 1945, the U.S. had conquered Okinawa, just 350 miles from Kyushu, the southernmost of Japan's four main islands. LeMay's bombers set those islands aflame. From March to May, enormous sections of Tokyo, Osaka, Nagoya, Kobe, Kawasaki and Yokohama were incinerated. The raids on Tokyo had to be called off after May because scarcely any major targets were left. Of the carnage, LeMay said, "No point in slaughtering civilians for the mere sake of slaughter." He was after military production. But, he added, "the entire population got into the act and worked to make those airplanes or munitions of war . . . We knew we were going to kill a lot of women and kids . . . Had to be done."

The U.S. Army and Navy, meanwhile, were reconstituting mechanisms from the Nazis' V-1 guided missiles, which had wrought such tremendous damage on England in the waning months of the European war. The result was the JB-2 jet bomb, a low-altitude missile. The Army had requisitioned 1,000 JB-2s by the end of July 1945 as part of an eventual plan to hit Japan with up to 500 such missiles a day. The Navy hoped to do the same with its version, called the Loon. But by that time, more alarming technologies were ready to close out the war.

By the end of May, MacArthur had outmaneuvered his rival, U.S. Admiral Chester Nimitz, to lead the invasion of Japan as commander in chief of U.S. Army Forces Pacific. The plan consisted of two parts: first, Operation Olympic, scheduled for Nov. 1, 1945, would land the largest invasion force in history—nearly 340,000 soldiers and Marines—on the island of Kyushu; then, as early as March 1946, Operation Coronet, involving up to 2 million men, would target the island of Honshu and the Kanto plain, on which Tokyo lies.

The Emperor's strategists also prepared for an invasion of Kyushu. Allied intel-   25
ligence estimates in late April put 84,200 Japanese troops in southern Kyushu. In fact, by late July almost 600,000 Imperial troops were on the island. That balance of Japanese to American fighting men portended a cataclysm. At Okinawa, until then the Pacific's largest land battle, 278,000 U.S. troops fought 83,000 Japanese. The Americans considered a worst-case scenario requiring three attempted landings to achieve victory. Meanwhile, Tokyo had issued orders to its troops—decrypted by U.S. intelligence, which long before had broken the Japanese ciphers—that a ferocious repulsion of the invasion was necessary. "Every soldier should fight to the last moment believing in the final victory." No one would be allowed to retreat; 13 million civilians were mobilized to fight with sticks and shovels if need be. One teenage girl was told, "If you don't kill at least one enemy soldier, you don't deserve to die."

U.S. casualty predictions ranged from 31,000 to 220,000. The Joint Chiefs of

Staff offered three different sets of estimates. The worst case: as many as 500,000 Americans killed or wounded. It was assumed that millions of Japanese defenders, military and civilian, would perish.

By tradition, the emperor kept silent during high-level strategy meetings. But on June 22, Hirohito spoke. His words were cloaked in the subtle and elliptical language of the court, but his meaning was clear: an effort must be made to negotiate an end to the war. The words provided no clear direction for his government. Though officials were eager for peace, few were willing to sue for it, certainly not with the U.S. Military factions were ready to stage assassinations or a coup if bureaucrats tried such a move. Japanese diplomats approached the Soviet Union, then neutral in the Pacific, seeking mediation and proffering an alliance. That intelligence caused concern in the U.S., already worried about the Soviets, so utterly triumphant over Germany. Thus, as Japan's peace seekers meandered, America's leaders pondered the obstacles to–and expediences of–victory.

Already the empire was ashes. "Nights of strong wind were chosen, and bombs were dropped to windward in great quantity," wrote Foreign Minister Mamoru Shigemitsu in his memoirs. "The area encompassed by a wall of flame then became the target for the next wave, which systematically bombed the whole. The area became a sea of flame." Kokura, Niigata, Nagasaki and Hiroshima seemed to have been spared; but they were on a special list. "Day by day, Japan turned into a furnace from which the voice of a people searching for food rose in anguish," wrote Shigemitsu. "And yet the clarion call was accepted. If the Emperor ordained it, they would leap into the flames." On Okinawa, Marine Private Eugene Sledge and his compatriots prepared for the invasion "with complete resignation that we would be killed."

Shortly after Pearl Harbor, Japanese propagandists crowed about the empire's people, the "100 million," and a national cohesiveness that could achieve anything it was directed to do: "100 million hearts beating as one," "100 million people as one bullet," and "100 million advancing like a ball of fire." No one expected the last to be a prophecy. For more terrifying wonders would come out of the heavens: the sun turned to darkness, the moon to blood.

The Responsive Reader

1. Some historians trace the origin of war to economic rivalry, others to the clash of ideologies. What is the keynote in Chua-Eoan's initial characterization of the war against Japan? What for him was "the nature of the war" that led to the use of the atomic bombs?

2. What does Chua-Eoan do to remind his readers of the brutality and carnage of

the war? What details, what figures, stand out in your mind as you look back over the article? (Was this a war different than any other?)

3. What does Chua-Eoan stress in his account of Japanese history? What do you learn here about Japanese nationalism? What do you learn about the ideology or mentality of the Japanese enemy? What here is familiar, and what is new?

4. Chua-Eoan places the war in the larger context of the history of European and American colonialism in Asia. How, and with what effect? How does he link the Pacific war with the tradition of American imperialism? What role did racist stereotypes about the Japanese play in the war?

5. Japan's imperialist expansion was touted by Japanese propaganda as championing the people of Asia against Western imperialist domination. According to Chua-Eoan, what went wrong? Where does he stand on the question of atrocities charged against the Japanese?

6. Toward the end, Chua-Eoan makes his readers see the final months of the war through the eyes of America's former enemy. With what effect?

For Discussion or Writing

7. Traditional treatments of war have stressed the themes of heroism and sacrifice. Are there any traces of this perspective in this article?

8. Chua-Eoan stresses the gulf separating the two alien civilizations. Can you nevertheless see parallels? Which features of Japanese history or culture described here have possible parallels in the American experience?

9. Today's historians are often charged with revisionism—rewriting history in accordance with a current ideological agenda. Does Chua-Eoan's article succeed in making you see the war between Japan and the United States less as a conflict between good and evil and more as a clash between different civilizations? Why or why not?

Collaborative Projects

10. There is a huge market for movies, TV programs, and books recreating past wars in lifelike detail. Why? What is their appeal? What is their audience? Working with a group, you may want to investigate the treatment of war in current television fare. Are there recurrent themes? Is there a marked contrast between war movies old and new?

Reading, Writing, Research

8

Reading Strategies

No one works in a vacuum. Much writing is part of an ongoing dialogue; it builds on or is triggered by the author's reading. A writer may read several articles attacking affirmative action–and then feel moved to come to its defense. An economist may have studied a proposal for stringent new emissions standards–and feel motivated to explain the prohibitive costs. Experts establish their authority by reading and digesting a wide range of material in their field. Much research picks up the thread where previous research left off and concludes with recommendations for further research ahead. If you show that you are a good reader, your audience may find it easier to take your work seriously and to take your ideas or data into account.

CLOSE READING: RESPONDING TO CLUES

How good a reader are you? You may find yourself doing two kinds of reading: When checking out promising sources, you will often skim–reading opening paragraphs, dipping into several of the pages, looking at the conclusion. Checking out a book, you will glance at the preface, study the table of contents, perhaps look up some key terms in the index.

However, to digest and make good use of your reading, you will have to develop the habit of close reading. You will have to be willing to pay attention–close attention. Alert readers pay attention not just to what an author says but also to how the author thinks. They catch on early to the writer's agenda. They are quick to grasp the outline of an author's thoughts, taking in the sequence of major points or following the major steps in an argument. They size up the evidence that backs up the author's claims. They read between the lines, sensing an author's allegiances and antipathies by picking up telltale phrases and revealing asides.

Focus

An experienced writer knows the first question in the reader's mind: "What is this about?" If after the first few paragraphs a central issue or question has not come into focus, writer and reader are both likely to be in trouble. The title is of course your first clue, especially if it is truly informative:

The Family Out of Favor

A New Kind of Patriotism

Pornography and the First Amendment

However, a title may also be meant to be intriguing or witty, as when an article on alternatives to the nuclear family is called "Non-nuclear Proliferation."

Often an opening example or case history raises the central issue. For instance, the introduction may discuss a pioneering court decision recognizing the right of terminally ill patients to end their suffering. You are likely to conclude that the article will focus on questions of the "right to die with dignity" and very probably the question of assisted suicide. Often an introduction will lead up to a key question: If strict environmental regulations are enforced, who will pay the cost–the taxpayers or the polluters? Does violence in the media mirror a violent society–or does it help create a more violent society?

Thesis

As you become aware of the focus of an article or report, you will start looking for an answer to the next basic question: "What is your point?" What is the central claim the author is making? What is the author trying to prove? Alert readers early on start looking for a thesis statement like the following:

> *Thesis*: For most Americans, the nuclear family is a thing of the past, but our ways of thinking and our laws have not kept pace with the pervasive changes in family life.

If this statement is truly the thesis (and not just a point mentioned in passing), the writer is likely to *reiterate* it–not just repeating it but reinforcing it, coming back to it from perhaps a slightly different angle. The conclusion will often restate it one more time, in a slightly different or more emphatic form:

> *Conclusion*: Laws lag behind changes in attitudes and social mores. Your community may still have laws on the books that forbid liquor sales during church hours on Sunday morning or that regulate how married couples may make love. It is up to our generation to bring the laws into harmony with the changing realities of family life.

Often the thesis will offer a preview of key points to be covered. It will spell out the program or chart the itinerary. A statement like the following tells the reader what to look for and what to expect:

> *Thesis:* As the nuclear family ceases to be the norm, more and more house-holds are composed of unmarried couples, single-parent families, gay and lesbian couples, and other family arrangements.

There is of course no law requiring a writer to take a stand, to spell out a thesis, early on. The author may choose to bring a central question into focus but leave it open—exploring the pros and cons and then on balance preferring one side to the other. An author may choose to leave an issue unresolved.

Sequence of Ideas

How good are you at tracing an author's train of thought? Experienced readers have their radar on for major stages in a process, key causes or effects, arguments and counterarguments. Some subjects naturally subdivide into major areas or major stages, with the writer presenting familiar ones first and then working up to others more puzzling or controversial. Alert readers mentally or literally highlight key phrases that mark off the major stages in an article like the following:

THE ALTERNATIVE FAMILY

Are you part of a *traditional family?* How close was the family in which you grew up to the nostalgia-model of wage earner, homemaker, two or three children by the same parents, and a dog named Spot? For most Americans, the nuclear family is a thing of the past, but our ways of thinking and our laws have not kept pace with the pervasive changes in family life. . . .

There have always been alternatives to traditional marriage. *Long-time unmarried couples* "common-law" marriages—were for people who for some reason could not or would not assume the legal obligations of wedlock. By the same token they are still generally denied joint health insurance or pension benefits. . . .

Today growing numbers of young unmarried couples live together in *short-term or medium-term relationships.* . . .

A pervasive change in the traditional lifestyle occurred when economics or rising expectations made growing numbers of women look for work outside the home. The multiplying number of *two-wage-earner couples* drastically changed patterns of child rearing and domestic arrangements. . . .

A stagnant or slipping standard of living and the skyrocketing incidence of divorce became the twin threats to the stability of the traditional family. The *single-parent family* became a challenge especially for women and a scapegoat for many of society's ills. . . .

In a conservative political climate, much controversy swirls around the issue of *same-sex marriages* or domestic partnerships. Domestic partners are still often denied visiting rights in hospitals or denied the right to adopt children. . . .

In spite of the fulminations of politicians—the attacks on single welfare mothers or on deadbeat dads—there is no turning back. People are learning how to develop new patterns of *mutual support.* Close family friends become surrogate dads or grandmothers. . . .

Often, of course, the way a piece of writing is laid out does not reflect subdivisions inherent in the subject matter. Rather, it may reflect stages in the writer's plan of attack, say, for challenging the reader's preconceptions or disarming the opposition. Alert readers look for the clues that signal the writer's rhetorical strategy: What is the writer's strategy for convincing a reluctant reader? What is the author leading up to?

For instance, a well-known cultural anthropologist may be writing about how to deal with sexual harassment. She first documents the seriousness and widespread occurrence of belittling, condescension, suggestive remarks, and sexual exploitation. (This way perhaps even doubting Thomases will start paying attention.) She then examines a common answer to the problem: publishing official guidelines or passing ordinances. (In her view, these verbal solutions are not going to be much more effective than warning labels for cigarettes.) A second, more drastic solution is litigation—lawsuits that are often bitterly contested and may leave the plaintiff traumatized. Since by now two alternative solutions have already been weighed and rejected, the reader is ready to say: Give us a solution that will work! The writer then is ready to push her own favorite solution: pervasive changes in attitude through education, through the influence of parents, teachers, and preachers on the next generation.

Make it a practice to outline in your mind the way an article or presentation takes shape. Highlight turning points in an argument as you read. Draw up informal outlines as memory helps; use them when you draw on a source or argue with a writer's claims. Here is one reader's informal outline of an article by Karl Zinsmeister titled "Are Earnings Falling?" in *American Enterprise* for September/October 1995. The author, writing from a management or employers' point of view, wrote to counteract the widespread assumption that the real wages of American workers were falling while the compensation of top-level management was reaching unprecedented heights.

ARE EARNINGS FALLING?

Thesis: It is not true that American workers are in a cycle of declining prosperity.

1. Families are smaller than they were twenty years ago, so workers have to feed fewer family members.
2. Calculations to allow for inflation in comparing "real wages" are often faulty or biased.
3. Different groups of workers have fared differently. While it is true that the median income of white males dropped 4% between 1967 and 1992, the income of black women, for instance, rose by 57%.
4. Many workers are now receiving substantial multiple fringe benefits (like health insurance) that do not show in comparisons of wage levels.
5. The number of house owners under 35 has gone up by a third compared with a generation ago
6. As for other material indications of prosperity, American workers now take for granted a level of material possessions–cars, VCRs, other electronic equipment unheard of in earlier days

Development

How seriously we take an article or study depends on the quality of the supporting material. The alert reader keeps asking: What made the writer think so? What is being offered in evidence? How impartial or reliable are the sources? How convincing are key examples? A statement like the following alone carries little weight: "Much has happened in our society to suggest that our norms of family life must change." A critical reader will attach considerably more weight to the statement if it is **substantiated**–if it is supported with relevant data:

Those who demand that the norms of family life must change as alternative family arrangements become more popular point to eye-opening statistics. The average marriage today will last 6.9 years. More than twenty percent of all children are born to unmarried mothers. Almost half of children born in the eighties live mainly with single parents. Many gay and lesbian couples have children from previous marriages.

A critical reader will look closely at evidence brought in to document new trends or support debatable points:

- In reading an article on alternative families, you are likely to look closely at the implications of recent court cases involving lesbian lovers winning custody of a child or being allowed to adopt a child.
- In reading an article on the health hazards of smoking, you are likely to take a close critical look at the statistics being brought in–how were they

selected? What is their source–government agency, academic research, consumer activists, industry-funded research?

Continuity

In reading an article or a chapter in a book, do you ever ask yourself: "Where
are we headed? How did this get in here? What is next?" Audience-conscious writers furnish clues that keep the reader on track. Often **transitions** serve as guide-
posts, helping the reader get from here to there. For example, a transitional phrase
like *granted* or *it is true that* signals that the author is conceding a point, perhaps acknowledging a fact that is damaging to the argument and needs to be explained (or
explained away).

- Notice transitions that announce examples, illustrations, or cases in point: *for
  instance, for example, to illustrate.* A particularly strong or clinching example may
  follow an *in fact* or *indeed*: "Many successful and highly visible Americans
  have been immigrants; *in fact*, it is not unheard of for a secretary of state to
  be foreign-born."
- Notice transitions that signal "more of same"–the author is pursuing the
  same line of thought: *similarly, furthermore, along the same lines.* A similar function is served by phrases like "further evidence for this developing trend . . .";
  "If confirmation were needed . . ." ; or "Other preliminary results point in the
  same direction."
- Look especially for transitions that signal objections or complications. Often
  a pivotal *however, nevertheless,* or *on the other hand* turns an argument around. It
  may become a true turning point in an article in a report. Transitional sentences (or paragraphs) may serve the same function:

In spite of the impressive evidence accumulated by research correlating
high cholesterol and heart disease, such findings are by no means universally
accepted. . . .

Here is a rundown of transitional words and phrases that serve as traffic signals in much well-developed prose:

CONTINUITY:	and, also, additionally, furthermore, moreover, besides
ILLUSTRATION:	for example, for instance, to illustrate
LOGICAL RESULT:	so, therefore, consequently, hence, accordingly, as a result
OBJECTION:	but, however, nevertheless, on the other hand

CONCESSION:	granted, admittedly, it is true that, to be sure
REINFORCEMENT:	indeed, in fact, above all, in particular
ENUMERATION:	first, in the first place, second, third
CHRONOLOGY:	initially, next, soon, later, meanwhile, in the end
SUMMARY:	in short, in brief, to sum up
CONCLUSION:	finally, eventually, in conclusion, to conclude

Writers keep readers on track by **related terms** that keep the discussion focused on a key issue. A network of related terms like *lawlessness, disregard for the law, breakdown of police protection, near anarchy,* and *urban jungle* will signal to you that the writer is continuing to emphasize the breakdown of law and order in many communities. A network of terms like *citizen initiative, personal responsibility, neighborhood watch,* or *self-help groups* will signal that the writer has shifted the focus to attempts to turn the tide.

Weighted Language

How good are you at reading between the lines? An author's language carries attitudes and judgments that may not be spelled out in so many words. Both advocates and opponents of a proposal or project may use **connotative**, emotionally charged language to steer the reader's reactions. (Are you more likely to approve a proposal that is called a "project" or one that is called a "scheme"?)

Suppose you are reading an article about a large-scale desalinization project in a Third-World country. If the author from the beginning uses belittling terms like *well-intentioned, well-meaning, untested,* and *remains to be seen,* you will sense that this writer's evaluation of the project is likely to be negative. (It is likely to be more aggressively negative if terms like *do gooders, bureaucrats, pencil pushers, far-fetched,* and *fresh out of Harvard* creep in.) On the other hand, the verdict is likely to be positive if from the beginning you notice uplifting terms like *far-reaching, bold, innovative, timely,* and *challenging.*

Formal Outlines

For an exceptionally close study of an article or a report, you may be asked to prepare a formal outline. The traditional formal outline shows a hierarchy of main headings and subheadings, using Roman numerals (I, II, III), capital letters, Arabic numerals (1, 2, 3), and sometimes lower-case letters. Often, first-level heads (Roman numerals) and second-level subheads (capitals) will be sufficient. For more elaborate analysis, you may have to use third-level and fourth-level subheads as needed. Here is a schematized view of an outline that charts each subtopic and subsubtopic of a piece of writing.

YOUR TITLE HERE

THESIS: Your thesis sentence appears here.
  I. Roman numeral for first major division
     A. Capital for first subdivision
        1. Arabic numeral for third-level subhead
        2. Arabic numeral for third-level subhead
     B. Capital for second subdivision
        1. Arabic numeral for third-level subhead
           a. Lower-case for fourth-level subhead (if any)
           b. Lower-case for fourth-level subhead (if any)
        2. Arabic numeral for third-level subhead
 II. Roman numeral for second major division
     A. Capital for first subdivision
        1. Arabic numeral for third-level subhead
           a. Lower-case for fourth-level subhead (if any)
           b. Lower-case for fourth-level subhead (if any)
        2. Arabic numeral for third-level subhead
     B. Capital for second subdivision
        1. Arabic numeral for third-level subhead
        2. Arabic numeral for third-level subhead
        3. Arabic numeral for third-level subhead
III. Roman numeral for third major division
     (and so on)

Here is a sample outline of an article:

The Long Road to Pay Equity

THESIS: While some traditional obstacles to equal pay have weakened, patterns of professional advancement will have to change before true equity can be achieved.

  I. Progress toward increased earning power for women
     A. Changing assumptions about "men's work" and "women's work"
        1. Police work
        2. Management
        3. Medicine
     B. Improved educational opportunities for women
     C. Increasing acceptance of women as long-term employees

II. Continuing obstacles to professional advancement
  A. Crucial role of the 25–35 age span
    1. Identification of junior management
    2. Work toward advanced degrees
    3. Job switching and networking
  B. Continuing family responsibilities for many younger women
    1. Extended absences from the labor force
    2. Necessity of part-time jobs

III. The need for flexibility
  A. New patterns of family leave
  B. Flexible work schedules

TAKING NOTES

Efficient and reliable note taking is a survival skill for any communicator or researcher. Professionals have their own way of gathering potentially useful material. They are likely to have their own filing system for material downloaded from data banks, for photocopied pages from key sources, and for clippings from newspapers or magazines. The ability to retrieve key passages from material on your computer screen and feed them into your notes without the need for keyboarding has greatly reduced the time needed for preparing extensive notes.

Whatever your system of filing background material, you need an efficient system for *pulling out* from your reading (and listening or viewing) material relevant to a current project. Typically, you will start a computer file or a set of note cards. Useful advice: Start each entry with a heading that shows you at a glance what section of a project or subtopic of a paper the entry relates to. Try to limit each entry to one key point—so that later you can move the entry around and feed it into your project at the right spot without having to break up an entry ranging over different points.

Very important: Enclose everything you copy word for word in quotation marks. Include complete publication data with the entry—or key it to a master list of sources. (For instance, use a numerical key or short author-title identification.)

Here are sample entries from a computer file or set of note cards. The student writer is investigating new perspectives on the rise in juvenile crime. He is recording essential input:

- authoritative statistics documenting the rise in youth crime
- comments on the failure of conventional approaches
- definition of a key concept (youth gangs redefined)

Note that the student writer has already done much of the sifting and adapting that is getting the material ready for use in a first draft. For instance, revealing statistics (showing a doubling of youth crime in ten years) have been selected. Exact quotes have been pulled out on policies meant to look "tough" on sexual assaults and other attacks in prison and on repeat offenders.

JUVENILE CRIME—STATS

In 1981, youths were charged with 53,240 violent crimes.
In 1992, the figure was 104,137.

Federal Bureau of Justice

JUVENILE JUSTICE

Trying juvenile offenders as adults and locking them up for long periods of time "looks tough but is shortsighted." Institutions for adult criminals are useless when it comes to crime prevention or rehabilitation. "Juveniles in adult institutions are five times more likely to be sexually assaulted, twice as likely to be beaten by staff, and 50 percent more likely to be attacked with a weapon than youths in a juvenile facility." "Three different studies conducted over a ten-year period . . . show significantly higher recidivism rates for youths tried in adult courts compared to those tried in juvenile courts."

Michael E. Saucier, national chair of the Coalition for Juvenile Justice, speech before Congress March 1994—check issue of *Congressional Record*

REDEFINING GANGS

"Despite conventional thinking, gangs are not anarchies. They can be highly structured, with codes of honor and discipline. For many members, the gang serves as family, as the only place where they can find fellowship, respect, a place to belong. You often hear the word *love* among gang members. Sometimes the gang is the only place where they can find it." (p. 58)

"Sociopathic behavior exists within the framework of a sociopathic society. Under these circumstances, gangs are not a problem; they are a solution, particularly for communities lacking economic, social, and political options." (p. 58)

Luis J. Rodriguez, "Rekindling the Warrior," *Utne Reader* July/August 1994, pp. 58–59.

DRAWING ON A TEXT: Quotation and Paraphrase

How well do you use material from written and oral sources? Study the ways experienced writers introduce quotations. Look for models of the right mix of word-for-word quotation and paraphrase. In **direct quotation**, you produce material verbatim, word for word. You enclose the author's exact words in quotation marks. You signal clearly all omissions (by spaced periods) or additions (by square brackets). In a **paraphrase**, you use extended indirect quotation. You put the author's ideas and information into your own words (no quotation marks). Note that often words like *that, why,* or *how* introduce indirect quotations.

> **Direct:** The candidate for mayor said, "If elected, I promise to make the homeless people on our city streets my top priority."

> **Indirect:** The candidate for mayor promised that if elected she would make the homeless on the city's streets her top priority.

If you repeat it too often, the "he says" or "she says" pattern may sound too mechanical. You can draw on a full range of other credit tags, or introductory phrases, ranging from *according to* or *in the words of* to *as Senator Whalen said.*

> According to Susan Faludi, author of *Backlash*, the dialogue in these women's films "probes the economic and social inequities of traditional wedlock."
>
> To quote psychologist Hilda Ignes, "Neurosis is the condition where an individual's emotional elevators go to the top floor when least desired."
>
> As Judith Guest says in *The Mythic Family*, "I have often been asked why it is that I only write about dysfunctional families. The answer that comes to mind is, what other kinds are there?"

Note that after a tag like "he says" or "the author states," a colon may replace the more usual comma before a long or formal quotation:

> In his extended critique of the recovery movement, David Rieff says: "It is a measure of the continued economic success of the United States that so many of its citizens could be so buffered from the real harshness of the world that they can spend their time anatomizing their own feelings."

Study the ways experienced authors set the stage for quoted material and put it to good use:

Credit Tag

An informative credit tag briefly answers one or more questions like the following: Who is talking? Where or when? What are the person's credentials? How is the quoted material relevant to your discussion? What is the main point?

> Ann Smith, director of a Pennsylvania family service clinic, wrote *Grandchildren of Alcoholics* to "bring this group of people out of hiding and into recovery."
>
> Lauren Teague is a clinical psychologist and vocal critic of the recovery movement. In an article called "Are We All Victims?" he says, "By concentrating on the psychological scars of affluent white Americans, we ensure that the real victims in American society will not get the attention they need to improve their lives."
>
> Dr. Charles Whitfield's "Recovery Potential Survey" in his *Healing the Child Within* includes questions ranging from the familiar "Do you find it difficult to express your emotions?" to the more probing "Do you respond with anxiety to authority figures and angry people?"

Key Quotation

You will often use direct quotation to reproduce a key concept, a central thesis, or a crucial charge or claim. Use a sentence or more of direct quotation to highlight a strong statement. Quote at first hand a startling or provocative idea that might make a reader say: "Are you sure you are reading this right?" By using verbatim quotation, you are signaling to your reader: "This is what the person actually said."

> Advocates of recovery groups claim that almost everyone is in some sense a victim—mostly, of abusive parents. "What we are hearing from the experts," John Bradshaw told an interviewer, "is that approximately 96 percent of the families in this country are dysfunctional to one degree or another."

Interwoven Quotations

To present an author's train of thought efficiently, you will often weave partial quotations organically into your own text. A passage with verbatim quotation interwoven with your own explanations might look like this:

> According to Charles Whitfield, one of the most successful authors in the recovery movement, only between 5 and 20 percent of Americans grew up "with a healthy amount and quality of love, guidance and other nurturing." The rest did not receive enough psychological reinforcement to "form consistently healthy relationships, and to feel good about themselves and what they do." The result may be substance addiction like drink or food, but it may also be "process addiction" taking the form of too much interest in an activity or too much dependence on another person.

Quoted Phrases

Short quoted phrases can give your readers a sense not only of the literal ideas but also of the tone and mindset of authors you have read:

> Traditionally, "child abuse" has meant sexual violation or physical violence. Today, leaders in the recovery movement use the term in a much broader sense. They talk of mental abuse, of parents abusing their children by "invalidating their experiences," even of abusers who "thwart the child's spirituality."

Paraphrase

When are you going to use paraphrase? Putting an author's ideas into your own words gives you greater flexibility than direct quotation. You can shorten a lengthy passage, highlighting key points. You can clarify important ideas by using more accessible language instead of highly technical terms. At the same time, you make sure you do not misrepresent the original author by changing the emphasis or by omitting crucial ifs and buts. (Note that even in an extended paraphrase, you may include short phrases quoted verbatim for an authentic touch.)

Paraphrase: As David Rieff says in an article on the recovery movement in *Harper's,* Americans, unlike Europeans, have always felt that they can make themselves over to become something new. The great American tales, from Cooper's *Deerslayer* to Mark Twain's *Huckleberry Finn,* are about busting loose. Their heroes throw off the bonds of family and tradition, striking out for new territories in order to achieve a new identity.

Paraphrase with Partial Quote: As David Rieff says in an article on the recovery movement in *Harper's,* Americans, unlike Europeans, have always felt that they can make themselves over to become something new. The great American tales, from Cooper's *Deerslayer* to Mark Twain's *Huckleberry Finn,* are about busting loose. Their heroes find a way "of shucking off the bonds of family and tradition," striking out for new territories in order to achieve a new identity.

Omission

If you shorten a quotation (to make key points stand out better, for instance), you need to signal the omission. Use an **ellipsis**–three spaced periods, or four if the omission follows a period marking the end of a sentence. (Much word processing software now substitutes a single-stroke set of three unspaced periods for the traditional ellipsis.)

As Monroe says, "The point of all these self-help books . . . is to give someone the *means* to recover."

As Bradshaw says, "I believe there are moments of great readiness in collective human consciousness. . . . If we were to use a new Jungian archetype to characterize our time it would be the wounded child."

Insertion

When you interrupt a quotation to correct or explain, you need to put your insertion between **square brackets** as shown on the following page.

As Linda Gregg says in *The Self-Help Ethos,* "In California, the state motto–
Eureka ["I have found it"] still reflects the original optimistic, euphoric spirit of the
new settlers."

Block Quotation

When reproducing three or more lines of quoted material, you will set them
off as a **block quotation.** You then do *not* put the block in quotation marks. You
indent one inch or ten typewriter spaces–with no further indenting for a paragraph break at the beginning of the block. (Indent an additional half inch or five
typewriter spaces for a second and any subsequent paragraphs in your block quotation.) Use such chunks of quoted material sparingly–they can give a lumpy quality to your prose, and they may tempt hurried readers to skip them.

John Bradshaw traces most of the ills of modern society to the breakdown of
family life. He says:

> Our family life is killing the souls of human beings. . . . Most families are
> dysfunctional because our rules for normalcy are dysfunctional. . . . The
> important issue is to find out what species of flawed relating your family
> specialized in. Once you know what happened to you, you can do some-
> thing about it.

Quote-Within-Quote

You need *single* quotation marks to signal that the author you quote is in turn
quoting someone else.

In the words of Mayor Garcia, "It is not enough to shout 'Three strikes and
you're out' at youngsters living in the world of crack."

SYNTHESIS: Correlating Texts

How good are you at fitting many different parts together to make a meaningful whole? To make efficient use of your reading, you need to learn how to integrate material from different sources. You extrapolate from each what is most
relevant to your presentation or argument. You then introduce the material from
each source in such a way as to anticipate the queries of readers who ask: "Why is
this here? How does this fit into your overall argument? How does this take your
article a step forward?"

A well-developed paragraph will often integrate material from several sources to offer substantial support for a key point. In an article like the following, the writer draws on supporting evidence at each step in the argument. Note the network of sentences that introduce each chunk of quoted material and relate it to the author's trend of thought:

WHOSE CHILD?

In dealing with questions of child custody, media coverage tends to focus on the most unusual or sensational cases. This year's most publicized lawsuit centered on the case of a mother who had given up her child for adoption and then years later changed her mind. *Newsweek* and *Time* both gave the case full treatment. Under the headline, "Whose Child?" Clint Doherty said in a *Newsweek* article . . .

In the past, other things being equal, mothers could count on being awarded custody. In "Women and Children Last," Lenore J. Weitzman studied patterns of divorce and child support based on the assumption that the divorced father would leave the ex-wife and children to start a new life. . . .

Increasingly, fathers sue for custody and win. A study by two sociologists at Columbia University found . . .

Custody cases turn ugly when one party charges the other with being an unfit mother or father. Psychologist Norma Menendez interviewed several women who emerged from such court battles bruised and traumatized. In her article "The High Price of Custody," she says . . .

Is joint custody the answer to the bruising tug-of-war between contending parties? How does it work out in practice? Brent Hartz, Director of Family Counseling at the Broadmoor Institute, talked to children living under joint-custody arrangements . . .

WRITING WORKSHOP: Using Your Sources

The following is an excerpt from an article in *Business Weekly* for July 10, 1995. What sources does the author use? How does he put them to use? What is the mix of oral and printed sources? How does the author introduce quotations—how does he put them in context and establish the credentials of his sources? Where does he use direct quotation; where does he use paraphrase? Where does he use quoted phrases, buzzwords, or the like?

NEEDED: A TWO-WAY SOCIAL CONTRACT IN THE WORKPLACE

Robert Kuttner

America's best corporations are caught between two opposite first principles.   1
One prizes the engaged, empowered employee. The other views employees as expendable costs. Reconciling these views is like squaring the circle.

It is hard to pick up a business magazine without encountering compelling tales of companies that improved productivity through the "high road"–a policy of empowered employees, teams, and high-performance work. This model implies a reciprocal commitment between management and employees, but in an economy of relentless downsizing something appears to be lacking. The company can only insist that high-performance work is necessary to stay in business: It does not guarantee that high performance will be rewarded or even that the employee will keep a job. The corporate social contract in America today, says Anthony P. Carnevale, chairman of the National Commission on Employment Policy, "is the sound of one hand clapping."

You might think this one-sided social contract would have costs to employee morale and hence to productivity. But, evidently, fear is a powerful motivator. In his study of corporate loyalty, *White Collar Blues*, Charles Heckscher was granted access to middle managers at eight large corporations undergoing major restructurings, including General Motors, Dow Chemical, and AT&T. Heckscher, who chairs the labor studies and employment relations department at Rutgers University, found that employees were highly dedicated but had scant confidence that their devotion would be repaid. Yet they retained a surprising degree of loyalty. "Perhaps the principal puzzle in companies undergoing the shock of change," he concluded, "is that it produces so little conflict and disintegration."

GLOWING REPORT

At another conference at the Jerome Levy Economics Institute of Bard College, the keynote speaker was Frank P. Doyle, executive vice-president of General Electric Co. Doyle confirmed Heckscher's portrait. GE today does three times the business it did in 1980–with half the workforce. To get there, Doyle said, "we did a lot of violence to the expectations of the American workforce. . . . We downsized. We de-layered. And we outsourced."

GE is among the most dynamic of U.S. companies, with a deep commitment to   5
imaginative human-resource strategies. For its core employees, GE is an attractive place to work. However even the best of our corporations cannot guarantee career

security, no matter how dedicated its workforce. If this is the core, heaven help the periphery.

At a conference at the Radcliffe Public Policy Center, there was much talk about a "new economic equation" to reconcile work and family life. Another corporate manager with a strong commitment to core employees, Robert E. Boruff, vice-president for manufacturing at Saturn Corp., gave a glowing report about how his company offers subsidized child care, flexible hours, and help to workers pursuing more education. But even Saturn uses outsourcing and contingent workers, who do not receive all these benefits.

HIGH-MINDEDNESS?

Corporate America is littered with companies that once prided themselves on generous fringe benefits and no-layoff policies–companies that now devalue health benefits and jettison faithful employees by the thousand. Although they talk a good game, America's most successful companies seem to have decided that a workplace compact is necessary only for their most valued workers. So a humane corporate culture for the entire workforce cannot be anchored in the high-mindedness or even the enlightened self-interest of the corporation.

READING ON-LINE

Reading on-line gives you instant access to a wide range of data, background information, news, and commentary. Today people can do much work at their home computers, bypassing the limitations of conventional library materials–which may be incomplete, missing, vandalized, or checked out. The isolated reader of the past becomes part of a larger audience of like-minded participants: Visitors to a web site like the Whole Earth 'Lectronic Link (WELL) can follow special-interest material tracked by many people.

Tasks that used to require hours of footwork or rifling through pages become easy:

- A reader zeroing in on a trend big in current economic news can punch in key words like OUTSOURCING or DOWNSIZING or FLEXIBLE SCHEDULING or TEMPS (for temporaries)–and call up a range of current coverage, downloading promising material for future use.

- For a researcher in the humanities, searching the great literary classics for relevant citations ceases to be an incredibly time-consuming chore. With Melville's *Moby Dick* available on disk, a researcher can instantly identify all passages mentioning BLUBBER, for instance, in the great mythic novel about whalers and whales.

- With rich materials assembled on a CD-ROM, reading turns into a multi-media experience. An art history student may be taking a virtual-reality trip through a Paris museum, stopping in front of a favorite impressionist paint-ing, zooming in for a close-up view, clicking on biographical material about the painter or critical discussion of the work.

Some readers are already reading the Sunday edition of the *New York Times* on-line. Books and articles are beginning to be published simultaneously in hardcover and electronic versions. Encyclopedias—from *Grolier's* to the *Britannica*—are available on-line and save the user the trek to a library. A minor growth industry is devel-oping navigational aids that promise to help users find their way around the Inter-net. Manuals ranging from *How to Navigate the Internet* to *Internet for Dummies* guide newcomers in their search for specific resources.

The flexibility of working on the computer allows you to develop your own personal working style. Articles you have downloaded are yours for future use and do not have to be returned to the library. You can make the print bigger or smaller or change fonts. You may be able to interact with the authors, addressing queries to them. You can print out hard copy for close reading and annotation.

Remember cautions like the following:

- *Articles you read on-line may be adapted from the original.* They may be digests or abridgments, with inadequate information about authorship or the origin of the materials.

- *Quality of materials can vary tremendously.* Unlike print publishing, the Internet does not have editors, reviewers, or critics who filter the flow of material—and keep much of it from seeing the light of day. One researcher reported that he had to wade through files ranging from expert testimony to an eighth-grader's library paper. Historical or scientific "facts" you have tracked down may be inaccurate or out of date.

- *You may miscalculate the required investment in time and money.* Inexperienced users may underestimate access or utilization costs. (A librarian may be able to help you estimate costs for accessing research resources.) Newcomers may not be prepared for delays or interruptions in times of user overload. Wait-ing for the computer to assemble images may prove frustratingly time-consuming.

- *Questions of copyright remain undecided.* Will users of the Internet respect others' intellectual property? Will original authors earn royalties based on how many users log in? Will publishing contracts have to be rewritten to assure residual rights?

9

Writing as Process

A successful piece of writing is the end result of a process. Successful writers know how to take a writing project through its stages. They do justice to key dimensions of the writing process: purpose–audience–input–organization–drafting–revision–editing. These phases of the process are not separate or self-contained. They overlap; they intermesh. While drafting the second or third major part of a paper, you may already be going back for some needed revision in the first part, making adjustments necessitated by what came up later. During final revision, you may still be looking for additional input: a striking example or quotation to bolster a weak point.

DISCOVERING YOUR PURPOSE

What are you trying to do? What is your purpose? A successful piece of writing cannot be an empty exercise; it has to start with something you wanted to do or something that needed to be done. You may set out to accomplish one or more of the following, refining or clarifying your purpose as you go along:

Sharing Information

What is the truth about job loss and job creation? What is the truth about declining employment in high-paying manufacturing jobs or middle-management positions? Are downsizing and massive layoffs continuing? What new jobs are being created in other sectors of the economy? An investigative writer ferrets out reliable statistics and secures candid testimony from authoritative sources. Those who want to know or need to know will welcome well-researched, up-to-date information laid out in an accessible pattern.

Writing to Explain

How do viral infections work? Why is TB making a comeback? How is the AIDS virus different? In vital areas of public health, we turn to writers who can cut through the fog of prejudice or hysteria. We need them to explain processes and causal relationships that we have to understand before we can make informed decisions.

Investigating a Trend

Much writing sheds light on a current trend. In the following planning report, a student writer maps out a trend–watching paper:

Planning Report: After spending two summers as a leader for the city's drop-in summer program, I have noticed that children today seem more violent than children I grew up with. Since I plan to continue working with children, I believe that studying the effect of television violence on younger children would help me with my future career. I plan to talk with teachers and counselors, and I am look-ing for relevant articles and reports on current studies. Today's children are differ-ent because of the lack of parental guidance and because of television becoming the babysitter. I am not trying to condemn parents for their lack of time and funds because often both are working (and some at two jobs) to support the family. I want to concentrate on why children playing in schoolyards are more likely today to raise their fists to a teacher if the teacher tells them no than they were fifteen years ago. We can see the rise in children's violence in expulsions from schools, in the constant reprimands by counselors and administrators, and, when young people grow up, by the increase in violence and gang warfare.

Correcting a Misunderstanding

People write with special motivation when they set out to correct a misunder-standing. They may write to correct misleading and damaging information. They may write to counteract a stereotype that harms members of their group. (Are all Americans of Scandinavian descent unemotional, uptight, or repressed? Do all African Americans have natural rhythm? Do all women have a strong nurtur-ing side?)

Writing to Define

What does the term *modern* mean in "modern art" and "modern" literature? What timeframe are we talking about? What assumptions would modern thinkers, writers, or artists share? Part or all of an article may focus on defining such a key term–on staking out the territory it covers:

The modern era, from the deep perspective of the student of human thought, began after the Renaissance, or possibly with the Enlightenment, or at any rate whenever ideas such as technological progress and the discovery of knowledge through reason and science began to undermine the authority of religion. . . . "To be modern," wrote Marshall Berman, "is to find ourselves in an environment that promises us adventure, power, joy, growth, transforma-tion of ourselves and the world–and, at the same time, threatens to destroy everything we have, everything we know, everything we are. . . . To be modern is to be part of a universe in which, as Marx said, 'all that is solid melts into air.'"

BENJAMIN WOOLLEY, *Virtual Worlds*

Arguing a Point

Should authority for wiretapping by public agencies like the FBI extend to new forms of electronic communication? What is the past record of such agencies in observing the stipulations of court orders? What are the misgivings of organizations like the American Civil Liberties Union? Do we want Big Brother agencies to pry into our e-mail or institute surveillance of electronic bulletin boards?

Writing to Persuade

Persuasion aims at results. Sometimes the result sought is a change in attitude, but more often the writer wants something concrete from the reader: a vote, an endorsement, a sale. Logical argument is often part of persuasion, especially when you are writing for readers who want to make up their own minds. But the secret of persuasion is to *motivate* your readers–to appeal to their personal interests, to get their emotions involved, to appeal to their shared interests as members of a group, or to mobilize shared values.

WRITING FOR AN AUDIENCE

Who is your audience? Your estimate of your intended audience affects both what you say and how you say it–it affects both substance and style. For instance, not just what is said but also *how* a writer discusses nicotine and tar in cigarettes will vary considerably depending on the intended reader. Is the communication intended for a cigarette ad for young smokers, for testimony before a congressional committee, for an internal memo in a tobacco company's public relations department, or for a symposium with fellow scientists?

Degrees of Formality

From the beginning of a writing project, you need to ask yourself: On a given subject, for a given audience, how formal and tightly structured will your writing be expected to be? Or, how informal can it be, with a more natural flow and with an occasional lighter touch? How personal or how impersonal will your writing be expected to be? How **objective** should it be–staying close to verifiable data? Or, how much room will there be for **subjective** impressions–anecdotal (more or less casual) observation, tentative conclusions or even hunches, personal likes and dislikes?

Here are accounts of two writing projects representing different levels of formality–different bands of the spectrum that goes from the personal to the impersonal:

- Suppose you are writing an art history paper about Picasso's famous painting of the Guernica bombing during the Spanish civil war. You are likely to adopt a **moderately formal** style with a strong personal dimension. You may be expected to be fairly objective about aspects of the composition–lines and textures, and features of the cubist painting style of which Picasso was a leading creator. (You need to show that you are knowledgeable about the technical aspects of your subject.) But ultimately your main concern may be the personal emotions of horror, helplessness, or rage the painting arouses in the viewer. These would be hard to discuss in a dry impersonal style. The words *I, me*, or *my* (first person pronouns) might appear naturally in your discussion, even though they were once frowned on in a strictly formal academic style.

- Suppose you are preparing a report on a scientific experiment for fellow researchers. You are likely to conform to a highly structured format and a **formal** impersonal style. Personal preferences and personal problems of the researcher would distract and interfere. Others regardless of background, gender, or personality–have to be able to verify information, replicate experiments, or produce the same results. Formal purpose statements and formal summaries may be required to spell out intentions, procedures, and findings. The impersonal effect is likely to be reinforced by the use of passive constructions–not "I made these arrangements" but "arrangements were made."

Peer Group and Popular Audience

Much research published in scientific journals aims at a small peer audience of experts in a limited specialty. Readers are likely to be familiar with both standard sources and new challenging perspectives in their field. They are going to be prepared for a detailed justification of research methods or detailed analysis of statistics. They will expect personal comment or personal anecdote to be kept out or kept to a minimum.

By contrast, a writer treating the same subject in a popular science journal is likely to spend much more time bringing the subject to life for the reader. The writer may feel a need for explaining key terms or for using analogies that help the lay audience visualize important concepts. Personal comments may illuminate the writer's personal background or fascination with the subject, as in Stephen Hawking's widely read discussions of issues in modern astronomy.

The General Reader

Much writing aims at a general audience cutting across regional, occupational, and gender lines. Newspapers assume a reader is informed enough to know where Bosnia is or why people owning stocks clamor for a reduced tax rate on capital gains. A local academic journal publishing articles by faculty from different disciplines may assume an audience with the equivalent of a college degree. Contributors may expect readers to know who John Steinbeck was and what role his *Grapes of Wrath* played in American literature of the Depression era. They may assume some knowledge of early leaders in the women's movement, like Susan B. Anthony or Sojourner Truth.

Your classmates will usually be a cross-section of general readers somewhere between a high school and a college degree. However, even when writing mainly for your classmates, you know that reader response may vary considerably depending on the composition of the class. When you are writing about immigration, welfare, or single mothers, it will make a difference whether most of your classmates are from affluent middle-class neighborhoods or from a minority background. Class, gender, race, ethnicity, party affiliation, religion, sexual orientation— all these may affect how your readers respond to your data and your arguments.

In-Group Audience, Neutral Audience, Hostile Audience

Do you think of your reader as friend or enemy? Your writing strategy will vary depending on the allegiances and commitments of your readers. Are you addressing an in-group sharing many of your own commitments? Or are you targeting an uncommitted or neutral audience—readers who need to be persuaded but might be open to new ideas? Or are you writing for an unfriendly or downright hostile audience—where you would have to try hard to find common ground and to present arguments that your readers would not reject out of hand?

- Writing for an in-group audience of fellow educators, a college teacher is likely to assume basic shared values: a commitment to the free exchange of ideas, the value of lifelong learning, the importance of funding for research, the need for support of libraries. The writer might then devote less time on proving need (which might be preaching to the already converted). More effort could go into developing strategies for filling these needs or for overcoming obstacles in times of budget crunch or public apathy.

- An advocate of free trade policies might be addressing an unfriendly audience with strong sympathies with organized labor. Among the questions that would have to be faced: How to address serious reservations about opening the borders to the products of cheap foreign labor? How to deal with resentment of countries that practice "free trade" with the United States while sealing off internal markets?

WORKING UP MATERIAL

How do you work up the material for a writing project? Experienced writers draw on a full range of resources. As appropriate to a particular task, they draw on first-hand observation, past experience, past or current reading, and informal or formal research. They collect relevant data, excerpt and interpret statistics, and get input from experts, insiders, or people in the know. They may utilize questionnaires, organize a minisurvey, or conduct informal or formal interviews. Skimpy input makes for thin and unconvincing writing. Experienced writers will often sift a wealth of possibly useful material and gradually narrow their choice to what is most relevant and effective.

To generate promising material, use or adapt prewriting techniques like the following:

Brainstorming

For many topics, a good first step is to take stock of what you already know. **Brainstorming** is a fast-moving method of calling up memories, observations, and associations. You jot down anything that comes to mind concerning a key word or central issue—whether saving the forests, victim feminism, or backlash politics. You conduct a quick search of the memory banks of the brain, letting one thing lead to another. You jog your memory for striking images, revealing incidents, high points of an article, important statistics, quotable quotes. You include any questions that arise or tentative ideas. At this stage, you don't edit the material. You are trying to work up a fund of possibly useful material, to be sorted out later.

The following are brainstorming notes for a paper on gun control. What happened when the writer decided: "Think guns"? What kind of paper might result if the writer followed up some of the points included here? What might be the writer's focus, strategy, and key evidence?

Brainstorming:

Guns Kill

my best friend has a gun

I don't like guns in the house, especially near kids

GUNS KILL PEOPLE, regardless of what NRA says

yes, people would still die without guns around, but not so easily what do most criminals use? guns

more men are obsessed with guns than women, why?

people collect guns (ok as long as you don't provide bullets)

children die from guns going off accidentally

sawed-off shotguns—are some guns bad, others good?

hunting guns

uzis—outgunned police

background checks not enough

you can't do a drive-by shooting if you don't have a gun

why are guns such a big deal in our society?

children at play shoot each other

WORKSHOP 1

Jot down a similar set of brainstorming notes for one of the following: women's sports, battered wives, assisted suicide, sexual harassment, hate speech, jocks. Try to include concrete images, actual incidents, specifics from your reading or viewing.

Clustering

Clustering makes lines of association branch out from a core meaning or core issue. You put a key work or key concept at the core of the cluster. You then pursue different lines of thought, letting a network of thoughts and images take shape. Clustering is a form of "brainstorming-plus": Even while it calls up images and ideas from your mental memory banks, it lays them out in a pattern. A pattern takes shape that can help you structure a passage, a paper, a presentation, or a script for a speech.

The cluster on the following page maps thoughts and associations that thinking about immigration brought to one writer's mind. What kind of paper do you see taking shape as you study the cluster? How might the writer proceed? What would be major areas covered?

WORKSHOP 2

Cluster the same term on which you did a brainstorming exercise or another term like *immigration, racism, violence, fundamentalism,* or *censorship.*

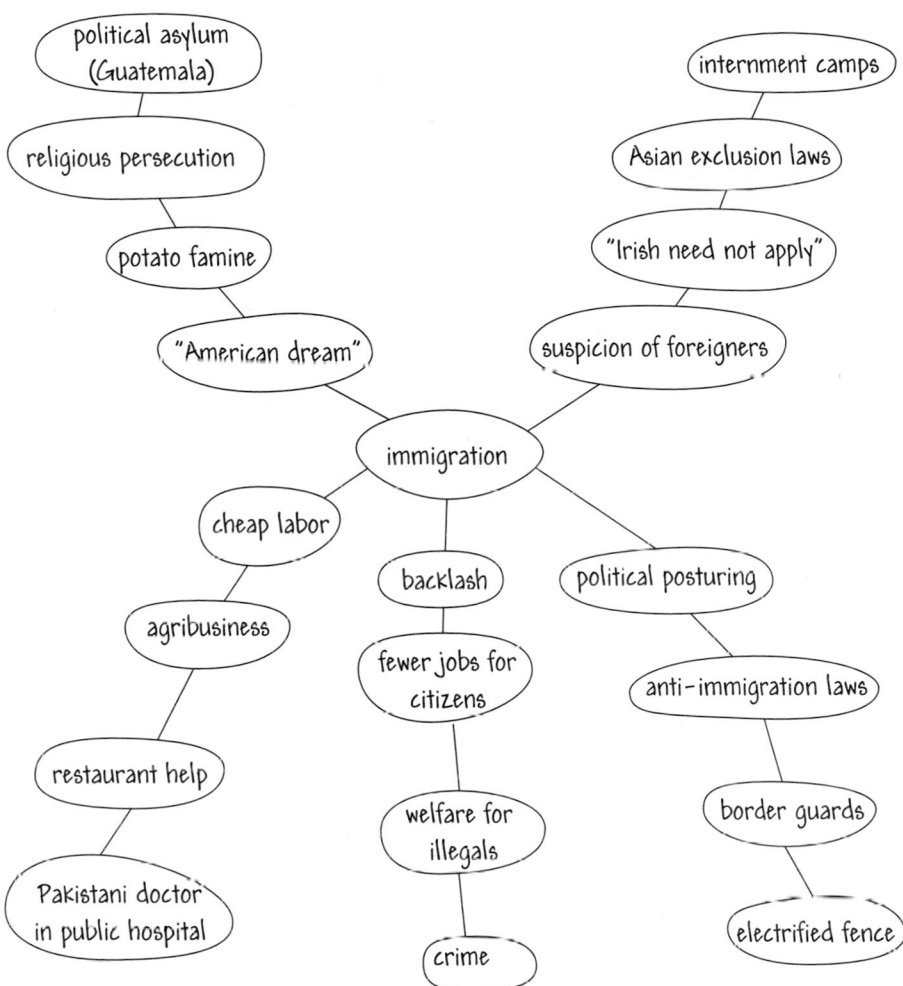

Discovery Frames

Discovery frames are sets of questions that help you explore a topic. They map out a program for checking out relevant material. For instance, in exploring a current issue, you can usually make headway by asking yourself questions like the following: Have I recently seen newspaper or magazine articles relevant to this issue? Have I watched a movie or television program related to my topic? What buzzwords, slogans, or clichés are likely to come up when this issue is discussed? Where has this issue touched my own life or the lives of people I know?

To work up material on a current issue, try adapting for your own purposes a set of questions like those on the following page.

Discovery Frame:

1. *What is the issue?* What is at stake? What striking incident, quotation, or statistic could dramatize the issue for your readers?

2. *How are the media dealing with the issue?* What examples of media coverage do you remember? Where have you seen the issue treated in articles, editorials, talk shows, movies, or documentaries?

3. *What popular misconceptions cloud the issue?* What prejudices does it bring into play? What are familiar or predictable misunderstandings?

4. *What do the experts say?* Who are the authorities on this subject? What can you learn from insiders or people in the know?

5. *What is your personal connection with the issue?* Where has it touched on your own experience? What difference has it made in your own life or the lives of people you know well?

6. *What lies ahead?* Where do current trends point? What are major options? Is the outlook promising or discouraging?

Here is a discovery frame focused on a current trend. Like other discovery frames, this one sets up a rough possible framework for a paper. A writer filling in a paragraph or two for each slot would have a rough first draft.

Staying Fit

1. *Surface Symptoms*: Where do you observe signs of the fitness movement? What signs of it do you see in your neighborhood or on campus? What role does it play in advertising and more generally in the media? (Do you see joggers in the streets? Are you aware of special events–Saturday morning races, marathons, bicycle competitions? Do you see ads for exercise bikes, rowing machines, running shoes?)

2. *A First-Hand Look*: Are you or people you know working out? How did you become personally involved? Have friends or family members taken up body building, weight lifting, or aerobics:? How has it changed their lives?

3. *Background Facts*: Do you read articles about health and fitness? Have you seen statistics on the benefits of exercise? What do experts say about weight control, stress reduction, or the prevention of heart disease?

4. *Deeper Causes*: Why is keeping in shape a major goal of today's young people? What values in our culture drive people toward more awareness of their bodies? Do we have a cult of youth in our society?

5. *Second Thoughts*: Have you seen any signs of a backlash against the fitness cult? Have you read warnings about the dangers of excessive or inappropriate exercise? Do you know people who have become disillusioned?

WORKSHOP 3

Use or adapt one of the discovery frames you have just studied for a topic that you have previously used for prewriting on another topic of your choice. (For instance, choose volunteers, violence, sexual harassment, affirmative action, hate speech, jocks, immigration, prejudice, violence, guns, or censorship.) Fill in one or two paragraphs of material under each heading in your discovery frame.

SHAPING A FIRST DRAFT

How do you get from a stack of promising material to a first draft? You will be asking yourself two intertwining questions: First, how does it all fit together—how am I going to organize my material and lay it out? Second, what does it all prove—what is going to be my overarching point or unifying **thesis**?

Generating a Working Outline

As you work up your material, you look for clues on how to structure it. How will you organize the material you have gathered? From the beginning, you try to sort things out. You group together related information; you note comments that point in the same direction. You note questions that you hear asked more than one time. As you think about your subject, read up on it, or talk to other people about it, you look for points that tend to come up again and again.

Here are examples of how a rough working outline might take shape:

- Why is immigration or especially illegal immigration a hot-button issue in current political campaigns? In exploring current anti-immigration sentiment, you several times read about job insecurity felt by working-class Americans. There is a widespread feeling that immigrants work cheaply and take jobs away from already hard-pressed native-born citizens. At the same time, people purporting to speak for the hard-pressed taxpayer stoke resentment of rising welfare costs. Is it true that illegal aliens cross the border to go on welfare? Law-and-order politicians play on the fear of crime—crime attributed to jobless illegals.

A rough outline for your paper on anti-immigration sentiment is already beginning to emerge here:

job insecurity
resentment of welfare costs
fear of crime

Reading an assigned chapter in your American history text or watching a television special may alert you to the fact that the country has experienced earlier waves of anti-immigrant feeling. You consider starting your paper with some historical perspective. However, you then decide you should first dramatize the issue by pointing to such current symptoms of anti-foreign sentiment as English-Only legislation or opposition to bilingual education. Your adjusted working outline might look like this:

Immigrants Go Home

symptoms of anti-foreign sentiment
    English-only
    opposing bilingual education
earlier anti-immigration cycles
    anti-Irish feeling
    Chinese Exclusion Act
root causes of current anti-immigration feeling
    job insecurity
    resentment of welfare costs
    fear of crime

- Why do recent immigrants seem to assimilate less easily or less completely than earlier waves of immigrants? Why does the "melting pot" theory of American society no longer seem to work the way it used to in the past? As you sort out a range of observations and comments, major reasons might come into focus as follows:

The New Unmeltable Immigrants

wide differences in ethnic identity
    not "Asians" but Koreans, Japanese, Filipino, Vietnamese
    divergent cultures: Ethiopians, Afghans
wide differences in social class
    Mexican agricultural workers and Mexican American engineers
    Vietnamese shopkeepers and Chinese computer specialists
increasing isolation in ethnic ghettos

A working outline is just what its name implies: It is a tentative itinerary. You may need to revise it as additional data or testimony point your paper in a slightly different direction. This last example might look like the outline on the following page when expanded and reformatted as a traditional formal outline.

The New Unmeltable Immigrants

I. The traditional melting pot

II. Obstacles to assimilation
    A. Wide differences in ethnic identity
        1. Not "Asians" but Koreans, Japanese, Vietnamese
        2. Divergent cultures: Ethiopians, Afghans
    B. Wide differences in social class
        1. Mexican agricultural workers and Mexican American engineers
        2. Vietnamese shopkeepers and Chinese computer specialists
    C. Increasing isolation in ethnic ghettos

III. The new American mosaic

Pushing Toward a Thesis

At the same time that you are trying to get your material under control, you will be pushing toward a unifying central idea, or thesis. As your paper begins to take more definite shape, what might have been at first a working hypothesis or trial thesis should evolve into the overarching thesis for your paper as a whole. For the first of the two papers on different aspects of the immigration issue, your trial thesis might have been:

> *Trial Thesis:* Current anti-immigration sentiment is rooted in worry about jobs, welfare costs, and crime.

However, your final thesis will explain more if you put cause and effect in its historical context:

> *Thesis:* The latent suspicion of foreigners becomes aggravated when hard times make voters worry about jobs, welfare costs, and crime.

For the second paper, the final thesis might read like this:

> *Thesis:* The melting pot theory no longer works for many of today's ethnically diverse, economically unequal, and increasingly isolated new immigrants.

Such a thesis works as a program for your paper; it already previews major points or major parts of the paper. If your thesis stays too vague or general, your readers will not have a good sense of the direction your paper is likely to take.

Sharpen or refine thesis statements that suggest too open an itinerary or too un-formed a program:

Too Open: New patterns of acculturation are changing the ways immigrants relate to American society.

Sharpened: Immigrants today can become integrated into American society without denying their roots; they are no longer forced to close one chapter and start a new.

Developing Your Points

As you start writing your draft, each point in your outline will turn into a commitment to the reader. In filling in the major slots in your overall plan, your agenda is to follow up each key point with authentic examples or supporting evidence. Remember that the less experienced writer tends to underestimate the reader's need for backup, follow-up, development, or support. In the paper on ob-stacles to assimilation, you would follow through with details like the following:

> One major obstacle to easy or rapid assimilation is the great ethnic and cul-tural diversity of recent immigrants. The new immigrants are often divided by age-old nationalistic loyalties and resentments. "White America" might apply the same familiar stereotypes to all Asians. However, Filipinos, Pakistanis, and Indonesians come from very different cultures. Chinese and Vietnamese, like Japanese and Ko-reans, have a long history of warfare or colonial exploitation. In the words of a history professor, "It was not until I worked with two Asian students, one Korean and one Filipino, that I realized the strength of national pride with the so-called Asian community. We do them a disservice by lumping the different groups together" . . .

Here, from a paper on a different topic, is an example of a well-developed paragraph following up one key point:

> Even though mass production and automation were supposed to turn us all into faceless robots, today's consumer is actually given an incredible range of choice. It is not just that visitors from former socialist countries look in awe at store shelves filled with cereals offering every possible mix of ingredients–bran, shred-ded wheat, corn flakes, dried fruit, and vitamins, and on and on. Everything from cars to bicycles and stereo sets is customized, personalized, and individualized. In the 1920s, Henry Ford built about two million identical cars a year, joking that a customer could have any color as long as it was black. Today, the sales represen-tative in the automobile showroom (which the customer has selected from a dozen others on automobile row) punches in preferred colors and accessories so that the plant can produce a "made-to-order" car to the customer's requirements.

Jeremy Rifkin, in The End of Work, reports that a Japanese bicycle maker using a computerized design system can turn out a totally customized bicycle (complete with the customer's name) in three hours–although the company holds up delivery for a few days so the customer can savor "the joy of anticipation."

WORKSHOP 4

Write a first draft of a paper on a topic you have explored during earlier prewriting activities. Prepare to share it with your classmates to discuss especially your overall plan, your thesis, and your use of supporting material.

REVISING AND RETHINKING

How attuned are you to the need for revision? For writers in the real world, revision is a fact of life. Memos are rewritten after input from colleagues and superiors. Important brochures are critiqued by concerned members of the organization. Textbooks are rewritten and revised in response to criticism from editors, reviewers, and users.

Revision is the time for second thoughts. It gives you a chance to strengthen the promising parts of a paper and to deal with what is weak or doubtful. Effective revision can make your key points emerge more clearly. It can fill in striking examples or statistics to bring the subject to life. It may rearrange major sections of your paper for a clearer flow. Effective revision builds on the strength of an earlier draft: It makes the material you had in your first draft show to better advantage. It makes the arguments you presented more convincing.

Instructor's Feedback

Every writing project is different. However, suggestions like the following come up again or again in editorial comments on manuscripts or in instructor's feedback on student writing:

1. *Check your introduction, or lead.* Does it do enough to arouse the interest and focus the attention of the busy reader? Dramatize the issue: Start with a detailed striking example, or with a provocative insider's quotation, or with thought-provoking statistics.
2. *Provide a stronger preview or overview.* Give your readers a sense of direction; alert them to the major waystations in your paper.

Uninformative: We will examine three of what are increasingly becoming common variations on the traditional family and some of the problems they create.

(What are the three? Can your preview make them interesting or plausible for your reader?)

3. *Scale down sweeping generalizations.* Are you making exaggerated claims? Sometimes the strategic use of a phrase like "on the whole" or "by and large" can protect you against charges of oversimplification. Scale down a thesis that promises your readers more than you can deliver.

4. *Build up details and examples.* Select one or more examples for a closer look. Perhaps treat one test case in enough convincing factual detail so that your readers will respect you as an authority on your subject. Add an example or evidence from a wider range to forestall charges of having relied on an unrepresentative sample.

5. *Reassess your overall strategy.* If necessary, shuffle material for a better flow from the familiar to the new, or from the simple to the more controversial. In your first draft, you may have looked at alternative living arrangements in the following order: unmarried couples–mixed marriages–same-sex partnership. As you rethink this arrangement, you might ask yourself: Is your middle category the least frequent and perhaps still most controversial? Perhaps you should *lead up* to it:

Overcoming Prejudice

- unmarried couples–an alternative to traditional marriages that was once frowned upon but is now widely accepted
- same-sex relationships–still often objected to but slowly becoming more familiar as the result of media acceptance and gay advocacy
- racially mixed marriages–still often skirted in popular entertainment

6. *Recognize apparent exceptions or countertrends.* Don't simply sweep complications under the proverbial rug. Anticipate and defuse objections. Where appropriate, use a pattern like "It is true that . . . however, a closer look reveals . . ."

7. *Furnish better handles or labels for key divisions of your paper.* It will be hard for your reader to visualize actual people when you use labels like "cohabiting couples" or bureaucratic phrases like "persons of opposite sex sharing living quarters." Readers will have an easier time grasping and remembering your overall scheme if you use labels like the following:

Non–Nuclear Lifestyles

- unmarried couples
- single-parent families
- "blend families"–new family units that combine or blend parts of earlier families dissolved by divorce
- same-sex partnerships–gay or lesbian couples

8. *Check for uneven treatment of major categories.* For instance, there has been much publicity concerning same-sex domestic partners. Much has been written about initiatives and counter-initiatives to give or deny them the same legal rights–pension rights, health care privileges, hospital visitation rights–as heterosexual couples. Discussing recent test cases and court decisions under this heading, you might have unintentionally shortchanged your other major categories. To restore the balance, you may have to build other parts of your paper up with case histories, insider testimony, striking statistics.

9. *Conclude with a stronger punchline.* It is too easy to conclude with a pious hope: "Family arrangements considered unconventional today may well be considered normal tomorrow." Try to make your conclusion offer something more positive and concrete:

> The big question becomes: "How important was the traditional nuclear family?" Professor Calero, anthropologist, says, "It is a good idea for people to grow up with a strong sense of family, of belonging, of knowing who they are." He continues, however, "it does not have to be a traditional nuclear family; it could be any family." What is important for the development of an individual is to receive affection–if not from the traditional family then from some other "family"–relatives, church groups, neighborhood groups, or women's associations.

Peer Review

Experienced writers are audience-conscious. They have learned to anticipate the reactions–positive or negative–of their readers. In your writing class, you may be able to profit from peer criticism or peer review. In turn, you may be asked to respond to fellow students' work. Aim at balance: Be sure to address the larger questions of strategy or adequate support as well as more specific or localized problems of sentence structure, punctuation, or spelling that damage a writer's credibility.

The following is a sample format for peer review.

PEER REVIEW

Title of paper _____

Name of reviewer _____

1. PURPOSE   What does the writer set out to do? What for you is the main point? Does it come through clearly enough? Why or why not?
2. ORGANIZATION   What is the author's strategy for tackling the subject? Is the

(Continued)

organization easy or hard to follow? Does it make sense? Is it anywhere
unclear or confusing? (Include a brief outline of major points or sections.)

3. FOLLOW-UP   Where does the author turn for material? Is there a good mix
   of sources? Which examples or what evidence do you consider effective?
   Are examples or support anywhere weak or missing?

4. BEGINNINGS AND ENDINGS   Is the title effective? Does the introduction get
   you involved in the subject? Does it bring the subject to life? Why or why
   not? Does the conclusion leave you with a strong impression? Why or why
   not?

5. STYLE   Is the writing awkward or a pleasure to read? Are there any images
   or phrases that stick in your mind? (Do you anywhere want to write in the
   margin "well put" or "well said"?) Are there any passages that seem murky,
   wordy, or confused? Does the author anywhere fall back on clichés?

6. MECHANICS   What matters of spelling, punctuation, or grammar need attention? Are any especially distracting or damaging to the writer's credibility?

7. READER RESPONSE   Where do you agree and where do you disagree? Are
   some issues played down or ignored? Do some issues get too much attention? What questions would you like to ask the author?

8. OPTIONAL COMMENTS   Do you have any other advice or personal comment
   for the author?

WORKSHOP 5

Prepare a peer review of the following early draft of a student paper. Pool
your reactions with those of your classmates. How effective is the paper? What
needs work?

Speech and the Debate

"Why do blacks have sex on their minds?" cracked a student broad-
caster at the University of Michigan while on the air. "Because they have
their pubic hair on their heads." The First Amendment states that Congress shall make no law abridging the freedom of speech or of the press.
Is it a violation of the First Amendment to try to curb such vulgar, crude,
and crass language and jokes on college campuses, or should it be considered as a step towards eliminating the abuse of our freedom and
rights? In the words of a writer in *The Chronicle of Higher Education*, should
"the rights of insensitive, viciously motivated members of college and
university communities be placed above victims' rights to an education
untainted by bigoted animosity?"

As the old adage goes: "Sticks and stones may break my bones, but
words will never hurt me." We hear vulgar language and see obscene
messages on T-shirts every day. However, as another writer said in *The*

Chronicle of Higher Education, the popular adage may be misleading: "The broken bone may heal. But the harm of being identified as 'nigger' or 'fag' or 'broad' will not fade." Hate speech, or fighting words as they are often called, have found a home in many places, including college campuses. Although hate speech is often not considered socially acceptable in today's society, many feel that we live in a free country and that the enforcement of "politically correct" speech interferes with their basic rights as Americans.

Although I have encountered numerous derogatory or offensive comments about women, gays, and various ethnic groups, I personally have not had any "hate speech" directed toward me. There seems to be a "fine line," a freshman of Portuguese descent told me, "between hate speech and just joking around." For instance, I myself have on numerous occasions called my often cheap and stingy Chinese friend a "chink"– derived from the sound a stingy person might make when counting his or her coins. This is not taken offensively, because I am also Chinese American and my friend knows that I do not mean it to be derogatory. However, if my friend and I were to say some of the potentially racial things we say to each other to a stranger, it would be considered offensive.

According to an editorial in the campus daily, the First Amendment is supposed to protect only speech that contributes to the exchange of ideas. Therefore, speech that incites violent acts is not protected. However, John Seigenthaler, in an article in *Editor and Publisher*, finds the enforcement of politically correct speech "offensive to the traditional concept that the academy should be an open forum." Hate speech codes are designed to protect "African Americans, women, gays, Jews, Native Americans, Hispanics, Asians, and other minorities." However, Seigenthaler feels that "if there is no hope for the academy but suppression of thought and speech, there is no hope."

Words that Seigenthaler recognized as being "hateful, mean-spirited, insulting, personally demeaning and emotionally debilitating" should have no rights on college campuses or in public displays because they are of malicious intent and make no constructive contributions to our society. However, within the confinements of one's own private home or living space (including dormitories) no institution should be able to regulate your speech.

EDITING AND PROOFREADING

Before you send anything out for feedback or publication, you want to edit it carefully to make sure it meets accepted standards of written English. Generally, written English or print English has become less conservative, moving closer to the rhythms of natural speech. Nevertheless, you want to edit carefully for anything that might make your readers think of you as careless or uneducated, undermining your credibility.

Sexist and Insensitive Language

Most institutions and publications have guidelines for avoiding sexist and other offensive or insensitive language. Many labels for occupations are unisex or gender-neutral: *senator, scientist, manager, editor, carpenter*. However, avoid expressions showing that in your mental universe politicians, bosses, doctors, or pilots are stereotypically male and secretaries, nurses, or cabin personnel stereotypically female. Avoid condescending or belittling terms like *lady Ph.D., poetess,* and *coed*.

Gender-Specific	Gender-Neutral
policeman	police officer
Congressman	Representative, member of Congress
mailman	mail carrier
fireman	firefighter
foreman	supervisor
chairman	chair, chairperson
businessman	merchant, businessperson
spokesman	voice, spokesperson
stewardess	flight attendant
waitress	server

How to deal with the "pronoun dilemma"? English does not have a gender-neutral pronoun (like *s/he*) that could take the place of both *he* and *she:* You can solve the problem by omitting pronouns or changing the whole sentence to the plural. When you talk about several or all doctors and nurses, the pronoun *their* is gender-neutral:

> **Sexist Pronouns:** A doctor should give *his* nurse specific guidelines for *her* work. (assumes that doctors are male, nurses female)

> **Gender-Neutral:** **Doctors** should give **nurses** specific guidelines for **their** work.

Be wary of generic labels. *Mankind* and the *family of man* theoretically stood for both men and women, but *humanity* and *humankind* are more clearly gender-neutral. *Manpower* has become *labor force* or *workforce*.

Avoid intentional or unintentional slurs and stereotypes—no dumb Swedes, no woman drivers or inscrutable Orientals, no African Americans with natural rhythm or natural athletic ability. Be sensitive to labels preferred by spokespersons for ethnic or cultural groups, such as *Native Americans,* or *Asians* instead of *Orientals.* Try *people with disabilities* instead of *the disabled,* or *people with a mental illness* instead of *the mentally ill,* to show that in your thinking someone's disability or illness is not the only thing that matters about the person.

Wordiness and Redundancy

Try to make every word carry its weight. Trim a sentence like "The unemployment *situation* was *kind of* getting out of hand" so that it says "Unemployment was getting out of hand." Unnecessary duplication is called **redundancy**; it clogs the arteries of your prose. *Newly renovated* is redundant, because *to renovate* already means *to make new.* Make your writing less wordy or roundabout by looking out for expressions like the following:

Wordy	*Brief*
because of the fact that	because
at the present time	now
at a period of time when	when
in the not too distant future	soon
in this time and age	today
ask the question whether	ask whether
a true and logical fact	a fact
the basic fundamentals	the basics
consensus of opinion	consensus

Try to replace roundabout transitions with a simple *therefore* or *however:*

Wordy: In considering the situation, we must also take into account the fact that many local residents do not share the mayor's enthusiasm for large-scale development.

Edited: Many local residents, **however,** do not share the mayor's enthusiasm for large-scale development.

Informal English and Slang

In college-level writing, you need to shift gears from chatty **informal** everyday talk to a more formal academic style. Edit for telltale signs of informal English: tags like "Well, . . ." and "Yes, . . ."; the informal *you* for people in general rather than strictly "you the reader" (not "When you make a million in the stock market . . ."); folksy references to *kids, folks, guys,* or *gals;* abbreviations like *doc* and *prof;*

contractions like *isn't, won't,* and *couldn't;* expressions like *could care less, had it in for me, rub it in, cut it out.* Extremely informal English shades over into **slang:** *gyp the customers, shaft the voters, pig out.*

Clichés and Buzzwords

Clichés may at one time have been catchy but by now everyone is tired of them. *In a very real sense,* they are *a far cry* from *being a sure winner* in the *hearts and minds* of men and women *from all walks of life* and, *to be brutally frank,* the *bloom is off* such expressions (*to coin a phrase*), and *in the final analysis, when all is said and done,* they *do more harm than good.* Do without all these and without *believe it or not, the last straw, off the beaten track, a shot in the arm, sink or swim,* and *the tip of the iceberg.*

While many clichés are *as old as the hills,* many **buzzwords,** or fashionable current clichés, are *state of the art.* Everyone *looks at the big picture,* waits for *the window of opportunity* to open, and looks at *the bottom line.* Everything has to be *cost-effective* and *user-friendly.*

Try fresh, attention-getting ways of saying what you have to say:

Trite: You will never rise to the top of the heap if every setback makes you *throw in the towel.*

Fresh: You will never be truly successful if every setback makes you **think of defeat as inevitable, like the rain.**

Grammarchecks and Stylechecks

It is still chancy to trust stylecheck software in matters of sentence structure or English grammar. The computer does not understand what you are saying, so it cannot judge debatable expressions according to context, intention, or idiom (the natural way of saying something in English). If you are shaky on matters like subject–verb agreement or pronoun form, you may have to consult a handbook of composition.

Faulty Agreement: Production of computer chips have started to move back stateside from overseas facilities.
(What has started to move? *Production has started* to move.)

Edited: **Production** of computer chips **has started** to move back stateside from overseas facilities.

Wrong Pronouns: Cassat met the French painter Degas, and *him and her became* close friends.
(Who became friends? *He* did, and *she* did.)

Edited: Cassat met the French painter Degas, and **he and she became** close friends.

Spelling Traps

Spellchecks help people who are not sure how to spell *accommodate* or *definite.* Watch out for shibboleths–telltale signs that may make your readers think of you as uneducated. For instance, do without *it's*–because half of the time it's wrong. Use *its* (without the apostrophe) when you mean *of it* or *belonging to it* (the government and *its* agents). Use *it is* when you mean *it is.* Use **memory aids** to help you with other familiar spelling traps: When you *accept* something, you take it *in* (as in an acceptance speech). When you *except* something, you take it *out* (you make an exception). When something *affects* you, it has a *partial* impact. When an army *effects* a withdrawal, it brings something about; it changes the *whole* situation.

A paper you have just finished keyboarding is likely to look deceptively finished and letter-perfect on the screen. Put some distance between yourself and the paper before you proofread–come back to it with a fresh and wary eye. If possible, proofread twice—once on-screen and once on hardcopy.

COMPUTER WRITING, COLLABORATIVE WRITING, INTERACTIVE WRITING

New patterns of communication and cooperation are changing how and why people write. Leapfrogging advanced technology and new patterns of networking have greatly broadened the base of people using written communication on a near daily basis. For many users, e-mail has superseded the telephone as the medium of instant off-the-top-of-my-head communication. Desk-top publishing of quasi-professional quality has turned many contributors to newsletters or other special-interest publications into published authors.

Computer Writing

Writing on the computer brings your writing process closer to the way you think. The text on the screen can be indefinitely massaged, allowing you to work in instantly your second thoughts and newly discovered data. You can feed in material from another document when you become aware of a previously unnoticed connection. Your thinking does not go through clearly marked off stages, where you say to yourself: "Input phase finished; start output." Instead, even while driving to school or taking out the garbage, your mind is still "cooking"; it is working on half-formed thoughts until they take more definite shape. Writing on the computer allows you to keep up with this process of thinking and rethinking.

Computers are becoming linked in networks in classrooms, dorms, or libraries.

Students exchange drafts of papers with peers; instructors provide electronic feedback to student writing.

Collaborative Writing

Both in an academic context and in the world outside, collaboration is often a major part of a writer's work. Many experiments, studies, and reports require teamwork. Many articles and books are co-authored. Many official documents or business communications are worked up in preliminary form by the worker bees and then reworked and finalized with the benefit of input from colleagues and supervisors.

Collaborative writing projects or oral presentations can give you valuable experience in various dimensions of collaboration: defining the overall goals of a project, defining the roles and responsibilities of contributors, farming out assignments in accordance with the contributors' special areas of interest or expertise, coordinating the work, setting up workable schedules, helping critique preliminary results, pushing the final product.

How do collaborating authors work together? How do they interact? Alleen Nilsen Pace, co-author of an article on computer jargon, described the collaboration as follows:

> I had the interest in language but limited expertise in computer science, and my collaborator, a professor of computer science, had the computer expertise but no special background in language. I approached him by phone about collaborating on an article on computer jargon. We then switched to e-mail and began to pass our ideas back and forth. E-mail allowed us to communicate rapidly. It generated momentum; in the exchange, the idea of one triggered new ideas in the other until there was a snowball effect. Since the article was my idea, I sent him my handful of tentative untechnical ideas on the metaphoric aspects of computer jargon. I reminded him that when hearing him talk to someone also in computers, I had felt left out of the loop. What does it mean to say: "You shake hands with the printer"? To fill in gaps, my coauthor scouted a dictionary of jargon terms, such as "the bleeding edge" (he sees himself on the bleeding edge of computer science) and faxed them to me. I, in turn, made a list of terms I wanted to explore and e-mailed them back to him. He immediately e-mailed back additional ideas which gave me enough substance to write a rough draft. In reading my draft, he was able to provide the sample sentences. By now we were bouncing ideas back and forth, shaping and refining our text. This collaborative process led to a product which gave us both much pleasure.

Guidelines like the following can prepare you for fruitful collaboration:

- *Collaboration requires a meeting of minds.* People with different personalities and sometimes differing agendas have to work together. You may have to make necessary adjustments in your own thinking and procedures.
- *Collaboration requires an understanding of respective roles.* Will you and your collaborator or collaborators be equal partners, with disagreements settled by discussion or by vote? Will someone be chosen as senior partner or project director on the basis of experience or expertise? With a larger group effort, will there be a steering committee or editorial committee coordinating everyone's efforts?
- *Collaboration requires clear definition of goals.* Will the final product pool contributions representing different styles or perspectives–but essentially lay them out side by side? Or will an editor (or editorial committee) synthesize the materials–eliminating repetition, ironing out discrepancies, making them conform to a common style?
- *Collaboration requires commitment to the group effort.* You will naturally hope to receive credit for the contribution you have made. But often the reality of the situation is that you will share in the success or failure of the collaborative effort as a whole.

Interactive Writing

In the view of some observers, on-line communication is changing the nature of writing and the writing styles of the future. On-line writing becomes a hybrid speak-write. The writer is thinking out loud, throwing out preliminary or unfinished ideas. Instant feedback from others will often help ideas to take shape–drawing out the writer, causing the writer to reveal personal background or to show the reasoning behind the points made. Hostile feedback may change the direction of an argument or cause the writer to head off negative criticism.

The give-and-take of interactive computer writing is developing its own vocabulary. A topic may "drift" as a participant goes off on a tangent. "Flames"–personal attacks–can short-circuit discussion. A "screed" is the result of someone getting on a soapbox–and perhaps causing others to log off. A participant not joining in and perhaps biding his or her time is said to "lurk."

Interactive computer writing is like written conversation–preserved or discarded as the participant decides. Computer gurus predict that growing participation in interactive on-line communication will push conventional writing toward greater immediacy, spontaneity, and flexibility.

10

Writing / Thinking Strategies

What kind of thinking goes into organizing your writing? How do you sort out data so that they will make sense to your reader? How do you structure a paper, a report, or a presentation? Familiar thinking strategies will help you structure your observations and experiences–help you organize your data or chart a course of action. For instance, you may trace the stages in a process, so you can show what leads to what. What is first, and what is the next step? You may classify, putting things that belong together in the same bin. What goes with what? You may compare and contrast, so you can help the reader make intelligent choices. How are things different, and how are they alike? You may trace cause and effect, so you can help your readers predict consequences or plan remedial action. What are the consequences if they do A, and what will happen if they do B?

These thinking strategies have many different applications, cutting across disciplines and occupations. A person who can analyze a problem or find the common denominator in a series of events can put the same intellectual equipment to work on a range of different tasks.

TRACING THE PROCESS

Some of the thinking patterns that organize reality for us seem to be built into the nature of things. In discussing the aging process, it seems natural to mark off stages: infancy, adolescence, young adulthood, mature middle age, the onset of age, and advanced old age. In nature, of course, these stages are part of a *continuum*. (The transition from one to the other is not announced by the ringing of a bell.) However, to get things into focus, to get a handle on how something works, we mark off stages. We work out a meaningful sequence.

Thinking in terms of major stages enables you to focus on one thing at a time–all the while seeing it as part of a larger whole. You can do justice to characteristic features and concerns that seem important during a particular phase without losing sight of the whole. One writer charted the life cycle of the salmon in the following manner:

The Last of the Wild Salmon

PHASE ONE: THE SALMON RUN Salmon fight their way upstream, motivated by a powerful instinctual drive. In prodigious leaps, they overcome waterfalls and manmade obstacles.

PHASE TWO: THE SPAWNING GROUNDS Lacerated by their upstream fight, the salmon reach the spawning grounds. They lay and fertilize a myriad eggs.

PHASE THREE. NEW LIFE The parents die, but after an interval fingerlings are in evidence everywhere, which eventually begin their journey downstream.

PHASE FOUR: TRANSITION The young salmon stay in the delta–they live in a sweetwater environment for a time, until they are ready for the saltwater environment of the ocean.

PHASE FIVE: RETURN TO THE OCEAN The adult salmon live in the ocean for a number of years–until a powerful urge propels them to seek the spawning grounds of their birth and the cycle begins anew.

Tracing a process or process analysis has a wide range of applications:

- We get a handle on manufacturing processes by dividing them into stages that enable us to focus on one major step at a time. Not all such processes are linear–we often need to chart how different lines of development meet and converge–the ways small creeks and rivers feed into a stream.
- Astronomers trace the birth of new suns from swirling clouds of cosmic dust that gravity causes to compact until the nuclear furnace is lit, burning fiercely until eventually the fuel is exhausted and gravity makes the star collapse on itself into a black hole.

SAMPLE OPTIONS FOR WRITING–PROCESS

1. Trace for your readers a natural process that goes through complicated and astonishing stages, for instance, the life cycle of a butterfly.

2. Introduce your readers to a manufacturing process that demands sophisticated skills. For instance, make them see what is involved in the making of a silicon chip.

3. Customers complain when instructions in user manuals are difficult to follow. Write exceptionally clear and foolproof instructions for upgrading a computer, hooking up schoolrooms with the Internet, or a similar task.

GENERALIZING: Charting the Trend

Among the reasoning processes that our minds employ to process data, the generalizing kind of thinking is the most basic. We constantly generalize on the basis of what we have experienced and observed. We lay related examples end to end; we begin to see a pattern. For instance, we see a companion get ill shortly after eating a new unfamiliar kind of mushroom we gathered in the woods. A few weeks later, a dinner featuring the same mushrooms makes several dinner companions sick. If it weren't for our ability to generalize, people would not learn from experience and would go on eating poisonous mushrooms, with dire results.

The generalizing kind of reasoning is traditionally called **induction**, or inductive thinking. It moves from an essential stage of data-gathering to general conclusions. It moves from fact to inference—from facts to insights that the facts warrant.

What kind of thinking goes into an inductive paper? For example, you may have noticed that many of the people you talk to have part-time jobs. Is this part of a larger trend? After a few days of informal research, these might be some of your notes:

- A newspaper article reports that the Bank of America is converting all tellers' jobs to part-time jobs without benefits.

- According to retail clerks I talked to at Sears, many (most?) of them are part-timers with variable hours, with income changing from week to week according to the varying need of the company for their services. During slow months they may average less than twenty hours a week; as retail sales step up when the holiday season approaches, they may clock 34–35 hours a week.

- An article in *Business Week* that tracks the tendency toward outsourcing. It reports, for instance, that IBM handed over much of its office or secretarial work to an outside firm paying lower wages and granting reduced benefits and employing many part-time employees. The savings per employee are estimated at $12,000 a year.

By the time you are this far into your investigation, you are likely to conclude that the part-time tellers at the bank were not a fluke or an aberration. They were part of a general pattern that is changing the way Americans try to make a living. You conclude that there is a powerful trend away from costly permanent full-time employment. Businesses reduce their labor costs by restructuring, flexible scheduling, outsourcing, and the like.

This conclusion becomes your working hypothesis, or trial thesis. How sound is it? You do not want to be guilty of hasty generalization. You will not want to jump to conclusions. With this topic, however, you will not have to look far for corroborating evidence:

- A call to the personnel office of a software company reveals that many of its contributors and debuggers are part-time employees, or "independent contractors," as they are called.
- The Sunday Supplement of the local newspaper prints the personal testimony of an employee who is trying to make ends meet with part-time pay and facing the uncertainties of employment that offers no job security, health care, or chance of promotion.

Even so, you will try to guard against basing your generalizations on an **unrepresentative sample.** Is part-time employment perhaps a special feature of secretarial work or work in retail? It would be good to go farther afield and bring in some relevant evidence from other areas:

- Several of my college instructors are untenured part-time help, and according to older students the college employs more part-timers than it used to.

Obviously, you are beginning to build up an array of examples that will convince many readers. What would it take to convince skeptics? You might decide to recognize apparent exceptions: Some of your friends complain about unscheduled overtime and overloads. Apparently, heavy overtime for a smaller core of full-time employees allows companies to hedge their bets by not going on a hiring spree in terms of growing demand. Companies may prefer to get extra work out of employees already on the payroll rather than sign on new employees requiring costly paperwork, orientation, on-the-job training, and the like.

In the first draft of your paper, your overarching generalization becomes your promise to the reader. If you state it early in your paper as your **thesis**, it stakes out a claim. You then marshal your examples to support the claim you make. (Sometimes you may decide to reverse the usual thesis-and-support order. You present your examples or your evidence first, *leading up* to the conclusion they warrant.) Your thesis gives you a chance to sum up your thinking in a pointed way that will have an impact on the reader:

Thesis: To reduce labor costs, American business is relying on part-time help on a large scale.

The following might be the rough working outline for your first draft. The strategy here is to move from the familiar to the new: from traditional ways to newer ways of putting employees on part-time status:

Working Part of the Time

part-time help
> part-time tellers at Bank of America
> part-time retail clerks at Sears
> a part-timer's story

outsourcing
> "independent contractors" in the software business
> farming out secretarial work to outside companies

an apparent countertrend
> overtime in a part-time world

Reaching cautious generalizations after studying a range of related data is the basic strategy guiding research and publication in a wide range of areas:

- Medical researchers may study cases of tuberculosis, outbreaks of cholera, and reported cases of polio. They may warn us of a potentially dangerous trend: Diseases long thought to be under control are making a comeback, both in Third-World countries and in disadvantaged, low-income neighborhoods in the industrialized countries of the West.

- Anthropologists generalize about behavior patterns in other cultures that offer thought-provoking parallels or contrasts to our own. For instance, in some cultures they find much hugging, stroking, and kissing among people who are not lovers. Other cultures are more reserved; people seem to shrink from the touch of others.

WRITING WORKSHOP: A Paper for Peer Review

The following sample paper explores a current question asked in many relationships: Is the American male becoming less macho and more sensitive? Critiquing this paper alone or as a member of a group, answer questions like the following: Does this issue mean anything to you? Why or why not? Where has this writer turned for material? What is her mix of sources? Do they sound authentic or authoritative to you? Is she generalizing cautiously, or is she jumping to conclusions? How do her conclusions compare with your own experience and observation? What questions would you like to ask the writer? (This paper is a second draft, with some further copy-editing for awkward transitions and confusing attribution of sources.)

The Sensitive Male: Reality or Myth?

Hollywood has come a long way from depicting super macho characters like Arnold Schwarzenegger, who a decade ago played the action hero in movies like *Commando*, brazenly and fearlessly shooting his way through the plot, not offering much dialogue other than a few grunts and moans. Currently many male characters in the movies are undergoing dramatic transformations; movies today more often bestow on their heroes moral consciences as well as physical prowess. In *Terminator II*, the hero listens patiently and sympathetically to a young boy who laments about growing up without his mother's presence. Moreover, at the end of the movie the hero sacrifices his own life to save the world from nuclear disaster.

How accurately does Hollywood reflect the changing attitudes of men? Have men's attitudes, especially toward women, really changed? Unlike Schwarzenegger's character, many men in real life experience difficulty adjusting to their new roles as nurturers. Mathilda Carter, a psychologist, is quoted in an article in the *U.S. News and World Report* as saying that "many men are confused and searching for their identity, as they struggle to blend vestiges of traditional masculinity with what are regarded as softer, or feminine traits." Some experts express optimism that eventually men will achieve a successful balance between their nurturing sides and their masculinity. Phyllis Bronstein, a psychologist quoted in the article in the *U.S. News and World Report*, maintains that "a less rigid definition of masculinity will emerge that enables men to be more at ease with whatever paths they choose. We're at the awkward stage right now."

Some television shows, such as *Party of Five*, appear to capture the current awkwardness that some men grapple with. In one episode Charlie (who at one time was an irresponsible playboy) is shown being urged by his girlfriend to bond with his baby brother by reading a nursery story to him. After a few moments of discomfort Charlie puts down the book and achieves intimacy with his brother by reading an electrical manual to him instead.

While television characters such as Charlie may do a good job capturing the ambivalence that men may wrestle with, some men complain that the media sensationalize or exaggerate this trend of the new sensitive male. For instance, in one episode of *Party of Five*, the oldest brother, Charlie, who is appointed legal guardian to his brothers and sisters after his parents are killed in a car accident, is shown taking his baby brother to an all-father's group. At this gathering, each father, teary-eyed and voice wavering with emotion, recalls the extraordinary moment when he first bonded with his baby. Commercials follow the trend: In one commercial, an empathetic husband tenderly looks at the camera and earnestly tells the audience how his wife, a dedicated gymnastic coach, overcomes her muscle pain by taking Aleve pain medication.

One of the men I interviewed, James Le Roy, a retired homicide and police officer, claims that such male characters produce a "manufactured emotion." He says that films such as *Legends of the Fall* sensationalize the ideal image of the sensitive man. James feels that the camera unnecessarily zooms in on Brad Pitt whenever he cries. He also feels that although television and Hollywood seem to exaggerate the sensitive male, they also at the same time still depict "jerks" like Tim Allen in *Home Improvement*. This character is excessively sarcastic to his wife and often appears ignorant of her feelings.

Some men that I spoke with claimed that men in real life need to improve their sensitivity toward women. Many of my male friends assert that men in real life are nothing like the sensitive male characters portrayed in television programs, who share their most intimate feelings. "Although I consider myself very sensitive, I'd say that over half of my male friends do not want to show any of their emotions," claims David Mussomeli, a twenty-eight-year-old accountant, "because they are afraid of being branded wimps." Alma M. Garcia, Associate Professor of Sociology and Director of Women's Studies at Santa Clara University, feels that when men are in small groups among themselves they are more likely to vent their hostilities about women. "Behaviors change before ideas do," she says.

While some men may modify their behavior in the public eye, others openly resist change. According to psychology professor Mathilda Carter, who was interviewed for the article in the *U.S. News and World Report*, some men react to the current confusion over the changes of gender roles by rejecting pressure from women to be more open. Moreover, she claims, "others take refuge in what has been called the new macho. . . . They contend that real men don't eat quiche or change diapers but instead swig beer."

Traces of old machismo can still be found in popular sitcoms such as *Married with Children*; in this show, the husband, Al Bundy, plays a shoe salesman who prefers to hang around the television set, drinking beer rather than conversing with his wife. In one episode he totally ignores his wife while conspicuously ogling other women at the supermarket. Most television shows are not this extreme; however, some sitcoms almost appear as the antithesis of the sensitive male. In the *Seinfield* show, the male characters appear to look down on marriage or long-term commitments. In one episode Jerry breaks up with his girlfriend after only a few weeks because of the way she eats her peas.

Thus, varying attitudes concerning sensitive males are reflected in a plethora of television and Hollywood movies. Although there is debate over how realistically the entertainment industry portrays men in society, clearly men have come a long way from their traditional roles as breadwinners and providers. As men and society adjust to these changes perhaps we should examine the way that we define strength and masculinity. Perhaps there is no such thing as being too sensitive. As Art Bohart, Professor of Psychology at California State University at Dominguez Hills observes in *USA Today*, "to be sensitive you have to be open and vulnerable. So to be strong at the same time means you have to develop a different kind of strength."

SAMPLE OPTIONS FOR WRITING: Generalization

1. Media watchers chart and document such trends as increasingly brutal violence on TV, male bonding in films, or increased personal abuse on talk shows or on the Internet. Examine one such trend on the basis of your own close first-hand observation.

2. For a time, women entering careers or trying to "dress for success" were admonished not to be "feminine." Is this trend continuing, or has it been modified or reversed?

3. Is society (or the part of it you know best) becoming more accepting of gays or the gay or lesbian subculture? How does your own observation compare with trends you observe in politics or in the media?

CLASSIFICATION: Sorting Out

Classification–sorting things out into categories–is a basic way of orienting ourselves in the world in which we live. To order an array of data, we ask: What goes with what? Schools classify and track students according to IQ aptitude, or test results. Insurance companies classify potential clients as low-risk, high-risk, and uninsurable.

Systems of classification become outdated when they no longer provide a good fit for shifting realities. Political scientists long worked with an analysis of the class structure derived from a traditional European model:

- aristocracy (the descendants of the robber barons and local warlords of the feudal age, often intermarrying with wealthy commoners)
- bourgeoisie (a well-to-do middle class of property owners, shopkeepers, factory owners, and public functionaries)

- proletariat (the working class of impoverished factory workers and peasants; "the masses," in Marxist terminology)

However, as the result of wars and revolutions, the hereditary aristocracy became increasingly obsolete, surviving today mainly in gossip columns about individuals like Prince Charles and Lady Di. A new upper class of wealthy entrepreneurs and top managers (and the sons and daughters of wealthy parents) became the new élite. In a time of strong labor unions and postwar prosperity, well-paid factory workers started to move up into the middle class and vote Republican. Gradually, when the manufacturing base started to erode as the result of cheap foreign labor and automation, a new underclass of the chronically unemployed and welfare-dependent started to develop. Today, a sociologist might set up a scheme of classification like the following:

ARE YOU UPWARDLY MOBILE?

- upper class (families of large inherited wealth and the corporate elite)
- upper middle class (mid-level managers, professional people, successful business people)
- lower middle class (lower-echelon employees, office workers, teachers, nurses, owners or marginal businesses)
- underclass (dropouts, chronically unemployed, long-term welfare cases)

As immigration resurfaces as a hot political issue, you might be asked to do some basic sorting out to help readers understand the current meaning of the phrase, "a nation of immigrants." Walt Whitman said that here is "a nation of nations." Obviously, the history, characteristics, and prospects of all immigrants are not the same. Can you set up some major categories? On the basis of your personal observation and reading, you might start with a set of unsorted impressions like the following:

Brainstorming:

large Polish communities in heartland cities like Chicago and Detroit

the Boston Irish (New England or New Ireland?)

Willa Cather writes about Czech immigrants in Nebraska

strong Jewish tradition in New York City (delis, garment district, banking and law, politicians)

anti-Castro Cubans in Miami

Puerto Ricans (*West Side Story*)

Mexicans crossing the border and battling *la migra* (the immigration service) doctors from India and Pakistan

Korean groceries downtown

Vietnamese businesses and restaurants

The following scheme of classification sorts out immigrants partly in terms of chronology; partly in terms of geography, and partly in terms of major causes of migration. Can you find a slot for yourself or for your family in this scheme?

Working Outline: A Nation of Nations

- "First-Wave" Northern European stock
  - English Puritans
  - Boston Irish
  - English-Scottish Influence in the South
  - Pennsylvania Dutch
  - Scandinavians in Minnesota
- "Second-Wave" Eastern and Southern European migration
  - Polish-Americans and Italian Americans
  - Czechs in Nebraska
  - Russian Jews
- Refugees from America's wars and the Cold War
  - "Displaced Persons" after World War II
  - anti-Castro Cubans in Florida
  - Vietnamese boat people
- "South-to-North" migration from Central and South America
  - Puerto Ricans in New York
  - Mexicans in California and Texas
- "New Wave" Asian immigration
  - professionals and shopkeepers from India and Pakistan
  - Chinese and Japanese influx ("model minority")
  - Korean businesses in black communities
  - Filipino and Pacific Islands arrivals

The need to classify, and the problems of classification that may result, surface in many areas:

- Filing systems and library catalogs would be impossible without a system of classification, good or bad.
- Biologists in the eighteenth and nineteenth centuries set up an elaborate

system of classification, or **taxonomy**, to make sense of the profuse variety of life on our planet. For instance, horses are part of a family that includes many breeds. All of these in turn are part of a genus that also includes close cousins like zebras and donkeys. All these again ultimately belong to the class of mammals—warm-blooded animals that suckle their young. According to the logic of the biologist's system of classification, whales are mammals and not fish; human beings are primates along with our cousins the apes.

- Census takers or college admission officials grapple with the question of whether and how to classify Americans by race or ethnicity. (What if people object to being identified by race? What if people whose ancestors left Europe behind centuries ago object to being classified as "European"? Do Mexican Americans count as white? How many Native American grandparents does a Native American have to have to be classified as a Native American?)

SAMPLE OPTIONS FOR WRITING: Classification

1. Many different kinds of immigrants have come into the country in recent years. How would you sort them out, setting up major categories?

2. In recent decades, many alternative living arrangements and lifestyles have come to compete with or take the place of the traditional nuclear family. Can you sort out current variations on the theme of living together?

3. The composition of the student body at many American colleges has changed substantially over the years. Can you sort out different kinds of students, including especially nontraditional kinds of students?

STRUCTURING A COMPARISON

We compare and contrast to guide our choices and to help us find our bearings. We compare new software or a new car with an earlier version to see if a change would be an improvement.

Constructing a comparison or contrast, you need to lay out your material in such a way that your readers can clearly see important similarities, crucial differences, or both. You have to make your readers see the connections between what is being compared, helping them establish the mental cross-references between one and the other. Sometimes, you will focus on important similarities first but then go on to differences that should not be overlooked. Or you may start with surface differences—but then go on to essential similarities. For a detailed, systematic comparison, however, you will often compare two things point by point, establishing similarities or differences under each heading.

How would a **point-by-point** comparison structure a paper? In October

1995, O. J. Simpson, former football legend accused of murdering his ex-wife and a friend, was found not guilty by a jury of nine blacks, one Latino, and two whites. He had been in custody for fifteen months as the single suspect in the case and was now set free. According to many observers, the verdict polarized the American public, dramatizing the split between the African American community and the white community. There was a flood of reactions, commentary, and testimony, ranging from stunned silence by many whites to cheering and celebrations by African American students at Howard University and elsewhere. Here is a working outline for one writer's point-by-point comparison of the different reactions in our racially polarized society:

Justice in Black and White

history of domestic abuse
> (white) familiar pattern of cumulative escalating violence
> (black) irrelevant to current charges

validity of scientific evidence
> (white) cumulative evidence of blood, fiber, footprints
> (black) contaminated evidence and official incompetence

extent of police bias
> (white) individual "bad cop" with record of police brutality
> (black) police conspiracy to frame the defendant

future action
> (white) case closed, with guilty man set free
> (black) reward for finding unapprehended killer

However, note that a different observer might have been more skeptical of the media coverage of both the trial and the aftermath. After sampling reactions from a range of both whites and African Americans and looking for comparable reactions in printed sources, one student writer focused on *similarities* rather than differences in black and white reactions. The resulting paper, however, also proceeded point by point. Here is a working outline:

Across the Racial Divide

media polarization of black and white attitudes

areas of agreement:

- condemnation of spousal abuse
  (reactions from both white and black sources)
- money talks–wealthy defendant and high-priced lawyers
  (reactions from both white and black sources)
- shared distrust of police
  (reactions from both white and black sources)

An alternative to the point-by-point treatment is the **parallel-order** comparison. To give your readers an adequate account of an alternative proposal for a senior citizens' residence, you may decide not to jump back and forth between the two options. You want to give your readers a sense of how the different parts of a proposal *work together*. However, while treating each proposal separately, you will try to take up comparable points in roughly the same order.

PROPOSAL A
    zoning issues
    acquisition costs
    community acceptance
    proximity to health services

PROPOSAL B
    zoning issues
    acquisition costs
    community acceptance
    proximity to health services

Conducting a systematic comparison and contrast is a skill with many uses and applications:

- Economists contrast American and Japanese management styles to see if we can learn something from our competitors.
- Psychologists compare today's youthful criminals with yesterday's juvenile delinquents, looking for clues to increased juvenile crime and for possible solutions.
- Virologists compare and contrast the behavior of viruses in order to chart strategies for dealing with frightening new epidemics.
- Consumer publications compare and contrast the maintenance records of foreign and domestic cars and advise their readers accordingly.
- Personnel managers compare and contrast the qualifications of applicants, and they base their evaluations or recommendations on their findings.

SAMPLE OPTIONS FOR WRITING: Comparison/Contrast

1. Compare and contrast a large-scale and a small-scale operation. For instance, compare/contrast agribusiness and family farm, grocery chain and mom-and-pop store, or small private school and large public institution.

2. Compare and contrast two cultural or ethnic traditions that you know well or have the opportunity to observe. Focus on one major point. For instance, focus on conventions of courtship, ways of expressing affection, traditions of disciplining children, or tolerance for individuality.

3. Compare and contrast traditional and modern (or modern and "postmodern") architecture in a setting that you know well or can study at first hand.

CAUSE AND EFFECT: Problem to Solution

Much analysis of social, historical, or psychological phenomena aims at identifying cause and effect. Once we understand what caused a problem, we may be able to work toward a solution. Once we recognize the causes of a bad situation, we may be able to keep from repeating the same mistakes. With a better understanding of what causes successful students to learn, we may be able to create conditions favorable to improved academic performance for others.

A typical cause-and-effect analysis might probe the unexpected results or "unintended consequences" of what seemed at one time a promising development. For instance, first California and then other states moved toward no-fault divorce. There was no more need to prove the marriage partner a bad human being. Bitterness and vindictiveness would be reduced, and legal costs would stay within bounds. Women would be recognized as equal partners, entitled to half of the property acquired during the marriage.

However, when experts looked at the results ten or fifteen years later, they found that for many women the promise of the no-fault system had not come true. Many found themselves with insufficient child support, with only a few years of alimony (often hard to collect), and with a family home that had had to be sold so property could be divided. Many, if not most, divorced women experienced a drastic decline in their standard of living. Why?

Lenore J. Weitzman, a professor of sociology at Harvard, identified the causes somewhat as follows:

1. While treating women as theoretical equals, courts ignored the drastically unequal earning power of a man who had built a career and of a homemaker or part-time worker trying to enter the labor force after many years of marriage.

2. The "equal" division of property is in fact unequal if the property is divided between one person (usually the male) and three or four other people (the mother and children).

3. The elimination of misconduct as grounds for divorce eliminated the bargaining power that women used to have when men would make economic concessions in order to obtain the "innocent" partner's consent to a divorce.

4. Dividing tangible property such as money and real estate did not, at least at first, take into account such intangible assets as advanced degrees, pension rights, insurance entitlements, or business contracts.

Detailed analysis of cause and effect often leads to suggestions for remedial action:

- Sociologists and social workers probe the causes of homelessness or domestic violence and recommend programs designed to alleviate the problem.
- Educators study high dropout rates in schools in low-income neighborhoods with a view toward raising graduation rates.
- Efficiency experts study the reasons for excessive downtime of an assembly line or a bank's central computer system in order to minimize breakdowns.

WRITING WORKSHOP: A Paper for Peer Review

The following final draft of a student paper explores a much-debated causal relationship: Does the steady diet of brutal violence to which American youngsters are exposed translate into an escalation of violence in real life? How does the writer of the following student paper answer this question? Critiquing this paper alone or as a member of a group, answer questions like the following: Does the student writer succeed in getting you involved in the issue? Where or how does she stake out her claim? What kind of evidence does she turn to? How convincing or authoritative is it? How convincing is this writer's analysis of the problem? How persuasive is her suggested solution? Where do you agree with the writer; where would you take issue with her?

Is Television Violence Inflaming Our Youth?

Three weeks ago, Channel Four News reported a disturbing incident where an eight-year-old girl stabbed her seven-year-old playmate over a Barbie doll. The eight-year-old girl reportedly did not want to share her doll with her friend and when the friend refused to give the doll back, the eight-year-old sprinted to her home and returned with a kitchen knife. She stabbed her seven-year-old playmate several times. When asked why she resorted to stabbing her friend, the eight-year-old, innocently rubbing her eyes with her hands, sobbed and stated that she did not want to share her doll. Where does an eight-year-old get this kind of problem-solving style?

A few years ago, an incident involving little boys was reported in Michigan. Two young boys set their parents' house on fire. The boys had watched a cartoon show where an angry Beavis and Butthead had set a house on fire (the cartoon characters' way of solving problems). The young boys thought it was a cool act, and since they were angry with their parents over some unknown issue, they copied Beavis and Butthead. One might think that the two children that set their parents' house on fire had psychological problems, or had experienced some severe trauma, or had been abandoned and therefore were driven to commit this act–that is incorrect. These youngsters were from a middle-class, loving family. Life had been great for them and everything was fine, according to the parents. It came as a surprise to the parents that their kids had set their family home ablaze!

What is happening? The perpetrators of these crimes are getting younger. An increasingly large percentage of our children are becoming violent and dangerous. "There is more and more violent crime being committed by younger and younger kids," says Bob Hargis, a teacher as Osborn School inside Santa Clara County Juvenile Center. What is driving these kids to act this way? Could television violence be a contributor to our youth's behaviors and actions today?

One might say that the main cause of violence by our youth is the breakdown of the family structure with a tremendous growth in single-parent families and gang involvement–that could be true, but what about the two little boys whom I will call James and John McDowell? They came from a decent home with no guns, no drugs, no gang activity. James and John were too young (approximately six years old) to wander off on their own in the streets getting involved in gangs or illegal activity. These were two innocent and fresh boys–they had not been exposed to the tough world except through television. We know from newspaper sources that the boys watched several hours of television a day.

According to Dr. Jan Allen, a professor of child and family studies at the University of Tennessee at Knoxville (U.T.K.), kids are influenced by what they see on television. Children imitate what they see and hear– this is how they learn. She states that "violence on television is absorbed and imitated particularly by children into our lives and into our culture." Dr. Allen concludes that many children will imitate what they see on television whether or not their parents condone violence, because children need adventure and power.

The McDowells admitted to letting their kids watch several kids' pro-grams–like the *Teenage Mutant Ninja Turtles*, the *Terminator*, *Dennis the Menace*– all shows that depict violent behavior as cute and endearing. The parents did not have a strong influence in their kids' television watching. So does it come as a surprise that the kids would imitate some of the television shows? In 1972, when concern about rising violence in America was simmering, the Surgeon-General's advisory committee on television and social behavior decided to look further. Researchers assembled a group of four-year-olds. Some were shown violent cartoons while others were shown neutral and positive films. When the two groups were put to-gether, the children who had seen the violent cartoons were more likely to become aggressive.

Another study conducted by the American Psychological Association's commission on violence and youth concluded in 1993 that "there is absolutely no doubt that higher levels of viewing violence on television are correlated with increased acceptance of aggressive attitudes and increased aggressive behavior." One might think that the above studies were done for a short period of time and therefore cannot be conclusive or reliable–that could be true; however another study was performed over a longer period.

A well-known study reported in the August 1994 *Economist* tracked the viewing habits and behavior of a group of American school children starting in 1960 when they were eight years old. Follow-up interviews with the children were conducted in 1971 and 1982. The researchers found that there was a correlation between the amount of television violence watched and aggression among the eight-year-olds. There was also a correlation between watching violence at eight years and aggressiveness at nineteen years of age. By the time the guinea pigs had reached age thirty, those who had watched more television violence as children tended to have thirty percent more criminal convictions; they tended to be seventy percent more likely to batter their spouses and, in their turn, to have more aggressive children.

Dr. Allen tells us that very young kids, which includes preschoolers, kindergartners, and first and second graders, have more difficulty in differentiating between fantasy and reality. Very young children are not far enough along cognitively to know the difference between fantasy and reality. Something that is make-believe is hard for them to distinguish and therefore this might inspire them to copy violent scenes on television. One might understand that it is difficult for young kids to differentiate reality from fantasy, but what about the teenagers?

One estimate found that by the time youngsters graduate from high school, many of them will have watched television for twenty-two thousand hours, compared to only half that number for hours spent in school. By age eighteen, young people will have been exposed to as many as eighteen thousand televised murders and eight hundred suicides, according to a 1992 study by Fred Hechinger of the Carnegie Council on Adolescent Development. The evidence is overwhelming that the impact of being bombarded with violent images ranges from an overall desensitization, to consequent acceptance of violence, to increasingly violent behavior.

Violence has become an integral part of television in the United States, and this television violence is creating big problems for our communities and America. I am not saying that television violence is the sole cause of violence and crime in our community. However, it is definitely one of the main factors contributing to our inflamed youth and increasing crime in our society. A growing percentage are no longer disturbed by grotesque acts on television. It seems funny or cool to them. An example I remember is when some high school kids were ejected from a movie theater for laughing at Jews being tortured in the movie *Schindler's List.* I have also witnessed some high school kids just laughing and giggling away when someone is being brutalized on television shows.

Are our youth corrupted by the blood-and-guts rubbish they watch on television, on videos and video games? Yes, I believe that screen violence does indeed foster actual violence and has contributed to the rise in crime amongst our youth. To what degree? I do not know. Violence is contributing to the moral decline of society because of this alarming lack of sympathy. Some of our youth have become numb to the sight of violent acts and so are not affected by terrible, brutal acts of violence. Unfortunately, studies also show that television violence is increasing incredibly despite all its effects on our youth. A study conducted by the Center for Media and Public Affairs recorded a forty-one percent increase in the number of violent scenes shown on television from April 1992 to April 1994. Bob Lichter, the director of the media affairs center, said that what the study showed was that "the television industry has tried to minimize violence where it is most obvious and visible, but otherwise it's been business as usual."

Television violence is on the upswing. Legislators and concerned organizations call for censorship of television violence. I feel that instead of censorship to fight television violence, there should be more information that helps parents to monitor and control what their children watch on television. Parents should also actively participate in teaching children the harmful effects of television violence–this could have made a difference in the McDowell case. Just as aspirin and bleach come with health warnings and hard-to-open tops, so should violent videos and television programs. With increased information, parents can take some measures to monitor and control their children's television-watching habits.

SAMPLE OPTIONS FOR WRITING: Cause and Effect

1. What are the causes of high dropout rates in local high schools? What, if anything, can be done?

2. Is it true that young couples get married later and have fewer children? If so, why?

3. According to many observers, the real wages of American workers have declined during the last ten or fifteen years. Why? What major causes can you identify?

4. There have been many initiatives designed to wean Americans away from the automobile and induce them to use public transport. What are the obstacles? What works, and what doesn't, and why?

WEIGHING PRO AND CON

We often make up our minds after giving due weight to the arguments pro and con. Ideally, voters make an informed decision after studying the argument pro and con a ballot proposition. Ideally, a planning commission approves or vetoes a proposed development after studying the arguments of developers and of citizen groups opposed to runaway growth. Much effective writing presents a balanced conclusion reached by the writer after giving due weight to the arguments on both sides.

Pro-and-con thinking goes from thesis to **antithesis** and then to **synthesis**– from statement to counterstatement and then to a balanced conclusion. After an unprecedented increase in immigration in recent decades, many Americans are questioning their traditional willingness to accept the "huddled masses" escaping from poverty or oppression. Pro-and-con thinking like the following might go into a balanced paper on the subject:

The Rising Tide

CON

immigrants take work away from Americans

they swell the welfare rolls

their children overburden cash-strapped schools

they bankrupt public health services

they stick to themselves

increasingly they keep their own language and customs

some come from countries opposed to American values

terrorists are often aliens given resident status

   PRO

   most Americans are descended from immigrants

   immigrants do menial jobs Americans don't want

   many immigrants are strongly motivated to succeed

   they maintain family values and religious ties

   Asian immigrants revitalize inner-city neighborhoods

   they have a strong work ethic and respect for education

fewer Mexican Americans than Anglos are on welfare

contact with other cultures enriches our own

BALANCED CONCLUSION

legal immigration has always proved an asset in the long run

however, the current flood of illegal immigration exceeds our ability to
absorb and assimilate newcomers

Genuine pro-and-con writing requires you to give equal time or equal weight to the arguments on both sides. If you incline to one side, true pro and con requires you to listen to people on the other side—and perhaps learn from them. It requires you to represent the views of the other side fairly—as you would want your own views represented fairly if the roles were reversed. (You may have to curb the natural tendency to give short shrift to opponents or undercut them with belittling remarks.)

A pro-and-con approach can help in situations where being self-righteous or adversarial is not likely to produce a balanced, reasonable conclusion. Here are some examples:

- When a major public hospital is running at an unacceptable deficit, what is the answer? Can taxes be raised to close the gap? Or should the hospital be privatized and run on a for-profit basis?

- In order to alleviate the spiraling cost of a college education, should colleges aim at a three-year bachelor's degree?

- Should taxpayers' money be used to subsidize public broadcasting, making possible programs like *Sesame Street* and *Masterpiece Theater*?

OPTIONS FOR WRITING

1. Has there been debate on your campus concerning an issue like removing ROTC, denying recognition to a gay or lesbian student group, or expelling students on charges of hate speech? What were the arguments pro and con? What for you was a reasonable solution?

2. Are there pro-growth and anti-development factions in your community or region? What are the arguments on both sides? Who do you think is more nearly right?

3. Courts and juries are beginning to decriminalize assisted suicide. But many continue to have grave objections. What are the arguments pro and con? On balance, to which side of the argument do you incline?

DEFINING A KEY TERM

Often you will define a key term in passing:

Dialectic–*the playing off of thesis and antithesis, of force and counter force*–became a major intellectual schema in the nineteenth century.

However, when a key term has a complicated history, creates confusion, or has become a fighting word, you may feel the need for an **extended definition**. To clarify the term–to stake out what the term marks off–you may decide to explore dimensions like the following:

History

The early American feminists were often suffragists–fighting for women's right to vote. *Feminism* in its early stages thus focused on a clear and overt instance of legal and political discrimination against women (which had nothing to do with their "nurturing" side or obligation to family).

Key Criteria

There may not be a single clue to a definition of *fascism*. You may decide criteria like the following help define the term:

- fervent nationalism as a reaction against the cosmopolitanism of the Enlightenment
- celebrating the leadership principle, looking for salvation to a strong leader brooking no opposition
- a paramilitary organization of society, with the state controlling the media and many areas of citizens' cultural and private lives
- as part of the nationalistic anti-foreign mentality, an often virulent and paranoid anti-Semitism

Significant Complications

Although many people lump together many tendencies of the left under the umbrella term *socialism*, the socialist movement early split into two major contending camps–a social-democratic branch (represented by many of the socialist parties of Western Europe) and a totalitarian communist branch (until recently represented by the communist party of the Soviet Union).

Key Examples

A definition may remain too abstract unless you show how it applies to test cases or key examples. When and where do politicians or the media use the term *terrorism*? What are striking recent examples? Where would you draw the line?

WRITING WORKSHOP: Defining a Key Term

- How well does the following paper define the central term for you? What major areas does it cover? What, in your judgment, does it leave out?
- What strategy did the writer work out for sequencing the material? Where does she sum up her definition? What are the major stages of the paper?
- Where and how do major transitional sentences take the reader from one part of the paper to the next?
- Where and how does the writer use material from her reading or listening?
- Who would be the ideal audience for this paper? Is it written for women only?

We Have Had to Come a Long Way

What does it mean to be a feminist today? Young women interested in women's issues hear contradictory voices. Traditionally, feminists have envisioned the women of the future as strong, self-reliant partners in all areas of life. They have envisioned "liberated women" holding their own in politics, in the executive suite, or on the construction site. Today, however, books like *Who Stole Feminism?* warn of a trend toward "victim feminism" that projects an image of women as weak and in need of protection, constantly vulnerable to oppression and exploitation. Similarly, many feminists champion a woman's right to choose career over family. As the author of a recent letter to the editor said, "If a man wants to be totally devoted to his career and not take on the responsibility of children, does he get lectured about family values? Then why should a woman?" However, others speak up for women who want to balance family and work. In the opinion of Joanne Jacobs, a columnist for the *Mercury-News,* "most women want a feminism that represents women who want to marry, raise children, balance family and work, balance personal fulfillment with commitment."

Are the disagreements among different wings of the women's movement obscuring the movement's basic goals? What is the core meaning of feminism? Feminism exists because women recognize that society does not serve their needs. A feminist need not be female but could be anyone–male or female–who believes in equal rights for both sexes. The feminist movement is designed to help women discover their own powers and their own self-worth. Its aim is to help women achieve equality in all areas of life–private, artistic, social, economic, and political.

The growing awareness promoted by today's feminist movement has strong historical roots. The first major stage of feminism lasted from 1850 to 1920 and ended when women won the right to vote with the

Nineteenth Amendment. Susan B. Anthony was an outstanding organizer of the National Woman Suffrage Association; Elizabeth Cady Stanton early spoke up for property rights for women. Sojourner Truth, a freed slave, said at the Women's Rights Convention in 1851: "I think that between the Negroes of the South and the woman at the North all talking about rights, the white men will be in a fix pretty soon." Amelia Earhart, the first woman to pilot a plane across the Atlantic, said: "Women must try to do things as men have tried. When they fail, their failure must be but a challenge to others."

My own belief in independence and equality goes back to my experience in high school. A black woman teacher said to me: "Every woman should be a feminist because she is a woman." However, I grew up with girls whose parents were leading them down the road to housewifery, motherhood, or low-paying jobs by not urging them on to excel in the way they did their sons. The brother went out for varsity sports; the sister became a cheerleader. I remember being one of only a few girls in a trigonometry class. Two of them dropped out, with little effort on the part of the teacher to change their minds.

How much progress has our society made toward feminist awareness? The images of women projected by current movies, TV shows, or advertising present us with contradictory evidence. Today in order to cash in on the enormous female market, advertisers increasingly cater to the image of the confident woman who is in control of her life. However, many of the new images seem ambiguous or dishonest. The underwear model may now be a career woman. The female pilot looks like a Clairol model and sells deodorant. Movies in which angry women take revenge on males may also be ambiguous. The women are tough, but do they also confirm stereotypes of women as irrational and destructive?

Although women today are constantly bombarded by the media with visions of their presumed great strides toward equality, there is much more to be accomplished. Feminism will fight on as long as a patriarchal society denies women equality in their private, social, economic, and political lives.

SAMPLE OPTIONS FOR WRITING: Extended Definition

1. What is a *neoconservative?* (How is a neoconservative different from an old-style conservative?) Or, what does the term *liberal* mean to people who consider themselves liberal? Or, what role has the term *radical* played in American history or politics?

2. What is "welfare dependency"? Is it more than a fashionable political slogan? What is being done to deal with it?

3. What is the "religious right"? Is it a movement? an attitude? a media creation? What are its guiding principles? What is its influence?

4. What is "math anxiety"? Is it real? Is it gender-specific? Are there ways of dealing with it?

ARGUMENT: Making Your Case

When you advance a serious argument, you are asking your readers to listen to reason. You have thought the issue through, and you trust them to do the same. Here is a brief review of lines of reasoning that often prove convincing:

Induction

You show a pattern by assembling data that point in the same direction. If your readers feel that you have given a fair sampling of the evidence, they may accept your conclusions. Perhaps you are presenting examples to show that women are more "people-oriented" and therefore better managers than men. Your conclusion, even though you will typically present it early in your paper, is the result of a generalizing process, of **inductive** thinking.

Dialectic

You play off opposing views and weigh their merits. Ideally, from the play of **pro and con,** a less one-sided, better informed position will emerge. Are immigrants a drain on the public treasury? Or do they revitalize our dying cities, take jobs others don't want, start family businesses, and broaden the tax base? After your readers have looked at both sides of the argument and given due weight to different facets of the issue, they have a chance to arrive at a balanced conclusion.

Deduction

You argue from principle. You start from assumptions that you expect your audience to share. You then build an argument on them that proceeds by logical steps. The basic logical pattern is "If A is true, and if B is true, then C will also be true." If only A students are eligible for the honor society, and if you are a B student, then it follows that you are not eligible. The same basic pattern underlies arguments on many public issues:

IF: The U.S. Constitution separates church and state, religion and
       government.

AND IF: The nativity scene is a religious symbol.

THEN: The nativity scene should not be displayed on government prop-
            erty, for example, in a city park.

Such **deductive** arguments spell out conclusions already implied in the premises. Your **premises** are the shared assumptions providing the foundation on which your argument rests. A sound argument takes the reader from accepted premises through a chain of logical reasoning to a valid conclusion. In a paper presenting a deductive argument, you will often apply a general rule or a general principle to a specific instance:

- If the laws forbid discrimination on the basis of gender, will we see the end of all-male military academies or of all-male business clubs downtown? Will we see the end of women being excluded from combat roles? Will we see the end of women's colleges?
- If the laws forbid discrimination on the basis of race, are racial preferences in college admission or in hiring and promotion dead?

Traditional logicians have charted a deductive argument as a three-step pattern. Such a three-step argument, moving from two accepted premises to a valid conclusion, is called a **syllogism**:

FIRST PREMISE: All full-time students are eligible for the loan program.

SECOND PREMISE: You are a full-time student.

CONCLUSION: Therefore, you are eligible.

FIRST PREMISE: Only residents will be hired for the police force.

SECOND PREMISE: I am not a resident.

CONCLUSION: Therefore, I need not apply.

In each of these syllogisms, the conclusion necessarily follows because the premise includes or rules out *all* members of a group. In practice, many arguments are not true syllogisms. Arguments that use *some* or *many* instead of *all* or *no* in the first premise warrant only a *probable* conclusion:

IF: Most members of the Achievement Club are business majors.

AND IF: Cecily is a member of the Achievement Club.

THEN: Cecily is likely to be a business major.

Deductive reasoning provides the logical underpinnings for many papers that argue from principle or appeal to the reader's basic values. An argument like the following starts from widely accepted assumptions about justice and then brings them to bear on the current controversy about capital punishment:

IF: A basic principle of justice requires that the justice system be
            ready to correct its mistake.

AND IF: Capital punishment makes it impossible for the justice system to correct judicial error, since it has literally already buried its mistake.

THEN: Capital punishment violates a basic principle of justice.

WRITING WORKSHOP: A Paper for Peer Review

What assumptions underlie the following student paper? What premises provide the foundation for the writer's argument? Can you chart the writer's arguments according to the *if-and if-then* pattern? Are you carried along by the logic of the argument? If not, where or why would you take issue with the writer?

Justice Denied

"On the subject of crime, all politicians are demagogues," says a columnist in a recent issue of the *New Republic*. Playing to the public fear of violent crime, legislators everywhere are advocating stiffer sentencing laws and more and bigger prisons. The death penalty, which was in abeyance in the seventies and eighties, has made a comeback. The courts are shortening the appeals process that has kept many convicted criminals on death row for ten, twelve, or fourteen years. However, in spite of the strong grassroots support for the revival of the death penalty, capital punishment violates several basic principles underlying the American system of justice.

The weakness of passionate last-minute appeals for clemency is that they tend to focus on the special circumstances of the individual case. A murderer was the victim of child abuse. A rapist suffered brain damage. By focusing on the individual histories of those waiting on death row, we run the danger of losing sight of the principles at stake when a civilized society reinstitutes capital punishment.

Most basic to our legal system is the commitment to even-handed justice. We believe that equal crimes should receive equal punishment. However, the death penalty has always been notorious for its "freakish unfairness." In the words of one study, "judicial safeguards for preventing the arbitrary administration of capital punishment are not working." Some murderers walk the streets again after three or five or seven years, whereas others—because of ineffectual legal counsel, an ambitious prosecutor, or a hanging judge—join the inmates waiting out their appeals on death row. Judges and juries apply widely different standards. In one celebrated case, two partners in crime were convicted of the same capital crime on identical charges. One was executed; the other is in prison and will soon be eligible for parole.

We believe that all citizens are equal before the law. Justice should be blind to wealth, race, or ethnic origin. However, poor defendants are many times more likely to receive the death penalty than wealthy ones. Rich defendants are protected by highly paid teams of lawyers whose maneuvers stymie the prosecution. Defendants with millions to spend bring in an array of experts who baffle the jury. Minority defendants convicted of capital crimes have a much higher statistical chance of being executed than white defendants.

Finally, fairness demands that the judicial system correct its own mistakes. If someone has been unjustly convicted there should be a mechanism for reversing the verdict and setting the person free. No one doubts that there are miscarriages of justice. Witnesses admit to mistaken identification of suspects. A convict confesses on his deathbed to a crime for which someone else was convicted. A woman withdraws a rape charge years after the accused was sent to prison. However, in the case of the death penalty, any such correction of error is aborted. The judicial system buries its mistakes. We are left with futile regrets, like the prosecutor who said: "Horrible as it is to contemplate, we may have executed the wrong man."

PERSUADING YOUR AUDIENCE

Writing designed to enlist support or produce action will test your powers of persuasion. Much analysis, much argument, does not proceed from disinterested curiosity. Instead, it supports a project, advances a point of view, or serves a cause. The more important the payoff is—the sale, the vote, the subscription, the sign-up for membership in your group—the more you will concentrate on *motivating* your audience. What shared values can you invoke? What sympathies or antipathies should you try to arouse? What apprehensions may you have to play to? What objections do you have to defuse?

Suppose your task is to prepare a proposal to allow development of high-priced housing on acreage originally left to the city for use as a park. Your audience includes city officials, members of the planning commission, and concerned citizens. You might chart your written and oral presentation as follows. You concentrate on the problems your proposal will solve. You emphasize the benefits it offers. You anticipate and defuse objections that are likely to come up.

In Support of Growth

History: The acreage was deeded to the city by a public-spirited citizen for possible use as a park.

Problems: Tight city budgets did not allow development of the property as a park. The bequest did not include money for continuing maintenance, so that the property has been neglected and presents an eyesore.

The bequest was made when much other land was available for construction, whereas now there is a scarcity of land suitable for development.

Benefits: Economic benefits will accrue to local contractors and local businesses. The city will derive much-needed tax revenue by broadening the tax base to include numerous upscale homes.

Development will end the drain on the city treasury from unavoidable maintenance costs.

Concerns: Low density will minimize traffic congestion.

Developers will set aside funds as contribution to the city's plan for senior citizen housing.

Experienced promoters, proposal writers, or advocates of causes employ strategies of persuasion ranging from tried and-true to new and ingenious. One time-tested strategy, for instance, proceeds by **eliminating alternatives**. When you examine two or three proposed solutions to a problem and then find them wanting, your readers will hope that the third or fourth proposed solution will provide the answer. You can chart this strategy as follows:

PHASE ONE: first alternative examined and rejected

PHASE TWO: second alternative examined and rejected

PHASE THREE: third alternative examined and recommended

For example, let us assume you are checking out the current backlash against bilingual education. First, you examine a proposed return to English-only, sink-or-swim instruction that would apparently "mainstream" even students with little or no English—whether they understand what the teacher is saying or not. You document the discipline problems and horrendous dropout rates in schools where many students cannot keep up with the instructional program. You then look at conventional bilingual programs—offering students instruction in geography, math, and other subjects in their own first language so that they will not hopelessly fall behind. You document much-publicized objections: Although these are intended as transitional programs, many students stay in them too long—and they are kept from the kind of total immersion in an English-language environment that would make possible true proficiency in English as their second language. Your readers should then be ready for a third and more promising alternative. Perhaps you will recommend subject-matter courses taught in English by

English-as-a-second-language specialists, supplemented by intensive English-as-a-second-language instruction.

Effective persuasion is the key to success not only in politics but also in many other areas. However, persuasion sooner or later raises questions of ethics. There is a fine line between presenting your case in the best light and manipulating the audience. The more vulnerable the intended audience is, the more a promoter or propagandist may be tempted to use familiar ploys. These might include sales pitches sent out in official-looking envelopes, endorsements from celebrities and fake authorities, inflated or manipulated statistics, scare tactics, and exploitation of religious or patriotic sentiment. The more experienced and wary an audience is, the more likely such tactics are to backfire. Even so, it is an open question whether consumer education and voter education can keep up with ever more sophisticated tactics of persuasion used by campaign strategists or public relations and advertising experts.

OPTIONS FOR WRITING: Playing the Advocate

1. Citizens often raise an outcry against publicly commissioned art that they consider too avantgarde or nontraditional. Or they object to the tearing down of a theater or other landmark to make way for another sterile office building. If there has recently been a similar case in your community or elsewhere in the news, write a letter to the editor championing the side you favor.

2. Addressing yourself to the concerned voter, attack or defend the use of public money for an institution like the National Endowment for the Arts, the National Endowment for the Humanities, the Public Broadcasting System, or the Voice of America.

3. There have been recent unsuccessful attempts to make the health care system and insurance companies recognize mental disorders or biochemical malfunctions of the human brain as on a par with other physical illnesses. If you care about this issue, prepare a plea to be presented to state or national legislators.

4. If you have strong views for or against pay equity or comparable pay for women, prepare a strong plea to an audience of concerned voters. Or, if you have strong views on the minimum wage, prepare a presentation to the local chamber of commerce.

11

Practical Prose Forms

Much of the writing in the world of scholarship and in the world of work conforms to established conventions. You write to an established format. For a given task or in a given area, you are expected to follow established ways of introducing and laying out material. Your readers may expect to see first a summary of your findings, then a review of previous research, then an account of your procedures, and finally a detailed interpretation of your results. Most professions or academic disciplines have style sheets, style manuals, or editorial guidelines for the newcomer. For the initiated, the conventions spelled out there have become second nature, like driving on the right side of the road.

Conventions change over the years. For instance, business letters have become considerably less stodgy and formula-ridden. Lawyers hire writing consultants to bring their legalese closer to plain English. Research paper styles in the humanities increasingly reflect the fact that students are likely to be working at the computer instead of typing on a Smith-Corona.

ABSTRACT, CONDENSATION, SUMMARY, REVIEW

Various kinds of summaries give a brief preview or overview of a lengthy document or an extended passage. Getting at the meat of an article or highlighting key points in a proposal is an important skill. Readers, managers, and coworkers often ask: "What's the gist of it? What does it boil down to?" Pointed summaries can help get the attention of a hurried reader or make salient points easily accessible to people in a position to make decisions.

Abstracts

Reports and monographs (extended treatments of a single subject) are often preceded by an **abstract** that provides a quick overview. The abstract sums up the author's purpose or thesis, charts major stages or key points, and often spells out implications for future work or for future research. Reading the abstract, the reader should have a clear idea of what the author sets out to do, what ground the author covers, and what key points the author makes. The reader consulting a reference work like *Sociological Abstracts* or browsing a database that includes abstracts can decide whether the abstracted source is relevant to current work and whether to consult it or not.

What if the student author of the research paper on chaos theory (Chapter 7) had been asked to include an abstract at the beginning of the paper? The abstract would start with a definition of chaos theory and the "butterfly effect." It would then summarize the application of chaos theory in four major areas: economics, ecology, medicine, new products. It might conclude by summing up the promise and the obstacles facing the theory.

Abstracts may be prepared by the author or by someone cataloguing the article, report, book, videotape, or the like. The following is a nonauthor abstract of a videotape listed in the database SPORT discus.

SilverPlatter 3.11   SPORT Discus – June 1994

TI: Girls and sports : the winning combination

AU: Drachkovitch,-R

CA: Women's sports foundation

SO: Women's Sports Foundation, New York 1991, 1

videocassette : sd., col. ; 20 min

PY: 1991

Digests and Summaries

Many organizations or institutions have a need for information digested or boiled down for internal use. Since a condensation will keep much of the original wording without quotation marks, it is very important to identify the shortened version clearly as a condensation or abridgment, using for instance a phrase like "condensed from . . ." or "abridged from . . ."

When you condense a document, keep guidelines like the following in mind:

- *Focus on the main trend of thought.* What sentence sums up the thesis of an essay? What sentences sum up the key ideas of successive paragraphs? What transitions—a crucial *therefore, however,* or *on the other hand*—signal a major turning point in an argument?

- *Cut down explanations and examples to a minimum.* Condense lengthy explanations. Keep maybe one key example out of three given by the author. Keep only key details or crucial statistics.

- *Keep essential qualifications.* Cutting out an important *if* or *but* will seriously distort and misrepresent the original source. Do not blur the difference between *will* and *might.*

- *Use the most economic wording.* Write "investigate" instead of "conduct an investigation." Write "fortunately" instead of "it was a fortunate coincidence that . . ."

Study the difference between a full-length passage, a condensed version, and a brief summary:

Original: Running is one of the primal human acts, and the particular human form it takes, using a bipedal stride in a fully upright stance, has played an essential part in shaping our destiny. It was once believed that our hominid ancestors were rather pitiable creatures compared with the other animals of the jungles and savannas; lacking the fangs, claws, and specialized physical abilities of the predators, the hominids supposedly prevailed only because of their large brains and their ability to use tools. But there is now compelling evidence that our direct ancestors of some four million years ago had relatively small brains, only about a third the size of ours. What these hominids *did* have was a fully upright stance with the modern, doubly curved spine that enters the skull at the bottom rather than the back (as is the case with the apes). The upright stance increased the field of vision and freed the forelimbs for use in inspecting and manipulating objects, thus challenging the brain to increase in capacity through the process of natural selection.   John Leonard, *Born to Run*

Digest: The way we run—fully upright, with bipedal stride—has shaped our human destiny. Our hominid ancestors were once thought pitiable compared with the fangs and strength of other predators, which, however, lacked large brains and tools. But evidently, four million years ago our ancestors had only one-third our brain size. They did have a full upright stance, with a larger field of vision, forelimbs free for manipulating objects, and gradually increasing brain capacity through natural selection. Their athletic ability assured survival, even without tools and high intelligence.

Summary: Early human beings, with relatively small brains, gained a competitive edge over other animals as the result of their fully upright bipedal stance, which increased their field of vision and freed the forelimbs for manipulating objects.

When does condensation shade over into interpretation? Dealing with a difficult or technical text, the person making a text more easily accessible will often do more than extrapolate key points. The writer may be expected to explain and interpret as well. Popularizers, textbook authors, and aides to important persons are good at showing not only what a text says but also what it means. Look at what has happened to *primal human acts, bipedal stride, hominid ancestors,* and *predators* in the following rendering of Leonard's passage. While using mostly paraphrase–putting the original author's ideas into the adaptor's own words–a few phrases quoted verbatim and put in quotation marks give the passage an authentic touch:

Interpretation: According to John Leonard in *Born to Run,* the way we run–fully upright, striding on two feet–has shaped our human destiny. Our near-human ancestors were once thought "rather pitiable creatures," lacking the fangs and claws of wild animals and surviving only because of their larger brains and ability to use tools. Actually our ancestors had brains only one-third the size of ours. However, they stood upright, could see farther, and used their hands to manipulate objects, "thus challenging the brain to increase its capacity" through natural selection.

INTERVIEWS

Experienced interviewers do their homework. For instance, before interviewing a VIP, they try to find out something about the person's homebase, career, and views as expressed in speeches or articles. They chart an agenda, preparing a set of questions that will keep the interview from meandering or petering out. At the same time, they prepare to be flexible–to adjust as one question strikes a spark and another proves a dud.

A strategy that often works is to start with questions that show a sympathetic interest in the subject's work. A good way to get people to talk is to show a willingness to listen to their problems or concerns. The interviewer might then push on to more probing questions that prod the subject into going beyond dutifully repeating an official line. The following might be your agenda for an interview with a social worker:

What brought you to social work?

What is your work routine like on a typical day?

What difficult or unusual cases have you recently worked on?

What do you like best about your job?

What do you like least about your job?

What is your answer to charges that social workers are bogged down in red tape?

What is your answer to charges that social workers don't really communicate with the people they work with or understand their problems?

If you had five minutes before the Board of Supervisors or before a committee of the state legislature, what would you tell them about social problems in your community?

WORKSHOP 1

Study the Oliver Sacks interview in Chapter 1. What shows that the interviewers had done their homework? How much do they seem to know about the person interviewed and the subject matter of the interview? How would you chart the course of the interview?

PROPOSAL WRITING

Proposal writing is a basic survival skill in the worlds of business, government, science, and education. People write proposals to secure approval for a project or to line up funding for an initiative. Researchers write proposals to conduct experiments. Management consultants propose to simplify the organizational chart of a company, to streamline a production process, or to establish better liaison among departments. Social workers design proposals for experimental projects to reach members of youth gangs. Educators develop proposals for an experimental on-line course or for innovative instruction in English as a second language. Artists and authors write proposals to secure support from foundations or endowments.

Preparing Your Proposal

Proposals may range from a plan for reorganizing office space at an insurance company to a bid to build and launch a new kind of communications satellite. Whatever the scope, when you write a proposal, your assignment is to convince those in charge or those with the say-so that you know what you are doing and that it is worthy of support. As with many other writing projects, the final outcome depends in large part on the quality of your preliminary spadework. Do your homework! Pay attention to parameters like the following:

Format   How much leeway do you have in matters of format? Proposals range from a proposal presented in an internal office memo to a carefully structured document submitted in response to a call for proposals issued by a company or agency. Is yours going to be an informal proposal, with you structuring it in the most effective way? Or is there a prescribed format to follow? What elements of the proposal do you have to include? How many copies do you have to file? What are the deadlines for submission? In addition, are there special requirements? For instance, does an agency or organization require "blind" submissions (with personnel identified only in a separate cover letter), so that in the proposal itself there will be no indication of gender or ethnicity that might activate bias on the part of evaluators?

Audience   Who is going to approve or reject the proposal? Remember that they who pay the piper call the tune. Experienced proposal writers are good at "scoping" or psyching out their intended audience. They check announcements and memos from the target organization or agency. They listen to informal comments by insiders. For instance, do the people running an agency or organization think of themselves as "hard-nosed" practical people, who want to see short-term measurable, quantifiable results? Or are they people who pride themselves on encouraging creativity, looking for imaginative or experimental approaches?

Past History   What proposals has the target organization or agency approved in the past? What proposals were turned down, and why? Can you gain access to ratings of past proposals or to letters justifying rejection of proposals found unsatisfactory?

Structuring Your Proposal

In presenting a proposal, you will typically be competing with others for attention, funding, or support. It's up to you to show that what you propose is desirable, feasible, and rewarding. A promising proposal is likely to include all or most of the following elements (not necessarily in this exact order):

Summary   What, briefly, are you proposing to do? What is the problem or need? How are you proposing to deal with it? What will it take to do the job? What are the major benefits?

Personnel   Why are you or your team qualified to do what you are proposing to do? What expertise qualifies you to give advice or propose solutions? Put relevant coursework or practical experience in a good light. If you can, point out your track record with similar work or comparable projects.

Need   What need are you trying to fill? Document the problem that needs solution, or demonstrate the gap that needs to be filled. For instance, in a proposal for a new youth activities center, bring in testimony from officials, teachers, and affected teenagers to show that in your community there is no place for adolescents to go, that there are no organized activities to motivate them. Show a pattern of vandalism, shoplifting, and confrontations with police involving bored and alienated youth. Point to other communities that have had good success with model programs.

Procedure   What exactly are you proposing? Be specific about your plans, whether it be planning an experiment, setting up a meeting, planning a conference, or polling working mothers. Or give advice concrete enough so that it can be successfully implemented by those concerned. Focus on what is supposed to happen and how it is going to be done.

Logistics   What money, equipment, and time are needed to implement your proposal? Spell out needed funding, specifying projected expenditures. Identify needed equipment and supplies, indicating availability or possible sources where appropriate. Set up a timetable: Is there a definite final deadline, and are there intermediate deadlines for stages of the project?

Benefits   What will the proposed project do for the company, for the community, or for the targeted population? Here is the payoff–convince your audience that what you propose is worth doing.

Evaluation   Often a company or funding agency will have established procedures for evaluating performance. There may be requirements for interim evaluation or progress reports. At other times, you yourself may want to propose arrangements for review of results. For instance, you may suggest **expert review**–the use of outside evaluators with special expertise in the field. Or you may suggest **community involvement**–the bringing in of a citizen committee for feedback from the community. You may propose the use of follow-up questionnaires or of telephone interviews.

Study the model proposal on the following page from Fred E. White, *Communicating Technology: Dynamic Processes and Models for Writers* (1996). Does the proposal identify the problem effectively? Are needs and procedures clearly spelled out? Do any details remain fuzzy? Are possible difficulties or obstacles addressed? Would you vote to fund the proposal?

WORKSHOP 2

Working alone or with a group, work up a proposal for a project like the following:

- developing a less cumbersome arrangement for recycling or waste disposal in your area
- planning better landscaping for your campus

A PROPOSAL TO IMPROVE RECREATIONAL FACILITIES
AT THE GRANDVIEW RESIDENCE FOR RETIRED CITIZENS,
GRANDVIEW, MICHIGAN

Prepared for the Board of Directors,
Grandview Residence
By
Alan Medina, Nurse's Aide

January 10, 1994

[Letter of Transmittal]

GRANDVIEW RESIDENCE

1055 Overlook Drive
Grandview, Michigan 48977

January 10, 1994

Gerald Larson, M.D., President
Grandview Residence

Dear Dr. Larson:

I am pleased to submit my proposal for conducting a study
to improve the recreational opportunities at Grandview
Residence.

As you know, the purpose of my proposed investigation is
to find a way to enhance the quality of life for our residents. Lack of physical and mental stimulation can seriously undermine the general health and well-being of
these senior citizens. By finding a cost-efficient means of
enriching their lives during their residency here, our
reputation as leaders in residential care for the aged
will be assured.

I am grateful to my supervisor, Mary Ortiz, R.N., for her
valuable assistance, and to you, Dr. Larson, for your
support and encouragement.

Sincerely,

Alan Medina

Alan Medina
Nurse's Aide

ABSTRACT

Recreational opportunities for the senior citizens at Grandview Residence are inadequate. The majority are forced to spend much of their time being inactive: watching TV or napping excessively. Because there are clear connections between lack of activity and deterioration of mental and physical health among the aged, a feasibility study urgently needs to be conducted to determine the best strategy for improving recreational opportunities. Such a study can be conducted within a month and at a relatively low cost.

Purpose of this proposal

The senior citizens of Grandview Residence lack adequate recreational facilities. The purpose of this proposal is to request funding to conduct a formal feasibility study that would determine which recreational improvements would work best for our residents.

Nature of the problem

For a facility that is responsible for the welfare of sixty residents, most of whom are emotionally stable and intellectually alert, Grandview possesses seriously inadequate recreational opportunities. It is common knowledge that lack of mental stimulation often results in physical dysfunction. According to Mary Ortiz, R.N. (my supervisor), "Prolonged inactivity can aggravate existing cardiovascular and respiratory problems and lead to debilitating muscular atrophy." Lack of the kinds of stimulation that recreational activities afford can also lead to depression and diminishment of cognitive abilities.

This proposal will first describe the existing recreational opportunities at Grandview, then describe the kind of feasibility study that would determine how best to improve these opportunities. Finally, the cost of such an investigation will be discussed.

Existing Recreational Opportunities at Grandview

For our sixty residents, we have one television, two

decks of playing cards, one checkers set, one chess set, one croquet set, and about thirty paperback books (mostly novels) in tattered condition. Clearly, these materials are inadequate, even if we had larger quantities of them on hand.

What a formal feasibility study of the problem can accomplish

The goal of the study will be to take as much guesswork as possible out of determining which recreational activities our residents would truly find useful and stimulating. A formal study will involve interviewing the residents, discovering what recreational activities are available, visiting other facilities for the aged to observe their recreational facilities, and finally, acquiring some recreational equipment for a trial run.

Cost analysis

A feasibility study of the best ways to improve the recreational facilities at Grandview would incur the following costs:

- Assistant to help conduct survey to determine residents' preferred recreational activities .....,$50.
- Catalogues of recreational equipment and supplies ....75.
- Local travel to other health-care facilities to discover how others have dealt with this problem ...50.
- Three assistants to supervise trial activities ....150.
- Purchase of trial equipment ....200.
- Preparation of the feasibility report ....50.

TOTAL ....$575.

Timeframe

Research..............3 weeks
Trial activities......1 week
Writing the report....2 weeks
          TOTAL .....6 weeks

- asking your college to fund a one-day conference on racial divisions, violence against women, or alternative lifestyles
- organizing a voter registration drive in your community
- organizing a program to help foreign students become part of the campus community
- introducing students in a local school to the Internet

REPORT WRITING

Reports are a basic form of communication in the world of work and of research. Reports keep your superiors or your peers informed of your performance–of what you have attempted and what you have accomplished. Reports give managers or coworkers a basis for determining future needs and planning future action. At the same time, businesses, organizations, or agencies use reports as a means of holding people accountable–reports give an accounting of how time and money was spent.

The following reading selection is a report on an experiment involving measures to ensure the survival of the whooping crane. This formal report illustrates elements that, with appropriate variations or adaptations, are found in many similar reports on experiments, fieldwork, or initiatives. This is the authors' definitive accounting of what they undertook and what they accomplished. Study the following elements of the report:

Abstract

The report starts with an abstract of about 200–250 words. The authors give a succinct account of their purpose, method, and results. They summarize the need for the experiment, include exact numbers to fix the scope of the experiment, sum up their methodology, summarize their findings, and conclude with a concise statement of their recommendations.

Discussion of the Literature

The authors show their familiarity with the field and with previous research. They cite about eight sources, starting with general discussions of efforts to reintroduce captive specimens of endangered species into the wild. They then narrow the subject, going on to the history of efforts to assist recovery of the specific species that is the subject of their experiment. Finally, they state their purpose, showing their experiment to be a logical and needed next step in an ongoing joint effort.

Acknowledgments

The authors express their thanks for the assistance of individuals and institutions who facilitated the experiment.

Methodology

The authors give an exact accounting of their contrasting procedures for reintroducing two experimental groups of birds into the wild. They describe their procedures for monitoring the results.

Results

The authors document in considerable detail the results of the experiment. They spell out complications to be considered in achieving comparable results for the two experimental groups. They analyze factors accounting for varying survival rates. They provide statistical tables and maps showing dispersal of the two populations.

Discussion

The authors put their results in a larger context, comparing their results, for instance, with the results of related studies.

Recommendations

Here are the suggestions for future research or future work.

How would you describe the intended audience for the report? How would you summarize its findings? How would you estimate their significance? Which elements of the report seem to you particularly well developed?

SURVIVAL AND MOVEMENTS OF GREATER SANDHILL CRANES EXPERIMENTALLY RELEASED IN FLORIDA

Stephen A. Nesbitt AND *James W. Carpenter*

Abstract: *The potential reintroduction of a population of whooping cranes (Grus americana) in Florida depends on having an effective introduction technique. We tested 2 experimental release techniques to evaluate post-release survival, dispersal, and the innate predilection to migration in cranes as a preliminary step in the establishment of a non-migrating population of whooping cranes. Thirty-four eggs of migratory greater sandhill cranes (GSHC) (G. canadensis tabida) were exchanged for the clutches in 23 nests of Florida sandhill cranes (FSHC) (G. c. pratensis), a non-migratory subspecies; 5 young were fledged from these introductions. Concurrently, 27 captive-reared, subadult GSHC were soft-released in the same area of north-central Florida. Movements and survival of both release groups were assessed through radio telemetry. In general, dispersal was similar to normal, subadult FSHC. The experimental birds tended to move south in autumn, but did not move north in the spring; frequency of southern movements was not different in control and experimental groups. Survival differed (P >0.005) between experimental groups; 56% for captive-reared young (for the first year following release) and 39% for foster-reared young (from hatching to leaving natal home range). Our data suggest that captive-rearing and soft-release should be used as the primary reintroduction strategy for future releases of whooping cranes.*

The restoration into former range or the augmentation of depleted populations are integral steps to the recovery of many endangered or threatened species (Carpenter and Derrickson 1981; Griffith et al. 1989, 1990). Introduction into the wild of captive–produced individuals or eggs, in conjunction with other management techniques, has been used or recommended as a strategy to accomplish these steps (Carpenter 1983, Kleiman 1989, Griffith et al. 1990). Before any endangered species is released, the effects of captive-rearing and wild release should be tested on a similar but more abundant species or subspecies. Sandhill cranes served as experimental surrogates for whooping cranes in early captive management studies (Erickson 1968, Derrickson and Carpenter 1983, U.S. Fish and Wildl. Serv. 1986). FSHC were used successfully as surrogates for Mississippi sandhill cranes (*G. c. pulla*) (U.S. Fish and Wildl. Serv. 1991) because both are non–migratory and have similar habitat requirements.

The Whooping Crane Recovery Plan calls for the establishment of 3 separate, self-sustaining flocks for downlisting from endangered status (U.S. Fish and Wildl. Serv. 1986). Efforts to achieve recovery in the wild began in 1975 with an experiment to establish a migratory population of whooping cranes in Idaho using GSHC as foster parents. This whooping crane population, although not self-sustaining, migrates along a well-defined corridor in the Rocky Mountains with its foster sandhill crane population (Drewien and Bizeau 1978, U.S. Fish and Wildl. Serv. 1986). Although whooping cranes once occurred as both migratory and non-migratory populations (Allen 1952), the reestablishment of a non-migratory population might be problematic because no representatives of the non-migratory whooping cranes remain; they last occurred in Louisiana in the 1940's (Lowrey 1974). Thus, we introduced eggs and captive-reared young GSHC (from migratory stock) in Florida, using FSHC as foster-parents or behavioral role models, to determine if cranes of migratory parentage will become non-migratory when they do not associate with parents that migrate.

We gratefully acknowledge S. R. Derrickson, D. H. Ellis, and S. G. Hereford, Patuxent Wildlife Research Center (PWRC), for their assistance in providing eggs and captive-produced GSHC for this study. Additionally, staff of the International Crane Foundation, Baraboo, Wisconsin, provided eggs from wild GSHC nests in Wisconsin. The Wisconsin Department of Natural Resources assisted with collection of eggs from the wild. S. T. Schwikert, K. S. Williams, and R. D. Bjork assisted with monitoring crane movements, and C. T. Moore assisted with analysis of movements. Funding for this project came from the Florida Game and Fresh Water Fish Commission and the U.S. Fish and Wildlife Service (USFWS) through section 6 of the U.S. Endangered Species Act (PL 93-205). The facilities and procedures used at PWRC and in Florida were in accordance with the Animal Welfare Act.

METHODS

Foster-Rearing

Half (17 of 34) of the eggs used in our study were laid by captive GSHC at PWRC; others were obtained from wild GSHC in Idaho ($n = 7$) or Wisconsin ($n = 10$). Eggs were removed from nests after 10–14 days of natural incubation, artificially incubated for 1–2 days, and transported to Florida in a portable incubator case (Erickson 1981) maintained at 34.4–37.8 C. Prior to transfer into nests, the eggs were maintained in a Roll-X, RX3A incubator (Marsh MFG. Inc., Garden Group, Calif.) at 85–90% humidity and 37.6 C. Usually eggs were transferred to nests of marked pairs of FSHC (Nesbitt 1988) in Florida within 24 hours of arrival, but occasionally, when nests were unavailable, up to 10 days elapsed. We checked nests within 24 hours after transfer to ascertain incubation status. Because of a disparity between the availability of GSHC eggs and peak nesting of FSHC in the study area, most of the eggs were transferred into second, third, or even fourth clutches (Nesbitt 1988). Young produced from these clutches were captured before fledging (60–65 days), uniquely color-banded, and instrumented with solar-powered leg-band transmitters (Melvin et al. 1983).

Soft-Release

Soft-release, the gradual transition of captive-produced animals to unsup-   5
ported, free-ranging life in the wild (Derrickson and Carpenter 1983, 1987), was used to evaluate the suitability of captive-reared migratory cranes for use in establishing a non-migratory population. We constructed an open-topped, 1.5-ha enclosure, comparable to the facilities used successfully to soft-release Mississippi sandhill cranes (Zwank and Derrickson 1982). The enclosure, subdivided to maintain the birds in the separate cohorts established at PWRC, incorporated examples of the feeding, roosting, and loafing habitats used by FSHC. Birds were banded with USFWS tags and individually color-marked at the pens before being introduced. The cranes were rendered flightless by wing brails (Ellis and Dein 1991), which were alternated between wings at 2-week intervals to prevent stiffness of the carpometacarpal joints (Derrickson and Carpenter 1983). Four to 6 weeks after arrival, the cranes were instrumented with radio transmitters and the brails removed allowing them to move freely in and out of the pen. The commercially available pelleted diet (Ziegler Bros., Inc., Gardners, Pa.) that had been used at PWRC was provided ad libitum while birds were in the pen and after release until they no longer used it.

Movements

The location, general behavior, and social interaction of each individual was monitored at least once weekly for ≥18 months (usually daily for the first 9 months) after dispersal from the pen or their natal home range. This ensured observation through 2 spring migration periods (Feb–early Apr). After the second spring migration season, we attempted to recapture survivors. Six individuals were reinstrumented and monitored for an additional 12–24 months. GSHC were not allowed to successfully reproduce with FSHC; whenever possible they were removed from the wild, or sexually neutered and returned to the wild. Eggs from FSHC were substituted for any clutches produced among mixed pairs to compare parenting ability of the captive-produced birds with that of wild FSHC.

As a control, the movements of 12 subadult (1 to 2 year olds) FSHC were monitored for ≥18 months following their departure from their natal home range. Movements of the 3 groups (soft-release, foster-reared, and control) were compared for 3 periods (Feb–May, Jun–Sep, Oct–Jan). For all movements >5 km, locations were plotted on 1:24,000 scale maps. Such movements took the bird into a new daily range. Because the experimental birds were from migratory stock we assumed that if they exhibited a dispersal pattern different from the control group, it would likely be a disproportionate number of north-south oriented movements during the February–May or October–January periods (corresponding to the spring and autumn migration periods for the wild GSHC). We calculated the proportion of total movements within each season that were directed either north (azimuth 0–45°) or south (azimuth 135–225°) for each individual or cohort (while the birds remained together). We tested for differences in proportions among the 3 groups, by season, with the Kruskal-Wallis test. For the foster-reared and soft-released groups, the survival rates were determined by the Kaplan-Meier procedure (Pollock et al. 1989).

RESULTS

Survival

Foster-Rearing.—Clutches consisting of 34 GSHC eggs were substituted into 23 FSHC nests during 1982–87. Of the transferred clutches, 17% were immediately abandoned, 26% were incubated and abandoned without hatching, 35% hatched ≥1 egg but fledged none, and 22% fledged young (Table 1). In 1982 and 1983, we observed that incubating birds, if disturbed from the nest, often did not return immediately (>30 min), thereby reducing embryo viability in eggs exposed to direct sunlight. Hence, we preferred to transfer eggs during early morning and early evening hours with cooler ambient temperatures.

TABLE 1. Hatching, fledging success, and survival of greater sandhill crane eggs per young cross-fostered to Florida sandhill cranes, Alachua County, Florida, 1982–87.

Eggs and nests	Eggs transferred[a]		Nests		Young fledged and surviving	
	No.	%	No.	%	>6 months	>1 year
Unsuccessful						
Abandoned immediately	8	24	4	17		
Incubated but abandoned before hatching	6	18	6	26		
Successful						
Hatched ≥1 egg but none fledged	12	35	8	35	5	4
Hatched ≥1 egg and ≥1 fledged	6	18	5	22		
Second egg of 2-egg clutch not hatched	2	6				
Totals	34		23		5	4

[a] Sources: 17 Patuxent Wildlife Research Center, 10 Wisconsin, 7 Idaho.

The 5 foster-reared GSHC left their natal territory 9–10 months after hatching, the same age at which juvenile FSHC typically separate from their parents (Nesbitt 1992). After leaving the natal home range, the birds functioned as solitary individuals for 1–4 weeks until they began associating with FSHC in a group situation. These groups often included some GSHC that had not yet begun spring migration. Survival rate for the period from hatching to leaving the natal home range was 0.39; from leaving the natal home range to 1 year post-dispersal, it was 0.80.

Soft-Release.–Seven 9- to 10-month-old GSHC arrived as 1 cohort in Florida on 14 February 1986; a second cohort of 8 birds arrived on 20 February. They were all released 4 April. All were capable of sustained flight except one with worn primary feathers. The impaired bird was caught 1 May, and 10 primary stubs were pulled (4 right, 6 left) to stimulate replacement of the worn feathers. By August, the feathers had grown back and the bird was able to fly. In early December 1986, 14 additional 9- to 10-month-old GSHC, in 2 cohorts, arrived in Florida. Twelve flew normally and were released 2 January 1987. Two were unable to fly; both birds had injured their right carpometacarpus. This may have occurred during shipment or during confinement in Florida. Twelve of the 27 soft-released cranes died during the first year post-release (Table 2). Predation was the largest single source of mortality (6 of 12 losses) with bobcats (*Lynx rufus*) suspected in five of the losses) (Table 2). For both releases, the pooled first-year survival rate was 0.56. Two-thirds of the first year post-release mortality occurred within 6 months after release.

TABLE 2. Number, survival, and source of mortality among 27 (4 cohorts) subadult greater sandhill cranes soft-released in Florida, 1986–87.

Variable	Cohort				
	1[a]	2[a]	3	4	Total
Arrival date	Feb 86	Feb 86	Dec 86	Dec 86	
n	7	8	6	8	29
Release date	Apr 86	Apr 86	Jan 87	Jan 87	
n	7	8	5	7	27
Survival					
≥6 months	11		3	5	19
≥1 yr	7		3	5	15
Alive/at large at end of study	0		3	5	8
Mortality					
Predation (bobcat)	5				5
Predation (other)			1		1
Collision (fences or powerlines)	1		1	1	3
Shot	1				1
Mycotoxicosis	1				1
Unknown/disappeared				1	1
Total	8		2	2	12

[a] These 2 cohorts joined as one after release.

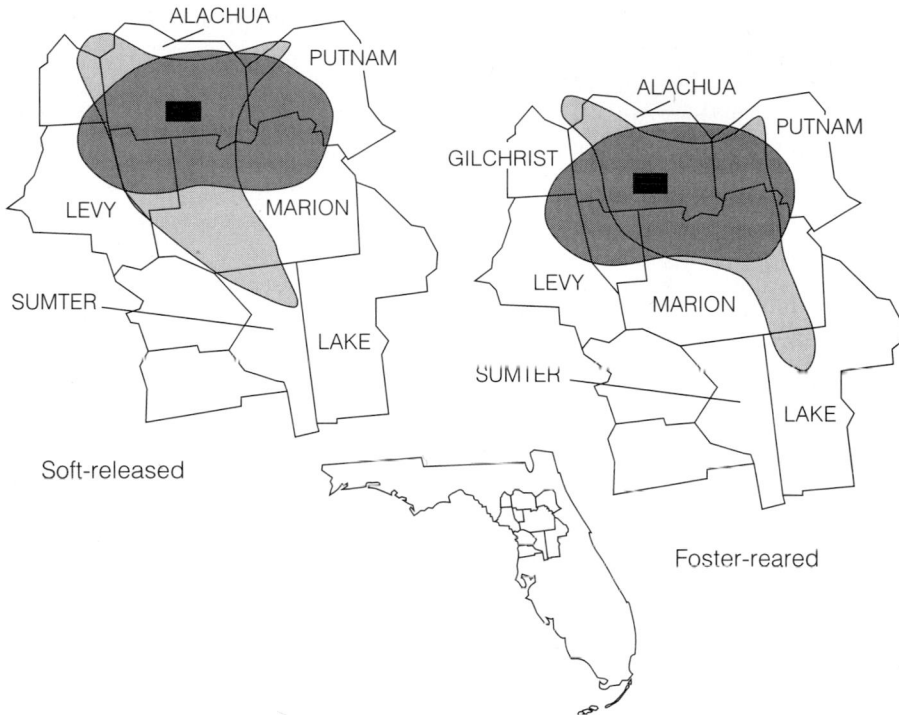

FIGURE 1.   Dispersal of experimentally released greater sandhill cranes (larger cross-hatching) and control Florida sandhill cranes (smaller crosshatching) in Florida, 1986–88. Closed rectangle denotes release/introduction site.

Movements

The foster-reared GSHC all left their natal home range and began post-independence dispersal between early January and mid-February. A subsequent pattern of movement 5–20 km away from the natal home range with periodic returns was characteristic of the dispersal behavior of both the foster-reared and control group. A foster-reared bird that disappeared after the first spring migration period apparently died. It was last encountered 40 km north of the release area in mid-April 1987. Only one of the 5 foster-reared GSHC exceeded the normal dispersal range described by the control FSHC group. That bird moved some 70 km south to Lake County (Fig. 1) in mid-December of the first post-independence year and remained there for 2 years. The other 3 foster-reared GSHC remained within 20 km of their natal home range throughout the second post-independence year.

For each of the 2 years that soft-release occurred, the birds were released in 2 cohort groups (groups established at PWRC). Both 1986 cohorts moved together as a flock, although the 2 cohorts remained distinguishable, even within larger mixed flocks, throughout the first post-release year. The only movement of a soft-released flock that exceeded the normal dispersal range for the control group occurred on 4 December 1986 when the 1986 release flock moved 120 km south to Sumter County (Fig. 1). The 7 survivors (two died after moving to Sumter County) returned north in mid-January 1987 and on 13 January they were 50 km west-northwest of the release area. The 2 cohorts separated in February 1987; 1 cohort (4 birds) had returned to the area of the release pen by 19 February, and remained there until June 1987 when they were recaptured. The other cohort of 3 birds moved to within 30 km west-northwest of the release area also on 19 February; contact with this group was lost when the last transmitter failed shortly afterward. Although we monitored the areas frequently by this cohort, it was never relocated, and we presumed all eventually died.

The 2 cohorts (12 birds) released in 1987 remained in the general release area for 4 months, where they regularly associated with wild cranes. On 4 March, 1 cohort (5 birds) moved 40 km south to near Reddick in Marion County (Fig. 1). On 25 March, the other cohort (7 birds) moved 50 km east to an agricultural area in Putnam County. They remained there for the remainder of the first post-release year. The 3 surviving birds from the first dispersing cohort returned to the release area on 14 May and remained there throughout the rest of the first post-release year.

No differences ($P \geq 0.635$) were detected among treatment group mean ranks for the proportion of north or south movement for the spring or autumn period (Table 3). Individual cohorts remained cohesive after release, and all but one of the surviving birds remained within their cohort for 12–14 months after release. The exception was a bird that moved about 10 km east from the release area in June 1986 and was killed by a predator. As the surviving birds approached 20 months of age, the cohorts began to separate into individuals or sub-groups and disperse.

TABLE 3. Mean rank (R) of proportions of total bird movements that were oriented either north or south for 3 treatment groups of sandhill cranes in Florida, 1986–88.

	Treatment group						
	Control[a]		Foster-reared[b]		Soft-release[c]		
Season	n	$\bar{R}$	n	$\bar{R}$	n	$\bar{R}$	P[d]
Spring	12	14.4	5	13.8	9	12.1	0.767
Summer	11	11.0	3	3.0	5	10.2	0.300
Autumn	7	7.6	2	7.8	7	9.6	0.635

[a] Wild subadult Florida sandhill cranes
[b] Greater sandhill cranes reared by wild Florida sandhill crane foster parents
[c] Captive-reared greater sandhill cranes
[d] P for test of group differences in mean rank; Kruskal-Wallis test for difference among bird types

Nine of 15 cranes that survived 1 year following release returned to the release area during the second spring. Five were captured and taken into captivity. Two males attracted FSHC mates and began to establish nesting territories on Kanapha Prairie. In 1989, one of these males (46 months old) and its wild mate nested twice, although no young were produced. All reproductive pair formation observed in the soft-released birds occurred with wild FSHC. No pairs formed between members of release cohorts. First pairings occurred within the soft-released and foster-reared groups at about the same age, which was similar to the mean age of first pairing among FSHC (20.6 months; Nesbitt and Wenner 1987).

Four of the 5 foster-reared young that fledged survived for ≥1 year after dispersing from their natal home range. Fifteen of 27 of the soft-released birds survived ≥14 months. Mortality among the soft-released group occurred primarily just after release or after a large (>5 km) movement. Survival rate (0.556) for the soft-released birds was similar to that (0.566) for FSHC from hatching to independence (Nesbitt 1992).

DISCUSSION

Dispersal of the experimentally introduced GSHC was generally within the range for the control FSHC. The December 1986 shift southward to Sumter County by the 1986 soft-release cohorts and the movement to Lake County by 1 foster-reared bird were 20–30 km beyond the normal dispersal range of the control group. Neither foster-reared nor soft-released GSHC showed a greater propensity to move north in spring than the control group. The tendency, although inconsistent, for the birds to move south in autumn, beyond the normal dispersal range for FSHC, was perhaps a response to the southward passage of GSHC migrating through northcentral Florida. Both 1986 soft-release cohorts and one of the foster-reared young moved southward coincidently with the movement through the area of migrating GSHC. Dispersal of the experimentally released cranes was usually to areas known to support FSHC; they probably followed other cranes to these areas. The only exception was the move to the Reddick area where cranes had not been known to occur.

The area in southcentral Florida identified as having the potential for successful introduction of whooping cranes (Bishop 1988) is at the southern extreme of the wintering range for GSHC in Florida; (Williams and Phillips 1972, Walkinshaw 1982). Fewer wintering GSHC would limit the exposure of introduced whooping cranes to the sight and sound of crane migration. Additionally, autumn migration, to which (based on the results of this study) introduced whooping cranes would more likely respond, would not proceed much farther south than the release location. Therefore, we believe that any dispersal related to autumn migration exhibited by introduced whooping cranes would be limited.

Hatching success (41%) and fledging per egg hatched (38%) were lower than those from foster-reared whooping cranes in Idaho (70.6% and 42.8%, respectively) (U.S. Fish and Wildl. Serv. 1986). Only 5 young (15%) of the 34 eggs transferred survived to fledging. Transferring eggs into forced renests (Nesbitt 1988) meant that most of the transfers were occurring late in the nesting season when water levels were normally declining, and nesting and brood-rearing conditions in Florida were no longer optimal. Under suboptimal conditions, the propensity of the foster pairs to desert or inadequately incubate the transferred clutches increased. Under better circumstances, the survival of transferred clutches from time of transfer to hatching and foster-reared young from hatching to dispersal from natal home range would perhaps be equivalent to survival of soft-released birds from release to 1 year post-release. Mortality among the soft-released birds was probably an inevitable consequence of their lack of experience.

MANAGEMENT IMPLICATIONS

Our data on introduced migratory GSHC suggest that neither cross-fostered nor soft-released whooping cranes introduced in southcentral Florida would demonstrate any appreciable tendency to migrate. The choice between the 2 techniques used to introduce whooping cranes would be influenced more by the post-release behavior and the respective costs. Lewis (1990) suggested that cross-fostering of whooping cranes by sandhill cranes may have affected pair formation in the Idaho population. This possibility and the difficulty of synchronizing whooping crane egg availability with nesting FSHC militated against cross-fostering whooping cranes in Florida. Soft-release of captive-produced, parent-reared, or isolation (puppet)-reared whooping cranes (Urbanek and Bookhout 1992), appeared to be the best introduction technique available. Thus, 14 captive-produced whooping cranes were soft-released in Florida in February 1993. We hope to similarly release additional birds as the number of captive-produced whooping cranes permits.

LITERATURE CITED

Allen, R. P. 1952. The whooping crane. Natl. Audubon Soc. Res. Rep. 3. 246pp.

Bishop, M. A. 1988. Factors affecting productivity and habitat use of Florida sandhill cranes: an evaluation of three areas in central Florida for a nonmigratory population of whooping cranes. Ph.D. Thesis, Univ. Florida, Gainesville. 109pp.

Carpenter, J. W. 1983. Species decline: a perspective on extinction, recovery, and propagation. Zoo Biol. 2:165–178.

——, and S. R. Derrickson. 1981. The role of propagation in preserving endangered species. Pages 109–113 in R. Odom and J. W. Guthrie, eds. Proc. nongame and endangered wildl. symp. Ga. Dep. Nat. Resour., Tech. Bull. WL5.I.

Derrickson, S. R., and J. W. Carpenter. 1983. Techniques for reintroducing cranes to the wild. Annu. Proc. Am. Assoc. Zoo Vet. 1983:148–152.

—, and —. 1987. Behavioral management of captive cranes–factors influencing prop-agation and reintroduction. Pages 483–511 *in* G. W. Archibald and R. F. Pasquier, eds. Proc. 1983 int. crane workshop. Int. Crane Found., Baraboo, Wis.

Drewien, R. C., and E. G. Bizeau. 1978. Cross-fostering whooping cranes to sandhill crane foster-parents. Pages 201–222 *in* S. A. Temple, ed. Endangered birds: manage-ment techniques for preserving threatened species. Univ. Wisconsin Press, Madison.

Ellis, D. H., and F. J. Dein. 1991. Flight restraint techniques for captive cranes. Pages 447–451 *in* J. Harris, ed. Proc. 1987 int. crane workshop. Int. Crane Found., Baraboo, Wis.

Erickson, R. C. 1968. A federal research program for endangered wildlife. Trans. North Am. Wildl. Conf. 33:418–433.

—. 1981. Transport case for incubated eggs. Wildl. Soc. Bull. 9:57–60.

Griffith, B., J. M. Scott, J. W. Carpenter, and C. Reed. 1989. Translocation as a species con-servation tool: status and strategy. Science 245.477–480.

—, —, —, and —. 1990. Translocations of captive-reared terrestrial vertebrates, 1973–1986. Endangered Species Update 8:10–14.

Kleiman, D. G. 1989. Reintroduction of captive mammals for conservation: guidelines for reintroducing endangered species into the wild. Bioscience 39:152–161.

Lewis, J. C. 1990. Captive propagation in the recovery of whooping cranes. Endangered Species Update 8:46–48.

Lowrey, G. H. 1974. Louisiana birds. Louisiana State Univ. Press, Baton Rouge. 651pp.

Melvin, S. M., R. C. Drewien, S. A. Temple, and E. G. Bizeau. 1983. Leg-band attachment of radio transmitters for large birds. Wildl. Soc. Bull. 11:282–285.

Nesbitt, S. A. 1988. Nesting, renesting and manipulating nesting of Florida sandhill cranes. J. Wildl. Manage. 52:758–763.

—. 1992. First reproductive success and individual productivity in sandhill cranes. J. Wildl. Manage. 56:573–577.

—, and A. S. Wenner. 1987. Pair formation and mate fidelity in sandhill cranes. Proc. North Am. Crane Workshop 4:117–122.

Pollock, K. H., S. R. Winterstein, C. M. Bunck, and P. D. Curtis. 1989. Survival analysis in telemetry studies: the staggered entry design. J. Wildl. Manage. 53:7–15.

Urbanek, R. P., and T. A. Bookhout. 1992. Development of an isolation-rearing/gentle re-lease procedure for reintroducing migratory cranes. Proc. North Am. Crane Work-shop 6:120–130.

U.S. Fish and Wildlife Service. 1986. Whooping crane recovery plan. U.S. Fish and Wildl. Serv., Albuquerque, N.M. 97pp.

—. 1991. Mississippi sandhill crane recovery plan. U.S. Fish and Wildl. Serv., Atlanta, Ga. 42pp.

Walkinshaw, L. H. 1982. Greater sandhill cranes wintering in central Florida. Fla. Field Nat. 10:1–8.

Williams, L. E., Jr., and R. W. Phillips. 1972. North Florida sandhill crane populations. Auk 89:541–548.

Zwank, P. T., and S. R. Derrickson. 1982. Gentle release of captive, parent-reared sandhill cranes into the wild. Proc. North Am. Crane Workshop 3:112–116.

Received 5 June 1992.
Accepted 28 March 1993.
Associate Editor: Mannan.

SURVEYS AND QUESTIONNAIRES

Polls and surveys are everywhere in our society. Public opinion polls, consumer research, and sociological studies of all kinds generate a steady stream of questionnaires, telephone surveys, or person-in-the-street interviews. Researchers who make a claim to objectivity or quasi-scientific accuracy refine their techniques to guard against familiar charges. Even though surveying only a relatively small sample, they aim at a representative cross section. They aim at balanced representation according to gender, ethnicity, region, income, education, or other significant factors. They try to avoid leading questions suggesting a desired or favored answer.

One familiar type of questionnaire asks respondents to rate items on a scale going from "agree strongly" to "disagree strongly," or from "approve" to "disapprove." The following might be a section of a survey asking teacher candidates to rate skills in oral communication:

---

1. To what extent do you agree or disagree that students should master the following oral communications skills by the time they graduate?

   a. Expressing ideas clearly and accurately

         1   2   3   4   5

       agree   disagree

   b. Organizing messages so that others can follow

         1   2   3   4   5

       agree   disagree

   c. Using the speaking voice audibly and effectively

         1   2   3   4   5

       agree   disagree

   d. Using nonverbal communication effectively

         1   2   3   4   5

       agree   disagree

   e. Responding alertly to others in dialogue or debate

         1   2   3   4   5

       agree   disagree

(Continued)

f. Controlling communication apprehension or anxiety

   1   2   3   4   5

   agree   disagree

g. Using audio-visual aids effectively in presentations

   1   2   3   4   5

   agree   disagree

WORKSHOP 3

Is a student evaluation form used for the evaluation of faculty on your campus? Does it include both a numerical rating and questions asking for written responses? If you were part of a committee to evaluate such forms, would you endorse it as it is or recommend changes? How would you support your recommendations? If you were part of a committee to draw up a new form, what form would you design?

12

Research Strategies

FOCUSING ON A TOPIC

You research a topic when you want to *know*. You are not satisfied with partial information, second-hand opinions, or the special pleading of interested parties. You want to dig out the relevant facts. You want to listen to experts or insiders and weigh conflicting testimony. When you finish your project, you want to be able to say: "On this subject, I am somewhat of an authority. On this subject, I know more than the casual observer."

What topic should you choose for a research project? Your top priority should be to focus on a topic that will hold your interest and that of your reader. Ideally, you will choose a topic that has puzzled or intrigued you before. You have done some previous reading or have followed developments relevant to the issue. You know where to turn for promising leads or expert information. However, an alternative route is to discover a new area of interest that for you is uncharted and exciting territory. In either case, you should guard against starting your project with your mind already made up. The purpose of research is to find out. Research means testing preliminary hypotheses, challenging the conventional wisdom, searching for answers to unanswered questions.

Informal research goes into most writing projects. Remember three key features that make a formal research paper different from more informal papers:

Synthesis

You integrate material from a range of sources. In a serious investigation of a subject, you do more than a hit-and-miss search. You correlate information from a full range of relevant authorities. You weigh differing views and reconcile discrepancies. Your aim is to give your reader the best available information and thinking on your subject.

Documentation

You identify fully the sources of your material. In a formal research paper, you provide **documentation**–complete publication data. Who said what, when and where? You give the full who, what, when, and where, complete with exact page numbers.

In practice, this means following the documentation style of an academic area or discipline–whether humanities, social science, or biology.

Objectivity

You stay close to the evidence you present. A formal research paper allows little room for personal impressions, subjective preferences, or outright bias. Formulate your conclusions cautiously and support them well. Your stance toward your audience will be: "This is the evidence. This is where I found it. This is where it leads." As long as you provide the data, your reader can decide whether they warrant your conclusions.

WRITING WORKSHOP 1: Defining the Issues

The following topics of current concern are open issues. People are disputing the facts, searching for answers, or debating suggested solutions. What is at issue? What can you learn about the issue by exploratory reading and by talking to people in the know? You may want to choose one of these as the topic of a short documented paper (8–10 pages).

1. *Toward Parity in Women's Collegiate Sports*   Do women have the same opportunities to participate in college athletics as men do? How successful have colleges been in moving toward equal funding or equal support for men's and women's sports? What is the issue? What is the local situation? How does it compare with the national picture? What progress is being made?

2. *Minority Representation (or Representation of Women) on College Faculties*   Do African American or Hispanic college instructors still often find themselves the only minority representative in a mostly white department? Have affirmative action efforts improved representation of minorities or of women? What is the local situation, and how does it compare with the national picture? What are the prospects for the future?

3. *Race and the Jury System*   Police officers accused in the Rodney King beating were acquitted by a jury in a predominantly white jurisdiction but were later convicted of civil rights violations in a more mixed setting. Robert Shapiro, a prominent lawyer for the defense in the O. J. Simpson trial, accused his colleagues of "playing the race card." What do the experts say about the role the racial composition of juries plays in determining their verdicts? What role does race play in advice experts give about jury selection?

4. *Self-Defense as a Response to Violent Crime*   Is there a movement to teach citizens threatened by violence the art of self-defense? Should women especially learn self-defense skills? What is the official position of law enforcement agencies on the issue? What are the arguments pro and con?

5. *Trying Juvenile Offenders as Adults*   A vice-president of the National Association of Child Advocates said: "There aren't enough jails and facilities to lock up all
the poor kids in this country, but that's what we are on the way toward doing."
What's behind the movement to "crack down" on juvenile crime by trying more
juvenile offenders as adults? What are the implications? What are the likely consequences? What are the arguments pro and con?

6. *Cultural Bias in Standardized Tests*   Can standardized tests test ability rather
than the upbringing and cultural background of students? For instance, are IQ tests
weighted against lower-class students deprived of many amenities and cultural experiences middle-class families provide? Do SAT scores reflect students' exposure to
a world of books, news broadcasts and analysis, cultural experiences?

7. *From Welfare to Workfare*   Advocates of welfare reform have been touting
workfare as the answer to welfare dependency. What is the rationale of such proposals? What initiatives or experiments have been tried? With what results? What
are the obstacles or difficulties? What are the prospects?

Getting Started

Find a newspaper or magazine article that could serve as an introduction or
overview for one of these topics. Prepare a 300-word abstract.

WRITING WORKSHOP 2: Research across the Curriculum

Choose one of the following topics for a full-length research paper. Bring together authoritative information and commentary on your chosen topic from a full
range of sources. What are major issues or dimensions of your topic? Is there a
consensus among the experts? Present and interpret your findings. Push toward a
unifying thesis.

1. *Temporary Work and the Erosion of Job Security*   (Suggested questions: How
many permanent jobs have been or are being converted to temporary or part-time
jobs? What are the causes and dimensions of this trend? Is it continuing or have
there been signs of a turnaround? What is the effect on the workforce? What does
the future hold?)

2. *Cave Paintings and the Beginnings of Art*   (Suggested questions: In 1994, new
cave paintings were discovered in Europe that shed further light on the Stone Age
origins of art. What are the facts about neolithic cave paintings? What are leading
theories about their origin and significance? What possible light do they shed on
neolithic religion or ritual?)

3. *The Movement to Save the Whales*   (Suggested questions: What is the history of
whaling? What are the statistics on whales as endangered species? What is the history of the movement to save the whales? What are its successes and failures?
What are the prospects for the future?)

4. *The Threat of Global Warming*   (Suggested questions: What is the scientific basis for theories of global warming? What are projected scenarios and consequences? What strategies for prevention do scientists recommend?)

5. *The Crack Epidemic*   (Suggested questions: A supervisor in a public housing project has said: "We have only one disease here: crack." What is the history of the crack epidemic? What does it do to users, dealers, neighborhoods? What are the efforts to control it? How successful are they?)

6. *The Child as Consumer*   (Suggested questions: Children directly or indirectly control a large share of consumer spending. How large a share? How do advertisers reach them? How do advertisers influence the parents?)

7. *Banning Hate Speech*   (Suggested questions: Many colleges have or are considering speech codes aimed at controlling hate speech and offensive language. What is the history of such efforts? What are key issues? What are the pros and cons?)

8. *Distancing the Homeless*   (Suggested questions: Is homelessness on a large scale a new phenomenon? What are its chief causes? What are suggested solutions or remedies? Are there promising programs or initiatives?)

9. *Sexual Harassment and Institutional Liability*   (Suggested questions: What are the responsibilities of businesses for creating a harassment-free working environment? What are their liabilities? What recent test cases shed light on these questions?)

10. *Turning Negative on Affirmative Action*   (Suggested questions: What has affirmative action meant in the world of business? What has caused a backlash against affirmative action? What are the prospects for the future?)

INITIATING YOUR SEARCH

Where do you turn for material? Your sources may include articles from newspapers and periodicals, full-length books, and reference works. Input from nonprint sources may include material from interviews, radio and television programs, or lectures. You can draw on a seemingly unlimited range of sources instantly accessible from a home computer or computer in your dorm or library. Your material may come from sources first published in hard copy but also available on-line, material originally published on-line, or material available on CD-ROM.

Although the electronic era was predicted to spell the end of the print age, print media continue to proliferate. Books on innumerable specialty areas cram the bookshelves of bookstores and libraries. University presses and specialized presses publish monographs—extended treatments of a limited scholarly or scientific subject. New magazines and professional journals appear (and may disappear again). Newsletters, brochures, and zines (informal and often irreverent in-group publications) reach specialized audiences large and small.

Drawing on electronic networks and computerized data banks, you can track down material in a fraction of the time that used to be required. Your library is likely to be linked with other libraries nationally and internationally, so that you can compensate for the gaps in your library's holdings. Reference books like the *Encyclopaedia Britannica* are now available on CD-ROM, allowing you to call up an article by typing in a key word or a string of key words—or allowing you to type in a question and click for the answer.

Evaluating Your Sources

You will need to convince your readers that you have consulted authoritative sources. What are the credentials of an author you are quoting? What is an author's credibility? When evaluating promising sources, ask questions like the following:

- *Is the source an authority on the subject?* How much of a commitment does the author have to the field? What is the author's track record? Does the author draw on first-hand investigation? Has the author written or lectured on the subject? Is the author associated with a prestige institution? Is the author quoted or consulted by others?

- *Is the work a thorough study of the subject?* Does it recognize previous work in the field? Does it look in depth at case histories, relevant experiments, or key examples? Does it carefully present and interpret statistics? Does it take dissent and objections seriously, weighing the pro and con on debated issues?

- *Does the author turn to primary sources?* Reliable authorities do not simply accept hearsay, second-hand accounts, or "what everybody says." They often settle important questions by tracking down **primary sources**. They may consult legal documents, diaries and letters, or transcripts of speeches. They may turn to interviews with eye witnesses, reports on experiments, or detailed statistical studies.

- *Is the source up to date?* Does it show awareness of recent research or new facts? If it was first published ten or fifteen years ago, has the author updated the findings—in a later study or in a revised edition of a book? In areas from economics to electronics and from biochemistry to foreign affairs, an older study may have been superseded by new findings and new thinking.

- *Is the source impartial or biased?* How credible is research on the health hazards of smoking or alcohol if it was funded by a tobacco company or by a brewery? Are you going to be able to make allowance for a pro-business bias in material from the U.S. Chamber of Commerce or for a pro-labor bias in material from the AFL-CIO?

Searching for Articles

You will often turn for material to publications ranging from daily news-papers and weekly newsmagazines to popular science magazines and to scientific and technical journals. Periodicals may appear on a weekly, monthly, or quarterly basis.

- You may turn to leading newspapers like the *New York Times, Washington Post, Wall Street Journal, Christian Science Monitor,* or *Los Angeles Times* not only for authoritative news coverage but also for background studies, book reviews, or editorial opinion. Ranging from the conservative to the progressive, news-magazines and journals of commentary and opinion include *U.S. News and World Report, Time, Newsweek, Harper's, Atlantic, Commentary, New Republic, Mother Jones, Nation,* or *Ms.* magazine. You might turn to newspapers and news-magazines for material, for instance, on court cases involving breast implants, reports on cases of assisted suicide, prolonged labor disputes, or test cases for challenges to affirmative action.

- For seriously researched material presented in an accessible format, you may turn to experts, scholars, or scientists writing for the general public in publications like *Science, Scientific American, Psychology Today, Discover* magazine, or *National Geographic.* You may turn to such publications for material ranging from anthropologists' revisions of the hypothetical family tree of apes, hominids, and first true humans to archeologists' new insights into pre-Columbian cultures, like the Maya, Aztec, or Inca civilizations.

- You may be drawing on material in scientific, technical, or scholarly journals in areas like psychology, biology, physics, medicine, history, or art. For instance, for a study of collaboration in technical writing you may find relevant source material in a journal called *Technical Communication.* For a paper on the implications of right-brain/left-brain research for teachers, your sources might include articles in journals with titles like *New Scientist, Brain, Neurology, New England Journal of Medicine,* or *British Journal of Educational Psychology.* Often part of your assignment will be to bridge the gap between the language of the specialist and the general reader. Graphs or statistics may present a special challenge to the newcomer or outsider.

Computerized databases greatly facilitate your search for material in periodicals. Systems like INFOTRAC give you an instant listing of articles from hundreds of publications. (Remember to check years covered–INFOTRAC, for instance, started comprehensive indexing only in 1991.) By typing in key words or **retrieval codes,** you can call up an extensive listing of sources on subjects like child abuse, global warming, free trade zones, or illegal immigration. You can call up book reviews, articles by or about a person, or information about an institution or a company. When you are researching progress toward gender equity in collegiate athletics, for instance, the computer will call up articles whose titles include the words you have typed in as key words or as possible subject headings: women and athletics; women and sports; sports equity; women's physical education; women and college sports; funding for college sports; gender equality in sports.

Other large umbrella systems can lead you to specialized databases in areas like sociology, government policy, medical research, or education. These databases will guide you to articles published by experts and professionals. For instance, for a paper on how schools are dealing with challenges to bilingual education, you may turn to a specialized education database. You will be able to tap into a statistics database providing access to relevant government statistics.

A student researcher obtained a range of leads like the following from the newspaper index that is part of INFOTRAC when looking for newspaper coverage of women's progress toward equity in sports. Look at the format:

- After the title, this database often includes a brief parenthetical note on the focus or key point of the article.

Database: National Newspaper Index
Subject: sports for women

The girls against the boys; women have played pro ball before. But never against men. Is this exploitation, or feminism . . . or both? (Coors Silver Bullets; the first women's professional baseball team)

The Washington Post, April 24, 1994 v117 pF1 col 3 (82 col in).

Author: Laura Blumenfeld

Subjects: Baseball (Professional) - Analysis
Women athletes - Competitions

Features: illustration; photograph

AN: 15207085

- It then tracks the exact location of the item: publication, volume number, section and page, column (with length of article in column inches).
- It then gives the author's name and possible subject headings under which the item may be catalogued.

Often source information includes an abstract—a summary of the findings or ideas developed in an article. The following printout from a sports-centered database includes an abstract that could help you decide whether the source is worth following up.

SilverPlatter 3.11   SPORT Discus 1975 - June 1994

SPORT Discus 1975 - June 1994 usage is subject to the terms and conditions of the Subscription and Licensing Agreement and the Applicable Copyright and intellectual property protection as dictated by the appropriate laws of your country and/or by International Convention.

TI: Sport and the maintenance of masculine hegemony
AU: Bryson, -L
JN: Women's-studies-international forum- (Elmsford, -N.Y.) ;
10(4), 1987, 349-360 Refs:37
PY: 1987
AB: Discusses two fundamental dimensions of the support that sport provides for masculine hegemony: 1) it links maleness with highly valued and visible skills, and 2) it links maleness with the positively sanctioned use of aggression/force/violence. Examines four social processes through which women are effectively marginalized in their sport participation - definition, direct control, ignoring, and trivialization - using examples from the sports scene in Australia. Concludes that women need to challenge the definition of sport, take control of women's sports, persistently provide information and reject attempts to ignore women's sport, and attack the trivialization of women in sport.
AN: 213623

For articles published before the 1990s, you may have to search the printed multivolume periodical indexes in your library. The *Readers' Guide to Periodical Literature* indexes magazines for the general reader, from *Time* and *Newsweek* to *Working Woman*, *Science Digest*, and *Technology Review*. In the *Readers' Guide*, articles are listed twice—once under the author's name and once under a subject heading. Compare two entries for the same article:

AUTHOR ENTRY: **Harris, Michael**
Junk in outer space. il Progressive 42:16–19 N '78

SUBJECT ENTRY: **SPACE pollution**
Junk in outer space. M. Harris. il Progressive
42:16–19 N '78

The author entry starts with the full name of the author, the subject entry with the general subject: space pollution. The title of the article is "Junk in Outer Space," published in the *Progressive* magazine. (The *il* shows that the article is illustrated.) Note data that you will need when documenting your sources in your finished paper: The *volume number* for the magazine is 42, followed by *page numbers* for the article after a colon: 16 through 19. (If the symbol + appears after the last page number, it shows that the article is concluded later in the magazine.) The *date of publication* was November 1978. (For magazines published more than once a month, the exact date is given. For example "N 10 '78 means "November 10, 1978.")

Other guides to periodicals for the general reader:

Essay and General Literature Index
Popular Periodicals Index
Applied Science and Technology Index
Art Index
Biological and Agricultural Index
Business Periodicals Index
Education Index
Engineering Index
General Science Index
Humanities Index
Social Sciences Index

Several reference guides are especially useful for papers on political, cultural, or economic trends: *Facts on File* is a weekly digest of world news, with an annual index. *The New York Times Index* is a guide to news stories that appeared in the *New York Times*. The annual index to the *Monthly Catalog of the United States Government Publications* lists reports and documents published by all branches of the federal government. Looking for material on the "glass ceiling" encountered by women executives, you might find a transcript of a speech by Linda Winikow, titled "How Women and Minorities Are Reshaping Corporate America," in *Vital Speeches*.

As you track down promising sources, start a card file or computer file recording complete data for each item: author, complete title of articles, name of periodical, date, and page numbers. (Where appropriate, record the section of a newspaper or the volume number of a magazine.) Include brief **annotation** as a reminder. A source record annotated by you might look like this·

----

periodical   Guterson, David. "Moneyball! On the Relentless
room   Promotion of Pro Sports." *Harper's Magazine*
               Sept. 1994: 37–46

The author is a contributing editor of *Harper's Magazine.* "I was not always so disgusted with sports; I was not always an aging crank," Guterson pleads before launching into a litany of the excesses of today's sports.

WRITING WORKSHOP 3: A Computer Search for Articles

Do a computer search for articles on AIDS education for young people. Try key words or headings like *safe sex education, safe sex teaching, AIDS education, AIDS prevention, AIDS and schools, AIDS and adolescents, AIDS and high school, AIDS and young adults, AIDS and youth.* (Follow instructions for making sure that the database you use will search for variant forms: *adolescents* and *adolescence* as well as *adolescent.*) Prepare a listing of the six most promising items, with complete description of each.

Searching for Books

Most libraries have converted their card catalogs to computerized indexes. Data given on traditional index cards and on computer listings are similar, although perhaps laid out differently. When you know of a promising book, you can look for it under the author's name or under the title. For instance, you would look under *Thurow* or under *Head to Head* for Lester Thurow's *Head to Head: The Coming Economic Battle Among Japan, Europe, and America*. However, when still looking for useful sources, you will check under subject headings. For instance, if you had not heard of Thurow's book you might be looking for books with a similar focus under subject headings like Economic Forecasting, Global Economy, International Economic Relations, U.S. Economic Policy, Japan–Economic Policy, or Trade Wars–U.S. and Japan.

Computer entries may look like the following **author card**. The **call number** will direct you or a librarian to the right section and the right shelf in the library.

```
Call #:    LB 2343.32 F54 1991

Author     Figler, Stephen K.

Title:     Going the distance:  the college athlete's guide to
           excellence on the field and in the classroom / by
           Stephen K. Figler. Princeton, N.J.: Peterson's
           Guides, 1991. xi, 208 p.: illus; 23 cm.

Notes:     Includes bibliography:  p. 203-208.

Subjects: College student orientation – United States
           College athletes – United States.

Add

Author:    Figler, Howard E.
```

A **title card** might look like the following:

```
            The American sporting experience
GV
583     Riess, Steven A.
R53         The American sporting experience / Steven A. Riess.
        New York:   Leisure Press, 1984.
            400 p.; 23 cm.

            Bibliography: p. 398-400
            ISBN 0-88011-210-7

            1.  Sports — United States — History — Addresses,
        essays, lectures.   I.  Title

GV583.R53                                       796.0973

                                                84-7188
```

When you have no definite leads, you may be looking at **subject cards** like the following:

```
GV
709     SEX DISCRIMINATION IN SPORTS
N44
            Nelson, Mariah Burton

        Are we winning yet?:  how women are changing
        sports and how sports are changing women, by Mariah
        Burton Nelson.
        1st ed.  New York:   Random House, 1991

        238 p.

        Bibliography:  pp. 215-225, and index
```

As with articles, you will want to prepare **source cards** or source entries giving complete publishing data for your record of promising sources.

HQ

1426   Wolf, Naomi. *Fire With Fire: The New Female*

W565   *Power and How It Will Change the 21st*

            Century. New York: Random House, 1993.

HQ

1426   Helgeson, Sally. *The Female Advantage: Women's*

H347   *Ways in Leadership.* New York: Doubleday, 1990.

To help you narrow your search to the most promising sources, you may check **book reviews** or abstracts. For example, the *Book Review Digest* excerpts reviews written shortly after publication of a book. Book reviews like the one on the page 621 are a feature of many general-interest periodicals and professional publications.

For many subjects, you can find a printed or computerized **bibliography**—a listing of important books and other sources of information. Shorter bibliographical listings often appear at the end of an entry in an encyclopedia or a chapter in a textbook. **Annotated bibliographies** give a capsule account of each source. The sample entry at the top of page 622 is from *An Annotated Bibliography of California Fiction 1664–1970* by Newton D. Baird and Robert Greenwood, 1971. Note that it lists two reviews written upon publication of the book.

Heimel, Cynthia. *Get Your Tongue Out of My Mouth, I'm Kissing You Good-Bye!*

Atlantic Monthly. Jun. 1993. c.192p. ISBN 0-87113-538-8. $20.   HUMOR

It's no surprise that the author of *If You Can't Live Without Me, Why Aren't You Dead Yet?* (LJ 4/15/91), *Sex Tips for Girls* (LJ 6/15/83), and *But Enough About You* (S. & S., 1986) has come up with another snappy eyebrow-raising title. Her brief essays here reflect the same satirical feminist wit that graces the pages of the *Village Voice* and *Playboy* magazine. Among the weighty issues Heimel tackles are boyfriends ("a woman needs a man like a fish needs a net"), dysfunctional family values ("PBS would be bankrupt if its fund-raisers didn't feature hours of John Bradshaw explaining to sobbing audiences how our families fill us with toxic shame and make it impossible for us to have anything other than lives of agony"), and living in L.A. ("Out here I have a car, and I don't know if anyone in Manhattan knows this, but a car is just a moving, giant handbag!"). Brash, hip, and very, very funny, Heimel is essential for all humor collections. [Previewed in Prepub Alert, LJ 2/1/93.]—Wilda Williams, "Library Journal"

1371   [Kerouac, John.]

ON THE ROAD.   By Jack Kerouac.   New York: Viking Press,

1957.   310 pp.

Two romantic anarchists, Sal Paradise and Dean Moriarty,

pursue a vaguely defined notion of purpose on the roads up and

down the North American continent, in stolen cars, in buses,

airplanes, and by hitch-hiking.   California, in part.

Commonweal 66:595 S 13 '57

San Francisco Chronicle p. 18 S 1 '57

WRITING WORKSHOP 4: Searching for Books

Search the main catalog of your library for books on endangered indigenous populations. Check subject headings like Indigenous People, Non-Western Cultures, Genocide, Aborigines, or Native Populations. Provide a listing of the six most promising sources, with complete publishing information on each.

Consulting Reference Works

Reference works, ranging from multivolume sets to compact manuals, provide detailed authoritative information on untold specialized subjects. Many are now available on line. For instance, the thirty-two volumes of the *Encyclopaedia Britannica*, which has been called "not only the largest but also the greatest of encyclopedias," are available on a single CD-ROM. Reviewers of the electronic *Britannica* have noted the loss of most photographs and graphics but also the advantage of a vastly expanded search capacity helping the researcher track elusive facts. You will find specialized reference works in a guide like Eugene P. Sheehy's *Guide to Reference Books*, published by the American Library Association. Here is a sampling of reference works that are often consulted:

Encyclopedias

- *The New Encyclopaedia Britannica* (founded in Scotland 200 years ago but long since an American publication), updated each year by the *Britannica Book of the Year*

- The *Encyclopedia Americana* with its annual supplement, the *Americana Annual*
- *Columbia Encyclopedia* in one volume

Biography

- *Who's Who in America*, a biographical dictionary with capsule biographies of outstanding living men and women
- *Who's Who of American Women*
- *The Dictionary of American Biography (DAB)*
- The *Biography Index*, a guide to biographical material in books and magazines

Specialized Reference Guides

- *American Universities and Colleges* and *American Junior Colleges*
- *Harper's Dictionary of Classical Literature and Antiquities*
- *The McGraw-Hill Encyclopedia of Science and Technology*, kept up to date by the *McGraw-Hill Yearbook of Science and Technology*
- *The Encyclopedia of Computer Science and Technology*
- The *Dictionary of American History* by J. T. Adams (in six volumes)
- Langer's *Encyclopedia of World History* (one volume)
- The *International Encyclopedia of the Social Sciences*
- *Grove's Dictionary of Music and Musicians*
- The *McGraw-Hill Encyclopedia of World Art* (fifteen volumes)
- The *Funk and Wagnalls Standard Dictionary of Folklore*
- *Vital Speeches of the Day*

WRITING WORKSHOP 5: Using Reference Tools

Check out one of the following often-consulted reference tools. Prepare a brief report on its scope, format, and usefulness. Provide helpful advice to prospective users.

1. *Books in Print*
2. *National Union Catalog (NUC)*
3. *Library of Congress Subject Headings*
4. *Sociological Abstracts*
5. *Contemporary Authors*
6. *Who's Who of American Women*
7. *Wall Street Journal Index*
8. *Historical Abstracts*

9. *Dictionary of Scientific Biography*

10. *Comprehensive Dictionary of Psychological and Psychoanalytic Terms*

11. *McGraw-Hill Dictionary of Art*

12. *Concise Encyclopedia of Living Faiths*

GATHERING: Taking Notes

As you bring your subject into focus, you will begin to take notes in a systematic, businesslike manner. At the beginning, you may spend much of your time browsing and skimming, looking for sources that might prove useful. However, even early in your search, you should start taking notes–recording data, transcribing quotable quotes, summarizing chunks of information. A central part of your task will be to build up a rich backlog of notes as input for your paper. You will be looking for needed background information, for evidence to support your tentative conclusions, or for material that helps clear up difficult points.

Assume your topic is the current trend toward "getting tough" on juvenile offenders. Perhaps you first became interested in the topic because of a schoolyard stabbing that shook up your community. Going beyond local newspaper coverage of the incident, you notice early that many observers are disturbed by the young age of perpetrators of violent crime. There are many articles, editorials, and columns with titles like "Criminals but Still Children" or "Old Enough to Kill" (the title of a column by a widely syndicated columnist). Your computer search yields a whole series of articles by a *New York Times* reporter whose beat seems to include the area of juvenile justice. In a little over a year, he published articles titled "Punishing Youths without Throwing away the Key," "Felon vs. Youth," and "Quirks in Juvenile Offender Law Stir Calls for Change." In journals dealing with law enforcement and in a collection of articles focused on juvenile crime, you find much related material.

On conventional note cards or as part of a computer file, you begin to take notes like the following. Note cards make it easy to shuffle material and to arrange it in order, guiding you in preparing your draft. Computer entries allow you to feed already typed material into your draft, merely adapting it instead of having to keyboard it again.

The first note summarizes factual information. It is mostly paraphrase (information passed on in your own words), with only one verbatim phrase in quotation marks. The second note includes a more extended direct quotation from the *New York Times* article. A quotation like this can later help you bring the incident to life in your actual paper. The quote-within-a-quote, directly from the accused juvenile, could later help you confront readers with the actual situation when they might be inclined to question or doubt a more second-hand account.

JUVENILE CRIMINALS—Age

Cameron Kocher, Cub Scout and only child, was nine years old when he allegedly shot and killed Jessica Carr. The prosecution decided to try the fifth-grader as an adult. The defense entered a plea of not guilty. The prosecutor said that the main goal of the prosecution was "psychiatric, not punitive" and that the decision to try the juvenile offender as an adult was influenced by the seriousness of the crime.

Quindlen, "Old Enough?" <u>NY Times</u> 1 Apr. 1990, B2.

JUVENILE CRIMINALS—Age

In the summer of 1993, 14-year-old Gregory Morris of Brooklyn, New York, badly wanted a bicycle. In Prospect Park, he and his friend spotted Allyn Winslow, a 42-year-old drama teacher, pedaling his blue mountain bike. "Gregory handed his .22 caliber revolver to a friend and shouted 'Get him! Get him!' The friend shot Winslow in the back, but the dying man managed to pedal away." Morris was convicted of felony murder and sentenced to a maximum of five years by the Brooklyn Family Court.

Hoffman, "Quirks," <u>NY Times</u> 12 July 1994, late ed.: B1.

Sometimes you will transcribe a whole especially revealing or important passage or paragraph word for word, for possible later use as a **block quotation.** Following is an example from notes for a paper on current economic trends.

OUTSOURCING—pressuring unions

"Temporary workers and outsourcing make up the bulk of today's contingent workforce—millions of Americans whose labor can be used and discarded at a moment's notice and at a fraction of the cost of maintaining a permanent workforce. Their very existence acts to drive wages down for the remaining full-time workers. Employers are increasingly using the threat of temp hiring and outsourcing to win wage and benefit concessions from unions—a trend that is likely to accelerate in the years ahead."

Rifkin, End of Work, p. 194

Other note cards or computer entries may summarize important background information or record important statistics. The following entry has extrapolated from detailed statistical tables the numbers the student researcher considered most relevant to her project:

ELECTION STATS—California

California voters are neither "traditionally Republican" nor "traditionally Democrat." In 1956, during the Eisenhower years, out of a total population of over ten million Californians with over five and a half million votes cast, Republicans got 55.4 percent and Democrats 44.3 percent of the votes cast in the presidential election. These percentages were reversed during the ascendancy of JFK and his successor Lyndon Johnson, with the Democrats in 1964 gathering 59.1 percent and the Republicans 40.8 percent of the votes. Twenty years later, when the "Great Communicator" Ronald Reagan ran for his second term, with a population of over twenty-three million and 9.5 million votes cast, the Republicans reached an all-time high of 57.5 percent vs. 41.3 for the Democrats.

Scammon, America at the Polls (1976), p. 78; (1994) pp. 109–117

Keep guidelines like the following in mind:

1. *Start each note with a heading showing a tentative subdivision of your paper.* For your paper on young offenders, you might be sorting out notes under headings like JUVENILE CRIMINALS–age, GETTING TOUGH–legislation, GETTING TOUGH–court decisions, and ALTERNATIVE APPROACHES.

2. *Limit each note to one key point or to closely related data.* This way you will be able to shuffle your notes and fit them into an early draft at the right place–without having to split up a quote or disentangle information.

3. *Distinguish clearly between paraphrase and direct quotation.* Put all material you transcribe word for word between quotation marks. Make sure unmarked quoted material will not slip into your paper, becoming confused with your own text.

4. *Identify the source, including exact page number(s).* If you are recording full source information in separate source entries (or on bibliography cards), abbreviate the information here.

5. *Err on the side of completeness.* It is much easier to discard unwanted material at a later stage than to have to return to a source to hunt for missing details.

SHAPING: Organizing and Drafting

How do you pull your material into shape? Your task is to sort out your material and set directions. You group together material that points in the same direction. You identify major parts of a problem or major stages in the development of a trend. You trace major currents and countercurrents, or you line up opinions pro and con. Your strategy will have to be two-pronged: You push toward a working outline, adjusting it or refining it as you go along. At the same time, you push toward an overarching thesis, summing up your findings.

From the beginning of your search you will be looking for recurrent themes. You will be alert for notes that are struck over and over, points that seem to come up again and again. Suppose you are investigating a trend toward treating juvenile criminals as adults, trying them in adult courts and sending them to adult jails. As you read current newspaper articles and treatments of the topic in general and in law enforcement journals, several points come into focus:

- There has been a general toughening of the public attitude toward crime. Liberal judges and liberal politicians are constantly being accused of being soft on crime. There has been a strong trend toward harsher sentences. (A case in point: A young white Southern male flying a large confederate flag and allegedly shouting "nigger" while driving past a group of young African Americans is pursued by a carload of young blacks and killed by bullets fired into his truck. Both the shooter and the friend who egged him on are sentenced to life imprisonment. Years earlier, people convicted of double murders could expect to be out on the streets within five or six years.)

- There is a growing impatience with and lack of sympathy for the young criminal. Phrases that keep cropping up include "coddling of young criminals," "young punks," "locking the door and throwing away the key," and "old enough to kill, old enough to be tried as adults."
- There has been a drumfire of articles and speeches on the alleged failure of liberal approaches. Many people seem to have given up on programs for rehabilitation, on protecting the young criminal (for instance, by withholding names from the press), or on giving young people in bad trouble a second chance.
- People are looking for an answer. Trying juveniles as adults appeals to the get-tough mentality of the times. You see many news reports with titles like "Teen Gets Life Term" and "Tougher Treatment for Juveniles."

As you sort out the material you are finding under roughly these four headings, you draw up a first scratch outline something like the following:

Scratch Outline: current get-tough mentality

sensationalizing juvenile crime

failure of "liberal" approaches

trying juveniles as adults

What is the upshot of your work so far? At this stage, your material points to a conclusion like the following:

Trial Thesis: As the public gets more impatient with crime, juvenile offenders are among the prime targets of harsher treatment.

As you consider this statement for a possible thesis, you realize that you are getting caught up in the pessimism and defeatism that is reflected in many of your sources. You decide to make a deliberate effort to look at the other side. You ask: Where are the advocates of more emphasis on prevention and rehabilitation? You remember and track down newspaper articles about priests, teachers, or counselors trying to keep young people out of jail, out of gangs. You take a closer look at articles with titles like "Jails or Jobs?" or "Alternatives to Hard Time." You track down accounts of work camps for juvenile offenders. You interview one or more members of your college faculty who are known for their interest in troubled adolescents.

This might be your revised and expanded working outline:

Working Outline:
conservative current climate
current get-tough mentality
sensationalizing juvenile crime
perceived failure of liberal approaches
getting tough on juveniles
trying juveniles as adults
harsh sentencing
searching for alternatives
emphasis on prevention (education, job training)
emphasis on rehabilitation (counseling, work camps)

Your new, more positive emphasis is reflected in your adjusted trial thesis:

New Trial Thesis: Although juvenile offenders are among the prime targets of a "get-tough" approach to crime, the search continues for approaches stressing prevention and rehabilitation.

Although you are satisfied with this more positive slant, you may wonder whether at this stage you have enough material to make this more positive stance convincing. You may be asking yourself: "Am I going to be a voice in the wilderness? Am I going to be accused of wishful thinking?" With much continuing clamor for clamping down on crime, you decide you need to bolster your case: How can you counter prevailing public sentiment? You decide to check out statistics on the alleged rise in juvenile crimes—how much is media hysteria? Is there any verdict on whether getting tough actually reduces juvenile crimes? What do counselors, law enforcement officers, and prison officials say on this subject? You insert a third major section focused on these questions in your working outline. (By now you have also come up with a working title.)

Rehabilitating Juveniles for a Better Society
conservative current climate
current get-tough mentality
sensational juvenile crimes
perceived failure of liberal approaches
getting tough on juveniles
trying juveniles as adults
harsh sentencing

second thoughts
    reexamining crime statistics
    effects on juveniles tried as adults
searching for alternatives
    emphasis on prevention (education, job training)
    emphasis on rehabilitation (counseling, work camps)

With your material laid out according to this plan, you feel your paper as a whole will effectively support a thesis like the following:

Thesis: Despite the clamor for "getting tough" on juvenile crime, the best hope for our society is on increased emphasis on education, prevention, and rehabilitation.

At this point, you feel you are ready to write a first draft. (Actually, many writers draft *sections* of a paper or chunks of an article while continuing their search for additional material.)

Presentation

In your finished paper, the opening page or pages will be crucial. How are you going to bring the issue into focus for your reader? How are you going to lead into the overarching thesis that the rest of the paper will clarify, elaborate, and support? For many papers exploring current issues in areas like politics, business, cultural studies, or popularized science, you cannot go far wrong if you heed traditional practitioners' advice: Start with a brief, pointed introduction leading directly into your **thesis statement:**

Newspaper readers have become used to stories about a teenager brutalizing a 4-year-old, or about teenage gangs going on a rampage of rape and murder. One of the most frightening trends in America is an increase in the severity of juvenile crime, and a decrease in the age at which children commit crimes. Public reaction, fueled by sensational stories in the media and by the law-and-order rhetoric of politicians, has been to subject young offenders to the harsher justice found in adult courts. Children are being tried in adult courts in more cases and at younger ages. Is being harsh with juvenile criminals in the best interest of the defendants? Is it in society's best interest, in terms of rehabilitating criminals, deterring and reducing crime, and justice? The alternative to treating juveniles as adults is a more rehabilitative approach. Some experts advocate more preventive efforts, as opposed to more punishment-oriented programs.

For research papers or research reports in some areas of study, you may be asked to open your paper with a formal **statement of purpose** like the following:

Experts, elected representatives, and the general public have been grappling with the issue of how to deal with juvenile crime, and treating youths as adults is currently a popular solution. The alternative to treating juveniles as adults I intend to treat in this paper is a more rehabilitative approach—some experts advocate more preventive efforts, as opposed to more punishment-oriented programs such as trying youths in adult courtrooms. In this paper, I intend to show the causes for the current sentiment toward trying youths as adults. Then I intend to argue that while juvenile crime is a problem, it may not be the epidemic that it has been made out to be, and that although it is necessary to be firm in dealing with juvenile criminals, the best way to deal with them may not necessarily be through adult courts and strictly "getting tough."

Development

Your basic task now is to develop each point in your working outline. At each step, you spell out clearly what point you are making, and you feed into your paper the data or the evidence to back it up. You lay out your material in such a way that your readers can see why each piece of evidence or supporting material fits into your paper at that particular spot. You pull out, adapt, or combine material from your notes. Note the emphasis on *adapt* here—on fitting material into your paper. (See Chapter 8 for additional detailed examples.)

At some points in your paper, your job may be to digest extensive input from a **single source**, pulling from your notes the most telling and the most relevant parts. Rather than quoting big chunks of undigested material, aim at a combination of direct quotation and paraphrase—or of summary and some partial quotation for the authentic touch. Here is a sample paragraph, drawing extensively on one of several articles by a *New York Times* reporter:

Individuals who work closely with juvenile criminals often support the idea of providing guidance and discipline. Being in close contact with young offenders, they come to know their motives and their needs. For instance, Justice Michael A. Corriero is a member of the New York State Supreme Court in Manhattan who tries to balance the need for punishment or deterrence with concern for the future life of the young offender. As Jan Hoffman of the *New York Times* reports, "Judge Corriero provides juvenile offenders hope for rehabilitation." Corriero gives juveniles the chance to earn a lighter sentence by placing them in "community-based intensive supervisory programs." In the judge's view, juveniles should not receive permanent felony conviction records–criminals convicted in adult courts have permanent records–since the juvenile "can't get a job with a felony conviction." And if the juvenile cannot contribute to society, Judge Corriero asks, "Have we really protected society?" ("Punishing Youths" B1).

Just as often, you will be pulling together related material from **several sources** to prove a point. You will be correlating or synthesizing input from different sources. Doing this effectively may well be the most important skill for the writer of a research paper. Here is a sample paragraph:

The justice system is generally moving toward trying juvenile offenders in adult courts. Marvin Owens of Virginia Beach, Virginia, was sentenced to life imprisonment by Circuit Judge Robert B. Cromwell, Jr. after a jury convicted Marvin of capital murder in the "execution-style slayings of his grandmother, a half-brother, and two cousins" ("Teen Gets Life" B7). Kevin Stanford was seventeen years old when he murdered Baerbel Poor in Jefferson County, Kentucky. After he had been transferred from juvenile court to adult court, the jury convicted Stanford of murder and sentenced him to death. When his case was appealed to the Supreme Court, Justice Scalia, in announcing the majority opinion, said that sentencing juvenile offenders to death did not violate the Eighth Amendment (*Stanford v. Kentucky* 316). A survey of 250 judges conducted by Penn and Schoen Associates and published in the *National Law Journal* found that "40 percent of the judges said the minimum age for facing murder charges should be 14 or 15, while 17 percent said it should be even lower, 12 or 13. The judges generally agreed that the criminal justice system should deal with young criminals more in the way it deals with adults" ("Tougher Treatment" A16).

Sequence

Caught up in the details of a well-researched paper, you need to remind yourself to take the reader along. In a well thought-out paper or article, the reader is able to highlight key sentences that together reveal the blueprint or skeleton of the paper. Look at the following network of **transitional sentences:**

Formal Outline

In many areas of study, instructions for your research paper may include a call for a **formal outline.** Here is a sample outline using a traditional outline format. Note Roman numerals for main headings, capital letters for subheadings, and Arabic numerals for sub-subheadings. (Fourth-level subheadings, if needed, would use lower-case *a., b.,* and *c.*)

Outline

THESIS: Despite the clamor for getting tough on juvenile crime, the best hope for our society remains an increased emphasis on education, prevention, and rehabilitation.

I. Changing views of the juvenile justice system
   A. Eric Smith's crime and trial
   B. Juvenile justice as promising alternative to adult courts
   C. Juvenile justice system seen as "soft on crime"

II. Reasons for trying children as adults
   A. Perceived failure of preventive measures
   B. Perceived rise of juvenile crime

III. Support for trying of juveniles as adults
   A. Officials within justice system
      1. Judges in juvenile justice system
      2. Probation workers supporting jail for youths
   B. Politicians and general public

IV. Questions about juvenile crime statistics
   A. Alarmist statistics and official testimony
   B. Dissenting views: statistics and testimony

V. Contradictory effects of treating juvenile offenders as adults
   A. Lax treatment in adult courts and prisons
      1. Youth centers worse than adult prison in California
      2. Youths getting light sentences in adult court
   B. Arbitrary or injust treatment in adult courts and prisons
      1. Conditions in adult prisons
      2. Wide discrepancies in sentencing

VI. Reservations about trying juveniles as adults
   A. Definitions of adult responsibility
   B. Failure to deter crime
   C. Turning youths into "hardened criminals"

VII. Alternative solutions to juvenile crime problem
   A. Effective traditional programs
      1. Educational programs
      2. Community-based intervention programs
      3. Boot camp
   B. Promising experimental programs
      1. Capital Offender Group in Texas
      2. Jacksonville program
      3. Colorado program

REVISING

There is no clear borderline between drafting and revising. Many writers tinker with a draft as they go along. However, you should try to schedule a major full-scale revision. Reread an early draft after a few days' cooling-off. Rereading your draft through the reader's eyes, you are likely to notice areas that need work. Often you will be able to profit from feedback from an instructor or from peers. This is the time for stock-taking and second thoughts. You should be able to spot missing links, incomplete or unconvincing evidence, awkward backtrackings, or unresolved contradictions.

Although every writing project is different, advice like the following will usually help you strengthen your paper:

1. *Do more to raise the issue.* Add an attention-getting **starter quote**, like the following from a paper on whether to try juvenile offenders as adults:

> "A 14-year-old with a gun is far more menacing than a 44-year-old with the same weapon. The teenager is more willing to pull the trigger–without fully considering the consequences." This is the way J. A. Fox and Glen Pierce highlight the menace of juvenile crime in "American Killers Are Getting Younger" in *USA Today.*

Or add a dramatic **opening example,** as did the author of a paper on the correlation between violence on the screen and violence in real life:

> In the sadistic thriller *Money Train,* a pyromaniac twice hoses New York City subway token clerks with gasoline through the money-change opening in their booths, strikes a match, and creates an instant crematorium. Four days after the premiere of the movie, two men set a 50-year-old token booth clerk ablaze by squirting him with a combustible fluid and then striking a match. The New York City Police Commissioner said that the crime appeared to be an imitation of the film.

2. *Do more to set directions for your paper.* Do more to create expectations. If your paper at the beginning seems to echo mainly current conservative complaints about the burgeoning cost of welfare, make it clear that your real focus is on hands-on attempts to get people off the welfare rolls. Early in your paper, provide more of a *preview* of your main concerns:

> We hear much about the "culture of dependency." We hear much about "able-bodied" welfare recipients who would rather live at the taxpayers' expense than go

to work. Proposals are labeled as "reforms" when their principal and perhaps only purpose is to save money. *What would it really take to move people from the welfare culture to the culture of work? How could we help people develop the skills and the work habits required by employers? How would we give high school dropouts a second chance at getting an education? What would we have to do to help welfare mothers with child care? How could we make up for the loss of health benefits that for many makes taking low-paying jobs a losing proposition?*

3. *Do more to signal turning points or major logical steps.* Do more to help your readers see the logical connection between one set of data or one batch of quoted material and the next. For instance, at the beginning of a new paragraph pick up the key idea of the preceding paragraph–and then show how it ties in with, leads up to, or contrasts with what is next:

. . . And if the juvenile offender cannot contribute to society, Judge Corriero asks, "Have we really protected society?" ("Punishing Youths" B1).

Other public officials, like Mayor Marion Barry of the District of Columbia, *follow Judge Corriero's line of argument.* Courtland Milloy, in an article in the *Washington Post,* says, "Barry knows as well as any one that the police are not the answer." . . .

4. *Do more to establish credentials or credibility of your sources.* To help your readers get their bearings, fill them in on the affiliation or allegiance of sources:

a report published by the Heritage Foundation, a *conservative think tank,* . . .
the *Nation,* a *magazine long associated with progressive causes,* . . .

5. *Avoid overreliance on any one source.* For instance, have you relied on one major authority to provide historical background? Have you relied on a single historian to assess the idealism, the struggles, the setbacks, and the achievements of the Civil Rights movement of the sixties and seventies? Try to bring in other authorities to corroborate or to challenge your main source. Draw on the testimony of people involved in the movement, of black activists and white liberals, of eye witnesses and historians looking back decades later. Show that you have done your own checking, your own thinking.

6. *Bundle quotations more effectively.* Do more to tie together related material. Do more to line up a second or third source that will confirm or corroborate the first.

7. *Break up block quotations.* Use block quotations sparingly. Use them at strategic points in your paper for strong testimonials or first-hand presentation of key evidence. If too many block quotations gave your first draft a lumpy, undigested quality, shift to a better mix of direct quotation and paraphrase.

8. *If you can, cite primary sources for greater authenticity.* For instance, at a strategic point, add an actual key quote from a Supreme Court decision on whether to try juveniles as adults.

9. *Conclude with a stronger punchline.* Save a striking dramatic example or a clinching quotation for the last. Or spell out the implications of your findings for future action. Try to leave your readers with a strong impression.

DOCUMENTATION STYLES (MLA, APA, AND OTHERS)

Documentation furnishes a full accounting of your sources. In a documented paper, you provide complete names, titles, publishing data, and page numbers. You show your readers where your material came from and where they can turn to verify your data, check your quotations, or find additional information. You will need to identify all sources that you quote directly. However, you need to give a source also when you paraphrase, summarize, or use someone else's facts and figures. In addition, you need to show the sources of ideas that are the result of someone else's effort or inspiration or of approaches someone else has developed. Respect other people's intellectual property–give credit to people whose ideas, data, or research findings you draw on or adapt.

Documentation styles vary from one area of study to another–and sometimes from one professional journal to another. They also vary from one edition of published guidelines to another, as editors try to modernize their styles and deal with new developments like on-line publication. Different areas of the curriculum use slightly different systems of coding information about sources. The skills you need to develop are a) following the basic outlines of a particular documentation format, and b) hunting down the instructions for documenting an unusual or out-of-the-way source.

- For papers in the humanities (English, philosophy), you will usually follow the documentation style of the Modern Language Association, outlined in the *MLA Handbook for Writers of Research Papers* (Fourth Edition, 1995).
- For papers in the social sciences (sociology, psychology, education), you will usually follow the APA style, outlined in the *Publication Manual of the American Psychological Association* (Fourth Edition, 1994).
- For papers in the sciences, you may be required to follow the style of the

Council of Biology Editors (CBE), the American Institute of Physics (AIP), or the American Chemical Society (ACS).

- For papers in journalism, the arts, and history, you may be required to follow the guidelines of the *Chicago Manual of Style* (CMS).

The most widely used documentation styles no longer use footnotes but instead use a system of two-track identification. In your text, you give minimal information about your sources in parentheses as **parenthetical documentation.** For instance, in the MLA style, you may simply give the page number if you have already identified the author in your text (11), or author and page number if not:

According to one estimate, "by the year 2020, less than 2 percent of the entire global workforce will still be engaged in factory work" (Rifkin 11).

In the APA style, you may give the date of publication in parentheses (1996) or author and date if you have not identified the source in your text (White, 1996).

At the end of your paper, you give a final complete listing and accounting of the works you have cited—labeled, for instance, "Works Cited" or "References." This final listing is your bibliography (literally "book list")—which today however is likely to include nonprint and electronic sources.

Entries in your final list of **Works Cited** (MLA) may look as follows:

Book:

Rifkin, Jeremy. <u>The End of Work: The Decline of the Global Labor Force and the Dawn of the Post-Market Era</u>. New York: Tarcher/Putnam, 1995.

Article:

Rifkin, Jeremy. "Civil Society in the Information Age: Workerless Factories and Virtual Companies." <u>Nation</u> 26 Feb. 1996: 11–16.

Entries in your final list of **References** (APA) may look as follows:

Book:

      Rifkin, J. (1995). <u>The end of work: The decline of the global labor force and the dawn of the post-market era</u>. New York: Tarcher/Putnam.

Article:

      Rifkin, J. (1996, February 26). Civil society in the information age: Workerless factories and virtual companies. <u>The Nation</u>, pp. 11-16.

A CHECK-SHEET FOR DOCUMENTATION STYLES

1. Separate title page required? formal outline required? abstract required?
2. What kind of running heads? (for example, "Rodriguez 2" flush right?)
3. What style for attribution of sources in your text? (Author mentioned in text with page numbers in parentheses? Data in text with author and date in parentheses? Code number for source in parentheses?)
4. What heading for final list of sources–"Works Cited"? "References"? "References Cited"?
5. Final list of sources to be alphabetized? numbered? arranged by code number?
6. Date of source given after name and title–or in parentheses immediately after author's name?
7. Caps or lower-case in titles? ("Correlates of Cocaine Use in Inner Cities" or "Correlates of cocaine use in inner cities"?)
8. Include or omit abbreviations like *p.* and *v.* for pages and volumes–in parenthetical documentation? in final list of sources?
9. What style for use and spacing of commas, periods, colons, parentheses with parenthetical documentation and in final list of sources?
10. What instructions for special indentation–for instance, for block quotations? What indentation in final list of sources? (For instance, first line of each entry indented or flush left?)

AVOIDING PLAGIARISM

Plagiarism is appropriating other people's intellectual work without acknowledgment. You plagiarize when you take over other writers' ideas, data, or exact words without acknowledging the source. Plagiarism can ruin a grade or academic record and badly damage a reputation. In blatant cases of plagiarism, someone copies whole passages (or sometimes a whole article) with perhaps only minor changes and then passes them off as his or her own. More commonly, plagiarism results from slipshod note taking, with chunks of material of dubious origin being fed into a paper.

Heeding advice like the following will help protect you against any suspicion of plagiarism:

- In your notes, include a *source tag* for all information or ideas.
- Put everything you copy word for word in *quotation marks*.
- When you paraphrase or summarize, change the wording enough so no one can point to a passage and say: "This does not sound like you–this sounds like someone else."
- Credit your source when you take over someone else's statistics, recently discovered facts, new theories, or personal point of view.
- Do not adopt someone else's *plan* or outline of key points without acknowledgment.

PARENTHETICAL DOCUMENTATION: MLA

When you follow the MLA style, you use parenthetical documentation and provide a final listing of **Works Cited.** You put page references and needed identification in parentheses in the text of your paper–not in separate notes. Study the following possibilities:

1. SIMPLE PAGE REFERENCE   You will often identify the author or the publication (or both) in the text of your paper. Your parenthetical page reference will then direct the reader to the right page. Put page number (or page numbers) in parentheses–*after* a closing quotation mark, *before* a final period:

Mark Trumbull, staff writer of the <u>Christian Science</u>

<u>Monitor</u>, claims, "All states have some provision for

sending youths to adult courts, and more than 20

states . . . have made their laws more strict since

1992" (3).

2. IDENTIFICATION BY AUTHOR   If you have *not* mentioned the author in your text, give the author's last name with the page reference:

```
Not everyone seems ready to give up on young criminals.

"Criminologists have questioned the concept of

rehabilitation for adult offenders, but in the juvenile

justice system, belief in rehabilitation is alive and

well" (Andrews 17).
```

3. IDENTIFICATION BY TITLE   If you are using more than one source by the same author, include a shortened form of the title. Enclose the title of an article (or other *part* of a publication) in quotation marks. Underline (or italicize) the title of a book or other *whole* publication.

```
Alex Comfort has frequently told us that the blunting

of abilities in the aged results at least in part from

"put-downs, boredom, and exasperation" ("Old Age" 45);

the changes we see in old people, according to him,

"are not biological effects of aging" (Good Age 11).
```

If you shorten a title, try to keep the *first word* (other than *The, A,* or *An*) the same in the shortened title, so that your readers can find the source in your alphabetical list of Works Cited.

4. IDENTIFICATION BY AUTHOR AND TITLE   If you use more than one source by an author not identified in your text, include the author's name and a short title. Put a comma between author and title, *no* comma between title and page number.

```
In France, Islamic immigrants from North Africa are

"increasingly resisting assimilation and integration"

(Belvedere, The Rise of Islam 187, 207-210).
```

5. REFERENCE WITHIN A SENTENCE   When it is needed for clarity, put page reference and identification part way through a sentence.

```
While homicide rates for people over twenty-five dropped

10 percent from 1990 to 1993 (Butterfield 7), the

homicide rate for 14- to 17-year-olds had gone up 165

percent over a period of ten years (Foxbury 89).
```

6. MORE THAN ONE AUTHOR   Include names of several authors with your page reference if you have not identified the authors in your test. For more than three authors, give name of first author and then put et al. (unitalicized), Latin for "and others."

> Tests are increasingly becoming the target of close
> scrutiny by right-wing groups (Beckers and Santos 134).
> In California, an ambitious new testing program was
> abandoned when religious groups claimed test questions
> "constituted an invasion of the students' privacy"
> (Verbrook et al. 79).

7. REFERENCE WITH BLOCK QUOTATION   At the end of a block quotation, put the parenthetical reference *after* final punctuation.

> Moeller in <u>Myths about Aging</u> tries to counteract
> familiar stereotypes:
>> Older people seem mentally slow or disoriented
>> when we deprive them of intellectual stimulus
>> and active involvement with other people.
>> Provided they remain active and are not
>> isolated or cast off, the majority of older
>> people remain mentally alert. Few of them show
>> signs of mental deterioration or senility,
>> and only a small proportion become mentally
>> ill. (114)

8. REFERENCE TO ONE OF SEVERAL VOLUMES   If in your Works Cited you are going to list several volumes of a work, use an Arabic numeral followed by a colon to specify the volume you have used:

> According to Trevelyan, the isolationist movement in
> America and the pacifist movement in Britain between
> them "handed the world over to its fate" (3:301).

9. REFERENCE TO A PREFACE   Use lower-case Roman numerals if you find them used in a book for the preface or other introductory material:

In her introduction to <u>Dancing on the Edge of the</u>

<u>World</u>, Ursula K. Le Guin says, "I try to limit myself

to topics on which, without claiming expertise or

wisdom, an effort to think honestly and feelingly might

do some good" (vii).

10. REFERENCE TO A LITERARY CLASSIC   Use Arabic numerals separated by periods for such divisions of literary works as act, scene, and line (*Hamlet* 3.2.73–76). However, some authors prefer the more traditional use of capital and lower-case Roman numerals (*Hamlet* III.ii.73–76).

In Shakespeare's <u>Tempest</u>, Gonzalo, who would prefer to

"die a dry death," fits this archetype (1.1.66).

11. REFERENCE TO THE BIBLE   Use Arabic numerals for chapter and verse (Luke 2.1), although some authors prefer to use a traditional style (Luke ii.1).

12. QUOTATION AT SECOND HAND   Show that you are quoting not from the original source but at second hand. Your Works Cited will then list only the second-hand source. (But quote from and cite the original source if you can.)

The composer was fond of saying that rather than his

symphonies being too long "the critics are too short"

(qtd. in Rasmussen 135).

13. REFERENCE TO NONPRINT MATERIALS   When drawing on an interview, a radio or television program, or a movie, make sure your text highlights the name of the interviewer, person being interviewed, director or producer, or scriptwriter whose name appears in your Works Cited. Sometimes you may identify a production or movie in parentheses to direct your reader to the right entry:

In an interview in 1994, Metaxas discussed the tendency

toward overt ideological statement in the visual arts.

A news special by a Chicago station brought the lawyers

for the tobacco companies out in force (<u>Hazard to</u>

<u>Health</u>).

ABBREVIATIONS FOUND IN SCHOLARLY WRITING

©   copyright (© 1996 by Naomi Wolf)

c. or ca.   Latin *circa*, "approximately"; used for approximate dates and figures (c. 1798)

et al.   Latin *et alii*, "and others"; used in references to books by several authors (T.V. Hudson et al.)

f., ff.   "and the following page (or pages)"

Ibid.   an abbreviation of Latin *ibidem*, "in the same place." (When used by itself, without a page reference, it means "in the last publication cited, on the page indicated.")

n.d.   "no date," date of publication unknown

op. cit.   short for *opere citato*, "in the work already cited"

passim   Latin for "throughout"; "in various places in the work under discussion" (See pp. 54–56 et passim.)

rev.   "review" or "revised"

rpt.   "reprint"; a reprinting of a book or article

---

14. REFERENCE TO MORE THAN ONE SOURCE   When identifying several sources in the same parenthetical reference, separate them by a semicolon:

```
After the dissolution of the Soviet Union, information
about Soviet spies working for the American government
became available to scholars with access to former
Soviet archives (Kaunas 128; Jablonski 24).
```

WORKS CITED DIRECTORY: MLA

A. ARTICLES IN PERIODICALS
     1. Standard Entry for Newspaper Article
     2. Standard Entry for Periodical Article
     3. Article by Several Authors
     4. Unsigned or Anonymous Article

(Continued)

A. Articles in Periodicals

1. STANDARD ENTRY FOR NEWSPAPER ARTICLE   Start with the last name of the author. Put the title of the article in quotation marks. Italicize (underline) the name of the newspaper. Go on to the date, separated from the complete page numbers by a colon. Abbreviate most months: 15 Dec. 1995. (But do not abbreviate months in the text of your paper.)

Where appropriate, specify the edition of the newspaper–early or late, east or west: *Wall Street Journal* 20 Nov. 1995, eastern ed.: A4. Identify sections of a newspaper by letters (B34) or by numbers (late ed., sec. 3:7):

> Nadler, David. "America, Playing to Its Own
>
>   Strengths." <u>New York Times</u> 2 June 1991, late
>
>   ed.: F11.

If an article is interrupted and continued later in the publication, use a plus sign to show that after the initial pages there is more later:

> Vartabedian, Ralph. "Chronic Joblessness after
>
>   Aerospace Layoffs." <u>Los Angeles Times</u> 8 June
>
>   1993: A1+.

Editor's Tip: In your list of "Works Cited," omit the article *The* in the names of publications like *The Wall Street Journal* or *The New Republic.*

2. STANDARD ENTRY FOR PERIODICAL ARTICLE   Start with the last name of the author. Enclose the title of the *article* in quotation marks. Italicize (underline) the name of the *publication*. Go on to the date (or month). Separate it from the *complete page numbers* by a colon.

> Gerlach, Michael L. "The Japanese Corporate Network:
>
>   A Blockmodel Analysis." <u>Administrative Science</u>
>
>   <u>Quarterly</u> Mar. 1992: 105–40.

3. ARTICLE BY SEVERAL AUTHORS   Give the full names of co-authors. If there are more than three, put et al. (Latin for "and others") after the name of the first author instead. (Or you may list all authors.)

> Gale, Noel H., and Zofia Stos-Gale. "Lead and Silver
>
>   in the Ancient Aegean." <u>Scientific American</u> June
>
>   1981: 176–77.

Martz, Larry et al. "A Tide of Drug Killings."

Newsweek 16 Jan. 1989: 44-45.

4. UNSIGNED OR ANONYMOUS ARTICLE   If the author of an article is unnamed, begin your entry with the title.

"Losing Its Way: Japanese Industry." Economist 18

Sept. 1993: 78-79.

5. ARTICLE WITH SUBTITLE   Use a colon to separate title and subtitle. Enclose both in the same set of quotation marks.

Claflin, Terrie. "Monumental Achievement: Twenty Years

after Vietnam, Invisible Vets Get Their

Memorial." Ms. Nov./Dec. 1993: 83-88.

6. ARTICLE WITH VOLUME NUMBER   For scholarly or professional journals, you will typically include the volume number, followed by the year in parentheses. (Usually page numbers are consecutive for the whole volume covering the issues for a year–the second issue will start with page 90 or page 137, for instance.)

Santley, Robert S. "The Political Economy of the

Aztec Empire." Journal of Anthropological

Research 41 (1985): 327-37.

7. ARTICLE WITH NUMBER OF VOLUME AND ISSUE   If page numbers are not continuous for the whole volume (each new issue starts with page 1), you may have to include the number of the issue. Add it after the volume number, separating the two numbers by a period (no space): 13.4.

Winks, Robin W. "The Sinister Oriental Thriller:

Fiction and the Asian Scene." Journal of Popular

Culture 19.2 (1985): 49-61.

If there is no volume number but only the number of the issue, treat it as if it were the volume number:

Bowering, George. "Baseball and the Canadian

Imagination." Canadian Literature 108 (1986):

115-24.

8. SIGNED OR UNSIGNED EDITORIAL   After the title, add the label: Editorial (no italics or quotation marks). If the editorial is unsigned, begin with the title.

Hernandez, Carlos. "Immigrants Are Not Aliens."

Editorial. <u>Harristown News</u> 27 Sept. 1994: 7.

"Giving Women a Sporting Chance." Editorial. <u>Los</u>

<u>Angeles Times</u> 23 Oct. 1993: B7.

9. LETTER TO THE EDITOR   After the name of the author, add the right label: Letter (no italics or quotation marks).

Nguyen, Long. Letter. <u>Los Angeles Times</u> 7 July 1993,

part II: 0.

10. TITLED OR UNTITLED REVIEW   Use the abbreviation *rev.* before the title of the work being reviewed. For unsigned reviews, start with the title of the review (if any) or the description of the review.

Harlan, Arvin C. Rev. of <u>A Short Guide to German</u>

<u>Humor</u>, by Frederick Hagen. <u>Brownsville Herald</u> 12

Nov. 1994: 89-90.

Rev. of <u>The Penguin Book of Women Poets</u>, ed. Carol

Cosman, Joan Keefe, and Kathleen Weaver. <u>Arts</u>

<u>and Books Forum</u> May 1990: 17-19.

11. COMPUTER SERVICE   For material obtained from a computer service, add the name of the system and access number or file and item number for the article you have used.

Schomer, Howard. "South Africa: Beyond Fair

Employment." <u>Harvard Business Review</u> May-June

1983: 145+. Dialog file 122, item 119425 833160.

12. INFORMATION SERVICE   Information services like ERIC provide both bibliographic listings and actual printouts of the documents themselves. If the material had been previously published elsewhere, provide standard publishing information, followed by identification of the service and an item number. If the material had not been previously published, cite it as a complete publication published by the service:

Kurth, Ruth J., and Linda J. Stromberg. <u>Using Word</u>

<u>Processing in Composition Instruction</u>. ERIC,

1984 ED 251 850.

B. Books (and other whole publications)

13. STANDARD ENTRY FOR A BOOK   Start with the *last* name of the author. Underline (italicize) the title. Enter place of publication, publisher's name, and date of publication. (Leave one space after periods.)

```
Kramer, Peter D. Listening to Prozac. New York:

     Viking, 1993.
```

Editor's Tip: Identification of publishers is heavily abbreviated: Harcourt (Harcourt Brace, Inc.); Morrow (William Morrow); Oxford UP (Oxford University Press); Acad. for Educ. Dev. (Academy for Educational Development).

```
Gates, Henry Louis, Jr. Loose Canons: Notes on the

     Culture Wars. New York: Oxford UP, 1992.
```

14. BOOK WITH SUBTITLE   Use a colon between title and subtitle. Italicize (underline) both the title and subtitle of a book.

```
Kozol, Jonathan. Amazing Grace: The Lives of Children

     and the Conscience of a Nation. New York: Crown,

     1995.
```

15. BOOK BY TWO OR THREE AUTHORS   For the first author, put the last name first. Then give full names of co-authors in normal order. With three authors, use commas between authors' names.

```
Gilbert, Sandra M., and Susan Guber. The Madwoman in

     the Attic: The Woman Writer and the Nineteenth-

     Century Literary Imagination. New Haven: Yale

     UP, 1979.

Wresch, William, Donald Pattow, and James Gifford.

     Writing for the Twenty-First Century: Computers

     and Research Writing. New York: McGraw, 1988.
```

16. BOOK BY MORE THAN THREE AUTHORS   Give the first author's name, followed by a comma and the abbreviation et al. (Latin for "and others"). Do not put a period after et, and do not underline or italicize.

```
Stewart, Marie M., et al. Business English and

     Communication. 5th ed. New York: McGraw, 1978.
```

17. LATER EDITION OF A BOOK   If you have used a book revised or brought up

to date by the author, identify the new edition the way it is labeled on its title page. After the title of the book, put 2nd ed. for second edition, for instance, or rev. ed. for revised edition.

> Zettl, Herbert. <u>Television Production Handbook</u>. 6th
>
> ed. Belmont: Wadsworth, 1997.

18. REPRINTING OR REISSUE OF A BOOK   If a work has been republished unchanged (for instance, as a paperback reprint), include the date of the original edition and then go on to full publishing data for the reprinting. If new material (like an introduction) has been added, include the information.

> Wharton, Edith. <u>The House of Mirth</u>. 1905. Introd.
>
> Cynthia Griffin Wolf. New York: Penguin, 1986.

19. BOOK WITH EDITOR'S NAME FIRST   If an editor has assembled the materials in the book, enter *ed.* after the editor's name. Use *eds.* if there are several editors.

> Hall, Nina, ed. <u>Exploring Chaos: A Guide to the New</u>
>
> <u>Science of Disorder</u>. New York: Norton, 1994.
>
> Kiernan, Karthy, and Michael M. Moore, eds. <u>First</u>
>
> <u>Fiction: An Anthology of the First Published</u>
>
> <u>Stories by Famous Writers</u>. Boston: Little, 1994.

20. BOOK WITH EDITOR'S NAME LATER   If an editor has edited the work of a single author, put the original author's name first if you focus on the *author's* work. Add ed. (for "edited by") and the editor's or several editors' names after the title. (Do not use *eds.*) However, put the editor's name first and the author's name later (after *By*) if the editor's work is particularly important to your project.

> Mencken, H. L. <u>The Vintage Mencken</u>. Ed. Alistair
>
> Cooke. New York: Vintage, 1956.

21. BOOK WITH TRANSLATOR'S NAME   Put *Trans.* followed by the translator's name (or translators' names) after the title. But put the translator's name first if the translator's work matters to your project.

> Freire, Paulo. <u>Pedagogy of the Oppressed</u>. Trans. Myra
>
> Bergman Ramos. New York: Seabury, 1970.
>
> Wilson, Marjorie Kerr, trans. <u>On Aggression</u>. By
>
> Konrad Lorenz. New York: Harcourt, 1966.

22. SPECIAL IMPRINT   A line of paperbacks, for instance, is often published

and promoted separately by a publishing house. Put the name of the line of books first, joined by a hyphen to the publisher's name: *Laurel Leaf-Dell, Mentor-NAL.*

> LeShan, Lawrence, and Henry Margenau. <u>Einstein's</u>
>
>   <u>Space and Van Gogh's Sky</u>. New York: Collier-
>
>   Macmillan, 1982.

23. UNSPECIFIED OR INSTITUTIONAL AUTHORSHIP   Reports issued by an organization and major reference works may list a group or institution as the author. Or they may not specify authorship.

> Carnegie Council on Policy Studies in Higher
>
>   Education. <u>Giving Youth a Better Chance: Options</u>
>
>   <u>for Education, Work, and Service</u>. San Francisco:
>
>   Jossey, 1980.
>
> <u>Literary Market Place: The Directory of American Book</u>
>
>   <u>Publishing</u>. 1984 ed. New York: Bowker, 1983.

24. WORK WITH SEVERAL VOLUMES   If you have used *one* volume of a multivolume work, add the abbreviation *Vol.* followed by an Arabic numeral for the number of the volume: Vol. 3. (You may add the total number of volumes and inclusive dates at the end.) If the separate volumes have their own titles, include the volume title as well as the title of the whole multivolume work.

> Woolf, Virginia. <u>The Diary of Virginia Woolf</u>. Ed.
>
>   Anne Olivier Bell. New York: Harcourt, 1977.
>
>   Vol. 1.
>
> Churchill, Winston S. <u>The Age of Revolution</u>. New
>
>   York: Dodd, 1957. Vol. 3 of <u>A History of the</u>
>
>   <u>English-Speaking Peoples</u>. 4 vols. 1956–58.

If you have used *more than one* volume, list the whole multivolume work, giving the total number of volumes: 3 vols.

> Trevelyan, G. M. <u>History of England</u>. 3rd ed. 3 vols.
>
>   Garden City: Anchor-Doubleday, 1952.

25. PART OF COLLECTION OR ANTHOLOGY   Identify first the article or other short piece (poem or story) and then the collection of which it is a part. Enclose the part title in quotation marks; underline (italicize) the title of the whole. Then enter the

publishing data for the collection. Conclude with inclusive page numbers for the part.

> Borges, Jorge Luis. "A New Refutation of Time." <u>The</u>
>
> > <u>Discontinuous Universe: Selected Writings in</u>
> >
> > <u>Contemporary Consciousness</u>. Eds. Sallie Sears
> >
> > and Georgianna W. Lord. New York: Basic Books,
> >
> > 1972. 208-23.

When you list several articles from the same collection, you may choose to list the whole collection separately. Then you **cross-reference** the individual selections to the whole collection, without repeating full publishing information each time. Items like the following would appear in appropriate alphabetical order in your Works Cited:

> Aufderheide, Patricia, ed. <u>Beyond PC: Toward a</u>
>
> > <u>Politics of Understanding</u>. Saint Paul, MN:
> >
> > Graywolf Press: 1992.
>
> Boyte, Harry C. "The Politics of Innocence."
>
> > Aufderheide 177-79.
>
> Brodkey, Linda, and Shelli Fowler, "What Happened to
>
> > English 306." Aufderheide 113-17.
>
> D'Souza, Dinesh. "The Visigoths in Tweed."
>
> > Aufderheide 11-22.

26. ENCYCLOPEDIA ENTRY   Put titles of entries in quotation marks. Page numbers and facts of publication may be unnecessary for entries appearing in alphabetical order in well-known encyclopedias or other reference books. Date or number of the edition used, however, should be included because of the frequent revisions of major encyclopedias. (Include author's name for signed entries. If only initials are given, you may find the full name in an index or a guide.)

> Politis, M. J. "Greek Music." <u>Encyclopedia Americana</u>.
>
> > 1965 ed.
>
> "Aging." <u>Encyclopaedia Britannica: Macropaedia</u>. 1983.
>
> "Graham, Martha." <u>Who's Who of American Women</u>. 14th
>
> > ed. 1985-86.

27. INTRODUCTION, FOREWORD, OR AFTERWORD   If you cite introductory material or an afterword by someone *other than the author* of the book, start with the contributor's name, followed by the generic description (*unitalicized, not* in quotation
marks): Introduction. Preface. Foreword. Afterword. Sometimes the introductory
material has separate page numbers, given as lower-case Roman numerals: v–ix or
ii–xvi.

> Bellow, Saul. Foreword. <u>The Closing of the American</u>
>
> > <u>Mind</u>. By Allan Bloom. New York: Simon, 1987.
> >
> > 11–18.
>
> DeMott, Robert. Introduction. <u>Working Days: The</u>
>
> > <u>Journals of</u> The Grapes of Wrath <u>1938–1941</u>. By
> >
> > John Steinbeck. Ed. Robert DeMott. New York:
> >
> > Viking, 1989. xxi–lvii.

28. GOVERNMENT PUBLICATION   References to entries in the *Congressional Record*
require only the date and page numbers. For other government publications, identify the government and the appropriate branch or subdivision. Use appropriate
abbreviations like *S. Res.* for Senate Resolution, *H. Rept.* for House Report, and *GPO*
for Government Printing Office.

> <u>Cong. Rec.</u> 28 Feb. 1993: 5833–48.
>
> California. Dept. of Viticulture. <u>Beyond Pesticides</u>.
>
> > Sacramento: State Printing Office, 1995.
>
> United States. Cong. Committee on Agriculture.
>
> > Subcommittee on Wheat, Soybeans, and Feed
> >
> > Grains. <u>Formulation of the 1990 Farm Bill</u>. 101st
> >
> > Cong., 1st Sess. 8 vols. Washington: GPO, 1990.

29. PAMPHLET OR BROCHURE   Treat a pamphlet or brochure the way you
would a book, but note that often author (and sometimes place or date) will not be
specified.

> <u>A Guide to Supplements</u>. Boston: Inst. for Better
>
> > Living, 1994.

30. PART OF A SERIES   If the front matter of a book shows its was published as
part of a series, include the name of the series (no italics, no quotation marks) before the publishing data.

Rose, Mike. <u>Writer's Block: The Cognitive Dimension</u>.

Studies in Writing and Rhetoric. Carbondale:

Southern Illinois UP, 1984.

31. BIBLE OR LITERARY CLASSIC   Specify the edition you have used, especially if different versions of the text are important, as with different Bible translations or different editions of a Shakespeare play. Put the editor's name first if you want to highlight the editor's contribution.

<u>The Holy Bible</u>. Revised Standard Version. 2nd ed.

Nashville: Nelson, 1971.

Hubler, Edward, ed. <u>The Tragedy of Hamlet</u>. By William

Shakespeare. New York: NAL, 1963.

32. QUOTATION AT SECOND HAND   List only the work where the quotation appeared:

Ibsen, Henrik. <u>Ghosts</u>. Ed. Kai Jurgensen and Robert

Schenkkan. New York: Avon, 1965.

33. TITLE WITHIN A TITLE   An italicized (underlined) book title may include the name of another book. Shift back to roman (*not* underlined) for the title within a title: *A Guide to James Joyce's* Ulysses.

Gordon, Jean. <u>A Guide to</u> Huckleberry Finn. New York:

Logos, 1984.

C. Nonprint Sources

34. PERSONAL INTERVIEW   Start with the name of the person you interviewed. Use the right label—unitalicized, *not* in quotation marks.

Silveira, Gene. Personal interview. 12 Oct. 1995.

Duong, Tran. Telephone interview. 22 Jan. 1994.

35. BROADCAST OR PUBLISHED INTERVIEW   Identify the person interviewed and label the material as an interview.

Asimov, Isaac. Interview. Science Watch. With Dorothy

Brett. KFOM, San Bruno. 19 Mar. 1986.

If an interview appeared in print, identify it as an interview, and then give standard publishing information about the printed source.

Asimov, Isaac. Interview. <u>Scientists Talk About</u>

<u>Science</u>. By Anne Harrison and Webster Freid. Los

Angeles: Acme, 1987. 94-101.

36. PERSONAL LETTER   For a letter you have received, name the letter writer and label the material as a letter. Give the date. For a published letter, use the name of the *recipient* as the title and then give full publishing data, with inclusive page numbers.

Phung, Diane. Letter to the author. 15 Jan. 1995.

Hemingway, Ernest. "To Lillian Ross." 28 July 1948.

<u>Ernest Hemingway: Selected Letters. 1917-1961</u>.

Ed. Carlos Baker. New York: Scribner's, 1981.

646-49.

37. TALK OR LECTURE   Name the speaker and give an appropriate label (Lecture, Keynote speech) and address (*with no* italics or quotation marks). If the talk had a title, use the title (in quotation marks) instead.

Kernan, Dorothy. Keynote speech. Opening General

Sess. New World Forum, Dallas. 8 June 1995.

Jacobi, Jean. "Television News: News from Nowhere."

Valley Lecture Series, Santa Clara. 29 Oct.

1994.

38. PRINTED SPEECH   If you had access to a printed version of a speech, add full publishing data to the usual information about a talk.

Partlet, Basil. "Yuppies and the Art of Cooking."

Western Chefs' Forum, Phoenix. 19 Aug. 1989.

Rpt. <u>West Coast Review</u> Spring 1990: 76-82.

39. TELEVISION OR RADIO PROGRAM   Underline (italicize) the title of a program. The title may be preceded by the name of a specific episode (in quotation marks) and followed by the name of the series (no italics or quotation marks): "The Young Stravinsky." *The Great Composers.* Musical Masterpieces. Identify network (if any), station, and city (with the last two separated by a comma: KPFA, Berkeley). Pull a name out in front to highlight a person's contribution.

<u>The Poisoned Planet</u>. Narr. Jean Laidlaw. Writ. and

prod. Pat Verstrom. WXRV, Seattle. 12 Feb. 1996.

Rostow, Jacob, dir. "The Last Bridge." <u>A Forgotten

   War</u>. With Eric Seibert, Joan Ash, and Fred

   Minton. KMBC, Sacramento. 12 Dec. 1987.

40. MOVIES   Underline (italicize) the title. Identify the director and production company, and give the date. Include further information as you wish about performers, scriptwriters, and other contributors. Pull a name out in front to highlight a person's contribution.

<u>Tom Jones</u>. Dir. Tony Richardson. Screenplay by John

   Osborne. Perf. Albert Finney, Susannah York,

   Hugh Griffith, Edith Evans, and Joan Greenwood.

   United Artists, 1963.

Zeffirelli, Franco, dir. <u>Romeo and Juliet</u>. By William

   Shakespeare. With Olivia Hussey, Leonard

   Whiting, and Michael York. Paramount, 1968. 138

   min.

41. VIDEOTAPES AND OTHER VISUALS   Label the medium: Videocassette. Filmstrip. Slide program (no italics or quotation marks).

<u>Creation vs. Evolution: Battle of</u> the Classrooms.

   Videocassette. Dir. Ryall Wilson. PBS Video,

   1982. 58 min.

42. COMPUTER SOFTWARE   Basic information includes writer of the program (if known), title of the program or material, distributor or publisher, and date. Because of frequent updatings of computer software, you may have to specify the version: Vers. 1.4. In addition, you may need to tell your readers what equipment and how much memory are required (in kilobytes: 128K).

Crighton, Irene. <u>Think/Write</u>. Vers. 1.2. Computer

   Software. Celex, 1989. Apple IIe, 128K, disk.

43. ON-LINE PUBLICATION/CD-ROM   Much printed material is now also available to you on-line or on CD-ROM. Give first the data for the print publication. Then add available data for electronic publication: database (italicized or underlined); electronic medium if applicable (CD-ROM); distributor or vendor; date of electronic publication. If there is no previous or parallel print publication, list the

electronic publication the way you would a print publication:

> Russo, Michelle Cash. "Recovering from Bibliographic
>
>   Instruction Blahs." RQ: Reference Quarterly 32
>
>   (1992): 178–83. Infotrac: Magazine Index Plus.
>
>   CD-ROM. Information Access. Dec. 1993.
>
> The CIA World Factbook. CD-ROM. Minneapolis: Quanta,
>
>   1992.

44. AUDIO RECORDING   Specify label of the recording company, followed by order number and date. (Use *n.d.* for "no date" if date is unknown.) Identify references to jacket notes or the like.

> Holiday, Billie. The Essential Billie Holiday:
>
>   Carnegie Hall Concert. Audiocassette. Verve,
>
>   UCV2600, 1969.
>
> Rifkin, Joshua. Jacket Notes. Renaissance Vocal
>
>   Music. Nonesuch, H–71097, n.d.

SAMPLE RESEARCH PAPER: MLA

The following student research paper observes the MLA guidelines for documentation. How well has the student writer researched the subject? How well does the paper accomplish its purpose–how effectively does it make and support its points? Does it help clear up questions you might have about the MLA format?

- Study the effectiveness of this paper as a *writing project*. What research has gone into this paper, and what use does the paper make of it? What is the writer's basic strategy or overall plan? How does the writer use direct quotation, paraphrase, and summary? Which points seem well supported? Do any seem weak or questionable? Does the paper change your thinking about the topic? Does the paper leave you with unanswered questions?
- Study this paper as a model for the *format* of your own paper. No separate title page is necessary (unless your instructor requires it). Double-spacing is used throughout, including block quotations and Works Cited (no quadruple-spacing after title or before and after paragraphs). Running heads (*Perry 1* and so forth) start flush right at the top of page one and continue through the Works Cited page. The indentation for a block quotation is one inch or ten typewriter spaces on the left–no extra space on the right.

James Perry

Professor Guth

English 176

21 November 1995

Child Criminals in Adult Courts—A Crime in Itself?

In August 1993, at a day camp in Savona, New York, Eric Smith, a 13-year-old, brutally murdered a 4-year-old. Eric grabbed the younger boy in a headlock, smashed his head with a rock, stuffed a napkin and a plastic bag in his mouth, and pummeled his body. After a long delay, despite his young age, Eric was tried as an adult, because of the severity of his crime and also because of a law allowing children as young as thirteen to be tried as adults when accused of murder (Nordheimer B5).

Smith's crime was indicative of some frightening trends in America—an increase in the severity of juvenile crime, and a decrease in the age at which children commit crimes. His trial also shows a current trend in American juvenile justice—children are being tried in adult courts in more cases and at younger ages. Experts, elected representatives, and the general public have been grappling with the issue of how to deal with juvenile crime, and treating youths as adults is currently a popular solution. Many questions arise in the debate over whether to try children as adults: How big a problem is juvenile crime? Is being harsh with juvenile criminals in the best interest of the defendants? Is it in society's best interest, in terms of rehabilitating criminals, deterring and reducing crime, and justice? Is treating child criminals as adults the most effective and most cost-efficient way of dealing with them?

The alternative to treating juveniles as adults is a more rehabilitative approach. Some experts advocate more preventive efforts, as opposed to more punishment-oriented programs such as trying youths in adult courtrooms. In this paper, I intend to show the causes for the current sentiment favoring trying youths as adults. Then I intend to argue that while juvenile crime is a problem, it may not be the epidemic that it has been made out to be, and that although it is necessary to be firm in dealing with juvenile criminals, the best way to deal with them may not necessarily be through adult courts and "getting tough."

The American justice system seems to be coming full circle. The nation's first juvenile court was established in 1899 in Cook County, Illinois, as a way to deal with young offenders in a more rehabilitative style, as opposed to the harsher justice found in adult courts (Andrews 17; Schwartz 150-151). However, by the 1960's, the public became more concerned about juvenile crime, as the youth population was growing and becoming more violent (Houghtalin and Mays 394). Americans have begun to question the "principles and effectiveness" of the current juvenile justice systems, and have argued in favor of harsher, firmer alternatives (Andrews 17). The 1966 U.S. Supreme Court case Kent vs. United States established guidelines for the transfer of young offenders to adult courts. The youths' threat to the safety of the public and amenability to treatments within the juvenile justice system were to be considered (Houghtalin and Mays 394). Since this time, more and more laws have been proposed and implemented to make it easier, and in some cases mandatory, for youths to be sent to adult courts for certain crimes, both violent and nonviolent. The public seems to want young criminals to be held responsible for their crimes and to be punished, and they believe that this can best be done in adult courts, where child criminals presumably will face harsher sentencing, often including time in adult prisons.

Measures to treat juvenile offenders as adults have been proposed and supported for several reasons in recent years. While some experts advocate more preventive measures, these are difficult to implement and would have more of a long-term effect, leaving Americans wondering "what we are supposed to do in the meantime" (Methvin 95). Bob Herbert argues that attempts to rehabilitate young offenders and treat them lightly are "well-intentioned" but "out of touch with the increasingly violent reality of juvenile crime" (E15). Other measures have failed to reduce juvenile crime; for instance, gun control laws are not believed to have a significant effect on violent crime by youths, since they tend to obtain the guns through illegal means anyway (Witkin 28). Although experts disagree as to the extent and seriousness of current juvenile crime, the fact is that the public feels that juvenile crime is a major problem, and they support measures to deal with it. An Assistant Maryland public defender feels that the public's focus on juvenile crime created the "political climate" that exists supporting anti-juvenile crime measures (qtd. in Stepp A12).

Many officials within the justice system feel that some young criminals should be treated as adults and tried in adult courts. A study published by the National Law Journal in August 1994 shows that many judges in the juvenile justice system feel that "the criminal justice system should deal with young criminals more in the way it deals with adults." For instance, two out of five judges surveyed feel child offenders should be eligible to receive the death penalty in some situations, and a majority felt that the minimum age for facing murder charges should be lowered ("Tougher Treatment" A16). Ira Schwartz, a former administrator of the Office of Juvenile Justice and Delinquency Prevention, feels that "juvenile court judges and youth probation workers are among the staunchest supporters of jailing for juveniles" (18).

Many legislators, and a large portion of the general public, share the sentiments of these justice authorities. Maryland Delegate Joseph F. Vallario, Jr. feels that "if [youths] want to do adult-type crimes, we're going to treat them like adults" (qtd. in Stepp A12). Another Maryland Delegate, Ulysses Curie, writes that because of the increasing violence and youth of juvenile offenders, "the juvenile system must be changed to respond to this reality" by treating youths more like adults (C8). Both Democrats and Republicans support measures to treat young criminals more like adults; both of the Maryland delegates quoted above are Democrats, and a major part of the Republicans' "Contract with America" was the "Taking Back Our Streets Act," which supported harsher punishment of crime ("Youth and Crime" 18). In recent years, many states have added legislation that lowered the ages at which youths can be tried as adults for certain crimes, added new crimes to those for which a juvenile may or must be tried as an adult, implemented mandatory sentencing for children convicted of certain crimes, and so on. For instance, in 1993, Louisiana added attempted murder and aggravated battery to the list of offenses for which a juvenile may be tried as an adult, and Maryland's legislature recently mandated adult trials for

Perry 5

youths over 15 for various crimes including carjacking (Stepp A12). In
an article in the New York Times Magazine, Alex Kotlowitz cites a recent
USA Today/CNN/Gallup Poll survey, in which 75 percent of those polled
felt that juveniles should be treated like adult criminals if they
commit a violent crime (40). Naturally, politicians have reacted to the
public's views regarding juvenile crime by supporting measures that
appear to "get tough" on young criminals.

    The public believes that juvenile justice is a problem of epidemic
proportions that must be dealt with in a strict manner. While no one
would deny that juvenile crime is a major problem, the actual size of
the problem is debatable. Some statistics support the view that youth
crime is a massive problem. In his article supporting getting tough
with juvenile criminals, Bob Herbert cites FBI statistics, indicating
that "one out of every six suspects arrested nationwide for murder,
rape, robbery or assault" is a minor (E15). Louis Sullivan, secretary
of the Department of Health and Human Services, points out that "during
every 100 hours on [America's] streets we lose more young men than were
killed in 100 hours of ground war in the Persian Gulf" (qtd. in Witkin
27-28). Some statistics also support the view that the juvenile justice
system isn't doing its job: Richard Woodbury cites a statistic that 60
percent of all juvenile offenders become repeat offenders (58).
Statistics show a decrease in the age at which children commit violent
acts; from 1982 to 1992, the number of young teenagers arrested on
murder charges increased from 2.7 per 100,000 to 4.9 per 100,000 (Stepp
A12).

    However, the experts and statistics do not unanimously support the
conclusion that juvenile crime is a growing epidemic. Laura Sessions

Stepp cites statistics that juvenile crime rates may be leveling off or decreasing (A12). Justice Department statistics show that a "crime wave" has occurred in recent years, but that adults are mainly responsible (Stepp A12). In 1994, the National Council on Crime and Delinquency predicted that the five-year arrest rates for "violent juvenile crime between 1990 and 1995 will be the second-lowest increase since 1965" (qtd. in Stepp A12). From 1991 to 1992, the juvenile arrest rate dropped (Stepp A12). Stepp believes that the public's preoccupation with juvenile crime comes more from the media's increased emphasis on juvenile crime than an actual increase. I do not mean to argue that juvenile crime is not a serious problem demanding attention and action; rather, I believe that it is not as big a problem as the public perceives it to be.

While many supporters of sending some children to adult courts feel this is a good way to "get tough" on crime, adult courts aren't always as "tough" on kids as many expect them to be. John Hurst, an investigative reporter for the Los Angeles Times, feels that the inmates in California's juvenile facilities are treated more severely than people housed in adult prisons; he says that "a young man [imprisoned in a youth facility] convicted of a crime cannot pay his debt to society safely" (qtd. in Schwartz 13). Many experts observe that young offenders often receive lighter or shorter sentences in adult courts than they would in the juvenile system (Kotlowitz 40-41, Houghtalin and Mays 395, Stepp A12). With the exception of violent offenders, young criminals sent to adult courts are often sentenced to probation, rather than incarceration (Houghtalin and Mays 395). Alex Kotlowitz feels that this occurs because many criminal courts are already overburdened with adult offenders, and lack the resources to deal with juveniles as well (41).

On the other hand, critics of trying of juvenile offenders as adults believe that justice is frequently not served for the opposite reason—adult courts and prisons are often too harsh for juveniles. Ira M. Schwartz depicts the ills that many juvenile prisoners in adult prisons face, including being held in old and dangerous prisons, inadequate supervision, sexual assault by other prisoners, and a lack of access to the amenities that adult prisoners enjoy such as books, television, visiting hours, and toilets (70-71, 81). Gordon McLean argues that a child imprisoned with adults is "a likely target for the more hardened criminal" and may face "sexual abuse, psychological torture, and death" at the hands of older inmates (13). Sentencing is often arbitrary: Schwartz cites statistics from Minnesota's prison system indicating that juveniles convicted of serious crimes often faced sentences similar to or shorter than those received by juveniles guilty of relatively minor infractions of the law (79).

Opponents of trying youths as adults call into question how appropriate it is to treat them as adults. Alex Kotlowitz brings up the story of fifteen-year-old "Brian H.," who was tried in an adult court for possessing and intending to sell drugs. Although it was his first offense, he was automatically transferred to adult court under state law because he was accused of selling drugs within 1,000 feet of a school. His father felt it was unfair for him to be tried as an adult, saying "how can you hold a kid at that age responsible for adulthood?" (qtd. in Kotlowitz 40). In 1992, in <u>Stanford v. Kentucky</u>, the Supreme Court sanctioned the imposition of the death penalty on a seventeen-year-old.

In his dissent, Justice Brennan cited an earlier court decision that said:

> The reason why juveniles are not trusted with the privileges
> and responsibilities of an adult also explains why their
> irresponsible conduct is not as morally reprehensible as
> that of an adult. Adolescents are more vulnerable, more
> impulsive, and less self-disciplined than adults. (335)

Some studies and experts have called into question the effectiveness of treating youths as adults in actually reducing crime, both in terms of deterring potential criminals from committing crimes and in terms of rehabilitating convicted youths. A 1991 Justice Department survey of youths tried as adults in New York and New Jersey showed that the youths tried as adults were arrested again more frequently, and sooner, than their counterparts who were tried in juvenile courts. Citing this survey in her article in the <u>Washington Post</u>, Laura Sessions Stepp claims that juvenile courts "do a better job of educating and training" young offenders than adult courts (Stepp A12). Alex Kotlowitz feels that children are more responsive to attempts at rehabilitation, because of their young age and their still-developing personalities, yet they are less likely to receive rehabilitation in adult courts than in juvenile courts (40). Many of those who convened at the 21st National Conference on Juvenile Justice in Boston during 1994 felt that "in most cases, transferring young offenders into the adult criminal-justice system achieves little in terms of public safety, and it extinguishes any likelihood of rehabilitation" (Andrews 17). Ira Schwartz believes that "the existing evidence suggests that there is little or no relationship between the

rates of serious juvenile crime and the rates of youth incarceration"
(29).

The threat of an adult jail sentence has a diminished effect on
young people for several reasons. Jill Smolowe argues in <u>Time</u> that
"popular wisdom has it backwards" regarding the effect of threats of
incarceration, because many young people believe that they won't get
caught (63). Douglas W. Nelson, the executive director of the Annie E.
Casey Foundation, believes that it is futile to threaten the liberty of
young people "who report they don't think they'll live until they're 21"
(qtd. in Stepp A12). Gordon Witkin argues that inner-city youths have a
"what the hell" attitude toward life and crime due to the conditions of
poverty and hopelessness that surround them (26).

Some have gone so far as to argue that sending young criminals to
adult prisons is not only ineffective in reducing crime and
rehabilitating the offenders, but that it may have the opposite effect.
A study comparing the recidivism of adults and minors released from
Florida's adult prisons indicated that not only were 60 percent of the
juveniles back in prison within four years, but that this rate was much
higher than the rate for repeat offenses by adults (Schwartz 51).
Gordon McLean, the youth guidance director for Metro Chicago Youth for
Christ, feels that sending a young criminal to adult prison is
"counterproductive," as the young criminal "returns to society more
hardened and embittered than when sentenced" (13). Senator Birch Bayh,
who chaired the U.S. Senate Subcommittee to Investigate Juvenile
Delinquency, feels that "the likelihood that a troubled child will
become an even more troubled adult" is increased by dealing with the
child harshly (xii). Ventura County Superior Court Judge Steven Perren

feels that the public's attitude towards juvenile criminals shouldn't be strict punishment without rehabilitation, because "there is a large segment here that is salvageable" (qtd. in Smolowe 64). Amos Dana, a probation officer with 33 years of experience, says that the facts "justify placing major emphasis on rehabilitation programs that help juveniles rather than sending them to adult prisons, where they could develop their criminal skills."

Many of the advocates of harsher penalties for juvenile offenders do not support other, more rehabilitative or preventive programs. Some feel that such programs are ineffective, others believe that we ought to focus more on punishment and justice than prevention, while many conservatives demand a decrease in the funding for such programs, calling them "pork" (Smolowe 64). However, evidence exists supporting that these types of programs may be better in several ways. Preventive measures tend to be much cheaper than incarceration. STARS, an academic and recreational program in Fort Myers, Florida, that has shown promising results including academic improvement among its participants, costs only $158 per child, much less than incarceration (Smolowe 64). The National Council on Crime and Delinquency believes that community-based intervention programs cost less than incarceration, and are more effective at preventing re-arrest (Stepp A12). A study by the National Recreation and Park Association indicates that recreation and training programs can have a direct impact on juvenile crime and arrest rates. For instance, a gang-intervention program in Dallas apparently resulted in a 26 percent drop in the juvenile arrest rate (Smolowe 63-64). Another popular remedy has often been suggested and implemented—the military-style boot camp. Although these camps are cheaper than conventional imprisonment, they haven't proven effective in reducing recidivism (Armstrong 4).

Besides more conventional, nonincarceration methods of dealing with young criminals, several promising programs exist across the country that incorporate both a get-tough philosophy and rehabilitative programs. Richard Woodbury reported in <u>Time</u> magazine on the Capital Offender Group program at the Giddings State Home and School near Austin, Texas. In the program, teenage killers are forced, through talk therapy, to feel the true effect of what they had done in order to prevent them from murdering again. Although many of the program's participants fail, only one of the 116 criminals who had passed the program at the time of Woodbury's article had killed again (58). An article by Clemence Fiagone in the <u>Christian Science Monitor</u> described a program in Jacksonville, Florida, that provides a highly successful "mixture of toughness and rehabilitation." Unlike many prison systems, Jacksonville is fortunate enough to have enough room to house its juvenile offenders for long periods of time, and keep them separate from adults, thus avoiding some of the inherent problems of incarcerating juveniles. The system's rehabilitative program includes counseling, classes, and a mentoring program. Jacksonville officials believe this program resulted in a 30 percent drop in child arrests in 1994, whereas Florida's statewide juvenile arrest rate rose by 23 percent (1, 14). Scott Armstrong reported in the <u>Christian Science Monitor</u> about a program in Colorado, which combined "boot-camp discipline" with "reformative counseling, education, and job-training." The program begins with a month-long, military-style boot camp in order to "break down [the inmates'] rebellious gang and street mentalities and begin to instill order and discipline," followed by an extended period of studying, and finished with the transition back into society (4).

Both modes of juvenile justice, the more rehabilitative, preventive mode associated with the juvenile justice system, and the harsher, more punitive mode associated with sending young offenders to adult courts, are well-intentioned. Those who support strict, adult-style sentencing do so in the name of punishment and public safety, while supporters of "softer" forms of justice champion the causes of preventing people from becoming criminals, and saving young offenders from becoming worse criminals before it's too late for them. While locking up criminals who deserve it is justifiable, measures should be taken to prevent the crime from happening in the first place. Ideally, new programs like those in Florida, Colorado, and Texas will continue to provide a successful blend of justice, prevention, and rehabilitation, and will serve as an example for other justice systems trying to cope with juvenile crime.

Perry 13

Works Cited

Andrews, James H. "Criminals, but Still Children." <u>Christian Science Monitor</u> 7 Mar. 1994: 17.

Armstrong, Scott. "Colorado Tries More Carrot and Less Stick in Punishing Juvenile Crime." <u>Christian Science Monitor</u> 7 Mar. 1994: 11.

Bayh, Birch. Foreword. <u>(In)justice for Juveniles: Rethinking the Best Interests of the Child</u>. By Ira M. Schwartz. Lexington: Heath-Lexington, 1989. xi–xiii.

Curie, Ulysses. "Reality Requires Tougher Responses to Juvenile Crime." <u>Washington Post</u> 6 Feb. 1994: C8.

Dana, Amos. Telephone interview. 17 Nov. 1995.

Fiagone, Clement. "Jacksonville's Tough Answer to Problem of Youth Crimes." <u>Christian Science Monitor</u> 13 Feb. 1995: 1, 14.

Herbert, Bob. "Little Criminals, Big Crimes." <u>New York Times</u> 24 July 1994, late ed.: E15.

Houghtalin, Marilyn, and G. Larry Mays. "Criminal Dispositions of New Mexico Juveniles Transferred to Adult Court." <u>Crime and Delinquency</u> 37 (1991): 393–407.

Kotlowitz, Alex. "Their Crimes Don't Make Them Adults." <u>New York Times Magazine</u> 13 Feb. 1994: 40–41.

McLean, Gordon. "Adult Prison Is No Place for a Kid." <u>Christianity Today</u> 12 Dec. 1986: 13.

Methvin, Eugene H. "Behind Florida's Tourist Murders." <u>Reader's Digest</u> Apr. 1994: 92–96.

Nordheimer, Jon. "Murder Trial Begins for Teen-Ager." <u>New York Times</u> 2 Aug. 1994, late ed.: B5.

Schwartz, Ira M. <u>(In)justice for Juveniles: Rethinking the Best</u>
     <u>Interests of the Child</u>. Lexington: Heath-Lexington, 1989.

Smolowe, Jill. "Going Soft on Crime." <u>Time</u> 14 Nov. 1994: 63-64.

Stanford v. Kentucky. 106 L Ed 2d 306. US Supreme Ct. 1992.

Stepp, Laura Sessions. "The Crackdown on Juvenile Crime—Do Stricter
     Laws Deter Youths?" <u>Washington Post</u> 15 Oct. 1994: A1+.

"Tougher Treatment Urged for Juveniles." <u>New York Times</u> 2 Aug. 1994,
     late ed.: A16.

Witkin, Gordon. "Kids Who Kill." <u>U.S. News and World Report</u>. 8 Apr.
     1991: 26-32.

Woodbury, Richard. "Taming the Killers." <u>Time</u> 11 Oct. 1993: 58-59.

"Youth and Crime." Editorial. <u>Christian Science Monitor</u> 10 Jan. 1995:
     18.

DOCUMENTATION STYLE: APA

Many publications in the social sciences follow the APA style of documentation, outlined in the *Publication Manual of the American Psychological Association* (Fourth Edition, 1994). You may be asked to follow this style in areas like psychology, linguistics, or education.

PARENTHETICAL CITATION

For brief identification of sources in the text of a paper, the APA format uses the **author–and–date** method. When using this style, include year or date of publication after the author's name: (Mineta, 1996). Do not repeat the author's name between parentheses if you have already mentioned it in your text (1996). Often, the APA style gives a source and the publication date of research without a page reference. Interested readers are expected to become familiar with the relevant research literature and consider its findings in context. However, give an exact page reference with all direct quotations.

Study the following sample citations. Note distinctive features like the use of commas, the abbreviations *p.* or *pp.* for "page" or "pages," or the symbol *&* (the ampersand) for *and*.

1. AUTHOR AND DATE ONLY–standard citation:

```
Anorexia nervosa is a condition of extreme weight loss
that results when young women compulsively starve
themselves (Grayfield, 1993).
```

2. DATE ONLY–author's name in your own text:

```
As defined by Grayfield, anorexia nervosa is a condition
of extreme weight loss that results when young women
compulsively starve themselves (1993).
```

3. PAGE REFERENCE–for direct quotation or specific reference:

```
Anorexia nervosa is "not really true loss of appetite"
but "a condition of emaciation resulting from self-
inflicted starvation" (Huebner, 1982, p. 143).
```

4. WORK BY SEVERAL AUTHORS   Name all co-authors. Use et al. (for "and others") only in second or later reference.

> Much advertising promotes miracle diets promising young
>
> women beauty and success (Bennings, Vasquez, & Theroux,
>
> 1994).
>
> The harmful effects of crash diets have been well
>
> documented (Bennings et al., 1994).

5. SAME AUTHOR   For several publications published by the same author in the same year, use *a, b, c,* and so on, in order of publication:

> Fyodor has published a series of studies challenging
>
> the tobacco industry's claims (1995, 1996a, 1996b).

6. REFERENCE TO SEVERAL SOURCES   List in alphabetical order, divided by semicolons:

> Unemployment statistics obscure the continuing increase
>
> of part-time and temporary work (Gutierrez & Vargas,
>
> 1994; Petersen, 1995).

7. UNKNOWN OR UNLISTED AUTHOR   Identify source by shortened title:

> Jury selection has become the subject of study for
>
> self-styled "experts" ("Psyching Out Prospective
>
> Jurors," 1996).

8. INSTITUTIONAL AUTHORSHIP   In general, use acronyms or abbreviations only in second or subsequent citation:

> Many promising drugs proved to have disastrous side
>
> effects (National Institute of Mental Health [NIMH],
>
> 1994).
>
> Research into the biochemistry of the brain has led to
>
> genuine breakthroughs in the treatment of emotional
>
> disorders (NIMH, 1994).

9. PERSONAL COMMUNICATIONS   Cite letters, memos, e-mail, or telephone interviews as personal communications. Include the date. Since they cannot be consulted or verified by the reader, do not include personal communications in your list of References.

Police officers tend to feel that the media tend to give a negative slant to police work (Victor Gomez, personal communication, March 17, 1995).

REFERENCES DIRECTORY: APA

Use the heading "References" for your final alphabetical listing of works quoted or consulted. Note the distinctive author-and-date sequence, with author identification followed by the date in parentheses:

Stefan, L. B. (1991). <u>Youth and the law: Getting tough on juvenile crime</u>. Boston: Benchmark Books.

Study distinctive features of the APA style: the use of initials (rather than first names) with authors' names, lower-case letters in titles, and the abbreviations *p.* or *pp.* for page numbers. Indent the *first* line of each entry one half inch (or five typewriter spaces).

A. Articles in Periodicals

1. STANDARD ENTRY FOR NEWSPAPER ARTICLE   Start with the last name of the author, followed by initials (not full first names). Then put the date in parentheses—do not abbreviate months (1996, September 21). Do not put titles of articles in quotation marks; use lower-case letters except for words you would normally capitalize in your text. Italicize (or underline) the name of the newspaper. Use *p.* or *pp.* for "page" or "pages." If appropriate, specify the edition of the newspaper—early or late, east or west: *The Wall Street Journal*, eastern ed., p. A3. (Keep the article *The* in the names of newspapers like *The Wall Street Journal* or *The New York Times*.)

Lipsyte, R. (1993, September 24). An immovable barrier in the fight for equity. <u>The New York Times</u>, p. B11.

2. STANDARD ENTRY FOR MAGAZINE ARTICLE   Start with the last name of the author. Go on to date, title of article, and name of publication. Include complete page numbers.

Parmelo, O. (1995, November). The discovery of x-rays. <u>Scientific American</u>, pp. 86–91.

If a newspaper or magazine article is concluded later in the issue, use a comma between the two sets of page numbers.

Miller, G. (1969, December). On turning

psychology over to the unwashed. <u>Psychology Today</u>,

pp. 53-54, 66-74.

3. ARTICLE BY SEVERAL AUTHORS　List the names of all co-authors, last names first. Put the *and*-sign (&) before the last author's name.

Cooper, J. C., & Madigan, K. (1995, July 10).

Consumers may be tight-fisted, but business isn't.

<u>Business Week</u>, pp. 29-30.

4. UNSIGNED OR ANONYMOUS ARTICLE　If the author of an article is unnamed, start with the title. Alphabetize by the first word of the title, not counting *The, A,* or *An.*

Losing its way: Japanese industry. (1993,

September 18). <u>Economist</u>, pp. 78-79.

5. ARTICLE WITH SUBTITLE　Use a colon between the title and subtitle.

Claflin, T. (1993, November/December).

Monumental achievement: Twenty years after Vietnam,

invisible vets get their memorial. <u>Ms.</u>, pp. 83-88.

6. ARTICLE WITH VOLUME NUMBER　Underline (or italicize) the volume number for a periodical, with complete page numbers following after a comma: *6, 152-169.*

Santley, R. S. (1985). The political economy of

the Aztec empire. <u>Journal of Anthropological</u>

<u>Research, 41</u>, 327-337.

7. ARTICLE WITH NUMBER OF VOLUME AND ISSUE　If page numbers are not continuous for the whole volume (each new issue starts with page 1), you may have to include the number of the issue. Put it in parentheses between the volume number and the page numbers: *6(3), 152-169.*

Steinhausen, H., & Glenville, K. (1983). Follow-

up studies of anorexia nervosa: A review of research

findings. <u>Psychological Medicine: Abstracts in</u>

<u>English, 13</u>(2), 239-245.

WORKS CITED IN DIRECTORY: APA

A. ARTICLES IN PERIODICALS
    1. Standard Entry for Newspaper Article
    2. Standard Entry for Magazine Article
    3. Article by Several Authors
    4. Unsigned or Anonymous Article
    5. Article with Subtitle
    6. Article with Volume Number
    7. Article with Number of Volume and Issue
    8. Signed or Unsigned Editorial
    9. Letter to the Editor
   10. Review of a Book
B. BOOKS (AND OTHER WHOLE PUBLICATIONS)
   11. Standard Entry for a Book
   12. Book with Subtitle
   13. Book by Several Authors
   14. Later Edition of a Book
   15. Book with Editor's Name
   16. Book with Translator's Name
   17. Several Works by Same Author
   18. Part of a Book
   19. Part of Collection or Anthology
   20. One of Several Volumes
   21. Unspecified or Institutional Authorship
   22. Encyclopedia Entry
C. ELECTRONIC AND NONPRINT SOURCES
   23. Computer Service
   24. On Line Publication
   25. Information Service
   26. CD-ROM
   27. Nonprint Media

8. SIGNED OR UNSIGNED EDITORIAL   After the date or title, add the label *Editorial* in square brackets. If the editorial is unsigned, begin with the title.

      Hernandez, C. (1994, September 27). Immigrants
are not aliens [Editorial]. <u>Harristown News</u>, p. 7.

      What is sacred? (1995, November/December).
[Editorial]. <u>Mother Jones</u>, pp. 3–6.

9. LETTER TO THE EDITOR   After the date or title, add the right label: Letter to the editor.

> Kosinski, L. (1996, November 12). Downsizing
>
> gets out of hand [Letter to the editor]. <u>The Los</u>
>
> <u>Angeles Times</u> part II: 7.

10. REVIEW OF A BOOK   Start with the author and title of the review. Include the title of the book reviewed in square brackets.

> Sheaffer, R. (1995, November). Truth abducted
>
> [Review of the book <u>Close encounters of the fourth</u>
>
> <u>kind: Alien abduction, UFOs, and the conference at</u>
>
> <u>MIT</u>]. <u>Scientific American, 273</u>(5), 102-103.

B. Books (and other whole publications)

11. STANDARD ENTRY FOR A BOOK   Use initials instead of the author's first name and middle name. Capitalize only the first word of the title or subtitle (but capitalize proper names that are part of a title as you would in ordinary prose).

> Gaylin, W. (1992). <u>The male ego</u>. New York:
>
> Penguin.

Use the full names of publishers, omitting tags like *Inc.* or *Co.*: Cambridge: Harvard University Press.

12. BOOK WITH SUBTITLE   Use a colon between the title and subtitle.

> Kozol, J. (1995). <u>Amazing grace: The lives of</u>
>
> <u>children and the conscience of a nation</u>. New York:
>
> Crown Publishers.

13. BOOK BY SEVERAL AUTHORS   Put the last name first for each of several authors. Use the *and*-symbol *&* (ampersand) instead of the word *and*.

> Minuchin, S., Rosman, B., & Baker, L. (1978).
>
> <u>Psychosomatic families: Anorexia nervosa in context</u>.
>
> Cambridge, MA: Harvard University Press.

> Boyer, P. S., Clark, C. E., Hawley, S. M., Kett,
>
> J. F., Salisbury, N., Sitkoff, H., & Woloch, N.

(1995). <u>The enduring vision: A history of the
American people</u>. Lexington: D. C. Heath.

14. LATER EDITION OF A BOOK   If you have used a book revised or updated by the author, identify the new edition the way it is labeled on its title page. After the title of the book, put *2nd ed.* for second edition, for instance, or *rev. ed.* for revised edition.

Zettl, H. (1997). <u>Television production handbook</u>
(6th ed.). Belmont, CA: Wadsworth.

15. BOOK WITH EDITOR'S NAME   Put the abbreviation for "editor" (*Ed.* or *Eds.*) in parentheses.

Hartman, F. (Ed.). (1973). <u>World in crisis:
Readings in international relations</u> (4th ed.). New
York: Macmillan.

Popkewitz, T. S., & Tabachnick, B. R. (Eds.).
(1981). <u>The study of schooling: Field based
methodologies in educational research and evaluation</u>.
New York: Praeger.

16. BOOK WITH TRANSLATOR'S NAME   Put the translator's name (or translators' names) followed by *Trans.* after the title.

Freire, P. (1970). <u>Pedagogy of the oppressed</u>
(M. B. Ramos, Trans.). New York: Seabury Press.

17. SEVERAL WORKS BY SAME AUTHOR   Repeat the author's name with each title; put works in chronological order.

Bruch, H. (1973). <u>Eating disorders: Obesity,
anorexia nervosa, and the person within</u>. New York:
Basic Books.

Bruch, H. (1978). <u>The golden cage: The enigma of
anorexia nervosa</u>. Cambridge, MA: Harvard University
Press.

18. ONE OF SEVERAL VOLUMES   Include the volume number.

> Davis, S. P. (1984). <u>History of Nevada</u>. Vol. 2.
> Las Vegas: Nevada Publications.

19. PART OF A BOOK   Use the appropriate label for a preface, introduction, afterword, or the like.

> Aufderheide, P. (1992). Preface. In
> P. Aufderheide (Ed.), <u>Beyond PC: Toward a politics</u>
> <u>of understanding</u> (pp. 1–4). Saint Paul, MN: Graywolf
> Press.

20. PART OF A COLLECTION OR ANTHOLOGY   Identify both the article (or other short item) and the collection of which it is a part. Reverse the initial and last name only for the author or editor of the part, not of the collection. If you cite several articles from the same collection, give full publishing information each time.

> Borges, J. L. (1972). A new refutation of time.
> In S. Sears & G. W. Lord (Eds.), <u>The discontinuous</u>
> <u>universe: Selected writings in contemporary</u>
> <u>consciousness</u> (pp. 208–223). New York: Basic Books.

21. UNSPECIFIED OR INSTITUTIONAL AUTHORSHIP   Reports issued by an organization and major reference books may list a group as the author or not specify authorship:

> American Psychological Association. (1982).
> <u>Ethical principles in the conduct of research with</u>
> <u>human participants</u>. Washington, DC: Author.

22. ENCYCLOPEDIA ENTRY   List an unsigned entry in an encyclopedia or other reference work under first word of entry. If the author of an entry is identified, include the name.

> Russia. (1994). In <u>The new encyclopedia</u>
> <u>Britannica</u> (15th ed.) (Vol. 10, pp. 253–255).
> Chicago: Encyclopedia Britannica.

C. Electronic and Nonprint Sources

23. COMPUTER SERVICE   For material published elsewhere but obtained through a computer service, include the name of the system and retrieval path (for

instance, name of file and item number). Do *not* put a period after retrieval numbers or access numbers.

> Schomer, H. (1983, May-June). South Africa:
>
> Beyond fair employment [On-line]. <u>Harvard Business</u>
>
> <u>Review</u>, pp. 145, 156. DIALOG File 122, Item 119425
>
> 833160

24. ON-LINE PUBLICATION   An availability statement replaces the name and location of publisher provided for print publications. The information needed may be a simple document number but may also be much more extensive. For an article by Bridgeman published in the on-line journal *Psychoioquy* and accessed through the File Transfer Protocol (FTP) the full availability statement after author, date, and title may read:

> Available FTP: 128.112.128.1 Directory:
>
> pub/harnad File: psych.92.3.26.
>
> consciousness.11.bridgeman

25. INFORMATION SERVICE   If the material had been previously published elsewhere, provide standard publishing information, followed by identification of the service and an item number. If the material had not been previously published, cite it as a complete publication published by the service:

> Kurth, R. J., & Stromberg, L. J. (1984). <u>Using</u>
>
> <u>word processing in composition instruction</u> [On-line].
>
> ERIC, ED 251 850

26. CD-ROM   Include source and retrieval number or similar information.

> Croft, F. S. (1995). Cruising in cyberspace [CD-
>
> ROM]. VocEd File: Item 875623

27. NONPRINT MEDIA   Include a label for the medium used (in square brackets). Do not list personal communications, such as unpublished letters, telephone interviews, e-mail messages, and similar materials that are not a matter of public record. Identify source and date in your parenthetical citation in your text, for instance (F. Ng, personal communication, June 7, 1996).

> Maas, J. B. (Producer), & Gluck, D. H.
>
> (Director). (1979). <u>Deeper into hypnosis</u> [Film].
>
> Englewood Cliffs, NJ: Prentice-Hall.

Clark, K. B. (Speaker). (1976). <u>Problems of freedom and behavior modification</u> [Cassette recording]. Washington, DC: American Psychological Association.

DiSanto, F. <u>Alienation</u> [Art work]. San Jose, CA: Institute of Mexican American Art.

Vitale, K. (Interviewer). (1996, May 6). Interview with C. Lobos. <u>Behind the news</u> [Radio program]. Washington, DC: Public Broadcasting Service.

SAMPLE RESEARCH PAPER PAGES: APA

The following pages are the opening pages of the juvenile justice research paper reformatted in the APA style. The sample pages are followed by the complete list of References. Note the use of the author–date style both in the brief parenthetic references in the texts and in the detailed list of References at the end. Note the use of specific page references for direct quotations.

Child Criminals in Adult Courts—A Crime in Itself?

James Perry

Professor Guth

English 176

21 November 1995

Child Criminals in Adult Courts—A Crime in Itself?

In August 1993, at a day camp in Savona, New York, Eric Smith, a 13-year-old, brutally murdered a 4-year-old. Eric grabbed the younger boy in a headlock, smashed his head three times with a rock, stuffed a napkin and a plastic bag in his mouth, pummeled his body with a rock, shoved a stick up his rectum, and poured a drink over his body. His trial began on August 1 in Bath, New York. Despite his young age, Eric was tried as an adult, due to the severity of his crime and also due to a law allowing children as young as thirteen to be tried as adults when accused of murder (Nordheimer, 1994, p. B5). His act was indicative of some frightening trends in America—an increase in the severity of juvenile crime, and a decrease in the age at which children commit crimes. His trial also shows a current trend in American juvenile justice—children are being tried in adult courts in more cases and at younger ages. Experts, elected representatives, and the general public have been grappling with the issue of how to deal with juvenile crime, and treating youths as adults is currently a popular solution. Many issues are relevant in the debate over whether to try children as adults—how major a problem is juvenile crime; is being harsh with juvenile criminals in the best interest of the defendants and in society's best interest, in terms of rehabilitating criminals, deterring and reducing crime, and justice; is treating child criminals as adults

Child Criminals 3

the most effective and most cost-efficient way of dealing with them; and
so on. The alternative to treating juveniles as adults I intend to
treat in this paper is a more rehabilitative approach—some experts
advocate more preventive efforts, as opposed to more punishment-
oriented programs such as trying youths in adult courtrooms. In this
paper, I intend to show the causes for the current sentiment toward
trying youths as adults. Then I intend to argue that while juvenile
crime is a problem, it may not be the epidemic it has been made out to
be, and that although it is necessary to be firm in dealing with juvenile
criminals, the best way to deal with them may not necessarily be through
adult courts and strictly "getting tough."

In a way, the American justice system seems to be coming full
circle. The nation's first juvenile court was established in 1899 in
Cook County, Illinois, as a way to deal with young offenders in a more
rehabilitative style, as opposed to the harsher justice found in adult
courts (Andrews, 1994). However, by the 1960's, the public became more
concerned about juvenile crime, as the youth population was growing and
becoming more violent. Americans have begun to question the principles
and effectiveness of the current juvenile justice systems, and have
argued in favor of harsher, firmer alternatives. The 1966 U.S. Supreme
Court case Kent vs. United States established guidelines for the
transfer of young offenders to adult courts. The youths' threat to the
safety of the public and amenability to treatments within the juvenile
justice system were to be considered (Houghtalin and Mays, 1991). Since
this time, more and more laws have been proposed and implemented to make
it easier, and in some cases mandatory, for youths to be sent to adult

courts for certain crimes, both violent and nonviolent. The public seems to want young criminals to be held responsible for their crimes and to be punished, and they believe that this can best be done in adult courts, where child criminals presumably will face harsher sentencing, often including time in adult prisons.

Measures to treat juvenile offenders as adults have been proposed and supported for several reasons in recent years. While some experts advocate and have implemented more preventive measures, these are difficult to implement and would have more of a long-term effect, leaving Americans wondering "what we are supposed to do in the meantime" (Methvin, 1994, p. 95). Bob Herbert argues that attempts to rehabilitate young offenders and treat them lightly are "well-intentioned" but "out of touch with the increasingly violent reality of juvenile crime" (1994, p. E15). Other measures have failed to reduce juvenile crime; for instance, gun control laws are not believed to have a significant effect on violent crime by youths, since they tend to obtain the guns through illegal means anyway (Witkin, 1991, p. 28). Although experts disagree as to the extent and seriousness of current juvenile crime, the fact is that the public feels that juvenile crime is a major problem, and they support measures to deal with it. Assistant Maryland public defender feels that the public's focus on juvenile crime created the "political climate" that exists supporting anti-juvenile crime measures (Stepp, 1994, p. A12).

Many officials within the justice system feel that some young criminals should be treated as adults and tried in adult courts. A study published in August 1994 showed that many judges in the juvenile justice system feel that "the criminal justice system should deal with

Child Criminals 5

young criminals more in the way it deals with adults." For instance,
two out of five judges surveyed feel child offenders should be eligible
to receive the death penalty in some situations, and a majority felt
that the minimum age for facing murder charges should be lowered
("Tougher Treatment," 1994, p. A16). Former administrator of the Office
of Juvenile Justice and Delinquency Prevention Ira Schwartz feels that
"juvenile court judges and youth probation workers are among the
staunchest supporters of jailing for juveniles" (1989, p. 18).

Many legislators, and a large portion of the general public, share
the sentiments of these justice authorities. Maryland Delegate Joseph
F. Vallario, Jr. feels that "if [youths] want to do adult-type crimes,
we're going to treat them like adults" (Stepp, 1994, p. A12). Another
Maryland Delegate, Ulysses Curie, writes that due to the increasing
violence and youth of juvenile offenders, "the juvenile system must be
changed to respond to this reality" by treating youths more like adults
(1994, p. C8). Both Democrats and Republicans support measures to treat
young criminals more like adults; both of the Maryland delegates quoted
above are Democrats, and a major part of the Republicans' "Contract with
America" was the "Taking Back Our Streets Act," which supported harsher
punishment of crime ("Youth and Crime," p. 18). In recent years, many
states have added legislation that lowered the ages at which youths can
be tried as adults for certain crimes, added new crimes to those for
which a juvenile may or must be tried as an adult, implemented mandatory
sentencing for children convicted of certain crimes, and so on. For
instance, in 1993, Louisiana added attempted murder and aggravated
battery to the list of offenses for which a juvenile may be tried as an . . .

Child Criminals 6

References

Andrews, J. H. (1994, March 7). Criminals, but still children. Christian Science Monitor, p. 17.

Armstrong, S. (1994, March 7). Colorado tries more carrot and less stick in punishing juvenile crime. Christian Science Monitor, pp. 1, 4.

Bayh, B. (1989). [Foreword.] In I. M. Schwartz, (In)justice for juveniles: Rethinking the best interests of the child (pp. xi-xiii). Lexington: Heath-Lexington.

Curie, U. (1994, February 6). Reality requires tougher responses to juvenile crime. The Washington Post, p. C8.

Fiagone, C. (1995, February 13). Jacksonville's tough answer to problem of youth crimes. Christian Science Monitor, pp. 1, 14.

Herbert, B. (1994, July 24). Little criminals, big crimes. The New York Times, late ed., p. E15.

Houghtalin, M. & Mays, G. L. (1991). Criminal dispositions of New Mexico juveniles transferred to adult court. Crime and Delinquency 37, 393-407.

Kotlowitz, A. (1994, February 13). Their crimes don't make them adults. The New York Times Magazine, pp. 40-41.

McLean, G. (1986, December 12). Adult prison is no place for a kid. Christianity Today, p. 13.

Methvin, E. H. (1994, April). Behind Florida's tourist murders. Reader's Digest, pp. 92-96.

Nordheimer, J. (1994, August 2). Murder trial begins for teen-ager. The New York Times, late ed., p. B5.

Child Criminals 7

Schwartz, I. M. (1989). <u>(In)justice for juveniles: Rethinking the best interests of the child</u>. Lexington: Heath-Lexington.

Stefan, L. B. (1991). <u>Youth and the law: Getting tough on juvenile crime</u>. Boston: Benchmark Books.

Stepp, L. S. (1994, October 15). The crackdown on juvenile crime—Do stricter laws deter youths? <u>The Washington Post</u>, pp. A1, A12.

Tougher treatment urged for juveniles. (1994, August 2). <u>The New York Times</u>, late ed., p. A16.

Witkin, G. (1991, April 8). Kids who kill. <u>U.S. News and World Report</u>, pp. 26-32.

Youth and crime. (1995, January 10). [Editorial.] <u>Christian Science Monitor</u>, p. 18.

Acknowledgments

JONATHAN ALTER, "The Cave on Tobacco Road" from *Newsweek*, September 4, 1995. Copyright © 1995 by Newsweek, Inc. All rights reserved. Reprinted by permission.

MARCIA ANGELL, "Science and the Law: Are Breast Implants Actually OK?" as it appeared in *The New Republic*, September 11, 1995. Copyright © 1995 by Marcia Angell. Reprinted by permission of The Martel Agency on behalf of the author. Marcia Angell, physician and executive editor of the *New England Journal of Medicine* is author of *Science on Trial: The Clash of Medical Evidence and the Law in the Breast Implant Case*, W. W. Norton, June 1996.

EDWARD BAIG, "A Cyberfest for Culture Lovers." Copyright © 1995 by the McGraw-Hill Companies. Reprinted from March 13, 1995 issue of *Business Week* by special permission.

CARL BERNSTEIN, "The Idiot Culture," abridged. Originally published in *The New Republic*, June 6, 1992. Copyright © 1992 by Carl Bernstein. Reprinted by permission of the author.

WENDELL BERRY, "The Peace of Wild Things" from *Openings*. Copyright © 1968 by Wendell Berry. Reprinted by permission of Harcourt Brace & Company.

DEBORAH BLUM, "The Monkey Wars" from *The Sacramento Bee*, 1992. Copyright © 1996 by The Sacramento Bee. Reprinted by permission of The Sacramento Bee.

SHANNON BROWNLEE, "Cancer's Bad Seeds" from *U.S. News & World Report*, December 11, 1989. Copyright © 1989 by U.S. News & World Report. Reprinted by permission.

ROBERT BRUSTEIN, "The Smashing of the Bell" from *The New Republic*, August 14, 1995. Copyright © 1995 by The New Republic. Reprinted by permission.

KAREN BURSTEIN, "Affirmative Action: What's Fair?" from *Ms. Magazine*, September/October 1995. Copyright © 1995 by Ms. Magazine. Reprinted by permission of Ms. Magazine.

FOX BUTTERFIELD, "Video of 'Racist' Event Challenged." Copyright © 1995 by The New York Times Company. Reprinted by permission.

RACHEL L. CARSON, "Our War Against Nature," excerpt from *Silent Spring*. Copyright © 1962 by Rachel L. Carson, renewed 1990 by Roger Christie. Reprinted by permission of Houghton Mifflin Company. All rights reserved.

LORNA DEE CERVANTES, "Refugee Ship" from a *A Decade of Hispanic Literature* (Arte Público Press–University of Houston, 1981). Reprinted by permission of the publisher.

GARY CHAPMAN, "Flamers" from *The New Republic*, April 10, 1995. Copyright © 1995 by The New Republic, Inc. Reprinted by permission of The New Republic.

HOWARD CHUA-EOAN, "The Clash of Cultures" from *Time Magazine*, August 7, 1995. Copyright © 1995 by Time Inc. Reprinted by permission.

AMY CORTESE AND KATHY REBELLO, "The Marketing of Windows 95" from *Business Week*, July 10, 1995. Copyright © 1995 by The McGraw-Hill Companies. Reprinted by special permission.

DEBORAH CRAMER, "Troubled Waters: Regulating the Fisheries," as first published in *Atlantic Monthly*, June 1995. Copyright 1995 by Deborah Cramer. Reprinted by permission of IMG Literary.

ALAN CRANSTON, "Dropping the A-bomb: The Non-Event" from *The New Republic*, August 21 & 28, 1995. Copyright © 1995 by The New Republic, Inc. Reprinted by permission of The New Republic.

STANLEY CROUCH, "Michael Jackson, Moby Dick of Pop" first published in *The New Republic*, August 21 & 28, 1995. Copyright 1995 by Stanley Crouch. Reprinted by permission of the author.

PHILIP ELMER-DEWITT, "Bards of the Internet" from *Time Magazine*, July 4, 1994. Copyright © 1994 by Time Inc. Reprinted by permission.

WILLIAM DOHERTY, "Private Lives, Public Values: The Future of the Family" from *Psychology Today*, May/June 1992. Reprinted by permission of Psychology Today.

PAULA DWYER AND WILLIAM GLASGALL, "The Lesson from Barings' Straits" from *Business Week*, March 13, 1995. Copyright © 1995 by the McGraw-Hill Companies. Reprinted by special permission.

BARBARA EHRENREICH, "The Next Wave," first published in *Ms. Magazine*, July/August 1987. Copyright © 1987 by Barbara Ehrenreich. Reprinted by permission of ICM on behalf of the author.

ELISSA ELY, "Dreaming of Disconnecting a Respirator," first published in *The Boston Globe*, July 1, 1989. Copyright 1989 by Elissa Ely. Reprinted by permission of the author.

LEA GARCHIK, "Astroturf Lobbyists Sprout All Over" from the *San Francisco Chronicle*, August 10, 1995. Copyright © 1995 by the San Francisco Chronicle. Reprinted by permission.

NANCY GIBBS, "The EQ Factor" from *Time* Magazine, October 2, 1995. Copyright © 1995 by Time, Inc. Reprinted by permission.

PAUL GRAY, "Doomsdays" from *Time* Magazine, August 7, 1995. Copyright © 1995 by Time Inc. Reprinted by permission.

HOWARD E. GRUBER, "Darwin's Imagery: The Tree of Nature," reprinted from *On Aesthetics in Science*, edited by Judith Wechsler, MIT Press 1978, Birkhauser 1988. Copyright © 1978, 1988 by Judith Wechsler. Reprinted by permission of the author and Judith Wechsler.

JESSICA HAGEDORN, "Asian Women in Film: No Joy, No Luck" from *Ms. Magazine*, January/February 1994. Copyright © 1994 by Jessica Hagedorn. Reprinted by permission of the author and her agent Harold Schmidt Literary Agency.

STEPHEN W. HAWKING, "Einstein's Dream," excerpt from *Black Holes and Baby Universes and Other Essays*. Copyright © 1993 by Stephen W. Hawking. Reprinted by permission of Bantam Books, a division of Bantam Doubleday Dell Publishing Group, Inc.

JEANNE A. HEATON AND NONA L. WILSON, "Tuning in Trouble: Talk TV's Destructive Impact on Mental Health," from *Ms. Magazine*, September/October 1995, adapted with permission from Jeanne Heaton, and Nona L. Wilson. Copyright © 1995 by Jossey-Bass, Inc., Publishers. Reprinted by permission.

ERIC HOFFER, "God and the Machine Age," original title, "Jehovah and the Machine Age" from *The Ordeal of Change* by Eric Hoffer. Copyright © 1952, 1953, 1954, 1956, 1958, 1959, 1961, 1962, 1963 by Eric Hoffer. Reprinted by permission of HarperCollins Publishers, Inc.

ROBERT HUGHES, "Why America Shouldn't Kill Cultural Funding" from *Time* Magazine, August 8, 1995. Copyright © 1995 by Time, Inc. Reprinted by permission.

JOANNE JACOBS, "Job One: Education" from *San Jose Mercury News*, Sunday, February 18, 1996. Copyright 1996 by San Jose Mercury News. All rights reserved. Reprinted by permission.

LEON J. KAMIN, Book Review: "Behind the Curve" from *Scientific American*, February 1995. Illustration data: National Longitudinal Survey of Labor Market Experience of Youth, 1980–1990. Copyright © 1995 by Scientific American, Inc. All rights reserved. Reprinted by permission.

YNESTRA KING, "The Other Body: Difference, Disability, and Identity Politics" originally appeared in *Ms. Magazine*, March/April 1993. Copyright © 1993 by Ynestra King. Reprinted by permission of the author. New York City.

PERRI KLASS, M.D., "Are Women Doctors Different?" from *Baby Doctor: A Pediatrician's Training*. Copyright © 1992 by Perri Klass, M.D. Reprinted by permission of Random House, Inc.

JONATHAN KOZOL, "Distancing the Homeless" abridged from *The Yale Review*, Vol. 77, Winter 1988. Copyright 1988 by Jonathan Kozol. Reprinted by permission of the author.

MARK KRAMER, "The Ruination of the Tomato." Copyright © 1980, 1987 by Mark Kramer (as in the original edition published by Harvard University Press). A slightly altered form appeared in *The Atlantic Monthly*. Copyright © 1979 by Mark Kramer. Reprinted by permission of Mews Books: Westport, CT.

ROBERT KUTTNER, "Needed: A Two-Way Social Contract in the Workplace" from July 10, 1995 issue of *Business Week*. Copyright © 1995 by The McGraw-Hill Companies. Reprinted by special permission.

RICHARD LACAYO, "Anatomy of a Disaster" from *Time* Magazine, August 28, 1995. Copyright © 1995 by Time Inc. Reprinted by permission.

LEON LEDERMAN, "Blackboard Bungle" from *The Sciences*, January/February 1995, published by The New York Academy of Sciences. Reprinted by permission of *The Sciences*.

ARTURO MADRID, "Diversity and its Discontents" from *Black Issues in Higher Education*, Vol. 5, No. 4, May 1988. Reprinted by permission of Arturo Madrid, Murchison Distinguished Professor of the Humanities at Trinity University. From 1984 until 1993, Madrid served as Founding President of the Tomás Rivera Center, a national institute for policy studies on Latino issues.

RANDALL MAJORS, "America's Emerging Gay Culture" from *Intercultural Communication:*

A Reader, Sixth Edition, edited by Larry A. Samovar and Richard E. Porter. Copyright © 1994 by Wadsworth Publishing Company. Reprinted by permission of the publisher.

LYNN MARGULIS, "Microorganism: Invisible Empire" from *The Sciences*, January/February 1995, published by The New York Academy of Sciences. Reprinted by permission of The Sciences.

NATHAN MCCALL, "Time" excerpt from *Makes Me Wanna Holler*. Copyright © 1994 by Nathan McCall. Reprinted by permission of Random House, Inc.

KATIE MONAGLE, "Work: Mable Dole Haden" from *Ms. Magazine*, September/October 1995. Copyright © 1995 by Ms. Magazine. Reprinted by permission of Ms. Magazine.

TONI MORRISON, Excerpt from "Cinderella's Stepsisters" first appeared in *Ms. Magazine*, September 1979. Copyright © 1979 by Toni Morrison. Reprinted by permission of the author and International Creative Management.

NINA MUNK, "Canada's Culture Cops," originally titled "Culture Cops" from *Forbes Magazine*, March 27, 1995. Copyright © 1995 by Forbes, Inc. Reprinted by permission of Forbes Magazine.

STEPHEN NESBIT AND JAMES CARPENTER, "Survival and Movements of Greater Sandhill Crane Experimentally Released in Florida" from *Journal of Wildlife Management*, Vol. 57, #4, October 1993, published by the Wildlife Society. Reprinted by permission.

JOYCE CAROL OATES, "Rape and the Boxing Ring," originally appeared in *Newsweek*, February 1992. Copyright © 1992 by Joyce Carol Oates. Reprinted by permission of John Hawkins and Associates, Inc.

SHARON OLDS, "The Possessive" from *Satan Says*. Copyright © 1980 by Sharon Olds. Reprinted by permission of the University of Pittsburgh Press.

WILLIAM OUCHI, "The Competitive Edge: Japanese and Americans," excerpted from *Theory Z: How American Business Can Meet the Japanese Challenge*. Copyright © 1981 by Addison–Wesley Publishing Company, Inc. Reprinted by permission of Addison–Wesley Publishing Company, Inc.

ORLANDO PATTERSON, "The Paradox of Integration" originally appeared in *The New Republic*, November 6, 1995. Copyright 1995 by Orlando Patterson. Reprinted by permission of the author.

PLATO, "Educating the Guardians" from *The Republic of Plato*, translated by F. M. Cornford (1941). Reprinted by permission of Oxford University Press/England.

ELLEN PAPAZIAN, "Are Nurses Being Phased Out?" from *Ms. Magazine*, September/October 1995. Copyright © 1995 by Ms. Magazine. Reprinted by permission.

SIDNEY PERKOWITZ, "Quantum Technology and Common Sense," excerpted from "Strange Devices" in *The Sciences*, January/February 1995, published by The New York Academy of Sciences. Reprinted by permission of *The Sciences*.

MARGE PIERCY, "Simple Song" from *Circles on the Water*. Copyright © 1982 by Marge Piercy. Reprinted by permission of Alfred A. Knopf, Inc.

SUSAN QUINN, "Marie Curie: A Life" from *The New Republic*, April 10, 1995. Copyright © 1995 by The New Republic, Inc. Reprinted by permission of The New Republic.

MARY ROBISON, "Yours" from *An Amateur's Guide to the Night*. Copyright © 1981, 1982, 1983 by Mary Robison. Reprinted by permission of Alfred A. Knopf, Inc.

OLIVER SACKS, "Red: The Mystery of Color," (Rätzel um die Farbe Rot). Interview with Oliver Sacks by *Der Spiegel*, #24, 1995. Originally in German, translated by Hans P. Guth. Copyright © 1995 by *Der Spiegel*. Reprinted by permission of The New York Times Syndicate/Paris and by Oliver Sacks.

PAUL SAMUELSON AND W. NORDHAUS, "Supply and Demand," excerpted from *Economics* 15/edition, 1995. Copyright © 1995 by McGraw-Hill Companies. Reprinted by permission of the publisher.

ARTHUR SCHLESINGER, JR., "Was America a Mistake?" originally appeared in *The Atlantic Monthly*, September 1992. Copyright 1992 by Arthur Schlesinger, Jr. Reprinted by permission of the author.

LISA M. SKOW, PH.D., "Cultural Patterns of the Maasai" by Lisa Skow and Larry Samovar from *Intercultural Communication* 6/e by Larry Samovar and Richard E. Porter, Wadsworth 1991. Reprinted by permission of Lisa M. Skow, Ph.D.

HEDRICK SMITH, "Preparing for Life in the Real World" from *Rethinking America*. Copyright © 1995 by Hedrick Smith. Reprinted by permission of Random House, Inc.

CHARLENE SPRETNAK, "Wholly Writ: Women's Spirituality" from *Ms. Magazine*, March/April 1993. Copyright © 1993 by Ms. Magazine. Reprinted by permission.

WILLIAM STAFFORD, "Traveling Through the Dark" from *Stories That Could Be True* (Harper & Row, 1977). Copyright © 1977 by William Stafford. Reprinted by permission of the Estate of William Stafford.

MYRON STOKES AND DAVID ZEMEN, "The Shame of the City" from *Newsweek*, September 4, 1995. Copyright © 1995 by Newsweek, Inc. All rights reserved. Reprinted by permission.

BRYAN SUN, "Chaos and Complexity: An Approaching Reality" from *Notes in the Margins*, Program in Writing and Critical Thinking, Spring 1994, Stanford University. Reprinted by permission of Notes in the Margins.

ROGER E. SWARDSON, "'Downsizing' Hits Home" from *The San Francisco Chronicle*, Sunday Edition, August 8, 1993. Reprinted by permission of Roger E. Swardson.

MAY SWENSON, "Question" from *The Complete Poems to Solve*. Copyright © 1954 by May Swenson; copyright © 1982 by May Swenson. Reprinted by permission of Simon & Schuster Books for Young Readers.

STUDS TERKEL, "On the Job," interview with Joe Gutierrez, from *Race* by Studs Terkel. Copyright © 1992 by Studs Terkel. Reprinted by permission of The New Press.

EVAN THOMAS AND W. COHN with V. SMITH, "Rethinking the Dream" from *Newsweek*, June 26, 1995. Copyright © 1995 by Newsweek, Inc. All rights reserved. Reprinted by permission.

AMOJA THREE RIVERS, "Cultural Etiquette: A Guide" originally appeared in *Ms. Magazine*, September/October 1991. Copyright 1991 by Amoja Three Rivers. Reprinted by permission of the author at Market Wimmin, Auto Rd., Auto: W.V. 24197.

LESTER C. THUROW, "The New Economics of High Tech" as it originally appeared in March 1992 Harper's Magazine, now in *Head to Head: Coming Economic Battles Among Japan, Europe and America* by Lester C. Thurow. Copyright © 1992 by Lester C. Thurow. Reprinted by permission of William Morrow and Company, Inc.

FRED E. WHITE, "A Sample Project" from *Communicating Technology: Dynamic Processes and Models for Writers* by Fred E. White, HarperCollins 1996. Copyright © 1996 by Fred E. White. Reprinted by permission of HarperCollins College Publishers.

CARL ZIMMER, "Emerging Secrets: Clues to Pre-Human Evolution," excerpted from "Coming Onto the Land" by Carl Zimmer from *Discover* Magazine, July/August 1995. Copyright © 1995 by The Walt Disney Company. Reprinted by permission of Discover Magazine.

Index of Authors and Titles

Index of Terms